MODERN ECONOMICS

Modern Economics

Semoon Chang
UNIVERSITY OF SOUTH ALABAMA

Allyn and Bacon
Boston London Sydney Toronto

Library of Congress Cataloging-in-Publication Data
Chang, Semoon, 1941–
    Modern economics.

    Includes bibliographical references.
    1. Economics.   I. Title.
HB171.5.C463   1990   330   89-18523
ISBN 0-205-12264-7

Printed in the United States of America
10 9 8 7 6 5 4 3 2 1   94 93 92 91 90

In memory of my late father

Contents

14   Fluctuations in the National Economy   296

15   Introduction to Macroeconomic Theories   321

16   The Keynesian Model of GNP Determination   343

17   Money, Banking, and Monetary Policy   370

18   Macroeconomics Since Keynes   390

PART FOUR   GLOBAL ECONOMY   417

19   Economics of Trade among Nations   419

Illustrations

Tables

Preface

On my bookshelf I see more than thirty books written for introductory economics courses. There must be a compelling motive to write a book in a market already crowded. My motive was the desire to write a book that would be substantive in coverage without being wordy and enjoyable to read without being cute. My business economic research and consulting convinced me of the need for a book that would interest students in learning basic economic tools and concepts that they can use in real life.

HOW IS THIS BOOK DIFFERENT?

Modern Economics covers all topics generic to economics taught at the one-semester college level. The presentation is thorough, but the straightforward writing style makes it easy for students to read and understand. The strength of my coverage of microeconomics draws on my experience in writing a managerial economics book, while the coverage of macroeconomics draws its strength from my balanced approach to alternative theories. In presenting alternative macroeconomic theories developed since Keynes, I introduce theories as advanced by economists who conceived them and then summarize critical reviews of these theories. This approach will challenge students to form opinions of their own.

Modern Economics' treatment of mainstream economics is illustrated with many everyday examples, such as daylight savings time, smoking and lung cancer, blue chip stocks, posthumous palimony, Ann Landers, and Garrison Keillor's Lake Wobegon. Many of the examples are historical: I present the origin of the ballpoint pen to explain barriers to entry, cite Schumpeter's claim that Adam Smith was not a classical economist, and point out that there is only one graph in Keynes's *General Theory*.

This book is written after extensive research. Where possible, the coverage is based on original sources. For example, instead of simply explaining exchange rate systems, as most books do, I indicate which countries have freely flexible exchange rates and which use a pegged exchange rate system.

ORGANIZATION OF THE TEXT

Modern Economics has twenty chapters: four chapters in Part I for introduction, eight in Part II, on microeconomics, six in Part III, on macroeconomics, and two in Part IV, on global economy. Each chapter contains an introduction, boxed articles, a chapter summary, discussion questions, and suggested readings. A thorough glossary is presented at the end of the text. The text is written in such a way that the author and the readers of the book are reasoning together in studying economic concepts.

TEXT SUPPLEMENTS

The text is accompanied by a *Study Guide* for students' use, and an *Instructor's Manual* containing test questions and optional materials that instructors may use to supplement the text. Answers to all end-of-chapter questions and problems are given in the *Instructor's Manual*. The *Instructor's Manual*, including the test bank, is also available on floppy diskettes, typed in popular word-processing softwares such as WordStar and WordPerfect.

I personally prepared both the *Instructor's Manual* and the *Study Guide*. Before the two were printed, I made sure that all the questions and problems in the two supplements were based on the textbook material and their answers were consistent and accurate. I did this by answering again all test items and self-test items, and then comparing my answers with those printed in the *Instructor's Manual* and the *Study Guide*.

Finally, all statistical tables in the main text will be updated in Spring each year, and mailed to instructors who adopt this book. A registration form that adopters can fill out to receive the updates is inserted in the *Instructor's Manual*. Materials on controversial policies such as changes in minimum wage regulation and the U.S.—Canada Trade Agreement will also be mailed to instructors.

ACKNOWLEDGMENTS

Admittedly, *Modern Economics* would not have been possible without help from a number of people. I am deeply grateful to the following professors who took time to read large parts of the manuscript and made valuable contributions:

Jack Adams, University of Arkansas–Little Rock
Saul Z. Barr, University of Tennessee–Martin
Wayne W. Clark, Brigham Young University
Richard Clemmer, Central Michigan University
John Dodge, Calvin College
Jamie Flores, Chabot College
Richard B. Hansen, Southeast Missouri State University
Stephen Jarrell, Bowling Green University
Phil King, San Francisco State University
Leonard W. Martin, Cleveland State University
Tommy C. Meadows, Austin Peay State University
Thomas M. Mitchell, Southern Illinois University–Carbondale
John Sherlock, Champlain College
David Swaine, Andrews University
James Aylesworth, Lakeland Community College

My colleague Philip R. Forbus read the entire manuscript and made numerous critical comments for improvement, and another colleague, A. Douglas Stutsman, read all chapters of Parts I, III and IV, and made suggestions for improvement. Anthony M. Basque, a well-known writing specialist, edited the entire manuscript before it was sent to Allyn and Bacon. Significant assistance was also received from the following persons: Kelley Saunders (editorial), Carolyn Harris (marketing), and Paula Carroll (production) all of Allyn and Bacon; Cynthia I. Benn, copyeditor; Cathleen Collins of Editorial Inc.; and, above all, Rich Wohl, executive editor at Allyn and Bacon.

MODERN ECONOMICS

PART ONE

INTRODUCTION

Economics deals with human behavior. The origin of economics can be traced as far back as written records exist. According to Joseph A. Schumpeter, one of the great economists, rudimentary economic analysis has been left to us by the Greek philosophers Plato (427–347 B.C.) and Aristotle (384–322 B.C.). Although their economic ideas failed to attain any distinctive status, they did discuss, as part of their general philosophy of state and society, concepts such as *oeconomicus,* the Greek word meaning the practical wisdom of household management. Aristotle's work was somewhat more advanced in that analytical intention was more conspicuous. Aristotle, for instance, (1) suggested the need for a medium of exchange beyond a barter system, (2) condemned interest charged on loans, and (3) made a distinction between value in use and value in exchange, thus explaining why products like diamond that have a lower use value may be more expensive than products like water that have a higher use value.

Our primary interest in this book is the study of modern economics to help us understand current economic problems. Keep in mind, though, that the development of analytical techniques in economics has been evolutionary. Understanding the contributions made by great economists of the past is important in understanding modern economics, although it is not necessary to go all the way back to the ancient Greek or Chinese era. The historical development of economic ideas will, therefore, be introduced throughout this book whenever the introduction helps our understanding of contemporary economic thinking.

Many economists consider the 1776 publication of *An inquiry into the nature and causes of the wealth of nations* by Adam Smith as the beginning of economics as a separate field of science. The leading theme of the *Wealth of nations* is economic development of nations through the division of labor and the interactions of individual members of the society who are motivated by self-interest. The development of major economic ideas during and after the days of Adam Smith will be traced in detail in later chapters. Our main task in the first four chapters is to lay a firm foundation for the following chapters by learning what economics is all about, glancing at how national economies work, understanding how the demand and supply model allows us to make predictions in the market when underlying conditions change, and studying the roles of government in the market economy.

1

What Is Economics?

Defining Economics

Economic Ways of Thinking

Scientific Methods

How Economics Can Help Us

PEOPLE WHO HAVE NEVER had an economics course or read a book on economics may not know how to define economics, but they all know what economic problems are. Economic problems that readily come to mind include unemployment, budget deficit, trade deficit, too little money, too much taxes, rising school tuition, and rising food prices. As these examples indicate, economic problems are a part of daily life. They either affect our personal affairs directly or are brought to our attention by the news media, which report these issues almost every day. In this first chapter we shall study only basic concepts that will influence our way of studying the remaining chapters of this book.

There are three learning objectives of this chapter. The first is to learn what economics is all about as it relates to our daily lives. The second is to equip ourselves with economic ways of thinking so that we can gain a better understanding of how economic problems develop and are solved. Economics is a science. Our knowledge of economics, like other sciences, has progressed through the use of scientific methods. Thus the third objective is noble: to learn how scientific methods are employed to improve human knowledge in a science.

DEFINING ECONOMICS

Economics is the science used to study aspects of human behavior that deal with the relationship between given wants and scarce resources that have alternative uses. These aspects of human behavior include production, distribution, and consumption of goods and services.

Scarcity

The key word in the definition of economics is the **scarcity** or *shortage* of resources that can be used for production of alternative products. Whenever there is a shortage of resources that requires their allocation among alternative uses, there is an economic problem. Suppose that there are shortages of study time for tests, medical doctors for patients in a rural area, jobs for the unemployed, homes for the homeless, tax revenues for helping the needy, and money for shopping. These shortages are economic problems, since the available time, doctors, jobs, homes, tax revenues, and shopping money are not enough to satisfy all of society's wants. Let us look closer at another example, daylight saving time (DST).

Daylight Saving Time
The U.S. Congress first imposed DST from April through October in 1918 to save fuel for World War I efforts. When the war ended in 1919, DST was discontinued. Year-round DST was imposed from 1942 to 1945, during World War II, and was called *war time*. Congress adopted the April to October DST in 1966, although not all states use DST at this time. DST lasts until the last Sunday of October. When we change clocks to daylight saving time at 2 A.M. on the first Sunday of April, most of us say either that we enjoy the extra hour of daylight or that we really don't care. But there is more to DST.

DST is an economic issue because there is not enough daylight time to make everyone happy. According to the Daylight Saving Time Coalition, when in 1987 Congress made a change in the starting day of DST from the last Sunday of April to the first Sunday of the same month, the sporting goods and leisure products industries were anticipating as much as $4 billion in added sales.[1] Those who were opposed to any extension of the period subject to DST included parents having to send their children to school bus stops, and operators of radio stations licensed to broadcast during daylight hours only. Parents opposed the extension because in the spring months their children would have to catch the bus when it was still dark early in the morning. Radio operators opposed the extension because they would miss some of their rush-hour audience who would have to leave home before the onset of daylight. DST is an economic good because it is scarce. An **economic good**, unlike a **free good,** such as air, which is not scarce, is one for which the desire exceeds the amount freely available.

Relative Concept
Scarcity is relative. Scarcity exists not because the absolute quantity of a resource available at this time is small, but because the available quantity of the resource is small in relation to the quantity of the resource that is wanted for all competing uses. Diamond would not be scarce if the combined quantity wanted for all competing uses were smaller than the available quantity. Even ocean water would be scarce if the economy wants more salt water than is available in all the oceans combined. Suppose that all members of the Daylight Saving Time Coalition who want an extension of period subject to DST and all those who oppose the extension change their minds and willingly accept the current DST arrangement. The hours of daylight available to the particular wants of the two groups remain unchanged, but the same hours are now sufficient to meet wants by both sides. In this case, DST is no longer an economic problem because it is no longer an economic good.

Opportunity Cost

The possibility that a given resource can be used to produce any one of a number of different products suggests another important concept in economics, an opportunity cost. **Opportunity cost** is the amount of other products that must be forgone to produce a given product. If a given quantity of a resource is used to build a new house, the construction of the house will necessarily require sacrifice of other products that could be produced with the same quantity of the same resource. The true economic cost of building the house, therefore, is not the money that is spent to build the house, but the value of alternative opportunities forgone due to the decision to build the house. Sometimes, the dollar outlays needed to produce a product are a good measure of the opportunity cost of producing the product. At other times, they are not.

Examples
Consider cash held at home. An economic cost incurs in keeping cash at home since the opportunity of earning interest on the cash is forgone. The opportunity cost of holding cash at home is the interest earnings forgone. Consider a self-employed businessman who spent $40,000 to run his business including the cost of goods that he sold. There are $40,000 worth of resources used by the businessman that could have been employed to produce other products. Suppose that total sales

---

[1]For more on daylight saving time, see Fern Schumer Chapman, Business's push for more daylight time, *Fortune,* November 12, 1984, pp. 149–162, and an Associated Press article by Randolph E. Schmid in the April 2, 1987, issue of the *Mobile Press.*

revenue was $50,000. The businessman made a profit of $10,000 according to his accountant. The opportunity cost of running his business, however, is likely greater than $40,000 since the money value of his time is not counted as cost. Assuming that he could easily have made $30,000 during the same year if he had worked elsewhere, the opportunity cost of running his business would have been $70,000. The $30,000 represents the businessman's time and effort used in the self-employed business. Economically speaking, he lost $20,000, rather than made $10,000 from his business.

Let us consider daylight saving time again. One of the strongest proponents of an extension of DST to additional weeks is Southland Corporation, the owner of 7-Eleven convenience stores. The company estimates that another seven weeks of DST would bring an additional $30 million in sales to the company, since more women would stop at 7-Eleven stores on their way home from work if there were still daylight. The American Association of Nurserymen estimates that beginning DST earlier by about seven weeks might increase the industry's sales by as much as $315 million per year, since people might start buying plants when DST comes, feeling that spring has arrived.[2] If sales of goods increase, more goods will be produced. If more goods are produced, more jobs will be created and more tax revenues will be generated. Why not extend DST for several more weeks and make many more people happy while helping the economy at the same time? Again, the concept of opportunity cost enables us to see the whole picture. The opportunity cost of generating additional sales activities by extending DST for several more weeks is not zero. Women who spend more money at 7-Eleven stores will spend less at supermarkets, while people who buy more plants early in spring will have fewer dollars to spend later in spring. Economic benefits from extending DST, therefore, are expected to be substantially smaller than the proponents of additional DST claim they will be.

Lesson
The lesson from studying the concept of opportunity cost is that when a course of action is considered, the full impact of the action should be evaluated carefully. There is a saying that there is no such thing as a free lunch. Few, if any, goods or services that satisfy our wants are free.

ECONOMIC WAYS OF THINKING

We study economics to improve our standards of living by enhancing our ability to make forecasts that help us take care of economic problems. We want forecasts in order to minimize fluctuations in the economy, avoid serious recessions, reduce the number of persons who are poor, and enjoy steady economic growth. To study economics properly, it is important to develop economic ways of thinking.

The Process of Optimization

There is no such thing as *the* economic way of thinking, since economic problems are as diverse as the capriciousness of human behavior, and solutions to these problems often require more than

---

[2]Chapman, Business's push for more daylight time, p. 150.

one approach. One economic way of thinking, however, underlies most, if not all, economic problems. It is called optimization.

The root of all economic problems is the scarcity of resources that makes rationing of resources unavoidable. The process of rationing scarce resources among alternative uses in order to attain some well-defined objective is referred to as **optimization**.[3] In production, managers of plants optimize by trying to produce a maximum quantity of output with given resources or produce a given quantity of output with minimum resources. In distribution, firms optimize by trying to select a combination of different modes of transportation so that the total delivery cost can be minimized. In consumption, consumers optimize by trying to purchase and consume a combination of goods and services that will give them the most satisfaction with a given budget. Economists use the term **utility** to represent the degree of satisfaction that consumers derive from consuming goods and services. Even in study, students optimize by trying to spend more time on subjects in which they feel rather weak or can score the most improvement for the same hours of study. Policymakers at the Federal Reserve Bank optimize by trying to increase money supply in such a way as to maximize the potential for economic growth and simultaneously minimize inflationary pressure.

The concept of opportunity cost helps us to optimize the use of resources by allowing us to see all aspects of a cost before making decisions.

Positive Economics and Normative Economics

The distinction between positive economics and normative economics was made over 100 years ago by the British economist John Neville Keynes. According to John N. Keynes, a **positive science** is a body of systematized knowledge concerning what *is,* whereas a **normative science** is a body of knowledge discussing criteria of what *ought* to be.[4] In other words, positive economics is, in principle, independent of value judgments of scientists and is an objective study of economics. The primary task of positive economics is to provide useful hypotheses or theories in order to make predictions. Normative economics is an art. Statements that arise from normative economics are based on subjective value judgments as well as findings of positive economics.

Let us go over minimum wages to illustrate the difference between positive economics and normative economics. The effective federal minimum hourly wage rate has remained at $3.35 since January 1, 1981. Suppose that the minimum wage rate increases by $1.00 to $4.35. What impact will there be on the labor market? A positive economic analysis tells us that the higher hourly wage rate will cause businesses to optimize the use of labor by employing fewer workers. The higher hourly wage rate, therefore, will tend to increase the number of unemployed persons, especially among teenage workers. A normative economic analysis may go beyond the findings of positive economics. Opponents of the higher minimum wage may claim that the minimum wage regulation should be abolished since it will cause an increase in the rate of unemployment. Proponents of the higher minimum wages, on the other hand, may claim that the minimum wage should be raised since it will reduce poverty by paying decent wages to those who benefit from the higher minimum wage rate.

[3]Optimization is also known as economizing.

[4]John Neville Keynes, *The scope and method of political economy* (London: Macmillan, 1891), pp. 34–35 and 46. John Neville Keynes was the father of the more famous John Maynard Keynes.

JOSEPH A. SCHUMPETER

Joseph Alois Schumpeter was born in 1883 in the Austrian province of Moravia (now Czechoslovakia) and was educated in law and economics at the University of Vienna. He served as finance minister in Austria, taught at the University of Bonn in Germany, and moved in 1932 to Harvard University. When Schumpeter died in 1950, he had spent the last nine years of his life writing the monumental *History of economic analysis,* which was finally completed by his wife, Elizabeth Boody Schumpeter, after her husband died. Schumpeter developed a theory that viewed profit as the reward for innovation by entrepreneurs, and predicted a drift of capitalism into socialism.

Since economics deals with human behavior, and those who study economics are human beings, it is not possible to completely free positive economics from value judgments of those who study economics as a science. Positive economics will always be influenced by value judgments of economists. Often it is not easy to make a distinction between positive economics and normative economics. We should not underestimate the importance of positive economics, however. The progress in positive economics will go a long way toward producing consensus in normative economics on many controversial economic issues.

SCIENTIFIC METHODS

Economics is a **social science.** It is *social* in that economics deals with behavioral aspects of human beings in groups or societies such as how producers respond to higher prices of their final products or how home buyers make decisions when mortgage rates rise. **Mortgage rates** are interest rates charged on loans that are intended to purchase homes, buildings, or land. Social science is different from physical science. Physical sciences deal with nonhuman objects such as atoms, superconductors, and plants, or with nonbehavioral aspects of human beings such as bones, muscles, and toothaches. The claim that *economics is a science* suggests that we need to study the scientific method. Scientific methods applicable to natural sciences such as biology, chemistry, and physics should also be applicable to social sciences such as economics.

What Is Science?

Schumpeter defines science as "any kind of knowledge that has been the object of conscious efforts to improve it." Alternatively, Schumpeter presents the practically equivalent definition by saying that "a science is any field of knowledge that has developed specialized techniques of fact-finding and of interpretation or inference (analysis)."[5] A more popular definition calls **science** a search to

[5]Both quotations are based on Joseph A. Schumpeter, *History of economic analysis* (New York: Oxford University Press, 1954), p. 7.

discover commonalities in the wide variety of human experience (for social sciences) and nonhuman phenomena (for natural sciences). Regardless of how science is defined, we should keep in mind that, for any field of knowledge to be established as a science, the field needs both to collect practical knowledge such as techniques and precise terminology unique to the field, and to develop theories exclusively for exploration of knowledge in the field.

The ultimate worth of studying economics as a positive science lies in the ability of those who study economics to develop practical knowledge and theories. Science is not simply a collection of factual statements; it is a collection of tooled knowledge and theories. There are many techniques and terms unique to economics, but the long-term influence of economics as a science depends on the development of worthy theories.

Hypothesis, Assumption, and Theory

To understand what the scientific method is all about, several terms need to be defined. These terms include *assumption, hypothesis, model, proposition, theory,* and *principle.* A review of studies that discuss these terms indicates that many of these terms are used interchangeably and in different contexts by different authors. The aim of this section is to develop definitions that are least objectionable.[6] The objective is not necessarily to present exact definitions of terms that are used in science, but to define terms so that we may have the least difficulty in communicating with others when using these terms.

Hypothesis
A convenient place to start is with the term *hypothesis.* A **hypothesis** is a proposition tentatively assumed in order to extract its logical or empirical consequences whose truthfulness can be tested against facts that are known or may be determined. In the case of hypotheses that explore historical data, it is possible to find facts that retroactively confirm predictions indicated by the hypothesis. **Proposition** is the *act* of suggesting something for discussion or development. A proposition also means *something* proposed or offered for consideration, acceptance, or adoption. A hypothesis is a special case of the proposition that is proposed for the purpose of prediction and can be proved false through an empirical test. A well-known proposition, which is clearly not a hypothesis, is Proposition 13, which Californians approved on June 6, 1978. Proposition 13 limited property tax on real estate to 1 percent of its market value. Scientists try to state hypotheses in a testable form so that their truthfulness can be verified empirically.

To illustrate how to state a hypothesis, let us reconsider daylight saving time and propose our own hypothesis. Our hypothesis is that an early start of DST generates significant net economic benefits. If the hypothesis were true, Congress might seriously consider adopting an earlier start of DST. Two terms in our hypothesis would need to be defined precisely, if the hypothesis were to be tested empirically. First, we may define an early start of DST as a start at least four weeks earlier than the first Sunday of April, each year. Second, significant net economic benefits may be defined as the difference in excess of $100 million between total economic benefits and total economic losses that incur annually in the entire U.S. economy.

---

[6]Definitions of some of the terms presented in this section were adapted from *Webster's third new international dictionary* (Springfield, Mass.: Merriam-Webster, 1986).

When hypotheses are proposed to add knowledge in any scientific field, the proposed hypotheses should not be trivial. Instead, they should contribute significantly to the existing body of scientific knowledge. Although not enormous in significance, our hypothesis on DST is certainly not trivial, since we already know that the hypothesis may cause potentially billions of dollars to change hands.

Assumption

Stating assumptions is important in developing hypotheses. **Assumption** is the *act* of taking for granted or supposing that a thing is true. An assumption is also *something* that is taken for granted. Some assumptions are so obvious that they are, for all practical purposes, tautologies, or needless repetitions. Tautologies should not be stated. Examples of such obvious assumptions are that sunrise remains unaffected by changes in DST, or that the rate of increase in consumers' income immediately after changes in DST will remain unchanged. Other assumptions are not so obvious and may have to be stated explicitly. An example of these less obvious assumptions is that advertising budgets of firms affected by changes in DST will not change when DST is moved forward.

The number of both obvious and less obvious assumptions that can be stated for a given hypothesis is virtually endless. We in economics, therefore, use an expression, *ceteris paribus,* in order to hold constant all factors that may affect the test of a hypothesis but are not stated explicitly. **Ceteris paribus** means "all other things being equal."[7]

Theory

What is a theory? **Theory** can be defined in several ways and means different things to different people. Let us present two most popular definitions. First, theory may be defined as an imaginative contemplation of reality. According to this definition, there is no essential difference between a theory and a hypothesis, since a hypothesis is also an imaginative contemplation of reality. It is not unusual to find that theory and hypothesis are used interchangeably by many, and this definition of theory certainly lends credence to such uses. Second, theory may be defined as a hypothesis whose truthfulness has already been proven empirically. This definition of theory, perhaps more acceptable to scientists, clearly requires observation of facts to support the claim made by the theory. Whether a hypothesis has to be proven empirically to become a theory or the term *hypothesis* can be used interchangeably with the term *theory* is not as important as understanding that the whole idea of studying hypotheses and theories is to promote a scientific way of thinking that is needed to extend and analytically refine human knowledge.

Finally, **principles** are propositions so well accepted that we do not consider challenging their validity. One of the principles on which our hypothesis is based is the profit-maximizing behavior of firms that are affected by changes in DST. Some economists dispute the principle by saying that the maximization of profits is unrealistic because firms cannot possibly know when

---

[7]Sometimes, assumptions can take off and have their own lives beyond reasonableness. A recent article by Gary S. Becker and Nigel Tomes on the distribution of income and intergenerational mobility contains an assumption: "We assume that children have the same utility function as their parents and are produced without mating, or asexually." For source, see Becker and Tomes, An equilibrium theory of the distribution of income and intergenerational mobility, *Journal of Political Economy* 87(December 1979):1153.

BIRTHDAY AND DEATHDAY

Testing a testable hypothesis can be fun. Professor David Phillips wanted to test a hypothesis claiming that a person's death month is related to the birth month in that some people postpone death in order to witness their birthdays. The hypothesis can be tested by comparing the date of death with the date of birth for a large number of people. If the comparison shows fewer deaths than expected just before the birthday, it may be concluded that some of the deceased postponed their death until after their birthdays.

The birth and death dates of more than 1,200 famous people were examined. Only the famous people were selected for the test because famous people's birthdays attracted public attention and gifts, and thus they were more likely to postpone their deaths than ordinary people. Also, birth and death records of famous people were more easily available. The sources of data included *Four hundred notable Americans, Who was who in America,* and *Royalty, peerage, and aristocracy of the world.* The study found a decrease in the number of deaths before the birth month and an increase in the number of deaths after the birth month. The dips and the rises in the number of deaths were much more than what might reasonably be explained by chance. The study also found that the more famous a group of individuals under investigation was, the larger were the death dips of its members before birthdays and their death rises after birthdays.

According to Professor Phillips, some people postpone their death in order to witness events other than their birthdays. There are fewer deaths than expected before the Jewish Day of Atonement in New York, where a large Jewish population resides. There is a dip in U.S. deaths before U.S. presidential elections. Both Jefferson and Adams died on July 4, 1825, fifty years after the Declaration of Independence was signed. Jefferson's last words as quoted by his physician were "Is it the Fourth?"

Source: David P. Phillips, Deathday and birthday: An unexpected connection, in Judith M. Tanur (ed.), *Statistics: A guide to the unknown* (San Francisco: Holden-Day, 1972), pp. 52–65.

profits are at a maximum.[8] When principles are challenged and challenged seriously, the principles are no longer principles but become testable hypotheses or theories that can still be falsified.

Induction and Deduction

Theories may be developed in one of two ways: inductive approach or deductive approach. **Induction** moves from observation of facts to development of a theory, whereas **deduction** moves from development of a hypothesis to observation of facts in order to empirically prove the

[8]For earlier writings on the challenge of the profit-maximizing principle of firms, see Kenneth E. Boulding, Implications for general economics of more realistic theories of the firm, *American Economic Review* 42(May 1952):35–44.

hypothesis. Realistically, a pure deduction is hardly possible since ideas will not simply pop into the mind even of a scientist if he knows absolutely nothing of the facts relating to these ideas. Whether a particular approach is an induction or a deduction is a matter of degree. The American economist Paul A. Samuelson states that "every science is based squarely on induction—on observation of empirical facts."[9] Economists in general have a tendency to use the deductive approach, tossing off an idea or two and trying to prove that the ideas are true by collecting empirical facts to support them. The main point is that observation of empirical facts underlies both inductive and deductive methods.

To understand that the difference between an induction and a deduction is a matter of degree, let us take one example, smoking.[10] Tobacco smoking is an ancient habit of humankind. Studies on the effects of smoking have appeared in medical journals over the last 100 years. Many physicians observed that most lung cancer patients were regular smokers of cigarettes. In 1927, for instance, Dr. F. E. Tylecote, an English physician, wrote that almost all of his lung cancer patients were cigarette smokers. Up to this point, the approach toward determining the relation between lung cancer and smoking was inductive. At some point, however, a deductive approach was needed. Physicians thus hypothesized that, for reasons yet to be known, people who smoked tended to get cancer more than people who did not smoke. Massive empirical studies were undertaken to test the hypothesis, including the one by E. Cuyler Hammond and Daniel Horn who, through the American Cancer Society, enlisted 22,000 female volunteers. Each of these volunteers was asked to select 10 healthy men between the ages of 50 and 69 and have each of them fill out a smoking questionnaire. About 200,000 were followed through a period of four years. According to Hammond and Horn, the lung cancer rate is 23.4 times higher among those who smoke more than one pack a day compared to nonsmokers. They also report that the death rate for heart and circulatory diseases is 1.57 times higher among heavy smokers than among nonsmokers.

HOW ECONOMICS CAN HELP US

In sports, it has been said that winning isn't everything—it is the *only* thing. In business, profits may not be the only thing, but they are just about everything. Economists may be a little too sophisticated to generalize like people in sports or business. How much economic knowledge can help those who study economics depends on their capacity and efforts to learn, digest, and apply economic knowledge.

Sound economic knowledge is important to us as citizens. In presidential election campaigns, the main issues tend to be more economic than political. Jobs, inflation, the federal budget, replacing old bridges, child care, and social security dominate political debate during an election year. Quite often, what politicians say they will do after being elected is exactly the opposite of what needs to be done to achieve the very objective that the politicians promote during the campaign. Consider financing of social security. Those who advocate protecting the integrity of the social security system by increasing benefit payments but who do so without proposing corresponding

[9]Paul A. Samuelson, Economic theory and mathematics—an appraisal, *American Economic Review* 42(May 1952):57.

[10]The example on smoking is based on B. W. Brown, Jr., Statistics, scientific method, and smoking, in Judith M. Tanur (ed.), *Statistics: A guide to the unknown* (San Francisco: Holden-Day, 1972), pp. 40–51.

increases in taxes are the ones who in the long run undermine the integrity of the system. Another example concerns foreign trade. Those politicians who try to protect domestic jobs by raising protective barriers such as import duties are the ones who in the long run undermine the very jobs they want to protect. This is because other nations may retaliate and buy less of domestically-produced goods and services. By studying economics, we as citizens are able to make better decisions on civic issues that affect our daily lives.

Economics is frequently classified into two categories: macroeconomics and microeconomics. **Macroeconomics** is the part of economics that is concerned with major aggregates or averages of the economy such as total output or inflation. **Microeconomics** is the part of economics that is concerned with individual units within the economy such as firms or individual markets. If we run a business, the knowledge of macroeconomics and forecasting should keep us from stockpiling inventories when the economy is about to enter a recession. If we run a business, our ability to evaluate the actions and motives of the Federal Reserve should keep us from borrowing a large amount of money when market rates of interest are about to fall. If we produce products for sale, the knowledge of microeconomics will help us determine, albeit not exactly, what price to charge and how much to produce in order to maximize profit.

Finally, understanding of the concept of opportunity cost should make us wiser in making our everyday decisions as typical consumers. We should not fall into "get rich quick" scams intended to exploit innocent persons, since the concept of opportunity cost tells us that nothing scarce is free. Our understanding of foreign exchange rates should help us prepare for vacation in foreign lands where purchases can be made only in local currency.

SUMMARY

Economics is a social science in which we study aspects of human behavior that deal with the relationship between unlimited wants and limited resources that can be used to satisfy alternative wants. Whenever there is a shortage of resources that requires their allocation among alternative uses, there is an economic problem. Scarcity is common to all economic problems. Scarcity exists because the quantity of a resource humans desire exceeds the quantity available. Opportunity cost is the amount of other products that must be forgone to produce a given product. The true economic cost of producing a product is measured by the opportunity cost. Solving economic problems is a process of optimization. Optimization means allocating scarce resources efficiently among competing uses. Positive economics is a body of economic knowledge concerning what is, whereas normative economics is a body of economic knowledge concerning what ought to be. In other words, positive economics is independent of value judgments and is an objective study of economics. Normative economics involves explicit value judgments. Science is a collection of tooled knowledge and theories. A hypothesis is a proposition that is tentatively assumed and requires empirical tests of its truthfulness. A theory is a hypothesis whose truthfulness has already been proven empirically. The whole idea of studying hypotheses and theories is to promote the scientific way of thinking that is necessary to nurture knowledge. Induction moves from observation of facts to development of a theory, whereas deduction moves from development of a hypothesis to observation of facts in order to empirically prove the hypothesis.

EXERCISES

1. The process of optimization underlies most, if not all, economic problems. What is meant by optimization and why is it important in economics?

2. Positive economics is stressed more than normative economics in the text because positive economics is more important than normative economics. Is this statement an accurate assessment of why positive economics is more popular among economists?

3. What are major differences between social sciences and natural sciences?

4. The first U.S. patent law was passed in 1790 to protect the invention of any useful art, manufacture, engine, machine or device, or any improvement thereon not before known or used. In May 1987 the U.S. Patent and Trademark Office announced that it would consider nonnaturally occurring nonhuman multicellular living organisms, including animals, to be patentable subject matter. The new patent policy is controversial because of the gene-splicing in biotechnology. Considering that biotechnology is a positive science that, unlike a normative science, is presumably free of value judgment, and considering that differences in value judgment are usually the source of controversy, why has the new patent policy been so controversial?

5. Some say that the present voluntary army system is too costly and suggest returning to the draft system. Economically speaking, is the voluntary army system more costly than the draft system? Why or why not?

6. How is a hypothesis different from a theory?

7. In the June 1, 1987, issue of *Newsweek* (p. 8), Fred Brock suggested that "the level of enrollment in a course correlates in inverse proportion to the level of intellectual energy required to pass it." Is this quotation a hypothesis, an assumption, a theory, or a principle? Briefly explain why your answer is the right choice.

8. When scientists state that there are black holes in the universe that absorb every object including light into them, is the statement an assumption, a hypothesis, or a theory?

9. Why are assumptions necessary in developing a theory? If assumptions do not hold true, will this necessarily make theories untrue?

10. Explain the difference between deduction and induction.

SUGGESTED READINGS

American Economic Review. (1952). 42(May). Boulding, K.E. Implications for general economics of more realistic theories of the firm (pp. 35–44); Knight, Frank H. Institutionalism and empiricism in economics (pp. 45–55); Samuelson, Paul A. Economic theory and mathematics—an appraisal (pp. 56–66).

These three articles deal with issues in scientific methodology in economics. Allen G. Gruchy and Fritz Machlup discuss the articles on pp. 67–73 of the same issue.

Brown, E. H. Phelps. (1972). The underdevelopment of economics. *Economic Journal* 82(March):1–10.

> A thoughtful article that explains why students are not learning what they should be learning and stresses the greater importance of collecting facts than developing abstract theories.

Friedman, Milton. (1935). *Essays in positive economics.* Chicago: The University of Chicago Press, esp. pp. 3–43.

> The Nobel Prize winning economist discusses scientific methods as they pertain to economics, including assumptions, hypothesis, and theory.

Galbraith, John Kenneth. (1987). *Economics in perspective: A critical history.* Boston: Houghton Mifflin.

> Claims that many economists for the past two and a half thousand years have developed theories that simply tell the people in power what they want to hear; and suggests that economists make value judgments to correct injustices in the current economic system.

Schumpeter, Joseph A. (1954). *History of economic analysis.* New York: Oxford University Press, pp. 14–20, Theory.

> Defines economic theory as a box of tools or gadgets, and discusses theory in economic science.

Hogarth, Robin M., and Reder, Melvin W. (eds.). (1987). *Rational choice: The contrast between economics and psychology.* Chicago: The University of Chicago Press.

> Prompted by the growing evidence showing exceptions to the rational choice paradigm, articles in this book assess the impact of these exceptions on economics.

2

An Overview of Economic Activities

Economic Circular Flow

Business Organizations

Corporations and Stock Market

Economic Systems

ECONOMIC ACTIVITIES ARE carried out by many people every minute of the day. Workers go to local Coca Cola bottling plants to produce Coke, while drivers filling up at gas stations purchase cans of Pepsi. Truckers transport beef and sesame buns to local McDonald's for distribution, while rock music and boxing promoters sell products called entertainment services. In fact, it is hard to name an activity that has no economic component.

Economic activities are carried out by individual agents such as housewives, factory workers, Pentagon officials, and importers. The first learning objective of this chapter is to group these individual agents into four categories and study their interactions in the context of the economic circular flow. Although all agents are important components of an economy, the business sector produces all goods and services and provides jobs to members of the household sector. The second learning objective of this chapter is to concentrate on the business sector and study how businesses are organized. A subsection on stock markets is also presented because of the important role that the stock market plays in managing personal as well as business finances. Depending on the extent to which the business sector is controlled by the public sector, economic activities can be organized in at least two different ways. The two predominant systems of organizing economic activities are capitalism and socialism. The third learning objective of this chapter, therefore, is to study different economic systems that different nations adopt for the management of their economic affairs.

ECONOMIC CIRCULAR FLOW

Broadly speaking, individual agents of an economy can be grouped into four major sectors: the household sector, the business sector, the government sector, and the foreign sector. Economic activities are essentially exchanges of goods and services between any two members who belong to one of the four main sectors of an economy. The essence of economic activity can be depicted schematically as a circular flow. **Economic circular flow** is the exchange between sellers and buyers of final products and the factors of production needed to produce these final products. **Factors of production** include (1) **land,** referring to land in its literal sense and minerals not yet excavated, (2) **labor,** meaning the time and effort of human beings exerted in the process of production activities, (3) **capital,** consisting of machines, producers' durable equipment, and buildings, and (4) **entrepreneurship** for the organization of the business enterprise and the assumption of the risk.

Simple Circular Flow

Simple economic circular flow, charted in Figure 2.1, is the movement of goods and services between the household sector and the business sector. The household sector, shown at left in the figure, refers to all households and nonprofit organizations in an economy. The business sector, shown at right in the figure, refers to all types of privately owned businesses that produce goods and services for profit. Two types of exchange occur between the two sectors. One type, shown in the upper half of Figure 2.1, involves the flow of final goods and services; the other, shown in the lower half of the figure, the flow of the factors of production needed to produce final goods and services.

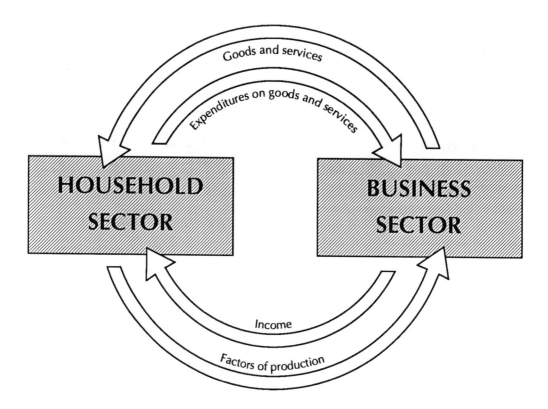

FIGURE 2.1 Simple Circular Flow. In the simple economic circular flow, there are two sectors: the household sector, which supplies the factors of production and purchases final goods and services, and the business sector, which buys the factors of production and uses them to produce final goods and services. Expenditures flow in the direction opposite to the flow of goods and services.

Members of the household sector, called consumers, need all types of final goods and services for everyday living. These products include groceries, housing, automobiles, chewing gum, aspirin, and what have you. These products are produced by firms in the business sector. The final products are sold by the business sector to the household sector as indicated in the upper half of Figure 2.1. Expenditures on final goods and services flow in the direction opposite to the flow of these goods and services. To pay for final products, consumers need money, and the most common way for consumers to acquire money is to earn income by providing the factors of production to firms in the business sector. The household sector provides land, labor, capital, and entrepreneurship to the business sector in exchange for payments that the members of the household sector use to purchase final goods and services. The exchange of the factors of production between the household sector and the business sector is illustrated at the lower end of Figure 2.1.

In brief, activities in the private sector of an economy consist of sale of the factors of production from the household sector to the business sector, production of final goods and services in the business sector, purchase of final goods and services by the household sector from the business sector, and consumption of final goods and services in the household sector.

Circular Flow with Government

The household sector and the business sector, together, make up the *domestic private* sector of an economy. The economy is private since government is not yet introduced into the flow, and the economy is domestic since foreign trade is excluded from our consideration. Figure 2.2 shows the economic circular flow for all of the *domestic* economy since it includes the government sector as well as the two private sectors. The government sector includes all three levels of government: federal, state, and local. Government provides goods such as space shuttles and local roads, and produces services such as public safety, national defense, and AIDS research. Government finances its production activities through taxation of the household and the business sectors. The role of government in the economic circular flow is indicated by the flow of taxes from both the household and the business sectors toward government and the flow of expenditures from government toward the household and the business sectors. Expenditures flow from government toward the household sector because, in such cases as AIDS research, government purchases services directly from the household sector and produces research directly. Expenditures also flow from government toward the business sector because, in cases like the space shuttle, government purchases goods that are produced by the business sector.

Circular Flow with Foreign Trade

An economic circular flow would not be complete without the foreign sector. The household sector buys final goods imported from foreign countries, and the business sector produces final goods that are exported to foreign countries. Imports are paid for with foreign currencies earned from the sale of exported goods.

Open Economy
The economic circular flow for the *open* economy is shown in Figure 2.3. An **open economy** is a domestic economy that trades with foreign countries. A domestic economy without foreign trade is called a **closed economy.** Imports flow from the foreign sector to the household sector as final goods, while exports flow from the business sector to foreign countries. Although not indicated in Figure 2.3, goods may also flow from the foreign sector to the business sector or from the business sector to the foreign sector as intermediate goods. **Intermediate goods** are produced goods that are used as inputs to produce other final goods. Payments for imports and exports flow in the direction opposite to the flow of goods and services.

Events that originate in one sector of the circular flow are likely to influence the flow of goods and services in other sectors of the economy. To illustrate, consider the impact of changes in the foreign exchange rate on the flow of goods in other sectors of the economy.

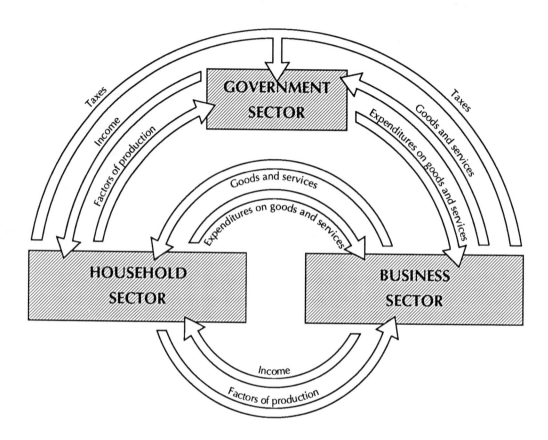

FIGURE 2.2 Circular Flow with Government. Government collects taxes from both the household sector and the business sector, and produces services for itself by purchasing the factors of production from the household sector, or buys final products from the business sector.

Example of the Interdependence

The currency used in Japan is the yen, while the currency used in the United States is the dollar. The price of one currency in terms of another is called the **exchange rate.** The exchange rate between the U.S. currency and the Japanese currency can be stated either as the price of yen in terms of dollars or as the price of a dollar in terms of yen. Assume that the exchange rate between yen and dollar is 200 yen per dollar. In other words, the price of one dollar in terms of yen is 200. Assume, also, that the price of a Nissan 300 ZX is 6 million yen in Japan. The price of the car in the United States then is $30,000 since 6,000,000/200 = 30,000. We assume that there are no **transactions**

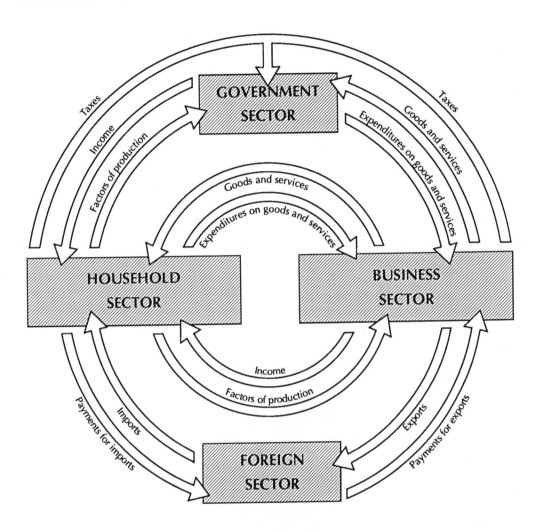

FIGURE 2.3 Circular Flow with Foreign Sector. Domestic goods and services are exported and foreign goods and services are imported through the foreign sector. Exports represent a leakage from the domestic circular flow, while imports represent an injection.

costs such as transportation or insurance costs that incur in the process of a trade. Suppose that, for some reasons, the value of the dollar falls by 50 percent, so that the exchange rate changes from 200 yen per dollar to 100 yen per dollar. In other words, the price of a dollar falls from 200 yen to 100 yen. What will happen to the U.S. economy?

Since the price of a Nissan 300 ZX in Japan is 6 million yen, Nissan Corporation will still want 6 million yen in Japanese currency. This earnings goal by Nissan means that the U.S. buyers of a 300 ZX will now have to pay $60,000 rather than $30,000, since 6,000,000/100 = 60,000. This higher price of a 300 ZX in the United States will cause imports of this car from Japan to the United States to fall. Since the price of the Japanese car is higher in the United States, the U.S. car buyers will have to settle for domestically produced cars, prompting General Motors, Ford, and Chrysler to increase production of their cars. The increased production and sale of domestic cars will increase the flow of goods from the business sector to the household sector (see Figure 2.3) and increase the flow of expenditures from the household sector to the business sector. The falling value of the dollar will lead to a decrease in imports from Japan to the United States, thus slowing the flow of imports and payments for imports. The increased demand for domestic cars will tempt domestic car manufacturers to raise the prices of domestic cars. Employment may increase but the higher prices of imports will lead to an inflationary pressure in the U.S. economy.

The falling value of the dollar also makes U.S. exports cheaper to the buyers of U.S. products in Japan. To see why the falling value of the dollar causes U.S. exports to be cheaper to foreign buyers, consider an example involving beer. Assume that a six pack of Michelob beer costs $4.00 in the United States. At the exchange rate of 200 yen per dollar, Michelob drinkers in Japan have to pay 800 yen for a six pack. At the exchange rate of 100 yen per dollar, however, Michelob drinkers in Japan need to pay only 400 yen for the same six pack, prompting Michelob drinkers in Japan to buy more Michelob and tempting drinkers of other alcoholic beverages in Japan to buy Michelob beer.

The economic circular flow is a simple representation of how an economy works through the interaction among its major sectors. The economic circular flow becomes the conceptual basis of developing macroeconomic theories in Chapters 13 and beyond.

BUSINESS ORGANIZATIONS

Goods and services are produced by firms in the business sector. There are approximately 16 million business enterprises in the United States, which have created over 100 million jobs. Anyone venturing to start a new business must first make a decision as to the form by which the business will be organized. There are three basic forms of business organizations: sole proprietorship, partnership, and corporation.

Sole Proprietorship

A **sole proprietorship,** or simply **proprietorship,** is a business in which the owner is self-employed. If a person performs services for a fee such as cleaning apartments, consulting, or washing cars, and is not an employee of the parties for whom he or she performs these services, then the person is automatically operating a sole proprietorship. Even a teenager mowing lawns for a fee is a sole proprietor.

Proprietorship is the simplest form of business organization and the easiest to organize, since there is nothing special to do to start a business. The business does not exist apart from the owner. Being his or her own boss, the proprietor has substantial freedom in making business decisions. The

TABLE 2.1 Numbers and Receipts by Type of
Business in 1985

Type of Business	Number (thousands)	Receipts ($billions)
Sole proprietorships	11,929	$ 540
Partnerships	1,714	368
Corporations	3,277	8,398
Total	16,920	$9,306

Note that receipts are total taxable receipts before deduction of cost of goods sold, cost of operations, and net loss from sales of property other than capital assets. Receipts include business receipts, interest, and receipts not specified.

Source: U.S. Department of Commerce, Bureau of the Census, *Statistical abstract of the United States, 1989,* 109th ed. (Washington, D.C.: U.S. Government Printing Office, January 1989), p. 516.

proprietor, however, often has limited financial resources for any large-scale enterprise, and is subject to unlimited liability. **Unlimited liability** means that if the business incurs a loss, the proprietor is risking not only the assets of the business but personal assets as well. In other words, all liabilities of the business are those of the owner.[1]

There are many sole proprietors, but the size of sole proprietorships is small relative to other forms of business organizations. Table 2.1 indicates that, in 1985, approximately 70.5 percent of businesses were sole proprietors, but business receipts of sole proprietors were no more than 5.8 percent of total business receipts.

Partnership

A **partnership** is a form of business organization existing between two or more persons who join together to carry on a trade or business. Each person contributes money, property, labor, or skills, and expects to share in the profits and losses of the business. The fact that two or more persons work together does not necessarily qualify them as a partnership. A joint undertaking merely to share expenses is not a partnership. There has to be a partnership agreement made in oral or written form as to the duties and rules of the partnership.[2] A partnership is similar to the sole proprietorship except

[1]To start a sole proprietorship, one needs to check whether the local government requires a business license, and to report income and expenses from business or profession on Schedule C of Form 1040. In addition, the proprietor's income is subject to social security tax. If an individual has another job such as full-time teaching or selling which pays at least as much as the social security wage base, there is no additional social security tax on his or her proprietor's income.

[2]For more on requirements for the three types of business organizations, read the annual publication by the Internal Revenue Service titled *Tax guide for small business.*

that it involves two or more persons sharing a business. Each partner is subject to unlimited liability by being personally liable for the debts of the partnership. When a partner withdraws from partnership, the partnership is dissolved. The most difficult part of organizing and running a business as a partnership is the personal relationship among partners. It is not unusual for the end of a partnership to be an unpleasant experience for partners of the business.

In 1985 partnerships constituted 10.1 percent of all business organizations and their receipts were only 4.0 percent of total business receipts.

Corporation

A **corporation** is a distinct legal entity that is owned by one or more stockholders. In principle, there is a separation of management from the ownership of corporations. Large corporations are usually managed by professional managers who are hired by stockholders. Small corporations are often managed by stockholders themselves. Since a corporation is a legal entity independent of stockholders, the stockholders of the corporation have **limited liability.** Unlike a sole proprietorship or a partnership, if the company gets into financial difficulties, the stockholders are not required to pay the corporation's liabilities out of their own pockets. Their losses are limited to the dollar value of their stock holdings.

There are two basic types of corporations. One is the regular corporation in which profits and losses accrue to the corporation itself and the corporation pays tax on any profits. The stockholders pay tax only when they receive dividends or upon the sale or liquidation of the business. The other type is the S corporation. A corporation with 35 or fewer stockholders may, under certain circumstances, elect S corporation status. Any profit or loss from the S corporation passes directly through to stockholders as though it were ordinary income from any other source. But the stockholders still benefit from the limited liability protection offered by corporate status. Table 2.1 indicates that, in 1985, corporations accounted for 19.4 percent of the total number of businesses, but their business receipts were no less than 90.2 percent of all business receipts.

Large corporations exert a significant market power. The long-term longevity of large corporations, however, is anything but secure. Table 2.2 presents the lists of the largest 25 U.S. industrial firms in 1917 and 70 years later. Only seven firms in the 1917 list were still on the 1986 list.

CORPORATIONS AND STOCK MARKET

Understanding the stock market is important not only to those who own financial securities such as stocks or bonds, but also to those who have been saving for retirement through programs at the place of work. Retirement funds of business and government employees and pension funds of labor unions are invested heavily in stocks and bonds. The stock market is one major place through which corporations raise funds when they need money and in which individuals put their nest eggs hoping that they are safe and their values grow. We are also reminded every day through the reporting of stock prices by television and newspapers that we are living in an environment that is dominated by corporations, if not stocks. In this section, we take a short excursion into the stock market so that

TABLE 2.2 Ranking the Largest 25 U.S. Industrial Firms and Their Assets in 1917 and in 1986

(Assets in $millions)

1917 Ranking		*1986 Ranking*	
1. U.S. Steel	$2,449.5	1. Exxon	$69,160
2. Standard Oil of New Jersey	574.1	2. General Motors	63,833
3. Bethlehem Steel	381.5	3. IBM	52,634
4. Armour and Company	314.1	4. Mobil	41,752
5. Swift and Company	306.3	5. AT&T	40,463
6. Midvale Steel and Ordnance	270.0	6. Chevron	38,899
7. International Harvester	264.7	7. Texaco	37,703
8. E.I. du Pont de Nemours	263.3	8. Ford Motor	31,604
9. U.S. Rubber	257.5	9. Shell Oil	26,528
10. Phelps Dodge	232.3	10. General Electric	26,432
11. General Electric	231.6	11. Amoco	25,198
12. Anaconda Copper	225.8	12. E.I. du Pont de Nemours	25,140
13. American Smelting and Refining Company	221.8	13. Tenneco	20,437
14. Standard Oil of New York	204.3	14. Atlantic Richfield	20,279
15. Singer Manufacturing	192.9	15. U.S. Steel	18,446
16. Ford Motor Company	165.9	16. Standard Oil	18,330
17. Westinghouse Electric and Manufacturing Company	164.7	17. Philip Morris	17,429
18. American Tobacco	164.2	18. R. J. Reynolds Industries	16,930
19. Jones and Laughlin	159.6	19. ITT	14,272
20. Union Carbide and Carbon	155.9	20. Phillips Petroleum	14,045
21. Weyerhaeuser Timber	153.2	21. Allied-Signal	13,271
22. B.F. Goodrich	146.1	22. Sun	12,923
23. Central Leather Company	145.3	23. Chrysler	12,605
24. Texas Company	144.5	24. Eastman Kodak	12,142
25. Pullman	143.3	25. Dow Chemical	11,830

Source: Steven Markman, 1916: The year of living dangerously, *Across the Board* 23(May 1986):44. The 1917 list, from *The visible hand* by Alfred D. Chandler Jr., was compiled from company reports, *Business history review* by Thomas Navin, and Moody's *Manuals of industrial securities.* The current list is from the *Fortune* 25 rankings by assets. Note that only seven of the 25 largest industrial firms today were in the top 25 about 70 years ago. (Standard Oil of New Jersey became Exxon, Standard Oil of New York became Mobil, and Texas Company became Texaco.)

HOW TO READ A STOCK MARKET QUOTATION

A typical stock market quotation reads as follows. The column numbers in the middle row of the quotation are inserted so that columns of the quotation can be explained.

(1)	(2)	(3)	(4)	(5)	(6)	(7)	(8)	(9)	(10)	(11)
52 Weeks				*Yld*	*P-E*	*Sales*				*Net*
High	*Low*	*Stock*	*Div.*	*%*	*Ratio*	*100s*	*High*	*Low*	*Close*	*Chg.*
46	34 3/4	BellSo	2.20	5.9	11	25592	39 1/4	37	37 1/4	1

Columns (1) and (2) show the highest and the lowest closing prices reported for the stock for the preceding 52-week period. Column (3) is the abbreviation of the company name. (BellSo is the BellSouth Corporation, a regional telephone company that was spun off AT&T on January 1, 1984.)

Column (4) indicates dividend rate, or the annual dividend. If no qualifier precedes the dividend, the stock is a common stock. Column (5) is the percent yield, and is calculated by dividing the dividend each share pays by its current market value, expressed in percentage. The higher the dividend rate, ceteris paribus, the better. Column (6) is the price-earnings ratio. It is computed by dividing the stock's selling price by the company's per share earnings for the most recent four quarters. Earnings per share are profits divided by the number of shares outstanding. Although a lower price-earnings ratio is preferable, ceteris paribus, differences may simply reflect company growth prospects, accounting policies, risks, and the stability of the earnings.

Column (7) is the trading volume for the day in hundreds. Whenever z precedes the volume number, the figure that follows represents the actual number of shares traded. For example, z20 means 20 shares, not 2,000 shares. Columns (8) and (9) indicate the trading price range of the stock on the previous day. Column (10) is the last trading price recorded when the market closed the previous day, whereas column (11) indicates the difference between the last closing price reported for the day and the last closing price reported for the preceding day. Financial pages of local newspapers may not print all 11 columns.

Source: Adapted from Dow Jones and Company, Educational Service Bureau, *How to read stock market quotations* (New York: Dow Jones, 1984).

we can understand its basics. Before we study stock markets, however, we need to look closer at the concept of the stock and another type of financial security related to the stock called the bond.

Stocks and Bonds

Common stocks, called simply **stocks** by many, represent shares in the ownership of a corporation. Actual stocks are no more than pieces of paper on which it is stated that the owner of the stock has a certain number of shares in the ownership of a corporation. Companies sell stocks to raise funds for their production activities. Investors buy them to earn dividends and to make money by selling the stocks if their prices rise in the future. **Dividends** are payments by corporations to their stockholders as a return for shares in the ownership of the corporations. Dividends are paid once a quarter (once every three months), but corporations may skip paying dividends if profits are not sufficient to pay them. Stockholders make major decisions on the management of their corporations through the board of directors that they select. Due to the large size of modern corporations, however, most stockholders rarely feel that they are the owners of corporations.[3]

A **bond** is a piece of paper on which the issuer promises the bondholder to pay back a loan, while making an interest payment periodically until the loan is paid back. A bondholder is a creditor, not an owner of the bond's issuing agency. Bonds are issued by a variety of borrowers, including corporations and agencies of governments. The rates paid on bonds vary according to the maturity of the loans and the financial health of the issuing agency. A bond familiar to most of us is the U.S. savings bond. Unlike the U.S. savings bond, which can only be *cashed* before or on the maturity date, however, bonds of corporations can be *bought and sold* among individual investors before the maturity date.

Stock Market

Like other products, stocks are traded in markets, called stock markets. There are two different types of stock markets: stock exchanges and over-the-counter markets. Stocks of relatively large corporations are traded at stock exchanges such as the New York Stock Exchange (known also as the **big board**) and the American Stock Exchange. Stocks of relatively smaller companies are traded through telephone networks of stock brokers, commonly known as the **over-the-counter (OTC) market.**

Buying a Stock
Unlike other products, stocks are traded through stock brokers. To purchase a stock or shares of a stock, one may wish to visit offices of stock brokerage companies such as Merrill Lynch, E. F. Hutton, and Payne Weber, or local depository institutions such as banks or savings and loan associations. There one deals with an individual broker called an **account executive.** If the amount

[3]For a fee, an investor may purchase an **option** to buy or sell a stock at a fixed price for a fixed time period. The option to buy is known as a **call.** If the stock price goes up by an amount greater than the fee, the trader who has a call makes a profit. The option to sell is known as a **put.** A profit on a put is made when a stock price falls by an amount greater than the fee to buy the put. For more on option trading, see James Greenleaf, Ruth Foster, and Robert Prinsky, *Understanding financial data in the Wall Street Journal* (New York: Dow Jones, 1983).

of money available for the purchase of stocks is rather small, one may consider opening a **sharebuilder's plan** offered by large stock brokerage firms. In a sharebuilder's plan, small amounts of money are submitted to the stock brokerage firm for the purchase of fractions of stocks. Unless the person who buys stocks is familiar with the market, account executives usually recommend the purchase of blue chip stocks. A **blue chip** refers to a company, or stocks of the company, that is a well-established leader in its industry and has a long history of dividend payment. Note that in poker playing and in casino gambling, the blue chip is usually the one with the highest value.

Stock Split

Sometimes, a stock is split in order to attract more investors for the stock. A **stock split** is an offering of additional shares of a given amount of stock with an intent to lower the per-share price of the stock. Stocks are split usually to attract additional buyers of the company's stocks. In spring 1987, for instance, there was a three-to-two split of BellSouth stocks. Those who owned 200 shares of the BellSouth stock were offered an additional 100 shares of the same stock so that the total number of shares after the stock split became 300. Shortly before the stock split, the price per share of BellSouth stock was about $60. Shortly after the stock split, the per-share price of the stock decreased to about $40.

Predicting Stock Prices

Perhaps one of the most interesting questions about the stock market is whether or not an accurate prediction of short-term stock prices can be made. Several hypotheses have been suggested. According to the **hemline hypothesis,** stock prices go up about six months after women's hemlines go up and stock prices go down about six months after women's hemlines go down. According to the **Super Bowl hypothesis,** stock prices rise during a given year if the winner of the Super Bowl is from the old National Football League, and stock prices fall if the winner is from the old American Football League. On a more serious note, Professor Burton Malkiel of the Yale University School of Organization and Management proposed a **random walk theory.** A random walk is defined as one in which future steps or directions cannot be predicted on the basis of past actions. When the term is applied to the stock market, it means that short-run changes in stock prices cannot be predicted. Taken to its logical extreme, it means that a blindfolded monkey throwing darts at a newspaper's financial pages could select a portfolio of stocks that would do just as well as one carefully selected by the experts.[4]

Price of a Bond and Interest Rate

Prices of stocks are influenced by numerous factors, but there is one main determinant of the price of a bond: the market rate of interest. Consider a corporate bond whose market price is $1,000. Assume that the market rate of interest is 10 percent, and that the bondholder receives $100 per year as a return for the ownership of the bond. What the company issuing the bond promises the bondholder is the periodic payment of a fixed amount, not the periodic payment of a fixed percentage of the bond price. There is no incentive for the bondholder to buy more bonds or sell the bond since a $1,000 investment is expected to yield a $100 return at the 10 percent interest rate. Suppose that the market rate of interest falls to 5 percent. To enjoy a $100 return at the 5 percent

---

[4]For more on the random walk theory, see Burton G. Malkiel, *A random walk down Wall Street,* 4th ed. (New York: W. W. Norton, 1985), p. 16.

interest rate, we need $2,000 since 5 percent of $2,000 is $100. The price of a bond fluctuates, while the promised annual return, $100, does not. The market price of the bond that promises a $100 return per year, therefore, will rise to $2,000. There is an *inverse* relation between the price of a bond and the market rate of interest. In reality, the price of a bond may change inversely with the *expected* changes in interest rates rather than *actual* changes in interest rates.

ECONOMIC SYSTEMS

One meaning of **institution** is an accepted way of doing things in a given society. Institutions, therefore, include marriage, driving on the right-hand side of the road, and other traditions to which a society is accustomed. Economic systems are typically classified according to economic institutions or practices in a given society.

Institutions that are of concern to students of economics are those that affect how resources are allocated among competing uses. For instance, societies have to answer such questions as whether to produce more military goods or more civilian goods, and how much more. Societies should also decide whether to increase the production of automobiles or the construction of housing units. The U.S. economy may need to make decisions on whether or not additional Old River control structures should be built to keep the Mississippi River from changing its course to Atchafalaya, or on whether future needs for electricity should be met with coal or nuclear power. Broadly classifying, there are two institutions through which decisions on resource allocation are made: the market and the government. All societies utilize both the market and the government for the allocation of resources. Economic systems are classified depending on how important the market is as a means of allocating resources in comparison to the government in a given society.

Types of economic systems mentioned frequently by many include capitalism, socialism, fascism, and communism. On May 13, 1987, for instance, Earl Nightingale made comments of the following nature on a CBS radio show: "If democracy is combined with private ownership of resources, we have capitalism. If democracy is combined with public ownership of resources, we have socialism. If dictatorship is combined with private ownership of resources, we have fascism. And if dictatorship is combined with public ownership of resources, we have communism." The reality is that no two economists are likely to agree on which institutions are needed to define each of the four systems, and how many, if any, of the four systems are economic systems rather than political or economic *and* political systems. Keeping this difficulty in mind, let us study the essentials of the four systems.

Capitalism

Institutions that characterize **capitalism** are private ownership of productive resources, free competition, price system, and limited government.

Private Property
Private ownership of productive resources means that individuals in a given economy have the right to buy, sell, and control productive resources such as land, labor, capital, and entrepreneurship. If an individual has resources or the financial ability to acquire resources, the individual may

DOW JONES AVERAGES

Charles Henry Dow and Edward D. Jones started Dow Jones and Company in 1882. Dow started computing an average of stock prices in 1884. The first index included only 11 stocks, of which nine were railroad stocks, reflecting the importance of railroads in those days. Over time, the roster of the index was expanded to 30. The first publication of an average comparable to today's 30 industrial stocks was made on October 1, 1928. The widely quoted Dow Jones Industrial Average is one of four stock averages compiled by the *Wall Street Journal*. Others are Dow Jones Transportation, composed of 20 transportation issues, Dow Jones Utility, composed of 15 utilities, and a composite of all 65 stocks. Stocks are selected in such a way as to represent the broad market or the industry that these stocks belong to.

When the averages were first computed, the index was obtained by adding the prices of selected stocks and dividing the total by the number of stocks included in the index. Suppose that there are three stocks priced at $5, 10, 15 each. The index then is $(5 + 10 + 15)/3 = 10$. The divisor is 3. As stocks are split and the roster of companies included in the index changes over time, the divisor no longer represents the number of stocks. Suppose that the $15 stock is split three for one, which would make the new share sell for $5. If the same method is used, the index will be $(5 + 10 + 5)/3 = 6.67$. Adjustment, therefore, is made so that the average remains at 10 after the stock split. The formula to calculate a new divisor is

$$\frac{\text{former divisor}}{\text{former total value}} = \frac{\text{new divisor}}{\text{new total value}}$$

That is,

$$3/30 = x/20$$
$$30x = 60$$
$$x = 2$$

The new index after the stock split is

$$(5 + 10 + 5)/2 = 10.$$

The divisor at this time is less than 2, and it does not remotely resemble the number of stocks included in computing the index. The latest change in the roster of the Dow Industrial Average occurred in October 1985 when General Foods Corporation and American Brands, Inc., were dropped and in their places Philip Morris and McDonald's were added. Of the companies in the original 30-stock index, 14 are still there, although some such as Exxon are listed under names different from the original ones.

Source: Adapted from Dow Jones and Company, Educational Service Bureau, *The Dow Jones averages: A non-professional's guide,* rev. ed., 1986.

produce any product that he or she wants to produce. In a system of private ownership of productive resources, a person may work in any field that the person wishes to work in. In reality, however, the right to buy, sell, and control resources is somewhat restricted even in a capitalistic economic system by the tradition of social groups or government regulation. A person's right to work is restricted by the availability of jobs in the desired field.

Free Competition

Free competition in capitalism is based on self-interest: the profit motive for producers and the motive of maximum utility for consumers. The power or ability of goods and services to satisfy consumers' wants is called **utility.** Capitalism is a highly efficient economic system because it provides a strong incentive for individual members of the economy to work hard. Capitalism allows producers to freely pursue greater profits, and allows consumers to freely pursue greater utility. When producers and consumers are allowed to pursue their own self-interest and keep the rewards of their efforts, they are expected to do their best.

Price System

Private property and free competition need an environment in which they can interact for maximum efficiency. The environment is provided by the price system, in which demand and supply forces freely interact to properly signal shortages and surpluses through changing prices. As a shortage develops in an industry, the price of the product rises and the profits of businesses that operate in the industry increase. As profits increase in the industry, more businesses move into the industry and make the market more competitive. If a surplus develops in an industry, the reverse chain action occurs.

Government

Capitalism even in its pure form cannot exist without government. The role of government in capitalism, however, is limited in comparison to other systems. People known as conservatives claim that in capitalism the government should pursue a policy of *laissez faire* with respect to economic activities, whereas those known as liberals claim that the role of government should be expanded to solve many social ills. **Laissez faire** (*let* people *do* as they please) refers to a doctrine that opposes government interference in economic affairs beyond the minimum necessary for the maintenance of law and order.

There are many capitalist countries, including the United States, but no country is purely capitalistic. Competition among sellers without any interference or threat of interference from the government may create markets that are highly concentrated among a few sellers. Some markets become concentrated because if left alone, certain firms become more efficient than others and can produce products at a lower unit cost as their size increases. Other markets become concentrated because larger firms buy smaller ones in the same industry. As markets are concentrated into a few large firms in an industry, competition is not likely to remain free. The very nature of competition requires a certain extent of government intervention to preserve competition. In capitalistic economic systems such as the U.S. economy, government plays an increasingly larger role in preserving competition, promoting social welfare, and regulating the private sector of the economy. Hence, economic systems such as ours are sometimes called **mixed economies** rather than capitalist economies.

Other Systems

Three noncapitalistic systems are briefly introduced in this section: socialism, fascism, and communism.

Socialism

Socialism is characterized by public ownership of productive resources. Ideas of socialism have been promoted to construct a system that would modify alleged weaknesses of capitalism. Institutions of socialism beyond the public ownership of productive resources, therefore, vary, depending on the extent of modification that different socialists envision.

In pure socialism, the rights of private property are limited to consumption goods. Productive resources such as land and capital are owned by the government. In countries such as France, Greece, and Britain, whose economies are sometimes called socialistic economies, the public ownership of productive resources is limited to key large-scale industries such as banks, railroads, coal, and aluminum industries. Most socialists agree that private individuals should be allowed to own and operate small farms and stores, while others suggest that industries beyond the key large-scale industries should be left to the private sector. Socialism also retains the price system, but decisions on the kinds and quantities of major products traded in the price system are made by the government. Socialists claim that prices in the capitalist system reflect not the desires of the people, but the desires of those who have large sums of money.

Fascism

Fascism is an economic and political system that, like capitalism, allows private ownership of productive resources, but is run by one political party that is determined to perpetuate its own power. Fascism is illustrated by Mussolini's Italy, Franco's Spain, Peron's Argentina, Marcos's Philippines, and Hitler's Germany. Fascists typically oppose communism, prompting some people to quip that opposing communism is the only good thing about fascism. At least in the beginning, fascist governments encourage the private ownership of productive resources. One problem with fascism is the tendency of a long-term alliance to develop between the government and large businesses. The alliance inevitably breeds corruption. A variation of fascism is an economic system in which there is one ruling party that permits one or more opposition parties whose political activities are free so long as these activities do not threaten the power of the ruling party. Economic systems in this type of fascism are basically capitalistic in that most decisions are made by the private sector. Because of the absence of political freedom, however, a long-term coalition tends to develop between the ruling party and leading businesses.

Communism

The idea of modern communism was developed by Karl Marx, and is thus called Marxian communism. Marxian communism emerged as a major political idea when Lenin's Bolsheviks took power away from the moderate but inept Czarist government of Russia.

THE IDEA. In capitalism, Marx claimed, there are the **bourgeoisie** (capitalists), who own property or capital, and the **proletariat** (workers), who own only their labor. Workers are paid wages that are at the subsistence level. Capitalists receive the rest of what is produced in the economy. Some products are purchased by workers as consumption goods and others are purchased by capitalists as capital goods as well as consumption goods. Since workers' wages are suppressed by the

KARL MARX

The idea of modern communism originated with Karl Marx. Marx was born on May 5, 1818 at Trier, Prussia, which is now part of West Germany. Marx wrote a doctoral dissertation titled *The difference between the Democritean and Epicurean philosophies of nature* and received his Ph.D. at the University of Jena in 1841. After living in Germany, Paris, and Brussels, where his views were treated with suspicion, Marx and his family settled in London in the fall of 1849. The *Communist manifesto* was published in London in February 1848 and *Capital, Volume one* was published in 1867. Marx predicted the collapse of advanced capitalism and the coming of socialism and communism. The Marxian view of communism has been interpreted in many different ways, and predictions made by Marx have not been accurate. For reasons that are more political than economic, Marxism still influences about a third of the world population. Marx died on March 14, 1883.

capitalists at the subsistence level and are not enough to purchase products that are unsold, occasional and sometimes prolonged economic depressions are unavoidable. As competition for more profit among capitalists intensifies, the income difference between the smaller size bourgeoisie and the expanding proletariat increases and depressions reach the crisis level. In the Marxian view, the profit-oriented production mechanism of capitalism is highly efficient.

The very mechanism that makes capitalism successful, however, unintentionally promotes its own demise through an insufficient demand for the products produced in the economy. Eventually, the workers topple the bourgeoisie government, abolish private ownership of productive resources, and establish a socialist state under the leadership of the proletariat. Capitalism is converted to socialism, which then becomes **communism** in which, according to Marx's ideal, there are no problems of government, scarcity, or conflicting classes. Individuals work according to their abilities and consume according to their needs.

THE REALITY. The reality of communistic systems did not quite develop as Marx envisioned. According to Marx, capitalistic nations that are most industrialized will turn to communism through the uprising of workers. The first communistic revolution, however, came in Russia, which was devastated by World War I, not in industrialized European nations. Eastern European countries such as Poland, Hungary, and East Germany became communistic countries not because they were advanced capitalistic economies, but because communism was forced upon them following World War II. Other countries, such as China and Cuba, that turned to communism after World War II did so not because they were industrially advanced, but because of internal corruption.

THE FUTURE. Looking to the future of communism, the 1990s loom as one of the most important periods in the history of communism, if not in the history of economic systems. In December 1978 China held the third plenum of the Eleventh Communist Party Central Committee, during which Deng Xiaoping consolidated his power as the overall leader. China then began a modernization movement that centered on people and the conditions necessary for creativity of individuals. The new policy freed peasants from collective farming, provided incentives for factory workers and managers, and established special industrial zones that offered tax breaks and cheap land for foreign investors. Since the 1980s China has also experimented with the market determination of prices for a wide range of goods and services.

Similar changes are also being attempted in the USSR under the banners of *perestroika* (restructuring) and *glasnost* (openness), the policies of Mikhail Gorbachev, who became General Secretary of the Communist party in 1985. Perhaps the most interesting question regarding these significant changes occurring in China and Russia is how far this economic freedom can be stretched without a concomitant broadening of political freedom in these two countries that are basically dictatorial. A telling evidence that this concern is real occurred on June 3, 1989, when the 27th Army soldiers of China killed students of the democracy movement and their supporters at Tiananmen Square in Beijing. The number of deaths remains unknown but is believed to be in the thousands.

SUMMARY

Economic exchange occurs in a circular flow between sellers and buyers of final products and the factors of production needed to produce these final products. The economic circular flow includes foreign trade as well as trade within a domestic economy. The exchange rate of the currencies of the trading countries affects the amount of exports. For example, if the price of the dollar in terms of yen falls, imports from Japan to the United States decrease and exports from the United States to Japan increase. There are three basic forms of business organizations: sole proprietorship, partnership, and corporation. Sole proprietorship is a business in which the owner is self-employed. A partnership is a form of business organization in which two or more persons join together to carry on a trade or business. A corporation is a legal entity that is owned by one or more stockholders who, unlike sole proprietors and partners, are subject to limited liability. A bond is a piece of paper on which issuers promise the bondholder to pay back the loan and to make a fixed interest payment periodically until the loan is paid back. There is an inverse relation between the price of a bond and the market rate of interest. Stocks of relatively large corporations are traded on stock exchanges, while stocks of relatively smaller companies are traded through the over-the-counter (OTC) market. A blue chip refers to a company, or stocks of the company, that is a leader in its industry and has a long history of dividend payment. Stock split is an offering of additional shares of a given amount of stock with an intent to lower the per-share price of the stock. An accurate prediction of short-term stock prices cannot be made.

Institutions of capitalism are private ownership of productive resources, free competition, the price system, and limited government. The laissez faire doctrine opposes government interference with the private sector such as regulation or subsidy in economic affairs beyond the minimum necessary for the maintenance of property rights. Socialism is characterized by public ownership of major productive resources such as banks, railroads, and the coal industry. Fascism allows private ownership of productive resources under one political party that perpetuates its power. The idea of modern communism was developed by Karl Marx. According to Marx, the very mechanism that makes capitalism successful promotes its own demise.

EXERCISES

1. List the three types of business organization, and define each.

2. Explain what is meant by limited liability in business organizations.

3. How are stocks different from bonds?

4. When news media report on daily changes in the Dow-Jones index, what do the changes measure?

5. What lessons can be learned from the economic circular flow that encompasses all four sectors—household, business, government, and foreign sectors?

6. What are the major institutions of capitalism? How is socialism different from capitalism?

7. In *Economics and the public purpose,* published in 1973 by Houghton Mifflin, Professor John Kenneth Galbraith presents a *liberal* view of the size of the American government, the view that the government has not become too big. Reasons cited by Professor Galbraith include (1) government must take action to minimize unemployment and inflation, (2) government must provide those things that are not available from the private sector, and (3) government must protect individuals from circumstances with which they cannot contend. Presented in the same text is the view of Professor Tibor Scitovsky that the role of government has become too large, known as the *conservative* view. Taking an example of welfare programs in general, what seems to be the major difference between the conservative view and the liberal view?

8. Someone once said, "Capitalism is highly efficient but not very equitable." Assuming that the term *equitable* means a relatively equal distribution of income among the residents of an economy, how can capitalism be made more equitable?

9. In Denmark, Norway, Sweden, and Finland, the idea that the government should provide a wide range of services, especially in health care and education, is so popular that it is not unusual for the public to demand and receive more welfare spending, but with the conflicting idea of placing a cap on tax increases. Are the economic systems of these countries capitalistic or socialistic?

10. If the price of the dollar in terms of Mexican pesos falls, how will the falling value of the dollar affect the trade between the United States and Mexico?

SUGGESTED READINGS

Chandler, Alfred D., Jr. (1977). *The visible hand: The managerial revolution in American business,* Cambridge, Mass.: Harvard University Press.

A Pulitzer Prize winning book discussing the rise of modern business enterprise and the ascendancy of the manager.

Dow Jones and Company, Educational Service Bureau. *The Dow Jones averages: A non-professional's guide,* revised ed. (1986); *How to read stock market quotations* (1984); and *Understanding financial data in the Wall Street Journal* (1963). New York: Dow Jones.

These three publications explain the stock market in easy-to-read lay terms.

Malkiel, Burton G. (1985). *A random walk down Wall Street*. New York: W. W. Norton.

Explains investment strategies above and beyond the random walk theory.

Scitovsky, Tibor. (1980). Can capitalism survive? An old question in a new setting. *American Economic Review* 70(May): 1–9.

The Richard T. Ely lecture presented at the 1979 meeting of the American Economic Association; discusses the inflexibility of modern capitalism.

Weber, Max. (1958). *The Protestant ethic and the spirit of capitalism*. Translated by Talcott Parsons. New York: Charles Scribner's Sons.

An important reference explaining the contribution made by Protestant ethics during the early stage of development of modern capitalism.

3

Demand, Supply, and Market Equilibrium

Market Demand

Market Supply

Market Equilibrium

Shifts in Demand and Supply Curves

Price Ceilings and Price Floors

WHEN WE ARE HUNGRY, we think of McDonald's or Godfather's Pizza. When we actually go to these fast food places, we never worry about whether they will have enough Big Macs or pizzas for us. Shouldn't we worry about it? How do they know that we are coming? Of course, they do not know that *we* are coming, but they know that someone will. In a market economy, stores tend to carry products that customers want and customers usually find products that they want at their favorite stores. A market economy is one in which competition works through the interaction of supply and demand. Individual sellers pursue private interests by selling the quantity and charging the price that will maximize their profits. Individual buyers, on the other hand, pursue private interests by selecting the bundle of goods and services that will maximize their satisfaction. There is no order imposed from above, but there is a sense of orderliness in the market.

The price system does more than provide orderliness. Given an appropriate environment that promotes competition in the market, the price system is capable of harmonizing private interests with the society's interests. The spontaneous harmony of the potentially conflicting interests of society and the individuals who comprise the society is explained by Adam Smith as the workings of an **invisible hand.** These days, the invisible hand is known as the mechanism of demand and supply. The structure of economic systems may be different among nations, but the mechanism of demand and supply works in much the same way in different economic systems. In this chapter, we study the concepts of demand and supply, how demand and supply determine the market price and the quantity of goods and services exchanged in the market, and how the market responds to governmental actions that thwart the rationing function of the price.

MARKET DEMAND

A **market** is an arrangement in which sellers of a good or service interact with buyers of the good or service. Some markets are centered in a particular location that allows personal contact between buyers and sellers, while other markets are organized through an indirect contact between buyers and sellers. Markets of the first type include the New York Stock Exchange, the French Market in New Orleans, Quincy Market in Boston, and any store in the neighborhood. Markets of the second type include mail-orders and facsimile orders across nations. In both types of markets, there are suppliers who are willing to produce and sell a given good or service and demanders who have money and are willing to buy the good or service.

What Is Demand?

Demand is said to exist when consumers capable of paying for a good or service are willing to buy the good or service in order to satisfy their wants. When consumers desire a product but do not have money, their demand is not effective since transactions are not possible without the means to pay.

Market demand refers to the quantities of a good or service that are demanded by all buyers in any given market at various prices. A schedule that shows the relation between different prices and the quantities demanded at these prices in a market is called a market demand schedule. Although market demand consists of individual demands, market demand is more important than individual demands for two reasons. One is that market demand tends to be more consistent than individual demands in exhibiting rational economic behavior such as the law of demand, and the other is that market demand, when it is combined with market supply, determines market price and the quantity exchanged.

Law of Demand

At any given time, there is a definite relation between the price of a good or service and the quantity of it demanded. The relation is *inverse,* which means that as the price of a good or service increases, the quantity of the good or service demanded is expected to decrease. Also, as the price of a good or service decreases, the quantity of the good or service demanded is expected to increase. This inverse relationship between the price of a product and the quantity of the product demanded is observed with such regularity that it is called the **law of demand.** Let us illustrate how the law of demand can be applied in consideration of policy alternatives affecting society.

Illustration One
The first illustration relates to water. We drink it, use it to wash, and use it to grow farm products and manufacture goods. We almost take for granted that rain will replenish whatever amount of water we may use up. Water, however, is no longer the infinitely renewable resource that we once thought it was. Consider the giant Ogallala aquifer, which stretches nearly 800 miles under eight states from the Texas panhandle to South Dakota.[1] The aquifer provides about 30 percent of the total irrigation needs in the United States and serves as the water source for 200,000 wells in 180 counties and for 40 percent of the nation's beef cattle. Water is being drawn from the Ogallala aquifer eight times faster than nature can replenish the supply, creating huge sinkholes in the Texas panhandle. Economists believe that part of the problem is that water has traditionally been underpriced. The law of demand indicates that a higher price of water will reduce the quantity of water used. One solution for the rapidly decreasing water resources, therefore, would be to make it more expensive for consumers to use the water.

Illustration Two
Another illustration of the law of demand and its impact on society relates to raising the minimum drinking age.[2] In 1984 Congress passed a law that would reduce federal highway funds to states that did not raise their minimum drinking age to 21 by 1986. The question is whether it is proper to discriminate against young adults by denying them legal access to alcoholic beverages when they are old enough to vote and, well, go to war.

Studies by Michael Grossman and his associates at the National Bureau of Economic Research confirm what the law of demand tells us: that higher prices cause a cutback in drinking, especially by young adults. The government cannot raise the price of alcoholic beverages, but it can raise taxes on alcoholic beverages so that consumers pay more for them. A 10 cent increase in the price of a bottle of beer has been found to reduce young adults' drinking by as much as a one-year increase in the minimum drinking age. Raising taxes instead of minimum drinking ages would reduce drinking by young adults and raise tax revenue at the same time. Keep in mind, though, that the solution of raising taxes to reduce drinking by young adults is favored by free market economists, but not necessarily by liberal economists.

[1]Berkeley Rice, Water shocks of the '80s, *Across the Board* 23(March 1986): 17–23.
[2]Gary S. Becker, Don't raise the drinking age, raise taxes, *Business Week,* November 25, 1985, p. 21.

TABLE 3.1 Price per Ounce of National
Brand FCOJ and Ounces of National Brand
FCOJ Demanded per Consumer per Week

Combination	Price per Ounce of FCOJ in Cents	Ounces of FCOJ Demanded per Consumer per Week
A	34.84	0.00
B	20.00	4.90
C	8.80	8.60
D	5.00	9.85
E	0.00	11.50

Demand Curve

The inverse relation between the price of a good or service and the quantity of the good or service demanded can be presented on a simple graph. To illustrate a demand curve, let us take the example of the frozen concentrated orange juice (FCOJ) market in the United States.

The orange juice industry has tried for about 40 years to manufacture a processed juice that tastes as fresh as if it came directly from an orange. Four types of processed orange juice are available: (1) FCOJ, the processing of which preserves some of the fresh orange quality; (2) canned juice, the processing of which requires high heat, leaving behind little of the fresh orange quality; (3) chilled juice, most of which is made from FCOJ; and (4) boxed juice, which is packed in a germ-free environment and tastes about the same as canned juice. Of the four, a demand function has been estimated for FCOJ. A **demand function** is an algebraic statement of the relation between the quantity of a product demanded and the determinants of its quantity demanded. Price of the product is most important of these determinants. An *estimated* demand function is a demand function that is tested against actual price and quantity data of a product.

Using survey data collected from 9,552 consumers during July 1981 through June 1982, Lee, Brown, and Schwartz estimated a linear demand function of national brand frozen concentrated orange juice.[3] The relation between price per ounce of national brand FCOJ in cents and the quantity

---

[3] The empirical demand function of frozen concentrated orange juice presented in this chapter was adapted from Jong-Ying Lee, Mark G. Brown, and Brooke Schwartz, The demand for national brand and private label frozen concentrated orange juice: A switching regression analysis, a working paper by the Florida Agricultural Experiment Station, 1986, published later in the *Western Journal of Agricultural Economics* 11(July 1986):1–7. The demand function for national brand FCOJ estimated by Lee, Brown, and Schwartz is simplified below with price as the only independent variable:

$$Q = 11.5 - 0.3301\, P,$$

where Q is the quantity of FCOJ in ounces purchased per person during the person's weekly shopping trip and P is the price per ounce of FCOJ. The demand schedule presented in Table 3.1 is obtained by plugging selective price figures into the equation and computing quantities that correspond to the alternative price figures.

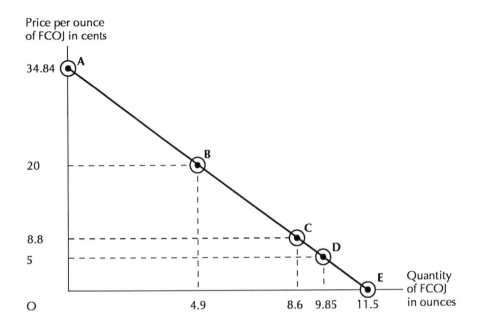

FIGURE 3.1 Demand Curve for FCOJ. As the price per ounce of FCOJ decreases from 34.84 cents to zero, the quantity of FCOJ demanded per consumer for any given week increases from zero to 11.5 ounces.

of national brand FCOJ in ounces demanded per consumer during the consumer's weekly shopping trip is summarized in Table 3.1 on the basis of their estimated demand function. Five combinations are shown in the table. These combinations range from a zero price, at which 11.5 ounces of FCOJ are demanded, to a price of 34.84 cents per ounce, at which no FCOJ is demanded.

The demand curve for FCOJ is graphed in Figure 3.1. The procedure for drawing the demand curve is as follows. First, draw two lines, one vertical and the other horizontal. Second, write "Price per ounce of FCOJ" on top of the vertical line to measure price on the vertical line, and write "Quantity of FCOJ in ounces" at the end of the horizontal line to measure quantity on the horizontal line. Third, write values obtained in Table 3.1 in such a way that combinations A, B, C, D, and E can be identified clearly in the graph. When the five combinations are connected, the demand curve for FCOJ is obtained. The demand curve reveals the same information that Table 3.1 contains. When price per ounce of FCOJ is 5 cents, the quantity of FCOJ demanded is 9.85 ounces per consumer per week. When price is 8.8 cents per ounce, the quantity of FCOJ demanded is 8.6 ounces. The inverse relation between price and quantity is indicated by the *negative* slope of the curve. If a curve is negative, it slopes downward to the right.

MARKET SUPPLY

If demand is one blade of the scissors that is the market, market supply is the other. Just as the two blades of a scissors must work together to cut paper, so are the price of a product and the quantity of the product traded in the market determined only if information is available on both market demand and market supply.

What Is Supply?

Supply refers to the quantities of a good or service that a seller is willing and able to make available for sale in the market at various prices. A schedule that shows the relation between different prices and quantities supplied at these prices is called a market supply schedule. **Market supply** is a summation of all supply schedules of individual firms in any given market. Although market supply consists of supply schedules of individual firms, market supply is more important than individual firms' supply schedules for two reasons. One is that market supply tends to be more consistent than individual firms' supply schedules in exhibiting rational economic behavior such as the law of supply, and the other is that market supply, when it is combined with market demand, determines market price.

Law of Supply

At any given time, there is a definite relation between the price of a good or service and the quantity of it supplied. The relation is *direct*. This means that as the price of a product increases, the quantity of the product supplied is expected to increase as well. As the price of a product decreases, the quantity of the product supplied is expected to decrease. This direct relation between the price of a product and the quantity of the product supplied, although observed with less regularity than the law of demand, is called the **law of supply.**

Supply Curve

The direct relation between the price of a good or service and the quantity of the good or service supplied can be presented on a simple graph. Consider again the frozen concentrated orange juice market, and assume that the quantity of FCOJ supplied depends solely on the price of FCOJ. A market supply schedule showing the relation between price per ounce of national brand FCOJ and the quantity of national brand FCOJ in ounces supplied per week by its average supplier is presented in Table 3.2.[4] The table shows five combinations of the price of FCOJ and the quantity of FCOJ

---

[4]The law of supply does not work as well as the law of demand, explaining in part why there is such a paucity of estimated supply functions. The supply schedule of FCOJ in Table 3.2 is based on a hypothetical supply function that is derived in such a way as to generate the price and the quantity of FCOJ exchanged as indicated in the study by Lee, Brown, and Schwartz. The hypothetical supply function is

$$Q = -4.6 + 1.5\,P.$$

TABLE 3.2 Price per Ounce of National
Brand FCOJ and Ounces of National Brand
FCOJ Supplied per Seller per Week

Combination	Price per Ounce of FCOJ in Cents	Ounces of FCOJ Supplied per Seller per Week
F	3.07	0.00
G	5.00	2.90
H	8.80	8.60
I	10.00	10.40
J	15.00	17.90

supplied. The combinations range from a price of 3.07 cents per ounce, at which the quantity of FCOJ supplied is zero, to a price of 15 cents per ounce, at which the quantity supplied is 17.9 ounces.[5]

The supply curve for FCOJ is graphed in Figure 3.2. The procedure for drawing the supply curve is the same as for drawing the demand curve. The supply curve reveals the same information that Table 3.2 contains. When price is 5 cents per ounce, the quantity of FCOJ supplied is 2.9 ounces. When price is 8.8 cents per ounce, the quantity of FCOJ supplied is 8.6 ounces. The direct relation between price and quantity supplied is indicated by the *positive* slope of the curve. If a curve is positive, it slopes upward to the right.

MARKET EQUILIBRIUM

In any given market, demand for a good or service interacts with supply of the good or service, resulting in a price that clears the market. Clearing the market means that the price equates the quantity demanded and the quantity supplied for the good or service. The price that equates the quantity of a product demanded and the quantity of the product supplied is called the **equilibrium price.** The quantity exchanged at the equilibrium price is called the **equilibrium quantity.** Equilibrium means an equality between opposing forces. In a market equilibrium, the opposing

---

[5]The examples of market demand and market supply in this chapter are presented for the average consumer and the average supplier. The use of these examples rather than demand by all consumers and supply by all suppliers in the market is due partly to the fact that the empirical demand function for FCOJ was estimated for the average consumer, and partly to consideration of the readability of these examples to students. The quantity of FCOJ demanded by the average consumer and the quantity of FCOJ supplied by the average supplier are converted to demand by all consumers and supply by all suppliers in the market, if the two quantities are multiplied respectively by the number of consumers and the number of suppliers in the market.

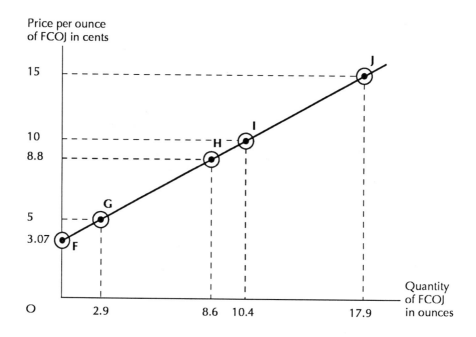

FIGURE 3.2 Supply Curve for FCOJ. As the price per ounce of FCOJ increases from 3.07 cents to 15 cents, the quantity of FCOJ supplied per week by the average supplier of FCOJ increases from zero to 17.9 ounces.

forces acting on price are balanced, so that there is no tendency of price to move up or down. The market equilibrium is achieved through a balancing act between too much demand, which tends to raise price, and too much supply, which tends to lower price. In this section, we study how the mechanism of demand and supply enables the market to achieve equilibrium.

Equilibrium Price and Quantity

To see how a market equilibrium is achieved, let us bring demand for and supply of FCOJ together by superimposing the demand curve graphed in Figure 3.1 and the supply curve graphed in Figure 3.2. The two curves are superimposed in Figure 3.3.

A market is in equilibrium when quantity demanded equals quantity supplied. The point where demand and supply curves intersect is called the equilibrium point. The equilibrium price is located when a line is drawn horizontally from the equilibrium point until the line reaches the vertical price line. The equilibrium price in Figure 3.3 is 8.8 cents per ounce. The equilibrium quantity is located when a line is drawn vertically from the equilibrium point until the line reaches the horizontal quantity line. The equilibrium quantity in Figure 3.3 is 8.6 ounces per week. In other

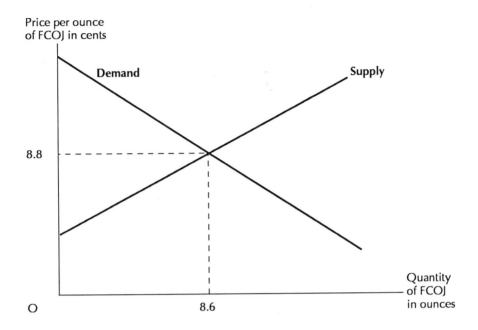

FIGURE 3.3 Market Equilibrium of FCOJ. Market equilibrium is located where demand and supply curves intersect. The equilibrium price is 8.8 cents per ounce, and the quantity exchanged between the average consumer and the average supplier at the equilibrium price is 8.6 ounces per week.

words, at the equilibrium price of 8.8 cents per ounce of FCOJ, the quantity of FCOJ demanded and the quantity of FCOJ supplied are equal to each other at 8.6 ounces per person per week.

If, for some reason, the market price of FCOJ were pushed below the equilibrium price to, say, 5 cents per ounce, the quantity of FCOJ demanded would be greater at 9.85 ounces per week than its quantity supplied at 2.9 ounces. When consumers want more than is made available by suppliers, the price of the product is expected to rise. If the market price of FCOJ were pushed above the equilibrium price, the quantity of FCOJ supplied would exceed its quantity demanded. When the quantity of a product made available by suppliers is greater than the quantity that consumers are willing and able to buy, the price of the product is expected to fall. It may be that no one will ever know what the equilibrium price and the quantity exchanged at the equilibrium price are for any given market. Markets, however, continue to move toward the elusive equilibrium point.

Equilibrium price (and quantity) conveys no value judgment. In a highly competitive market, the market price may well be the equilibrium price. Some buyers may feel that equilibrium prices are too high for their liking, while some sellers may feel that equilibrium prices are too low for their liking. Potential buyers are excluded from buying a given product when its equilibrium price is too high for their income, while some suppliers may go out of business when the equilibrium price is

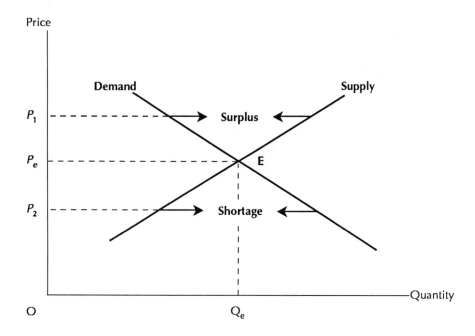

FIGURE 3.4 Generalizing Market Equilibrium. In a given market, market equilibrium is located where the demand and supply curves intersect. A surplus develops at a price higher than the equilibrium price, and a shortage develops at a price lower than the equilibrium price.

too low to cover their cost of production. The meaning of the equilibrium price remains unchanged, however. Equilibrium price is the level of price at which the quantity of a product demanded is equal to the quantity of the product supplied so that the market is cleared.

Signaling Shortages and Surpluses

Let us generalize what we have found in Figure 3.3 by drawing in Figure 3.4 demand and supply curves that are unrelated to any specific product.

The negative slope of the demand curve in Figure 3.4 reflects the law of demand, while the positive slope of the supply curve reflects the law of supply. The demand curve and supply curve intersect at point E, which is the equilibrium point. Any price above the equilibrium level, such as

P_1, creates a *surplus*, since at P_1 the quantity supplied is greater than the quantity demanded by the distance indicated as surplus. Any price below the equilibrium level, such as P_2, creates a *shortage*, since at P_2 the quantity demanded is greater than the quantity supplied by the distance indicated as shortage.

When a surplus develops in a market, sellers will find unsold goods piling up in their storage rooms or have difficulty attracting customers. The existence of a surplus forces sellers to lower the price of their goods or services toward the equilibrium price. When a shortage develops in a market, sellers will find goods selling too fast and inventories disappearing rapidly from their storage rooms. The existence of a shortage forces sellers to raise the price of their goods or services toward the equilibrium price. Changing prices signal the existence of a surplus or a shortage.

SHIFTS IN DEMAND AND SUPPLY CURVES

As long as the determinants of demand and supply do not change, the equilibrium price and the quantity exchanged at the equilibrium price are not expected to change. There are so many determinants affecting demand for and supply of a given product, however, that it is unlikely that all these determinants will remain unchanged for any length of time. In this section, we study the major factors that influence demand and supply, and learn how changes in these factors affect the demand and supply model presented in the preceding section.

DETERRENT EFFECTS OF CAPITAL PUNISHMENT

Economic theory suggests that individuals respond to incentives and penalties embodied in the criminal justice system. Stated in simple terms, increases in the severity of punishment are expected to diminish homicidal behavior. If execution is the most severe punishment, it will be the greatest deterrent. Wolpin developed a model similar to a demand function to analyze the pattern of homicides in England and Wales from 1929 to 1968. His findings indicate that executing one additional murderer, ceteris paribus, reduced the number of homicides by 0.0932 per million population. Evaluated at the average population of England and Wales, this finding means that each execution of a convicted murderer has a deterrent effect equivalent to 4.08 potential victims. If the deterrent effect of capital punishment found in Wolpin's study for England and Wales were applicable to the United States in direct proportion, each execution of a convicted murderer in the United States would save about 21 to 22 lives.

Source: Kenneth I. Wolpin, Capital punishment and homicide in England: A summary of results, *American Economic Review* 68(May 1978):422–427.

Determinants of Demand

In presenting a simple demand and supply model, it was assumed that the quantity of a good or service demanded depended on the price of the good or service (P_x) alone. In reality, the quantity of a good or service demanded depends on many factors in addition to the price of the good or service. These factors include money income of consumers (Y), taste or preference of consumers regarding the good or service (T), number of consumers in a given market (N), prices of goods and services that are related to the good or service under consideration (P_r), and other determinants like the education level of consumers, age, types of neighbors, and more (O). Stated in algebraic form, the relationship between the quantity of a good or service demanded and its determinants may be expressed as

$$Q_x = f(P_x; Y, T, N, P_r, O). \tag{3.1}$$

The expression "$= f(\ )$" reads as "is a function of" and means that the dependent variable (Q_x) depends on the independent variables presented in the parentheses. Let us find out the exact relationship between the quantity of product X demanded and the factors that influence the quantity. In discussing the relationships, keep in mind that when one determinant is allowed to change, all other determinants are assumed to remain unchanged. The Latin phrase *ceteris paribus* ("other things being equal") is used in economics to express the assumption that all other factors remain constant.

Price of X (P_x)
The relation between the price of product X and the quantity of product X demanded is inverse. This relation was explained as the law of demand.

Money Income of Consumers (Y)
Demand for most goods and services is expected to increase as income increases. The relation between demand for product X and consumers' income, therefore, is direct. When demand for a good or service increases as income rises, the good or service is called a **normal good.** Demand for certain goods or services decreases as income rises. These goods or services are called **inferior goods.** Inferior goods have preferred substitutes that are more expensive. Further, a good may be an inferior good to one person, but a normal good to another person. Goods that are frequently mentioned as examples of inferior goods include potatoes, dry powdered milk, hamburgers, and margarine. Unless stated specifically as an inferior good, all products mentioned in this book are normal goods.

Taste or Preference (T)
Demand for product X will increase as more consumers like the product. The relation between demand for product X and its taste or preference (T), therefore, is expected to be direct. An interesting controversy regarding the impact of consumers' taste on demand for a product arose in the 1980s with the advent of colorization, a process of applying color to old black and white movies. The idea, of course, is to make money by increasing the demand for old movies through colorization. The Screen Actors Guild, the American Film Institute, and the American Society of Cinematographers have denounced the practice, claiming that colorization turns art such as the classic *Casablanca* into junk. An opposing view, of course, is that since our culture produces

megatons of junk every year, why not let the market decide? The critics' real fear is not that colorization is bad, but that colorization will win the market. "My, my," one observer quipped, "an industry that feeds teenagers three helpings of *Porky's* and six of *Friday the 13th* now complains about the corruption of tastes."[6]

Consumers (N)

As the number of consumers of product X increases in a given market, demand for the product is expected to increase also. For most products, demand increases as more people move into the area. The relation between demand for product X and the number of consumers, therefore, is expected to be direct.

Prices of Related Goods or Services (P_r)

There are two types of goods or services that are related to product X: substitutes and complements.

Substitutes are products other than product X that can satisfy human wants almost as well as product X does. Examples of substitutes include different brands of a product such as Minute Maid Country Style, Florida Gold 100% Valencia, and Citrus Hill Select orange juices. Substitutes for product X are competitive with product X. The relation between demand for product X and the prices of its substitutes, therefore, is expected to be direct. The direct relation means that as the price of a substitute for product X decreases, the demand for product X is expected to decrease as well, since more consumers will buy the substitute, which is now cheaper. As the price of a substitute for product X increases, on the other hand, the demand for product X is expected to increase, since product X is now relatively cheaper.

Complements are goods or services that are used together. Examples include tennis racquets and tennis balls, automobiles and tires, coffee and cream, and notebooks and pencils. The relation between the price of a complement to product X and demand for product X itself is expected to be inverse. The inverse relation means that as the price of a complement decreases, the demand for product X is expected to increase, since the lower price of a complement means a lower total cost of consuming product X and its complement. As the price of a complement to product X increases, the demand for product X is expected to decrease.

Shifts in Demand Curve

Reconsider demand function (3.1):

$$Q_x = f(P_x; Y, T, N, P_r, O). \tag{3.1}$$

According to the law of demand, a decrease in the price of product $X(P_x)$ increases the quantity of product X demanded (Q_x). In Figure 3.5, this change is tracked from point A to point B of the same demand curve. The change along a given demand curve is called a **change in quantity demanded.** An increase in the price of a product causes a decrease in the quantity of the product demanded, while a decrease in the price of a product causes an increase in the quantity of the product demanded. Changes in the quantity demanded are caused solely by the change in the price of the product.

---

[6]Charles Krauthammer, Casablanca in color? I'm shocked, shocked! *Time,* January 12, 1987, p. 82.

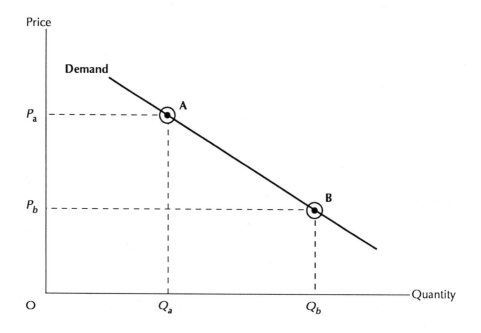

FIGURE 3.5   Change in Quantity Demanded. A change in the price of a product causes a change in the quantity of the product demanded and leaves a given demand curve unchanged.

Suppose that there is an increase in consumers' income. The quantity of product X that consumers demand will also increase even if the price of the product remains unchanged. This change is shown in Figure 3.6. Point C is no longer on the original demand curve. The reason why point C does not remain on the same demand curve is that the demand curve represents a relation between the price of the product and its quantity demanded, while all factors that influence demand other than price are assumed to remain unchanged. If these other factors change, a demand curve is said to have shifted.

When demand curves shift, economists say that there is a **change in demand,** as opposed to changes in the quantity demanded that represent a movement along a given demand curve. If a demand curve shifts to the right, there is an increase in demand. If a demand curve shifts to the left, there is a decrease in demand. Panel (a) in Figure 3.7 illustrates the impact of an increase in demand on market equilibrium price and quantity exchanged while supply remains unchanged. The impact is a higher price and an increased quantity exchanged. Panel (b) in Figure 3.7 illustrates the impact of a decrease in demand on market equilibrium price and quantity exchanged while supply remains unchanged. The impact is a lower price and a decreased quantity exchanged.

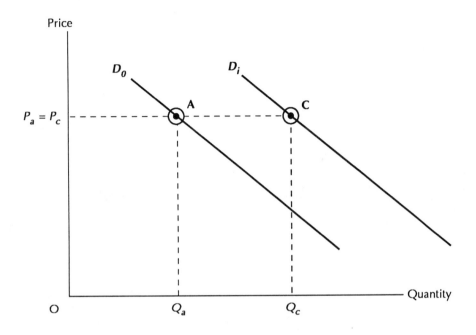

FIGURE 3.6 Change in Demand. A change in any factor or any combination of factors, except the price of the product, that influence demand causes the demand curve to shift. When a demand curve shifts, there is a change in demand.

The study on frozen concentrated orange juice by Lee et al. found that the demand for national brands increases with income, but the demand for private brands (store brands and "generic" products) decreases with income. These findings suggest that national brands are normal goods, but private brands are inferior goods. Further, the study found that, ceteris paribus, the demand for national brands is lower the greater the number of years of education that the female consumer has, while demand for private brands rises with education. Changes in both income and education level cause the demand curve for FCOJ to shift.

Determinants of Supply

In drawing a supply curve, it was assumed that the quantity of a good or service supplied depended on the price of the good or service alone. In reality, the quantity of a product supplied depends on many factors other than the price of the product. These determinants include resource prices (R), production technology (H), and other such determinants as taxes and subsidies and the number of sellers (O) in a given market. Stated in algebraic form, the relation between the quantity of a good or service supplied and its determinants may be expressed as

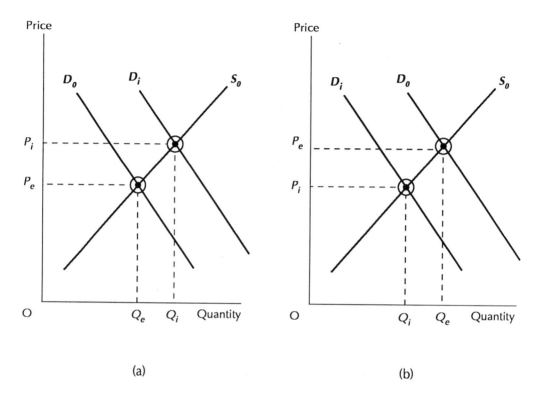

FIGURE 3.7 Changes in Demand and Market Equilibrium. In panel (a) an increase in demand causes a higher price and an increased quantity exchanged. In panel (b) a decrease in demand causes a lower price and a decreased quantity exchanged.

$$Q_x = f(P_x; R, H, O). \tag{3.2}$$

Let us determine the exact relation between the quantity of product X supplied and the factors that influence the quantity of product X supplied.

Price of X (P_x)
The relation between price of product X and the quantity of product X supplied is direct. This relation was explained as the law of supply.

Resource Prices (R)
Supply of a product presupposes its production. The production of a product typically requires the use of several resources. These resources are called input factors, or simply inputs. If prices of

resources decrease while the price of the product remains unchanged, the profit of the producer increases, motivating the producer to increase the supply of the product. The relation between the supply of a product and resource prices, therefore, is inverse.

Production Technology (H)

An improvement in production technology has the same impact as a decrease in resource prices. Assuming that the product price remains unchanged, an improvement in production technology increases the profit of the producer, motivating the producer to increase the supply of the product. The relation between the supply of a product and production technology, therefore, is direct.

Shifts in Supply Curve

Let us consider again the supply function (3.2):

$$Q_x = f(P_x; R, H, O). \tag{3.2}$$

According to the law of supply, an increase in the price of product $X(P_x)$ increases the quantity of product X supplied (Q_x). In Figure 3.8, this change is tracked from point A to point B of the same supply curve. The change along a given supply curve is called a **change in quantity supplied.** An increase in the price of a product causes an increase in the quantity of the product supplied, while a decrease in the price of a product causes a decrease in the quantity of the product supplied. Changes in the quantity supplied are caused solely by the change in the price of the product.

Suppose that there is a decrease in resource prices. The quantity of product X that producers supply is expected to increase even if the price of the product remains unchanged. This change is illustrated in Figure 3.9. Point C is no longer on the given supply curve. The reason why point C does not remain on the same supply curve is that in drawing the supply curve all factors that influence supply other than the price of the product are assumed to remain unchanged. If these other factors change, a supply curve is said to have shifted.

The shift in a supply curve is called a **change in supply** as opposed to changes in quantity supplied that represent a movement along a given supply curve. If a supply curve shifts to the right, there is an increase in supply. If a supply curve shifts to the left, there is a decrease in supply. Panel (a) in Figure 3.10 illustrates the impact of an increase in supply on market equilibrium price and quantity exchanged while demand remains unchanged. The impact is a lower price and an increased quantity exchanged. Panel (b) in Figure 3.10 illustrates the impact of a decrease in supply on market equilibrium price and quantity exchanged while demand remains unchanged. The impact is a higher price and a decreased quantity exchanged.

Simultaneous Shifts in Demand and Supply Curves

Over a long period of time, demand and supply tend to change simultaneously. When there is an increase in demand, there is no reason for supply to remain unchanged. When both demand and supply change at the same time, the result of the change on market equilibrium price and quantity exchanged is not known until relative changes between demand and supply are known. Two cases

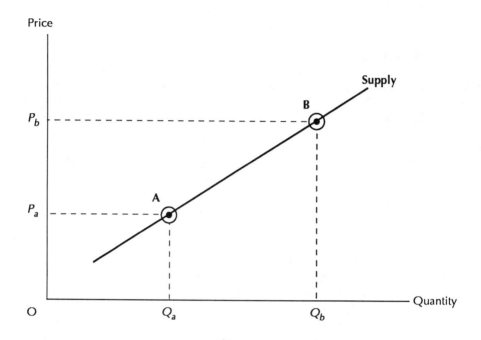

FIGURE 3.8 Change in Quantity Supplied. A change in the price of a product causes a change in the quantity of the product supplied and leaves a given supply curve unchanged.

of simultaneous increases in demand and supply are illustrated in Figure 3.11 and two cases of simultaneous decreases in demand and supply are illustrated in Figure 3.12.

In Figure 3.11(a), both demand and supply have increased, but the increase in demand is greater than the increase in supply. The result of these simultaneous increases in demand and supply on market equilibrium price and quantity exchanged is a higher price and an increased quantity exchanged. In Figure 3.11(b), both demand and supply have also increased, but the increase in demand is smaller than the increase in supply. The result of these simultaneous increases in demand and supply on market equilibrium price and quantity exchanged is a lower price and an increased quantity exchanged.

In Figure 3.12(a), both demand and supply have decreased, but the decrease in demand is greater than the decrease in supply. The result of these simultaneous decreases in demand and supply on market equilibrium price and quantity exchanged is a lower price and a decreased quantity exchanged. In Figure 3.12(b), both demand and supply have also decreased, but the decrease in demand is smaller than the decrease in supply. The result of these simultaneous decreases in demand and supply on market equilibrium price and quantity exchanged is a higher price and a decreased quantity exchanged.

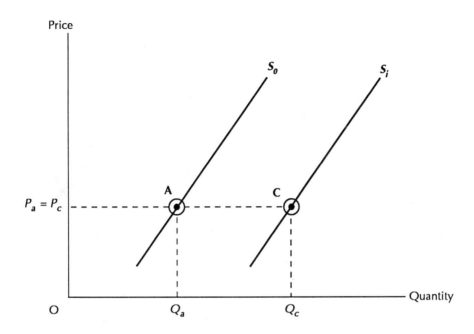

FIGURE 3.9 Change in Supply. A change in any factor or any combination of factors, except the price of the product, that influence supply causes the supply curve to shift. When a supply curve shifts, there is a change in supply.

PRICE CEILINGS AND PRICE FLOORS

The mechanism of demand and supply signals a shortage through a rising market price. The higher price rations scarce products toward those consumers who are willing to pay the most and induces firms to produce more of the good or service. The mechanism of demand and supply signals a surplus through a falling price, which motivates consumers to increase their purchasing and induces firms to produce less of the product. The rationing function of the price can no longer work if prices are arbitrarily kept below or above equilibrium levels. Establishing a market that does not permit the rationing function of price is the intent of price ceilings or price floors.

Price Ceilings

Price ceilings refer to maximum prices that are legislated to be below the equilibrium market prices. When price ceilings are imposed, the normal functioning of the market is thwarted, but the force

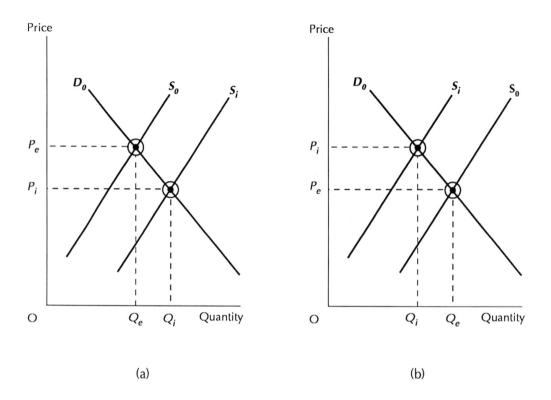

FIGURE 3.10 Changes in Supply and Market Equilibrium. In panel (a) an increase in supply causes a lower price and an increased quantity exchanged. In panel (b) a decrease in supply causes a higher price and a decreased quantity exchanged.

of demand and supply cannot be contained totally. It is this aspect of price ceilings that provides an interesting ground for discussion.

Examples

There are several examples of price ceilings. Mandatory price controls during World War II, the Korean War, and the waning years of the Vietnam War are examples of price ceilings. When price ceilings are imposed on a wide variety of goods and services, certain sellers and buyers devise their own rationing mechanism by creating a black market. **Black markets** are arrangements in which buyers and sellers trade at prices above the legal ceiling price.

Other examples of price ceilings include rent controls in large cities such as New York. Rent controls are intended to benefit the poor, who would not be able to rent housing units in the absence of rent controls. When rent controls last over a number of years, however, owners of housing units subject to rent control have no incentive to maintain the units, much less improve them. Rent

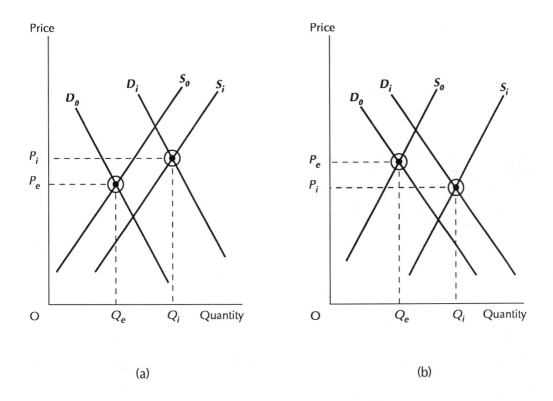

(a)   (b)

FIGURE 3.11 Simultaneous Increases in Demand and Supply. In panel (a) an increase in demand is greater than an increase in supply, thus causing a higher price and an increased quantity exchanged. In panel (b) an increase in demand is smaller than an increase in supply, thus causing a lower price and an increased quantity exchanged.

controls, therefore, eventually cause a decrease in the number of housing units supplied and hurt the poor who were the reason for rent controls in the first place. Studies have confirmed that the quality of the existing supply of rental housing units deteriorates in response to rent controls since landlords can increase profits only by reducing maintenance.[7]

Interest on Credit Card Debt
Let us study another example of price ceilings. Most interest rates had fallen substantially in the mid-1980s, but interest rates on credit card debt had fallen little, if at all, during the same period.

---

[7]See John C. Moorhouse, Optimal housing under rent controls, *Southern Economic Journal*, 39(July 1972):93–106.

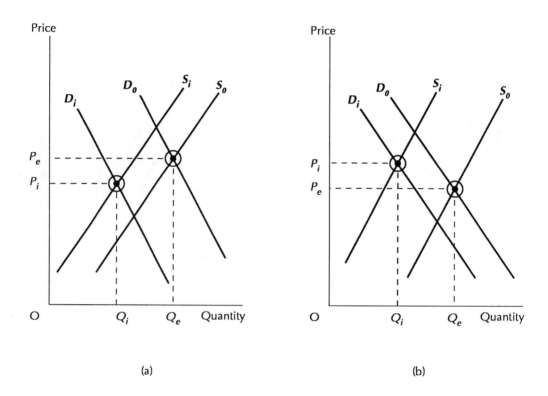

FIGURE 3.12 Simultaneous Decreases in Demand and Supply. In panel (a) a decrease in demand is greater than a decrease in supply, thus causing a lower price and a decreased quantity exchanged. In panel (b) a decrease in demand is smaller than a decrease in supply, thus causing a higher price and a decreased quantity exchanged.

The relatively high interest rates on credit card debt led Congress to consider several bills that would have imposed a nationwide rate ceiling on credit card accounts.[8]

Consumer surveys indicate that credit card users are of two types: convenience users who usually pay off credit card balance in full during the grace period, and borrowers who usually do not pay off their balance in full during the grace period, thereby incurring finance charges. Surveys made in 1977 and also 1983 indicate that about half of all families that used bank or retail credit cards were convenience users and the other half, borrowers. Figure 3.13 indicates that as ceiling

[8]This example on interest rate ceiling on credit card debt is based on Glenn B. Canner, James T. Fergus, Patricia A. Boerschig, Julia A. Springer, and Janice S. Westfall, The economic effects of proposed ceilings on credit card interest rates, *Federal Reserve Bulletin* 73(January 1987):1–13. For more studies on the subject, see Douglas F. Greer, Rate ceilings and loan turndown, *Journal of Finance* 30(December 1975):1376–1383.

RESPONSE THRESHOLD OF QUANTITY TO CHANGES IN PRICE

When economists draw demand and supply curves, these curves are drawn as if the quantity demanded or supplied is responsive in direct proportion to a price change even when the change in price is very small. If this assumption does not hold true, the demand or supply curve would not be a straight line. The assumption is not expected to hold true. Consider Weber's law.

Weber's law states that the amount of increase in stimulation that is just noticeable by a human observer is a constant proportion of the starting level of stimulation. For example, suppose that someone carrying a 50-pound load can detect the addition of one more pound to the load. Additions of less than one pound are not noticed. The just noticeable difference is one pound. This difference is also called the difference threshold. It takes a change of one pound in 50 to produce the difference threshold; so the ratio is

$$1/50 = .02 \text{ or 2 percent.}$$

Weber's law states that regardless of the starting weight, it will take a 2 percent increase in weight to be just noticeable. The fraction, 1/50, is called the Weber fraction, and it is a measure of how sensitive we are in various judgments.

Consider automobiles. If the price of an automobile is lowered by one or two dollars, potential automobile buyers are not expected to notice the price decrease and respond to the price decrease. Consider also changes in money supply. An increase in the nation's money supply by $1 million will attract no one's attention. Although Weber's fractions were not computed for economic variables, there are examples of Weber's fraction in the field of psychology:

Dimension	Weber Fraction	Percent Change Needed to Notice a Difference
Brightness of a light	1/62	1.6
Lifted weight	1/53	1.9
Amount of rubber smell	1/10	10.4
Pressure on the skin surface	1/7	13.6
Amount of salty taste	1/5	20.0

The potential use of Weber's fractions in business and economic decision-making appears unlimited.

Source: Lyle E. Bourne, Jr., and Bruce R. Ekstrand, *Psychology: Its principles and meanings,* 3rd ed. (New York: Holt, Rinehart and Winston, 1979), p. 19.

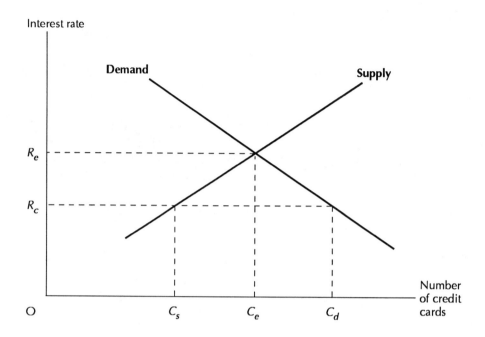

FIGURE 3.13   Ceiling Rates on Credit Card Debt. Imposing ceiling interest rates (R_c) on credit card debt below the equilibrium interest rates (R_e) will keep credit card companies from issuing credit cards to applicants who barely qualify.

rates (R_c) are imposed below the prevailing market rate, the number of credit cards issued is expected to decrease.

If the interest rate ceiling imposed on credit card debt is below the prevailing rate, credit card issuers will take cost-cutting measures. The most obvious such measure would be to tighten credit standards so as to reduce collection costs and charge-offs (uncollectable or "bad" debts). This measure would have the greatest adverse effect on marginal card applicants who barely meet the current minimum requirements. These applicants tend to have a lower income, a shorter employment tenure, and a relatively poor credit record. Another measure that credit card issuers may take is to reprice credit card services through imposing a higher annual fee or shortening the grace period. These measures will hurt convenience users. The only group of card users that would benefit from regulations to reduce interest rates on credit card debt would be those who are qualified to obtain cards which they use for borrowing rather than for convenience.

Price Floors

Price floors refer to minimum prices that are imposed above equilibrium market prices. Like ceiling prices, floor prices also thwart the normal functioning of the market, but the force of demand and supply will try to react to the floor price.

Minimum Wage Regulation: Theory

An interesting application of price floors is the minimum wage regulation. The Fair Labor Standards Act of 1938 and subsequent amendments of the Act have provided minimum hourly wage rates applicable to most nonsupervisory employees in the U. S. economy. The minimum wage was 25 cents in 1938; it has been raised to $3.35 on January 1, 1981.[9]

The effect of the minimum wage regulation is graphed in Figure 3.14. In the absence of minimum wages, the market equilibrium wage rate would be W_e and the number of workers employed would be N_e. As wage floors are imposed at W_m, the number of workers who are willing to work increases to N_s, while the number of workers employers are willing to hire decreases to N_d. Since the number of persons who actually have jobs is determined by the demand for workers, not by the supply of workers, the level of employment decreases from N_e to N_d.

The total number of unemployed persons $(N_s - N_d)$ owing to higher minimum wages may be greater than the number of persons $(N_e - N_d)$ who *lose* jobs due to higher minimum wages. Let us see why. As the minimum wage rate increases from W_e to W_m, some workers $(N_e - N_d)$ will lose their jobs and become unemployed. The higher wage rate W_m may also induce persons $(N_s - N_e)$ who had been outside the labor force at wage rate W_e to seek employment at the higher wage rate. The combined number of unemployed persons, therefore, is increased to $(N_s - N_d)$. Over time, some unemployed persons give up looking for jobs, causing the unemployment rate to decrease. When unemployed persons do not actively seek jobs, they are no longer counted as unemployed in official unemployment statistics.

Minimum Wage Regulation: Practice

Does an increase in the minimum wage actually reduce employment? Economists do not necessarily agree on the answer. A recent summary of empirical studies found that a 10 percent increase in the minimum wage would reduce teenage employment by a magnitude of 1 to 3 percent.[10] Some economists, including Lawrence Klein of the University of Pennsylvania, John Kenneth Galbraith of Harvard University, and Lester Thurow of the Massachusetts Institute of Technology, dispute the finding. In a February 1988 letter to a subcommittee of the House Education and Labor Committee that considered raising the minimum hourly wage from $3.35 to $4.65, those three economists and 51 others claimed that there was no evidence of significant employment and business disruption when the nation raised the minimum wage six times in the past.

---

[9]For the data on effective federal minimum hourly wage rates, see U.S. Department of Commerce, Bureau of the Census, *Statistical Abstract of the United States, 1989,* 109th ed., p. 411.

[10]For more on the impact of minimum wages, see Finis Welch, *Minimum wages: Issues and evidence* (Washington, D.C.: American Enterprise Institute for Public Policy Research, 1978); Thomas Gale Moore, The effect of minimum wages on teenage unemployment rates, *Journal of Political Economy* 79(July-August 1971):897–902; and Charles Brown, Curtis Gilroy, and Andrew Kohen, The effect of the minimum wage on employment and unemployment, *Journal of Economic Literature* 20(June 1982):487–528.

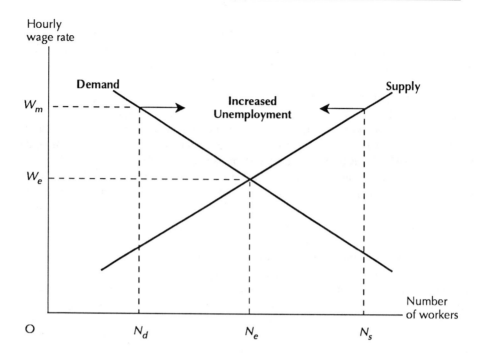

FIGURE 3.14   Effect of Higher Minimum Wages. As minimum wages are raised, the number of unemployed persons, especially among teenage workers, is expected to increase. The employment level decreases from N_e to N_d.

SUMMARY

A market is an arrangement in which sellers of a good or service interact with buyers of the good or service. Market demand refers to the quantities of a good or service that are demanded by all buyers in any given market at various prices. The inverse relation between the price of a good or service and the quantity of it demanded is called the law of demand. In drawing a graph, it is necessary to assume that all other things remain equal. The assumption "other things being equal" is expressed as *ceteris paribus*. Market supply refers to the quantities of a good or service that all producers in a market are willing and able to produce and make available for sale in the market at various prices. The direct relation between the price of a good or service and the quantity of it supplied is called the law of supply. The price that equates the quantity of a good demanded and the quantity of the good supplied is called the equilibrium price, and the quantity exchanged at the equilibrium price is called the equilibrium quantity. At equilibrium, the market is cleared. Any price above the equilibrium level creates a surplus. Any price below the equilibrium level creates a shortage. The existence of a surplus forces sellers to lower the price of their products toward the equilibrium price. The existence of a shortage forces buyers to bid up the price of the products toward the equilibrium price.

Determinants of demand for any given product include, besides the price of the product, money income of consumers, taste or preference of consumers regarding the product, number of consumers in a given market, prices of goods and services that are related to the product under consideration, and others. If factors other than the price of the product change, a demand curve is said to have shifted. When demand curves shift, there is a change in demand as opposed to changes in the quantity demanded that leave a demand curve unshifted. Supply of a product depends on the price of the product, resource prices, production technology, and other factors such as taxes and subsidies or the number of sellers in a given market. If factors other than the price of the product change, a supply curve is said to have shifted. The shift in a supply curve is called a change in supply as opposed to changes in the quantity supplied that signify no shift in the supply curve. Price ceilings are maximum prices that are imposed below the equilibrium market price. Price floors are minimum prices that are imposed above the equilibrium market price. Both ceiling prices and floor prices thwart the normal functioning of the market.

EXERCISES

1. What is the difference between a change in demand and a change in quantity demanded? What is the difference between a change in supply and a change in quantity supplied?

2. Why is it necessary to make a distinction between a change in demand and a change in quantity demanded and between a change in supply and a change in quantity supplied?

3. Suppose that an article is published in which the author says that by the year 2000, demand for oil is expected to exceed the supply of oil. What does this statement mean? Is a shortage of oil expected in 2000?

4. Regarding the illustration about the minimum drinking age cited in the text, is it wrong to raise the minimum drinking age? What is the illustration trying to say?

5. Economists claim that there is no shortage of any product in a competitive market. But we keep hearing of a shortage of oil, housing units, and what have you. How can the two views be reconciled?

6. Suppose that the price per gallon of gasoline is fixed at $1.00 by a government decree. Suppose also that the supply of gasoline decreases substantially due to an oil embargo by oil exporting countries. What are possible consequences in the retail gasoline market?

7. The marketing alchemists who mix psychology, sociology, and crystal ball gazing came up with the trend spotter's guide to the tastes of the 1990s shown as Table 3.3.

TABLE 3.3 Consumer Trends for the 1990s

Consumer Choices	1970s	1980s	1990s
Main course	Beef	Chicken	Beef
Fast food	Hamburger	Taco	Family cookin'
Electronics	VCR	Compact disc	Tiny TV
Exercise	Tennis	Aerobics	Walking
Relaxation	Den	Family room	Media room
Shopping	Department store	Specialty store	Boutique
Foreign car	Japanese	Korean	Brazilian
Alcohol	Beer	Wine cooler	Cocktails
Music	Disco	1960s rock	Big band

Source: Fortune February 2, 1987, p. 36. Copyright 1987 Time Inc. All rights reserved.

What would happen to demand curves for products listed as preferred goods in the 1990s?

8. The most significant political pressure for a higher minimum wage seems to come from organized labor, particularly the AFL-CIO. Few workers represented by the AFL-CIO ever receive the minimum wage because such skilled workers generally receive relatively high wages. Why would the AFL-CIO support and exercise its political influence for a higher minimum wage?

9. One of the firms that experienced difficulty in adjusting to the deregulated market in the 1980s was Eastern Airlines. Because of higher costs of operation, Eastern Airlines was finally sold to Texas Air in 1986. According to the February 2, 1987 issue of *U.S. News & World Report* (on p. 45), Eastern spent $490 an hour to service a 727 jet, while other airlines spent only $300 to $400 an hour for the same service. Explain, using the demand and supply model, the effect of the higher cost of service by Eastern on the company's status as a competitor.

10. Consider the price of oil and the quantity of oil supplied during the mid-1980s by stripper wells, each pumping 10 barrels or less per day but totaling 8 percent of the oil consumed in the United States. There were more than 400,000 stripper wells in the United States. The price of oil fluctuated widely in the mid-1980s. Between November 1985 and July 1986, for instance, the West Texas Intermediate spot price of oil dropped from $31.50 per barrel to about $12 per barrel. As the price of oil fell, most stripper wells stopped pumping oil. The price began to rise, passing $17.50 in December 1986. The price of oil was highly responsive to the policies of the Organization for Petroleum Exporting Countries (OPEC). OPEC's objective during the

period was to bring oil prices to $18 per barrel, but not much higher. What could be a possible explanation of OPEC's policy of limiting the price to $18 per barrel? Explain in terms of change in quantity supplied.

SUGGESTED READINGS

Bourne, Lyle E. Jr., and Ekstrand, Bruce R. (1979). *Psychology: Its principles and meanings,* 3rd ed. New York: Holt, Rinehart and Winston, p. 19 and p. 74.

Explains the Weber's law that economists may need to pay more attention to.

Gill, Richard T. (1976). *Great debates in economics,* vol. 2. Pacific Palisades, Calif.: Goodyear, pp. 175–227, The pros and cons of wage-price controls.

A good summary of the controversial topic, mandatory price and wage controls.

Lee, Jong-Ying, Brown, Mark G., and Schwartz, Brooke. (1986). The demand for national brand and private label frozen concentrated orange juice: A switching regression analysis. Florida Agricultural Experiment Station Journal paper.

A rare study that illustrates straight estimation of demand function without using natural logarithms.

Lewis, J. Parry. (1969). *An introduction to mathematics for students of economics,* 2nd ed. London: Macmillan.

One of the best introductory mathematics books for business and economics students.

Sheldon, Pauline J., and Mak, James. (1987). The demand for package tours: A mode choice model. *Journal of Travel Research* 25(Winter):13–17.

Illustrates an estimated demand function for package tours that identifies parties likely to purchase package tours and shows that travelers are responsive to price savings from package tours.

Walsh, Richard G., and Davitt, Gordon J. (1983). A demand function for length of stay on ski trips to Aspen. *Journal of Travel Research* 21(Spring):23–29.

An interesting study estimating the demand curve for length of stay on ski trips to Aspen, Colorado, and showing shifts in demand curve.

4

Government
and Taxation

**Division of Roles among Different
Levels of Government**

Public Expenditure and Public Choice

Principles of Taxation

Representative Tax System

GOVERNMENT IS AN ORGANIZATION formed for the purpose of exercising authority over individual members of a given society. The types of government, therefore, vary widely with the specific authority that individual governments are intended to exercise. At the national level, in the United States, there is the federal government. At the state level there are 50 state governments, and at the local level there are more than 80,000 governments including counties, municipalities, townships and towns, school districts, and special districts. Each of these governments produces goods and services, and the government production of goods and services requires the private sector to give up resources that could have been used to produce goods and services of the private sector. How large the role of government should be in the U.S. economy is an issue of great concern.

Studies on the role of government may be divided into two categories: those concerned with taxation and expenditure of government, and those concerned with regulation of the private sector that is intended to correct what are commonly known as market failures. The objective of this chapter is limited to introducing the subject of taxation and expenditure of government; market failures and government regulation are treated in Chapter 12.

DIVISION OF ROLES AMONG DIFFERENT LEVELS OF GOVERNMENT

The issue of which level of government should have what responsibilities has been highly controversial. In principle, those powers not explicitly assigned to the federal government rest with the state and local governments. Amendment X of the U.S. Constitution defines the rights of states by stating: "The powers not delegated to the United States by constitution, nor prohibited by it to the States, are reserved to the States respectively, or to the people." Significant powers expressly delegated to the federal government include national defense, printing money, and running the post office. There are numerous other responsibilities, however, that are shared by the federal and the state and local governments. In this section we study the major roles of different levels of government and how these roles are financed.

Federal Government

Major categories of receipts and expenditures by the federal government and the state and local government for the calendar year 1988 are summarized in Table 4.1. The calendar year is 12 consecutive months ending on December 31. For accounting of taxation and expenditure the federal government and the majority of state and local governments use a fiscal year running from October 1 through September 30. A **fiscal year** (FY) is also a 12-month period but selected arbitrarily for accounting of revenues and expenditures. A fiscal year may end on the last day of any month.

In 1988 the federal government collected $974.2 billion in taxes to be used for general administration, and in contributions for social insurance that are mostly earmarked. **Earmarking** means that the receipts must be spent for specific purposes by law. Among taxes, the personal income tax (called also individual income tax) generates the largest revenue, followed by the corporate profit tax and indirect business taxes. The **personal income tax** is a tax levied on taxable incomes of individuals and unincorporated firms such as sole proprietorships and partnerships, while the **corporate profit tax** is a tax levied on profits of corporations. Corporate profit tax is also

TABLE 4.1   Government Receipts and Expenditures, 1988 ($billions)

Receipt and Expenditure Categories	Federal Government		State and Local Government	
Receipts				
Personal tax and nontax receipts		$ 413.4		$ 176.9
Personal income tax	$404.0		$ 92.8	
Estate and gift tax	7.9		0	
Nontaxes	1.6		69.3	
Other	0		14.8	
Corporate profits tax accruals		110.3		30.8
Federal Reserve banks	18.8		0	
Corporate profit tax	91.5		30.8	
Indirect business tax and nontax accruals		56.8		332.2
Excise tax	33.2		0	
Customs duties	16.5		0	
Sales tax	0		158.8	
Property tax	0		129.6	
Other	7.2		43.8	
Contribution for social insurance		393.6		51.0
Federal grants-in-aid		0		110.4
Total		$ 974.2		$ 701.3
Expenditures				
Purchases of goods and services		$ 380.2		$ 583.4
Transfer payments		440.1		128.1
Net interest paid		154.2		−40.8
Grants-in-aid to state and local governments		110.4		0
Other		31.2		−23.3
Total		$1,116.1		$ 647.4

Source: Adapted from U.S. Department of Commerce, Bureau of Economic Analysis, *Survey of current business,* 69(January 1989), Tables 3.2 and 3.3 on p. 13.

called **corporate income tax. Indirect business taxes** are taxes that businesses pay to the government but treat as costs of producing a product and charge to consumers through higher prices. These taxes include the sales tax, excise tax, property tax paid by businesses, and license fees. The **sales tax** is often called a **general sales tax** or **retail sales tax** because it is usually collected at the retail level. The sales tax is also called a **gross receipts tax** because it is computed as a certain percentage of gross sales. An **excise tax** is a special type of sales tax. In the case of the sales tax, one tax rate applies to a wide range of goods and, sometimes, services. In the case of the excise tax, the tax rate varies with products on which the excise tax is levied. The excise tax is also called a **selective sales tax.**

Total expenditures of the federal government for 1988 were $1,116.1 billion. Note that expenditures for the year exceeded revenues by $141.9 billion. Unlike individuals, who have to pay off their debts sooner or later, and many state and local governments that by law have to maintain a balanced budget each year, the federal government can borrow without having to worry about paying back the debt in the near future. The next question is: Where does the federal government spend the tax revenue and the large amount of money it borrows?

Income security programs such as social security, retirement of military and civilian employees, and welfare programs require the largest amount of expenditures, followed closely by national defense and interest payments on the federal debt. Other federal programs include international affairs such as economic and military assistance, administration of justice, veterans benefits and services, maintenance of federal highways, subsidies to airports and local mass transit systems, and grants-in-aid to state and local governments.

State and Local Government

In 1988 state and local governments received $701.3 billion and spent $647.4 billion. Just as there are differences between state governments and local governments, there are differences among state governments, and also among local governments. Any generalization of revenue and expenditure patterns of state and local governments, therefore, is quite limited.

State governments in general receive most of their revenue from the income tax, sales tax, fees for various licenses, and the property tax. Several states, including Alaska, Delaware, Massachusetts, Minnesota, Montana, New York, Oregon, and Wisconsin, depend heavily on a state income tax as the major source of revenue, while other states such as Arizona, Connecticut, Florida, Indiana, Mississippi, New Mexico, South Dakota, Tennessee, Washington, and Wyoming depend heavily on a general sales tax. New Hampshire has neither a general sales tax nor a state income tax and derives a majority of its income from selective sales taxes. The property tax is not a major source of revenue to any of the 50 state governments. Unlike the federal government, there are few, if any, responsibilities that are carried out by the state government alone. State governments provide services for highways, public welfare, education, prisons, and industrial development.

Major sources of revenue for local governments vary considerably with types of local government, and even within the same type of local government. School districts derive a majority of their revenue from property taxes, while special districts derive a majority of their revenue from charges for their services. The major source of revenue for most county governments is the property tax, but major sources of revenue for municipalities (cities) vary widely. For instance, the property tax is the most important source of revenue for such cities as Boston, Buffalo, Honolulu, Indianapolis, Milwaukee, Minneapolis, New York City, and Portland, while the local income tax is the most important source of revenue for Cincinnati, Cleveland, Columbus, Louisville, Philadelphia, and Toledo. For Oklahoma City, Tulsa, and Mobile, the general sales tax is the most important source of revenue.

Major functions of the general purpose local governments such as cities and counties are mostly mundane and directly affect our daily lives. These services include public safety, fire protection, sanitation, parks and recreation, public welfare, libraries, and local roads. School districts provide services for public education, while special districts such as water and sewer boards provide services that are intended for individual special districts.

TAX FREEDOM DAY

Economists at the Tax Foundation annually calculate the tax freedom day to dramatize the size and weight of government that influence the economy. Earnings of taxpayers from January 1 to tax freedom day are paid to government as taxes, assuming that all earnings in the paycheck are paid as taxes to federal, state, and local government. Earnings for the remainder of the year are equivalent to after-tax incomes of taxpayers. If the tax freedom day is May 1, for instance, it takes from January 1 through April 30 to earn the money to pay the average American's tax bill for the year.

Tax freedom days for selected years 1930 to 1989 are as follows:

Year	Tax Freedom Day
1930	February 13
1940	March 8
1950	April 3
1960	April 17
1970	April 28
1980	May 1
1981	May 4
1982	May 3
1983	April 30
1984	April 28
1985	May 1
1986	May 2
1987	May 4
1988	May 5
1989	May 4

Source: Tax Foundation, *Tax Features* 30(April 1986):1, 32(April/May 1988):1, and 33(April 1989):1.

PUBLIC EXPENDITURE AND PUBLIC CHOICE

Different levels of government *produce* different types of goods and services that firms in the private sector may or may not be able to produce. Government may also *provide* goods and services to the public by purchasing them from the private sector. Many local governments, for instance, contract with private firms which, in turn, collect household and commercial refuse. No distinction is made in this section between production by the government sector and provision by the government sector, since both production and provision by the government sector represent public expenditure. In this section, we study the nature of goods produced by the public sector and introduce the decision-making process concerning how much of these goods should be produced by the public sector rather than the private sector.

Pure and Impure Public Goods

Public goods have two properties. One is that it is not possible to exclude the use of public goods from people who do not pay for the provision of these goods, and the other is that it is not desirable to exclude the use of public goods from those who do not pay even if it is possible to exclude them.

Pure Public Goods
Public goods are said to be **pure,** if it is totally impossible to exclude from use of these goods people who do not pay for them. Examples of pure public goods are rare, although national defense is often cited as an example. Since exclusion is not possible in consumption of public goods, many consumers of the good may not contribute to the cost of producing the good if the contribution is voluntary. Those who enjoy consumption of goods and services but are not willing to contribute to the cost of producing these goods are called **free riders.** If the production of pure public goods is left up to the private sector, firms will have no incentive to produce these goods since there will be many free riders. Goods such as automobiles and houses that can be consumed only by those who pay for them are called **private goods.**

Impure Public Goods
Many goods have varying degrees of excludability and undesirability of exclusion. **Impure public goods** are those goods from which free riders are neither totally excludable nor totally desirable of exclusion even if it is possible to exclude them.

Examples of impure public goods abound. National vaccination programs, for instance, are excludable by giving vaccination shots only to those who pay nominal fees. The vaccination programs would not be an effective *national* vaccination program, however, if those who do not want to participate are excluded. Exclusion from vaccination programs is highly undesirable. Highways, especially if they are uncongested, are another example. It is technically possible to set up toll booths at every entrance or exit but it is not desirable, since having additional drivers will incur little costs to the road. Local police and fire protection services are yet another example since it is practically impossible to exclude from protection those who refuse to pay taxes. Vaccination, highways, and public safety are all examples of impure public goods.

Who Produces Public Goods
Most public goods are produced by the public sector since government can avoid the free-rider problem by forcing the consuming public to pay for the provision of the public goods. Most private

goods are produced by the private sector since the profit motive of private producers makes them more efficient producers of the private goods.

Sometimes public goods are produced by the private sector. Radio and television signals are an example. Once the signals are on the air, it is neither possible to exclude people who are not willing to pay nor desirable to exclude them. Radio and television signals are clearly public goods but are produced by the private sector. Cable TV is a private good since the service is clearly excludable. Although most public goods are produced by the public sector, not all goods produced by the public sector are necessarily public goods. The public sector also produces several private goods. Examples of private goods that are produced by the public sector include flood insurance, deposit insurance, electricity produced by publicly owned utilities, and postal service.

Needs for the Public Sector

Let us imagine a community without a government. Suppose that the community's products are taken by the strongest in the community at the expense of its weak members, while the total amount of the community's products remains unchanged. Activities of this kind, in which there is a change in the distribution of products among members but the cumulative gains equal the cumulative losses, are called a **zero-sum game**. There will be a **negative-sum game** if cumulative gains are smaller than cumulative losses. Cumulative gains will be smaller than cumulative losses, if a fight breaks out among members of the community and some of the products are lost or destroyed during the fight. In the absence of a government, communities may well experience a negative-sum distribution.

With a government that has the authority to represent the collective preference of the community, communities will be able to enjoy at least a zero-sum distribution of products through the maintenance of law and order. A **positive-sum game** refers to an activity among two or more persons in which cumulative gains are greater than cumulative losses. Communities may experience a positive-sum distribution through the encouragement of specialization among members of the community. Even if all members of a community agree on the need for the public sector, a question still remains as to how much should be produced by the public sector and how much should be produced by the private sector.

Unlike the quantity of private goods whose optimal quantity is signaled by market price and thus is determined by market demand and market supply, there is no effective mechanism that determines the optimal quantity of public goods. Put differently, should there be more libraries, more parks, or more paved roads in the community? Should the nation develop and deploy the Strategic Defense Initiative (SDI)? Should more waterways be built? How much money should the nation spend on research on acquired immune deficiency syndrome (AIDS)?

To answer these questions, let us consider a municipal golf course. If there were no greens fee, there might be so many golfers playing on the course that the municipal government would hear loud complaints demanding that another golf course be built for residents of the city. Do these complaints really mean that the city does not have enough golf courses? The answer, of course, is no. By levying a greens fee, the golf course that was once in short supply may no longer be in short supply. In determining the greens fee, the city may consider fees charged by private country clubs that maintain comparable golf courses. In the case of national defense and public safety, there are no comparable private sector products that can be used as a guide in determining the optimal quantity. The theory of public choice is intended to address the questions of what public goods to produce and how much of these public goods to produce.

Public Choice under Political Democracy

Public choice is a field of economics that studies the decision-making process of government based on the assumption that the individual politically, like the individual economically, is rational, self-interested, and a utility maximizer. Put differently, public choice uses economic methods to study subjects that have traditionally been the domain of political science. The emphasis of public choice lies in the individual, not the class of individuals.

The Median Voter

In a political democracy, politicians make decisions on behalf of individual voters whom they represent. For simplicity, the preferences of individual voters may be averaged to the preference of the median voter. The **median voter** is the voter whose preferred expenditure for a public good is at the level where the number of individuals who prefer higher expenditure is exactly equal to the number of individuals who prefer lower expenditure. In principle, decisions on the production of public goods should be based on the preference revealed by the median voter. The median voter is not necessarily the one who has the median income. If there is a redistribution of income within a community so that the income of the median voter increases while the average income of the community remains the same, the demand for public goods in the community tends to increase.

The problem with the median voter concept is that elections are usually held not on a single issue, but on several issues simultaneously. The median voter on issue A is not necessarily the median voter on issue B. We do not know who the median voter is when all issues are combined. Without knowing who the median voter is, the process of determining the preference revealed by the median voter becomes more complicated, if not impossible. From the median voter, therefore, let us move toward all voters.

JAMES M. BUCHANAN

Buchanan has been a leading public choice theorist. Unlike most economists of 30 years ago, who were concerned with the workings of the private sector, Buchanan was determined to find out why the public sector makes decisions in the way it does. Buchanan used individuals as the foundation of the analysis by assuming that self-interested behavior prevails in the public sector as well as the private sector. For his contribution toward the public choice theory, Buchanan was awarded the 1986 Nobel Prize in Economics. Born in 1919, Buchanan taught at Florida State University, University of Virginia, University of California/Los Angeles, and Virginia Polytechnic Institute before he became general director of the Center for the Study of Public Choice at George Mason University.

Rational Ignorance Effect

In a democratic society like the United States, preferences on public goods, ideally, are revealed through voting by members of the society. Selecting and voting for a candidate is not like selecting a combination of goods and services that one buys at the marketplace. The difference arises from the fact that there are usually several issues that a candidate has to consider and favor. A voter is not likely to find a candidate whose stands on issues exactly match the voter's own. The difference between purchasing a combination of goods and services at the marketplace and selecting a candidate creates the potential for a major difference in behavior between consumers and voters. Let us see why.

Consumers search for information that can give them the most utility from the purchase of a combination of goods and services; voters' behavior tends to be the opposite. In the absence of a candidate whose stands exactly match those of individual voters, the public choice theory suggests that voters tend to vote for the candidate whose platform is perceived by these voters to give them a maximum economic gain. Maximum economic gains or losses are only *perceived* rather than known fully by voters, since candidates themselves frequently do not vote according to their platforms once they are elected. Because of the uncertainty of the outcome of voting for a particular candidate, voters have little incentive even to seek information. The lack of incentive for voters to obtain additional information that is needed to cast a more informed vote is called the **rational ignorance effect.** The result of this approach is that voters' preferences revealed through voting may not represent the true preferences of all voters.

The rational ignorance effect is not the only deficiency of the decision-making process under a political democracy. Public choice theory claims that there are other deficiencies in the political decision-making process, notably the special interest effect.

Special Interest Effect

Ideally, decision-makers in the public sector make decisions for the majority of the society. According to the special interest effect, the political process does not always promote the general welfare of the society.

Special Interest Groups

Public choice theory hypothesizes that politicians make decisions in such a way as to maximize their probability of winning an election. Issues proposed by special interest groups are attractive to politicians. **Special interest groups** are those that try to obtain substantial gains for their members at the expense of the larger number of nonmembers, who suffer small losses. Politicians feel that they will lose the votes of the members of special interest groups if they vote against the issues supported by special interest groups, but they will not lose the votes of the larger number of individuals outside the groups, who have only a little to lose from politicians' support for special interest issues. Individuals are usually not well informed on the issues supported by special interest groups, anyway.

The **special interest effect** refers to the support of special interest issues by politicians based on their judgment that their gains from supporting special interest groups will be greater than their losses from individuals who may not vote for the politicians because of the support that these politicians give for special interest groups.

The concept of the special interest effect suggests that politicians will support special interest programs even if these programs are not the most desirable programs from the society's point of view. Examples of the special interest effect are numerous. To find some, all one has to do is to read exemptions allowed in local sales tax ordinances or loopholes allowed in the Tax Reform Act of 1986. Other examples include pork barrel public works programs and tariffs on selected imports. **Pork barrel** means appropriations by government for political patronage especially to please legislators' constituents.

Logrolling

When pork barrel projects cannot be approved standing alone on their own merits, these projects may be *logrolled* with other significant laws such as tax reform acts or annual budget appropriation bills. In **logrolling,** congressional votes are used more as a way to win political support than as tools for serving the public interest.

Consider Citmoco Services, a firm that sold oil to a company in the Bahamas in 1973 and 1974 when the price of oil was controlled for all domestically traded oil. The Bahamian company delivered the oil back to the United States. The owner of Citmoco contended that the oil was exported and hence was not subject to price controls. The U.S. Department of Energy disagreed and sued. On appeal, the owner of Citmoco was ordered to repay his financial gain from the deal plus interest that totaled $20 million. The U.S. senator who represented the area in which Citmoco was located logrolled an amendment with the $600 billion federal appropriations bill. The amendment prohibited the Justice and Energy departments from spending money to collect the $20 million judgment from the owner of Citmoco.[1]

Public choice theory admits the superiority of capitalism based on political democracy and merely attempts to improve the decision-making process under the existing system. For instance, Professors Gwartney and Wagner propose (1) that a two-thirds approval of both houses in the U.S. Congress be required for passage of any legislation that affects taxation and debt limit and mandates spending by states, private businesses, or individuals, and (2) that the president of the United States be provided a line-item veto. The **line-item veto** permits the president to reduce the approved amount of, or eliminate, specific spending programs without vetoing the entire budget.[2]

PRINCIPLES OF TAXATION

Discussion of the government so far in this chapter has been concerned with the types of goods that government produces and the decision-making process by which democratic government under the capitalistic economic system produces these goods. In the remaining sections of this chapter, we study concepts and problems that pertain to financing the production of public goods, namely, taxation. First we need some basic concepts in taxation.

---

[1]For more on the story, see the *Wall Street Journal,* January 22, 1988, p. 26, and *Mobile Press Register,* January 23, 1988, p. 2B. For other examples of pork barrel, see What dollars can buy, *U.S. News & World Report,* November 7, 1988, pp. 23–24. This article lists the 15 most egregious congressional boondoggles in which congressmen put interests of the special interest groups ahead of those of the nation. *Boondoggle* means a valueless undertaking.

[2]James D. Gwartney and Richard E. Wagner, The federal budget process: Why it is broken and how it can be fixed (Tallahassee, Fla.: The James Madison Institute, Madison Papers Series, 1988).

ABOVE THE LAW

The United States Congress has exempted itself from a number of laws covering civil rights, minimum wages, and safety requirements and discrimination. One example is that the minimum wage regulation does not apply to about 15,000 persons working for Congress. Another example is that Michael Deaver and Lyn Nofziger, who were aides to the then President Reagan, were convicted of violating the Ethics in Government Law. The law, however, does not apply to congressmen and their staffers who become lobbyists and do the same things that Deaver and Nofziger did. Besides the Fair Labor Standards Act and the Ethics in Government Law, laws that do not apply to Congress include

> Civil Rights Act
> Equal Employment Opportunity Act
> Equal Pay Act
> National Labor Relations Act
> Occupational Safety and Health Act
> Freedom of Information Act
> Privacy Act

Illinois Congressman Henry Hyde said, "Congress would exempt itself from the laws of gravity if it could."

Sources: Adapted from Jerome Cramer, Above their own laws, *Time,* May 23, 1988, p. 18., and Florida State University, the James Madison Institute for Public Policy Studies, *The Madison Messenger* (Spring 1988):2.

Average Tax Rate and Marginal Tax Rate

The tax rate is the ratio of tax payments relative to the tax base. If total tax payments are divided by the total tax base, the result is an **average tax rate.** If additional tax payments are divided by changes in the tax base, the result is a **marginal tax rate.** Let us go over examples.

Average Tax Rate
The federal personal income tax had 15 taxable income brackets until 1986. A different tax rate was applied to each income bracket. The 1986 Tax Reform Act reduced the 15 taxable income brackets to only two, fully effective starting in 1988. There were five interim brackets in 1987, the transitional year. The 1988 taxable income brackets are presented in Table 4.2.

Consider two persons, Mr. P(oor) who is making $10,000 per year, and Mr. R(ich), who is making $100,000 per year. Assume that these earnings are taxable incomes, meaning that personal exemptions and all deductions have already been subtracted from gross income. Suppose that both Mr. P and Mr. R are married and file joint returns. Total tax payments by each of the two are shown below. Note that 15 percent means 0.15 in decimals.

Mr. P's tax payments

$10,000 x 0.15 = $1,500

Mr. R's tax payments

$$\begin{aligned} \$29,750 \times 0.15 &= \$\ 4,462.50 \\ (\$100,000 - \$29,750) \times 0.28 &= \underline{\$19,670.00} \\ \text{total} & \quad \$24,132.50 \end{aligned}$$

The average tax rates (ATR) for Mr. P and Mr. R are obtained by dividing total tax payments by their respective incomes. Note that 0.15 in decimals is converted to percentages by multiplying the decimals by 100.

Mr. P's ATR

$$= \frac{\text{total tax payments}}{\text{total taxable income}}$$

$$= \frac{\$1,500}{\$10,000}$$

$$= 0.15 \text{ or } 15\%.$$

Mr. R's ATR

$$= \frac{\text{total tax payments}}{\text{total taxable income}}$$

$$= \frac{\$24,132.50}{\$100,000}$$

$$= 0.241325 \text{ or about } 24.1\%.$$

TABLE 4.2 Taxable Income Brackets, 1988

Tax Rate	Joint Returns	Heads of Households	Singles
15%	0–$29,750	0–$25,300	0–$17,850
25%	Above $29,750	Above $25,300	Above $17,850

Marginal Tax Rate

The term *marginal* in economics has a unique meaning. **Marginal** in economics means a very small incremental change. To compute a marginal tax rate, therefore, there has to be a change in taxable income. Suppose that Mr. P's income increases by $1,000 from $10,000 to $11,000, while Mr. R's income increases by $5,000 from $100,000 to $105,000. The total tax payments for Mr. P and Mr. R are

Mr. P's tax payments

$11,000 x 0.15 = $1,650

Mr. R's tax payments

$$
\begin{array}{rl}
\$29,750 \times 0.15 = & \$\ 4,462.50 \\
(\$105,000 - \$29,750) \times 0.28 = & \$21,070.00 \\
\text{total} & \overline{\$25,532.50}
\end{array}
$$

The marginal tax rates (MTRs) for the two taxpayers are the following:

Mr. P's MTR

$$
= \frac{\text{changes in tax payments}}{\text{changes in taxable income}}
$$

$$
= \frac{\$1,650 - \$1,500}{\$11,000 - \$10,000}
$$

$$
= \ 0.15 \text{ or } 15\%.
$$

Mr. R's MTR

$$
= \frac{\$25,532.50 - \$24,132.50}{\$105,000 - \$100,000}
$$

$$
= \frac{\$1,400}{\$5,000}
$$

$$
= \ 0.28 \text{ or about } 28\%.
$$

The marginal tax rates for Mr. P and Mr. R are the same as tax rates presented in Table 4.2. The reason is that incomes have increased within the bracket that had the same tax rate. Consider Mr. S, who is neither poor nor rich but just struggling to move up the income ladder. Mr. S's income was $28,000 and rose to $32,000. What are Mr. S's ATRs at the two income levels and MTR between the two income levels? Mr. S's ATR at income level $28,000 is 15 percent. Mr. S's ATR at income level $32,000 is obtained as follows:

Tax payments

$$\begin{array}{rcl} \$29,750 \times 0.15 & = & \$4,462.50 \\ (\$32,000 - \$29,750) \times 0.28 & = & \underline{\$\ \ 630.00} \\ \text{total} & & \$5,092.50 \end{array}$$

Mr. S's ATR

$$= \frac{\$5,092.50}{\$32,000}$$

$$= 0.1591406 \text{ or approximately } 15.9\%.$$

Mr. S's tax payments at income level \$32,000 are \$5,092.50, while his tax payments at income level \$28,000 are \$4,200.00, 15 percent of his total income. Mr. S's MTR, therefore, is obtained as follows:

Mr. S's MTR

$$= \frac{\$5,092.50 - \$4,200.00}{\$32,000 - \$28,000}$$

$$= 0.223125 \text{ or approximately } 22.3\%.$$

Rate Structure of Taxes

There are three types of tax rate structures: progressive, proportional, and regressive.

A **progressive tax** is a tax characterized by a marginal tax rate that is greater than average tax rate. When a tax rate is progressive, the percentage of income paid as tax increases as income increases, and decreases as income decreases. The federal personal income tax illustrated in the preceding subsection is progressive, although it is not as progressive as it had been until the 1986 Tax Reform Act took effect. When a tax rate is progressive, those with more income do not simply pay more tax than those with less income; those with more income pay a larger percentage of their income as tax.

A **proportional tax** is a tax characterized by a marginal tax rate that is equal to the average tax rate. When a tax is proportional, the average tax rate remains unchanged as income increases. Under a proportional tax, the percentage of income that those with more income pay as tax is exactly the same as the percentage paid by those with less income.

A **regressive tax** is a tax characterized by a marginal tax rate that is lower than the average tax rate. When a tax is regressive, the average tax rate decreases as income increases. Under a regressive tax, the percentage of income that those with more income pay as tax is smaller than the percentage paid by those with less income.

Sales Tax on Food and Prescription Drugs

Sometimes, whether a tax is progressive, proportional, or regressive cannot be determined on the basis of appearance alone. A sales tax on food and prescription drugs is such an example.

Remember the two persons, Mr. P and Mr. R? Suppose that the two persons live in a community that levies a 5 percent sales tax on food purchased at supermarkets. Suppose also that Mr. P's family spends $5,000 per year on food purchased at supermarkets, while Mr. R's family spends $8,000 per year on food purchased at supermarkets. Mr. R's family is likely to spend more on food even if the number of family members is the same in both families because the wealthier family is expected to have parties more often and buy more expensive food items. Sales taxes paid by the two families, then, are as follows:

	Annual Income	Dollars Spent on Food Items	Sales Tax Paid (5%)
Mr. P's family	$ 10,000	$5,000	$250
Mr. R's family	100,000	8,000	400

Whether a tax is progressive, proportional, or regressive is determined by dividing the tax payment by income. Mr. P's effective tax rate, therefore, is 2.5 percent, obtained by dividing 250 by 10,000, whereas Mr. R's effective tax rate is 0.4 percent, obtained by dividing 400 by 100,000. The sales tax on food is clearly regressive in this case, since the tax rate falls as the level of income rises.

The **effective tax rate** is the tax rate obtained when actual tax payments are divided by income. The concept of the effective tax rate becomes an issue when, like the present example, the effective tax rate is different from the tax rate that applies to the amount of sales. Because of the regressive nature of the sales tax on food and prescription drugs, many states and municipalities exempt sales tax on prescription drugs and food purchased at supermarkets.

Tax Incidence

When a tax is levied, the person who makes the payment may not be the one who ultimately assumes the burden of paying the tax. Tax incidence is the burden of paying the tax. **Tax incidence** refers also to the final resting place of a tax burden, and the problem of tax incidence is the problem of identifying the tax incidence. Those who actually hand the tax dollars over to the government are not necessarily the same as those who ultimately bear the burden of paying the tax, because taxes may be shifted *forward* to consumers or *backward* to producers.

Personal income taxes and inheritance taxes usually are borne by those upon whom the taxes are initially levied. Tax incidence of the corporate income tax is not clear. If corporations operate in a market that is not highly competitive and are in a position to shift the tax to consumers by raising prices of their products, the real burden of the corporate income tax falls primarily on consumers. If, on the other hand, corporations operate in a highly competitive market and cannot raise prices of their products when the tax is levied, the real burden of the corporate income tax falls primarily on stockholders of corporations. The incidence of the corporate income tax in reality is likely shared by stockholders of a firm and the firm's customers.

Taxes are often classified into ad valorem tax and unit tax. **Ad valorem tax** is a tax levied on the monetary value of the tax base, whereas **unit tax** is a tax levied on the unit of the tax base. An example of a unit tax is a gasoline tax levied on the gallons of purchase, such as 8 cents per gallon. An example of an ad valorem tax is the property tax. In fact, the property tax is such a good example of an ad valorem tax that *ad valorem tax* and *property tax* are sometimes used synonymously. The incidence of tax on owner-occupied properties falls on the owners. The incidence of tax on rental properties, however, tends to shift forward to the tenant through higher rents.

Taxation and Equity

When the government levies tax and raises revenue, the taxation affects the distribution of income among taxpayers. When the distribution of income among individual members of a society is altered, an equity problem arises because different members of the society have different opinions as to whether or not the altered distribution of income represents an improvement for the society. There are two basic principles of taxation that have a direct bearing on the distribution of income. They are the ability-to-pay principle and the benefit principle.

The **ability-to-pay principle** is an approach to taxation that suggests taxes should be paid according to the ability of taxpayers to pay. The ability-to-pay is often defined in terms of income. The federal personal income tax is an example of a tax based on the ability-to-pay principle. Depending on what the decision-makers want, income does not have to be the only criterion for measuring ability to pay. Financial wealth such as stocks, bonds, and physical properties that a person owns can also be used as an indicator of the ability to pay. The **benefit principle** is an approach in taxation that suggests taxes should be paid by those who benefit from expenditures made possible from the particular tax revenue. An example of a tax based on the benefit principle is gasoline tax. The gasoline tax is paid by those who benefit from using roads.

The difference between the ability-to-pay approach and the benefit approach is not necessarily cut and dried. Consider local public schools. The primary source of revenue for these schools is property tax. When an increase in the property tax rate is considered for an additional revenue for local public schools, there are always those who oppose the proposal by claiming that the additional revenue should come only from those families with children who attend public schools. The reasoning behind this claim is the benefit principle. Benefits from public education, however, are believed to extend beyond those who attend public schools.

REPRESENTATIVE TAX SYSTEM

Whenever governmental units need additional revenue, policymakers ask themselves what taxes should be raised. The real questions are what is the ideal tax system and what taxes should be raised to bring the present tax system toward the ideal tax system. The problem is that there is no such thing as an ideal tax system that most people can agree on. Consider, again, Mr. P and Mr. R. Mr. P's ideal tax system is likely the one in which revenues are collected on a progressive tax basis, while the ideal tax system for Mr. R is likely the one in which tax payments are in direct proportion to one's income or expenditures. In other words, whether a tax system is ideal or not depends on the value judgment of the person who answers the question. This statement does not mean that policymakers should give up their attempt to search for an ideal tax system. First of all, there are desirable characteristics of a tax system, such as a minimum cost of administering the tax, that policymakers may consider.[3] Second, policymakers may consider consulting a second best alternative, the representative tax system.[4]

The **representative tax system** (RTS) was developed by the Advisory Commission on Intergovernmental Relations in order to find out what would be the total revenue of each of the 50 states if every state applied identical tax rates at the level of national averages to each of 26 commonly used tax bases. Table 4.3 provides a breakdown of the 26 tax bases and the average tax rate for each base levied by state and local governments combined. The RTS can be used as a yardstick for measuring the tax capacity of each of the 50 state and local fiscal systems plus the District of Columbia. The **tax capacity** in the RTS approach is defined as the revenue that each state would collect if it applied national average tax rates to the common set of 26 tax bases. The RTS approach also enables one to derive the tax effort of each state. The **tax effort** of a state is obtained when the state's actual tax collections are divided by the estimated tax capacity and the result is multiplied by 100. Let us illustrate.

In 1983 state and local governments in California collected as taxes $32,170,874,000 exclusive of federal aid. If the national average tax rates were applied to the 26 bases, California's tax revenue would have been $35,142,023,000. California's tax capacity, therefore, was $35,142,023,000, while California's tax effort index was 91.5 percent, obtained by dividing actual tax collections by tax capacity. The tax effort index of 91.5 means that overall California's tax rates were 91.5 percent of national averages in 1983. During the same year, New York's tax capacity was $19,826,188,000, while New York's actual tax collections were $32,211,714,000. New York's tax effort index for 1983, therefore, was 162.5. The tax effort index of 162.5 means that the higher than national average tax rates in New York yielded 62.5 percent higher revenues in New York than would have been collected if national average tax rates were applied in the state.

The RTS approach does not tell us anything about what is or is not an ideal tax system. The approach, however, does tell us what an average state-local fiscal system is doing in collecting revenues from local sources.

SUMMARY

The major sources of revenue to the federal government are the personal income tax, the corporate income tax, and indirect business taxes. Major responsibilities of the federal government are

---

[3]For desirable characteristics of a tax system, see Joseph E. Stiglitz, *Economics of the public sector* (New York: W. W. Norton, 1986), pp. 328–344. The characteristics include (1) economic efficiency, meaning that the tax system should not interfere with the efficient allocation of resources; (2) administration simplicity, meaning that the cost of administering the tax should be minimum; (3) flexibility, meaning that the tax system should respond easily to changing economic circumstances; (4) political responsiveness, meaning that tax burden should not be hidden and the true cost of the tax should be clear to all taxpayers; and (5) fairness by the community standards.

[4]For more on the representative tax system, see Advisory Commission on Intergovernmental Relations, *1983 Tax capacity of the states* (Washington, D.C.: ACIR, April 1986).

TABLE 4.3   Representative Tax Rates of State and Local Governments, 1983

Taxes	Description of Tax Base	Representative Tax Rate
A. General sales and gross receipts tax	Retail sales and selected services	6.6%
B. Selective sales taxes		
Parimutuel	Parimutuel turnover from horse and dog racing	4.87%
Motor fuel	Fuel consumption	$0.09/gallon
Insurance	Insurance premiums	1.73%
Tobacco	Cigarette consumption	$0.14/pack
Amusement	Receipts from amusement and entertainment	1.02%
Public utilities	Revenues from utilities	3.23%
Distilled spirits	Consumption of distilled spirits	$3.58/gallon
Beer	Consumption of beer in barrels	$6.25/barrel
Wine	Consumption of wine	$0.56/gallon
C. License taxes		
Vehicle operator	Motor vehicle operators' licenses	$3.29/lic.
Corporation	Number of corporations	$593.27/corp.
Hunting and fishing	Number of licenses	$8.01/lic.
Alcoholic beverages	Licenses for sale	$813.76/lic.
Automobiles	Private registrations	$30.10/reg.
Truck	Private truck registrations	$69.75/reg.
D. Personal income taxes		
	Federal income tax liability	20.03%
E. Corporate income taxes		
	Corporate income	8.45%
F. Property taxes		
Residential	Market value of residential property	1.34%
Farm	Market value of farm real estate	0.60%
Commercial/ industrial	Net book value of plant, equipment, and inventories	1.23%
G. Public utilities	Net book value of assets	1.49%
H. Estate and gift taxes	Federal estate and gift tax receipts	45.1%
I. Severance taxes		
Oil and gas	Value of oil and gas production	6.67%
Coal	Value of coal production	2.86%
Nonfuel mineral	Value of nonfuel mineral production	0.92%

Source: Advisory Commission on Intergovernmental Relations, *1983 Tax capacity of the states* (Washington, D.C.: ACIR, April 1986), p. 2.

income security, national defense, administration of justice, and international affairs. State governments in general receive most of their revenue from the income tax, sales tax, license fees, and property tax. State governments provide services for highways, public welfare, education, prisons, and industrial development. The major source of revenue for most county governments is the property tax, while major sources of revenue for municipalities vary widely among the property tax, sales tax, and the income tax. City and county governments provide police protection, fire protection, sanitation, parks and recreation, public welfare, libraries, and local roads. There is no effective mechanism that determines the optimal quantity of public goods.

Public choice uses economic methods to study subjects that have traditionally been the domain of political science. The median voter is the voter whose preferred expenditure for a given public good is at the level where the number of individuals who prefer higher expenditure exactly equals the number of individuals who prefer lower expenditure. The lack of incentive for voters to seek additional information necessary to cast a more informed vote is called the rational ignorance effect. The special interest effect refers to the support of special interest issues by politicians who judge that their gains from supporting special interest groups will be greater than their losses.

There are three types of tax rate structures. A progressive tax is characterized by a marginal tax rate that is greater than the average tax rate. A proportional tax is characterized by a marginal tax rate that is equal to the average tax rate. A regressive tax is characterized by a marginal tax rate that is lower than the average tax rate. Sales taxes on food and prescription drugs are regressive since those with more income pay a smaller portion of their income as tax. Tax incidence is the final resting place of a tax burden. The ability-to-pay principle is an approach to taxation that suggests taxes should be paid according to the ability of taxpayers to pay. The benefit principle is an approach to taxation that suggests taxes should be paid by those who benefit from expenditures made possible from the particular tax revenue. Whenever governmental units need additional revenue, policymakers of communities may consult the representative tax system as a second best alternative to an ideal tax system.

EXERCISES

1. Explain the differences between sales tax and excise tax.

2. What are the major sources of revenue to your city or town?

3. Comment on the statement that public goods are produced by the public sector and private goods are produced by the private sector.

4. What is meant by the median voter, and why can the concept of the median voter not be used in determining the optimal quantity of public goods to produce?

5. One of the main ideas that came from public choice theory is the rational ignorance effect of voters. Assuming that the rational ignorance effect exists, how does the effect influence the voting behavior of voters in revealing the true preference of all voters?

6. Pork barrel means appropriations by government for political patronage especially to please legislators' constituents. A good example of a pork barrel project is the

Tennessee-Tombigbee Waterway that connects the Tennessee River and the Tombigbee River through rural counties in Mississippi and Alabama. [For more on the waterway, see Semoon Chang and Philip R. Forbus, Tenn-Tom versus the Mississippi River, *Transportation Journal* 25(Summer 1986):47–54.] How does public choice theory explain the popularity in Congress of pork barrel projects such as the Tenn-Tom Waterway?

7. When those with more income pay a larger amount of tax than those with less income, the rate structure of the tax is progressive. Is this statement correct? Why or why not?

8. Sales tax rate is constant at, say, 4 or 6 percent regardless of the amount of purchase. Economists, however, call sales tax on food purchased at supermarkets a regressive tax. Why?

9. What is the incidence of indirect business taxes?

10. Suppose that the local water district wishes to construct a water treatment plant on a lot owned by an individual who plans to use the lot as a dirt pit, meaning that the soil from the lot is sold as dirt that is used to repair roads or fill potholes. According to the text, governments exercise authority over individual citizens. Assuming that the owner of the lot is not willing to sell the lot to the water district, discuss what the water district should do to build the water treatment plant on the lot.

SUGGESTED READINGS

Buchanan, James M., and Tullock, Gordon. (1962). *The calculus of consent.* Ann Arbor, Mich.: University of Michigan Press.

   One of the most important books on public choice: developed theories of constitutions, political behavior under alternative decision rules, special interest, and other concepts of public choice.

Collett, Iris Weil. (1988). *The ultimate rip-off: A taxing tale.* Sun Lakes, Ariz.: Thomas Horton and Daughters.

   A well-written, suspenseful novel explaining how the Internal Revenue Service enforces tax laws.

Mueller, Dennis C. (1979). *Public choice.* New York: Cambridge University Press.

   A good reference on many topics that pertain to the theory of public choice.

Mueller, Dennis C. (1976). Public choice: A survey. *Journal of Economic Literature* 14(June):395–433.

   A somewhat advanced survey of development and main points of the public choice theory.

Pechman, Joseph A. (1985). *Who paid the taxes, 1966–985.* Washington, D.C.: Brookings Institution.

   An extensive discussion of tax incidence in the United States.

Rockoff, Lisa E. (1985). The federal budget process: How it works. Federal Reserve Bank of Atlanta *Economic Review* 70(May):34–40.

   Explains the federal budget process and the Congressional budget timetable as well as the budget process terminology.

U.S. Department of Treasury, Financial Management Service, *United States Government annual report.*

   An easy to read, mostly graphic and tabular, summary of the annual financial report of the U.S. government.

PART TWO

MICROECONOMICS

Microeconomics is the part of economics that is concerned with individual units within the economy such as firms, industries, particular prices, and individual markets. Macroeconomics, on the other hand, is the part of economics that is concerned with major aggregates or averages of the economy such as total output, inflation, and unemployment. The study of microeconomics as a separate field from macroeconomics is a matter more of convenience than of necessity. When we attempt to solve real economic problems, we need tools developed in both macroeconomics and microeconomics. Also, the tools of analysis developed in microeconomics are an indispensable part of macroeconomic analysis. The eight chapters in Part Two are concerned with microeconomic topics, while the six chapters of Part Three are concerned with macroeconomic topics.

Economic ideas prevailing between 1776 to 1870 of Adam Smith and such British cohorts as Thomas R. Malthus (1766–1834), David Ricardo (1772–1823), and John Stuart Mill (1806–1873) are known collectively as Classical economics. Microeconomics during the Classical days was dominated by the theory of value, in which economists tried to answer the question of what determined the price of a product. The answer the Classical economists gave was the cost of production, meaning that their analysis was limited to the supply side. In the 1870s, other economists such as Leon Walras of Switzerland (1834–1910), Carl Menger of Austria (1840–1921), and Stanley Jevons (1835–1882) of Great Britain criticized the Classical theory of value and emphasized demand as the determinant of value, to the virtual exclusion of supply. These three economists and their followers are known collectively as marginalists or the marginalist school. These economists stressed marginal analysis, or the point of change where the decisions were made. It was not until the days of Alfred

Marshall that economists finally realized that the value of a product was determined by both the supply side stressed by the Classical economists and the demand side stressed by the marginalists.

Alfred Marshall, a British economist, published his *Principles of Economics* in 1890. The book has had a great impact on microeconomics through its introduction of many analytical concepts that became increasingly popular over time. These concepts include consumer's surplus, quasi-rent, internal and external economies, the distinction between the long run and the short run, and the elasticity coefficient. The elasticity concept is presented in Chapter 5, while the concepts of the long run and the short run are presented in Chapter 6. Although the demand and supply model has already been presented in Chapter 3, we have not yet studied how individual firms employ the model in their efforts to maximize profit under different market structures. This last topic is discussed in the remaining six chapters of Part Two.

5

Price Elasticity of Demand

Introducing the Price Elasticity of Demand

Properties of the Price Elasticity of Demand

Other Elasticities

Practical Applications

FIRMS PRODUCE PRODUCTS and sell them to make profits. To generate the maximum profit, owners of all businesses try to be careful in selecting the prices of their products. As a first step toward selecting the maximum-profit price, the owner may want to know how changes in price affect the firm's sales. Let us think of a neighborhood dress store. The owner of the store sometimes changes prices of dresses that she sells to increase the dollar volume of sales and, hopefully, increase profits. The owner would not want to lower the price below the wholesale price, since a price below cost means a loss to her. The owner would not want to raise the price too high either, since the quantity of sales may be too small to make profits at higher prices. Information on how responsive sales are to price changes would be beneficial to the store owner in selecting an optimal sales price, especially during holidays or other times when the store has excess inventory.

Managers of firms are not the only ones who want to know how responsive sales are to price changes. Government officials also need that information when tax increases are considered. An increase in the tax on a product is expected to increase the price of the product. Government would certainly not want to increase a tax on those products for which the quantities demanded decrease drastically with a slight increase in their prices. The responsiveness of sales to price changes is indicated by the price elasticity of demand.

The learning objective of this chapter is to understand the concept of price elasticity and learn how the concept can be used for day-to-day decision-making.

INTRODUCING THE PRICE ELASTICITY OF DEMAND

The price elasticity of demand is a practical and useful concept to those who make pricing decisions. Prices include not only prices of goods but prices of services as well. Determining fees for services such as a haircut or business consulting, for instance, is as important as determining prices of goods such as videotapes or computers.

Defining the Price Elasticity of Demand

The **price elasticity of demand** is an indicator of buyers' response, in terms of changes in the quantity demanded, to changes in the price of a good or service. The price elasticity is measured by the ratio of the percentage change in the quantity of a good or service demanded to the percentage change in the price of the good or service. That is, the price elasticity of demand (E_p) is defined as

$$E_p = \frac{\text{percentage change in quantity demanded}}{\text{percentage change in price}} \tag{5.1}$$

Expression (5.1) may be transformed into an operational definition. To do so, let

Q_1 = quantity before price change
Q_2 = quantity after price change
F_1 = price before change
F_2 = price after change

The operational definition of the price elasticity of demand is

$$E_p \;=\; \frac{Q_2 - Q_1}{Q_1} \;\div\; \frac{P_2 - P_1}{P_1} \qquad\qquad (5.2)$$

Computing the Elasticity Coefficient

Before we study more about the elasticity concept, let us study how to compute the price elasticity coefficient by considering the Ford Mustang. The introduction of the sleek Mustang in 1965 enabled its originator, Lee Iacocca, to become a prominent figure in the automobile industry.

An Illustration
Suppose that this year economists at the Ford Motor Company obtained the relation between the price of Mustangs and the number of Mustangs sold per week at each price level as indicated in Table 5.1.

To illustrate how the elasticity coefficient is actually computed, we take as an example the first two sets of price and quantity figures in Table 5.1. Assuming that the price has decreased from $15,000 to $14,000, data for P's and Q's in equation (5.2) are the following:

$$Q_1 = 10,000$$
$$Q_2 = 11,000$$
$$P_1 = 15,000$$
$$P_2 = 14,000$$

Plugging these values into equation (5.2), and solving the equation for the elasticity coefficient, we obtain

TABLE 5.1 Prices and the Number of Mustangs Sold

Price of a Mustang	Number of Mustangs Sold per Week
$15,000	10,000
14,000	11,000
13,000	12,000
12,000	13,000
11,000	14,000
10,000	15,000

$$E_p = \frac{Q_2 - Q_1}{Q_1} + \frac{P_2 - P_1}{P_1} \tag{5.2}$$

$$= \frac{11{,}000 - 10{,}000}{10{,}000} + \frac{14{,}000 - 15{,}000}{15{,}000} \tag{5.3}$$

$$= \frac{1{,}000}{10{,}000} + \frac{-1{,}000}{15{,}000}$$

$$= \frac{1{,}000}{10{,}000} \times \frac{15{,}000}{-1{,}000}$$

$$= -1.50 \tag{5.4}$$

The price elasticity of demand for the range of price change from $15,000 to $14,000 is –1.50.

Graphic Illustration
A graphic illustration of the elasticity concept is shown in Figure 5.1, in which the demand curve is drawn on the basis of the data contained in Table 5.1. We designate the point crossed by price $15,000 and quantity 10,000 as point A. The elasticity coefficient, –1.50, obtained in (5.4), is called the *point price elasticity of demand*, or simply the *price elasticity of demand*, at point A. To further clarify that the elasticity coefficient obtained in (5.4) is the elasticity at point A, let us take the same two sets of price and quantity figures in Table 5.1. This time, however, we assume that the price has increased from $14,000 to $15,000. Data for P's and Q's in equation (5.2) are now changed to

$$Q_1 = 11{,}000$$
$$Q_2 = 10{,}000$$
$$P_1 = 14{,}000$$
$$P_2 = 15{,}000$$

The elasticity coefficient for this *price increase* can then be computed using equation (5.2):

$$E_p = \frac{(10{,}000 - 11{,}000)}{11{,}000} + \frac{(15{,}000 - 14{,}000)}{14{,}000} \tag{5.5}$$

$$= -1.27 \tag{5.6}$$

The elasticity coefficient, –1.27, is the point price elasticity of demand at point B, which is crossed by price $14,000 and quantity 11,000. For a given set of price and quantity data, the price elasticity of demand is different depending on whether the price has increased or decreased.[1]

[1]The arc price elasticity of demand is sometimes used to compute the elasticity coefficient. The elasticity coefficient obtained using the arc elasticity formula is the coefficient at the midpoint between points A and B on the demand curve shown in Figure 5.1. The elasticity coefficient, therefore, is the same regardless of whether the price rises or falls for a given set of price and quantity data. The arc elasticity formula (E_a) is

$$E_a = \frac{Q_2 - Q_1}{Q_2 + Q_1} \div \frac{P_2 - P_1}{P_2 + P_1}$$

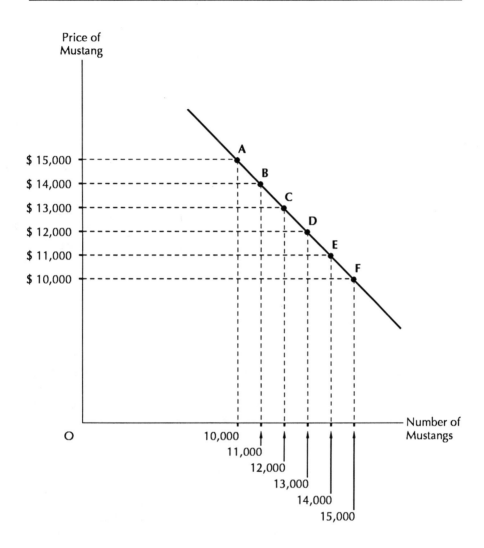

FIGURE 5.1 Hypothetical Demand Curve for Mustangs. The demand curve for Mustangs is based on hypothetical data presented in Table 5.1. The number of Mustangs demanded is 10,000 when the price of a Mustang is $15,000, and 15,000 when the price is $10,000.

Interpreting the Elasticity Coefficient

Once the elasticity coefficient is computed, we need to know what the computed elasticity coefficient means. The sign of the elasticity coefficient is determined even before the elasticity coefficient is computed. The sign is negative when the two variables, price and quantity demanded, change in the opposite direction. The sign is positive when the two variables involved change in the same direction. The elasticity between price and quantity supplied is expected to have a positive sign because a higher price is associated with a larger quantity supplied. So is the elasticity between income and demand since, as income increases, the demand for most goods and services is also expected to increase.

The elasticity coefficient –1.50 means that, at point A on the demand curve graphed in Figure 5.1, as the price of the product changes by 1 percent, the quantity of the product demanded changes by 1.50 percent in the opposite direction. If the price of a Mustang decreases by 1 percent from $15,000 to $14,850 (obtained as 15,000 minus 150, which is 1 percent of 15,000), the number of Mustangs sold is expected to increase by 1.5 percent. The number of Mustangs sold, therefore, is expected to increase from 10,000 to 10,150 (obtained as 10,000 plus 150, which is 1.5 percent of 10,000).

The elasticity coefficient –1.27 means that, at point B on the demand curve graphed in Figure 5.1, as the price of a Mustang changes by 1 percent, the number of Mustangs sold is expected to change by 1.27 percent in the opposite direction. If the price of a Mustang increases by 1 percent from $14,000 to $14,140, the number of Mustangs sold is expected to decrease by 1.27 percent, from 11,000 to 10,860.

Classifying the Price Elasticity of Demand

The concept of price elasticity of demand can be applied to a wide range of goods and services, even though no elasticity coefficients are actually computed. To use the elasticity concept for decision-making purposes, we need to classify the elasticity coefficients into five categories: completely elastic, relatively elastic, unitary elastic, relatively inelastic, and completely inelastic. Since the sign itself has no bearing on determining whether the demand for a given good or service is elastic or inelastic, the classification of elasticity coefficients is usually presented in absolute values. The **absolute value** of a number, denoted by two vertical bars on both sides of the number, is the value of the number without the positive or the negative sign. The absolute values of 5, –1.50, E, and –E, for instance, are respectively 5, 1.50, E, and E. The five categories of elasticity coefficients (E) are summarized in Table 5.2 and explained one by one in the remainder of this section. Figure 5.2 and Figure 5.3 are presented to elucidate the five categories of the elasticity coefficient.

Completely Inelastic
Let us start with the case of a completely inelastic demand, since this case is easy to understand. Let us reconsider the elasticity formula

$$E_p = \frac{\text{percentage change in quantity demanded}}{\text{percentage change in price}} \tag{5.1}$$

A **completely inelastic demand** means that the elasticity coefficient is zero. The elasticity coefficient is zero only if the value of the numerator is zero, which happens only if there is no change in the quantity demanded. Put differently, demand for a product is completely inelastic if the quantity of the product demanded remains unchanged, regardless of what happens to the price of

TABLE 5.2 Classifying Price
Elasticities of Demand

Elasticities	Demand
$\|E\| = \infty$	Completely elastic
$\|E\| > 1$	Relatively elastic
$\|E\| = 1$	Unitary elastic
$\|E\| < 1$	Relatively inelastic
$\|E\| = 0$	Completely inelastic

the product. In Figure 5.2, the demand curve that represents completely inelastic demand is the vertical one. The vertical demand curve points toward one quantity for different levels of the price.

Examples of products for which the demand is almost completely, if not completely, inelastic include insulin, boxes of salt, boxes of matches, certain medical procedures such as a heart bypass operation, and cigarettes to true smokers. The quantities of these products demanded are expected to change little, if any, when the prices of these products change by a *relatively small* amount.

Please keep in mind that price change has to be small relative to the product price in order for the demand for the product to be completely inelastic. Since demand reflects ability as well as willingness to pay, every demand schedule becomes elastic if prices change by a significant amount. Consider insulin. If the price of insulin increases significantly, many diabetics will not be able to buy the medicine no matter how badly they may need it.

Relatively Inelastic

If the percentage change in quantity demanded is smaller than the percentage change in price for a product, the absolute value of the elasticity coefficient is less than 1, and the demand for the product is said to be **relatively inelastic.** When price changes, and when the resulting percentage change in quantity demanded is not as large as the percentage change in price, demand for the product is relatively inelastic. Products for which the demand is relatively inelastic are sometimes called **necessities.**

Examples of products that are relatively price-inelastic include such products as city bus service, water, and bread in general rather than specific brands of bread. Products for which the demand is completely inelastic are also necessities. The demand curve that represents relatively inelastic demand is one comparatively, but not completely, vertical than other demand curves as shown in Figure 5.2.

Relatively Elastic

A **relatively elastic demand** is the opposite case of the relatively inelastic demand in that the percentage change in quantity demanded is greater than the percentage change in price. When demand for a product is relatively elastic, a small percentage change in the price of the product leads to a larger percentage change in the quantity of the product demanded. Products for which the demand is relatively elastic are sometimes called **luxury** or **luxurious goods.** Examples of these

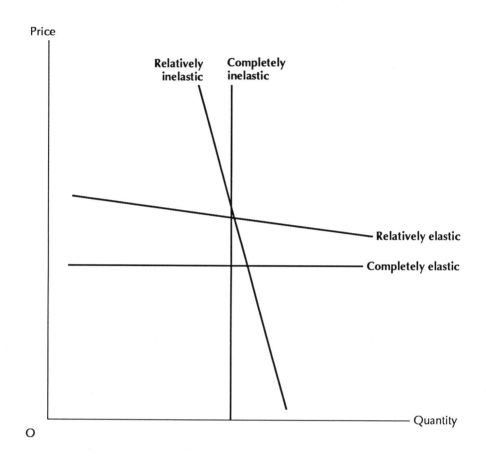

FIGURE 5.2   Demand Curves for Different Elasticities. Four of the five different elasticities are shown in this graph. The more vertical a demand curve is, the less elastic the demand that the curve represents.

products include fur coats, VCRs, and Johnnie Walker whisky.[2] The demand curve that represents relatively elastic demand is graphed in Figure 5.2 as one comparatively, but not completely, horizontal.

Completely Elastic
A **completely elastic demand** means that an infinitesimally small percentage change in price leads to an infinitely large percentage change in the quantity of the product demanded. The elasticity

---

[2]The word *whisky* spelled without the letter "e" refers to Scotch whisky, whereas *whiskey* spelled with an "e" refers to any whiskey, such as bourbon, that is not Scotch.

coefficient for completely elastic demand is infinity. Completely elastic demand, graphed as the horizontal demand curve in Figure 5.2, is a special case of relatively elastic demand. The more horizontal a demand curve is, ceteris paribus, the more elastic is the demand that the demand curve represents. A completely horizontal demand curve represents demand that is completely elastic. We utilize a completely elastic demand curve later when we study the pricing behavior of firms under perfect competition in Chapter 8.

Unit-Elastic
The elasticity coefficient for unit-elastic demand is 1. The elasticity coefficient will remain at one, only if a percentage change in price is offset by the corresponding percentage change in quantity demanded. If demand for a product is **unit-elastic,** percentage changes in the price of the product are offset by corresponding percentage changes in its quantity demanded, leaving the total revenue unchanged.

Let us go over Figure 5.3. Under the demand curve drawn in the figure, two different rectangles are indicated by a falling price and the rising quantity demanded that corresponds to the falling price. A percentage change in price is offset by the resulting percentage change in quantity, only if the area of a rectangle (OABC) formed by a given combination of price and quantity is exactly the same as the area of another rectangle (ODEF) formed by another combination of price and quantity.[3] Each of these rectangles represents total revenue, since the area of a rectangle is obtained by multiplying price, shown as the vertical distance such as OA or OD, and quantity demanded at a given price, shown as the horizontal distance such as OC or OF. Unit-elastic demand is such an exact case that products for which the demand remains unit-elastic for varying prices are not likely to exist.

PROPERTIES OF THE PRICE ELASTICITY OF DEMAND

The price elasticity of demand can be made more useful if the determinants of price elasticity are known, since this knowledge allows decision makers to influence the demand for a product. Price elasticity can also be made more useful if decision makers know how different elasticities affect total revenue when prices are changed, since this knowledge allows them to increase total revenue by changing prices. Determinants and other important properties of the price elasticity of demand are presented in this section.

Determinants of the Price Elasticity

There are three main determinants of the price elasticity of demand: the availability of substitutes, the proportion of the total expenditure for the product in the potential purchaser's (the demander's) budget, and time.

---

[3]A curve that results in rectangles of the same area under the curve is called a rectangular hyperbola. The demand curve drawn in Figure 5.3 is a rectangular hyperbola and represents a unit-elastic demand.

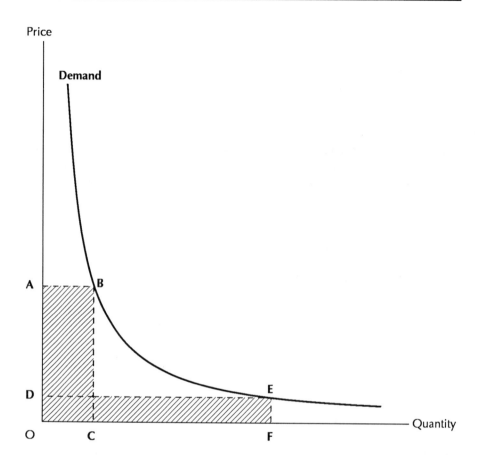

FIGURE 5.3   Unit-Elastic Demand. When the demand for a product is unit-elastic, different rectangles formed under the demand curve are equal in area to one another. A percentage change in price is exactly offset by the corresponding percentage change in quantity demanded.

Availability of Substitutes

Generally speaking, the larger the number of substitutes available for the product, the greater the price elasticity of demand for the product. Demand for Sunbeam bread is more elastic than demand for bread in general, because consumers can buy other brands of bread if the price of Sunbeam bread rises. Demand for Budweiser is more elastic than demand for beer in general, and demand for wood parquet is more elastic than demand for floor materials in general.

PRICE ELASTICITIES OF DENTAL CARE

As a person gets older, the person's need for dental care also increases. For children, on the other hand, dental care is still regarded by many as a luxury good. Assuming that this description is accurate, one would expect different price elasticities of demand for dental care between adults and children. To be specific, demand for dental care is expected to be inelastic for adults and elastic for children. This is exactly what Professors Willard Manning and Charles Phelps found in their study on the demand for dental care. According to Manning and Phelps, the price elasticities of demand for dental visits are –0.65 for adult males, –0.78 for adult females, and –1.40 for children.

Source: Willard G. Manning, Jr., and Charles E. Phelps, The demand for dental care, *Bell Journal of Economics* 10(Autumn 1979):503–525. Copyright 1979, American Telephone and Telegraph Company, reprinted by permission.

Consider demand for new automobiles. Price elasticities of demand for new automobiles have been computed by many economists.[4] The price elasticity of demand for new automobiles has been found by these economists to be near –1.2, ranging from –1 to –2. The empirical elasticity coefficients suggest that the demand for new automobiles in general is relatively, but not very, elastic. Demand for individual models of new automobiles, however, was found to be substantially more elastic. Professor F. Owen Irvine, for instance, found that the price elasticity of demand for Ford Mustangs was –8.42.[5] If the price of a Ford Mustang falls by 1 percent *with all other car prices remaining constant,* the number of Mustangs demanded is expected to increase by 8.42 percent, rather than by the 1.2 percent found for new automobiles in general. Individual new car models have many more substitutes available in other new car models and used cars than do new automobiles in general.

The elasticity –8.42 does not mean that in reality Ford *can* increase sales of Mustangs by 8.42 percent by unilaterally lowering its price by 1 percent. If Ford lowers the price of the Mustang, manufacturers of other cars that are substitutes for Mustangs are also expected to lower their prices. The lower prices of substitutes for Mustangs will prevent sales of Mustangs from increasing significantly.

[4]For empirical studies showing price elasticities of the demand for new automobiles, see Daniel B. Suits, The demand for new automobiles in the United States, 1929–1956, *Review of Economics and Statistics* 53(February 1971):1–10; Senate Subcommittee on Antitrust and Monopoly, The price elasticity of demand for automobiles, in Edwin Mansfield (ed.), *Microeconomics: Selected readings,* 2nd ed. (New York: W. W. Norton, 1975), pp. 73–81; and F. Owen Irvine, Jr., Demand equations for individual new car models estimated using transaction prices with implications for regulatory issues, *Southern Economic Journal* 49(January 1983):764–782.

[5]Irvine, ibid., p. 776.

Portion of Budget

The larger the portion of income spent on a product in a consumer's budget, the greater the price elasticity of demand for the product. Consider a house priced at $100,000. If the price of the house increases by 10 percent, the difference between the old price and the new price is no less than $10,000, which will surely be noticed by most home buyers. Consider a pound of Morton salt priced at 20 cents. If the price per pound of salt increases by 10 percent, the difference between the old price and the new price is no more than 2 cents, which will hardly be noticed by any shopper. If the low-priced item is bought in a large quantity, however, the portion of money spent on the item is large in a consumer's budget, and the demand for the product becomes more elastic.

Another way of finding out how the proportion of one's budget spent on products determines the price elasticity of demand is to see how families with different levels of income treat a given product. Demand for any given product may be price-elastic to low-income families who worry about the price of the product. The demand for the same product, however, may be price-inelastic to high-income families who do not have to worry about the price of the product. Demand for the same product also becomes less elastic to a given family as the family's income increases. Price elasticity falls with rising family income because a given price becomes less of a burden as the family's income rises. Let us invite the great economist Marshall to give us some examples:[6]

> *The current prices of meat, milk and butter, wool, tobacco, imported fruits, and of ordinary medical attendance, are such that every variation in price makes a great change in the consumption of them by the working classes, and the lower half of the middle classes; but the rich would not much increase their own personal consumption of them however cheaply they were to be had. In other words, the direct demand for these commodities is very elastic on the part of the working and lower middle classes, though not on the part of the rich. . . . A little while ago sugar belonged to this group of commodities: but its price in England has now fallen so far as to be low relatively even to the working classes, and the demand for it is therefore not elastic.*

Time

Demand for a product tends to be more elastic, the longer the time period under consideration. The effect of time on the price elasticity of demand works through the process in which consumers can find and possibly develop tastes or preferences for other products that can be used as substitutes for the high-priced product. The longer the time period, the better the opportunities for consumers to find substitutes for the high-priced product. Long-run elasticities, therefore, tend to be more elastic than short-run elasticities.

Short-run and long-run price elasticities for selected products are presented in Table 5.3. For some products such as jewelry, watches, and stationery, little difference exists between short-run and long-run elasticities, while differences in elasticities are large for products like tobacco, toilet articles, intercity bus travel, and foreign travel.

Elasticities on a Given Demand Curve

Let us reconsider the first two combinations of price and quantity in Table 5.1. The two combinations, reproduced below, are graphed in Figure 5.1 as points A and B:

---

[6]Alfred Marshall, *Principles of economics,* 8th ed. (London: Macmillan, 1956), pp. 88–89.

ALFRED MARSHALL

Marshall (1842–1924) studied mathematics at St. John's College, Cambridge University, and stayed on at Cambridge to teach mathematics. His strong feelings of compassion toward the poor, however, led him to study economics. Marshall was truly a great economist. Many of the concepts that he developed, including the familiar demand and supply curves, are now taken for granted. Today's microeconomics courses are said to be three-quarters Marshall, and a thorough examination of Marshallian contributions to economic theory would include nearly all contemporary economic theories. His major publication, *Principles of Economics*, was published in 1890 after more than 20 years of preparation. The book was the most dominant economics text until the 1930s. Marshall was quoted as having said, "The more I study economics the smaller appears the knowledge I have of it ... and now at the end of half a century, I am conscious of more ignorance of it than I was at the beginning."

Quotation cited in Joseph A. Schumpeter, *Ten great economists* (New York: Oxford University Press, 1965), p. 109.

Combination	Price	Quantity
A	$15,000	10,000
B	14,000	11,000

Both points A and B lie on the straight line demand curve. The elasticity coefficient at point A was –1.5, whereas the elasticity coefficient at point B was –1.27. It is obvious that the price elasticity of demand does not remain constant over different prices on the same straight line demand curve. Consider the last two combinations of price and quantity in Table 5.1:

Combination	Price	Quantity
D	$11,000	14,000
E	10,000	15,000

Assuming that the price falls from $11,000 to $10,000, the price elasticity of demand at point D is

TABLE 5.3   Short-Run and Long-Run Price
Elasticities of Demand

Item of Expenditure	Short Run	Long Run
Tobacco products	−0.46	−1.89
Jewelry and watches	−0.41	−0.67
Toilet articles and preparations	−0.20	−3.04
Stationery	−0.47	−0.56
Intercity bus fares	−0.20	−2.17
Motion pictures	−0.87	−3.67
Legitimate theater and opera	−0.18	−0.31
Foreign travel by U.S. residents	−0.14	−1.77

Source: Adapted from H. Houthakker and Lester D. Taylor, *Consumer demand in the United States: Analyses and projections* (Cambridge, Mass.: Harvard University Press, 1970), pp. 61–144, reprinted by permission.

$$E_p = \frac{(15,000 - 14,000)}{14,000} \div \frac{(10,000 - 11,000)}{11,000} \quad (5.7)$$

$$= -0.79 \quad (5.8)$$

As we move down along the demand curve from point A to point B to point D, the price elasticity in absolute value continues to decline from 1.50 to 1.27 to 0.79.

Elasticities at different points on the same demand curve are generalized in Figure 5.4. Demand is inelastic at low prices or points below the midpoint of the demand curve, because, at low prices, consumers are not as sensitive to a given percentage change in price as they are to the same percentage change at high prices. Demand is elastic at high prices or points above the midpoint of the demand curve, because consumers are more sensitive to a given percentage change in price when prices are high. Demand is unit-elastic at the midpoint of the demand curve. If, for instance, the price per pound of Morton salt increases by 10 percent from 20 cents to 22 cents, demand is expected to remain inelastic. Suppose that its price continues to climb until the price finally reaches, say, $100 per pound. If its price increases by the same 10 percent from $100 to $110, consumers will think twice before they buy the salt, and the demand for salt becomes elastic.

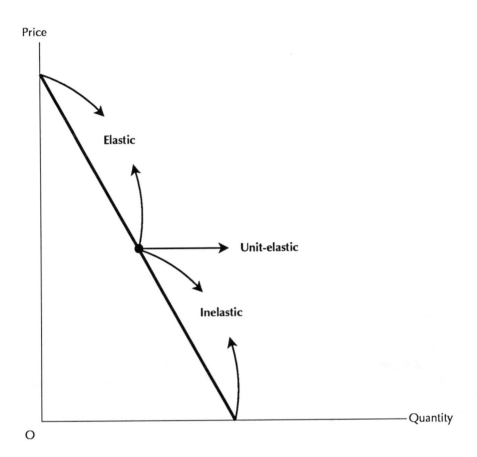

FIGURE 5.4   Different Elasticities for Different Prices. On a given straight line demand schedule, demand at prices above the midpoint of the demand curve is elastic, whereas demand at prices below the midpoint is inelastic.

Price Elasticities and Total Revenue

Total revenue is the dollar value of all sales and is obtained by multiplying price by the quantity of sales. If 10 compact disc (CD) players were sold at a price of $200 each, total revenue would be $2,000. When the price of the CD player increases from $200 to $300, total revenue will increase if the number of CD players sold remains the same. Total revenue will also increase if the higher price is enough to make up for the decreased number of CD players sold. Whether total revenue increases or decreases with a price rise depends on the relative decrease in sales, which, in turn, depends on the price elasticity of demand. The relationships between price elasticities and total revenue are summarized in Table 5.4, and are explained below.

TABLE 5.4   Price Elasticities and Total Revenue

Elasticity of Demand	Price Changes	Changes in Total Revenue
Elastic	Rise	Decrease
Elastic	Fall	Increase
Unit-elastic	Rise	No change
Unit-elastic	Fall	No change
Inelastic	Rise	Increase
Inelastic	Fall	Decrease

Inelastic Demand

If demand for a product is inelastic, an increase in price results in an increase in total revenue. As the price of the product goes up, consumers spend more on this product and less on others. A higher price will cause sales to fall, but the higher price is more than sufficient to offset the decrease in sales, thereby increasing total revenue. If demand is inelastic, a decrease in price results in a decrease in total revenue. A lower price will cause sales to rise, but the increased sales are not sufficient to offset the lower price; therefore, total revenue is lowered. For necessities such as food and other household items sold at supermarkets, consumers buy almost the same quantity when their prices change. Total revenue, therefore, rises with price increases and falls with price decreases.

Elastic Demand

If the demand for a product is elastic, an increase in the price of the product will result in a decrease in total revenue. A higher price will cause sales to fall, and the higher price is not sufficient to offset the decrease in sales; therefore, total revenue is decreased. If demand is elastic, a decrease in price will result in an increase in total revenue. A lower price will cause sales to rise, and the increased sales are more than sufficient to offset the lower price, thereby increasing total revenue.

Unit-Elastic Demand

The effect of price changes on unit-elastic demand has already been introduced in Figure 5.3. The area of a rectangle is obtained by multiplying the vertical distance and the horizontal distance of the rectangle. If the vertical distance of a rectangle is 10 and its horizontal distance 20, the area is 200. Likewise, if the vertical distance of the same rectangle is $10 (per unit) and its horizontal distance is 20 units, the area of the rectangle becomes $200. All rectangles under the demand curve graphed in Figure 5.3 represent total revenue, since the vertical distance of any of these rectangles measures price and the horizontal distance of any of these rectangles measures quantity. By the definition of unit-elastic demand, the areas of all rectangles under a unit-elastic demand curve are the same. When demand is unit-elastic, therefore, total revenue remains unchanged regardless of whether prices rise or fall.

Unit-elastic demand has an interesting property. Suppose that we start producing and selling a product. Suppose also that, in the absence of any comparable product, we have decided to charge a very low price in the beginning and raise the price gradually as the sales volume increases. At low prices, demand for our product is relatively inelastic. We raise price to increase total revenue. As the price reaches a level beyond the midpoint of the demand curve, demand for our product becomes elastic and total revenue starts declining. Total revenue is maximized when the demand for our product is unit-elastic.

OTHER ELASTICITIES

The price elasticity of demand is the most important elasticity concept. There are other important elasticities, however. The other elasticities mentioned often in business and economics are the price elasticity of supply, the income elasticity of demand, and cross elasticities.

Price Elasticity of Supply

The price elasticity of supply is calculated in the same way as the price elasticity of demand. The sign of the price elasticity of supply is positive, however, and unit-elastic supply appears to be simpler to understand than unit-elastic demand.

The **price elasticity of supply** measures suppliers' response in terms of changes in the quantity supplied to changes in the price of a product. The price elasticity of supply (E_p) is obtained by dividing the percentage change in quantity supplied by the percentage change in price:

$$E_p = \frac{\text{percentage change in quantity supplied}}{\text{percentage change in price}} \tag{5.9}$$

Like its counterpart in demand, the price elasticity of supply has the five classifications summarized in Table 5.5. No symbol for absolute value is necessary in Table 5.5 because the signs of the price elasticity of supply are positive.

TABLE 5.5 Classifying Elasticities of Supply

Elasticities	Supply
$E = \infty$	Completely elastic
$E > 1$	Relatively elastic
$E = 1$	Unitary elastic
$E < 1$	Relatively inelastic
$E = 0$	Completely inelastic

The five classifications of the price elasticity of supply are graphed in Figure 5.5. **Completely inelastic supply** means that the quantity supplied remains unchanged when price changes and is represented by the vertical supply curve. An example of products for which the supply is completely inelastic is genuine, not reproduced, antiques. **Relatively inelastic supply** means that the percentage change in quantity supplied is less than the percentage change in price, and is represented by the comparatively, but not completely, vertical supply curve. Examples of products for which the supply is relatively inelastic are farm products. A substantial increase in the quantity of farm products supplied is not likely until the next growing season, even if the prices of farm products increase substantially.

Relatively elastic supply is the opposite case of relatively inelastic supply. When supply of a product is relatively elastic, a small percentage change in the price of the product results in a large percentage change in its quantity supplied. Most manufactured goods may be cited as examples. **Completely elastic supply** is a special case of relatively elastic supply and, like completely elastic demand, has no practical examples. **Unit-elastic supply** means that a percentage change in the price of a product leads to the same percentage change in the quantity supplied. Unlike unit-elastic demand, which is represented by a curve, unit-elastic supply is represented by a straight line supply schedule of any positive slope that passes through the origin.

Income Elasticity of Demand

The **income elasticity of demand** measures buyers' response in terms of changes in demand for a product when consumers' income changes. Since demand for normal products usually increases with rising income, the income elasticity (E_y) is expected to have a positive sign. The formula for the income elasticity of demand is

$$E_y = \frac{\text{percentage change in quantity demanded}}{\text{percentage change in income}} \qquad (5.10)$$

Although the income elasticities for most goods and services are expected to have positive signs, not all income elasticities have positive signs. Let us see why. As income increases, demand for most goods and services also increases. Goods and services for which demand increases as income increases are called **normal** or **superior goods.** Goods such as automobiles, houses, ice cream, butter, opera tickets, and legal, accounting, and public safety services are normal goods. There are some goods and services for which the demand tends to decrease as income increases. Goods and services for which demand decreases as income increases are called **inferior goods.** Margarine, powdered milk, and cheap products in general that have preferred but more expensive substitutes are examples of inferior goods. For consumers who buy margarine for its lower cholesterol, margarine would be a normal good rather than an inferior good, since they will still buy margarine rather than butter regardless of their income.

Recall that the sign of elasticity is determined by the direction of the two variables that are involved in computing the elasticity. The income elasticity for normal goods has a positive sign, but the income elasticity for inferior goods has a negative sign, since income and demand for inferior goods move in the opposite direction.

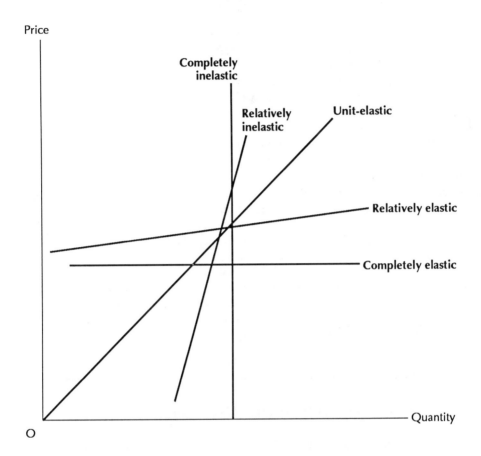

FIGURE 5.5 Supply Curves for Different Elasticities. Like demand curves, the more vertical a supply curve, the less elastic the supply that the supply curve represents. The only exception is the unit-elastic supply curve that passes the point of origin.

Cross Elasticities

The cross (price) elasticity of demand is an elasticity that involves two different products. Suppose that there are two products, A and B. If the two products are related in some way, a change in the price of product A will affect the demand for product B. The **cross elasticity of demand** between two products measures changes in demand for one product in response to changes in the price of the other product. The cross elasticity of demand (E_c) between products A and B, therefore, is

$$E_c = \frac{\text{percentage change in quantity of B demanded}}{\text{percentage change in price of A}}\qquad(5.11)$$

Unlike other price elasticities, the sign of cross elasticity has a meaning. The sign tells us whether the two products are substitutes or complements. A **substitute** for a good or service is another good or service that satisfies the same wants, whereas a **complement** for a good or service is a good or service that is consumed together with the good or service under consideration. If the two products are unrelated, the elasticity coefficient is zero. A zero cross price elasticity means that changes in the price of one product have no effect on the demand for the other product.

The Pulsar NX and Toyota FX16 are *relatively* inexpensive sports cars and considered by many as being substitutes for each other. If the price of the NX falls, the number of NX's demanded will increase but the demand for FX16's is expected to fall. The price of one product and the demand for its substitute product move in the same direction. Consider an example with rising price: Terradex and Radtrak are both detectors of radon, an odorless and colorless radioactive gas that causes lung cancer. Radon seeps into a house if a house is built on a lot that overlies uranium. The cross elasticity between Terradex and Radtrak is also positive because an increase in the price of Terradex results in an increase in demand for Radtrak.

Finally, consider golf clubs and a golf course, which are complements. The service of a golf course is priced by a greens fee. If the greens fee of a golf course is raised from $10 to $20 for 18 holes of play, the higher greens fee will have an adverse effect on the number of golf games played on the course and eventually on the number of new golfers. The higher greens fee will reduce the number of golf clubs purchased. The cross elasticity between fees for the service of a golf course

---

RESIDENTIAL DEMAND FOR WATER

Professors Henry Foster and Bruce Beattie of Texas A&M University estimated price and income elasticities of the urban residential demand for water. Their estimates are based on 1960 data of water quantity, price, and residents from 218 cities in the United States. The income elasticity of residential demand for water was 0.6274, positive but relatively inelastic. Apparently, demand for water increases as income increases but at a slower rate than the rate of increase in income. The price elasticity of demand for water is highly inelastic and varies from one region to another: Midwest (−0.0804), South (−0.0928), New England and Northern Atlantic Coast (−0.1180), Southwest (−0.1223), Plains and Rocky Mountains (−0.2261), and Northern California and Pacific Northwest (−0.2686).

The highly inelastic residential demand for water among all regions of the United States means that the vast majority of utilities may be able to increase total revenue by raising the price of water. Raising the price of water, however, may not be an effective way of reducing the quantity of water demanded if the object is conservation.

Source: Henry S. Foster, and Bruce R. Beattie, Urban residential demand for water in the United States, *Land Economics* 55 (February 1979):43–58.

and the number of golf clubs that golfers buy, therefore, is negative since the two move in the opposite direction. The sign of cross elasticity of demand for complements is negative.

PRACTICAL APPLICATIONS

Before we leave this chapter, let us look at two practical applications of the price elasticity of demand: one relates to identifying the incidence of an excise tax, and the other to the pricing behavior of a firm when its competitors lower their prices.

Incidence of a Sin Tax

A tax on alcoholic beverages or cigarettes is sometimes called a **sin tax.** When government needs additional revenue, the sin tax is a favorite source for many politicians, especially those who neither drink nor smoke. It is highly probable that, wherever we live, more than half the price that we pay for cigarettes and alcoholic beverages goes to the government. Demand for alcoholic beverages and cigarettes is believed to be relatively inelastic, although the high taxes on alcoholic beverages in selected communities may have pushed their prices to the range in which demand for alcoholic beverages has become elastic.

When demand for cigarettes is highly inelastic, the demand curve for cigarettes is almost vertical, as shown in Figure 5.6. An increase in the excise tax levied on sales of cigarettes at the retail level is an additional cost to the seller. The seller, therefore, will try to add the increased tax to the supply price of cigarettes. The increase in the excise tax shifts the supply curve upward.

Assume that the price per pack of cigarettes before tax was $1.00, and that the new excise tax is 20 cents per pack. This means that the vertical distance between the supply curve without the new tax and the supply curve with the new tax for all levels of quantity is 20 cents. The new price is determined by the demand curve and the supply curve with the new tax. The new price with tax is indicated in Figure 5.6 as $1.18. The incidence of the excise tax on smokers is 18 cents, which is the increase in market price from $1.00 to $1.18 per pack that the smoker pays, while the incidence of the new tax on cigarette suppliers is 2 cents, which represents the decrease in after-tax price from $1.00 to 98 cents per pack. The burden of a new tax on a product for which the demand is inelastic is borne mostly by consumers, whereas the burden of a new tax on a product for which the demand is elastic is borne mostly by suppliers. **Tax incidence** refers to the way in which the ultimate burden of paying a tax is shared among individuals.

Price Cut as a Defensive Strategy

Fashionique is our neighborhood dress store. Suppose that other dress stores in town that Fashionique competes against lowered the prices of the dresses that they sell. What should Fashionique do? Since competing stores sell substitutes for the Fashionique dresses, the lower prices at competing stores will lure customers away from Fashionique. The decreased demand for dresses sold at Fashionique shifts the demand curve for Fashionique dresses from AB to CD as shown in Figure 5.7.

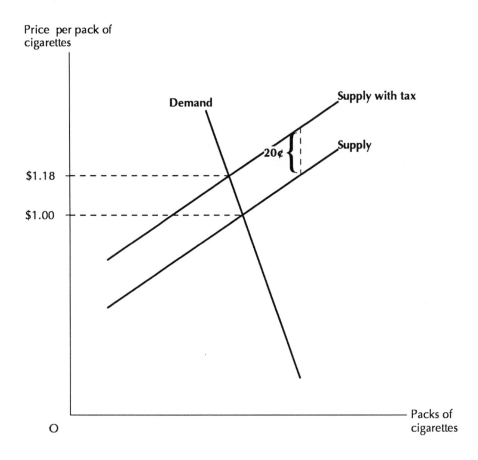

FIGURE 5.6 Incidence of an Excise Tax on Cigarettes. Demand for cigarettes is highly inelastic. When demand for a product is highly inelastic, an excise tax on the product is borne mostly by consumers of the product.

At the price that is currently charged by Fashionique, demand for Fashionique dresses becomes less elastic since the price is indicated comparatively at a higher point (Y) of the new demand curve CD than the point X indicated on the old demand curve AB. To dramatize the point, the current price level is selected in such a way that point X lies below the midpoint of demand curve AB, and point Y lies above the midpoint of the shifted demand curve CD. Demand for Fashionique dresses is more elastic at point Y on demand curve CD than at point X on demand curve AB. The elastic demand for Fashionique dresses at point Y on the shifted demand curve CD will provide an opportunity for Fashionique to lower the prices of its dresses if it wishes to increase total revenue.

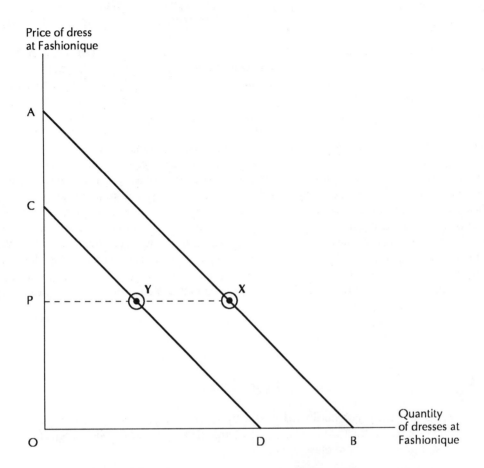

Price of dress
at Fashionique

FIGURE 5.7 Price Cuts and Price Elasticity. If competitors of Fashionique
lower prices, the demand curve for Fashionique dresses shifts to the left, and
the demand for Fashionique dresses at the present price becomes more
elastic, providing an incentive for Fashionique to cut its own price.

SUMMARY

The knowledge of the price elasticity of a product is used to select prices that maximize sales
revenue of the product. The price elasticity of demand is classified into five categories: completely
elastic, relatively elastic, unit-elastic, relatively inelastic, and completely inelastic. The more
responsive demand is to changes in price, the more elastic the demand is. The price elasticity of
demand depends on the availability of substitutes, the proportion of total expenditures for a product
in one's budget, and time. The larger the number of substitutes available for the product, the greater

the price elasticity of demand for the product. Demand for a given product becomes less elastic to a family as the family's income increases. This is because a certain price becomes less of a burden as the family's income rises.

Elasticities at different points on the same demand curve are different. Demand is inelastic at low prices or points below the midpoint of the demand curve, and is elastic at high prices or points above the midpoint of the demand curve. If demand for a product is inelastic, an increase in price results in an increase in total revenue. If demand is elastic, an increase in the price of the product results in a decrease in total revenue. When demand is unit-elastic, total revenue remains unchanged regardless of whether prices rise or fall. The price elasticity of supply measures suppliers' response in terms of changes in the quantity supplied when the price of a product changes.

The income elasticity of demand measures percentage changes in demand for a product in response to percentage changes in consumers' income. The cross elasticity of demand between two products measures percentage changes in demand for one product in response to percentage changes in the price of another product. Normal goods have a positive income elasticity, while inferior goods have a negative income elasticity. Substitutes have a positive cross price elasticity, while complements have a negative cross price elasticity. A new tax on a product for which the demand is inelastic is borne mainly by consumers, whereas a new tax on a product for which the demand is elastic is borne mainly by suppliers. Finally, if competitors cut prices, the demand curve for substitutes sold by the firm under consideration shifts to the left, and the demand for these substitutes becomes more elastic.

EXERCISES

1. According to a report published in 1958 by the U.S. Senate Subcommittee on Antitrust and Monopoly, the income elasticity of demand for new automobiles ranged from 2.5 to 4.2. Interpret these elasticity coefficients.

2. Explain the unit of measurement of the price elasticity of demand.

3. Suppose that Dairy Queen's cost of making and selling a Blizzard ice cream sundae remains the same for all realistic quantities of sale, and that the current price of the sundae is significantly above the cost. Assuming that the demand for the ice cream is highly elastic, what should Dairy Queen do to increase profit?

4. Determine the signs of the following elasticities:

   a. Price elasticity of supply
   b. Price elasticity of demand
   c. Income elasticity of demand for normal goods
   d. Income elasticity of demand for inferior goods
   e. Cross elasticity between two substitutes
   f. Cross elasticity between two complements
   g. Cross elasticity between two unrelated goods

5. Determine whether demand for the following products is likely to be price-elastic or inelastic:

   a. Movie tickets in general
   b. Tickets for the best movie of the year
   c. Sony color TV
   d. Reunite wine
   e. Textbooks

6. Why is it likely that demand for a product is inelastic when its price is low but becomes more elastic as its price rises?

7. Determine the signs of the cross elasticities between the following pairs of goods:

   a. Golf clubs and golf courses
   b. Automobiles and gasoline
   c. Vodka and balloons
   d. Parker pens and Cross pens
   e. Dunkin doughnuts and French doughnuts

8. A study by Rebecca L. Johnson and Daniel B. Suits on the demand for visits to U.S. national parks was published in the fall 1983 issue of the *Journal of Travel Research* (pp. 21–24). According to the study, the gasoline price elasticity of demand for visits to national parks is –0.427. What does this elasticity coefficient mean?

9. The same study by Johnson and Suits found that the income elasticity of demand for visits to national parks was negative 0.885. Assuming that this is an accurate estimate, what does the estimated income elasticity mean?

10. Studies have found that the cross elasticity of demand for butter with respect to the price of margarine is 0.81, but the cross elasticity of demand for margarine with respect to the price of butter is 0.67. How could the two elasticities be different?

SUGGESTED READINGS

Bell, Frederick W. (1968). The pope and the price of fish. *American Economic Review* 58(December):1346–1350.

   In February 1966 Pope Paul VI ended the ban on eating meat on Fridays for Roman Catholics. The study examines the effect of the end of the ban on the demand for fish in the northeastern United States, and presents the price elasticities of demand for various species of fish.

Chang, Semoon. (1984). *Practitioners' guide to econometrics.* Lanham, Maryland: University Press of America, pp. 91–98.

   Explains, step by step, how elasticities are computed by economists using the multiple regression method.

Houthakker, H. S., and Taylor, Lester D. (1970). *Consumer demand in the United States: Analyses and projections,* 2nd and enlarged ed. Cambridge, Mass.: Harvard University Press.

A widely cited study that contains empirical price and income elasticities for more than 80 different goods and services.

Taylor, Lester D. (1975). The demand for electricity: A survey. *Bell Journal of Economics* 6(Spring):74–110.

A survey of studies that contains a summary of estimated elasticities of demand for electricity.

6

Production and the Costs of Production

FARMING IS NOT such an easy profession as politicians retiring to the life of "gentleman farmer" would lead us to believe. Consider the relation between fertilizer and the crop yield per acre. As the amount of fertilizer applied to farmland increases, the yields tend also to increase. Too much fertilizer, however, will burn the crops. The process of planning, growing, and harvesting crops is the process of optimizing the use of farmland, farm labor, and other inputs including fertilizer. Like farming, firms optimize by trying to maximize the quantity of output for a given budget. Firms also optimize by trying to minimize the cost of producing a given level of output. The cost of production is the mirror image of production activities.

The learning objective of this chapter is to study basic concepts that relate to the production of goods and services and the costs of producing these goods and services. Just as the cost of production is the mirror image of production activities, so are the cost concepts the mirror image of production concepts.

PRODUCTION

Production refers to an act of creating a good or service that has an exchange value. Building airplanes and submarines is a production activity; so is packaging pickles and steak sauce. Production is not limited to goods. Teaching, legal services, accounting services, and commercial entertainment such as stage shows and boxing matches are also production activities.

Production Function

Production processes typically require many different types of inputs. These inputs are broadly classified into land, labor, capital goods, and entrepreneurship. Each of these broad categories of inputs may be classified into more specific inputs. Labor, for instance, may be divided into hourly workers and salaried managers. A **production function** describes the relation between the quantity of output (Q) and various amounts of inputs (V_i) needed to produce that quantity of output, given production technology. That is,

$$Q = f(V_1, V_2, ..., V_n),\tag{6.1}$$

where V_1, V_2, and V_n are different inputs.

In studies of production, inputs are classified into fixed inputs and variable inputs. **Fixed inputs** are those inputs whose quantity remains unchanged as the quantity of output changes. Fixed inputs include services of managers, physical plant capacity, and certain utilities such as safety lights and fixed monthly charges for telephone services. **Variable inputs** are those inputs that vary with the quantity of output. Variable inputs include most labor services and materials.

The presumption of the production function is that firms efficiently utilize all resources, including given technology, in order to obtain maximum output from given inputs. The relation between the quantity of output and inputs described in equation (6.1), therefore, is unique in that the quantity of output Q represents the maximum output that can be obtained from given inputs V_i. The assumption of maximum output for given inputs is what makes production an economic problem. The process of combining different inputs in such a way as to obtain the maximum quantity of output from given inputs represents an optimization process that is central to all economic problems. The process of actually making a product is purely an engineering problem.

Product Concepts

Three product concepts are introduced in this section: total product, average product, and marginal product. For the sake of simplicity, let us assume that all inputs with the exception of labor are fixed in quantity, and that the labor input is measured in the number of workers.[1] These assumptions considerably simplify our discussion by clarifying the amount of product that can be attributed to a particular input, labor.

Defining Product Concepts

Total product of labor is the maximum quantity of output obtainable from a given number of workers with given capital goods that the workers work with. The **average product of labor** is the quantity of output per worker, obtained by dividing the total quantity of output by the number of workers. The **marginal product of labor** is the change in total product that is attributable to a unit change in labor services. The marginal product of labor usually means the quantity of output produced by the last worker hired. The term *marginal* in economics means one additional unit or one last unit added.

An Illustration

Let us think of a small dressmaking business in the garment district of New York City. A hypothetical relation between the number of seamstresses working at the business and the number of dresses they make during a given year is presented in Table 6.1. The first column shows the number of seamstresses, while the second column shows the total number of dresses that all seamstresses make. Figures in column (2) are the total product of labor. Figures in column (3) are the average products of labor, obtained by dividing the figures in column (2) by the number of seamstresses in column (1). When there are two seamstresses, for instance, the total product of labor is 250 dresses per year, and the average product of labor is 125 dresses per year, obtained by dividing 250 by 2. Figures in column (4) are marginal products of labor, obtained by dividing changes in total products by changes in the number of workers.

Consider the marginal product of the third seamstress. Changes in total products from those for two seamstresses (250) to those for three seamstresses (390) are 140, while the change in the number of seamstresses from two to three is one. The marginal product of the third seamstress (MPL), therefore, is obtained as

---

[1]Labor input is typically measured in hours. A **man-hour** is the labor service provided by a person for production for one hour. A **man-year** is the labor service provided by a person for production for a year. Another term used interchangeably with man-year is the **FTE**, which stands for the **full-time equivalent** and measures the amount of labor service that is equivalent to a man-year. If one person works full-time during the first half of the year and another person works full-time for the second half of the year, the total labor service by both persons is one FTE.

$$\text{MPL} = \frac{\text{changes in total product}}{\text{changes in labor}} \qquad (6.2)$$

$$= \frac{390 - 250}{3 - 2}$$

$$= \frac{140}{1}$$

$$= 140 \qquad (6.3)$$

The marginal product of labor is the change in total product that results from a one-unit change in the quantity of labor. In Table 6.1, the number of seamstresses in column (1) increases by one. The marginal product of labor presented in column (4), therefore, can be obtained simply by subtracting the total product of a given number of seamstresses from the total product of the number of seamstresses that is one greater than the given number. The process is illustrated in brackets of column (4) in Table 6.1. The marginal product of the second seamstress, for instance, is obtained by subtracting 100, which represents the total product of one seamstress, from 250, which represents the total product of two seamstresses.

To economists, the term *labor productivity* may mean any of the three: total, average, or marginal products. To laypersons or mass media, labor productivity usually means the average product of labor. If the quantity of output per worker increases, labor productivity is said to be rising. If the quantity of output per worker decreases, labor productivity is said to be falling.

TABLE 6.1   Total, Average, and Marginal Products of Seamstresses

(1) Number of Seamstresses	(2) Total Product of Labor per Year	(3) Average Product of Labor per Year	(4) Marginal Product of Labor per Year
0	0	0	0 [= 0 – 0]
1	100	100	100 [= 100 – 0]
2	250	125	150 [= 250 – 100]
3	390	130	140 [= 390 – 250]
4	500	125	110 [= 500 – 390]
5	600	120	100 [= 600 – 500]
6	660	110	60 [= 660 – 600]
7	660	94	0 [= 660 – 660]
8	640	80	–20 [= 640 – 660]

SHORT RUN AND LONG RUN IN PRODUCTION

The business world is dynamic. Operators of businesses place orders for winter products in the middle of summer, and successful operators of dress stores work constantly to detect slight but ever-present changes in fashion. Operators of businesses should also consider expanding facilities when prospects for additional business look promising, and consider closing facilities when prospects are judged to be gloomy. To organize these changes in ways that can help individual businesses, it is necessary to make a distinction between the short run and long run in production.

The Short Run versus the Long Run

The difference between the short run and the long run in laypersons' conversation is relative: The short run is a relatively short period of time, while the long run is a relatively long period of time. Economists sometimes use the two terms as they are used in laypersons' conversation. In studies of production and costs of production, however, economists make a clear distinction between the two terms that cannot necessarily be measured in lengths of a time period.

The **short run** in production refers to a period of time during which at least one input is fixed in amount and at least one input is variable so that the rate of output can be changed. The **long run** in production refers to a period of time during which all inputs vary. Stated in simple terms, the productive capacity remains unchanged in the short run but changes in the long run. Let us explain the difference between the two.

A candy store and a hamburger shop are located adjacent to each other on Main Street in Anytown. Suppose that sales at the hamburger shop have been increasing rapidly during the past six months, but sales at the candy store have been very slow during the same period. As more customers come to the hamburger shop, the shop hires more workers to make more hamburgers and cater to the customers. Hiring more workers and selling more hamburgers with the given productive capacity are short-run changes.

Suppose that one day the owners of the hamburger shop decide to buy the adjacent candy store for expansion. From the moment that the decision to buy and sell the candy store has been signed by owners of the hamburger shop and owners of the candy store, the hamburger shop enters a long-run adjustment, which ends on the day when the expansion is completed and the expanded facility is open for business. Once the long-run change is over, the hamburger shop returns to the short-run operation.

The short run is an operating concept in that it involves day-to-day operations with a fixed capacity, while the long run is a planning concept in that the productive capacity is changed for increased production and possibly for lower unit costs of production. All inputs are variable in the long run since fixed inputs such as the size of a plant are no longer fixed during the long-run adjustment of a firm's expansion, or contraction, of its productive capacity.

Law of Diminishing Returns

An interesting question involving production in the short run is, what happens to the quantity of output when more units of a variable input such as labor are added to the firm's fixed inputs? The answer has already been given in the beginning sentences of this chapter. As use of fertilizer increases, crop yields increase, but not forever. If too much fertilizer is used, crops burn and crop yields actually decrease. In this section, let us formalize the answer by introducing the law of diminishing returns.

According to the **law of diminishing returns,** as successive units of a variable input are added to fixed inputs, the marginal product that is attributable to each additional unit of the variable input eventually declines. A numerical example of the law was introduced in column (4) of Table 6.1, Marginal Product of Labor. Given a limited-size room in which dresses are made, as more seamstresses are hired, the number of dresses that each additional seamstress makes may increase initially but eventually decreases as more seamstresses are hired and the room gets more and more crowded.

Since the law of diminishing returns requires the presence of fixed inputs, the concept is a short-run concept. In contrast, the concept of returns to scale, introduced below, is a long-run concept, since it assumes that the quantities of all inputs change.

Returns to Scale

An interesting question involving production in the long run is, what happens to the quantity of output when all inputs are varied simultaneously? Will the quantity of output increase at a faster or a slower rate than increases in inputs? When all inputs are varied simultaneously more or less in equal proportion, the **scale of production** is said to change. The primary concern in long-range planning is to find out what happens to the quantity of output as the scale of production changes. Changes in output that result from changes in the scale of production are called **returns to scale.**

The returns to scale in production are classified as increasing, constant, or decreasing returns to scale, depending on what happens to the quantity of output when the quantities of all inputs change in equal proportion. Suppose that the quantities of all inputs are doubled. If the quantity of output more than doubles, there are increasing returns to scale; if the quantity of output is also doubled, there are constant returns to scale; and if the quantity of output less than doubles, there are decreasing returns to scale.

A scale coefficient may be used to illustrate returns to scale. Let us define the **scale coefficient** (SCE) as the ratio of changes in the quantity of output to changes in the quantities of all inputs:

$$SCE = \frac{\text{changes in quantity of output}}{\text{changes in quantities of all inputs}} \tag{6.4}$$

The three classes of returns to scale are indicated using the value of SCE as follows:

SCE > 1;   increasing returns to scale
SCE = 1;   constant returns to scale
SCE < 1;   decreasing returns to scale

The returns to scale for many industries have been estimated by several economists, including Paul H. Douglas, John R. Moroney, and A. A. Waters.[2] These estimates indicate that production

---

[2]Paul H. Douglas, Are there laws of production? *American Economic Review* 38(March 1948):1–41; John R. Moroney, Cobb-Douglas production functions and returns to scale in U.S. manufacturing industry, *Western Economic Journal* 6(December 1967):39–51; and A. A. Walters, Production and cost functions: An econometric survey, *Econometrica* 31(January-April 1963):1–66.

exhibits approximately constant returns to scale, meaning that a proportionate increase in the quantities of all inputs leads to a proportionate increase in the quantity of output. If the quantities of all inputs double, for instance, the quantity of output approximately doubles. Specific scale coefficients estimated by Moroney on the basis of 1957 data of U.S. industries are presented in Table 6.2. Estimated scale coefficients for most industries are close to 1, ranging from 0.95 for the petroleum industry to 1.11 for the furniture industry.

COSTS OF PRODUCTION

The notion of costs in economics relates to the basic premise that resources are scarce and have alternative uses. Costs represent the other side of production and measure the opportunity to produce alternative goods and services that is forgone by producing a given product. Costs of production, therefore, are opportunity costs. *Opportunity costs* in production represent payments

TABLE 6.2 Scale Coefficients for Selected Industries

Industry	Scale Coefficient
Food and beverages	1.07
Textiles	1.00
Apparel	1.04
Lumber	1.04
Furniture	1.11
Paper and pulp	0.98
Printing	1.08
Chemicals	1.09
Petroleum	0.95
Rubber and plastics	1.06
Leather	1.04
Stone, clay, etc.	1.03
Primary metals	0.96
Fabricated metals	1.03
Nonelectrical machinery	1.02
Electrical machinery	1.03
Transportation equipment	1.02
Instruments	1.04

Source: Adapted from John R. Moroney, Cobb-Douglas production functions and returns to scale in U.S. manufacturing industry, *Western Economic Journal* 6(December 1967):46.

OPPORTUNITY COST OF COHABITATION: POSTHUMOUS PALIMONY

Alimony refers to the payment made to a former spouse upon divorce. Palimony is a payment of support to a former cohabitant to whom one was not married. *Palimony* is a judicial term that recognizes modern practices of cohabitation and attempts to deal with parties equitably. The legal recognition of palimony varies with individual states. In 1985, for instance, the Superior Court of New Jersey ruled that a woman could sue her deceased lover's estate for posthumous palimony by allowing Ms. Giammarco to present evidence to prove her allegation that Mr. Carroll promised to support her the rest of her life, and give her his home and 40 percent of his business.

In 1984, however, the Mississippi Supreme Court declined to recognize palimony for Margie who had lived with Sam over 33 years and buried him on her mother's lot. The Mississippi Supreme Court offered the following seven reasons for the denial of palimony: The parties could have drawn a deed or will; cohabitation is looked upon with disfavor; cohabitation is against public policy; the acts performed by the person seeking the support payment were done gratuitously; to allow palimony would be to revive common law marriage in Mississippi; in effect, Margie was a mistress not a spouse; and the legislature, not the court, should decide the issue.

Recognizing or declining to recognize palimony is an issue that is more judicial than economic. It suffices here simply to point out that cohabitation without marriage or prenuptial agreements incurs an opportunity cost that can be measured by the amount that the surviving partner could have received if she or he were married to the deceased partner or made a prenuptial agreement with the deceased partner.

Source: Adapted from Ernest W. King, 'Posthumous palimony': New Jersey takes the next step; Will Mississippi take the first step? *Business Insights* 6(Fall 1986):5–6.

---

that a firm must make to resource suppliers that the firm could otherwise have spent on production of alternative goods and services. It is in this sense that costs of producing a given product are said to measure the opportunities forgone for production of other goods and services. The concept of costs is introduced in this chapter from the viewpoint of one typical firm, not the whole industry.

Cost Function

Production of a good or service is not possible without incurring costs. This is because production requires use of resources that could be used to produce other goods and services. The relation between production and cost is almost like the two sides of a coin. When there is a production function, there is a cost function that corresponds to the production function.

A **cost function** describes the relationship between costs of production (C) and levels of output (Q). That is,

$$C = f(Q). \tag{6.5}$$

The presumption of the cost function is similar to that of the production function: that firms efficiently use resources to minimize the costs of producing a given output. The relation between costs and output described in equation (6.5) is unique in that the cost (C) represents the minimum cost needed to produce a given level of output.

Explicit versus Implicit Costs

Some production costs are explicit, while others are not. **Explicit costs** are the portion of the opportunity costs that is made in cash expenditures, while **implicit costs** are the portion of the opportunity costs that is not made in cash expenditures.

Consider $1,000 that is held at a firm, rather than deposited at a bank. There are costs involved in holding the money at a firm; the costs are the amount of interest earnings that are sacrificed by holding the money at a firm. The costs of holding cash at a firm are all implicit costs, since no cash expenditures are made for payment of interest earnings.

For another example, consider a small cosmetics store that Ms. Jones opened using $40,000 of her own money. Suppose that during the past year, total revenues from sales of cosmetics were $50,000, while total costs for running the business were $40,000. Total costs include purchases of cosmetics from the manufacturer, rent, utilities, supplies, and wages for all hired workers. For accounting and tax purposes, the owner of the store made a profit of $10,000 for the year. Although economists admit that this way of computing business profits serves a purpose, economists do not believe that the $40,000 accurately measures the real cost of running the store. Assuming (1) that the owner could easily have made $25,000 if she worked elsewhere last year, and (2) that banks pay 10 percent interest on deposits, total costs of running the cosmetics store were not $40,000, but $69,000, obtained by

	$40,000	cash expenditure
+	25,000	forgone wage income
+	4,000	10 percent of $40,000
	$69,000	

Of the total opportunity cost of $69,000, $40,000 is explicit cost and $29,000 is implicit cost. Implicit costs are just as real as explicit costs. According to the way economists measure the cost, Ms. Jones lost $19,000 rather than earned a profit of $10,000. The $19,000 is the difference between total revenue of $50,000 and total economic cost of $69,000.

SHORT-RUN COST CONCEPTS AND CURVES

Cost concepts that individual firms utilize in day-to-day operations to optimize use of scarce resources are all short-run costs. Short-run costs are costs of production in which the quantity of at least one input, known as the fixed input, remains unchanged as the level of output changes. In practical terms, short-run costs refer to all types of costs that vary with the level of output while the capacity of production remains constant. Short-run cost concepts and curves are utilized for studies on the behavior of firms and industries presented in the following several chapters.

Fixed versus Variable Costs

In our discussion of production, inputs were divided into fixed inputs and variable inputs. **Fixed costs** are the payments made in purchasing fixed inputs, while **variable costs** are the payments made in purchasing variable inputs. Fixed costs do not vary with the level of output, while variable costs do. Fixed costs are explicit if cash outlays are made in obtaining fixed inputs, and implicit if these costs represent the use of owners' resources without cash outlays.

Sunk Costs

Knowing whether a particular cost is a fixed cost or a variable cost is important because fixed costs are usually *sunk* in the short run and play a rather interesting role in determining the optimal course of action. **Sunk costs** refer to expenditures that are already made and thus are common to alternative decisions. Let us illustrate the use of sunk costs in making managerial decisions.

Suppose that the scientist employed in our environmental consulting firm spent $10,000 on equipment to write a grant proposal. The total amount of the grant requested is $25,000, but the granting agency is willing to offer only $20,000. Even if the scientist does not accept the grant, the $10,000 used to purchase the equipment has already been spent, or *sunk,* and cannot be recovered. In this case, the firm would be wise to accept any amount that is equal to or greater than $15,000. The amount of $15,000 is the difference between the total amount requested and the amount already spent to prepare the proposal. Put differently, the $15,000 represents cost estimates other than those for the equipment that is needed to carry out the project. Any amount exceeding $15,000, therefore, will contribute to the payment for the equipment that has already been made.

More on Fixed Costs

To illustrate exactly what fixed costs are, let us introduce operating costs, summarized in Table 6.3, of a towboat developed for a barge and towing (B&T) company located somewhere along the Mississippi River. Companies providing barge services are of three types: those that own both towboats and barges, those that own towboats to push barges owned by other companies, and those that own barges that are pushed by towboats owned by other companies. The B&T company in our example is of the second group, and owns towboats with different horsepowers, of which the 2800 horsepower boat profiled in Table 6.3 is the largest. Although the name of the company is changed, the operating costs in the table are based on actual data.

To estimate the short-run costs of barge services of the B&T company, certain assumptions need to be made, although these assumptions are more statements of facts at the time of study than assumptions. These assumptions are (1) that the salvage value of a towboat is 5 percent of its replacement cost; (2) that the service life of a towboat is 25 years; (3) that the company's required rate of return on investment is 15 percent; and (4) that fringe benefits are approximately 35 percent of wage payments. The computational procedure in Table 6.3 is self-explanatory, but selected items need clarification. Replacement cost is the price of a new 2800 horsepower towboat, while salvage value refers to the sale price of the towboat at the end of its useful life as a towboat. Depreciation is the allowance set aside each year for the declining value of the towboat due to usage and obsolescence.

TABLE 6.3 Operating Costs of 2800 Horsepower Towboat

Cost Items	Costs
To compute the present value:	
1. Replacement cost:	$2,160,000
2. Salvage value: (5% of replacement cost)	108,000
3. Accumulated depreciation:	82,080
4. Present value: [(1) minus (3)]	2,077,920
To compute annual capital cost:	
5. Return on investment: [15% of (4)]	311,688
6. Annual depreciation: [(1) minus (2) divided by 25]	82,080
7. Administration/supervision:	9,357
8. Annual capital cost: [sum of (5), (6), and (7)]	403,125
To compute annual operating cost:	
9. Total crew wages:	208,000
10. Fringe benefits: [35% of (9)]	72,800
11. Food/subsistence:	15,000
12. Transport to/from vessel:	6,650
13. Maintenance/repair:	150,000
14. Supplies:	26,000
15. Insurance on towboat:	38,080
16. Annual operating cost:	516,530
17. Capital and operating cost: [(8) plus (16)]	919,655

Source: Semoon Chang, Estimating short-run costs of a barge company, *Maritime Policy and Management* 15(January–March 1988):69.

In Table 6.3, fixed costs typically include (5) return on investment, (6) annual depreciation, (7) administration and supervision, and (15) insurance on towboats. Variable costs typically include (9) total crew wages, (10) fringe benefits, (11) food and subsistence, (12) transport to and from vessel, (13) maintenance and repair, and (14) supplies, along with costs of fuel and fuel tax not shown in the table. Fixed costs incur even when the towboat is idle, while variable costs incur only when the towboat is put to work.

The B&T company maintains a crew on standby basis by paying full wages even when the towboat is idle, as many barge and towboat companies do. All operating costs in the table, then, become fixed costs, and the only variable cost would be the cost of fuel and fuel tax. The traditional economic approach may imply that a clean distinction can be made between fixed cost and variable cost. Our study of Table 6.3, however, suggests that a given cost item may be treated either as a fixed cost or as a variable cost, depending on how the item is paid for by the particular company. The portion of the cost that is traditionally classified as a variable cost may be classified as a fixed cost by a firm if it remains invariant to short-run changes in the quantity of output.

Note also in Table 6.3 that there are no implicit costs. Costs that could easily be treated as implicit costs in small businesses are (5) return on investment, (6) annual depreciation, and (7) costs relating to administration and supervision. In small businesses, the three cost items are usually implicit and no cash expenditures are involved. The B&T company, however, is sophisticated enough to treat these costs as explicit costs by recognizing them as separate cost items.

Total, Average, and Marginal Costs

The primary objective of studying cost concepts is to improve our ability to optimize the use of resources by minimizing costs of producing a given quantity of output. For the purpose of optimization, firms usually employ production costs per unit of output, as shown in Table 6.4. Cost data presented in Table 6.4 are hypothetical, but when three zeroes are added, they closely resemble the actual cost data of the barge and towing company presented in Table 6.3.

TABLE 6.4 Total, Average, and Marginal Costs for an Individual Firm

Q	FC	VC	TC	AFC	AVC	AC	MC
0	400	0	400	—	—	—	—
1	400	100	500	400	100	500	100
2	400	180	580	200	90	290	80
3	400	246	646	133	82	215	66
4	400	304	704	100	76	176	58
5	400	355	755	80	71	151	51
6	400	402	802	67	67	134	47
7	400	448	848	57	64	121	46
8	400	496	896	50	62	112	48
9	400	576	976	44	64	108	80
10	400	700	1100	40	70	110	124

Hypothetical Cost Table
In Table 6.4, *Q* represents the quantity of output, which in our case is measured by the number of barges pushed by the 2800 horsepower towboat. Total fixed cost (FC) remains constant at $400, while total variable cost (VC) increases as the quantity of output increases. Total cost (TC) is the sum of fixed cost and variable cost. The average fixed cost (AFC) is obtained by dividing total fixed cost by the quantity of output, while the average variable cost (AVC) is obtained by dividing total variable cost by the quantity of output. The average cost (AC), also called the average total cost, may be obtained either by adding the average fixed cost and the average variable cost, or by dividing the total cost by the quantity of output.

The marginal cost (MC) is obtained by dividing changes in total cost by changes in the quantity of output. The marginal cost may also be obtained by dividing changes in total variable cost by changes in the quantity of output, since total fixed cost does not vary with the quantity of output. In the table, the quantity of output changes by one unit, making it possible to obtain marginal cost simply by subtracting total cost for a given output from total cost for an output one unit greater than the given output.

Summary of Relations
These relations among cost concepts are summarized:

$$TC = FC + VC \tag{6.6}$$

$$AFC = \frac{FC}{Q} \tag{6.7}$$

$$AVC = \frac{VC}{Q} \tag{6.8}$$

$$AC = AFC + AVC \tag{6.9}$$

$$AC = \frac{TC}{Q} \tag{6.10}$$

$$MC = \frac{\text{change in TC}}{\text{change in Q}} \tag{6.11}$$

It is interesting to see in Table 6.4 that the average cost of production declines until it reaches $108 for 9 units of output, and starts increasing again for output levels beyond 9. Fixed-cost items such as the capacity of production are most efficient when certain amounts of variable inputs are applied to these items. For instance, the 2800 horsepower towboat of the B&T company is designed to push nine barges in reality and thus incurs the lowest per-barge cost when it pushes nine barges. As the number of barges that the towboat pushes increases beyond the optimal number 9, the law of diminishing returns takes effect and the average cost rises.

Cost Curves in the Short Run

The short-run cost curves used most often in studying the pricing behavior of individual firms are those of average cost, average variable cost, and marginal cost. The average cost, average variable cost, and marginal cost curves are graphed separately in panels (a), (b), and (c) of Figure 6.1. All three curves are superimposed in Figure 6.2, in which the units of measurement are still preserved.

Figure 6.3 is a replica of Figure 6.2 except that the units of measurement are deleted to generalize the usage of these curves beyond the instance of the towboat and barges. Let us introduce the general characteristics of the three cost curves using Figure 6.3.

Reading the Graph
In Figure 6.3, we use the vertical axis to plot costs and the horizontal axis to plot the corresponding level of output. All three curves are said to have a U-shape for their decreasing and then increasing

---

ECONOMICS OF 55 MPH SPEED LIMIT

In 1974 Congress reduced the speed limit on interstate highways from 70 miles per hour (MPH) to 55 MPH to reduce oil consumption by 25 percent. Two major benefits from the lower speed limit were readily observed: reduced consumption of oil and reduced traffic fatalities. As the energy crisis of the early 1970s disappeared, numerous studies were made regarding the benefits and costs of reduced traffic fatalities from the lower speed limit. Driving near 55 MPH on interstate highways incurs costs since drivers have to spend more time driving, and at the same time it generates benefits by saving lives. The process of optimization, then, tells us to compare the dollar value of benefits with the dollar value of costs.

The dollar value of benefits depends on (1) the number of lives saved each year from the reduced speed limit, and (2) the estimated value of a human life. The number of lives saved varies widely from around 4,500 to 7,466, while the estimated value of human life varies widely also. One study concludes that the cost per life is no less than $1.3 million per year, while another study concludes that time must be valued at less than one-quarter of the average wage in order for the 55 MPH speed limit to be justified purely on economic grounds. Still another study claims that the lower speed limit did not save any lives since it is the variance of speed among drivers, not the higher speed, that causes traffic fatalities. All these studies concluded that the 55 MPH speed limit could not be justified based on a comparison of benefits and costs.

In 1987 Congress allowed states to raise the speed limit on rural interstate highways to 65 MPH.

Sources: Thomas H. Forester, Robert F. McNown, and Larry D. Singell, A cost-benefit analysis of the 55 MPH speed limit, *Southern Economic Journal* 50(January 1984):631–641; Charles A. Lave, Speeding, coordination, and the 55 MPH limit, *American Economic Review* 75(December 1985):1159–1164; and M. Anne Lowery, An economic analysis of the costs and benefits of driving 55 MPH, *Troy State University Business and Economic Review* 10(January 1986):7.

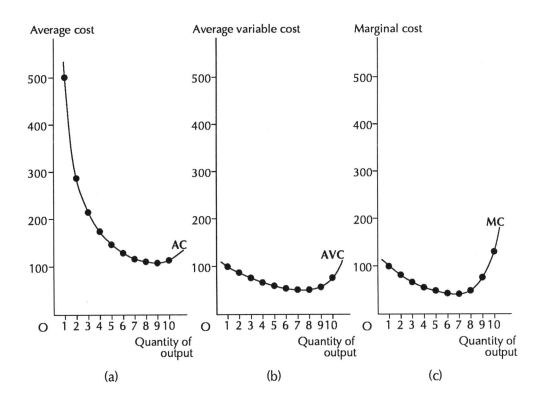

FIGURE 6.1 AVC, AC, and MC Curves of the B&T Company. AVC, AC, and MC curves are graphed separately based on cost data of a towing company presented in Table 6.4. All three curves exhibit declining costs until the quantity of output reaches an optimal level, and then increasing costs beyond it.

nature. Cost curves decrease until the amount of variable inputs is increased to the optimal level that fixed inputs require for their most efficient use. When the amount of variable inputs exceeds the optimal level, cost curves start rising because of the law of diminishing returns.

The vertical difference between the average cost curve and the average variable cost curve represents average fixed costs since average cost is the sum of average variable cost and average fixed cost. The average fixed cost decreases as the quantity of output increases, meaning that the vertical distance between the two curves becomes narrower as the quantity of output increases.

Relation between AC and MC Curves
Another interesting characteristic of the cost curves in Figure 6.3 is that the marginal cost curve crosses the lowest points of the average variable cost and the average cost curves. Let us concentrate

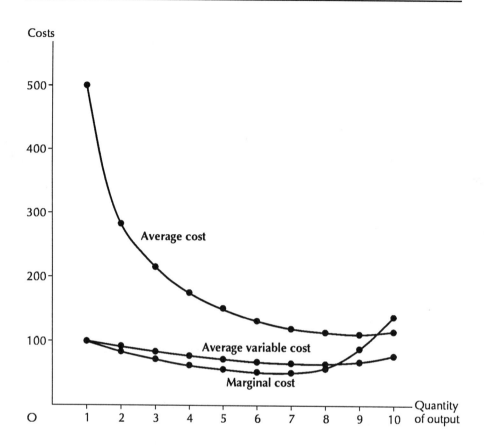

FIGURE 6.2   AVC, AC, and MC Curves Superimposed. AVC, AC, and MC curves in Figure 6.1 are superimposed in this graph to show the relation among the three curves.

on the average cost and the marginal cost curves to understand why the marginal cost curve crosses the lowest points of the cost curves.

The distance $0Q$ in Figure 6.3 represents the quantity of output that corresponds to the lowest point of the average cost curve. For output levels, such as $0C$, that are less than $0Q$, the vertical distance BC, which represents marginal cost, is smaller than the vertical distance AC, which represents average cost. Assume the marginal cost for an additional unit of output is smaller than the average cost of all preceding units of output. Also assume the additional unit is added to all preceding units to compute the new average cost. Then the average cost newly computed after the additional unit is added to all preceding units would be smaller than the average cost for all preceding units alone.

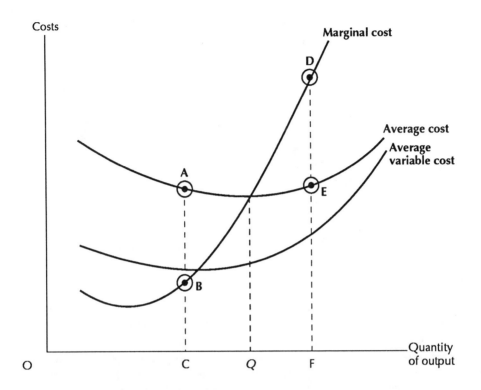

FIGURE 6.3   AVC, AC, and MC Curves Generalized. All three curves have a U-shape. The MC curve crosses the lowest points of the AVC and AC curves. The vertical difference between AC and AVC curves represents AFC.

For output levels, such as 0F, that are greater than 0Q, the vertical distance DF, which represents marginal cost, is greater than the vertical distance EF, which represents average cost. Assume the marginal cost for an additional unit of output is greater than the average cost of all preceding units of output. Also assume the additional unit is added to all preceding units to compute the new average cost. Then the average cost newly computed after the additional unit is added to all preceding units would be greater than the average cost for all preceding units alone.

Now let us generalize the relation between the average and the marginal. Suppose that the *average* weight of all of us in this classroom is 150 pounds. Suppose that another person enters our classroom, and she is Twiggy, weighing 80 pounds. When the *marginal* weight of Ms. Twiggy is added and the average weight of the entire class is computed again, the new average weight will be smaller than 150 pounds. Consider the opposite case. Suppose that the new person who joins us is not Twiggy but Mike Tyson, the youngest heavyweight boxing champion, who weighs 230 pounds. After Tyson's weight is added, the new average weight of the class will be greater than 150 pounds. To summarize, if marginal cost is smaller than average cost, the average cost declines; if marginal cost is greater than average cost, the average cost increases. The marginal cost curve, therefore, crosses the lowest point of the average cost curve, and at the lowest point of the average cost curve, the average cost is equal to the marginal cost.

Minimum Cost of Production

Recall the premise of the cost function: that firms efficiently utilize all resources in order to minimize costs in producing a given output. This means that every point on the average cost curve represents the minimum cost that is needed to produce the quantity of output indicated by the point. For instance, Table 6.4 indicates that the average cost of producing 9 units of output is $108, while the average cost of producing 10 units of output is $110. These cost figures mean that 9 units of output cannot be produced at a cost of less than $108 per unit, while 10 units of output cannot be produced at a cost of less than $110 per unit.

COSTS OF PRODUCTION IN THE LONG RUN

Short-run cost curves show minimum costs of production for given levels of output, provided that the capacity of production is fixed. Long-run cost curves, on the other hand, show minimum costs of production for given levels of output when the capacity of production is allowed to change. Put differently, long-run cost curves show minimum costs of production for different plant capacities. Long-run cost curves make practical sense if the demand for a firm's product is large enough to make alternative plant capacities worth considering. The main objective of studying long-run cost curves is to determine the optimal capacity of production as indicated by the lowest per unit cost of production. In this section we study two issues that relate to the optimal capacity of production.

Economies and Diseconomies of Scale

By definition, the long-run average cost curve and the long-run average variable cost curve are identical, since fixed-cost items such as plant size are allowed to vary, and thus there are no fixed costs in the long run. Figure 6.4 shows a long-run average cost curve.

Unlike the U-shape of short-run cost curves, which is explained by the law of diminishing returns, the U-shape of long-run cost curves is explained by economies of scale and diseconomies of scale. **Economies of scale** refer to decreasing average costs of production made possible by a larger scale operation, while **diseconomies of scale** refer to increasing average costs of production due to problems arising from a scale that is too large for efficient management. Factors that contribute to economies of scale include specialization of workers in job assignments, use of technologically efficient machines and equipment, possible use of by-products, and quantity discounts in purchase of inputs. All these advantages are made possible because of large-scale operation. If the scale of production is too large, however, diseconomies set in because of problems involving control and coordination of a firm's operations. The concept of economies of scale in costs corresponds to increasing returns to scale in production, whereas the concept of diseconomies of scale in costs corresponds to decreasing returns to scale in production.

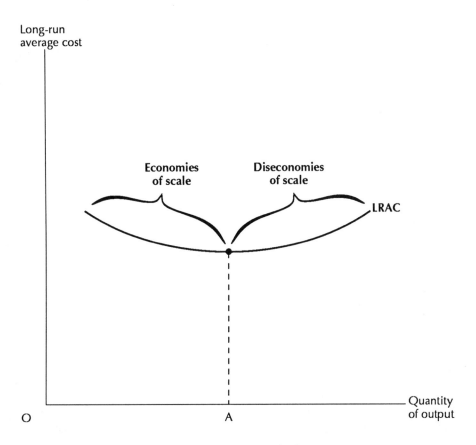

FIGURE 6.4 Long-Run Average Cost Curve. The long-run average cost curve is U-shaped due to economies from a large-scale production and diseconomies from a larger scale production.

Minimum Efficient Scale

As a firm expands its capacity of production, the per-unit cost of production is expected to decrease due to economies of scale. As a firm overexpands its capacity, however, the per-unit cost of production may increase due to diseconomies of scale. The production scale to which we turn our attention now is one at which per-unit cost of production is minimized, shown by the lowest point on the long-run average cost curve.

THE CONCEPT. The **minimum efficient scale** refers to the smallest level of output at which a firm's long-run average cost is minimized. The minimum efficient scale is indicated as 0A in Figure 6.4. For large manufacturing industries such as aluminum, automobile, coal, paper, and steel, the minimum efficient scale tends to be large. For other industries such as beauty salons, taverns, and electronics repair stores, the minimum efficient scale tends to be rather small. The concept of the minimum efficient scale is important because eventually the minimum efficient scale determines the number of firms surviving in a given area for any particular industry. If the minimum efficient scale is large relative to total market demand for the product, only a few firms are likely to survive competition in the long run. If the minimum efficient scale is small relative to total market demand for a product, there will be many firms or stores that sell similar products.

CHANGES IN THE MINIMUM EFFICIENT SCALE. Although many industries can easily be characterized by large or small minimum efficient scales, the minimum efficient scale of a given industry may change over time as technology improves. To see this trend of changing minimum efficient scales, let us consider the beer industry.

From 1950 to 1983, the number of independent U.S. brewing companies decreased from 369 to 33, while the sizes of surviving firms increased dramatically. The annual output of an average-sized firm increased from approximately 0.24 to 5.90 million barrels from 1950 to 1983 (one barrel of beer contains 31 gallons of beer). According to Professor Victor J. Tremblay, these changes caused the five-firm concentration ratio to increase from 23.4 to 83.5 percent.[3]

The reason for the increased size of an average firm was technological improvements in production, including faster packaging equipment and greater plant automation that caused scale economies to rise. For example, modern canning lines fill 2,000 twelve-ounce cans per minute, whereas a typical high-speed canning line operated at a rate of just 300 cans per minute in 1952. In order to keep canning lines operating efficiently, it is estimated that a brewer would have had to increase plant production from 0.3 million barrels in 1952 to 2.2 million barrels in 1986. The minimum efficient scale of a modern brewing company is expected to be larger than 2.2 million barrels, since there are other advantages such as advertising efficiency that can be realized with a large-scale operation.

The scale economies of a brewing company can be estimated by several different methods. One method that has actually been used to estimate the extent of scale economies at the firm level is the survivor test.[4] This test assumes that firms with efficient sizes will survive and gain market share over time, whereas firms with inefficient sizes will not survive. According to the survivor test, therefore, it is possible to determine the minimum efficient scale by observing the sizes of firms that have survived over a long period. Table 6.5 describes the market share distribution of nine firm-size classes of the brewing industry over seven time periods from 1950 to 1983. The trend toward larger firms is unmistakable. Firms with a capacity of 18 million or more barrels accounted for only about 3 percent in the mid-1960s, but have steadily increased to over 50 percent in the 1980s.

---

[3]The example of the scale economies of the brewing industry is based on Victor J. Tremblay, Scale economies, technological change, and firm-cost asymmetries in the U.S. brewing industry, *Quarterly Review of Economics and Business* 27(Summer 1987):71–86.

[4]For the survivor technique, see George J. Stigler, The economies of scale, *Journal of Law and Economics* 1(October 1958):54–71.

TABLE 6.5 Size Distribution of Firm Market Shares in Percent by Size of Class, 1950–1983

Size Class (million barrels)	Time Period						
	1950–53	*1954–58*	*1959–63*	*1964–68*	*1969–73*	*1974–78*	*1979–83*
0 – 0.999	54.948	41.011	29.855	19.590	14.459	13.554	—
1 – 1.999	11.526	16.318	13.643	8.351	5.698	0.775	—
2 – 2.999	10.316	12.539	11.792	7.717	4.695	1.992	12.674
3 – 3.999	5.932	14.029	8.095	7.976	12.045	4.604	4.330
4 – 4.999	5.996	2.856	10.452	16.224	4.403	5.455	0
5 – 5.999	5.982	8.986	12.623	6.617	10.142	4.664	0.596
6 – 8.999	5.300	4.261	9.696	10.386	6.905	5.508	3.181
9 – 17.999	0	0	3.844	19.888	18.112	19.747	26.191
>18	0	0	0	3.251	23.541	43.701	53.028

Source: Victor J. Tremblay, Scale economies, technological change, and firm-cost asymmetries in the U.S. brewing industry, *Quarterly Review of Economics and Business* 27(Summer 1987):71–86; table from p. 75. Note that the figure 12.674 in the last column measures the market share for size class 0–2.999.

SUMMARY

Production is the act of creating a good or service that has an exchange value. Inputs are classified into fixed inputs, of which the quantity remains unchanged as the quantity of output changes, and variable inputs, which vary with the quantity of output. There are three concepts of products: total product, average product, and marginal product. The short run in production means a period of time during which at least one input remains constant, whereas the long run refers to a period of time during which all inputs vary. The law of diminishing returns is a short-run concept, while the concept of economies or diseconomies of scale is a long-run concept. If output more than doubles when inputs double, there are increasing returns to scale; if output also doubles, there are constant returns to scale; and if output less than doubles, there are decreasing returns to scale.

Costs represent the other side of production and measure payments that a firm must make to resource suppliers in order to attract resources away from production of alternative goods and services. Costs are classified into explicit costs and implicit costs. Costs are also classified into fixed costs and variable costs. Sunk costs refer to expenditures that are already made and are thus invariant across alternative actions. Total cost is the sum of fixed cost and variable cost, whereas average cost is the sum of average fixed cost and average variable cost. The marginal cost is obtained by dividing changes in total cost by the corresponding changes in the quantity of output. The marginal cost curve crosses the lowest points of the average variable cost and the average cost curves.

The U-shape of the short-run cost curve is explained by increasing and diminishing returns, whereas the U-shape of the long-run cost curve is explained by economies of scale and diseconomies of scale. The minimum efficient scale refers to the smallest level of output at which a firm's long-run average cost is minimized. If the minimum efficient scale is large relative to total market demand, only a few firms are likely to survive competition in the long run in any given market. If the minimum efficient scale is small, many firms will sell similar products in any given market.

EXERCISES

1. The quantity of output specified in a production function is the maximum output that can be produced from various amounts of inputs with given technology. Why is it necessary to specify a production function as the *maximum* output rather than *any* level of output that can be produced from various amounts of inputs?

2. Suppose that the quantity of the total product increases by 100 as the number of workers increases by 2. In the absence of any other information, what would be the marginal product of labor?

3. What is the most important difference between the law of diminishing returns to a factor and the concept of diseconomies of scale?

4. It is often said that there are no fixed costs in the long run. Since costs are payments for inputs, the statement suggests that there are no fixed inputs in the long run. How can there be no fixed inputs in the long run?

5. Briefly explain each of the following cost concepts:

   a. Total fixed cost
   b. Total variable cost
   c. Average total cost
   d. Marginal cost
   e. Implicit cost
   f. Sunk cost

6. A firm can finance an expansion of its plant and equipment by borrowing funds at an annual interest rate of 12 percent or by using its own current net earnings without borrowing. Should the firm finance the expansion out of its current net earnings since no interest has to be paid? If not, why not?

7. Average cost curves of a firm may be U-shaped. The reason that an average cost curve is U-shaped is different, however, depending on whether it is a short-run average cost curve or a long-run average cost curve. What are the reasons for U-shaped average cost curves in the short run and in the long run?

8. Why does the marginal cost curve cross the lowest points of the average variable cost and the average cost curves?

9. Determine whether the following cost items are fixed costs or variable costs:

   a. Wages of hourly workers
   b. Office supplies
   c. Annual depreciation allowance
   d. Required return on investment
   e. Property tax paid by businesses

10. Define the minimum efficient scale of a plant and explain how it affects the number of firms in an industry.

SUGGESTED READINGS

Bassett, Lowell. (1969). Returns to scale and cost curves. *Southern Economic Journal* 36(October):189–190.

A brief article that clarifies returns to scale and per unit costs in economics.

Cobb, Charles W., and Douglas, Paul H. (1928). A theory of production. *American Economic Review* 18(March):139–165.

Introduces the famous Cobb-Douglas production function.

Douglas, Paul H. (1976). The Cobb-Douglas production function once again: Its history, its testing, and some new empirical values. *Journal of Political Economy* 84(October):903–915.

An update of the Cobb-Douglas production function with a good introduction written by one of the two inventors of the production function.

Johnston, J. (1960). *Statistical cost analysis*. New York: McGraw-Hill.

Summarizes features and conclusions of several statistical studies on cost functions; also presents critical evaluations of these studies.

Walters, A. A. (1963). Production and cost functions: An econometric survey. *Econometrica* 31(January–April):1–66.

A classic article on empirical cost functions that contains estimates of cost functions and an extensive list of references.

7

Foundations for Price and Output Decisions of Firms

Introduction to Market Structure

Revenue Concepts and Curves

MR = MC Rule for Profit Maximization

THE CENTRAL IDEA of classical economics that is still upheld by most economists in democratic capitalism is the superiority of the price system over any other system in allocating scarce resources among their competing demands. According to the idea, the supply and demand mechanism coordinates diverse self-interested actions of consumers and producers into something that is good for the society. Actions by consumers based on self-interest mean that consumers try to buy, subject to budget constraints, the combination of goods and services that gives them the most utility. Actions by producers based on self-interest mean that producers produce and sell goods and services in such a way as to maximize profits. The question that we would like to answer in the next three chapters is, what should producers do to maximize profits?

Producers, or potential entrepreneurs, should make decisions on a number of business matters before they realize any profits. Producers need to select products that they want to produce and sell, as well as the location where they will produce the products. Producers need to find someone who will finance the business venture and hire persons who will work as employees of the business. Producers also need to make decisions on promoting their products, managing the optimal quantity of inventory, and on all other mundane matters that any ongoing business experiences on a daily basis. Needless to say, maximum profits can be realized only when right decisions are made on all these matters. Although economists are concerned with all these different aspects of a business operation, economists are especially interested in two key decisions that producers make: *what price to charge* and *how much to produce.*

Pricing decisions depend significantly on the nature of demand for the product, introduced in Chapters 3 and 5. Output decisions, on the other hand, depend significantly on the nature of production and supply of the product, introduced in Chapters 3 and 6. Final decisions on pricing and the quantity of output, however, are made on the basis of *both* demand for, and costs of production of, goods and services. We combine demand and costs of production in the next three chapters. In this chapter, we complete the presentation of the analytical foundations for the next three chapters by introducing several important concepts: market structure, revenue, and the equimarginal rule for profit maximization.

INTRODUCTION TO MARKET STRUCTURE

Markets are everywhere. Pricing and output decisions of individual firms, however, are different from one market to the next. If a firm sells a product that no other firms sell and that has no close substitutes, the price of the product charged by the firm is expected to be higher than its price if it were sold in a market in which many other firms sell the same or similar products. **Market structure** is a description of the characteristics of demand and cost conditions that are common to firms within an industry. These characteristics influence, if not determine, the pricing and output decisions of firms. Broadly speaking, markets are classified into (1) perfect competition or perfectly competitive markets, and (2) imperfect competition or imperfectly competitive markets. We will start with working definitions of the two types of markets.

Perfect Competition

Somehow, the word *perfect* is scary. There are good movies but not perfect movies, although the original *Gone with the wind* may be close to one if there were such a thing as a perfect movie. There are good football players but not perfect football players. There are good violinists but not perfect violinists, although some may claim exceptions in Isaac Stern and Itzhak Perlman. Like these examples, perfect competition may not exist in reality. If perfect competition does not exist, why do we bother studying it? We study perfect competition for two reasons. One reason is that perfect competition lends itself as a role model by which advantages and disadvantages of other market structures can be compared. This comparison will enable us to think and generate ideas to improve real markets. The other reason is that some markets are sufficiently, although not perfectly, competitive such that the theories of perfect competition can be applied to them.

Perfect competition is defined as market conditions in which the demand for the output of every firm in a given industry is perfectly elastic, so that each firm is a price taker for all quantities of output it produces.[1] The most important characteristic of a perfectly competitive market is that sellers collectively affect the determination of the market price but individually have no influence on the market price. Sellers are **price takers,** which means they charge the price that is determined in the marketplace. This characteristic has an interesting consequence: Small companies in an industry that is dominated by one or several large companies also behave as takers of prices that are determined by larger companies. The theory of perfect competition is applicable to these companies at the competitive fringe, although the industries to which these companies belong are far from being perfectly competitive.

Imperfect Competition

Markets that are imperfectly competitive vary considerably with the degree of control that individual firms have over the determination of the market price. Depending on the degree of control, markets are divided into monopoly, oligopoly, and monopolistic competition.

Monopoly

A **monopoly,** also called **pure monopoly,** is a firm that supplies the entire market for a particular product. The product has no close substitutes in the monopoly market. Examples of a pure monopoly are as rare as examples of perfect competition.

Although markets in general refer to an economic relationship between sellers and buyers, they are usually defined for specific products. When a market is defined for one particular product, however, substitutes can almost always be found in one form or another. For a narrowly defined product such as travel by bus, for instance, substitutes are travel by automobile or airplane. If a market is defined for a broadly defined product, on the other hand, the concept of the market is not very useful. A broadly defined product such as travel in general contains two or more distinctive products, such as travel by train and travel by airplane, that should be studied separately for policymaking purposes. These examples illustrate the difficulty in defining a purely monopolistic market.

---

[1]The definition of perfect competition is discussed in detail in Chapter 8.

Oligopoly

Oligopoly refers to markets that are dominated by a few leading sellers. Oligopolistic markets include the automobile, steel, aluminum, and cigarette industries.

Two important characteristics of an oligopoly are mutual interdependence in pricing among oligopolists (the leading sellers), and barriers to entry into the industry. Sellers in an oligopolistic market always consider possible responses from rival sellers in the industry when contemplating price changes or other promotional actions. Knowing that it is not easy for other firms to enter the industry, sellers in an oligopolistic market may not engage in highly competitive practices. The barriers to entry include patents that legally preclude other firms from producing the same product, consumers' brand loyalty toward existing products such as Coca Cola and the Lincoln Continental, and high capital costs needed to start a business in the oligopolistic industry.

Monopolistic Competition

Monopolistic competition refers to markets in which a large number of firms sell products that are differentiated. **Product differentiation** means that consumers perceive given products as being different. Physical differences among products are important only to the extent that these differences affect the consumers' perception of these products. If consumers perceive McDonald's and Hardee's hamburgers as being different, the two hamburgers are differentiated. If consumers perceive Kentucky fried chicken and Popeye's fried chicken as being the same, the two brands of fried chicken are homogeneous, or not differentiated.

To further illustrate product differentiation, consider generic drugs. When a company develops a new drug, it obtains a patent that lasts for 17 years, during which only the company holding the patent has the right to manufacture the drug. Other firms may manufacture the drug only if they pay the patent holder a royalty. The new drug is given two names. One is the **generic name,** which is the name of the chemical compound that makes up the drug. The other is the **brand name,** or proprietary name, which is the name that the company chooses to call the new product. Once the patent expires, the drug may be produced and sold by other companies under different brand names. A generic drug is completely interchangeable with its brand name counterpart once the generic drug receives a *bioequivalent rating* from the Federal Drug Administration, which is required prior to its production. Prices of brand name drugs, however, can be substantially higher than prices of generic drugs because brand name drugs are usually differentiated through advertising. Product differentiation is important because consumers are willing to pay higher prices for differentiated products, which they perceive to be of higher value.

One important characteristic common to all imperfectly competitive markets is that sellers individually as well as collectively affect the determination of the market price. Unlike sellers under perfect competition, sellers under imperfect competition are **price makers.** This means that instead of charging the price that is determined in the market, they charge the price that can give them the maximum profit.

REVENUE CONCEPTS AND CURVES

Firms need to generate sufficient revenue from sales to make profits. Revenues, therefore, represent the other side of a coin if one side represents the costs of production. Eventually, costs of production and revenues from sales should be considered simultaneously in order to find the price and the

---

ODD PRICING: VERSION ONE

Professor Lee Kreul of Purdue University's School of Consumer and Family Sciences analyzed pricing practices in the restaurant business. Kreul reviewed 467 prices in advertisements placed by 242 restaurants in 24 newspapers. The review indicates that when a restaurant placed advertisements for meals that cost less than $7, the price usually ended with the number 9, such as the prices $3.99 or $4.99. The review also indicates that when a restaurant placed advertisements for meals costing $7 to $10, the price usually ended with the number 5, such as the prices $7.95 or $8.95. Kreul suggests that the pricing practices of restaurants are intended to provide a discount illusion. Restaurants change the ending number of a price from 9 to 5 as the price of meals increases beyond $7 because more than one cent is required to create the discount illusion for these higher priced meals. Kreul also suggests that patrons interested in meals costing more than $7 might perceive a price ending in the number 9 as indicating low quality or sloppy service.

Source: Jack C. Horn, The high-class nickel discount, *Psychology Today*, September 1982, p. 18. Reprinted with permission from *Psychology Today Magazine* Copyright 1982 (PT Partners, L.P.).

---

quantity of output that a firm should produce and sell for profit maximization. We studied costs in the preceding chapter. We now introduce the concept of revenue in this section.

Total, Average, and Marginal Revenue

Like costs, revenues from sales of goods and services are of three types: total revenue, average revenue, and marginal revenue. **Total revenue** (TR) is simply the dollar value of sales, obtained by multiplying price (P) by the quantity of sales (Q). **Average revenue** (AR) is total revenue divided by the quantity of sales. Average revenue is always the price of a product as long as all units of the product are sold at the same price. **Marginal revenue** (MR) is obtained when changes in total revenue are divided by the corresponding changes in the quantity of sales. To summarize,

$$TR \ = P \times Q \tag{7.1}$$

$$AR \ = \frac{TR}{Q} = P \tag{7.2}$$

$$MR \ = \frac{\text{changes in TR}}{\text{changes in } Q} \tag{7.3}$$

To illustrate a revenue schedule that shows total, average, and marginal revenues for different levels of sales, let us return, in Table 7.1, to the example of frozen concentrated orange juice. Suppose that the price per 12 ounce can of frozen concentrated pineapple-orange juice distributed by the Dole Packaged Foods Company in Honolulu, Hawaii is $1.25. Even if sales increase within a reasonable range, the price of the orange juice is expected to remain the same. Total revenues in column (3) are obtained by multiplying the product price in column (1) and the quantity of sales in column (2). Average revenues in column (4) are obtained by dividing total revenues in column (3) by the quantity of sales in column (2). Average revenue is the price per unit for a given quantity of sales. If price does not change, the average revenue will also not change and is equal to the price.

Marginal revenues in column (5) are obtained by dividing change in total revenue from column (3) by the corresponding change in the quantity of sales from column (2). Since the quantity of sales in column (2) changes by one unit, marginal revenues are obtained simply by subtracting total revenue of a given quantity of sales from total revenue of a quantity one unit larger than the given quantity of sales. Another way of looking at marginal revenue is that marginal revenue is the revenue that the seller receives when the quantity of sales increases by one more unit. So long as the product price remains constant, the revenue from sales of one additional unit will be equal to the product price. Marginal revenues in Table 7.1, therefore, are identical for different quantities of sales since the price of the product remains the same.

Revenue Curves under Perfect Competition

A word of caution is in order before we proceed. When competition is said to exist in a particular industry, it means that there is competition among individual firms within the industry. When a market is perfectly competitive, however, there are so many sellers relative to total market supply that an increase or a decrease in sales by one firm will have no effect on the market price. Assuming that the orange juice market is perfectly competitive, an increase in the supply of the juice by *all*

TABLE 7.1 Revenue Schedule for Dole Orange Juice under Perfect Competition

(1) Product Price	(2) Quantity of Sales	(3) Total Revenue	(4) Average Revenue	(5) Marginal Revenue
$1.25	0	0	—	—
1.25	1	$ 1.25	$1.25	$1.25
1.25	2	2.50	1.25	1.25
1.25	3	3.75	1.25	1.25
1.25	4	5.00	1.25	1.25
1.25	5	6.25	1.25	1.25
1.25	6	7.50	1.25	1.25
1.25	7	8.75	1.25	1.25
1.25	8	10.00	1.25	1.25
1.25	9	11.25	1.25	1.25
1.25	10	12.50	1.25	1.25

firms in the entire orange juice industry is expected to lower the price of the juice, but an increase in the supply of the juice by Dole *alone* is not expected to change its price. In other words, Dole is a price taker and charges the price that is determined by demand for and supply of the product in the market. The process in which Dole acts as a price taker is illustrated in Figure 7.1.

The price of the orange juice (P_e) is determined by its market demand and market supply. This process is shown in Figure 7.1(a). The price in our example is $1.25. Individual firms like Dole charge the market price. Individual firms under perfect competition have no incentive to raise the price above the equilibrium level, since consumers under perfect competition know exactly who is selling at what price, and not a single consumer will buy the product from the firm raising the price. Individual firms under perfect competition have no incentive to lower the price either, since the market price is the market clearing price, and individual firms will be able to sell all their products at the prevailing market price.

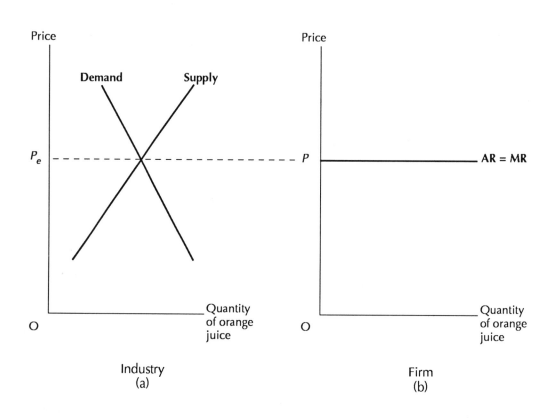

FIGURE 7.1 Average Revenue and Marginal Revenue of a Firm under Perfect Competition. The market price of the juice is determined by demand for and supply of the juice in the market. The price (P) is $1.25. Individual firms such as Dole charge the price determined in the market.

Let us take a careful look at Figure 7.1(b). The price of the orange juice charged by Dole for different quantities of sales remains constant at the level of the market price. The horizontal line at the level of the market price is the average revenue (AR) curve for Dole, since revenue from the sale of *each* unit by Dole is the same as price. The horizontal line is also the marginal revenue (MR) curve for Dole, since the change in total revenue from the sale of each *additional* unit by Dole is the same as price.

Recall that demand curves show the relation between different prices and quantities demanded at these prices. The horizontal line also shows the relation between prices and quantities demanded at these prices, in the special case where there is only one price. The horizontal line is a completely elastic demand curve. The demand curve is always the same as the average revenue curve because both show the relation between prices and quantities sold at these prices. At this point, we may recall the price elasticity of demand. The demand curve for a product that is completely elastic was a horizontal line. The demand curve faced by a firm under perfect competition is completely elastic, and represents the firm's average revenue curve as well as its marginal revenue curve.

Revenue Curves under Imperfect Competition

We have spent so much time studying the special case of the demand curve under perfect competition that by now we have almost forgotten how a normal demand curve looks. Firms operating under market conditions that are imperfectly competitive are faced with a normal-looking demand curve that has a downward slope to the right. A monopoly firm and other firms under oligopolistic and monopolistically competitive industries can adjust the price of their products for maximum profits. An increase in the price of their products does not come free, however. A price increase decreases the quantity of their products demanded, while a price decrease increases the quantity of their products demanded.

Relations among Different Revenues
The average revenue curve by definition is always the same as the demand curve, regardless of whether markets are perfectly competitive or imperfectly competitive. This means that the average revenue curve of firms under imperfect competition has a downward slope to the right. When the average revenue curve has a downward slope to the right, marginal revenue from the sale of one additional unit would not be equal to the average revenue, since sales of additional units are expected to lower the price and, thus, the average revenue. The relation among total revenue, average revenue, and marginal revenue under imperfect competition is illustrated in Table 7.2.

Table 7.2 is similar to Table 7.1 except that the price of the product is assumed to decrease in Table 7.2 as the quantity of sales increases. Total revenues in column (3) are obtained by multiplying price in column (1) by the quantity of sales in column (2). Average revenues in column (4) are again the same as product prices. Marginal revenues in column (5) are obtained when changes in total revenue are divided by the corresponding changes in the quantity of sales. Since the quantity of sales changes by one unit in column (2), marginal revenues are the differences between succeeding total revenues. There are two features in Table 7.2 that we should clearly understand: the relation between total revenue and marginal revenue, and the relation between average revenue and marginal revenue.

TABLE 7.2 Revenue Schedule for Dole Orange Juice under Imperfect Competition

(1) Product Price	(2) Quantity of Sales	(3) Total Revenue	(4) Average Revenue	(5) Marginal Revenue
$1.25	0	0	—	—
1.20	1	$1.20	$1.20	$1.20
1.15	2	2.30	1.15	1.10
1.10	3	3.30	1.10	1.00
1.05	4	4.20	1.05	0.90
1.00	5	5.00	1.00	0.80
0.95	6	5.70	0.95	0.70
0.90	7	6.30	0.90	0.60
0.85	8	6.80	0.85	0.50
0.80	9	7.20	0.80	0.40
0.75	10	7.50	0.75	0.30

Total Revenue and Marginal Revenue

First, we review the relation between total revenue and marginal revenue. When the quantity of sales increases by one successive unit, as indicated in column (2) of Table 7.2, marginal revenues are simply the differences between two succeeding total revenues. For instance, the marginal revenue for the second unit ($1.10) is the difference between total revenue for two units ($2.30) and total revenue for one unit ($1.20). Another way of looking at the relation is that total revenue is the sum of all marginal revenues for all preceding and current units of sales. For instance, total revenue for two units ($2.30) is the sum of the marginal revenue from the first unit ($1.20) and the marginal revenue from the second unit ($1.10). Total revenue for three units ($3.30) is the sum of the marginal revenue from the first unit ($1.20), the marginal revenue from the second unit ($1.10), and the marginal revenue from the third unit ($1.00). Similarly, total revenue for 10 units of sales ($7.50) is the sum of all marginal revenues listed in column (5) of Table 7.2.

Average Revenue and Marginal Revenue

Second, we now review the relation between average revenue and marginal revenue. When the market was perfectly competitive, average revenue was the same as marginal revenue. When the market is imperfectly competitive, marginal revenue beyond the first unit is always smaller than average revenue.

When there is only one unit of sale, price, average revenue, and marginal revenue are all equal to one another. The second unit of sale in Table 7.2 caused the price to decrease from $1.20 to $1.15. The lower price induced by the second unit of sale, however, applies to the first unit as well as the second unit. The 5 cent decrease in price from $1.20 to $1.15 in selling the second unit led the average revenue from the first unit of sale to decrease from $1.20 to $1.15 and caused total revenue to increase to $2.30. The amount of $2.30 represents the sum of $1.15 for the first unit of sale plus $1.15 for the second unit of sale. If the lower price for the second unit of sale applied only to the second unit, and if the first unit were still sold at $1.20, total revenue from the sale of the first two units would have increased to $2.35, $1.20 for the first unit of sale plus $1.15 for the second unit of sale. Because the lower price induced by the sale of the second unit applied to the first unit as well as the second unit, average revenue decreased by only 5 cents from $1.20 to $1.15, but marginal revenue decreased by 10 cents, 5 cents each from the first unit and the second unit. This property of Table 7.2, that marginal revenue decreases faster than average revenue, suggests that the marginal revenue curve should lie below the average revenue curve with a steeper slope as the quantity of sales increases.

Deriving MR Curve from AR Curve
The procedure of deriving the marginal revenue curve from a given average revenue curve is shown step-by-step in Figure 7.2. In Figure 7.2, AC is the average revenue curve, point A is the price at which the quantity demanded is zero, and point C is the quantity demanded at the zero price. The marginal revenue curve AB is obtained when 0C is bisected at point B, and points A and B are connected.[2]

MR = MC RULE FOR PROFIT MAXIMIZATION

Firms produce goods and services to make profits. When markets are competitive, making profits may not be sufficient to ensure the survival of these firms. A favorite behavioral assumption that economists make when studying production activities of firms is that firms optimize by trying to maximize, not simply make, profits. Profit is the difference between total revenue and total cost. Total cost refers to total economic costs, which include implicit as well as explicit costs. Profits are maximized by producing a level of output at which the difference between total revenue and total cost is the greatest. The profit-maximizing level of output can also be determined, more conveniently, by equating marginal revenue and marginal cost. In other words, the profit-maximizing level of output is determined by equating revenue and cost *at the margin*. Before we introduce the MC = MR rule for profit maximization, let us briefly review the history of the marginal revolution.

The Marginal Revolution

The main concerns of the Classical economists were those of long-run economic development, free competition, and the labor theory of price. The entire focus of economic analysis was changed, however, when William Stanley Jevons published *The theory of political economy* in 1871, Carl Menger published *Principles of economics* in 1871, and Leon Walras published *Elements of pure economics* in 1874. Unlike the earlier approach, in which productive resources were allowed to change, the new approach emphasized the search for the conditions that maximize the use of given productive resources among competing claims. Unlike the Classical value theory, that stressed the supply side of market price formation, the new approach stressed marginal utility and demand as determinants of market price.

[2]The proof that line AB is the marginal revenue schedule corresponding to the average revenue schedule AC is presented in the Study Guide that accompanies this book.

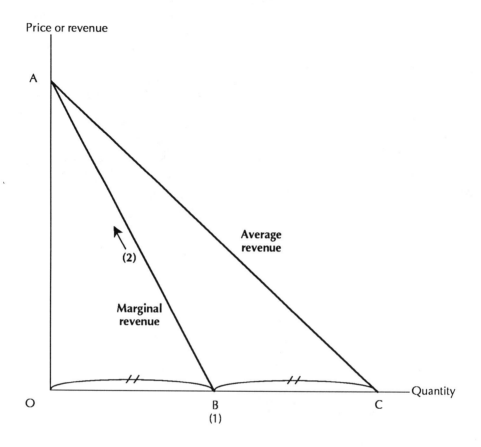

FIGURE 7.2   Deriving Marginal Revenue Curve from Average Revenue Curve under Imperfect Competition. First, bisect OC. Second, connect A and B. Line AB is the marginal revenue curve.

The new approach stressed the equimarginal principle, which relied on the concept of the *marginal*. Although the equimarginal principle was discovered about 33 years before the beginning of the marginal revolution, the marginal principle for profit maximization became an important part of modern economics. The word *marginal* in the term *marginal revolution* does not mean that the revolution was marginal in the sense of "insignificant." On the contrary, the marginal revolution means that the development of the new analytical tool, marginal analysis, was revolutionary in the history of economic ideas.

The equimarginal principle was further refined over the years. In 1838, for instance, the French economist Antoine-Augustin Cournot (1801–1877) published *Researches into the mathematical principles of the theory of wealth,* in which he proved that the monopolist could maximize

ODD PRICING: VERSION TWO

Quoted prices in department stores, catalogs, and televised advertising frequently are of the form $2.99, $399, and $1,098. The practice of ending a price in 9 or 8 cannot be explained by marginal cost pricing since the probability that most marginal costs end just one cent or one dollar below a round number is very small.

Professors Gabrielle Brenner and Reuven Brenner propose the hypothesis that the practice is based on the limited capacity of our brains for storing directly accessible information. When exposed to a continuous flow of information about prices, consumers store in their memories the most valuable message. In the case of quoted prices, the most valuable message is the first digit of a number. When a price is $398, for instance, the consumer tries to remember first that the price is $300, or perhaps that it is $390, but rarely does he or she remember that it is exactly $398.

The question is why consumers do not first round the number from, say, $398 to $400 and then store it. The answer, according to Brenner and Brenner, is that immediately after the message, consumers are exposed to additional information such as another advertisement, or a television or newspaper news item. The information on price, therefore, must be stored very quickly, and the quickest way to do so is by storing the first digits.

Source: Gabrielle A. Brenner and Reuven Brenner, Memory and markets, or Why are you paying $2.99 for a widget? *The Journal of Business* 55(January 1982):147–158. A revised and extended version of the article appears in R. Brenner *Rivalry*, Cambridge University Press, 1987.

profits by producing an output at which marginal cost equals marginal revenue.[3] In the next section, we introduce the equimarginal rule for profit maximization, using simple graphs instead of the calculus that Cournot used. The equimarginal rule enables firms to locate the level of output that maximizes profits. The rule is also highly practical, as explained later in this chapter.

How the MR = MC Rule Works

Marginal revenue is the revenue from production and sale of the last unit of output, while marginal cost is the cost of producing the last unit of output. The **MR = MC rule** states that profits are maximized when firms produce the level of output at which marginal revenue is equal to marginal cost. To understand how the equality between marginal revenue and marginal cost ensures maximization of profits for firms, let us superimpose in Figure 7.3 a typical marginal cost curve onto a horizontal marginal revenue curve derived from Figure 7.1. The horizontal marginal revenue curve means that the firms under our consideration operate under market conditions that are perfectly competitive. The following explanation holds equally true even if the demand curve is

[3]For more on Cournot and profit maximization, see Mark Blaug, *Economic theory in retrospect*, 4th ed. (Cambridge, England: Cambridge University Press, 1985), pp. 317–318.

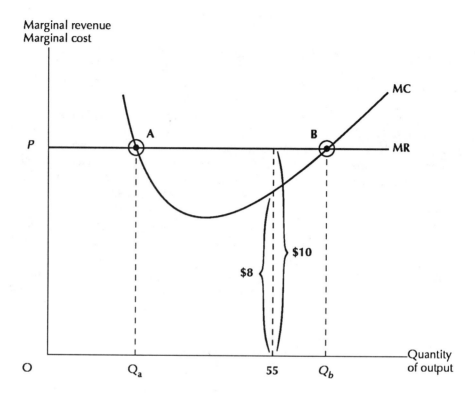

FIGURE 7.3 Profit Maximization under Perfect Competition. Firms maximize profits by producing the level of output (Q_b) at which marginal revenue equals marginal cost on its rising portion.

downward sloped rather than horizontal. The case of the downward-sloping demand curve is explained later, in Figure 7.4.

MR = MC Rule under Perfect Competition
The superimposed marginal cost and marginal revenue curves are shown in Figure 7.3. In the beginning stage of production, the fixed capacity of the firm is not yet used efficiently, and the average and marginal costs of producing the first several units are expected to be quite high. Marginal costs of producing the first several units, therefore, easily exceed marginal revenues from selling these units. This portion of production activities is indicated in Figure 7.3 from the origin to Q_a, at which quantity the declining marginal cost curve and the marginal revenue curve cross each other, as indicated by point A.

As the quantity of output produced continues to increase and as fixed inputs are put to a more efficient use in their relation to variable inputs, the cost of producing the last unit continues to

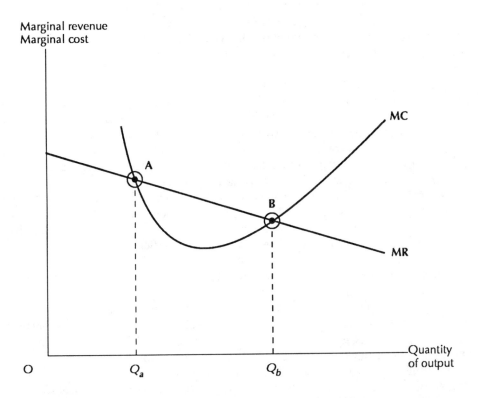

Marginal revenue
Marginal cost

MC

A

B

MR

Quantity
of output

O Q_a Q_b

FIGURE 7.4 Profit Maximization under Imperfect Competition. Firms under imperfect competition also maximize profits by producing the level of output (Q_b) at which marginal revenue equals marginal cost on its rising portion.

decline and the marginal cost becomes smaller than marginal revenue. This portion of production activities is indicated by the distance from point A to point B on the marginal revenue and marginal cost curves, or the distance between points Q_a and Q_b on the quantity axis. For these wide-ranging levels of output, marginal revenue is greater than marginal cost. When marginal revenue is greater than marginal cost for a particular unit of output, firms make profit on the unit, because revenue from selling the unit (MR) is greater than the cost of it (MC). The amount of profit on the unit is equal to the difference between marginal revenue and marginal cost.

Suppose that the firm in Figure 7.3 produces 55 units of output. The cost of making the fifty-fifth unit is $8, but the revenue from selling the fifty-fifth unit is $10. The firm realizes an addition to profit of $2 if it produces and sells the fifty-fifth unit. The firm can increase profits by increasing the level of production so long as revenue from producing and selling the unit (MR) is greater than the cost of making the unit (MC). The firm maximizes profits when it produces the level of output at which marginal revenue is equal to marginal cost. Technically speaking, the unit at which marginal revenue equals marginal cost neither generates a profit nor incurs a loss to the firm. That unit, however, is a convenient dividing point between the quantity of output that maximizes profits and larger quantities that may still generate profits but not the maximum profit. The quantity of output at which the firm maximizes profits is indicated as Q_b in Figure 7.3. At Q_b, marginal revenue equals marginal cost on its rising portion.

MR = MC Rule under Imperfect Competition

The MR = MC rule for profit maximization also applies to firms operating under market conditions that are not perfectly competitive. This is illustrated in Figure 7.4. The demand curve faced by firms operating under imperfect competition has a downward slope to the right. As derived in Figure 7.2, the marginal revenue curve for a declining demand curve is located below the demand curve and has the downward but steeper slope to the right. Beyond the slope of the respective marginal revenue curve, there is no difference between Figure 7.3 and Figure 7.4.

As was the case in Figure 7.3, firms operating under imperfectly competitive markets experience a declining marginal cost during the beginning stages of production, and marginal cost exceeds marginal revenue for the first several units of output. Sooner or later, the amounts of variable inputs are large enough to allow the firm to utilize fixed inputs more efficiently, and marginal cost falls below marginal revenue. The output levels between points Q_a and Q_b are those for which marginal revenue exceeds marginal cost. When the level of output reaches Q_b, at which the rising portion of the marginal cost curve crosses the marginal revenue curve, the firm maximizes profits.

A note of caution is in order. The MR = MC rule does not necessarily mean that the firm is making profits. What the rule says is that if the firm is making profits, the rule makes sure that the firm is maximizing profits; if the firm is losing money but continues to produce, the rule makes sure that the firm is minimizing losses. Whether the firm is making a profit or incurring a loss depends on the price of the product in relation to the average cost of production at the point where marginal revenue equals marginal cost. If the product price is greater than the average cost of production, the firm is maximizing profits. If the product price is smaller than the average cost of production, the firm is minimizing losses. The MR = MC rule is essentially a short-run rule, since no firm can survive long by only minimizing losses.

Practical Applications of the MR = MC Rule

Marginal revenue and marginal cost are concepts used almost exclusively by economists. Business managers typically use the term *profit contribution* to describe what is essentially the difference between marginal revenue and marginal cost.

Profit Contribution

The **profit contribution** of a product is the difference between revenue from sales of the product and the variable cost of its production. The profit contribution is usually expressed on the per unit basis:

$$PC = P - AVC \tag{7.4}$$

where

PC = profit contribution
P = price of product
AVC = average variable cost of production

ODD PRICING: VERSION THREE

Dear Ann Landers: I read your letter to E.A. in Riverside, the man who wanted to know why stores charge odd prices, such as $.99, $1.99, $29.99, etc. You answered: "It's a sales gimmick that's been around forever."

I am a 10-year-old boy and I think I have a better answer.

Around 1875, Melville Stone owned a newspaper named the *Chicago Daily News*. The price was a penny. Circulation was good, but after a while it began to drop off. He found that it was because pennies were in short supply. Mr. Stone persuaded Chicago merchants to sell their merchandise for a penny below the regular price. This put more pennies in circulation and it helped save the paper.

My source is: "Why didn't I think of that?" by Webb Garison.

—N.C. reader.

Source: Mobile Register, August 4, 1987, p. 7-B. Reprinted with permission from Ann Landers, Los Angeles Syndicate.

In the marginal analysis, the profit for the last unit of output (PLU) is the difference between marginal revenue (MR) and marginal cost (MC). That is,

$$PLU = MR - MC \qquad (7.5)$$

The question is, Under what conditions will the profit contribution (PC) in equation (7.4) be equal to the profit for the last unit (PLU) in equation (7.5)?

Consider firms in reality. Most firms do not change prices every day or even every week. So long as the price of a product remains constant, as it usually does for any reasonable range of sales, price (*P*) is equal to marginal revenue (MR). The average variable cost is also not likely to change as output changes within a reasonable range. If the average variable cost remains unchanged, the average variable cost (AVC) is equal to marginal cost (MC). The concept of profit contribution, therefore, is a good approximation of the difference between marginal revenue and marginal cost.[4] Because of its simplicity, it is profit contribution, not marginal revenue or marginal cost, that is used by managers of firms in making decisions. Let us observe how these concepts are practiced by firms for profit maximization.

Illustrations

In 1962 Continental Air Lines scheduled many flights on which only half the available seats were filled.[5] In those days, the total cost of a typical flight was $4,500, of which $2,500 was the flight's share of fixed costs such as interest payments and depreciation that would incur even if the flight

---

[4]For more on the relationship between profit contribution analysis and marginal analysis, see J. Ronnie Davis and Semoon Chang, *Principles of managerial economics* (Englewood Cliffs, N.J.: Prentice Hall, 1986), pp. 414–416.

[5]Airline takes the marginal route, *Business Week,* April 20, 1963, pp. 111–114.

were not made, and the remaining $2,000 was out-of-pocket or marginal costs. Revenue from a typical half-filled flight was approximately $3,100. By scheduling half-filled flights, each additional flight added $1,100 to the company's profits. Note that if all flights were half filled, the company would have lost money on every flight, and the company's total revenue would have been short of its total cost. The difference ($1,100) between marginal revenue ($3,100) and marginal cost ($2,000) increased the company's total profit because the MR = MC rule was applied to the airline's business *at the margin* only.

For another example, consider the Emperor Clock Company in Fairhope, Alabama, which specializes in making grandfather clocks. Suppose that the retail price of a typical grandfather clock is $800, the average variable cost of making the clock is $500, and the clock's share of fixed costs is $200, leaving the remaining $100 to net profits. Suppose that a traveler from Texas to Florida stops by the store and offers a final price of $600. If all grandfather clocks were sold below the full cost of $700, the firm would go out of business. For business at the margin, however, such as the traveler's offer of $600, the firm's profit would increase if the clock were sold at $600 to the traveler. The profit contribution from the sale would be $100 since the sale price is $600 and the average variable cost is $500. The profit contribution would be used toward paying the fixed cost. Remember that the traveler is not expected to tell the store's regular customers how much he or she paid for the clock and thus adversely affect the store's regular sales.

SUMMARY

Depending on the characteristics of demand and cost conditions that are common to firms within an industry, markets are classified into four major types: perfect competition, monopoly, oligopoly, and monopolistic competition. Perfect competition refers to market conditions in which the demand for the output of every firm in a given industry is perfectly elastic so that the firm is a price taker for all quantities of output it produces. A monopoly is a firm that supplies the entire market for a particular product with no close substitutes. Oligopoly refers to markets that are dominated by a few leading sellers. Oligopolistic markets are characterized by mutual interdependence in pricing among large firms and by barriers to entry. Monopolistic competition refers to markets in which a large number of firms sell products that are differentiated. Unlike sellers under perfect competition, sellers under imperfect competition are price makers, charging the price that can give them maximum profits.

The demand curve faced by firms operating under perfect competition is horizontal. The horizontal demand curve is the firm's average revenue curve as well as its marginal revenue curve. The average revenue curve of firms under imperfect competition has a downward slope to the right. When the average revenue curve has a downward slope to the right, the corresponding marginal revenue curve has a steeper slope than the average revenue curve. Total revenue is the sum of all marginal revenues for all preceding and current units of sales.

Economists assume that firms optimize by trying to maximize profits. Profits are maximized by producing a level of output at which the difference between total revenue and total cost is the greatest. The MR = MC rule states that profits are maximized when firms produce a level of output at which marginal revenue is equal to marginal cost. Because MR = MC, if a firm is making a profit it is also maximizing profits; when the firm is losing money but continues to produce, the MR = MC rule makes sure that the firm is minimizing losses. In reality, managers use the term *profit contribution* to describe what is essentially the difference between marginal revenue and marginal cost. The profit contribution of a product is the difference between price and average variable cost. If price and average variable cost remain unchanged, the profit contribution equals the difference between marginal revenue and marginal cost.

EXERCISES

1. Considering that there are few good examples of markets that are perfectly competitive, what are some possible reasons for studying perfect competition?

2. Economists, especially those specializing in antitrust economics, often use the term **workable** or **effective competition** to describe markets that are so highly competitive that no one seller or no group of sellers in concert has the power to control the market price to its advantage. [See, for instance, Henry Adler Einhorn and William Paul Smith, *Economic aspects of antitrust: Readings and cases* (New York: Random House, 1968), pp. 5–23.] Assuming that there are many sellers in an industry, will the industry necessarily be qualified for workable competition?

3. According to the May 4, 1987, issue of *Time* (p. 110), the first U.S. patent law was passed in 1790 to protect the invention of any useful art, manufacture, engine, machine, or device, or any improvement thereon not before known or used. In May 1987 the U.S. Patent and Trademark Office announced that it would consider nonnaturally occurring nonhuman multicellular living organisms, including animals, to be patentable subject matter. The new patent policy is controversial because of the development of gene-splicing in biotechnology. For instance, firefly genes can be introduced into tobacco plants, which then glow in the dark. In the extreme case, genes of two different animals might be combined to create an animal that does not now exist. Suppose that new multicellular living organisms are created and patented. What would be the most likely market structure for these organisms?

4. Are McDonald's and Hardee's hamburgers differentiated?

5. The demand curve for perfect competition is described as being horizontal. Assuming that the market for independent trucking (that is, trucking businesses owned by sole proprietors) is perfectly competitive, is the demand curve for the independent trucking industry horizontal? Why or why not?

6. When an average revenue curve is sloped downward to the right, as it usually is for firms that operate under imperfectly competitive market conditions, average revenue is greater than marginal revenue, causing the marginal revenue curve to lie below the average revenue curve. What could explain this?

7. Given a downward-sloping demand curve, explain the process of deriving the marginal revenue curve that corresponds to the given demand curve.

8. Suppose that a firm realizes marginal revenue that is greater than marginal cost for sales of all of its products. Does this mean that the firm is making a profit?

9. Under what conditions is the concept of the profit contribution equivalent to the difference between marginal revenue and marginal cost?

10. At Christie's London auction house in July 1987, a Vincent Van Gogh work called *The Bridge at Trinquetaille* was sold in just two tense minutes of bidding for $20.2 million, the second highest price paid for a painting at an auction at the time. The highest price paid ($39.9 million) as of July 1987 was for another Van Gogh work called *Sunflowers,* sold only three months prior to the sale of *The Bridge.* The 29-inch by 36-inch *Bridge,* painted in 1888 when Van Gogh lived in Arles, was sold by the family of New York banker Siegfried Kramarsky, who bought the painting in 1932. What are the total revenue, average revenue, and marginal revenue of keeping and selling *The Bridge?*

SUGGESTED READINGS

Davis, J. Ronnie, and Chang, Semoon. (1986). *Principles of managerial economics.* Englewood Cliffs, N.J.: Prentice Hall.

An extensive coverage of pricing methods and practices is presented in Chapter 11.

Earley, James S. (1956). Marginal policies of "excellently managed" companies. *American Economic Review* 46(March):44–70.

A rather old but widely quoted article that shows evidence that well-managed companies apply the MR = MC rule to making business decisions.

Haynes, W. Warren. (1964). Pricing policies in small firms. *Southern Economic Journal* 30(April):335–347.

Shows that pricing practices of many small firms are also based on marginalism. The findings are based on a questionnaire survey.

Oxenfeldt, Alfred R. (1960). Multi-stage approach to pricing. *Harvard Business Review* 38(July-August):125–133.

Presents a six-stage pricing process that minimizes the likelihood of error.

8

Price and Output Decisions of Firms under Perfect Competition

What Is Perfect Competition?

Price and Output Decisions in the
   Short Run

Issues on Competitive Pricing

PERFECT COMPETITION IS almost like Garrison Keillor's Lake Wobegon, the misty, imaginary Minnesota town that was the home for a show called *A Prairie Home Companion,* broadcast on public radio each Saturday for 13 years until 1987. What life was like in Lake Wobegon varied with the kind of dream that one wished to experience there. Just as Lake Wobegon provided some with an opportunity to dream of the kind of life that they wished they could have lived, so also does perfect competition provide some economists with an opportunity to dream of the kind of market that they wish that they could arrange. Elusive as that may be, it is still necessary to study perfect competition because it provides the basis for studying and, hopefully, for improving other more realistic markets.

All firms have to determine the price that they will charge for their product and the quantity of the product that they have to produce in order to maximize profits. Firms that operate in perfectly competitive markets are expected to make these decisions in a manner that is different from the manner in which firms operating under more realistic market conditions do. If we were to make markets increasingly more competitive, the way in which real firms determine their price and quantity of output would be more like the one in which firms in the conceptually perfect competitive market make their decisions on price and output. By studying price and output decisions of firms operating under perfect competition, we hope to present the basis for making a judgment as to whether or not it is desirable, or even possible, to move toward more competitive markets.

The first section of this chapter reviews the concept of perfect competition. The process through which firms operating under perfect competition determine the product price and the quantity of output is presented in the second section. Issues inherent to perfect competition such as marginal cost pricing, externalities, and income distribution are discussed in the third section.

WHAT IS PERFECT COMPETITION?

About 60 years ago, Edward Chamberlin made a distinction between pure competition and perfect competition.[1] According to Chamberlin, pure competition refers to market conditions that are *unalloyed* with monopoly elements, meaning that the demand for the output of each firm in a given industry is perfectly elastic. Chamberlin further claimed that perfect competition requires pure competition plus additional conditions such as product homogeneity, absence of uncertainty, and more. The usual requirements of perfect competition are

1. a large number of sellers and buyers each of whom handles quantities so small relative to the market as a whole that no one seller or buyer can control the market price;
2. no barriers to entry into the market or exit from the market;
3. homogeneity of products sold by different sellers in the market, meaning that consumers perceive all of these products to be basically identical;
4. perfect knowledge of the market by all buyers and sellers such that everyone knows who is selling which product where at what price; and
5. perfect mobility of resources.

Whether a market should be called pure competition or perfect competition depends on how

[1]Edward Chamberlin, *The theory of monopolistic competition* (Cambridge, Mass.: Harvard University Press, 1933), p. 5.

restrictively one wishes to characterize the competitiveness of the market. In 1938 Cournot stated that competition would be perfect if each seller provided so small a part of the total output of a product that the removal of one seller from the market would make no appreciable difference to market price. Following Cournot, we will characterize perfect competition as a market in which individual firms have no control over the market price. When individual sellers have no control over market price, the demand curve for the product must be horizontal, since a horizontal demand curve means that the firm is a price taker.

In this chapter, we will define **perfect competition** as market conditions in which the demand for the output of every firm in a given industry is so perfectly elastic that each firm is a price taker for all quantities of output it produces. This definition is essentially the same as pure competition as defined by Chamberlin and perfect competition as defined by another great economist, Joan Robinson.[2] Many economists use the notions of pure competition and perfect competition interchangeably, however.

A significant advantage of defining perfect competition as markets with horizontal demand curves for products produced by individual firms is that perfect competition does not have to be the Lake Wobegon that we imagine, but can be the Lake Wobegon that we live in every day. Other things being equal, markets are more competitive as the number of sellers increases and the market share of each seller decreases. Several markets, including those of most agricultural products and independent trucking, are sufficiently competitive and can be studied using the theory of perfect competition presented in this chapter.

PRICE AND OUTPUT DECISIONS IN THE SHORT RUN

Firms must make decisions on what price to charge and how much to produce. Since firms operating under perfect competition are price takers, these firms charge the price that is determined in the market. The focus of decision making in firms operating under perfect competition, therefore, is on determination of the level of output at which the firm maximizes profits.

Combining the Cost and Revenue Curves

Profits are obtained by subtracting costs from revenues. To graphically show the process of determining the profit-maximizing level of output, it is necessary to combine and superimpose cost curves and revenue curves. Cost curves and revenue curves of firms that operate under perfectly competitive markets are superimposed onto each other in Figure 8.2. First, it is necessary to know how to read rectangles formed by cost and revenue curves.

Reading Rectangles
Figure 8.1 is drawn to demonstrate how to read graphs on cost and revenue curves. To read Figure 8.1, it is necessary to understand that the area of a rectangle is obtained when the vertical distance is multiplied by the horizontal distance. Suppose that the vertical distance of a rectangle is 10 and

[2]For more on the definition of perfect competition, see Joan Robinson, What is perfect competition? *Quarterly Journal of Economics* (November 1934):104–120.

ECONOMICS MEETS THE GRAMMARIAN

Words ending in the suffix "-ics" (acoustics, politics, tactics, gymnastics, etc.) are regarded as either singular or plural, depending on meaning. When the word is being treated as a subject or science, it is construed as singular ("Tactics is among the subjects taught at West Point"). When the word denotes practical activities or qualities, it is construed as plural ("The tactics of the Battle of Gettysburg are studied at West Point"). . . . . Incidentally, economics is almost always construed as singular, perhaps because it is difficult to think of it in the sense of practical activities.

Source: Theodore M. Bernstein, Economics meets the grammarian, *Business Horizons* 30(January-February 1987):51.

---

its horizontal distance is 20. The area of the rectangle, then, is 200, obtained when 10 is multiplied by 20. This is illustrated in Figure 8.1(a). Suppose that the price is $10 per unit and the quantity of sales is 20 units, as shown in Figure 8.1(b). Total revenue is $200, exactly the same as the area of the rectangle in panel (a) of the figure.

Suppose that, in Figure 8.1(c), price is OA and the quantity of sales is OC. Total revenue is obtained by multiplying price and quantity. When the vertical distance was multiplied by the horizontal distance in panels (a) and (b), the result was the area of the rectangle. Likewise, total revenue in panel (c) is indicated by rectangle OABC, in which the vertical distance OA is price and the horizontal distance OC is quantity.

Introducing the Graph

The process by which a competitive firm makes decisions on price and the quantity of output is shown in Figure 8.2. Keep in mind that cost and revenue curves shown in Figure 8.2 are those for *one* representative firm under perfect competition, not for the industry.

In Figure 8.2, the average revenue (AR) and the marginal revenue (MR) curves are horizontal because the firm is a price taker. Being a price taker means that the firm simply charges the price that is determined by supply and demand in the market, and it determines the quantity of output based on the price. If the price is high, the firm increases the quantity of output it supplies. If the price is low, the firm decreases the quantity of output it supplies.

Price and Output Decisions Graphed

The height of the average revenue curve is the market price that is determined by demand and supply in the market. The price of the product, therefore, is OA. To find the quantity of output at which the firm maximizes profits, the MR = MC rule is applied. The point where marginal revenue equals marginal cost is D. To determine the quantity of output for profit maximization, we need to go to the horizontal axis that measures the quantity of output. We do this by drawing a line vertically from point D toward the quantity line. The point of intersection on the quantity line is G. The profit-maximizing quantity of output, therefore, is OG.

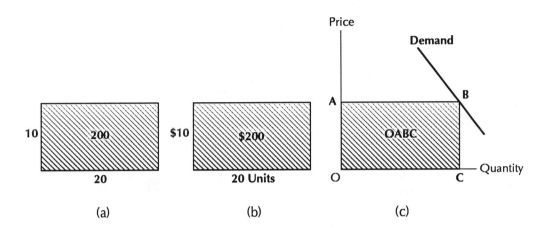

FIGURE 8.1   Reading Rectangles. The area of a rectangle is obtained when the vertical distance is multiplied by the horizontal distance.

It is easy to identify in Figure 8.2 total revenue, total cost, and economic profit all at the profit-maximizing level of output. Total revenue is OADG since OA is price and OG is quantity. To determine the total cost of producing and selling the quantity OG, we need to know the per unit cost of production. The production cost per unit is indicated as GE, since point E is on the AC curve, or OB since it is the same distance as GE. Total cost is OBEG, obtained by multiplying the average cost OB and the quantity OG. The difference BADE between total revenue OADG and total cost OBEG represents economic profit for the firm. Economic profit means profit beyond and above the normal profit. Rectangle BADE reveals an economic profit because cost curves represent economic costs inclusive of all explicit and implicit costs.

Total cost is the sum of fixed cost and variable cost. Fixed cost and variable cost can also be identified in Figure 8.2. The average cost at the output level OG is GE. The average variable cost at the output level OG is GF since F lies on the AVC curve, or OC since it is equal in distance to GF. Total variable cost is OCFG, obtained by multiplying the average variable cost OC by the quantity of output OG. Since GE is the average cost and GF is the average variable cost, and since average fixed cost is the difference between average cost and average variable cost, the distance FE or CB is the average fixed cost. To obtain total fixed cost, CB is multiplied by OG, resulting in CBEF. The fixed cost CBEF is also obtained by subtracting total variable cost OCFG from total cost OBEG.

To Summarize Readings of the Graph
All readings of Figure 8.2, explained above, are summarized in the following. These readings are unique since they relate to the profit-maximizing level of output.

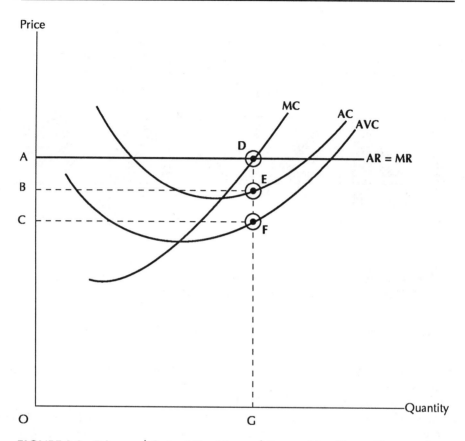

FIGURE 8.2 Price and Output Decisions of Competitive Firms. Firms under perfect competition charge the price OA determined in the market and produce OG units of output determined by the MR = MC rule.

price:	OA
average revenue:	GD or OA
marginal revenue:	GD or OA
quantity:	OG
total revenue:	OADG
average cost:	GE or OB
total cost:	OBEG
profit per unit:	ED or BA
profit:	BADE
average variable cost:	GF or OC
total variable cost:	OCFG
average fixed cost:	FE or CB
total fixed cost:	CBEF

Moving toward the Break-even Point

When firms in one industry make economic profits, firms in other industries begin to transfer resources to the market in which firms are enjoying economic profits. As more firms join the industry, the market supply curve shifts to the right and the market price falls. **Economic profits** are profits in excess of a normal rate of return. To understand how firms respond to changes in economic profits, we need to know what a normal rate of return is.

Normal Rate of Return

A **normal rate of return** is defined as the expected rate of return that the firm would expect to make if the same amount of resources were invested in production of other goods or services. A most practical definition of the normal rate of return is the average rate of return on investment in all other industries. To illustrate, suppose that firms manufacturing the gas pumps used at gas stations make 18 cents for every dollar invested before taxes are paid. The rate of return for these firms, then, is 18 percent. The rate of return on investment in U.S. manufacturing industries usually averages 10 to 15 percent on a pretax basis. Suppose that the average rate of return on investment in U.S. manufacturing industries is 12.5 percent. Firms manufacturing gas pumps are making economic profits of 5.5 percent, which is the difference between 18 percent for these firms and 12.5 percent for the average rate of return on investment in all industries.

If firms manufacturing gas pumps continue to make economic profits, more firms will join the industry, causing the supply of gas pumps to increase and their prices to fall. Likewise, if the production of computer software is profitable, more firms will produce software. If selling fur coats is profitable, more businesses will sell fur coats. If the rate of return on investment in the sale of fur coats falls below the average rate of return on investment in other industries, businesses selling fur coats will leave the industry.

Firms' Response to an Increase in Market Supply

The effect of an increase in the industry supply on individual firms within the industry is shown in Figure 8.3. In Figure 8.3, the price before additional firms enter the industry is OA. As more firms join the industry, the supply curve shifts to the right in panel (a) of the figure, and the market price falls from OA to OA'. As the market price falls, the average revenue curve for individual firms also falls as shown in panel (b).

If the market is highly competitive, the market price is expected to fall until it finally reaches the level that equals the lowest point of the average cost curve. At that lowest point all firms make no more than normal profits, that is, the same level of profit as firms in all other industries make on an investment. The firm in Figure 8.3(b) responds to the falling market price from OA to OA' by reducing the quantity of output produced from OG to OG'.

Production at the Break-even Point

Figure 8.4 is an expanded version of Figure 8.3(b). Suppose that the market price falls until it reaches C, the lowest point of the average cost curve. The firm charges price OA. To determine the profit-maximizing quantity of output, we draw a line vertically from point C, where marginal revenue equals marginal cost, until the vertical line reaches point E on the quantity line. The profit-maximizing quantity of output is OE. Since price is OA and the quantity of output produced and sold is OE, total revenue at the output level OE is OACE. The average cost at the profit-maximizing quantity of output is EC, since point E is on the AC curve, or OA, which is equal to EC. Total cost,

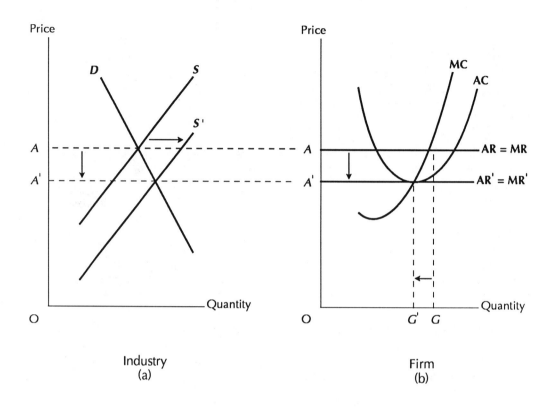

FIGURE 8.3   Effect of Falling Price in the Industry on Firms. As more firms enter the industry, the market price falls in panel (a), and the AR curve faced by individual firms falls toward the lowest AC level in panel (b).

therefore, is OACE, which is equal to total revenue. The firm described in Figure 8.4 receives total revenue that is equal to total cost. The lowest point C of the average cost curve is called the **break-even point,** because total revenue and total cost are equal to each other and the firm breaks even financially at this point.

Total cost in Figure 8.4 can also be divided into fixed cost and variable cost. The average variable cost at the output level OE is ED since D is on the AVC curve, or OB, which is equal to ED. Total variable cost, therefore, is OBDE, obtained by multiplying the average variable cost OB and the quantity of output OE. The difference DC (or BA, which is the same distance) between average cost EC and average variable cost ED is the average fixed cost. Total fixed cost, therefore, is BACD.

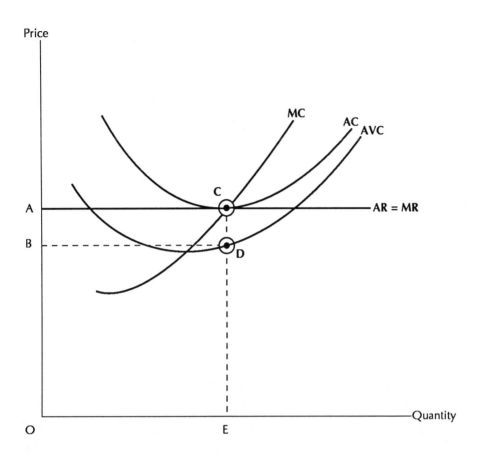

FIGURE 8.4 Operating at the Break-even Point. When competitive firms operate at the lowest point of the AC curve, firms' total revenue equals total cost. Point C is the break-even point.

Shutdown Point and Loss Minimization

Firms do not always earn profits. Even profitable firms sometimes have to survive hard times. When new firms enter an industry in which existing firms earn economic profits, there is no assurance that the influx of new firms will stop as soon as the price falls to the break-even level. In a market system in which decisions on production are made by individual firms rather than one central agency, it is likely that the market will overreact to economic profits and the influx of new firms will continue until price falls below the break-even level. When price falls below the break-even level, firms incur losses. Firms do not usually shut down simply because they incur losses. When firms do not make profits but are still in business, firms optimize use of their resources by trying to minimize their losses.

Optimal Use of Resources under Losses

Suppose that a firm incurring a loss shuts down operations temporarily. Even if the firm does not produce, there will be a loss since expenditures on all fixed inputs will still have to be made. Rent or mortgage payments on property, interest on loans, property taxes, salaries of managers, and some utilities will all have to be paid, unless and until the firm completely goes out of business. In other words, if the firm shuts down temporarily, the amount of loss is equal to fixed cost.

Assuming that the loss is judged to be only temporary, the firm will continue to produce so long as the amount of loss is equal to or less than the firm's fixed cost. If the loss exceeds the firm's fixed cost, the firm has two choices. One choice is to shut down. The other is to continue to operate in order to avoid the costs of return to production, since return would incur significant start-up costs in hiring new employees and attracting new customers. The next subsection illustrates the firm's response to falling prices based on the assumption that the firm will shut down as soon as the loss exceeds the firm's fixed cost.

Production at the Shutdown Point

The loss-minimization process of firms is graphically depicted in Figure 8.5. Suppose that in Figure 8.5 the price falls to a point as low as the lowest point of the average variable cost and the firm continues its production. The marginal revenue and marginal cost curves cross each other at point D. The price charged by the loss-minimizing firm would be OB or ED, and the quantity of output produced by the firm would be OE. Total revenue is OBDE, obtained by multiplying price OB and the quantity of output OE. To determine the total cost of production, draw a line vertically from point D until the line crosses the average cost curve at point C. The average cost of production for the output level OE is EC or OA. Total cost is OACE, obtained by multiplying average cost OA and the quantity of output OE. The amount of loss, therefore, is BACD.

The difference DC between average cost EC and average variable cost ED is the average fixed cost. When average fixed cost DC is multiplied by the quantity of output OE, total fixed cost is obtained at BACD, which is exactly the same as the amount of the loss. This review indicates that if the price is equal to the lowest average variable cost, the firm incurs a loss that is equal to the firm's fixed cost. If the price is lower than the lowest average variable cost, the firm's loss will be greater than the fixed cost. If the price is higher than the lowest average variable cost but lower than the lowest average cost, the firm still incurs a loss, but the amount of loss will be smaller than the fixed cost. In this case, a portion of the revenue from sales is used to pay for some of the fixed costs.

Point D is called the **shutdown point** because at a price below ED the firm minimizes losses by shutting down its operation. At a price equal to ED, the amount of loss is equal to the fixed cost regardless of whether the firm continues operation or shuts down.

Changing Product Prices and Output Decisions of Firms

When the market price of a product changes, the change is expected to affect the output decisions of firms. Firms are intuitively expected to increase the quantity of output produced as market price rises and decrease the quantity of output produced as market price falls. We will formalize in this section the relation between changes in market price and the output decisions of firms.

Graphic Illustration

The relation between changes in market price and quantities of the product produced by a firm operating under perfect competition is shown in Figure 8.6. Suppose that the market supply of a

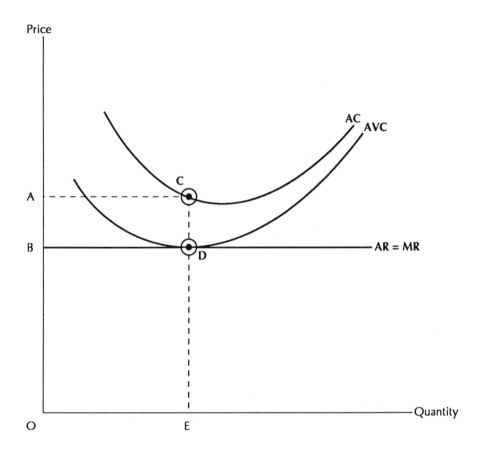

FIGURE 8.5 Operating at the Shutdown Point. When competitive firms operate at the lowest point of the AVC curve, the firm's loss equals the firm's fixed cost. Point D is the shutdown point.

product increases due, say, to an increase in income. As market supply increases, the market supply curve will shift to the right. As the market supply curve shifts to the right, as indicated in Figure 8.6(a), the market price falls from OP_1 to OP_2 to OP_3. The falling market price of the product causes the average revenue and the marginal revenue curves of a competitive firm to fall from OP_1 to OP_2 to OP_3 in panel (b) of the figure.

As the marginal revenue curve falls, the MR = MC point moves downward along the existing marginal cost curve from point A to point B, and finally to point C. As the MR = MC point falls from A to B to C, the quantity of output produced by the firm also falls from OQ_1 to OQ_2 to OQ_3. If the price falls below the shutdown point C in panel (b), however, the firm will not produce and

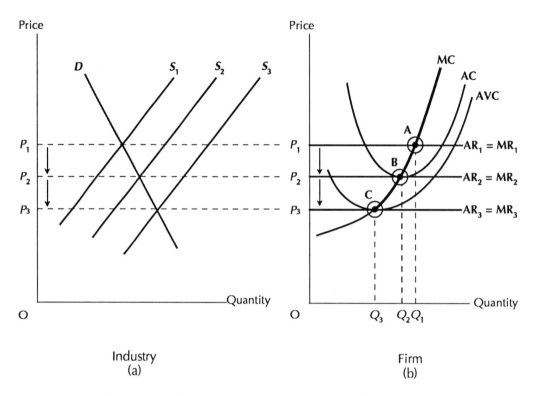

FIGURE 8.6 Changing Market Price and Output Decisions of Firms. As market price falls from OP_1 to OP_2 to OP_3, the quantity of the product supplied by the firm also falls from OQ_1 to OQ_2 to OQ_3. If the price falls below the lowest point of the average variable cost curve, the firm shuts down to minimize losses.

the quantity supplied will become zero. Point C is the lowest point of the average variable cost curve.

At a price below the lowest point of the average variable cost curve, we have concluded that the firm will shut down. It is important to understand that such a temporary shutdown will not always and inevitably occur whenever price falls below the lowest point of the average variable cost. A shutdown occurs in this case, however, because we are assuming that the firm will choose to shut down if the loss is greater than the firm's fixed cost. In reality, firms may continue to produce if these firms judge that the long-term loss from the temporary shutdown exceeds the short-term gain.

Supply Curve of the Firm
Figure 8.6(b) shows clearly that the segment of the marginal cost curve on or above the lowest average variable cost curve represents the relation between prices and quantities supplied at these

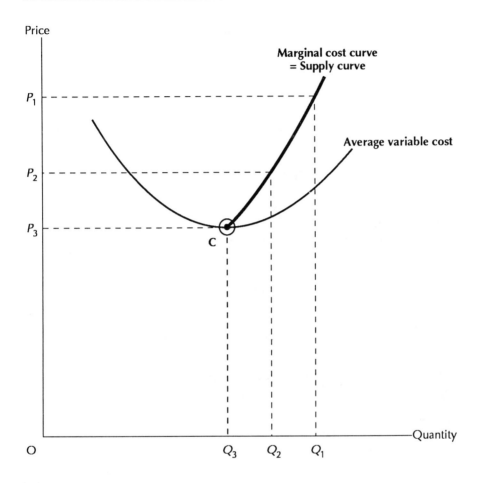

FIGURE 8.7   Supply Curve of Firms under Perfect Competition. The supply
curve of firms operating under perfect competition is the segment of the
marginal cost curve that lies on or above its average variable cost curve.

prices. At price OP_1, for instance, the quantity of the product supplied by the firm is OQ_1; at price
OP_2, the quantity supplied is OQ_2; and at price OP_3, the quantity supplied is OQ_3. The relation
between prices and quantities supplied at these prices is the definition of the firm's supply curve.
The segment of the marginal cost curve on or above the average variable cost curve, therefore, is
the short-run supply curve of firms that operate under perfect competition. Figure 8.7 is a
reproduction of the portion of the marginal cost curve in Figure 8.6(b) that represents the firm's
supply curve.

ADAM SMITH

Adam Smith was born in 1723 in the seaport town of Kirkaldy, Scotland. His father died before Smith was born. Smith attended Glasgow College at age 14, and in 1751 he became a professor of logic and later held the chair of moral philosophy at Glasgow College. When the *Wealth of nations* was published in 1776, Smith's fame was permanently established. In the book, Smith proposed that free exchange between buyers and sellers, motivated by their self-interests, is morally neutral and socially productive through the workings of the *invisible hand.* Since free exchange based on self-interests is in harmony with the interest of society, Smith preferred economic freedom to government control. A *laissez faire* (*let* people *do* as they please) policy thus was born. The impact of the *Wealth of nations* has been so substantial that English historian Henry Thomas Buckle declared that this book represented the most valuable contribution ever made by a single person toward establishing the principles of government. Much of Smith's income in the later years of his life was spent on charities, and shortly before his death in 1790, most of his manuscripts were destroyed in accordance with his wishes. There was no explanation of why he wished them destroyed.

ISSUES ON COMPETITIVE PRICING

Some interesting issues arise from the process through which competitive firms make decisions on price and the quantity of output for profit maximization. Three of these issues are marginal cost pricing, externalities, and distribution of income.

Marginal Cost Pricing

Economic efficiency is twofold: technical efficiency and allocative efficiency. **Technical efficiency** refers to the process of maximizing the quantity of output for given amounts of inputs, or minimizing the cost of producing a given quantity of output. **Allocative efficiency,** on the other hand, refers to the process of producing goods and services that are most valued by society. Producing a large amount of goods and services that few people want in any given society would not be an efficient use of scarce resources. It is the second definition of economic efficiency that we are interested in for our discussion of marginal cost pricing.

What Is Marginal Cost Pricing?
For firms operating under perfect competition, price is equal to average revenue, which in turn is equal to marginal revenue. The average revenue and marginal revenue schedules of firms operating under perfect competition are identical. Firms determine the profit-maximizing level of output by equalizing marginal revenue and marginal cost. In other words, profit-maximizing firms operating

under a completely elastic demand curve select price (P) at a level that is equal to marginal revenue, which in turn is equal to marginal cost (MC); that is, P = MC. The process of pricing a product according to the P = MC relation is known as **marginal cost pricing.**

Why Is It Economically Efficient?

Marginal cost pricing is said to be economically efficient. To understand what this statement means, consider a careful shopper who finally selects a cassette tape of Symphony No. 5 by Ludwig van Beethoven and pays $15 for it. The price of the cassette tape is the maximum price that the consumer is willing to pay for the product in order to satisfy his or her wants. The product price thus measures the maximum benefit or satisfaction that the consumer derives from purchasing the tape.

The marginal cost of making the cassette tape, on the other hand, measures the minimum cost for Polydor International of producing the last unit of Beethoven Symphony No. 5 albums on cassette tape. The minimum cost represents the minimum amount of resource that the society is willing to give up in order to produce the product. If price (P) is equal to marginal cost (MC) for a given product, the maximum price that consumers are willing to pay for the product is exactly equal to what the society has to forgo to produce the product.

If the price of a product is greater than the marginal cost of producing the product, consumers value the product more than the society is willing to sacrifice to produce the product, causing production of the product to increase. If the price of a product is less than the marginal cost of producing the product, the resources used to produce the product should be transferred to production of another higher priced product that consumers value more. When resources are transferred to production of another product that society values more, economic efficiency is improved. That is because the product valued more by the society is now produced instead of the product that the society values less.

To summarize, marginal cost pricing requires that demand price be made equal to marginal cost. Since resources are drawn away from alternative uses, marginal costs should accurately reflect the social opportunities forgone to produce a given product. The equality of price and marginal cost ensures that consumers equate marginal benefits from the use of given resources with the real alternatives forgone elsewhere. In a world of pure competition, the market mechanism would operate to ensure this equality.

Practical Evaluation of Marginal Cost Pricing

Several controversies surround the concept of marginal cost pricing. Of these, the most interesting concerns the possibility that the price based on marginal cost may not be sufficient to pay for the cost of production by the firm. In the long run, the product price has to be at least as large as the average cost of producing the product in order for the firm to survive. Marginal cost pricing ensures that price equals marginal cost, but it does not ensure that price is at least as large as average cost. We may illustrate this issue by using the example of bridge crossings.[3]

Suppose that once the bridge in question is built, the bridge is expected to last practically forever, and there are no additional costs associated with bridge crossings because the bridge is never so full as to give rise to crowding. The marginal cost to society of an additional crossing is zero. The economically efficient price for a crossing, therefore, is precisely zero. A positive price such as would discourage even a single crossing would cause allocation to be inefficient, since a

[3]Advisory Commission on Intergovernmental Relations, *Local revenue diversification: Income, sales taxes, and user charges* (Washington D.C.: ACIR, October 1974), pp. 65–66.

costless crossing that could make someone better off without hurting anyone else would remain unexploited. Yet it is equally evident that charging a price of zero for crossings will hardly raise sufficient revenue to cover the cost of building the bridge. Even if the bridge crossings were not costless, the proper charge for a bridge crossing based on marginal cost pricing is the associated increment in total cost, and charging by that rule is not expected to raise revenues sufficient enough to pay for the full cost of building the bridge. To do otherwise would be to deny use of the bridge to someone who is willing to pay the entire cost associated with a crossing.

The practical problem with marginal cost pricing is that although each user should pay only for the cost of what he or she consumes, all users should bear the total cost jointly. A suggested solution for the financing problem with marginal cost pricing is that if the capacity is fully utilized on some occasions and not on others, then there should be two prices: (a) a peak period price high enough to cover the cost of providing the capacity and the actual operating costs related to the use by the peak period group; and (b) a nonpeak period price covering only the actual operating costs related to the use by the nonpeak period users.[4] Consider, for example, a medium-sized Midwest town that plans to construct a natural gas distribution facility. The town's peak demand for natural gas for heating will occur during the winter period December through March of the following year. The cost of building a facility large enough to meet the town's peak demand is $10 million. The suggested application of marginal cost pricing is that all households using natural gas in the period December through March should share the construction cost, but that each household using natural gas in the remaining eight months should pay its marginal cost only.

The contention by economists that resources are most efficiently allocated when price is equal to marginal cost is based on certain conditions. The most important of these conditions is that there are no important spillover effects in production and consumption of the product that are not reflected in the marginal cost of producing the product.[5] If there were spillover benefits, marginal cost would overestimate the true cost of producing the product; if there were spillover costs, marginal cost would underestimate the true cost of producing the product. The meaning of these statements is not easy to understand but is explained in the next paragraphs.

Externalities

One of the major advantages of having markets that are perfectly competitive is that under perfect competition, price (P) accurately measures other goods and services (MC) that society must sacrifice to produce the product under our consideration. When there are spillover effects, price no longer measures marginal cost accurately.

Defining Externalities

Consider chloroflorocarbons (CFC). CFC is widely believed to destroy the earth's ozone layer. Once released, CFC remains in the atmosphere for about 100 years, destroying the atmosphere's

[4]Ibid., p. 66.

[5]Other conditions are that the current distribution of income be acceptable or certainly not biased toward the particular measurement of prices and costs; and that deviations from $P = MC$ elsewhere in the economy not require compensating adjustments in this sector. This last condition is the problem of the theory of the second best. For more on these conditions, see Jerome W. Milliman, Beneficiary charges—toward a unified theory, in Selma J. Mushkin (ed.), *Public prices for public products* (Washington, D.C.: The Urban Institute Washington, 1972), p. 34.

ozone layer. The disappearance of the ozone layer is expected to increase the earth's temperature, cause more fires, cause skin cancer, and break the food chain, thereby reducing food production. Scientists believe that CFC is released through the burning of fossil fuels or the use of spray cans utilizing CFCs as a propellant.

An interesting economic problem stemming from these theories about CFC is that CFC affects not only the firms that use fossil fuels and consumers who buy their products but also persons who are not a party to the trade. When firms using fossil fuels do not remove CFC before it is released into the atmosphere, the market prices of products produced by these firms underestimate the true cost of their production. Effects of a trade between sellers and buyers on a third party who is not part of the trade are called **spillover effects** or **externalities.** In the case of flu shots or pesticides, the spillover effects are beneficial to society and thus are called **spillover benefits** or **external benefits.** In the case of water or air pollution and CFC, the spillover effects are detrimental to society and thus are called **spillover costs** or **external costs.**

An Illustration

We can see how spillover effects such as pollution affect the allocation of resources by supposing that a power company pollutes water in the process of generating electricity. If the power company were to clean the water and add the cost of cleaning the water to the price per kilowatt hour of electricity, the price of electricity would be higher than it is now. In other words, when the power company is allowed to pollute water, the price of electricity is lower than it should be, and consumers are expected to use more electricity than they would be using if the price were higher. Allowing the power company to pollute water is equivalent to society allocating more resources to the generation of electricity than would have been allocated in the absence of externalities.

The effect of pollution on resource allocation both before and after pollution is indicated in Figure 8.8. Supply curve S represents the supply schedule of electricity when the power company is allowed to pollute the water. If the company is forced to clean the water by installing pollution abatement equipment and then adds the cost of the equipment to the supply price, the supply curve shifts to the left from S to S'. The leftward shift of the supply curve means that the supply price of a given quantity of electricity is higher. The shift in supply to the left thus causes the price to rise from OP to OP' and the amount of electricity used to fall from OQ to OQ'. Allowing the power company to pollute the water, in effect, keeps the price of electricity lower than it would have been without pollution by the amount indicated as PP', and, as a result, the amount of electricity used is higher than it would have been without pollution by the amount indicated as Q'Q. The water pollution by the power company may be said to lead to an overconsumption of electricity. Economists would say that there was an overallocation of resources to the generation of electricity.

When firms pollute the environment, this does not necessarily mean that owners or managers of these firms are bad people. In a market that is highly competitive, the extra expenditure by one firm on cleaning up the pollution may influence the survival of the firm unless the expenditure is matched by other firms in the industry that also pollute the environment. The existence of externalities, therefore, invites government to interfere with operations of the private sector. Government may force all firms to *internalize* external costs in a number of ways, including regulation by the Environmental Protection Agency and sale to firms of a *permit to pollute* the environment. Revenues from the sale of permits to pollute can then be used to clean up the environment.

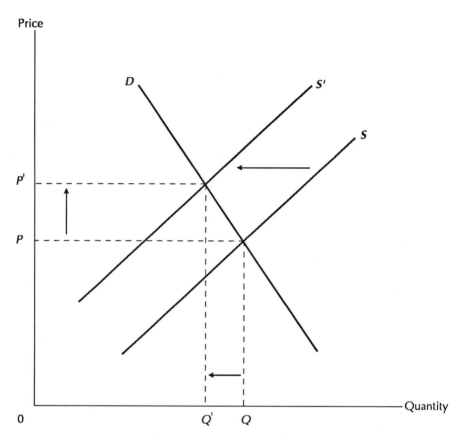

FIGURE 8.8 Effect of Antipollution Measures. As firms are forced to install pollution abatement equipment, price rises and the quantity exchanged falls.

Income Distribution

Another controversy that surrounds competitive markets is that a competitive market is likely to result in an unequal distribution of income among the members of society. If all people were exactly alike with respect to their capacity to make a living, income would be distributed equally among all people. However, the capacity of individuals to earn income differs from one person to another. There are many reasons why different people have different capacities to earn income. These reasons include differences in the level of education of workers, differences in the amount of inherited wealth of individuals, different intelligence levels of individuals, and many more. A competitive price system rewards individuals according to their ability, leaving those who have little capacity to earn further behind those who have greater capacity. Once the difference in the capacity of individuals to earn income is given, a competitive market system of itself has no mechanism to correct the difference.

RISING INCOME AND POVERTY LINE

The official census income level below which households are classified as poor is based on the assumption that the poor spend approximately one-third of their incomes for food. The poverty line originally consisted of three times what the Department of Agriculture in 1955 ascertained to be the minimum food consumption requirement for a family of four. Assuming that there is no inflation, the absolute minimum income level below which households are classified as poor should not change, but it does over time, according to Robert W. Kilpatrick, so far as public opinion is concerned.

Assuming that there is no inflation, does the poverty line which supposedly indicates the minimal income for a family's survival rise or remain the same as family income increases? By hypothesizing that growth in average income increases the poverty line but by less than the same proportion, Kilpatrick developed a model

$$PI = f(Y),$$

where PI is the poverty line income and Y is the median family income. The model was estimated on the basis of 10 Gallup poll results taken between 1957 and 1971 in which the poll asked, "What is the smallest amount of money a family of four needs each week to get along in this community?"

The result of Kilpatrick's study was presented in the form of an elasticity coefficient, 0.547. The figure is the ratio of the percentage increase in poverty line income relative to the percentage increase in median family income. According to the study results, a 1 percent increase in family income leads to a 0.547 percent increase in the poverty line income. The hypothesis that the poverty line rises with average income but by less than the same proportion is thus accepted.

Source: Robert W. Kilpatrick, The income elasticity of the poverty line, *Review of Economics and Statistics* 40(August 1973):327–332. Copyright, President and Fellows of Harvard College.

Equity versus Efficiency

The issue of income distribution is often stated as a trade-off between equity and efficiency. The basic argument in favor of an equal distribution of income is that an equal distribution of income maximizes a society's total utility. In other words, a more equal distribution is alleged to raise the overall happiness of the entire society. According to this view, an equal distribution of income improves the equity of the society.

The basic argument against an equal distribution of income is that an equal distribution of income reduces the incentive to work. In other words, why should anyone work hard if everyone receives the same amount of income regardless of how hard he or she works? According to this view, an equal distribution of income allegedly hurts the efficiency of the economy by preventing the economy from producing the maximum output that it can produce. Like other economic problems, there is no generally accepted answer to the question of what is the optimal trade-off between equity and efficiency. It may safely be stated that modern democratic societies are not likely to accept either the absolutely equal distribution of income or the distribution of income based solely on the ability of individuals.

The Issue of Poverty

Perhaps the most important issue regarding the distribution of income pertains to poverty. The U.S. government began measuring poverty in 1964 when Mollie Orshansky, then at the Social Security Administration, suggested that a reasonable measure of a poverty-level income would be that income sufficient to purchase a minimally adequate amount of goods and services. The poverty-level income for a nonfarm family of four, and the number and percentage of persons below the poverty level for selected years since 1959, are summarized in Table 8.1. The poverty level income is based on the economy food plan developed by the U.S. Department of Agriculture.[6]

There are problems associated with defining the poverty threshold income. Some of the important problems follow.

1. Noncash benefits such as Medicare, Medicaid, food stamps, nutrition assistance, housing assistance, and employer-provided fringe benefits such as health insurance are not included in defining the poverty threshold.
2. Because of the significant increase in real incomes, current families spend approximately one-fifth, rather than one-third, of their income for food.
3. The poverty count applies to poor families and individuals, but not to poor households, meaning that multiperson households are counted as a single unit only if all persons in the household are related.

A continuous improvement in defining the poverty threshold income is important, since a number of federal programs to assist low-income families are based on the Office of Management and Budget (OMB) poverty guidelines, published in February or March of each year. These programs include Head Start, food stamps, the Job Corps, the national school lunch program, low-income home energy assistance grants, community services block grants, and the migrant and seasonal farmworker program.

Regarding public assistance to the poor, the opinions of the public are of two types. One view is that poverty is the fault of the poor themselves, and the other is that poverty is the result of forces external to the poor. According to the first view, the poor do not deserve public assistance, and if society provides public assistance to the poor at all, the process of receiving such assistance should be stigmatized by making it shameful to the poor. According to the second view, welfare should be regarded as a right. This view was behind the drive that began in the mid-1960s to deliver welfare payments with dignity. Even in this second view, the American public has made it clear that it is willing to provide to the poor **in-kind aids** such as basic housing, food, and health care but is not willing to give the poor the cash to buy these items themselves.

---

[6]For more on measuring poverty, see Daniel H. Weinberg, Measuring poverty, a technical analysis paper prepared for the Department of Health and Human Services, SHR-0012350, December 1984.

TABLE 8.1   Poverty Level Income and Percentage of Persons below the Poverty Level

Year	Income Cutoffs for Nonfarm Family of Four	Number of Persons below Poverty (Millions)	Percentage of Persons below Poverty
1959	$ 2,973	39.5	22.4%
1960	3,022	39.9	22.2
1966	3,317	28.5	14.7
1969	3,743	24.1	12.1
1970	3,968	25.4	12.6
1975	5,500	25.9	12.3
1976	5,815	25.0	11.8
1977	6,191	24.7	11.6
1978	6,662	24.5	11.4
1979	7,412	26.1	11.7
1980	8,414	29.3	13.0
1981	9,287	31.8	14.0
1982	9,862	34.4	15.0
1983	10,178	35.3	15.2
1984	10,609	33.7	14.4
1985	10,989	33.1	14.0
1986	11,203	32.4	13.6
1987	11,611	32.5	13.5

Source: U.S. Department of Commerce, *Statistical abstract of the United States,* 109th ed. (Washington, D.C.: U.S. Government Printing Office, January 1989), p. 452.

SUMMARY

Perfect competition refers to market conditions in which the demand for the output of every firm in a given industry is so perfectly elastic that the firm is a price taker for all quantities of output it sells. Firms under perfect competition charge the price that is determined by market demand and market supply. Firms make output decisions by equalizing marginal revenue and marginal cost. Economic profits are profits that exceed a normal rate of return, whereas the normal rate of return means the average rate of return on investment in all other industries. When firms in one industry make economic profits, firms in other industries will transfer their resources to the profitable industry. As more firms join the industry, market price falls. The market price is expected to fall until it reaches the level that equals the lowest point of a firm's average cost curve. Firms at this stage of production are operating at the break-even point. If the price is equal to a firm's lowest average variable cost, the firm incurs a loss equal to the firm's fixed cost. The lowest point of the average variable cost curve is the firm's shutdown point. The marginal cost curve of firms operating under perfect competition that is at or above the lowest point of the average variable cost curve is the firm's short-run supply curve.

Marginal cost pricing requires that the demand price be equal to marginal cost. The product price measures the maximum benefit or satisfaction that the consumer derives from consuming the last unit of a given product. Marginal cost measures the minimum amount of resource that society is willing to forgo to produce the product. If price is equal to marginal cost for a given product, the maximum price that consumers are willing to pay for the product is exactly equal to what society has to sacrifice to produce the unit. Under perfect competition, price at the profit-maximizing level of output equals marginal cost. Price overestimates the cost of production when external benefits exist, whereas price underestimates the cost when external costs exist. Finally, competitive markets tend to result in an unequal distribution of income among the members of society.

EXERCISES

1. Perfect competition is frequently defined as a market in which there is a large number of sellers. How large should the number of sellers be in order for a market to become perfectly competitive?

2. In practical terms, what is meant by a horizontal average revenue schedule?

3. The break-even point in production is defined as the point at which total revenue is equal to total cost, or price is equal to average cost. Are firms that are operating at the break-even level of output and are expected to operate at the level in the foreseeable future likely to continue to produce or, rather, leave the industry?

4. Fox coats are usually less expensive than mink coats. Suppose that equal numbers of fox and mink coats are sold each year and the profit margin per fox coat is greater than the profit margin per mink coat. How will the industry react to the difference in the two profit margins?

5. The lowest point of the average variable cost is called the shutdown point. Assuming that price is lower than the lowest average variable cost, will rational firms shut down operations to minimize loss in the short run?

6. Suppose that the pretax rate of return on investment in the local bakery is 16 percent, while the pretax rate of return in all industries averages 14 percent. Does the local bakery earn an economic profit? If it does, by how much?

7. What is meant by marginal cost pricing? Also, marginal cost pricing is said to be economically efficient. Why?

8. Suppose that an AIDS antivirus is manufactured by many pharmaceutical companies, and its price is determined competitively in the market. Are AIDS shots using this antivirus likely to be overpriced or underpriced from the society's viewpoint?

9. The issue of income distribution is perceived as being the problem of a trade-off between equity and efficiency. Explain this statement.

10. There are two views on the issue of poverty. One view is that poverty is the fault of the poor, and the other is that poverty is the result of forces external to the poor. What difference will the two views make in terms of providing assistance to the poor?

SUGGESTED READINGS

Aaron, Henry J. (1984). Six welfare questions still searching for answers. *The Brookings Review* (Fall). Washington, D.C.: The Brookings Institution.

A thoughtful article on welfare discussing such questions as who should be eligible for aid, what obligations the recipients of assistance owe to society, and to what extent the rising incidence of single-parent families is traceable to increased assistance.

Nolan, Joseph, and Nolan, David. (1986). Better corporate citizens: The path to social responsibility. *Across the Board* 23(May):54–58.

An interesting article written by a father and his son about the way corporate leaders have handled major crises; contains many interesting quotations including one from John F. Kennedy, who said, "My father always told me that all businessmen were sons of bitches," and one from Andrew Carnegie, who said, "The man who dies rich dies disgraced."

Robinson, Joan. (1934). What is perfect competition? *Quarterly Journal of Economics* (November):104–120.

Introduces and critically evaluates definitions of perfect competition made by the then leading economists.

Scherer, F. M. (1980). *Industrial market structure and economic performance.* 2nd ed. Chicago: Rand McNally.

Presents a comprehensive coverage of market structures and pricing.

U.S. House of Representatives, Committee on Ways and Means, Subcommittees on Oversight and on Public Assistance and Unemployment Compensation. (1983). *Background material on poverty,* Committee Print 98-15, October 17.

A good reference to serve as a starting point for those interested in studying poverty.

William, Jerome W. (1972). Beneficiary charges: Toward a unified theory. In Mushkin, Selma (ed.), *Public prices for public products.* Washington, D.C.: The Urban Institute, pp. 27–66.

Contains a good coverage of marginal cost pricing.

9

Price and Output Decisions of Monopoly Firms

Sources of Monopoly Power

Price and Output Decisions of Monopoly Firms

Issues of Monopoly Markets

Price Discrimination

MOST PEOPLE IN BUSINESS dream of being the only supplier of goods and services in the industry. If there is only one person selling hamburgers, cutting hair, building homes, or writing romance novels, each of these persons will soon become a millionaire. A market in which one firm produces and supplies a product that has no close substitutes is called a **monopoly.** Monopoly is the opposite of perfect competition. The one firm that produces the product is called a monopoly, monopolist, or a monopoly firm.

In this chapter, we study how monopoly firms make decisions on price and output for profit maximization. Although we are interested in studying the pricing behavior of a pure monopoly, the term *monopoly* in this chapter encompasses not only pure monopolies but also **near monopolies,** which are firms with substantial but not complete monopoly power. Additional issues that we study in this chapter include natural monopoly and price discrimination. Examples of pure monopolies are as rare as examples of perfect competition. But the economic principles based on pure monopolies are applicable to the more realistic near monopolies as well as pure monopolies.

SOURCES OF MONOPOLY POWER

One interesting question that arises from studies of monopoly markets is, how can some firms sustain monopoly power while others cannot? To answer this question, we need to look at the scope of a market for a given product. The existence of a monopoly product depends on how closely substitutes are defined in relation to the given product, and the barriers to entrance of new firms into the monopoly market.

Monopoly and the Scope of a Market

Although examples of a pure monopoly are rare, examples of firms with substantial monopoly power are not as rare. The degree of monopoly power in a given market depends on how a product is defined. Frequently, the scope of a market is defined in terms of geography.

Monopoly in the Local Market
In a small town where there is only one movie theater, for instance, the theater is a monopoly only if the product is defined as large screen entertainment. If the product is defined as watching a movie not limited to a large screen, the theater is not a monopoly, not a pure monopoly anyway. VCRs can be a good substitute for the movie theater to many potential moviegoers.

Utility companies servicing the local market are often called monopolies. **Utility companies** are firms that supply public utilities such as electricity, natural gas, telephone, water, and sewer services. Strictly speaking, utility companies are not pure monopolies. Electric power companies compete with gas companies to attract customers, especially in the market for heating new homes under construction. The local telephone service has substitutes, albeit poor, in mail and messenger or delivery services. Tap water has a substitute in bottled water sold at supermarkets.

The geographic area is not the only way a market can be defined. Markets may also be defined in terms of other characteristics such as hours of service and the income level of buyers. If in a neighborhood the only store that is open 24 hours a day is the 7-Eleven store, the 7-Eleven store enjoys a certain degree of monopoly power. If there is only one department store in a town that carries products purchased mostly by upper income consumers, the store also enjoys a certain degree of monopoly power.

Monopoly in the National Market

When the scope of a market is defined in terms of the national market, examples of monopolies are harder to come by. Prior to World War II, for instance, the Aluminum Company of America (ALCOA) was the only predominant manufacturer of aluminum. Being the predominant producer of aluminum, ALCOA was a monopolist of aluminum, but was not a pure monopoly because it did have competition from producers of other metals that, to varying degrees, were substitutes for aluminum. Although pure monopolies are rarely found, some companies have occasionally enjoyed market power so substantial that these companies were, for all practical purposes, pure monopolies. These companies include Western Electric, producing telephone equipment until the 1984 deregulation of American Telephone and Telegraph; IBM, whose market share for general purpose digital computer systems fluctuated around 80 percent in the 1960s and 1970s; and Xerox, with about 80 percent market share for electrostatic copier machines during the 1960s. Other products that reached monopoly status from time to time include nickel, magnesium, and Pullman railroad cars.

These days, DeBeers is often cited as a good example of a monopoly firm. The DeBeers diamond syndicate controls about 80 to 85 percent of the world's supply of diamonds. If the product is defined as precious stone instead of diamond, DeBeers is far from being a monopolist. There are numerous other precious stones such as emerald, ruby, sapphire, and other gems. The scope of market is discussed further in the next chapter when we present concentration ratios of manufacturing industries.

Barriers to Entry

A monopoly firm can sustain monopoly power only if there are barriers to entry that prevent other firms from entering the same market. **Barriers to entry** are the factors that keep other firms from entering a given market. If firms in a certain industry earn economic profits, firms in other industries will be attracted to this profitable industry, and the supply of the product is expected to increase. As more firms enter the industry, economic profits disappear and any advantage that existing firms had disappears also. The only way for existing firms to retain their monopoly power is to maintain a shield of barriers to other firms that wish to enter the industry. Barriers to entry provide potential monopoly firms with a source of monopoly power. Barriers to entry include ownership of an essential raw material, patents, economies of scale, government policies that impose barriers, and market imperfection.

Ownership of an Essential Raw Material

One major barrier to entry is the ownership or control of an essential raw material by the monopolist. The source of ALCOA's monopoly power before World War II was the control of bauxite, the key ingredient needed to produce aluminum. The source of DeBeers' monopoly power is the control of the diamond mines, especially in South Africa. Mergers of large companies are often triggered by the ownership of essential raw materials such as oil, coal, or platinum reserves by the company that is merged.

Patents

A **patent** is the exclusive right to produce a certain product or use a certain production technology. An interesting example that illustrates how a patent works to sustain monopoly power is the ballpoint pen.[1] The ballpoint pen was invented by Milton Reynolds in 1945 and was patented by the Reynolds International Pen Company, which started production of the ballpen on October 6, 1945. The initial price was $12.50 when, in fact, the cost of production was estimated to be only 80 cents per pen. A patent does not guarantee complete monopoly power, however. High economic profits by Reynolds prompted other competitors to enter the market with ballpoint pens that were similar, but not similar enough to violate patent laws. By December 1946, approximately 100 firms were making and selling ballpoint pens for as little as $2.98. By mid-1948, ballpoint pens were selling for as little as 39 cents and costing 10 cents to make. A patent gives a firm temporary monopoly power and enables the firm to charge high prices, but sooner or later the free market disperses economic profits of the monopoly firm to later entrants to the market.

Economies of Scale

Economies of scale refer to cost advantages originating from large-scale operation. The so-called **heavy industries** such as the steel, automobile, and oil refinery industries, which require a large amount of expenditure on fixed inputs, are characterized by economies of scale. This means that larger firms can produce products at a lower unit cost than smaller firms. In industries characterized by economies of scale, firms that start on a small scale are not likely to survive because the small scale of operation results in a higher average cost of production. Economies of scale, therefore, effectively limit the number of potential entrants to the industry.

Government Imposition of Barriers

The government may legally allow certain firms to be monopolists. Examples of these firms are local water and sewer boards, local telephone services, and power and natural gas companies. The reason for the government to allow public utilities to operate as legal monopolies is the requirement of a large expenditure on fixed inputs such as telephone poles, transmission cables, and water treatment plants. The hypothesis is that one firm can produce utilities at a lower unit cost than several smaller firms can. When one firm is allowed to supply the entire market, however, the lack of competition becomes a problem and the monopolist may be tempted to raise prices. For this reason, most states maintain agencies that regulate prices and other operating aspects of utility companies.

Market Imperfection

The lack of perfect information in the market can also be a source of monopoly power. If a firm earns economic profits but keeps this fact hidden from other potential competitors, the firm will be able to enjoy monopoly power until other firms become aware that the firm has been earning economic profits. A temporary monopoly power arising from lack of market information tends to prevail in firms that can easily conceal prices of their goods or services from competitors.

---

[1]Where are they now? The amphibious pen, *New Yorker*, February 17, 1951, p. 39ff.

PRICE AND OUTPUT DECISIONS OF MONOPOLY FIRMS

Monopolists, like firms operating under competitive markets, need to determine the price of the product and the quantity of the product to produce for profit maximization. Unlike firms in competitive markets that charge the market price and select the profit-maximizing level of output subject to the market price, monopoly firms may set the prices of their products and, as a result, vary the quantity of these products produced.

Pricing Behavior of Monopoly Firms

The ability of monopolies to set price does not mean that these firms charge the highest price that they can. If these firms wished to charge the highest possible price, they could probably do so by selling only one unit. The highest price would not lead to maximum total profit. Monopoly firms determine price and the level of output in such a way as to maximize total profit.

To find out how monopoly firms determine price and the level of output for maximum profits, we combine revenue curves and cost curves of monopoly firms as we did for firms operating under perfect competition. Cost conditions are essentially internal to the firm, meaning that the shapes of cost curves are the same for monopoly firms and competitive firms. What really makes the difference between monopoly firms and competitive firms is the difference in the market conditions under which these firms operate.

Stated simply, the firm operating under perfect competition is faced with competition from other firms in the same market that forces the firm to charge the market price, whereas monopoly firms are not faced with competition from other firms and, thus, can set their own price. The only constraint that the monopolist needs to consider in determining the product price is the law of demand. Higher prices will reduce the amount of sales, and lower prices will increase the amount of sales. The law of demand means that both the average revenue and marginal revenue curves for monopoly firms are sloped downward to the right.

Graphic Illustration

The process by which a monopolist makes price and output decisions for profit maximization is shown in Figure 9.1. Like profit-maximizing firms in competitive markets, the monopolist also makes price and output decisions according to the MR = MC rule. In Figure 9.1, marginal revenue equals marginal cost at point G, since at point G the marginal revenue curve and the marginal cost curve cross each other. The profit-maximizing level of output is OH, located by drawing a vertical line from point G until the line reaches the quantity line. The profit-maximizing price of the product that the monopolist charges is obtained by drawing a line vertically from point G until the line reaches the average revenue curve. The profit-maximizing price, therefore, is HD or OA. Note that the price is not found by drawing a horizontal line from point G until it crosses the price line. Price is not OX or HG. The price that consumers are willing to pay is always indicated somewhere on the average revenue (demand) curve.

The monopolist shown in Figure 9.1 is earning an economic profit because price OA is greater than the average cost of production OB. The profit is the difference between total revenue and total cost. Since total revenue is OADH and total cost is OBEH, the monopolist's profit is BADE. Total cost OBEH is the sum of variable cost OCFH and fixed cost CBEF.

Monopoly firms do not necessarily make profits all the time. Suppose that we invent a product for which no close substitutes are currently available. By definition, we are a monopolist. Suppose that our new product is not terribly useful and no one is willing to pay the price that we need to

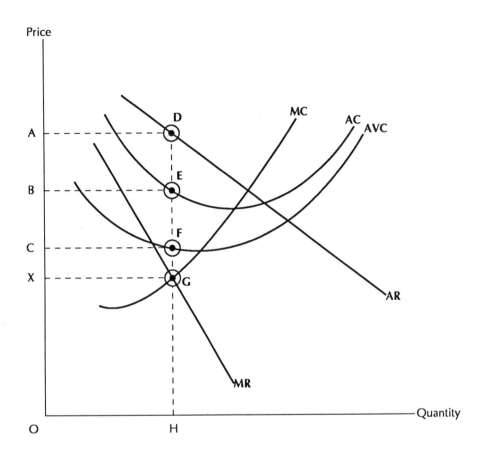

FIGURE 9.1 Price and Output Decisions of a Monopoly. Monopolists determine price and the level of output according to the MR = MC rule. The level of output OH is found on the horizontal axis. Price OA is found by extending the line from the MR = MC point G vertically to the AR curve.

recover the cost of making the product. We incur loss. The price that consumers actually pay for a product depends not only on the cost of producing the product by the firm, but also on the amount of satisfaction that consumers expect to derive from consuming the product. If the price that consumers are willing to pay for the monopoly product is equal to the average cost of production, monopoly firms break even.

A monopolist that operates at the break-even point is shown in Figure 9.2(a). If the price is smaller than the average cost, the monopolist incurs a loss. A monopolist incurring a loss is illustrated in Figure 9.2(b). In panel (a), price OA is equal to the average cost of production DB. Total revenue, therefore, is equal to total cost at OABD. In panel (b), price OB is smaller than the

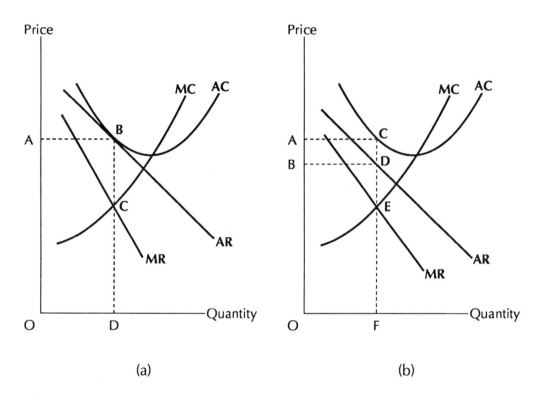

(a)   (b)

FIGURE 9.2 Monopolies Breaking Even or Incurring a Loss. Monopolists break even in panel (a) where price equals the average cost of production, while monopolists incur a loss in panel (b) where price is lower than average cost at all quantities of output.

average cost of production FC. Total revenue OBDF is smaller than total cost OACF, resulting in a loss BACD.

ISSUES OF MONOPOLY MARKETS

The idea of optimization that underlies all economic problems is to promote efficiency in allocation of scarce resources among competing uses. Studies of monopolies raise some interesting social questions concerning matters of economic efficiency. One of these questions is whether or not competitive markets are any more efficient than monopoly markets in allocating scarce resources. If competitive markets were more efficient than monopoly markets in allocating scarce resources, we would have the theoretical basis for promoting more competition in the economy. If not, there would be little use for promoting more competition in the economy. Another issue concerns the fact

SIC

When products are classified for whatever reasons there may be, one needs to consult the *Standard Industrial Classification Manual*. The U.S. government's standard industrial classification (SIC) defines industries in accordance with the composition and structure of the economy and covers the entire field of economic activities. It is revised periodically to reflect the changing industrial composition of the economy. Major revisions were made in 1957, 1972, and also in 1987. Anyone who is involved in industrial and marketing studies needs to keep a copy of the *Manual* handy.

The SIC has 12 broad divisions denoted A through K. Division D, for instance, is manufacturing. Within each division, there are several major groups called two-digit SICs. All together, there are 99 two-digit SICs. Major Group 27 that belongs to Division D represents printing, publishing, and allied industries. Within SIC 27, there are 9 three-digit SICs: SIC 271 to SIC 279. SIC 275, for instance, represents commercial printing within which there are 3 four-digit SICs. Four-digit SICs are the specific classifications of industries that are widely used. Summarizing the SIC for printing, publishing, and allied industries:

    Division D Manufacturing:
        SIC 27 Printing, publishing, and allied industries:
            SIC 275 Commercial printing:
                SIC 2752 Commercial printing, lithographic
                SIC 2754 Commercial printing, gravure
                SIC 2759 Commercial printing, not elsewhere classified

The SIC *Manual* is prepared by the Office of Management and Budget (OMB) and can be purchased from the National Technical Information Service in Springfield, Virginia.

Source: Executive Office of the President, Office of Management and Budget, *Standard industrial classification manual 1987* (Springfield, Va.: National Technical Information Service, 1987).

that it is clearly advantageous to have a natural monopoly in certain industries. We study both topics in this section.

The section concludes with a discussion of contestable markets, a relatively recent idea in studies of monopoly that had a significant impact on the movement toward deregulation early in the 1980s. The terms *monopoly* and *competitive markets* are used in a loose sense in the remainder of this section. Monopoly refers to a firm with substantial, but not necessarily total, market power, whereas competitive markets refer to market conditions that are highly, but not necessarily perfectly, competitive.

Comparing Monopoly with Competitive Markets

Are competitive markets better than monopoly markets? To judge whether one is better or worse than the other, we need a basis on which to compare the two. In economics, the basis for comparing two different market structures is economic efficiency, also called allocative efficiency. In studies of market structures, **economic efficiency** characterizes one market structure if its prices are lower and the quantity of output it produces and sells is larger than those of other market structures. If prices are lower and, as a result, the quantity of output traded is larger in market A than in market B, market A is said to be economically more efficient than market B.

The Hypothesis
Obviously, the hypothesis is that competitive markets are more efficient than monopoly markets. If this hypothesis were true, the price of a product would be lower and the quantity of the product traded would be larger under competitive markets than under monopoly markets. Our objective here is to find out whether competitive markets are, ceteris paribus, really more efficient than monopoly markets and, if they are, how much more efficient.

Graphic Illustration
Figure 9.3 is presented to clarify the basis for comparing the two market structures. In Figure 9.3, the average cost curve for individual firms of a given industry is drawn as a horizontal line based on the assumption that the average cost tends to vary little for a normal range of output. The average revenue curve in the figure is one for the industry and, thus, has a downward slope exhibiting the law of demand for both competitive and monopoly markets. Assuming that the market is competitive, firms earn no more than a normal rate of return, suggesting that the competitive price P_c is equal to the average cost of production. At the competitive price P_c, the quantity demanded would be Q_c.

   If the entire market is supplied by a monopolist, the monopolist will make decisions according to the MR = MC rule. Since the average cost curve (AC) is horizontal, the corresponding marginal cost curve (MC) should be the same as the average cost curve. The monopolist, therefore, charges the monopoly price P_m, which is obtained by drawing a vertical line from point B, at which marginal revenue equals marginal cost. The monopoly price P_m is higher than the competitive price P_c. At the monopoly price P_m, the quantity demanded would be Q_m, which is smaller than the quantity demanded Q_c under a competitive market. Figure 9.3 strongly suggests, but does not necessarily prove, that competitive markets are more efficient than monopolistic markets.

An Example
In 1986, 11,453,000 new passenger cars were sold in the United States, of which 8,215,000 cars were produced domestically and 3,238,000 were imported. The price of a medium-sized two-door coupe was approximately $11,000. Suppose that in 1986 the automobile industry was far from being competitive. In Figure 9.3, the values of monopoly price P_m and monopoly quantity Q_m are approximately $11,000 and 11,453,000. Suppose that the average cost of producing automobiles, including a normal rate of return on investment, is 10 percent below the retail price. The competitive price P_c, then, becomes $9,900, which is obtained by multiplying $11,000 by 0.9.

   Studies have found that the price elasticity of demand for new cars is –1.2. This elasticity coefficient means that when price falls by 10 percent, from $11,000 to $9,900, car sales are expected to increase by 12 percent, from 11,453,000 to 12,827,360 (obtained by multiplying 11,453,000 by

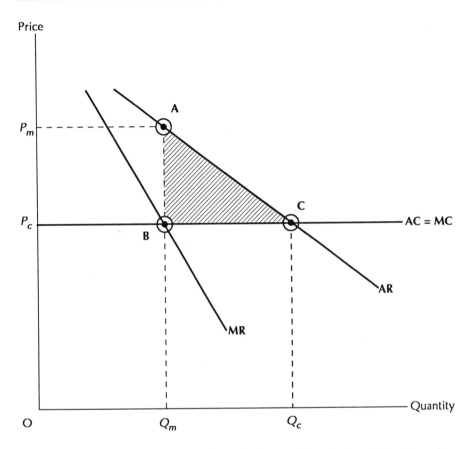

FIGURE 9.3 Comparing Monopoly and Competitive Markets. Price P_m under monopoly markets is higher than price P_c under competitive markets, while the quantity of sales Q_m under monopoly markets is smaller than the quantity of sales Q_c under competitive markets. The triangle ABC is called the deadweight welfare loss.

1.12). If our assumptions are true, the number of automobiles Q_c that would have been traded in competitive markets in 1986 is 12,827,360. The difference AB in Figure 9.3 between the monopoly price ($11,000) and the competitive price ($9,900) is $1,100. The difference BC in Figure 9.3 between the quantity traded (12,827,360) in a competitive market and the quantity traded (11,453,000) in a monopoly market is 1,374,360. We continue this example to estimate the deadweight welfare loss.

Estimating the Deadweight Welfare Loss
Let us isolate the triangle ABC in Figure 9.3 and reproduce it as Figure 9.4. The area of the triangle ABC represents a loss to society's welfare by having a monopoly market in the automobile industry

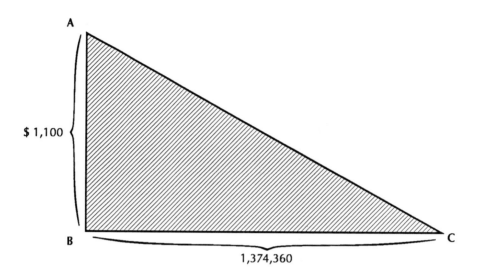

FIGURE 9.4   Deadweight Welfare Loss. The loss in welfare from having a monopoly market in the automobile industry is estimated as the area of the triangle ABC, which represents $755,898,000.

as opposed to a competitive market. The triangles ABC in Figure 9.3 and in Figure 9.4 are called **deadweight welfare loss** (DWL) by economists. Deadweight means something that is lost permanently and, thus, not recoverable. Economic welfare is often measured in terms of the dollar value of goods and services consumed. The triangle ABC represents a loss in economic welfare, since the triangle represents the additional dollar value of automobiles that consumers have to pay for having a monopoly market in the automobile industry. The deadweight welfare loss is not an abstract concept, but can actually be measured.

The deadweight welfare loss in our automobile example is obtained by multiplying the price difference ($1,100) and the quantity difference (1,374,360) between the two market structures, and dividing the product by 2 since ABC is a triangle rather than a rectangle. That is,

$$\text{DWL} = \frac{1,100 \times 1,374,360}{2} \tag{9.1}$$

$$= 755,898,000$$

According to equation (9.1), the loss to society's welfare from having a monopolistic market in the automobile industry rather than a competitive market was approximately $756 million in 1986, equivalent to about 0.6 percent of the total dollar value of passenger car sales for the year.

Empirical Studies of the Deadweight Welfare Loss

The next question, then, is, What have economists found about the magnitude of the deadweight welfare loss in the entire economy? A substantial amount of deadweight welfare loss would indicate that society suffers substantially from allowing markets to be monopolistic. If this were the reality, it would be valuable to promote competition in the economy. A small amount of deadweight welfare loss would indicate that we gain little from promoting competition in the economy, and perhaps from studying economics itself.

After reviewing several studies which demonstrated that the welfare loss due to monopoly is small, R. A. Mundell suggests that unless there is a thorough theoretical re-examination of the validity of the tools by which these studies are founded, "someone inevitably will draw the conclusion that economics has ceased to be important!"[2] Like other empirical studies in economics, estimates of the deadweight welfare loss vary, although evidence points more toward a rather small loss. The welfare loss is typically presented as a percentage of national income. If the loss is 1 percent, for instance, the loss of income due to monopoly is 1 percent of the national income. An estimate by Arnold C. Harberger indicates that the loss is no more than 0.07 percent, while an estimate by D. Schwartzman is even lower, at 0.01 percent.[3] Critics of the Harberger study have calculated the welfare loss in the range of 4 to 6 percent.[4]

X-Efficiency

At least one economist hypothesizes that the amount to be gained from making the market more competitive and thus improving allocative efficiency is trivial, while the amount to be gained by increasing X-efficiency is significant.[5] X-efficiency is so called because the type of efficiency later defined as X-efficiency was initially undefined and was proposed for discussion purposes. According to Harvey Leibenstein, who proposed the hypothesis, the current operation of most, if not all, businesses is suboptimal regarding the use of technology, existing capital stock, and especially human resources belonging to these businesses. Leibenstein claims that "for a variety of reasons people and organizations normally work neither as hard nor as effectively as they could."[6] For instance, workers may come to work *around* 8 o'clock in the morning rather than *by* 8 o'clock, when they are supposed to start working. Also, the consideration of personal relations among workers sometimes keeps workers from being assigned to places where they are most efficient. The fact that firms are not as efficient as they could be in utilizing resources under their control is called **X-inefficiency.**

The main source of a firm's X-efficiency can be traced ultimately to managerial efficiency, since managers determine not only their own productivity but also the productivity of all cooperating units in the organization. A substantial reduction in unit costs can be realized when the X-efficiency of a firm improves. According to Leibenstein, the X-efficiency depends significantly on the degree of competitive pressure. The hypothesis of X-efficiency is another indictment against

[2]R. A. Mundell, Free trade, protection, and customs union, *American Economic Review* 50(June 1962):622.

[3]Arnold C. Harberger, Monopoly and resource allocation, *American Economic Review* 44(May 1954):77–87; D. Schwartzman, The burden of monopoly, *Journal of Political Economy* 68(December 1960):727–729.

[4]David R. Kamerschen, An estimation of the "welfare losses" from monopoly in the American economy, *Western Economic Journal* 4(Summer 1966):221–236.

[5]Harvey Leibenstein, Allocative efficiency vs. "X-efficiency," *American Economic Review* 56(June 1966):392–415.

[6]Ibid., p. 413.

monopoly markets, since the pressure needed to improve X-efficiency is greater in competitive markets than in monopolistic markets.

Natural Monopoly

A **natural monopoly** is a firm whose average cost of production declines over the entire range of market demand. Industries that are conducive to the creation of a natural monopoly are those in which the economies of scale are so large that the largest firm has the lowest per-unit cost of production and is able to drive its smaller competitors out of the market. Natural monopoly is *natural* in that the declining long-run average cost gives an added advantage to the largest firm in the industry.

Creating a Natural Monopoly
To see how a natural monopoly may be created, we send 10 entrepreneurs to a remote island with $1 million each and ask them to produce a certain product. Suppose that production of the product is characterized by economies of (large) scale. The only condition that we require from the entrepreneurs is that we will buy the product at a price equal to the average cost from only the producer who produces the product at the lowest cost. As soon as one of the 10 businesses has a slight edge in the cost of production, we start buying the product from the low-cost business. As the quantity of sales increases, the low-cost business expands its facilities. As it does, the average cost of the low-cost business decreases even more because of the assumption that production of the product is characterized by economies of scale. The low-cost firm effectively emerges as the monopoly firm.

The example of a natural monopoly is not limited to a remote island. So long as the market in an area is relatively small and highly competitive, and firms in the industry require large expenditures on fixed inputs, conditions are favorable for the creation of a natural monopoly. Good examples of natural monopolies are firms that produce public utilities such as electricity, natural gas, water, sewer, and telephone services.

Graphic Illustration
Usually, one telephone company provides local telephone service in any given area. Suppose that the average cost, and thus the price, of providing local telephone service to a household is $20 per month, including normal profits. What would happen to the monthly rate for telephone service if more than one company were allowed to provide telephone service in the area? The answer is given in Figure 9.5.

The long-run average cost of providing local telephone service by one telephone company declines over the entire range of market demand, indicated as OH_1. Assuming that the telephone company charges a monthly rate equal to the average cost of providing the telephone service, the monthly rate charged by one company is $20. As two companies are allowed to share the market, both companies will have to operate with fixed facilities, resulting in a higher average cost. The monthly rate increases to, say, $30. The idea of allowing natural monopolies to operate as legal monopolies is to prevent competition that hurts consumers as well as the companies.

Problems with Natural Monopolies
When natural monopolies such as utility companies are allowed to become legal monopolies, there is a possibility that these companies may abuse the monopoly power. The monopoly power can be

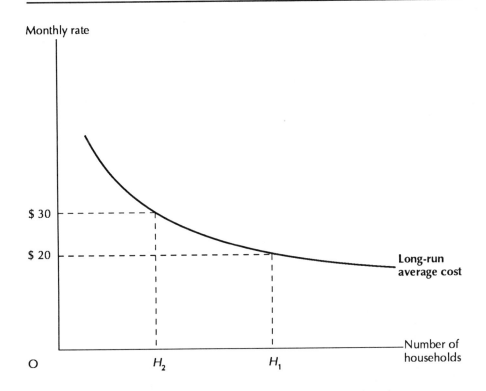

FIGURE 9.5 Two Telephone Companies Sharing the Market. Because of the declining long-run average cost curve, the monthly rate for telephone service may increase as the number of telephone companies serving the market increases.

abused by providing services only to the point at which marginal revenue equals marginal cost, and charging the profit-maximizing price. To keep utility companies from charging the profit-maximizing price, all states maintain agencies that regulate the pricing behavior of utility companies. There are many problems in regulation of public utilities, but few answers. The problems include the determination of an optimal rate of return on investment in utility companies, the determination of an optimal price, identification of all costs and revenues in a form that can be readily compared, and the determination of rates when, for instance, electricity is sold to neighboring states experiencing a temporary shortage.

Another problem of allowing utility companies to operate as legal monopolies is the possibility that these companies may have a tendency to overexpand their production capacities. State regulatory agencies generally use the fair rate of return approach by which utility companies are allowed to earn what the regulatory agencies consider to be the average rate of return on investment in plant and equipment. The rate base under the fair rate of return approach is the capital (plant and equipment) of utility companies. Under the fair rate of return approach, utility companies may be tempted to expand their plants and equipment, since the expanded capacity along with the current level of revenue will effectively lower the rate of return below the predetermined fair rate. To restore the fair return based on the expanded capacity, regulatory agencies will have to allow utility companies to raise utility rates.

The hypothesis that firms subject to rate of return regulation tend to overexpand their facilities is called the *Averch-Johnson* **effect.**[7] Empirical studies that have tested the *Averch-Johnson* effect have mixed results, however.[8]

Contestable Markets

In presenting the theory of contestable markets at the 94th meeting of the American Economic Association, William J. Baumol, then president of the Association, said, "I must resist the temptation to describe the analysis I will report here as anything like a revolution."[9] The judgment of whether the theory is revolutionary or an aberration will be made by economic historians. The theory of contestable markets was advanced in several studies during the 1970s.[10] Policy implications of the theory are significant, especially when it is applied to markets characteristic of a natural monopoly.

Defining Contestable Markets

According to the **theory of contestable markets,** potential entry or competition for a monopolistic market disciplines the behavior of monopoly firms as effectively as actual competition would within the market. There are two key elements for market contestability. One is free entry and costless exit, and the other is the price flexibility that allows potential entrants to the market to undercut current suppliers. When these two conditions are met, markets are said to be *contestable* because of their vulnerability to hit-and-run operations by new firms in the industry. Contestable markets are readily subject to competitive forces, even when the markets are supplied by one or several firms. The number of sellers is not important according to the theory of contestable markets, because any economic profit in the industry will attract new entrants, which enter the market freely, charge prices below the level charged by existing firms, and exit the market costlessly as soon as economic profits disappear.

[7]H. Averch and L. Johnson, Behavior of the firm under regulatory constraint, *American Economic Review* 52(December 1962):1052–1069.

[8]For empirical results of the Averch-Johnson effect, see R. M. Spann, Rate of return regulation and efficiency in production: An empirical test of the Averch-Johnson thesis, *Bell Journal of Economics and Management Science* 5(Spring 1974):38–52; and W. J. Boyes, An empirical examination of the Averch-Johnson effect, *Economic Inquiry* 14(March 1976):25–35.

[9]William J. Baumol, Contestable markets: An uprising in the theory of industrial structure, *American Economic Review* 72(March 1982):1–15; the quotation is from page 1.

[10]Besides Baumol's article in *American Economic Review,* see Elizabeth E. Bailey, Contestability and the design of regulatory and antitrust policy, *American Economic Review* 71(May 1981):178–183; and Michael Spence, Contestable markets and the theory of industry structure: A review article, *Journal of Economic Literature* 21(September 1983):981–990.

Contestable Markets Different from Perfect Competition

If firms in contestable markets behaved as if they were in competitive markets, what would be the difference between perfectly competitive markets and contestable markets? Perfect competition requires a relatively large number of firms that behave as price takers, whereas a large number of firms is not a requirement for contestable markets. For a large number of firms to survive in a market for a long period of time, no firm should be able to enjoy economies of scale. If a firm enjoys large economies of scale, the firm can reduce the average cost as production increases. If the firm can reduce the unit cost of production by increasing the capacity of production, the firm's market share will eventually grow to dominate the market. The main difference between the theory of perfect competition and the theory of contestable markets, therefore, is that the former is not compatible with the existence of industries characterized by economies of scale, whereas the latter is.

According to the theory of perfect competition, firms in an industry that is dominated by several large firms will no longer behave as price takers. Instead, these firms will charge a higher price and produce a lower quantity than they would under perfect competition. According to the theory of contestable markets, the existence of economies of scale is irrelevant so long as expenditures, known as sunk costs, on the large capacity of production are borne by an entity other than the firm itself. This point is crucial to understanding the usefulness of the theory of contestable markets, as shown in the following examples.

Examples

Consider the proposed merger between Texas International and National Airlines late in the 1970s.[11] The Houston–New Orleans market shares for the 12 months ending June 30, 1978, were 27 percent by National, 24 percent by Texas International, 23 percent by Delta, 17 percent by Continental, and 7 percent by Eastern. The U.S. Department of Justice opposed the merger based on the 51 percent market share of the two airlines if they were allowed to merge. The Civil Aeronautics Board (CAB) recommended approval of the merger based on the theory of market contestability. In the airline industry, the largest sunk cost relates to the airport facility. If the New Orleans or Houston airports were owned by Texas International or National Airlines, the market would not have been contestable. In reality the airport facility is not owned by any one airline company. The facility is owned by an entity such as the local airport authority that is independent of airline companies serving the area. Any new airline that plans to enter the Houston–New Orleans market will have to pay only a landing fee and rent for use of the airport terminal.

When a market is contestable, large market shares held by a selected few firms are not important, since the market is vulnerable to competitive forces. Existing firms are expected to behave as if they were in a competitive market. About a year later, a small regional carrier, Southwest Airlines, entered the market with a low-fare turnaround service and ended up offering about 25 percent of the capacity of the market. Proponents of the theory of contestable markets claim that the fast growth of Southwest Airlines supported the hypothesis that the Houston-New Orleans market was contestable.

For another example, suppose that one cable television company is allowed to install cables in every corner of the town. The company is a monopolist and will set monthly fees according to the MR = MC rule. If a town wishes to make the market competitive, the town may make the local cable TV market contestable in one of two ways. One way is to install cables for itself and charge an access fee to any cable company that wants to do business in the town. The other is to require

---

[11]This example is based on Bailey, Contestability and the design of regulatory and antitrust policy, p. 181.

the lone cable company to permit access by other potential entrants to the company's cables and charge for the access.

As we study in Chapter 12, the theory of contestable markets played an important role in the deregulation of industries. Not all economists accept the practical value of the theory, however.[12]

PRICE DISCRIMINATION

Firms with monopoly power may discriminate prices for maximum profits. **Price discrimination** refers to charging different prices for the same product that are not justified by cost differences. Different prices may be charged to different buyers in different markets or to one buyer for different units of the same product.

Charging different prices to different buyers in different markets is quite common. Charges for local telephone service vary between commercial customers and residential customers. Charges for long distance telephone service are discriminated in favor of those who make calls in the evenings and weekends. Those who go to movies during the daytime are treated favorably with discount prices, while bus fares are often reduced for students and senior citizens. Psychiatrists are known to charge higher hourly fees for those with a higher income than for those with a lower income. Neighborhood dentists may charge higher fees for the same service to those who have dental insurance than to those without dental insurance. All these practices are intended to increase profits by charging different prices to different consumers for the same service.

Requirements for Successful Price Discrimination

If a firm is to succeed in increasing profits through price discrimination, three conditions have to be met. First, the firm has to have a monopoly power, since firms operating under competitive markets will be unable to change prices. Second, markets in which different prices are charged must be segmented with no possibility of resale. Markets may be segmented in terms of location, time of day, income, age, sex, race, and so on. Third, consumers in segmented markets must be willing to pay different prices. Put differently, consumers in segmented markets must have different price elasticities of demand for the identical product. If, for instance, a person feels that his or her mental depression is serious enough to require counseling by a psychiatrist, but if the person is financially poor, the psychiatrist will have to lower the fee to have the poor person as a paying patient. If the person is wealthy, the psychiatrist can charge a high fee and still have the person as a paying patient. The price elasticity of demand for psychiatric services is high for the poor but low for the rich.

Prices may be discriminated among markets across nations. Intuitive reasoning tells us that imported products should be more expensive in the United States than in the exporting countries because of transportation costs and import duties in the United States. This is not necessarily true. Some products are more expensive in the United States than in the exporting countries, but other products may be cheaper in the United States than in the exporting countries. Foreign firms may charge a lower price in the United States than in exporting countries for the same product, because the U.S. market is more competitive by allowing imports of similar products from many other countries. In this case, the price elasticity of demand for the product is higher in the United States

---

[12]For articles critical of the theory of contestable markets, see William G. Shepherd, Contestability vs. competition, *American Economic Review* 74(September 1984):572–587.

EASING THE IMPACT OF COMPANY SHUTDOWNS

When we study monopolies, profit maximization, and the like, we may feel that all businesses are making profits and that any trouble businesses may have is only temporary. This is not true. Each year, businesses fail, plants are closed, and approximately 200,000 workers lose their jobs because of plant closings, employers going out of business, and layoffs from which they are not recalled. When plants are closed, large companies often try to ease the impact of their shutdowns, in part due to self-imposed social obligations, and in part to keep workers from filing lawsuits.

Policies and practices for plant closure typically include advance notice; generous severance and pension rights; extension of health care benefits; outplacement assistance; and counseling of displaced workers. Companies involved in a closure affecting a large number of employees may seek government assistance. Title III of the Job Training Partnership Act (JTPA) of 1982, which replaced its controversial predecessor, the Comprehensive Employment Training Act (CETA), is a principal funding mechanism for federal aid to displaced workers. JTPA authorizes the states to use this financial assistance to aid individuals in obtaining unsubsidized employment through various means including job search assistance, job training, and relocation assistance.

There have been cases in which companies did a great deal of planning to ease the impact of plant closings. These cases, along with the closing dates and the number of workers affected, include the International Harvester plant in Louisville, Kentucky (August 1984; 727); the Levi Strauss Jeans-wear plant in Denison, Texas (October 1984; 296); the GTE-Lenkurt facility in San Carlos, California (March 1983; 1,000); the ARMCO Steelworks plant in Houston, Texas (January 1984; 2,000); and the Ford Motor Company plant in San Jose, California (May 1983; 2,386). The quoted numbers of workers are probably an underestimation, however. By the time a plant is actually closed, the number of workers who have worked at the plant is usually reduced to a bare minimum.

Source: Ronald E. Berenbeim, *Company programs to ease the impact of shutdowns,* research report 878 (New York: The Conference Board, 1986).

than in the exporting countries. If exporting countries lower the price of a product in importing countries below the cost of production, exporting countries are said to be **dumping** the product. Newly industrialized countries (NICs) may dump products in foreign markets to earn foreign exchange that they need for the purchase of imports they need.

Consumer's Surplus and Price Discrimination

When prices are discriminated against one buyer for different units of a given product, the seller is in fact taking the consumer's surplus away from the buyer. The **consumer's surplus** is the difference between the amount the consumer is willing to pay for units of a product and the amount the consumer actually pays. Consider a thirsty jogger who has just jogged six miles on a hot summer day. A nearby snack stand sells carbonated soft drinks in small cups. The jogger needs about three cups to quench his or her thirst. Knowing this, the operator of the snack stand may negotiate with the jogger and charge $1.25 for the first cup of soft drink, which is the maximum price the jogger is willing to pay for the first cup, $0.75 for the second cup, which is the maximum price the jogger is willing to pay for the second cup, and finally the regular price of $0.50 for the third cup. Total revenue to the operator is $2.50 for sale of the three cups rather than the $1.50 that the operator could have received if the regular price were charged for all three cups. The consumer surplus is $1.00, which is the difference between what the consumer was willing to pay and what the consumer would normally pay if the regular price were charged for all three cups of soft drink. In this example, the seller took the consumer's surplus away from the consumer by charging different prices for different units of the same product.

In reality, consumers usually pay the same price for different units of a product, meaning that consumers keep the consumer's surplus.

A special case of price discrimination against one buyer for different units of a product is a Dutch auction. In the commonly used **English auction,** the price of an item is successively raised until only one bidder remains. The successful bidder pays slightly more than what the second most eager buyer is willing to pay. In a **Dutch auction,** the auction price starts very high and is reduced gradually until a person accepts the bid price. In a Dutch auction, the successful bidder pays the maximum that he or she is willing to pay without knowing how much any other buyer is willing to pay. The successful bidder in the Dutch auction may lose the entire consumer's surplus, whereas the successful bidder in the English auction may still enjoy the consumer's surplus. The word *auction* is derived from the Latin *augere,* which means "to increase."

SUMMARY

Monopoly firms sustain monopoly power only if there are barriers to entry that keep other firms from entering the same market. Barriers to entry include ownership of an essential raw material, patents, economies of scale, government imposition of barriers, and market imperfection. Firms operating under a competitive market charge the market price and select the profit-maximizing level of output subject to the constraint that firms are price takers. Monopoly firms can set the prices of their products as well as the quantity of these products supplied. Whether competitive markets are any more efficient than monopolistic markets depends on empirical estimates of the deadweight welfare loss. The deadweight welfare loss is the loss to society's welfare by having a monopoly market as opposed to a competitive market. The welfare loss is usually presented as a percentage of national income. Estimates range from 0.01 percent or less to about 6 percent. According to Harvey Leibenstein, the amount to be gained by increasing X-efficiency is significant. Industries conducive to the creation of a natural monopoly are characterized by economies of (large) scale. When the rate of return is regulated in such a way that it is based on the amount of a firm's capital, the firm may have a tendency to overexpand its production capacity.

According to the theory of contestable markets, potential entry or competition for the monopolistic market disciplines the behavior of monopoly firms as effectively as actual competition would within the market. Two conditions for market contestability are free entry and exit, and price flexibility. Price discrimination means charging different prices for the same product that are not justified by cost differences. Three conditions have to be met for successful price discrimination. The firm has to have monopoly power; markets must be segmented; and consumers in segmented markets must have different price elasticities of demand. When prices are discriminated against one buyer for different units of a given product, the seller is taking the consumer's surplus away from the buyer. The consumer's surplus is the difference between the amount the consumer is willing to pay for units of a product and the amount the consumer would normally pay if the regular price were charged. In an English auction, prices are bid upward. In a Dutch auction, the auction price starts very high and is reduced gradually until a person accepts the bid price. The successful bidder in a Dutch auction may lose the entire consumer's surplus, whereas the successful bidder in a conventional auction may still enjoy the consumer's surplus.

EXERCISES

1. Does a 7-Eleven store in the neighborhood have any monopoly power? If it does, what is the source of its monopoly power?

2. When U.S. Steel Corporation was merged with the Marathon Oil Company and the Texas Oil and Gas Corporation, it changed its name from U.S. Steel to USX Corporation. Besides the two oil companies, USX owns a division called Diversified Business, under which USX owns American Bridge Division, Cyclone Fence, Oilwell Division, Quebec Cartier Mining Company, Transportation Subsidiaries, U.S. Agri-Chemicals, USR Realty Development, U.S. Steel Mining Company, and USX Engineers and Consultants. In view of this complex structure of a conglomerate like USX, what lessons should one draw in defining a monopoly product?

3. Barriers to entry refer to the factors that keep other firms from entering a given market. What are the five barriers to entry discussed in the text?

4. Summarize the similarities and differences in pricing and output decisions between firms operating under perfect competition and monopoly firms.

5. An important hypothesis underlying studies of market structure is that competitive markets are more efficient than monopoly markets. How do economists measure whether one market structure is more efficient than another market structure?

6. What is the deadweight welfare loss, and how is the deadweight welfare loss computed? Assuming that the deadweight welfare loss is very small, what policy suggestions can be derived from the assumption?

7. Biometrics is the science of quantifying a biological characteristic. One practical field of biometrics is quantifying a fingerprint that can be used for all kinds of industries concerned with security. Fingerprints may eventually replace credit cards. The fingerprinting biometric industry is still very young and is dominated by only a few firms such as Fingermatrix of White Plains, New York, and two California firms, Stellar Systems of San Jose and Identix Inc. of Palo Alto. Contrary to expectation, none of

these firms made any profit during their early years of operation. What is a possible explanation for their failure to make profits?

8. Why are natural monopolies such as public utilities an economic problem?

9. What is a contestable market, and what conditions are necessary for markets to be contestable?

10. Why do firms discriminate prices, and what conditions are necessary for firms to successfully discriminate prices?

SUGGESTED READINGS

Bailey, Elizabeth E. (1981). Contestability and the design of regulatory and antitrust policy. *American Economic Review* 71(May):178–183.

An article on contestable markets written in easy-to-understand terms.

Daniel, Coldwell, III. (1970). *Mathematical models in microeconomics,* Boston: Allyn & Bacon.

Basic models of microeconomics are developed step by step.

Harberger, Arnold C. (1954). Monopoly and resource allocation. *American Economic Review* 44(May):77–87.

Widely cited; one of the first studies on measuring the deadweight welfare loss.

Shepherd, William G. (1984). Contestability vs. competition. *American Economic Review* 74(September):572–587.

An article critical of the theory of contestable markets, claiming that contestable markets are not found in any real markets having significant market power.

10

Price and Output Decisions of Firms in Reality

Monopolistic Competition

Issues of Monopolistic Competition

Oligopoly

Pricing Practices of Firms in Reality

As BEST AS IT CAN be remembered, this is the story Earle Nightingale told his radio audience on May 11, 1988, through CBS radio affiliates: There was a flood in a small town. It was a bad flood, sweeping away practically everything in its path. One man was barely surviving on the roof of his home. When a boat came by whose operator asked the man to jump in, the man waved the boat off saying that he was a religious person and that God would save him. While he was praying, another boat came by and the man waved this boat off also, saying again that God would save him. Later, a helicopter hovered above him and was dropping a rope for him to climb up. The man waved the helicopter off, however, telling the crew not to worry since God would save him. He drowned. Later he was standing at the gate of Heaven, and he asked the gatekeeper why God did not save him. The gatekeeper responded, "Didn't you have two boats and a helicopter trying to save you?"

When studying perfect competition and pure monopoly, one shouldn't be so literal-minded as the stubborn old man in the story, who believed that God would personally come down from heaven and save him from drowning. The reality is more complicated than that. Real markets are neither perfectly competitive nor purely monopolistic. In practically all industries, there is more than one producer of a product, but the number of firms is not large enough to make all firms price takers. Most real markets lie between perfect competition at one extreme and monopoly at the other. Economists classify markets between the two extremes into monopolistic competition and oligopoly. The main learning objective of this chapter is to study the pricing behavior of firms operating under monopolistic competition and oligopoly.

MONOPOLISTIC COMPETITION

In 1933, two books were published on imperfect competition, representing a significant advance in the development of economic ideas. One was *The economics of imperfect competition* by Joan Robinson, and the other was *The theory of monopolistic competition* by Edward H. Chamberlin. Both attempted to explain the pricing behavior of firms by using the downward-sloping demand curve of a monopolist that is affected by the behavior of other monopolists. In addition, Chamberlin introduced the concept of product differentiation as an important characteristic of the real market. For this contribution, the credit for the development of the theory of monopolistic competition was given more to Chamberlin than to Robinson. Chamberlin (1899–1967) submitted his Ph.D. thesis on the theory of monopolistic competition to Harvard, and the thesis was awarded the departmental prize as the best thesis for the year 1927. In 1933 the thesis was published as a book that became one of the most important studies on microeconomics.[1]

In this section, we first define monopolistic competition as the term is used by modern economists. The definition is followed by a discussion of product differentiation and a study of the usual price and output decision process of firms operating under monopolistic competition. We then discuss selected issues of monopolistic competition, with special reference to the difference in economic efficiency between monopolistic competition and perfect competition.

---

[1]Edward H. Chamberlin, *The theory of monopolistic competition* 8th ed. (Cambridge, Mass.: Harvard University Press, 1976).

Monopolistic Competition Defined

Pharmaceutical companies that develop new brand-name drugs are called innovator drug companies. Innovator drug companies spend a large sum of money to develop a drug. When a new drug is tested and finally approved by the Food and Drug Administration (FDA) for public use, the company gives it a brand name as Hoffmann-LaRoche did when it gave the name Valium to diazepam, a tranquilizer it developed. The innovator acquires a patent and becomes the only producer of the drug for the duration of the patent. When the patent expires, any pharmaceutical company can apply for approval by the FDA to make its own version of the drug and market it under the drug's generic name, such as diazepam rather than Valium. This means that innovator drug companies make many generic drugs as well as all brand-name drugs. In fact, about 80 percent of generic drugs are manufactured by approximately 60 brand-name drug companies, and the remaining 20 percent are manufactured by about 300 smaller drug companies. Generic diazepam, for instance, is produced by more than a dozen companies to compete with Hoffmann-LaRoche's Valium.[2]

The main competition to brand-name drugs comes from smaller companies that produce generic drugs and charge lower prices for them. Generic drugs are expected to work as effectively as brand-name drugs because generic drugs must pass a *bioequivalence test* before the FDA will grant approval for production. Because manufacturers of brand-name drugs promote them heavily, brand-name drugs are priced substantially higher than generic drugs. Prices of some of the most frequently prescribed brand-name and generic drugs are summarized in Table 10.1. As shown by these examples, prices of brand-name drugs are about 70 percent higher than prices of generic drugs. Why are consumers willing to pay a higher price for brand names? It is because they believe the advertised promotions. Consumers differentiate brand-name drugs from generic drugs, perceiving the brand-name items to be of a better quality, even if studies indicate that they are of equal quality. So long as consumers perceive brand-name drugs to be superior to generic drugs, manufacturers of brand-name drugs can charge higher prices for their products than can those who manufacture generic versions of the same drugs.[3]

Based on this illustration, we are now ready for a more precise definition of monopolistic competition. **Monopolistic competition** refers to markets or market conditions in which a large number of sellers produce and sell differentiated products. The production of prescription drugs is monopolistically competitive in that there are many drug manufacturers producing differentiated drugs. Please note that monopolistic competition in our example relates to competition existing among manufacturers of prescription drugs, not necessarily to drugstores retailing prescription drugs. The key element of markets that are monopolistically competitive is differentiation of similar products produced by many different firms. Each seller operating under monopolistic competition has an absolute monopoly on its own product but is subject to competition from more or less imperfect substitutes produced by other sellers.

Notice that product differentiation alone does not characterize monopolistic competition. If differentiated products are sold by only a small number of sellers, the market is oligopolistic, not

[2]For more on generic and brand-name drugs, see The big lie about generic drugs, *Consumer Reports* 52(August 1987):480–485.

[3]The laws in all 50 states allow pharmacists to substitute a less expensive generic version when the doctor prescribes by brand, unless the prescribing doctor writes "dispense as written" or signs one of two lines dictating the prescription of brand-name drugs.

TABLE 10.1   Prices of Brand and Generic Drugs

Prescription Drug		Dosage	Retail Price	
Brand Name	Generic Name	(mg)	Brand	Generic
Amoxil	amoxicillin	250	$21.46	$15.29
Ativan	lorazepam	1	31.99	17.99
Darvocet-N 100	propoxyphene	100	28.01	17.89
	acetaminophen	650		
Dilantin	phenytoin	100	7.49	5.79
EES 400	erythromycin ES	400	17.99	14.97
Inderal	propranolol HCL	40	19.56	10.49
Keflex	cephalexin	250	77.34	48.99
Lasix	furosemide	40	10.74	5.89
Motrin	ibuprofen	600	18.23	9.93
Tylenol No. 3	acetaminophen	300	14.89	6.88
	with codeine	30		
Valium	diazepam	5	27.47	8.49

Source: The big lie about generic drugs, *Consumer Reports* 52(August 1987):481. Copyright 1987 by Consumers Union of United States, Inc., Mount Vernon, NY 10553. Reprinted by permission from *Consumer Reports,* August 1987.

monopolistically competitive. Only if differentiated products are sold by many sellers is the market monopolistically competitive. Good examples of monopolistic competition include markets for women's dresses, fur goods, wood furniture, and fasteners such as nuts and bolts.

Product Differentiation

Product differentiation means that consumers perceive two or more products satisfying the same wants to be different and thus prefer one to the other. If the consumer perceives the two or more products to be the same, these products are said to be *homogeneous.* Whether any two similar products are homogeneous or differentiated depends ultimately on individual consumers' perceptions of the products, although the dominant opinion in the market is often generalized to indicate whether the two products are differentiated or homogeneous.

Examples
To most people, McDonald's and Burger King hamburgers are differentiated, and so are different brands of cigarettes. To many others, Coke and Pepsi are differentiated, and so are different brands of beer. Sometimes, two products that are different may be regarded as being homogeneous. For instance, the taste of Kraft's Miracle Whip is widely believed to be different from the taste of

Hellman's mayonnaise. So long as one believes that the taste of the two brands of spread is different, Miracle Whip and Hellman's are differentiated. The two brands would not be differentiated to those who have no preference between the two and feel like eating whichever they can get their hands on first. At other times, products that are identical for all practical purposes are regarded as being differentiated. Pure aspirin is such an example.

The Case of Pure Aspirin

There are over 400 brands of pure aspirin sold in the United States. This number does not include such painkillers as Tylenol, Advil, Bufferin, and Anacin. These painkillers are not pure aspirin. According to publications such as *Consumer Reports,* all standard aspirin tablets contain 5 grams per tablet of acetylsalicylic acid and are equally effective.

Through advertising, however, Bayer has convinced consumers that Bayer aspirin is superior to other brands. In other words, Bayer has succeeded in differentiating its product from other brands of pure aspirin. It is widely known that Bayer charges a higher price for the same quantity of aspirin while still enjoying the largest market share. If consumers believe that all brands of pure aspirin are equally effective, aspirin is not differentiated to these consumers.

Product differentiation is not simply economists' jargon. When firms are successful in differentiating their products, the demand for these products becomes less elastic and firms take advantage of the reduced price elasticity of demand by charging higher prices.

Nonprice Competition and Product Differentiation

Broadly speaking, firms employ nonprice competition to differentiate their products from products produced by their competitors. Nonprice competition involves two approaches: a promotion policy and a product policy. Both approaches are called nonprice competition because firms compete through means other than lowering the price of the product.

The promotion policy of firms refers to public announcements such as advertising intended to persuade consumers to buy their products. Advertisements by firms are usually more *persuasive* than informative and are intended to attract more customers. Advertisements by government or other nonprofit agencies are usually more *informative* than persuasive. The product policy of firms refers to changes in the product—an improvement of the product's quality, new and more attractive packaging, or an improvement in the delivery of services, that are intended to persuade consumers to buy their products.

Effects of Product Differentiation

An interesting question relating to product differentiation is, What are its effects? A more practical question is whether or not product differentiation through such means of nonprice competition as advertising is desirable from society's viewpoint. To answer this question, we need to delineate two issues. One is that product differentiation by its very definition suggests the availability of a large number of similar products that satisfy essentially the same want. The other is that advertising may or may not increase the cost of production and subsequently the price of the product. Even if we assume that price is higher because of advertising, many people may still prefer the freedom of choice of having an option at the expense of higher prices. Car buyers would certainly prefer to have alternatives in the selection of new cars. No one who enjoys the freedom of choice will want to drive a Yugo, or even a Mercedes, all the time.

When products are differentiated which are practically the same, such as different brands of aspirin or generic drugs, the answer becomes a little more complex. The difference in price in these cases represents a benefit that is more psychological than real. What consumers get out of product differentiation is a **placebo effect,** meaning that when a person believes that the medicine works, it may actually work. A **placebo** is a medicine devoid of effective chemical ingredients that is given merely to comply with the mood of the patient. From the viewpoint of public policy, there is little that anyone can do beyond educating the public that there are alternatives which cost less.

Price and Output Decisions

The process by which a monopolistically competitive firm determines the price and the quantity of output for profit maximization is explained in Figure 10.1. A monopolistically competitive firm has a certain degree of monopoly power in its market because of product differentiation. Since the firm has some monopoly power, the demand or the average revenue curve faced by the monopolistically competitive firm is not horizontal. Instead, it has a downward slope to the right. Although the demand curve is not completely elastic, it is not expected to be highly inelastic either. It has a downward slope to the right only to the extent that the firm has monopoly power on its market. The slope of the demand curve is relatively horizontal since, unlike a pure monopoly, the monopolistically competitive firm faces competition from other firms in the industry that produce close substitutes.

In Figure 10.1, the price and the level of output for profit maximization are determined according to the MR = MC rule. Marginal revenue and marginal cost are equal to each other at point E. The quantity of output is determined by drawing a line from point E vertically down to the quantity line at point F. The distance OF represents the profit-maximizing level of output. The price is determined by drawing a line from point E vertically up to the average revenue curve at point C. The profit-maximizing price is FC, since C crosses the demand curve, or OB, which is equal to FC. Total revenue at the profit maximizing level of output is OBCF, obtained by multiplying price OB by quantity OF. Total cost is OADF, obtained by multiplying average cost OA and quantity OF. Economic profit ABCD is the difference between total revenue OBCF and total cost OADF.

Figure 10.1 describes the short-run price and output decisions of a monopolistically competitive firm. The existence of economic profit, however, will induce long-run changes by prompting existing firms to expand their capacity of production and by attracting new firms to the industry. As these long-run changes occur, competition in the industry becomes more intense. Less successful firms may adopt promotional policies to capture a part of the more profitable firms' market share, while profitable firms adopt promotional policies to hold on to their market share.

The long-run changes and the added competition that come about due to the existence of economic profit may eventually cause economic profits to disappear, and all firms in the industry may earn zero economic profit. In perfect competition, firms are price takers and as such have no defense against the long-run tendency of zero economic profit. In monopolistic competition, however, firms do have a certain degree of defense against the long-run tendency of zero economic profit. The defense, of course, lies in the ability of these firms to undertake nonprice competition. The result of the long-run adjustment by a monopolistically competitive firm is shown in Figure 10.2.

As usual, the firm described in Figure 10.2 determines price and the level of output for profit maximization according to the MR = MC rule. The profit-maximizing quantity of output is OD, and the profit-maximizing price is OA, which equals the average cost of production DB. Total revenue is OABD, which is also total cost. The firm earns normal profits only. Although Figure 10.2 is drawn

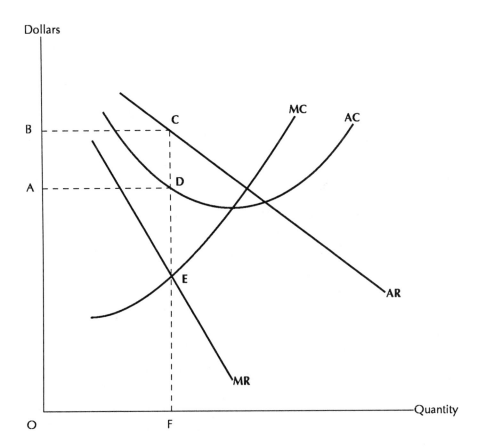

FIGURE 10.1 Price and Output Decisions of a Monopolistically Competitive Firm. The firm described in the figure charges price equal to OB, produces the level of output equal to OF, and earns an economic profit equal to ABCD.

to describe the long-run equilibrium of a monopolistically competitive firm, it also describes a monopolistically competitive firm that happens to be breaking even in the short run.

ISSUES OF MONOPOLISTIC COMPETITION

Is monopolistic competition any good? In other words, should society leave monopolistically competitive markets alone or try to make these markets more competitive? To answer the question, we need to discuss two issues: how realistic monopolistic competition is, and how efficient the market is in comparison to perfect competition.

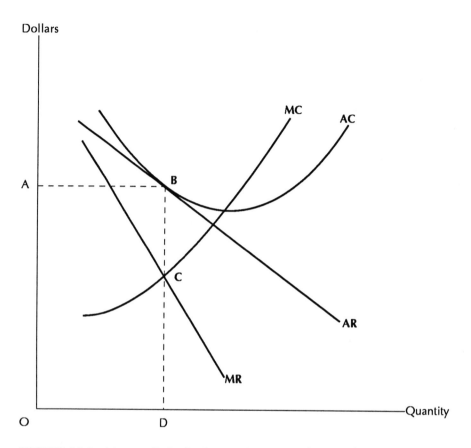

FIGURE 10.2 Monopolistically Competitive Firm That Breaks Even. The firm described in the figure charges price equal to the average cost of production. The firm is either breaking even in the short run or is in long-run equilibrium.

Large Number of Sellers

How realistic monopolistic competition is depends on how strictly monopolistic competition is defined.

The Symmetry Assumption

Suppose that a certain number of sellers are selling products that are differentiated but have close substitutes. When Chamberlin developed the theory of monopolistic competition, he made a key assumption concerning the market in which the group of sellers operates. The assumption is that any adjustment of price or of product by a single producer spreads its influence over so many of his competitors that the impact felt by any one is negligible. This assumption is known as the

THE DEPENDENCE EFFECT

One intriguing question in modern affluent societies is whether the desire of a poor consumer to obtain bare necessities is any more urgent than the desire of a wealthy consumer to obtain a mink coat or an expensive home. Economics is concerned with allocating limited resources among alternative uses for production of goods and services that satisfy human wants. Regarding human wants, no distinction is made between wants such as hunger that originate within individual consumers and wants such as the desire for an opal ring that are contrived for individual consumers. Consider that automobile manufacturers started making automobiles to meet transportation needs of the public. Over the years, the auto makers added numerous gadgets and equipment that consumers probably did not even know that they needed. These additions include white-wall tires, vinyl tops, turbo engines, and a gadget designed to avoid police detection for speeding. Sometimes, automobile manufacturers had to attach the logo LX outside the body of a car to tell car buyers that it is a luxury model. All these additions satisfy new wants created through advertising and salesmanship in the process of satisfying the original wants—that is, basic transportation needs.

The process in which new wants are created by production that is supposed to satisfy the original wants is called the **dependence effect.** The fact that one man's consumption becomes his neighbor's obsession clearly illustrates that the process by which wants are satisfied is also the process by which new wants are created. A man who is hungry never needs to be told of his need for food, whereas contrived wants or created wants need a reminder. According to Professor Galbraith, the emphasis of an economy should be more on satisfying innate wants and less on production that creates wants. The attitudes and values that make production the central achievement of our society have some exceptionally twisted roots.

Source: John Kenneth Galbraith, *The affluent society,* 2nd ed. (New York: Times Mirror, New American Library, 1969), ch. 11, pp. 139–145.

symmetry assumption. The symmetry assumption implies that a monopolistically competitive market has to have a large number of sellers selling differentiated products. In fact, the number of sellers that Chamberlin had in mind in defining monopolistic competition is so large that a price change by one seller has no perceptible influence on other sellers. The way monopolistic competition is defined by Chamberlin, therefore, shows little difference between monopolistic competition and perfect competition. Viewed this way, examples of monopolistic competition may be almost as rare as those of perfect competition.[4]

[4]For more on critical evaluation of monopolistic competition, see Mark Blaug, *Economic theory in retrospect* 4th ed. (Cambridge, England: Cambridge University Press, 1986), pp. 391–396; and George Stigler, Monopolistic competition in retrospect, *Five lectures on economic problems* (New York: Macmillan, 1950), pp. 12–24.

Modern Interpretation

Modern interpretation of monopolistic competition is quite loose. Monopolistic competition refers to markets in which a large number of sellers sell differentiated products without defining, or elaborating on, the number of sellers. The advantage of the modern interpretation is that many practical markets can be classified as monopolistic competition. One problem with the modern interpretation is that there appears to be little difference between monopolistic competition and oligopolistic markets selling differentiated products. The difference between monopolistic competition and oligopolistic markets selling differentiated products is somewhat arbitrary, so far as the number of sellers is concerned. The key difference between the two types of markets is not necessarily the number of sellers but the existence or absence of a significant mutual interdependence, especially in pricing, among leading sellers.

Mutual interdependence refers to a market situation in which decisions on price and nonprice strategies of a firm are based on the assumption that other firms in the industry will react to these decisions. If mutual interdependence is significant, the market is an oligopoly, whereas if mutual interdependence is negligible, the market is monopolistically competitive. Mutual interdependence is more significant in markets that have fewer sellers.

Market Concentration Ratio

Many economists prefer to measure the degree of market competition in terms of market concentration ratios. The **market concentration ratio** refers to the share of the total activity of an industry that is accounted for by its largest companies.[5] Concentration ratios are typically presented in groups of four companies or more to avoid disclosure of the operations of any individual firms.

Concentration ratios vary with how the scope of a given market is defined. To be specific, the measured level of market concentration tends to rise the more narrowly a product is defined. Consider steel. There is no market for steel as such. There are separate markets for separate steel products such as structural shapes, tinplates, and rails. Concentration ratios for the steel industry as a whole tend to be lower than concentration ratios estimated separately for each of the steel products, since many steel products cannot be substituted for one another.

If the product is defined so narrowly that substitutable products are excluded, concentration ratios will overstate the actual level of concentration. Consider containers. When concentration ratios are computed, fabrication of metal cans is classified as one industry and production of glass containers is classified as another industry. Concentration ratios of each industry will clearly overstate actual concentrations in these markets, since metal cans and glass containers are substitutes for each other.

In summary, concentration ratios of a market vary with how broadly the product sold in the market is defined. If the product is defined broadly, there will be more substitutes available, and measured concentration ratios tend to understate actual concentration. If the product is defined narrowly to the extent that its substitutes are excluded, measured concentration ratios tend to overstate actual concentration.

It may also be pointed out that the scope of a market is not the only determinant of market concentration ratios. If the price of a product increases substantially, many products that were not

---

[5]The discussion of market concentration ratios in this section is based on U.S. Department of Commerce, Bureau of the Census, *1982 census of manufacturers: Concentration ratios in manufacturing,* MC82-S-7 (Washington, D.C.: U.S. Government Printing Office, April 1986), pp. IX and X.

previously considered as substitutes for the product will now be considered as such. If the price of wine goes up significantly, for instance, wine drinkers are likely to consider beer as a substitute for wine. As the price of a product increases in relation to other prices, market concentration ratios for the product overstate actual concentration.

Market concentration ratios are based on a census of the nation's business and industrial establishments that the U.S. Census Bureau conducts every five years. Examples of market concentration ratios are presented in Table 10.2. Concentration ratios in the table are the percentages of the value of shipments in selected manufacturing industries. Motor vehicles, tires, organic fibers, and guided missiles are manufactured by firms in highly concentrated industries. These industries are clearly oligopolies. Commercial printing, fluid milk, and periodicals, on the other hand, are manufactured in market conditions that are more monopolistically competitive than oligopolistic. Certain products such as newspapers are produced in an industry that is monopolistically competitive only if the scope of the market is defined nationally.

Economic Efficiency

Since the theory of perfect competition was developed to provide us with a model of an efficient market, we know that monopolistic competition cannot be as efficient as perfect competition. The question is, How can we be sure that monopolistic competition is not as efficient as perfect competition? Figure 10.3 helps us answer this question.

Graphic Illustration

Suppose that a firm earning normal profits operates under a perfectly competitive market. The firm then operates as a price taker and is faced with a horizontal demand curve AR_1 in Figure 10.3. In the figure, the price charged by the competitive firm is OA, and the quantity of output produced by the firm is OF. Suppose that the same firm operates under a monopolistically competitive market. Due to the market power on its product, the demand curve faced by the now monopolistically competitive firm is no longer horizontal. The demand curve AR_2 is drawn tangent to the average cost curve to make sure that the firm is also earning no more than normal profits.

The price of the product charged by the firm operating under monopolistic competition is OB, which is higher than OA charged by the same firm operating under perfect competition. The quantity of output produced by the firm operating under monopolistic competition is OD, which is smaller than OF produced by the same firm operating under perfect competition. Economic efficiency is measured by a lower price and a larger quantity of output. Figure 10.3 indicates that even if the firm makes only the normal rate of return in either market, the price is higher and the quantity of output is smaller under monopolistic competition than under perfect competition. We thus conclude that monopolistic competition is not as efficient as perfect competition.

Product Differentiation and Economic Inefficiency

The extent of the inefficiency associated with monopolistic competition is indicated in Figure 10.3 by the distance AB vertically and the distance DF horizontally. Distance AB represents a higher price due to monopolistic competition, whereas distance DF represents a smaller quantity due to monopolistic competition. The magnitude of the inefficiency appears sizable in Figure 10.3, not necessarily because it is sizable in reality, but because of the way the average revenue curve is drawn in the figure. The less differentiated the products are, the flatter the average revenue curve becomes.

TABLE 10.2 Concentration Ratios in Manufacturing, Selected Industries, 1982

Industry Code	Industry	Number of Companies	Percentage of Shipments by the Number of Largest Companies			
			4 Firms	8 Firms	20 Firms	50 Firms
2011	Meatpacking plants	1,658	20	43	61	75
2026	Fluid milk	853	16	27	48	66
2051	Bread, cake, and related products	1,869	34	47	60	73
2086	Bottled and canned soft drinks	1,236	14	23	39	56
2111	Cigarettes	8	(D)	(D)	(X)	(X)
2421	Sawmills and planing mills, general	5,810	17	23	34	46
2621	Papermills, except building paper	135	22	40	71	93
2711	Newspapers	7,520	22	34	49	66
2721	Periodicals	3,143	20	31	49	64
2751	Commercial printing, letterpress	10,211	7	10	16	24
2752	Commercial printing, lithographic	17,332	6	10	17	24
2821	Plastics materials and resins	263	22	38	64	89
2824	Organic fibers, noncellulosic	44	77	91	99	100
2834	Pharmaceutical preparations	584	26	42	69	90
2841	Soap and other detergents	642	60	73	83	90
2844	Toilet preparations	596	34	49	71	88
2911	Petroleum refining	282	28	48	76	93
3011	Tires and inner tubes	108	66	86	98	99+
3312	Blast furnaces and steel mills	211	42	64	82	95
3321	Gray iron foundries	801	29	37	53	69
3465	Automotive stampings	566	61	66	74	82
3523	Farm machinery and equipment	1,787	53	62	69	77
3531	Construction machinery	817	42	52	69	81
3573	Electronic computing equipment	1,520	43	55	71	82
3585	Refrigeration and heating equipment	730	34	46	65	80
3661	Telephone, telegraph apparatus	259	76	83	92	97
3662	Radio and TV communication equipment	2,083	22	35	57	73
3711	Motor vehicles and car bodies	284	92	97	99	99+
3714	Motor vehicle parts and accessories	2,000	61	69	77	84
3721	Aircraft	139	64	81	98	99+
3761	Guided missiles and space vehicles	86	71	96	100	(X)
3861	Photographic equipment and supplies	723	74	86	91	94

Source: U.S. Department of Commerce, Bureau of the Census, *Statistical abstract of the United States,* 109th ed. (Washington, D.C.: U.S. Government Printing Office, January 1989), p. 725. D means "withheld to avoid disclosure," while X means "not applicable."

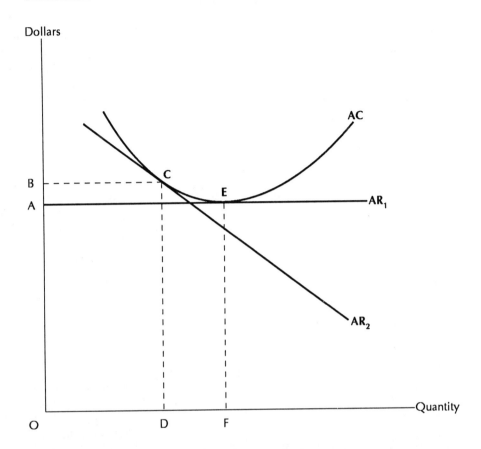

FIGURE 10.3 Monopolistic Competition and Perfect Competition. The price is higher in monopolistic competition (OB) than in perfect competition (OA), and the quantity of output produced is smaller in monopolistic competition (OD) than in perfect competition (OF).

If the average revenue curve representing monopolistic competition is almost horizontal, the magnitude of the inefficiency becomes insignificant. In Figure 10.3, the portion CE on the average cost curve represents the capacity of production of a firm that is not used because the firm is operating under monopolistic competition. The unused capacity becomes smaller the less differentiated the products are.

The main contribution of the theory of monopolistic competition lies in its finding that if markets are monopolistically competitive, free markets will not necessarily result in an optimum allocation of productive resources. Graphically speaking, this statement means that the downward-sloping demand curve will not allow profit-maximizing firms to produce at the lowest point of the average cost curve.

OLIGOPOLY

Some industries have a small number of firms. Other industries have a large number of firms but are dominated by a small number of firms. Both types of market are oligopolistic in nature. The exact number of firms small enough to constitute an oligopoly is a matter of opinion. Some industries are so highly concentrated that practically everyone agrees that these industries are oligopolies. These industries include motor vehicles, chewing gum, cigarettes, typewriters, laundry equipment, and others indicated by high concentration ratios in Table 10.2. The microeconomic definition of an oligopoly in the following subsection is followed by two explanations of the pricing behavior of firms operating under oligopolistic markets.

Oligopoly Defined

Unlike the term *monopolistic competition,* which appeared in the economic literature in the 1930s, the term *oligopolium* appeared in the economic literature as early as 1516, when Sir Thomas More stated in his book *Utopia* that for competition to prevail it is not sufficient that a commodity be sold by more than one seller.[6]

Textbook Market

An interesting example of an oligopoly is the textbook market. A trade is basically an exchange of goods and services between a buyer and a seller. Whenever another party interferes with the exchange, the interference is usually bad news for consumers. Consider the market for textbooks. Students who actually buy textbooks are not the people who select these books. Professors are the ones who select textbooks. When professors select a textbook, they usually do not even know what its price is. The demand for textbooks, therefore, is price-inelastic because the level of demand is determined by professors, who care more about the content of the books than about their price, not by students, who actually worry about the price. This unique aspect of demand for them explains, in part, why textbooks are so expensive. As long as the demand for textbooks is inelastic, publishers can raise the prices of textbooks, *provided that* the number of publishers is limited to a few who recognize mutual interdependence in pricing and other business practices among themselves. If the small number of publishers behave as if they belong to competitive markets or contestable markets, the prices of textbooks may not be as high as they are now.

Typical costs of publishing a textbook average $31.80 in 1990 dollars, which consists of plant overhead ($5.68), printing and binding ($5.11), editorial costs ($2.27), company overhead and marketing ($12.49), and profit ($6.25). Students pay around $40 to allow for the profit ($7.95) by the bookstore.[7] Prices of many textbooks are even higher because university bookstores may add a monopoly premium, raising their cost-plus margin by more than $7.95.

What Is Oligopoly?

An **oligopoly** is a market dominated by a small number of firms selling either homogeneous products or differentiated products. A market supplied by a large number of sellers is still an oligopoly if the market is dominated by a few large firms. Firms in an oligopolistic market recognize

---

[6]Joseph A. Schumpeter, *History of economic analysis* (New York: Oxford University Press, 1966), p. 305.

[7]Adapted from Timothy Tregarthen, The market for principles of economics texts, *The Margin* 2(March 1987):15.

that their success depends not only on how well they run their own businesses individually, but also on how other firms respond to pricing and other promotional decisions that any one firm undertakes. If firms under oligopolistic markets compete, their price and output decisions resemble those of firms operating under competitive markets. If they act in concert, their price and output decisions resemble those of monopolistic firms. The key element of an oligopolistic market, therefore, is the recognition of mutual interdependence among oligopolists in pricing and other promotional strategies.

Why are certain industries prone to develop as oligopolies? Why do other firms not enter the oligopolistic market? And why do oligopolistic markets persist without being broken up by an additional entry into the market? The answer lies in economies of scale. Successful oligopolistic markets are characterized by economies of scale. Because of savings in unit cost from large-scale production, any outside firm contemplating entry into an oligopolistic market may have to spend several billion dollars for investment in machines, equipment, and buildings before any profit is realized. When the outcome of a business venture appears uncertain because the venture requires a substantial amount of initial investment, economies of scale become a serious barrier to entry.

Price and Output Decisions

The development of the theory of oligopoly for nearly the past 500 years has centered on *conjectural interdependence* among oligopolists. **Conjectural interdependence** means that price and other promotional decisions of a firm are based on the firm's guess as to how its competitors would react to its decisions. Two different versions of conjectural interdependence among oligopolists are presented in this section: kinked demand curve and price leadership. Theories of oligopoly are not

---

PRICING GUIDELINES

You're gouging on your prices if you
Charge more than the rest.
But it's unfair competition
If you think you can charge less.
A second point that we would make
To help avoid confusion:
Don't try to charge the same amount.
That would be collusion!
You must compete. But not too much,
For if you do, you see,
Then the market would be yours
And that's monopoly!

Source: R. W. Grant, *Tom Smith and his incredible bread machine,* quoted from Earl L. Bailey (ed.), *Pricing practices and strategies* (New York: The Conference Board, 1978), p. 18.

as exact as those developed for other market structures, because any successful oligopolistic product or promotion policy must be unpredictable. Rivalry in the oligopoly market is a complex game in which each player tries to figure out other players' strategies while keeping his or her own ambiguous.

Kinked Demand Curve

The most widely known model of an oligopoly is the kinked demand curve, developed in the 1930s by Paul Sweezy.[8] The location and shape of a demand curve faced by a firm operating under oligopolistic markets depend on how the firm's rival firms in the industry react to a price change initiated by the firm. There are two possibilities. One possibility is that rival firms match whatever price changes are initiated by the firm. The demand curve based on this assumption is drawn as CF in Figure 10.4. Demand curve CF is comparatively less elastic than demand curve BG. Demand curve CF indicates that when the oligopolistic firm lowers price the quantity of sales increases only modestly because rival firms also lower their prices and keep the firm from enjoying a substantial increase in sales.

The other possible reaction by rival firms is that they may simply ignore any price change initiated by the firm. In this case, the firm that lowers price will be able to increase the quantity of sales substantially. The demand curve faced by the oligopolistic firm under this assumption is comparatively horizontal, indicating the more elastic nature of the demand curve. The demand curve based on the assumption that rival firms do not match price changes initiated by the firm is BG in Figure 10.4.

The kinked demand curve explanation of an oligopoly is based on the middle ground of the two extreme possibilities. According to the **kinked demand curve,** price decreases of an oligopolist are matched by rival firms, but price increases are not matched. The demand curve faced by an oligopolist, therefore, is BDF with a kink at point D. The BD portion of the demand curve explains the behavior of an oligopolistic firm that will not raise price, fearing that the price increase will not be matched by rival firms and will thus lead to a loss in sales. The DF portion of the demand curve explains the behavior of an oligopolistic firm that will not lower price, fearing that the price decrease will be matched by rival firms and will thus nullify any advantage that the firm expects from lowering the price. The only rational pricing behavior of the oligopolistic firm then is to maintain the present price OA and sell the present quantity OE. The hypothesis suggested by the kinked demand curve is that the price in an oligopolistic market tends to be rigid.

Whether or not prices in oligopolistic markets are any more rigid than prices in other market structures is essentially an empirical question. If prices in oligopolistic markets are not any more rigid than prices in other markets, the kinked demand curve is simply an unsuccessful attempt to explain the pricing behavior of oligopolists. Some studies suggest that prices in oligopolies are no more rigid than prices in other markets.[9] Another problem with the kinked demand curve is that the curve explains why prices in oligopolistic markets tend to be rigid but does not explain how the existing price level is determined. The kink on the kinked demand curve occurs at the existing price and sales level. Because the kinked demand curve cannot explain how the existing prices and quantities of output are determined, the kinked demand curve hypothesis is not a model of price and output determination.

[8]Paul Sweezy, Demand under conditions of oligopoly, *Journal of Political Economy* 47(August 1939):568–573.

[9]For a critical evaluation of the kinked demand curve, see George J. Stigler, The kinky oligopoly demand curve and rigid prices, *Journal of Political Economy* 55(October 1947):432–449; and Julian Simon, A further test of the kinky oligopoly demand curve, *American Economic Review* 59(December 1969):971–975.

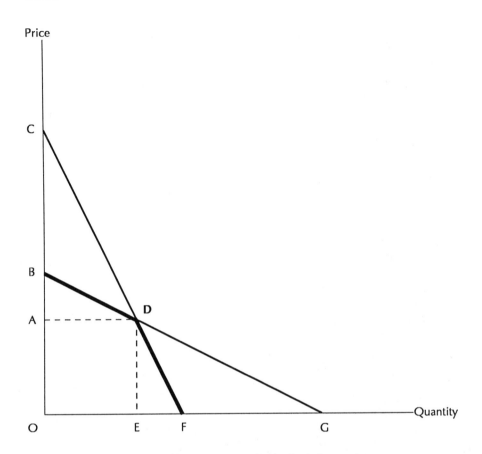

FIGURE 10.4 Kinked Demand Curve. The kinked demand curve assumes that competitors follow price decreases of an oligopolist but do not follow price increases. The price in an oligopolistic market tends to be stable at OA.

Price Leadership

Another way of explaining the mutual interdependence in pricing among firms operating under an oligopolistic market is price leadership. **Price leadership** refers to the practice in which one firm in the industry initiates a price change and other firms in the same industry follow the price leader by more or less matching the price change. Firms that lead the price change in oligopolistic markets are usually firms that can produce products at the lowest cost per unit. These firms tend also to be the most dominant firms in the industry. Price leaders in the recent past include U.S. Steel (now USX) in the steel industry, ALCOA in the aluminum industry, General Motors in the automobile industry, and R. J. Reynolds in the cigarette industry. When the dominant firm initiates a price change, the price leadership model hypothesizes that rival large firms and other small firms on the competitive fringe follow suit and change prices more or less proportionately.

PRICING PRACTICES OF FIRMS IN REALITY

Let us pause for a moment and reflect on what we have learned about pricing practices of real firms. Regardless of market structure, the basic premise of our discussion has been that firms attempt to maximize profits, and to do so firms set price according to the MR = MC rule. As explained in Chapter 7, the concept of profit contribution is used in pricing products, but only by businesses at the margin. The profit contribution approach is similar to the MR = MC rule when price and the average cost of production do not change with output. An interesting question is, How do businesses price their products?

Obviously, pricing is very important. William T. Moran, former president of Admar Research Company, states, "There is more money won and lost each year through price and price-promotion actions than through all other marketing decision areas combined."[10] Other business leaders have stated that all of the following factors should be considered when making price decisions:[11]

> market conditions
> competitive prices
> product differentiation
> phase of the product life cycle
> growth rate of the market
> status of other prices: whether rising, stable, or falling
> the firm's market share
> the market's ability to pay
> the market's expectations about prices
> competitors' typical responses to price changes
>   in the industry

In addition, managers of firms consider: **loss leader pricing,** in which a firm prices a product below its cost in order to attract customers; **predatory pricing,** in which a firm cuts price in order to drive competitors out of the market; and **limit pricing,** in which a firm prices a new product below the minimum average cost of production in order to prevent new entries into the market for the product.

The problem is that none of these terms and pricing strategies appears to suggest that MR = MC pricing is the pricing method that firms pursue for profit maximization. How then do we explain the seeming absence of any relation between the MR = MC pricing method and other pricing methods that firms seem to follow on a day-to-day basis? This is an empirical question. Two studies surveyed pricing practices of firms: one on well-managed companies and the other on small businesses.[12] Both studies concluded that, although different terms were used by these firms, prices actually charged by successful firms were essentially based on the MR = MC principle.

[10]William T. Moran, Insight from pricing research, in Earl L. Bailey (ed.), *Pricing practices and strategies* (New York: The Conference Board, 1978), p. 7.

[11]S. E. Heymann, Cost considerations, in Earl L. Bailey (ed.), *Pricing practices and strategies* (New York: The Conference Board, 1978), p. 40.

[12]The two studies are James S. Earley, Marginal policies of "excellently managed" companies, *American Economic Review* 46(March 1956):44–70; and W. Warren Haynes, Pricing policies in small firms, *Southern Economic Journal* 30(April 1964):335–347.

SUMMARY

Most real markets are best described by either the model of monopolistic competition or the oligopoly model. Monopolistic competition refers to markets in which a large number of sellers produce and sell differentiated products. The key elements of monopolistically competitive markets are product differentiation and the existence of many sellers selling close substitutes. Product differentiation means that consumers perceive two or more products satisfying the same wants to be different, and they prefer one to the other. Product differentiation causes the demand for these products to become less elastic, and firms take advantage of the reduced price elasticity of demand by charging higher prices.

Due to the relatively inelastic demand for their product, monopolistically competitive firms that break even tend to produce a smaller quantity of output at a higher cost than do perfectly competitive firms that break even. Monopolistic competition is said to be less efficient than perfect competition. Many economists measure the degree of market competition in terms of market concentration ratios. Concentration ratios are typically presented in groups of four companies or more to avoid disclosure of the operations of any individual firms. Concentration ratios vary with how the scope of a given market is defined. The level of market concentration tends to rise the more narrowly a product is defined. If the product is defined broadly, there will be more substitutes available, and measured concentration ratios understate actual concentration. If the product is defined so narrowly that its substitutes are excluded, measured concentration ratios overstate actual concentration. Concentration ratios depend also on price.

Oligopoly refers to a market that is dominated by a small number of firms selling either homogeneous products or differentiated products. In terms of pricing behavior, the main characteristic of firms operating under oligopolistic markets is mutual interdependence, especially in pricing decisions. The kinked demand curve hypothesizes that prices in an oligopolistic market tend to be stable. The kinked demand curve model is based on the assumption that price decreases by an oligopolist are matched by rival firms, but price increases are not. Another explanation of the pricing behavior of an oligopoly is price leadership. According to the price leadership model, one firm in the industry initiates a price change, and other firms follow the price leader by matching the price change.

EXERCISES

1. When the patent of a brand-name drug expires, any drug company can produce the drug under its generic name once its version of the drug passes a bioequivalence test and wins approval from the FDA. What is the market structure that best describes the drug manufacturing industry?

2. What are the major differences between monopolistic competition and oligopoly?

3. How do firms try to differentiate their products from those produced by rival firms?

4. When Edward H. Chamberlin developed the theory of monopolistic competition, he made a key assumption called the symmetry assumption. What is the symmetry assumption, and what is the significance of the assumption?

5. Economists sometimes talk about the *waste* of monopolistic competition by claiming that monopolistic competition is not as efficient as perfect competition. How do economists determine that monopolistic competition is less efficient than perfect competition?

6. Why are textbooks likely to be overpriced?

7. According to the September 1, 1986, issue of *Fortune* (p. 27), the share of the U.S. wine market is divided as indicated in Table 10.3. What would be the most appropriate description of the structure of the U.S. wine market?

TABLE 10.3   Share of the U.S. Wine Market

Company	Market Share
E. & J. Gallo Winery	26.1%
Seagram & Sons	8.3
Canandaigua Wine	5.4
Brown-Forman	5.1
National Distillers	4.0
Heublein	3.7
Imports	23.4
All others	24.0
Total	100.0%

8. Why are certain industries likely to develop as oligopolies?

9. What is the assumption underlying the kinked demand curve, and what is the major criticism against the kinked demand curve analysis?

10. The October 6, 1987, issue of *Financial World* selected the 10 worst-managed companies in America based on many criteria including poor judgments in assessing their own industries, undertaking a debt burden that is too large, overexpansion, and a lack of ideas or convictions. These companies included the Cannon Group, MCI, Texas Air, and Adolph Coors, among others. If these companies were indeed managed as poorly as *Financial World* claimed, how do they still survive?

SUGGESTED READINGS

Chamberlin, Edward H. (1976). *The theory of monopolistic competition.* 8th ed. Cambridge, Mass.: Harvard University Press.

The book that proposed the theory of monopolistic competition and often called revolutionary in the development of the price theory.

Hicks, John R. (1935) Annual survey of economic theory: The theory of monopoly. *Econometrica* 3(January):1–20.

A widely read survey article on monopoly, bilateral monopoly, and monopolistic competition.

Moran, William T. (1978). Insight from pricing research. In Earl L. Bailey, (ed.), *Pricing practices and strategies.* New York: The Conference Board.

A monograph containing several articles on pricing, all written by those who make pricing decisions at major firms.

Nicholls, William. (1951). *Price policies in the cigarette industry.* Nashville: Vanderbilt University Press.

An interesting study on price leadership in the cigarette industry.

Stigler, George J. (1978). The literature of economics: The case of the kinked demand curve. *Economic Inquiry* 16(April):185–204.

An excellent summary of articles on the kinked demand curve.

11

Economics of Productive Resources

In Chapters 7–10 we were mainly concerned with determining the quantity of output and the product price of profit-maximizing firms under differing market conditions. In other words, the main concern of the preceding four chapters was output. In this chapter, we focus on inputs and introduce concepts and theories that relate to the optimal use of inputs. Our primary interest in studying inputs is twofold. One objective is a rather obvious one: We would like to find out how firms determine the optimal quantity of a given input factor for cost minimization. The other objective is less obvious but just as important as the first: We want to know how the compensation to the owners of productive resources is determined. That is, we want to know why some people are making more money than others. Chapter 1 classified the factors of production broadly into four groups: labor, land, capital, and entrepreneurship. Returns to these factors of production are, respectively, wages, rent, interest, and profit. The first section of this chapter presents a theory of demand for productive resources in general, which is followed by studies of wages, rent, interest, and profit.

DEMAND FOR PRODUCTIVE RESOURCES

Inputs, input factors, factors of production, and productive resources are all synonymous and are used interchangeably. Firms use productive resources to produce other goods and services. In this section, we introduce ideas about how firms determine the optimal quantity of productive resources for production of final products.

Derived Demand

When we study productive resources, it is important to understand that firms demand productive resources because these resources are needed to produce final products. Demand for productive resources is called a **derived demand** because demand for inputs results from demand for final products that these resources help produce. Labor, land, and capital are not useful unless these resources are combined to produce products that consumers want. Demand for lumber is a derived demand because it is a consequence of the demand for houses and other buildings. Demand for rubber is a derived demand because it results from the demand for tires and other industrial components made of rubber.

Because the demand for productive resources is a derived demand, the market value of a productive resource depends on the value of final products that the resource is used to produce. If there is no industrial use for diamonds, the price of industrial diamonds is expected to decline. If there is no demand for convertible automobiles, all the cloth and frames used to make the convertible tops will command little value in the market. The determination of the optimal quantity of productive resources demanded is based on the value of final products that these resources help produce. The higher the value of final products that these resources help produce, the greater the demand for these resources.

Optimal Demand for Productive Resources

Stated plainly, profit-maximizing firms are expected to employ a given unit of a productive resource so long as the additional revenue generated by the use of the unit is equal to or greater than the cost of employing the unit. Suppose that we apply for a job at a local department store. The store will hire us only if the revenue that we are expected to generate is at least as large as the wages that the store is willing to pay us. Let us formalize this hypothesis by using labor input as an example.

Illustration

Consider a small software firm producing interactive software that converts files on a 5 1/4 inch diskette to and from files on a 3 1/2 inch diskette. Suppose that the firm already has machines, equipment, and a laboratory, and has just started to hire workers. The number of workers is shown in column (1) in Table 11.1. In the table, a worker's input is measured by a day's work. As more workers are added to other existing inputs of the firm, the quantity of the software that the firm produces increases. The **total physical product of labor,** presented in column (2), is the quantity of output produced by all workers, measured in physical units. The **marginal physical product of labor,** shown in column (3), refers to the change in the quantity of physical output as one more worker is added to other existing productive resources of the firm. Figures in column (2) are selected arbitrarily but are subject to the law of diminishing returns as indicated in column (3). The marginal physical product of labor in column (3) declines with additional units of labor services.

The firm under consideration is very small, with a maximum capacity of only a few employees. The market price of the software is $10, and the price is not expected to change as the number of software packages produced by the firm increases. The product price in column (4), therefore, remains constant at $10. Notice that we are not making the assumption of perfect competition to keep the product price stable at $10. The only assumption we are making is that the firm is a price taker. Our firm may well be a small firm on the competitive fringe of an oligopoly.

TABLE 11.1   Marginal Revenue Product of Labor

(1) Units of Labor	(2) Total Physical Product	(3) Marginal Physical Product	(4) Product Price	(5) Marginal Revenue Product
0	0	0	$10	$ 0
1	25	25	10	250
2	45	20	10	200
3	60	15	10	150
4	70	10	10	100
5	75	5	10	50
6	75	0	10	0

Marginal Revenue Product of Labor
The **marginal revenue product** of labor in column (5) is the change in total revenue resulting from a one-unit change in the use of labor service. In other words, the marginal revenue product represents the additional revenue that the worker who is hired last brings to the firm. The marginal revenue product in the table is obtained when marginal physical product in column (3) is multiplied by product price in column (4). How many workers the firm hires depends to a large extent on the marginal revenue product of labor schedule.

From the viewpoint of the firm, the optimal number of employees is that number which generates the maximum profit for the firm. The cost of hiring the last unit of a productive resource is called the **marginal factor cost** or the **marginal resource cost.** To determine the optimal number of workers, the firm compares the marginal revenue product of labor with the cost of hiring the worker. The process of determining the optimal number of workers is indicated in Figure 11.1.

In Figure 11.1, the marginal revenue product of labor is indicated as declining as the number of workers hired increases. The cost of hiring a worker, measured in daily wage rate, is $150. The wage rate is assumed not to change as the firm hires additional workers. The wage rate schedule, therefore, is horizontal. The firm will hire three workers, since the marginal revenue product of the third worker is equal to or greater than the cost of hiring the third worker. The firm will not hire the fourth worker because the revenue ($100) that the fourth worker brings to the firm is smaller than the wage rate ($150). In fact, the firm will hire three workers so long as the daily wage is $150 or lower, but greater than $100. The marginal revenue products of labor, shown in column (5) of Table 11.1 and drawn in Figure 11.1, are the software firm's demand schedule of labor. The marginal revenue product schedule shows the relation between daily wages and the number of workers demanded by the firm at these wages.

Marginal Productivity Theory

Reconsider the process of determining the optimal number of workers for the software firm. The very process that the firm uses to determine the optimal number of workers for profit maximization also determines how much workers get paid. According to the theory of demand for productive resources, the owner of a productive resource is paid the marginal revenue product of the resource. This process of determining the income distribution among resource owners on the basis of their marginal revenue products is known as the **marginal productivity theory of income distribution.** The notion that "you get paid what you are worth" underlies the marginal productivity theory. The marginal productivity theory is not necessarily self-evident in Table 11.1.

Wage Share of Total Revenue Product
Our example in Table 11.1 indicates that the wage rate is $150 and the firm hires three workers at this wage rate. The third worker gets paid the marginal revenue product since the worker's marginal revenue product is $150. What about the first and the second workers? Does the marginal productivity theory suggest that they get paid $250 and $200, since these are their respective marginal revenue products? The answer is no. The three workers in our example perform the same work. The only reason that the first worker's marginal revenue product is the highest is that the first worker was hired first and thus was able to use a larger number of machines and equipment. If only one worker were hired, the marginal productivity theory would suggest that the worker be paid $250. When the second worker is hired, the second worker's marginal revenue product is lower

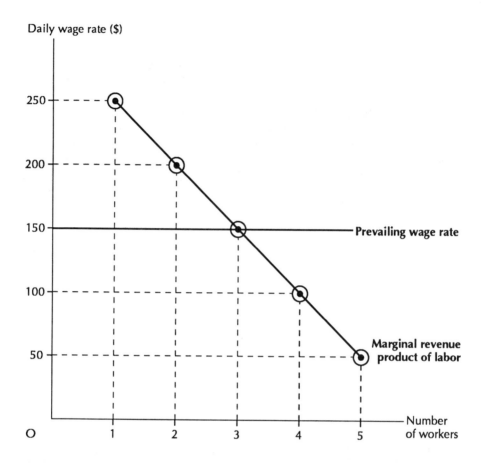

FIGURE 11.1   Determining the Optimal Number of Workers. A profit-maximizing firm determines the number of workers (3) at the level where the marginal revenue product of labor ($150) is equal to the wage rate ($150).

($200) than the first worker's ($250). The sum of marginal revenue products of the two workers is $450 ($250 + $200). The sum of marginal revenue products of all workers is called the **total revenue product.** In this case, the marginal productivity theory suggests that both workers get paid $200 each.

When two workers are hired, total wages are $400, and the total revenue product that the two workers bring for the firm is $450. The difference of $50 between total wages of $400 and total revenue product of $450 represents marginal revenue products of other productive resources such as capital and entrepreneurship that were also used to produce the software. When three workers are hired, all three workers are paid $150 each. In this case, total wages are $450, total revenue product is $600 ($250 + $200 + $150), and marginal products for productive resources other than workers are $150, which is the difference between total wages and total revenue product.

Marginal Revenue Productivity Theory in Practice

Are actual incomes distributed according to the marginal productivity theory? Whether or not incomes are distributed according to the marginal productivity theory depends on whether or not the assumptions underlying the theory hold true in reality. There are two important assumptions underlying the marginal productivity theory of income distribution.

One assumption is that the market is perfectly competitive. Suppose that product markets are dominated by monopolistic firms, and the labor market is highly competitive. Labor unions either do not exist or are weak if they do exist. In this type of economy, wages are likely to be smaller than workers' marginal products, since the bargaining power of workers is limited. If the product market is highly competitive and all workers are unionized, on the other hand, wages may exceed the marginal products of workers. The bargaining power of workers is substantial in this economy. Many markets in reality are not highly competitive. This means that the actual distribution of income does not necessarily approximate that of the marginal productivity theory.

Another assumption underlying the marginal productivity theory of income distribution is that there are no spillover effects. If a worker works in a firm that generates a significant amount of external diseconomies such as pollution, the worker's marginal revenue product overestimates the worker's true productivity from society's viewpoint. If, on the other hand, a worker generates a significant amount of external economies such as vaccine against flu, the worker's marginal revenue product underestimates the worker's true productivity. The existence of spillover effects, unless these were compensated properly, would make it difficult to apply the marginal productivity theory to the actual distribution of income.

Even if the actual distribution of income approximates that of the marginal productivity theory, critics argue that the marginal productivity theory is not equitable. According to the marginal productivity theory, those who possess (a) a large amount of capital, (b) exceptional intellectual or other skills, or (c) market power through being a monopoly firm will be rewarded with a large amount of income. Many individuals do not possess these resources for reasons beyond their control. For instance, some of us receive little, if any, inheritance, while others forgo a higher education due to inadequate family income. Those who do not possess these resources may not be able to compete on equal terms with those who possess these resources.

WAGES

The determination of the optimal quantity of a productive resource was discussed in the preceding section with labor input as an example. In this section we generalize the determination of wages discussed in the previous section.

Determination of Wages

Wages are the price paid for the use of labor services. Like other prices, wages are also determined by supply and demand. The determination of wages is illustrated in Figure 11.2. The demand curve

---

EULER'S THEOREM

Consider the firm in Table 11.1 with two employees. If the two employees are paid according to their marginal revenue products at $200 each, the total revenue product of $450 ($250 + $200) is greater than the sum of $400 ($200 + $200) of the marginal revenue products of the two employees. Will the leftover $50 ($450 – $400) in revenue be exactly equal to the marginal revenue product of the owners? If the amount leftover were greater than the owners' marginal revenue product, an income distribution based on the marginal productivity theory would favor the owners of the firm. If the amount leftover were smaller than the owners' marginal revenue product, the theory would not be practical since the owners of the firm would reject the theory as a means of income distribution.

Suppose that all owners of productive resources are paid their marginal products. Will the sum of all incomes (or marginal productivities) paid to these owners be equal to the money value of total products produced in the economy? The issue of a possible difference between the total income of a society and the sum of incomes of individual resource owners of the society was probed by a Swiss mathematician named Leonhard Euler (1707–1783) long before economists proposed the marginal productivity theory. According to a theorem developed by Euler, if each input factor is paid the amount of its marginal product, the money value of the total product will be exactly exhausted by the distributive shares of all the input factors, *provided that* the economy is operating under conditions of constant returns to scale. This property of the marginal productivity theory of income distribution under conditions of constant returns to scale is called **Euler's theorem.** When incomes are distributed according to the marginal productivity theory under conditions of constant returns to scale, all input factors are paid their respective marginal products.

---

is the market demand curve, which is the sum of the marginal revenue product of labor schedules of all firms in a given industry. The supply curve is the relation between wages and the quantity of labor available for work at these wages. Unlike the wage curve in Figure 11.1, the supply curve in Figure 11.2 has an upward slope to the right. The wage curve was horizontal in Figure 11.1 because an increase in employment by one firm was assumed not to raise wages. The supply curve in Figure 11.2 has an upward slope to the right because in any given industry the quantity of labor available for work is expected to increase as wages increase. The equilibrium wage and the quantity of labor employed are determined by the intersection between demand and supply curves.

Wage Differences

Figure 11.2 explains the principle underlying the determination of wages, but it does not necessarily explain why wage differences exist among different occupations and among different individuals within the same occupation. Numerous hypotheses have been suggested to explain wage differentials. These hypotheses include level of education, immobility of workers, and equalizing differences. Labor unions, which may also affect wage differentials, are discussed separately.

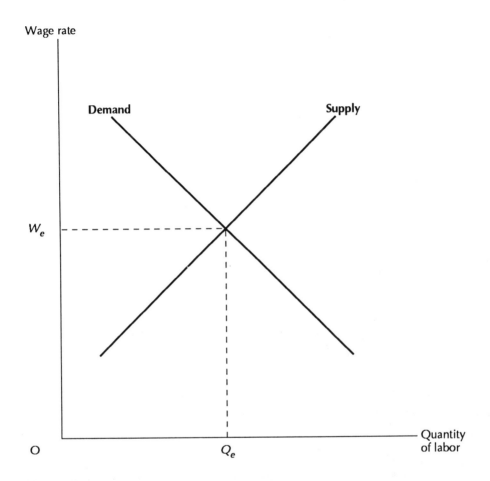

FIGURE 11.2 Determination of Wages. Wages (W_e) are determined by the demand curve of labor and the supply curve of labor in the market. The demand curve of labor is the sum of the marginal revenue product of labor schedules of all firms.

Education

The educational attainment of individual workers directly affects the productivity of workers and thus their earnings. The relation between educational attainment and median income is clear and direct. The median income of households and the educational level of the householder for 1986 are presented in Table 11.2. Those who had only an elementary level education had a household income of $13,231. The household income increased to $24,271 for those who had graduated from high school. The household income of those householders who had at least four years of college education was $41,677, more than three times that earned by those who had graduated from

TABLE 11.2 Median Income of Households and
Education Level of Householder in 1987

Educational Attainment of Householder	Total Households (000s)	Median Income
Elementary School:	11,500	$11,730
less than 8 years	6,437	10,884
8 years	5,063	12,999
High School:	41,037	23,382
1 to 3 years	10,476	16,727
4 years	30,561	25,910
College:	33,301	38,337
1 to 3 years	14,294	31,865
4 years or more	19,007	43,952

Source: U.S. Department of Commerce, Bureau of the Census,
Statistical abstract of the United States, 1989, 109th ed. (Washington, D.C.:
U.S. Government Printing Office, January 1989), p. 441.

elementary school only. Workers are sometimes classified into skilled and unskilled workers. The most common basis for making such a classification is the level of education attained by these workers.

Immobility of Workers
The immobility of workers is of two types: immobility in relocation and immobility among jobs. Some workers are not willing to move to another location because they value the nearness of friends and relatives, while others are not willing to relocate because they are afraid of not surviving in a new environment. The immobility of workers among jobs refers to the difficulty a person experiences in moving from one occupation to another. The immobility among jobs may be due to discrimination in sex, race, or age. It may also be caused by unions that restrict their membership. Whatever the reasons may be, when workers are not willing or able to move to another location for the same occupation or another occupation with higher pay, wage differentials tend to persist.

Equalizing Differences
Some wage differentials are equalizing differences in the sense that the difference in wages enables employers to attract workers to occupations that are not attractive. Construction workers in the deep South or in the extreme North frequently have to work in hostile weather conditions; they require premium pay as compensation for these hardships. Those who perform hazardous duties also require premium pay to compensate for adverse working conditions. The reverse is also true in that jobs with nonmonetary amenities command less pay.

MARGINAL REVENUE PRODUCTS OF HOCKEY PLAYERS

When there is only one buyer in the player market, exploitation of players is expected such that players' salaries are smaller than their marginal revenue products (MRPs). (A one-buyer market is known in economics as a **monopsony**.) When competition occurs through, say, intraleague competition for free agents, salaries are expected to approximate players' MRPs. J. C. H. Jones and W. D. Walsh tested this hypothesis using salary data of National Hockey League (NHL) players. As a monopsonist, the NHL has not experienced interteam competition for players except during the seven-season existence (1972–1978) of the World Hockey Association (WHA), which apparently transformed a monopsonistic situation into a competitive one characterized by interleague competition for players. The data for the test were drawn from a cross-section time-series sample of 12 teams for the three seasons, 1975–76 to 1977–78; and a sample of 274 players for the 1977–78 season.

The major conclusion of the study is that the data fail to reject the hypothesis. In fact, the converse is true. Stated in simple terms, data show that when competition exists, salaries either approximate, or are greater than, the MRPs of the players. Marginal revenue products and salaries of selected hockey players are summarized in Table 11.3 The negative sign of a player's salary in the last column means that the player is overpaid.

TABLE 11.3 Marginal Revenue Products and Salaries of Selected NHL Players, 1977–78

Names of Players	MRP	Salary	Exploitation (MRP – Salary)
P. Esposito	$205,671	$325,000	–119,329
Guy Lafleur	192,836	180,000	12,836
M. Dionne	191,908	320,000	–128,092
B. Clarke	175,516	160,000	15,516
J. Rattelle	153,712	150,000	3,712
D. Potvin	149,426	150,000	– 574
B. Park	129,624	250,000	–120,376
Pitt Martin	117,990	140,000	–22,010
D. Lever	107,784	120,000	–12,216
R. Middleton	104,073	100,000	4,073
L. Robinson	94,591	125,000	– 30,409
S. Sedlbauer	78,402	80,000	–1,598
B. Gainey	54,897	80,000	–25,103
H. Snepts	35,643	70,000	–34,357

Source: J. C. H. Jones and W. D. Walsh, The World Hockey Association and player exploitation in the National Hockey League, *Quarterly Review of Economics and Business* 27(Summer 1987):87–101; table adapted from p. 95.

LABOR UNIONS

Although the number of workers who belong to labor unions has increased steadily, the percentage of union membership relative to the total civilian labor force peaked in 1954 and has continued to decline ever since. Admittedly, some workers like labor unions, while others hate them. Regardless of whether one likes or hates labor unions, we all agree on the significant role that labor unions have played in the history of the American labor movement. No study of wage determination would be complete without some study of labor unions.

History of the Union Movement in the United States

Charles Robert Darwin (1809–1882) observed in the struggle for existence among life forms that favorable variations were preserved, while unfavorable variations were destroyed. The Darwinian theory of evolution suggests that the process of natural selection tends to favor the survival of those species whose peculiarities render them best adapted to their environment. The progress of American unionism is a good example of social Darwinism. Labor unions in the United States have been supportive of the nation's political democracy. Labor unions that did not support political democracy were not fit for survival.

Early Union Movement
The first union in the United States was the Federal Society of Journeymen Cordwainers, formed in 1794 by shoemakers, who were called cordwainers at the time. Like all union movements in early American unionism, the Society was a craft union. A **craft union** is a union of skilled workers. The central labor practice around the turn of the eighteenth century was that organized journeymen made a *list* of unit prices for various product items such as boots, workshoes, and women's shoes. They then gave a "take it or leave it" choice to the master workman who employed them.

When shoemakers in Philadelphia jointly imposed their list on their employers, they were charged with criminal conspiracy. In 1806 the presiding judge ruled that the combination of workmen who were trying to raise their wages was illegal because the combination benefited workers themselves and because the combination injured those who did not join the Society. Labor unions have since come a long way toward improving the welfare of their members.

In 1869 Uriah Stephens and six other tailors organized the Noble Order of the Knights of Labor, a national labor union that lasted until 1917. The Knights of Labor advocated labor legislation for such modern programs as health and safety, equal pay for equal work for both sexes, shorter hours, and arbitration of industrial disputes. One problem with the Knights of Labor was that they pushed for the idea of one big union that would have effectively ended the dependence of workers on private employers and rejected the wage system. The idea of one big union appealed neither to the skilled workers nor to the then political climate of the nation.

In 1881 a new national body that adhered to craft unionism was organized in the Federation of Organized Trades and Labor Unions. The Federation changed its name in 1886 to the American Federation of Labor (AFL). The leader of the new union was Samuel Gompers, who pursued such conservative goals of craft unionism as autonomy of each national union, exclusion of government from the affairs of the labor union, and collective bargaining as the sole method for negotiation.

After a brief flirt with communism by the Industrial Workers of the World (1905–1920s), the union movement reached another milestone in the 1930s. With the death of Samuel Gompers in

1924, several leaders of the AFL began to take advantage of the changed environment by organizing industrial unions. **Industrial unions** are labor unions that encompass both unskilled and semi-skilled workers. Best known among the new leaders was John L. Lewis, president of the United Mine Workers of America.

The true industrial unionism for mass production workers was born when the Congress of Industrial Organizations (CIO) was organized on November 10, 1935, under the leadership of John L. Lewis. At the time the CIO was organized, the CIO unions were still under the umbrella of the AFL. It was early in 1937 when the CIO unions were finally expelled from the AFL.

AFL-CIO
Late in 1952, the leaders of both unions, William Green (AFL) and Phillip Murray (CIO), died, and so did the animosity between the two organizations. The new leaders, George Meany of the AFL and Walter Reuther of the CIO, made a commitment to a merger to avoid raiding each other's jurisdictional domains and to establish a more powerful voice for unions. Prior to the merger, two issues were keeping the two unions apart: alleged communists in the CIO and corruption in the AFL. When the CIO was accused of housing unions with suspected communists, the CIO expelled these unions, to the satisfaction of the AFL. When the AFL was accused of corruption, the AFL cleaned it up, to the satisfaction of the CIO.

In 1955 the two unions were merged into the American Federation of Labor–Congress of Industrial Organizations (AFL-CIO). Not all unions belong to the AFL-CIO, however. A notable exception is the United Mine Workers of America, with about 300,000 members, which withdrew from the CIO in 1942 as a result of a dispute between John Lewis of the United Mine Workers and Phillip Murray, who was the president of the CIO at the time. The International Brotherhood of Teamsters, with almost 2 million members, was expelled from the AFL-CIO in 1957 for refusing to answer allegations of corruption. Effective November 1, 1987, the Teamsters union was admitted again to the AFL-CIO. The AFL-CIO wanted the Teamsters to bolster its membership, while the Teamsters wanted the AFL-CIO to make it politically unpalatable for the federal government to take legal action against the Teamsters for its alleged corruption charges.

Labor Laws

Labor unions cannot survive for long without the support of society through labor legislation. There are several labor laws that played an important role in the progress of the union movement in the United States. These laws include the Davis-Bacon Act, the Norris-LaGuardia Act, the Wagner Act, the Taft-Hartley Act, the Landrum-Griffin Act, and the Civil Rights Act.

Davis-Bacon Act
In 1931 Congress passed the Davis-Bacon Act, which required contractors and subcontractors of federally financed projects to pay employees wage rates established by private industry, or *prevailing,* in the locality. The *prevailing wages* usually are tied to the union wage scale in the area. The law was intended to assist depressed areas by keeping contractors from importing low-wage workers to these areas. The Davis-Bacon Act is still in force and has an effect of precluding nonunion contractors from bidding on projects financed by the federal and, in many states, the state government.

Norris-LaGuardia Act

An **injunction** refers to a court order that requires one to refrain from doing a specified act. The Norris-LaGuardia Act of 1932 changed the role of the U.S. courts from one of employers' ally to a neutral one by ending an injunction against union activities. The Act states that no court of the United States shall have the jurisdiction to issue any restraining order on temporary or permanent injunction in a case involving a labor dispute. Stated plainly, the Act allows unions to freely engage in such activities as peaceful assembly, organizing, picketing, and striking.

The Act also ended yellow dog contracts. A **yellow dog contract** is a contract that stipulates as a condition of employment that employees not join unions. The yellow dog contract was used by employers to discourage workers from joining labor unions.

Wagner Act

The clear foundation of modern union power was laid in the National Labor Relations Act of 1935, also known as the Wagner Act. According to the Wagner Act, employees have the right to organize, join, or assist labor organizations, and to bargain collectively through representatives of their own choosing. The Wagner Act prohibited discrimination against members of unions either in hiring or in tenure of employment, and made illegal any refusal to bargain collectively with a union certified to represent a majority of the employees. The Wagner Act created the National Labor Relations Board to protect these rights. Over the next 12 years, however, the pendulum swung against labor unions.

Taft-Hartley Act

In 1947 Congress passed the Labor Management Relations Act, also called the Taft-Hartley Act. The Taft-Hartley Act brought pressure to bear on unions to bargain in good faith by declaring many union activities illegal. Among the activities declared illegal by the Taft-Hartley Act are forcing an employer or an independent businessman to join a union; coercing employees into joining a union or a strike; using a closed shop to ensure the security of a union; and having a union shop that was not accepted by the majority vote of the employees in the unit.

A **closed shop** requires union membership as a condition of employment, while a **union shop** requires workers to join a union *after* they are hired. Other arrangements include an open shop and an agency shop. In an **open shop**, workers are not required to join a union even after hiring. At least in principle, workers in states that maintain an open shop have the freedom to join or not to join a union. Workers in these states are said to *have the right to work*. An **agency shop** does not require workers to join a union before or after employment but does require workers to pay union dues to stay on the job.

The opposite of a strike is a **lockout,** in which the employer withholds employment from workers at the expiration of an existing contract. Both strikes and lockouts are legal unless the president of the United States declares, as authorized in the Taft-Hartley Act, that the work stoppage threatens national security.

Landrum-Griffin Act

The Labor-Management Reporting and Disclosure Act, known commonly as the Landrum-Griffin Act, was passed in 1959 to deal with corrupt practices of labor unions. The provisions of the Landrum-Griffin Act include secret ballot election of union officers; the right of each worker to have a copy of the collective bargaining agreement affecting the worker; the requirement that a union have a constitution; and the requirement that financial reporting be made to the U.S. secretary of labor. The Landrum-Griffin Act was hailed as the bill of rights for union members, and opened the door for federal regulation of the internal affairs of unions.

Civil Rights Act

The rights of minority workers were not fully protected until the passage of the Civil Rights Act in 1964. Title VII of the Civil Rights Act made illegal any discrimination against workers based on race, color, religion, sex, or national origin.

Economics of Labor Unions

Leaders of labor unions try to improve the welfare of union members in many ways. Of these, perhaps the most important is to increase wages. There are basically three ways in which unions attempt to raise the wages of their members: (1) restriction of the supply of workers in a given occupation, (2) an increase in demand for labor service that can be provided by union workers, and (3) an outright demand for higher wages. These three approaches to increasing union wages are illustrated in Figure 11.3.

The impact of restricting the supply of workers in a given occupation is shown in Figure 11.3(a). As the supply curve of workers shifts from S to S_u, the equilibrium wage rate increases from W_e to W_u. Unions may employ such strategies as a strict apprenticeship period or an entrance examination before a worker is allowed to work in a given occupation. Professional associations such as the American Medical Association, although not labor unions, may also restrict the supply of workers by requiring strict conditions for accreditation of medical schools.

The impact of an increase in demand for labor service is shown in Figure 11.3(b). As the demand for services of union workers increases from D to D_u, the equilibrium wage rate increases from W_e to W_u. In recent years, unions have seldom used featherbedding as a strategy for increased demand for their services. **Featherbedding** refers to preserving a job no longer needed. Instead, unions have tried to obtain concessions from management in such a way that certain tasks, such as repairing a broken crane, can be performed only by machine workers who are authorized to repair it. This requirement of *no switch* in job assignment becomes an important issue, especially when the nature of the breakdown is so simple that any worker can repair the crane. By allowing only certain workers to repair the crane, unions in fact increase the demand for their services, resulting in high production costs.

When unions are industrial in nature rather than craft, they may simply ask for higher wages for their members. In Figure 11.3(c), unions are shown to demand wages W_u that are higher than equilibrium wages W_e. Realistically, union wages in excess of equilibrium wages are often supported by a reduced level of employment from E_e to, say, E_u, as shown in panel (c).

ECONOMIC RENT

Rent in ordinary conversation means money that landlords collect from tenants for use of their properties. Rent in economics is quite different. **Economic rent** is that part of a payment to the owner of a productive resource over and above the amount that this resource could command in any alternative use. In other words, economic rent is a receipt in excess of opportunity cost. To clarify

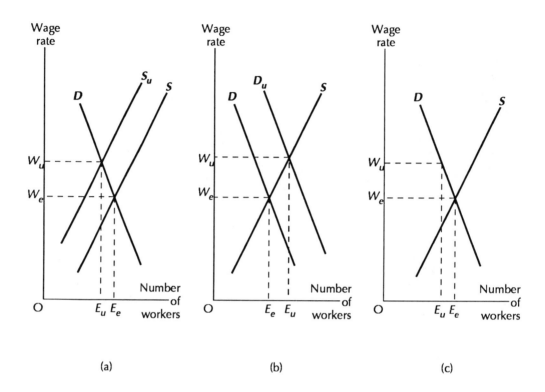

FIGURE 11.3 Three Approaches to Increasing Earnings of Union Members. Labor unions attempt to improve the earnings of their members through a restriction of membership in panel (a), an increase in demand for union workers in panel (b), and an increase in wages per member at the expense of jobs in panel (c).

the meaning of economic rent, suppose that our current salary is $25,000, and the salary that we could receive at our next preferred job is $20,000. The difference, $5,000, is an economic rent. Note that we would still remain at our current job even if any or all of the $5,000 was taken away from us. In this sense, economic rent is a payment that plays no role in allocating resources. Stated in simple terms, this amount is not necessary to attract our services to the current employment.

There are two interesting issues involving economic rent: the concept of a single tax on land, and rent-seeking behavior.

Single Tax on Land

In 1879 Henry George published a book called *Progress and poverty* in which he proposed the idea that land rent might be taxed away completely without reducing the productive potential of the

SUPPLY CURVE FOR PHYSICIANS' SERVICES

Economist Martin Feldstein used time series data for the period 1948 to 1966 to estimate a supply equation for physicians' services in the United States. The supply equation relates the quantity of services supplied per physician to (1) the price of these services, (2) the cost per unit of service provided, (3) the relative significance of net income from private practice, and (4) the number of "interesting cases." The supply equations, obtained by Feldstein, are all backward bending (that is, negative in slope) in the observed range. The backward bending supply curve means that as physicians' fees and their earnings increase, the quantity of physicians' services supplied decreases, not increases. This evidence suggests that regulations that depress a physician's price, such as fee schedules in insurance plans or government ceilings, will increase, rather than decrease, the quantity of the physician's services supplied.

Source: Martin S. Feldstein, The rising price of physicians' services, *Review of Economics and Statistics* 52(May 1970):121–133. Copyright. President and Fellows of Harvard College.

economy. To attract popular support for his ideas about land taxation, George proposed that a tax on land rent be the only tax levied by the government. Thus was born what is known as the single-tax movement. One of the few surviving single-tax colonies is the 4,300 acre Fairhope Single Tax Corporation in Baldwin County, Alabama. The area was organized as a single–tax colony in 1894 and formally became a corporation in 1904. Interestingly enough, nowhere in the leases and lease applications is the Henry George theory mentioned.

Critics of the single-tax movement claim that the idea is not workable for several reasons. First, a tax on land alone would not generate enough revenue to finance all governmental activities. Second, for existing buildings with piecemeal improvements, it would be almost impossible to differentiate pure economic rent from payments for capital improvements. Third, capital gains from the ownership of land are not any different from capital gains from the ownership of other assets such as stocks, bonds, and all collectible items whose value appreciates over time. If a method can be found to separate the pure economic rent owing to the ownership of land from payments for capital improvements, however, Henry George's idea of a single tax on land may be an effective tool for revitalizing sagging parts of communities. The tax on economic rent could be used to punish those who hold onto land solely for the appreciation of its value, and reward those who try to improve properties on the same land.

Rent-Seeking Behavior

One of the most interesting applications of economic rent relates to studies of rent-seeking behavior. Let us see what rent-seeking behavior is all about.

Profit-Seeking

Businesses try to maximize profit by producing goods or services that other competitors have not yet produced. In competitive markets, economic profits disappear through the entry of new firms into the profitable industry. The entry of new firms dissipates profits that existing firms enjoy. So long as there are no barriers to new firms entering an industry, resources are allocated toward industries producing products valued most by society, as indicated by their larger profits. The process of competition, therefore, ensures an efficient allocation of resources. Economic profit in a competitive market is a return to the monopoly power of firms that lasts only until new firms in the industry dissipate the profit through competition. This, of course, is the way a market system is supposed to work. The profit-seeking behavior of firms is the foundation of growth and development in a market economy.

Rent-Seeking

When the profit-seeking behavior of firms or individuals in an institutional setting generates social waste rather than social gain, the behavior is called **rent-seeking behavior.**[1]

Caviar is the processed salted eggs of a fish that are still in the fish's ovarian membrane. Suppose that we somehow convince the government of the health threat to the general public of the handling of caviar by many different firms. Suppose also that we are concerned more with making money than with the public health. We succeed in obtaining the sole license to sell all caviar imported from other countries. Due to the increasing popularity of caviar in the U.S. market, we make a large amount of economic profit. The profit can be viewed as an economic rent since it is a return to the ownership of our monopoly power that is fixed in supply through government license.

The profit-seeking behavior in a competitive market is economically efficient because it reallocates resources toward production of goods and services that are valued more by consumers. Our profit-seeking behavior based on government license, however, is economically inefficient for two reasons. One is that the price of caviar that we charge is higher than the price that might prevail should other firms also sell imported caviar, and the other is that the higher price will reduce the quantity of caviar consumed. Our profit-seeking behavior is also socially wasteful. The arrangement by which we are the only seller of imported caviar adds nothing of net value to the national product. Other firms interested in selling imported caviar in the U.S. market will not simply sit passively, but will invest time, effort, and even bribery to take the license away from us. These activities are clearly socially wasteful and constitute rent-seeking behavior.

If the license to sell imported caviar sounds rather far-fetched, consider the federal licensing of television and radio stations, the local licensing of taxicabs, ambulances, and cable TV suppliers, and many import quotas and licensing practices in newly industrialized countries. When a license is required to engage in a business such as selling alcoholic beverages or dispatching ambulances, the entry of new firms into this business is effectively closed. Only those businesses possessing a license can operate in the industry. The license constitutes a barrier to entry.

In India licenses for imports of intermediate goods were issued in proportion to firms' capacities. Intermediate goods are the goods used to produce other final goods. This mechanism of import licensing led firms to expand their capacity to compete for a greater share of import licenses when, in fact, the expanded capacity was unused.[2] All these activities restrict supply

---

[1]The introduction of the term *rent seeking* is attributed to Anne O. Krueger in her article, The political economy of a rent-seeking society, published in *American Economic Review* 64(June 1974):291–303.

[2]Jagdish Bhagwati and Padma Desai, *Planning for industrialization: A study of India's trade and industrial policies since 1950* (Cambridge, England: Cambridge University Press, 1970).

arbitrarily, raise prices, and cause economic rents to accrue to those who secure the right to engage in these activities. These activities, although competitive in their own right, are purely rent-seeking and represent a waste of resources that could have been used productively elsewhere.

One solution to the rent-seeking problem is for the government to auction these valued *rights* among prospective entrants into the market. The auction effectively converts the licenses into private property rights that can be marketable, thereby eliminating rent-seeking.[3]

INTEREST

Interest is the price that one pays for use of money owned by others, and is expressed in percentage terms. The money borrowed is called the principal. An annual rate of interest of 10 percent on $1,000 of principal is $100. Like other prices, the rate of interest is determined by demand for money available for loan and supply of money available for loan.

Determination of the Interest Rate

The amount of money available for loan is called **loanable funds.** The determination of interest rates is shown in Figure 11.4. The vertical axis represents interest rates, while the horizontal axis represents loanable funds. The market rate of interest OA is determined by the equilibrium between demand for loanable funds and supply of loanable funds. The demand for loanable funds comprises different levels of government financing deficits, business investment, and household credit purchases. The sources of loanable funds include budget surpluses, especially by state and local governments; business and household savings; and an increase in money supply by the banking system.

All interest rates vary with the risk and the length of each loan. In general, interest rates are higher the riskier the loans are and the longer the duration of the loans. The reason for higher long-term rates is the uncertainty about future rates of inflation. To compensate for possible unexpected inflation in the long run, long-term rates of interest are usually set higher than short-term rates.

Selected Interest Rates

There are three interest rates that are widely watched by the general public: the discount rate, the mortgage rate, and the prime rate. The **discount rate,** changed occasionally by the Federal Reserve System, is the interest rate levied by the Federal Reserve Bank on loans made to depository institutions such as commercial banks and savings and loan associations. (The Federal Reserve System is explained in detail in Chapter 17.)

A **mortgage rate** is an interest rate charged on loans made to purchase real properties such as a house or land. Home builders also pay the mortgage rate on money they borrow to build houses. If the mortgage payment is guaranteed by the Veterans' Administration, the mortgage rate is called a *VA-insured* rate. If the mortgage payment is insured by the Federal Housing Administration, the mortgage rate is called an *FHA-insured* rate. If the mortgage rate is freely determined by supply and

---

[3]Types of rent-seeking behavior are wide ranging, and general theories of rent seeking are yet to emerge. An excellent reference on rent-seeking behavior is Buchanan, James M., Robert D. Tollison, and Gordon Tullock (eds.), *Toward a theory of the rent-seeking society* (College Station, Texas: Texas A&M University Press, 1980).

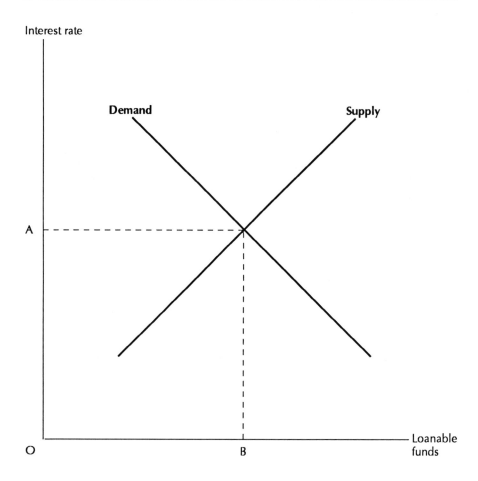

FIGURE 11.4 Determination of the Interest Rate. The interest rate (OA) in a competitive market is determined by demand for and supply of loanable funds. Sources of the demand and supply of loanable funds are discussed in the text.

demand, it is called a *conventional* mortgage rate. The conventional mortgage rate typically applies to the purchase of houses that are relatively expensive.

The **prime rate** is the interest rate that a bank charges on loans made to its most creditworthy business customers. Prime rates are determined by individual banks but show a significant uniformity because of competition among banks in securing loanable funds and in attracting prime customers. Prime rate is discussed further in Chapter 17.

Nominal versus Real Rate of Interest

Interest rates may be classified as nominal or real, depending on how inflation is treated. The **nominal rate of interest** is the rate of interest calculated on current dollars. Practically all interest rates quoted in business transactions are nominal rates. The **real rate of interest** is the nominal rate of interest adjusted for the effects of inflation. As a practical matter, the real rate of interest is obtained by subtracting the rate of inflation from the nominal rate of interest.[4] Economists believe that it is the real rate of interest, not the nominal rate of interest, that determines the level of economic activities. Other things being equal, borrowers are expected to borrow more money when the nominal rate of interest is 10 percent and the expected rate of inflation is 8 percent, than when the nominal rate of interest is 5 percent and the expected rate of inflation is, say, 1 percent. The real rate of interest for the former case is 2 percent, obtained by subtracting 8 percent from 10 percent, whereas the real rate of interest for the latter is 4 percent, obtained by subtracting 1 percent from 5 percent.

Historical rates of real interest are obtained by subtracting the historical rates of inflation from the nominal rates of interest for the corresponding periods. The nominal rate of interest for future years, economists argue, should be based on the underlying real rate of interest plus the *expected,* rather than *current,* rate of inflation. The real rate of interest, therefore, is obtained by subtracting the *expected* rate of inflation from the nominal rate of interest. There is no such thing as *the* real rate of interest. Reason must prevail in determining the long-term real rate of interest. A negative real rate of interest or a very high real rate of interest is clearly a short-term aberration. Various studies suggest that the long-term real rate of interest ranges between 1 and 3 percent.[5]

PROFITS

Economic profit is a return on the entrepreneurial contribution to production. Economic profit is obtained by subtracting total cost from total revenue in which total cost is the sum of explicit and implicit costs. The concept of cost, therefore, includes a normal rate of return. A practical definition of the **normal rate of return** is the average rate of return on investment in all industries. An **economic profit** is realized when a firm or firms in an industry earn profits that are greater than the average rate of return on investment in the economy.

The average return on investment in a given industry is called the **profit norm.** Data on profit norms at the industry level have a wide range of applications.[6] Profit norms allow us to evaluate a company's profitability by comparing it with that of its peers in terms of size and geographic area.

---

[4]According to the Fisher effect, if lenders and borrowers anticipate identical rates of inflation, then the nominal rate of interest is equal to the real rate of interest plus the rate of anticipated inflation. For more on the Fisher effect, see Irving Fisher, *The theory of interest* (New York: Macmillan, 1930).

[5]Selected references on the real rate of interest include: Holland, A. Steven, Real interest rates: What accounts for their recent rise?, The Federal Reserve Bank of St. Louis *Review* 66(December 1984):18–29; Angelo Mascaro and Alan H. Meltzer, Long- and short-term interest rates in a risky world, *Journal of Monetary Economics* (November 1983):485–518; and James A. Wilcox, Why real interest rates were so low in the 1970s, *American Economic Review* 73(March 1983):44–53.

[6]A standard reference for industrywide profit norms is the set of *Industry norms* books published by Dun & Bradstreet in New York. A briefer and less extensive reference on profit norms is *Annual statement studies,* published by Robert Morris Associates, a national association of bank loan and credit officers located in Philadelphia.

The comparison enables financial companies to determine the creditworthiness of firms before loans are made to these companies. The comparison may also be used by firms that plan to grow through mergers and acquisitions of other firms, and by firms that are targets of such takeovers. Firms that are considering a merger with another firm may want to examine the profitability of the target firm, while target firms for merger may use profit norms to identify firms with which a merger is more desirable. The idea at the heart of using profit norms for financial analysis is to identify regularities of the industry and potential irregularities of individual firms.

There is no single predominant theory that explains the source of economic profits. Proposed sources include business ventures undertaking uninsurable risks, business innovations such as new products or new marketing strategies, and the existence of monopoly power. What is clear, however, is the role that economic profits play in allocating scarce resources among alternative uses. Resources continue to be transferred from industries suffering losses or experiencing smaller economic profits to industries enjoying greater economic profits.

SUMMARY

Profit-maximizing firms are expected to employ a productive resource so long as the marginal revenue product of the resource is equal to or greater than its marginal factor cost. According to the marginal productivity theory of income distribution, owners of productive resources are paid according to the marginal productivity of the resource. Wage differences among workers are explained by their level of education, the lack of mobility of workers, equalizing differences, and the existence of active labor unions. The progress of American unionism is a good example of social Darwinism. Labor unions that did not support political democracy did not survive. The Federation of Organized Trades and Labor Unions was organized in 1881 and changed its name in 1886 to the American Federation of Labor (AFL). Industrial unionism for mass production workers was born when the Congress of Industrial Organizations (CIO) was organized on November 10, 1935. In 1955 the two unions were merged into the American Federation of Labor–Congress of Industrial Organizations (AFL-CIO). The existence of labor unions requires the support of society through labor legislation. Important labor laws include the Davis-Bacon Act (1931), the Norris-LaGuardia Act (1932), the Wagner Act (1935), the Taft-Hartley Act (1947), the Landrum-Griffin Act (1959), and the Civil Rights Act (1964).

Economic rent is a payment to the owner of a resource fixed in supply. Economic rent is an allocatively unnecessary payment, since this payment is not necessary in attracting resources to their current employment. Henry George spearheaded a single tax on land movement through the publication of *Progress and poverty* (1879), a book in which he proposed the idea that land rent might be taxed away completely without reducing the productive potential of the economy. When firms or individuals in an institutional setting engage in profit-seeking behavior that only generates social waste, such behavior is called rent-seeking. Interest is the price that one pays for use of money owned by others and is determined by demand for and supply of loanable funds. Interest rates are higher proportionate to increasing risk and increasing length of loans. The real rate of interest is the nominal rate of interest from which the expected rate of inflation is subtracted. The long-term real rate of interest ranges between 1 and 3 percent. Economic profits play a critical role in allocating scarce resources among alternative uses by transferring resources to industries that enjoy economic profits.

EXERCISES

1. What is meant by derived demand?

2. To profit-maximizing firms, the optimal quantity of inputs demanded means the quantity of inputs that leads to the maximum amount of profit. How do profit-maximizing firms determine the optimal quantity of inputs?

3. What is the marginal revenue product?

4. What is the marginal productivity theory of income distribution, and what problems would result if the theory were applied throughout the economy?

5. What are some reasons for the differences in wages that individual workers earn?

6. Briefly explain each of the following labor laws:

   a. Davis-Bacon Act
   b. Norris-LaGuardia Act
   c. Wagner Act
   d. Taft-Hartley Act
   e. Landrum-Griffin Act

7. A recent development in studies of economic rent relates to the rent-seeking behavior of individuals. What is rent-seeking behavior, and what is the major cause for such behavior?

8. What is the difference between the nominal rate of interest and the real rate of interest?

9. According to the April 15, 1985, issue of *Fortune* (pp. 105–106), University Patents, Inc., of Westport, Connecticut, is owned publicly, and promotes the commercial potential of faculty research of professors from eight universities. About 40 percent of royalties received from users of patents held by University Patents goes to the company, 15 to 30 percent to faculty inventors, and the remainder to the universities. Think about the 30 to 45 percent of royalty income submitted to the universities. Does that portion of income represent wages, interest, economic rent, or economic profit?

10. Presented in Table 11.4 are nominal and real rates of interest. The 90-day T-bill is a bill issued by the U.S. Department of Treasury that expires in 90 days. On the basis of the table, what can be said about the difference between the nominal rate and the real rate of interest?

TABLE 11.4 Nominal (*N*) and Estimated Real (*R*) Interest Rates, 1953–1990

	Interest Rates (%)						
	90-Day T-Bill Rate		Prime Rate		New Home Mortgage Yield		Inflation Rate
Year	N	R	N	R	N	R	
1953	1.94	1.19	3.17	2.42	4.30	3.55	0.75
1954	0.95	0.58	3.05	2.68	4.60	4.23	0.37
1955	1.75	2.12	3.16	3.53	4.65	5.02	−0.37
1956	2.66	1.17	3.77	2.28	4.65	3.16	1.49
1957	3.26	−0.05	4.20	0.89	4.65	1.34	3.31
1958	1.84	−1.01	3.83	0.98	5.49	2.64	2.85
1959	3.41	2.72	4.48	3.79	5.49	4.80	0.69
1960	2.95	1.23	4.82	3.10	6.16	4.44	1.72
1961	2.38	1.37	4.50	3.49	6.16	5.15	1.01
1962	2.78	1.44	4.50	3.16	5.60	4.26	1.34
1963	3.16	2.17	4.50	3.51	5.84	4.85	0.99
1964	3.55	2.24	4.50	3.19	5.78	4.47	1.31
1965	3.95	2.34	4.53	2.92	5.74	4.13	1.61
1966	4.88	1.71	5.63	2.46	6.14	2.97	3.17
1967	4.33	1.56	5.63	2.86	6.33	3.56	2.77
1968	5.34	1.15	6.28	2.09	6.83	2.64	4.19
1969	6.69	1.23	7.95	2.49	7.66	2.20	5.46
1970	6.44	0.72	7.91	2.19	8.27	2.55	5.72
1971	4.34	−0.04	5.70	1.32	7.59	3.21	4.38
1972	4.07	0.86	5.25	2.04	7.45	4.24	3.21
1973	7.03	0.81	8.02	1.80	7.95	1.73	6.22
1974	7.87	−3.17	10.80	−0.24	8.92	−2.12	11.04
1975	5.82	−3.31	7.86	−1.27	8.75	−0.38	9.13
1976	5.00	−0.76	6.84	1.08	8.76	3.00	5.76
1977	5.27	−1.23	6.82	0.32	8.80	2.30	6.50
1978	7.22	−0.37	9.06	1.47	9.30	1.71	7.59
1979	10.04	−1.31	12.67	1.32	10.48	−0.87	11.35
1980	11.61	−1.89	15.27	1.77	12.25	−1.25	13.50
1981	14.08	3.76	18.87	8.55	14.17	3.85	10.32
1982	10.72	4.56	14.86	8.70	14.47	8.31	6.16
1983	8.62	5.41	10.79	7.58	12.20	8.99	3.21
1984	9.57	5.25	12.04	7.72	11.87	7.55	4.32
1985	7.49	3.93	9.93	6.37	11.12	7.56	3.56
1986	5.97	4.11	8.33	6.47	9.82	7.96	1.86
1987	5.83	2.18	8.20	4.55	8.94	5.29	3.65
1988	6.67	2.53	9.32	5.18	8.81	4.67	4.14
1989	8.12	3.30	10.80	5.98	9.56	4.74	4.82
1990	7.21	3.34	9.24	5.37	9.85	5.98	3.87

Sources: Business Conditions Digest and DATADISK from Cambridge Planning, Cambridge, Mass. Figures from 1989 are estimates.

SUGGESTED READINGS

Buchanan, James M., Tollison, Robert D., and Tullock, Gordon (eds.). (1980). *Toward a theory of the rent-seeking society.* College Station, Texas: Texas A&M University Press.

A collection of 21 provocative articles by 18 economists on the concept of rent-seeking behavior of individuals and groups that seek a transfer of wealth toward themselves through an organization.

Espenshade, Thomas J. (1984). *Investing in children.* Washington, D.C.: The Urban Institute Press.

Presents estimates of parental expenditures on children from birth to age 18. Expenditures are found to vary widely with the parents' socioeconomic status, number of children, and the wife's employment status.

Gregory, Charles O. (1961). *Labor and the law.* 2nd ed. New York: W. W. Norton.

A good reference on labor laws and the history of labor unions.

Hildebrand, George H. (1979). *American unionism: An historical and analytical survey.* Reading, Mass.: Addison-Wesley.

A good summary of the development of the union movement in the United States.

Martin, Gerald D., and Clay, William C., Jr. (n.d.). *How to win maximum awards for lost earnings: A guide to estimating damages fairly and proving them in court.* Englewood Cliffs, N.J.: Executive Reports Corporation.

A good introductory book if one is interested in working as an economic expert witness or as a lawyer specializing in wrongful death and injury cases.

12

Correcting Market Failures

Market Failures and Needs for
  Regulation

Deregulation of Industries

Antitrust Laws

THE REGULATION OF PRIVATE FIRMS by the government is a fact of life. In employment practices, firms pay attention to the rules of the Equal Employment Opportunity and the National Labor Relations Board. In corporate financing, firms should follow rules formulated by the Internal Revenue Service, the Securities Exchange Commission, and the Small Business Administration. In manufacturing, firms need to meet standards established by the Occupational Safety and Health Administration, the Environmental Protection Agency, and the U.S. Army Corps of Engineers if production involves use of a waterway. In pricing and marketing, firms must consider antitrust laws as well as the rules of the Federal Trade Commission, the Food and Drug Administration, and the Consumer Product Safety Commission. Underlying this maze of rules and regulations of governmental agencies, there has to be some coherence that can be expressed in terms of hypotheses or theories as to why government regulates the private sector. This chapter is concerned with such hypotheses.

MARKET FAILURE AND NEEDS FOR REGULATION

Suppose that a shortage of paper towels develops. In a competitive market, the shortage causes the price of paper towels to increase, signaling the shortage of the product. As the price of paper towels increases, existing firms will increase the quantity supplied of paper towels including Bounty, Job Squad, Viva, Brawny, and ScotTowels. New firms may also enter the industry, further increasing the supply of paper towels in the market. If a surplus develops, the opposite reaction will occur in the market. Most existing firms will reduce the quantity of the product they supply, while others will leave the industry.

Markets may not work as smoothly as they are described here, however. When price fails to signal shortages or surpluses of a product, the market fails to reallocate resources from one industry with surplus products to another industry experiencing a shortage of its product. **Market failure** occurs when price does not signal shortages and surpluses of a product in a given market.

Types of Market Failure

Broadly speaking, there are two types of market failure: competitive and contrived. Competitive market failures are the types of failures that occur in a competitive market through the profit-maximizing behavior of firms. Competitive market failures are the by-products of competition in the market and occur even if firms have no intention of monopolizing the market. Competitive market failures are further classified into two groups: natural monopoly and externalities. These two groups are discussed in this section.

The other type of market failure is contrived in the sense that firms act with an intent to create monopoly power through monopolization, price fixing, and other measures of unfair competition. Contrived market failures are discussed in the second half of this chapter under antitrust laws.

Natural Monopoly

A **natural monopoly** is a firm that can supply the entire market demand on the declining portion of the firm's long-run average cost curve. Natural monopolies tend to develop in markets in which economies of scale are so large that the largest firm can supply the product at the lowest cost per unit. Figure 12.1 graphically illustrates a natural monopoly. The long-run average cost curve of a firm declines for the entire market demand (*OQ*). If two or more firms share the market, the cost of production will increase above the level *OC*.

When a market is characterized by a natural monopoly, the largest firm will eventually be able to drive its smaller competitors out of the market. Once the monopoly status has been established, the natural monopoly will have the monopoly power to restrict output, raise prices, and earn monopoly profits.

Government has two choices in dealing with natural monopolies. One choice is to *do nothing*—allowing competition to work itself out and the natural monopoly to dominate the market. If the natural monopoly charges the full-cost price that only permits a normal rate of return to the firm, the price charged by the natural monopoly will be lower than the price that would prevail when several other firms are also allowed to operate in the same market. A more likely outcome is that the price charged by the natural monopoly will be higher than the price that would prevail when several other firms are also allowed to operate in the same market. This outcome is likely because the natural monopoly is expected to exert its monopoly power to increase profits.

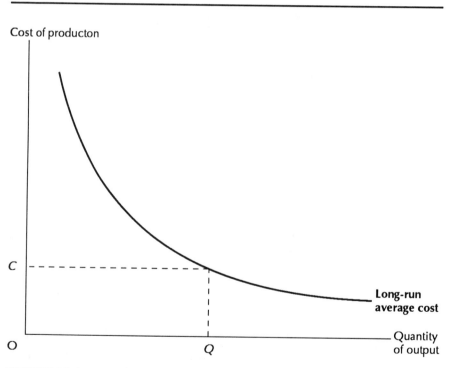

FIGURE 12.1 Natural Monopoly. If an industry is characterized by a natural monopoly, one firm can produce products (*OQ*) at a lower cost (*OC*) than many firms can.

The other choice in dealing with natural monopolies is to minimize the potential waste of resources by allowing only one firm to operate in the market but to regulate that firm's rate of return on investment. This is the usual approach taken by the state and local government. Public utilities such as electricity, natural gas, water and sewer, and local telephone services are allowed to operate as a monopoly subject to state and local regulation.

Externalities

To understand externalities, consider air. No one owns the air. Since no one has property rights to the air, no one has control over its use. Air in fact is a free input into the production process. Firms will use air as much as they can because it is free. This is how the market works, but the result is air pollution. Unfortunately, air pollution affects not only the firms that pollute the air, but the general public as well.

Defining Externalities
Externalities refer to the effects of production on parties other than the immediate buyer and seller. If externalities benefit the third party, **external benefits** or **external economies** are said to exist. If externalities harm the third party, **external costs** or **external diseconomies** are said to exist. Externalities are also called **spillover effects**. Examples of external benefits include a road paved and used by a firm and made available for use by the general public, or flu shots made by a drug company that benefit the entire society. Examples of external costs include all types of pollution.

Graphic Illustration
Figure 12.2 shows how externalities affect resource allocation. The demand for and supply of a product produced by a firm that incurs external costs such as air or water pollution are indicated as D and S. The market price and the quantity of the product traded are OP and OQ. Assuming that the firm cleans up pollution before it is discharged, the average cost of production goes up by the distance AB. Distance AB represents external costs measured on the per-unit basis. In other words, the supply curve without pollution is S'. The price without pollution is OP', which is higher than OP because the new price OP' includes the cost of cleaning up pollution. The quantity traded without pollution is OQ', which is smaller than OQ because consumers will buy a smaller quantity at a higher price.

When there exist external costs such as water or air pollution, the supply curve of the product does not account for such costs incurred by society, and thus the market price tends to underestimate the social cost of production. **Social cost** measures the amount of other goods and services that society as a whole sacrifices to produce a given product. Social cost, therefore, includes both the firm's private cost of production and externalities. When external benefits exist, the demand curve of the product does not account for the benefits received by society, and thus the market price tends to underestimate the true value of the product.

What to Do about Externalities
Government has several options in dealing with the problem of externalities. For production of goods and services, such as flu shots, that benefit the general public, the government may provide a subsidy for research and development. The subsidy encourages production of these products by

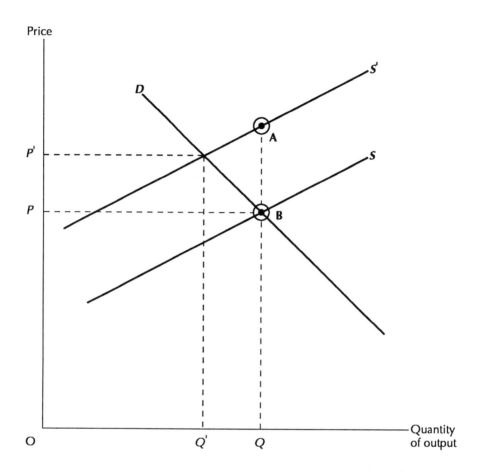

FIGURE 12.2 Effects of External Diseconomies. If a firm is forced to clean up pollution before it is discharged, the price of the product increases from *OP* to *OP'*, and the quantity of the product traded decreases from *OQ* to *OQ'*.

private firms that are not in a position to recover costs of producing the portion of benefits that accrues to the general public.

For goods and services whose production generates external diseconomies such as water or air pollution, the government may force firms to *internalize* the external costs through the levy of a pollution fee or direct regulation by the Environmental Protection Agency. In this case, the government regulation causes the supply curve of the product to be shifted upward so that the supply curve can accurately measure the true costs of production to society. The government may also levy a tax on firms according to the amount of pollution that these firms emit and then use the tax revenue to clean up the pollution. In this case, the new tax also causes the supply curve of the product to be shifted upward and accurately measure the social cost of producing the product.

Theories of Government Regulation

Two theories are proposed to explain why government regulates the private sector of the economy. One is the public interest theory and the other is the capture theory.

Public Interest Theory

According to the **public interest theory of regulation,** government regulates industries in response to public demand for correction of market failures. To view the public interest theory in proper perspective, let us classify government regulation into two broad groups: economic regulation and social regulation. **Economic regulation,** also called **industrial regulation,** refers to government regulation of specific industries such as airlines, trucking, taxi service, railroad, community-antenna television (CATV), now called cable TV, and others. In economic regulation, government is concerned with the overall economic performance of these industries separately. **Social regulation,** on the other hand, refers to government regulation across industries. In social regulation, government is concerned with issues such as safety and pollution that are common to many industries. The public interest theory appears more appropriate in explaining social regulation than economic regulation.

Richard A. Posner, of the University of Chicago Law School, reviewed a large number of studies on regulation and concluded that regulation was not positively correlated with the presence of monopolistic market structure.[1] If economic regulation is unrelated to the monopoly power of markets, economic regulation is not addressing the most important issue in government regulation, which is to make the market more competitive by reducing the monopoly power of firms. Posner claims that there is nothing intrinsic that requires government regulation in such industries as airlines, trucking, stock brokerage, ocean shipping, taxi service, and other heavy industries.

Capture Theory

The alternative to the public interest theory is the capture theory of regulation. The capture theory is more appropriate for explaining regulation of specific industries. According to the capture theory, government regulates industries not to protect public interest but to protect and promote the interests of the industries that are regulated.[2] The capture theory claims that government regulation is provided in response to the demand by firms in the regulated industry to maximize their profits. Regulatory services provided to firms in the regulated industries include price fixing, route fixing, restriction on entry through a license, and subsidies. Firms operating in a regulated industry are often protected from any cutthroat price competition or an erosion of market share by new entry into the industry. Regulations of this type are usually justified in terms of promoting the quality of service or the safety of consumers.

---

[1] Richard A. Posner, Theories of economic regulation, *Bell Journal of Economics and Management Science* 5(Autumn 1974):335–358.

[2] For the capture theory, see George J. Stigler, The theory of economic regulation, *Bell Journal of Economics and Management Science* 2(Spring 1971):3–21; and Sam Peltzman, Toward a more general theory of regulation, *Journal of Law and Economics* 19(August 1976):211–240.

DEREGULATION OF INDUSTRIES

Many government regulations began during the Great Depression years of the 1930s and continued to expand until the mid-1970s. The number of pages of the *Federal Register*, which publishes all proposed and adopted regulations, was no more than 2,599 in 1936, but increased to 14,479 in 1960,

---

A STORY OF COMMERCIAL PARKING OPERATORS

In a city not far away there was a stadium used for football games played on Saturday afternoons by the local university team. On football afternoons, many people not in the parking lot business went into the parking lot business by directing cars into their driveways. One day, commercial parking lot owners operating in the vicinity organized the Association of Professional Parking Lot Employers, or APPLE. Every member of APPLE pledged $1.00 per parking space for something called a slush fund, but it was never made clear whose slush would be bought with these funds. Several months later, however, a resolution was adopted by the city council requiring licensing for anyone in the parking lot business. Requirements for a license included liability insurance, bonding for each car parked, and more.

On their way to the stadium for the next big game, drivers encountered a large number of police officers informing them that it was illegal to park at unlicensed parking lots. Long lines of waiting cars appeared at the commercial parking lots located within 12 blocks of the stadium. Little by little, cars started appearing again in residential driveways for car washes on football afternoons. Car washes were popular, especially on rainy days! In the meantime, traffic at commercial parking lots was extremely bad and getting worse.

Political pressure by drivers on the city council was mounting to do something about the traffic jams at commercial parking lots. The city council sent a stern note to APPLE, which in turn recruited a team of consulting faculty from the local university's computer science department. The study group concluded that what was needed was more computers, and recommended that all members of APPLE be hooked into one computer to facilitate the logistics of moving cars to the most accessible spaces. Many commercial parking lot operators bought new computers and began arguing that they needed higher parking fees to cover higher operating costs. The city council granted a 10 percent increase in parking fees.

Many people started using city buses and stayed home to watch the football games on TV. Complaints about parking were so bad that students and faculty put severe pressure on the university administration, which finally dropped intercollegiate football altogether and converted the stadium into a park for underprivileged children.

Source: Adapted from Henry G. Manne, The parable of the parking lots, *The Public Interest* 23(Spring 1971):10–15.

finally reaching a peak of 87,012 in 1980. Late in the 1970s, a forceful movement toward the deregulation of industries took place. In this section, we study the mid-1970s to the mid-1980s, an important period in the history of government regulation.

Why Deregulate?

Perhaps the most important question concerning deregulation of industries is, why bother? What are we trying to achieve through deregulation? The primary objective of deregulating industries is to improve economic efficiency by allocating resources toward production of goods and services that are valued more by society. Specific objectives are (1) lower prices and increased quantities of products traded, (2) improved quality of services, and (3) improved managerial efficiency. Whether or not deregulation of industries has been successful, therefore, should be judged on the basis of how many of these objectives have been achieved by deregulation. We may also anticipate a concentration of market shares to develop in the process of achieving these objectives. The concentration of market power may negate at least some advantages of deregulation.

Theory of Contestable Markets

Let us pause for a moment and think about whether or not deregulation is likely to achieve these objectives. It would not be prudent to deregulate industries without thinking through what the likely results of the deregulation would be. The major theoretical basis for the deregulation of industries is the theory of contestable markets, presented earlier in Chapter 10.

The **theory of contestable markets** hypothesizes that firms in a highly concentrated market behave as if the market is competitive so long as the entry to and the exit from the market are costless. When markets are deregulated, a concentration of market share among a few firms is expected. According to the theory of contestable markets, the market concentration is not a problem so long as government ensures the free entry of new firms into and their free exit from the market.

Evaluating Market Concentration

The hypothesis that market concentration does not matter in contestable markets does not mean that market concentration has no influence on economic efficiency. To clarify this statement, we classify market concentration into two types.

One type of market concentration is based on the concept of the economies of large-scale operations. According to this explanation, firms are merged to take advantage of decreasing long-run average costs of production through economies of scale. When firms are allowed to merge through deregulation for the purpose of taking advantage of the scale economies, the optimal sizes of the merged firms are determined by the minimum efficient scale. An increased market concentration would be consistent with the theory of contestable markets only to the extent that the scale of merged firms does not exceed the minimum efficient scale. If the scale of production of merged firms were greater than the minimum efficient scale, the benefits of deregulation accruing to society would not be maximized through mergers.

The other type of market concentration is based on monopolization. According to this explanation, there are no cost advantages from a merger, and firms are merged to create a firm that has a larger market share and thus greater market power. If firms are merged for the purpose of monopolizing the market, the concentration is expected to have a detrimental effect on society. Antitrust laws are designed to prevent firms from monopolizing the market.

Later in this section, we study whether or not deregulation led to the fulfillment of the objectives that promoters of deregulation had in mind. Before that, however, let us go over the trends of deregulation during the mid-1970s to the mid-1980s.

Trends of Deregulation

Deregulation is the process of dismantling a regulation that is already in force. Since most regulations have been accumulated over a long period of time, it is difficult to say when regulation of a given industry started.

Legal Basis for Deregulation

Table 12.1 illustrates how regulations have a tendency to accumulate. Although this example is rather extreme, the table shows that numerous safety measures had been taken from 1968 to 1982. These measures added $1,600 to the cost of making an automobile in 1982 prices.

Significant laws and events that led to the regulation and deregulation of selected major industries are summarized in Table 12.2. The major laws that deregulated the airline, bank, natural gas, railroad, ocean shipping, telephone, and trucking industries were all passed between 1978 and 1984, clearly indicating the importance of that seven-year period in the history of government regulation.

Verdict on Deregulation

By 1986 at least a partial verdict on the deregulation of industries was in. Studies point out that prices in 1986 were lower than the prices that would have prevailed without deregulation in such industries as airlines, railroads, trucking, barge transportation, and long-distance telephone services.[3] Lower prices mean that the quantity of goods or services traded is greater than would have been traded without deregulation. Studies also indicate a trend toward concentration in industries characterized by the economies of scale, such as airlines and railroads. In railroads, for instance, the number of large rail-freight carriers decreased from 13 in 1978 to only 6 in 1986. The 6 carriers were controlling 86 percent of the rail-freight market in 1986. When industries were not characterized by the economies of scale, however, the number of new firms entering an industry increased. In trucking, for instance, no less than 17,000 new firms entered the industry between 1978 and 1986, but 6,470 firms in the industry failed during the same period, indicating the volatility of the market following deregulation. The turmoil in the trucking industry was concentrated mostly on the *truckload* (TL) part of the industry, which offers simple point-to-point haulage. In the *less-than-truckload* (LTL) part of the industry, which routes small lots through terminal networks, the 10 largest firms controlled 60 percent of the LTL shipments.

The deregulation of the telephone industry was the one least liked by the public. On July 8, 1982, Federal District Court Judge Harold H. Greene approved the consent decree that ordered the American Telephone and Telegraph (AT&T) company to reorganize. Until that time, AT&T had been a government-approved natural monopoly. On January 1, 1984, AT&T became a private firm specializing in long-distance telephone service whose market was no longer protected by the

---

[3]Early articles on the effects of deregulation include Is deregulation working?, *Business Week*, December 22, 1986, pp. 50–54; Stephen Koepp, Rolling back regulation, *Time*, July 6, 1987, pp. 50–52; and Kenneth Labich, Why bigger is better in the airline wars, *Fortune*, March 31, 1986, pp. 52–58.

Table 12.1 Increase in Retail Price of Automobiles Due to
Federal Requirements

Year of Regulation	Action	Estimated Current Cost (1982 dollars)
1968	Seat and shoulder belts, standards for exhaust emissions	$ 62
1968–69	Windshield defrosting and defogging systems, door latches and hinge systems, lamps, reflective devices, and associated equipment	19
1968–70	Theft protection (steering, transmission, and ignition locking and buzzing systems)	16
1969	Head restraints	35
1969–73	Improved side-door strength	27
1970	Reflective devices and further emissions standards	20
1971	Fuel evaporative systems	37
1972	Improved exhaust emissions; seat-belt warning system and locking systems on retractors	55
1972-73	Exterior protection	123
1973	Reduced flammability of interior materials; locations, identification, and illumination of controls improvements	11
1974	Improved exhaust emissions and interlock systems	172
1975	Additional safety features and catalytic converter	189
1976	Hydraulic brakes, improved bumpers (less savings from interlock removal)	54
1977	Leak-resistant fuel system	27
1978	Redesign of emissions controls	13
1979	Emissions and safety standards	21
1980	Redesign of emissions controls, bumper damage standards	144
1981	Emissions controls and improved fuel economy	490
1982	Improved fuel economy	85
	Total	$1,600

Source: Murray L. Weidenbaum, *Business, government, and the public,* 3rd
ed. (Englewood Cliffs, N.J.: Prentice Hall, 1986), p. 70.

Table 12.2 Laws for Regulation and Deregulation

Industry	Basis for Regulation	Basis for Deregulation
Airline	Civil Aeronautics Act (1938)	Airline Deregulation Act (1978)
Banks		Depository Institutions Deregulation and Monetary Control Act (1980)
Natural Gas	Natural Gas Act (1938)	Natural Gas Policy Act (1978)
Railroad	Interstate Commerce Act (1887)	Staggers Rail Act (1980)
Shipping	Interstate Commerce Act (1887)	Shipping Act (1984)
Telephone	Federal Communications Commission (1934)	Consent decree of AT&T divesture (1982) and AT&T break-up (1984)
Trucking	Interstate Commerce Act (1887)	Motor Carrier Act (1980)

government. Since AT&T was a monopolist, many expected its market share to decrease substantially after deregulation. By 1986, however, AT&T still controlled 82 percent of the long-distance market. Only MCI and U.S. Sprint had more than 1 percent market shares. Before the 1984 break-up of AT&T, it was widely believed that local telephone service was subsidized by incomes that the company earned from its long-distance telephone service. Within three years after the break-up, long-distance rates were lowered by 20 percent, local rates were raised by approximately 35 percent, and the overall telephone bill increased by 25 percent. Since the break-up, however, the number of telephone makers selling to the U.S. market has increased from 25 to more than 200.

Prospects for More Deregulation
The movement toward deregulation may continue for years to come. Several industries that are currently regulated may be ripe for deregulation. These industries include electricity service, local telephone service, satellite communications, and investment banking.[4]

The service of electrical power delivery is a natural monopoly in that the cost of delivering a kilowatt hour of electricity tends to be lower when one company supplies a given local market. The potential for deregulation lies in the generation of electricity, which can be separated from the delivery service of electricity. The delivery service, therefore, may remain regulated, but generation

---

[4]A good summary on the issue of industries that may be ripe for deregulation was made by Levinson in Marc Levinson, The verdict of deregulation, *Dun's Business Month*, November 1986, pp. 30–34.

can be made competitive by allowing local distribution companies to buy electricity on the open market. The seed for deregulation in the generation of electricity may have been sown already. In many rural areas, relatively small electricity co-operatives have long been delivering power that they do not generate. Certain manufacturing plants generate their own electricity under an arrangement called **cogeneration,** by which these plants sell excess electricity to the local power company.

The monopoly power of local telephone companies has steadily been eroded through the availability of cellular phones and satellite transmitters that allow large users of local telephone services to bypass local telephone systems. In the case of communications satellites, all communications satellites are owned by the International Telecommunications Satellite Organization, a consortium of over 100 countries, while telephone and telex transmission companies lease space on Intelsat's satellites. Eventually, private companies may construct their own satellite systems and compete with Intelsat in carrying nonvoice traffic. This added competition would effectively limit Intelsat's ability to subsidize service to developing countries with revenues from high-traffic routes.

Finally, federally regulated banks are currently barred from securities underwriting. **Securities underwriting** means that a bank or a securities firm sells securities to the public on behalf of the firm or agency that issues the securities. Already, American bank holding companies are underwriting securities abroad, and foreign banks do the same in the United States. Early in 1989, the Federal Reserve Board authorized subsidiaries of Federal Reserve member banks to underwrite a limited range of securities. These securities include (1) municipal revenue bonds, which local governments issue to assist local industrial development, and (2) commercial papers that corporations issue to borrow money.

The Case of the Airline Industry

For some unknown reason, the deregulation of the airline industry has attracted a disproportionate amount of attention from those studying the effects of deregulation.[5] During the time between the passage of the Civil Aeronautics Act of 1938 and the Airline Deregulation Act of 1978, the Civil Aeronautics Board (CAB) maintained control over the two important decisions airlines had to make: where to fly and how much to charge. This meant that airlines could compete with one another only through nonprice competition such as offering more frequent flights or free drinks during flights. Air fares were higher under regulation because nonprice competition was costly and the CAB's policy of maintaining the financial health of the industry led airline companies to raise fares. This hypothesis was corroborated by studies which found that the interstate carriers subject to CAB regulation marked up fares 20 to 95 percent more than the intrastate carriers not subject to CAB regulation for similar routes.[6]

---

[5]Our summary of the effects of deregulation on the airline industry is based mainly on two articles written by Paul W. Bauer of the Federal Reserve Bank of Cleveland: "Don't panic": A primer on airline deregulation, Federal Reserve Bank of Cleveland *Economic Review,* Quarter 4, 1986, pp. 17–24; and Competition, concentration, and fares in the U.S. airline industry, Federal Reserve Bank of Cleveland *Economic Commentary,* September 15, 1987, pp. 1–4.

[6]T. E. Keeler, Airlines regulation and market performance, *Bell Journal of Economics* 3(Autumn 1972):339–434. See also a report by the General Accounting Office (GAO) to the Congress entitled *Lower airline costs per passenger are possible in the United States and could result in lower fares,* February 1977, p. 11. The report claimed that passengers could save up to $2 billion or more per year with competitive fares.

Contestability Hypothesis

Those who advocated deregulation of the airline industry suggested that the airline industry was contestable and that any market concentration under a deregulated market was nothing to worry about. The contestability hypothesis of the airline industry was based on the observation that inputs used by the airline companies were mobile and did not constitute heavy fixed expenditures. For instance, airline companies can quickly shift planes from one route to another as needs arise. Further, there is a ready secondary market for used aircraft, suggesting that planes are fairly mobile from one carrier to another. Even ground facilities are usually rented, making them easily disposable. The proponents of deregulation predicted lower coach fares, increased numbers of passengers, reduced flight frequency, and no more concentration in the industry.

Results of Deregulation

The results of deregulation show that the average fare that passengers actually paid after adjusting for inflation fell about 20 percent following deregulation. The prediction of reduced frequency, however, did not turn out to be correct. Following deregulation, airlines developed what is known as a *hub-and-spoke* system. In the hub-and-spoke system, airlines organize their routes in such a way that most of their flights converge on one or two hubs. These hubs collect traffic from the *rim* cities; then the passengers change planes at the hub to go out on other flights to their final destination. Well-known airlines and their hubs in the late 1980s included Allegheny (Pittsburgh), Continental (Houston), Delta (Atlanta), Northwestern (Minneapolis), Republic (Memphis), TWA (St. Louis), and United (Chicago). Due to the hub-and-spoke system, flight frequencies actually increased after deregulation.

In short, how much is deregulation of the airline industry worth to consumers? A study by Steven Morrison and Clifford Winston indicates that the total benefit of deregulation to consumers is approximately $5.7 billion a year.[7] For the average passenger, the benefits per trip are $11.08 and come from the following sources: a gain of $4.04 from lower fares, a loss of $0.96 from slightly increased travel time, and a gain of $8.00 from increased flight frequency. Morrison and Winston further estimate that airline profits are $2.5 billion higher (or losses are $2.5 billion lower) than they were under regulation.

The last question relates to whether the public should be concerned about the trend toward concentration following deregulation. The July 6, 1987, issue of *Time* states that the market share of the six largest airline companies increased from 76 percent in 1978 to 81 percent in 1986. There would be little to worry about if the industry were highly contestable. The airline industry does not appear highly contestable, however. One reason for the lack of competition on some routes is that entry into these concentrated markets was not as easy as was first expected. Many airports across the country had severe problems with traffic congestion. Obtaining gates and takeoff and landing slots at these airports was difficult. Since gates and landing rights were "grandfathered" to the airline holding them as long as they were used, the airlines that owned these scarce resources were able to earn monopoly returns from them. When a right is **grandfathered,** those who are holding the right at the time laws and regulations are changed are not affected by the change.

---

[7]Steven Morrison and Clifford Winston, *The economic effects of airline deregulation* (Washington, D.C.: Brookings Institution, 1986).

To Preserve Gains from Deregulation
Several steps can be taken to ensure that the gains from deregulation are not lost and that the costs of adjustment to deregulation are minimized. First, airport expansion is needed to help reduce one of the few barriers to entry that remain in the industry. Deregulation, by greatly increasing air travel through lower fares, made the congestion worse. The solution is not to reduce air travel, but to expand the system by enlarging the gate space and avoiding long-term leases of the gate space. Airlines that do not fully utilize their gate space should not be allowed to keep it. Second, airport authorities should adopt peak load pricing. By charging higher landing fees during the busy hours, airport resources can be used more efficiently. Third, the U.S. Departments of Transportation and Justice should continue to enforce existing antitrust laws. Finally, allowing foreign air carriers into the U.S. domestic market should be considered as a way of further increasing industry competition.

ANTITRUST LAWS

Earlier in this chapter, market failures were classified into two groups: competitive market failures, such as externalities and natural monopoly, and contrived market failures. Competitive market failures represent weaknesses of the market system that develop, even if firms have no intent to monopolize a market. Contrived market failures, on the other hand, represent weaknesses of the market system that are caused by the intent of firms to monopolize the market. Antitrust laws are concerned mainly with the behavior of firms that relate to contrived market failures. Laws that deal with anticompetitive conduct and structure of firms are called **antitrust laws.**

Selected Antitrust Laws

The term *trust* in antitrust means a combination of several corporations under the trusteeship of a single board of directors that manages these corporations jointly. Stockholders surrender their voting stock certificates in exchange for nonvoting trust certificates. Since profits are expected to be higher through the trust arrangement, the number of trusts grew rapidly in the late 1800s. Although the term *antitrust* was derived from the trust arrangement in the 1800s, the modern signification of the term is simply *antimonopoly*. Until 1890 there was no nationwide antitrust statute, and rulings on antitrust matters were based on common laws.

Sherman Antitrust Act
The Sherman Antitrust Act was the first nationwide antitrust act in the United States. The Sherman Antitrust Act, named after the Ohio senator who proposed it, John Sherman, was signed into law on July 12, 1890. The Sherman Antitrust Act is one of the shortest laws and contains only eight brief sections, of which only the first two are substantive and the remaining describe more or less procedural matters.

Section 1 of the Act declared illegal any contract that restrained interstate trade, while Section 2 of the Act declared any attempt to monopolize a market illegal. The language of these two sections is straightforward, but what the law tried to say was far from clear. Regarding restraints of trade in Section 1, the Act did not clarify either what was and was not an interstate business or what specific acts constituted restraint of trade. For instance, does the transmission repair done at the local

THE SHERMAN ANTITRUST ACT

An Act to protect trade and commerce against unlawful restraints and monopolies.

Be it enacted by the Senate and House of Representatives of the United States of America in Congress assembled.

Sec. 1. Every contract, combination in the form of trust or otherwise, or conspiracy, in restraint of trade or commerce among the several States, or with foreign nations, is hereby declared to be illegal. Every person who shall make any such contract or engage in any such combination or conspiracy, shall be deemed guilty of a misdemeanor, and, on conviction thereof, shall be punished by fine not exceeding five thousand dollars, or by imprisonment not exceeding one year, or by both said punishments, in the discretion of the court.

Sec. 2. Every person who shall monopolize, or attempt to monopolize, or combine or conspire with any other person or persons, to monopolize any part of the trade or commerce among the several States, or with foreign nations, shall be deemed guilty of a misdemeanor, and, on conviction thereof, shall be punished by fine not exceeding five thousand dollars, or by imprisonment not exceeding one year, or by both said punishments, in the discretion of the court.

Sec. 3. Every contract, combination in form of trust or otherwise, or conspiracy, in restraint of trade or commerce in any Territory of the United States or of the District of Columbia, or in restraint of trade or commerce between any such Territory and another, or between any such Territory or Territories and any State or States or the District of Columbia, or with foreign nations, or between the District of Columbia and any State or States or foreign nations, is hereby declared illegal. Every person who shall make any such contract or engage in any such combination or conspiracy, shall be deemed guilty of a misdemeanor, and, on conviction thereof, shall be punished by fine not exceeding five thousand dollars, or by imprisonment not exceeding one year, or by both said punishments, in the discretion of the court.

Sec. 4. The several circuit courts of the United States are hereby invested with jurisdiction to prevent and restrain violations of this act; and it shall be the duty of the several district attorneys of the United States, in their respective districts, under the direction of the Attorney General, to institute proceedings in equity to prevent and restrain such violations. Such proceedings may be by way of petition setting forth the case and praying that such violation shall be enjoined or otherwise prohibited. When the parties complained of shall have been duly notified of such petition the court shall proceed, as soon as may be, to the hearing and determination of the case; and pending such petition and before final decree, the court may at any time make such temporary restraining order or prohibition as shall be deemed just in the premises.

Sec. 5. Whenever it shall appear to the court before which any proceeding under section four of this act may be pending, that the ends of justice require that other parties should be brought before the court, the court may cause them to be summoned, whether they reside in the district in which the court is held or not; and subpoenas to that end may be served in any district by the marshal thereof.

(continued)

continued

Sec. 6. Any property owned under any contract or by any combination, or pursuant to any conspiracy (and being the subject thereof) mentioned in section one of this act, and being in the course of transportation from one State to another, or to a foreign country, shall be forfeited to the United States, and may be seized and condemned by like proceedings as those provided by law for the forfeiture, seizure, and condemnation of property imported into the United States contrary to law.

Sec. 7. Any person who shall be injured in his business or property by any other person or corporation by reason of anything forbidden or declared to be unlawful by this act, may sue therefor in any circuit court of the United States in the district in which the defendant resides or is found, without respect to the amount in controversy, and shall recover threefold the damages by him sustained, and the costs of suit, including a reasonable attorney's fee.

Sec. 8. That the word "person," or "persons," wherever used in this act shall be deemed to include corporations and associations existing under or authorized by the laws of either the United States, the laws of any of the Territories, the laws of any State, or the laws of any foreign country.

Approved, July 2, 1890

Source: Antitrust laws with amendments, 1890–1970 (Washington, D.C.: U.S. Government Printing Office, 1971), pp. 1–2.

AAMCO constitute interstate business or intrastate business? Do local car dealers who charge higher prices to people speaking with accents engage in restraint of a trade? Although laws cannot be completely specific, the Sherman Antitrust Act did not even attempt to address these issues.

Regarding Section 2, the Act did not make clear whether it forbade certain types of business *conduct* only, or certain market *structures* as well as certain types of business conduct. For instance, the Act did not make clear whether the monopoly status of a firm that was obtained through internal efficiency and growth was illegal, as was the attempt to monopolize the market. The attempt to monopolize represents business conduct, whereas monopoly status represents a business structure.

Clayton Act

The Clayton Act, signed into law on October 15, 1914, was designed to correct the deficiency of the Sherman Act (1) by spelling out some of the major types of behavior of firms that constituted restraints of trade, and (2) by strengthening the powers of antitrust prosecutors. There are certain practices that the Clayton Act declared illegal, if their effects were to reduce competition substantially. Section 2 prohibits price discrimination. Price discrimination based on differences in the cost of selling or transportation is not illegal. Section 3 prohibits **tying contracts,** which require a buyer to purchase unwanted products as a stipulation of the purchase of products that he or she does want, and **exclusive contracts,** which require the buyer not to deal with competitors of the seller. Section 7 prohibits monopolization through purchase of stocks of another company, if such an acquisition lessens competition substantially. Section 8 prohibits **interlocking directorates,** meaning that a person cannot be a director of two or more competing corporations. Section 8 has been largely unenforced.

There are a couple of other interesting sections in the Act. Section 4 allows private parties injured by violations of the Sherman and Clayton acts to sue for treble damages. If one can prove that the amount of the damage was $1 million, the award would be $3 million. Section 6 specifically exempts labor unions and agricultural organizations from the Sherman and Clayton acts.

It is interesting to note that the Clayton Act did not create criminal offenses. This means that the U.S. Department of Justice attorneys cannot bring charges under the Clayton Act unless Sherman Act violations are also alleged. This explains in part why many of the alleged violations of antitrust laws are brought to court on the basis of both the Sherman Act and the Clayton Act.

Federal Trade Commission Act

The Federal Trade Commission (FTC) Act, signed into law on September 26, 1914, created the Federal Trade Commission and charged it with the exclusive authority to enforce Section 5 of the Act, stating that unfair methods of competition in or affecting commerce, and unfair or deceptive acts or practices in or affecting commerce, are unlawful. The exclusive authority to enforce means that private individuals have no standing to sue to enjoin violations of the FTC Act or to seek damages for such violations.

One of the interesting aspects of the FTC Act is the language of Section 5, which is so broad that it gives the FTC a semilegislative authority to determine what methods of competition are undesirable. Certain types of business conduct that do not necessarily violate antitrust laws may be judged unfair acts of competition by the FTC. The FTC holds hearings if law violations are suspected. If the FTC determines that a given business practice violates the FTC Act, it may either negotiate with the company to stop the practice, or initiate a legal procedure to force the company to *cease and desist* the practice. Some past activities of the FTC include negotiations with automobile manufacturers to force correction of defects of automobiles for improved safety, and initiation and enforcement of the freedom by professionals such as doctors and lawyers to advertise their services.

Other Antitrust Acts

The three major antitrust acts (Sherman Act, Clayton Act, and FTC Act) have been amended numerous times since their enactment.[8] When amendments are significant, these amendments carry their own names. Two of these significant amendments relate to the Clayton Act.

The 1936 amendment of Section 2 of the Clayton Act is known as the Robinson-Patman Act. Section 2 of the Clayton Act prohibits price discrimination. The Robinson-Patman Act was intended to protect small, independent wholesalers and retailers from large chain stores by prohibiting discounting to large buyers not justified by cost differences. The Robinson-Patman Act also prohibits discounting by a large seller among different localities if such discounting lessens competition substantially.

The 1952 amendment of Section 7 of the Clayton Act is known as the Celler-Kefauver Act. Section 7 of the Clayton Act prohibits purchase of stocks of another company for the purpose of monopolization. To avoid violation of the Clayton Act, firms had purchased plants and equipment, instead of stocks, for monopolization. The Celler-Kefauver Act closed this loophole of Section 7 by prohibiting the purchase of assets such as the plant and equipment of another firm for the purpose

---

[8]*Antitrust laws with amendments 1890–1970* (Washington, D.C.: U.S. Government Printing Office, 1971).

of monopolization. Section 7 prohibits stock acquisitions, whereas its 1952 amendment prohibits asset acquisitions, if such acquisitions reduce competition substantially.

Antitrust Issues and Policy

Antitrust laws are designed to achieve certain policy objectives. We discuss major policy objectives of antitrust laws in this section by classifying them into several subject categories such as monopolization, mergers, price fixing, and unfair methods of competition. Before we study these policy issues, however, we need to clarify the concept of interstate commerce.

Intrastate or Interstate Commerce

When a business practice allegedly violating antitrust laws is tried under federal antitrust statutes, the practice must be judged to be *interstate* in nature rather than *intrastate*. If the practice is judged as intrastate commerce, it should be tried under state laws, not federal laws. Sometimes it is not easy to make a clear distinction between intrastate commerce and interstate commerce. Court rulings on whether any commerce is intrastate or interstate are usually based on the substantial effect doctrine. The **substantial effect doctrine** holds that any intrastate business practice exerting a substantial economic impact on interstate commerce falls under federal regulatory power.[9] The trend is that more activities that appear local in nature have been ruled as being interstate.

In *Katzenbach* v. *McLung,* for instance, the court allowed federal antitrust laws to be brought to bear on restaurants serving interstate travelers or serving food that moved across state lines.[10] In *Associated Press* v. *United States,* on the other hand, the condition that a business practice be interstate in nature was satisfied by the fact of interstate dissemination of news.[11] Concerning the amount of interstate trade relative to total trade of a firm, the court ruling in *United States* v. *Yellow Cab Co.* shows a liberal interpretation of the substantial effect doctrine by stating that the amount of interstate trade affected by the conspiracy is immaterial, since Section 1 of the Sherman Act outlaws unreasonable restraints of interstate commerce regardless of the amount of commerce affected.[12]

In *Oglesby and Barclift, Inc.* v. *Metro MLS, Inc.,* one of the early cases involving local real estate brokerage services, the court held that fixing a minimum commission and the percentage split of commissions by Metro MLS, Inc., violated the Sherman Act.[13] The ruling was based on the facts (1) that about 25 to 30 percent of home financing had been insured under VA and FHA programs, (2) that the members of Metro MLS advertised beyond the state line, and (3) that many members of Metro belonged to national referral organizations located outside the state.[14]

---

[9]*Wickard* v. *Filburn,* 317 U.S. 111 (1942).

[10]379 U.S. 294 (1964).

[11]326 U.S. 1 (1945).

[12]332 U.S. 218, 225 (1947).

[13]*Oglesby & Barclift, Inc.* v. *Metro MLS, Inc.,* 1976-2 CCH Trade Cases No. 61,064.

[14]For more on the difference between intrastate and interstate commerce and other antitrust issues of multiple listing services, see Semoon Chang, Multiple listing services: The antitrust issues, *Real Estate Law Journal* 10(Winter 1982):228–246.

Monopolization

Section 2 of the Sherman Act forbids the *act* of monopolization. For monopolization to be illegal, two requirements must be met. One is the possession of monopoly power in a relevant market, and the other is a purposeful or deliberate act to acquire or maintain monopoly power. Monopoly power means the ability to control prices and exclude competition from the relevant market. Main issues of monopolization relate to definitions of market share and relevant market.

Courts typically use market share as a measure of monopoly power. In the ALCOA case, for instance, Judge Hand held that a 90 percent market share was sufficient to constitute monopoly power, but 60 percent would be insufficient.[15] In the United Shoe case, on the other hand, Judge Wyzanski held that a 75 percent market share was sufficient.[16] The main problem with the use of market share as a measure of monopoly power is that the concept does not take into consideration either the availability of substitutes or the contestability of the market, which measures how easy it is for new firms to enter the industry.

Defining a relevant market is equally or even more difficult. As a rule, the more narrowly defined a market is, the easier it is to prove that the company has monopoly power. For instance, the cellophane market may be defined broadly as one for flexible wrapping material rather than as one for cellophane wrapping material.[17] Or, professional *championship* boxing matches may be judged to constitute a market that is distinct from professional boxing matches in general.[18] There is no general rule beyond that which holds that commodities reasonably interchangeable by consumers for the same purposes make up that part of the trade or commerce. What is meant by *reasonably interchangeable* is subject to court interpretation.[19]

Mergers

A **merger** refers to the purchase of assets of a firm by another firm such that the two firms can be operated under one ownership. There are three types of mergers: horizontal, vertical, and conglomerate. A **horizontal merger** is a merger between two firms selling the same or similar products in the same market. A **vertical merger** is a merger between two firms that are related as supplier and buyer of a product. A **conglomerate merger** is a merger between two firms selling products that are unrelated.

One important case involving corporate mergers is the Brown Shoe decision.[20] The proposed merger was between the Brown Shoe Company and the G. R. Kinney Company. Both were shoe manufacturers that maintained separate retail outlets. The case, therefore, involved both horizontal and vertical mergers. Brown Shoe was the fourth largest domestic shoe manufacturer in 1955, with only about 5 percent of the national market. Kinney was the twelfth largest domestic shoe manufacturer, with only 0.5 percent of the national market. The proposed merger between Brown Shoe and Kinney was declared illegal by the Supreme Court. The Court cited two trends for its decision. One was the acquisition of retail outlets by a manufacturer and subsequent increases in purchases of shoes by the retail outlets from the merged manufacturer. The other trend was a

---

[15]*U.S.* v. *Aluminum Co.*, 148 F.2d 416, 424.

[16]*U.S.* v. *United Shoe Machinery Corp.*, 110 F.Supp. 295.

[17]*U.S.* v. *E. I. duPont*, 351 U.S. 377, 1956.

[18]*Boxing Club* v. *U.S.*, 358 U.S. 242, 1959.

[19]*U.S.* v. *E. I. duPont*, 351 U.S. 377, 1956.

[20]The summary of the Brown Shoe case is based on J. Ronnie Davis and Semoon Chang, *Principles of managerial economics* (Englewood Cliffs, N.J.: Prentice Hall, 1986), pp. 469–470.

declining number of shoe manufacturing plants. The Court viewed the proposed merger between Brown Shoe and Kinney as one instance in a series of mergers that would result in an oligopoly if left unchecked.

The importance of this case lies in the opinion of the Court, which stressed the intent of Congress to prevent oligopolies and to protect small locally owned businesses, even if this intention resulted in higher costs and prices from the maintenance of fragmented industries and markets.

Firms attempting a merger may consult merger guidelines prepared by the U.S. Department of Justice. The original guidelines were published in 1968 in order to determine whether or not to challenge corporate acquisitions and mergers. Revised guidelines were released by the Department of Justice on June 14, 1982. The revised guidelines are concerned more with market concentration and the likelihood of successful collusion among firms in a given market than with the overall size of the companies attempting a merger.[21]

Price Fixing

The Supreme Court ruled in the *Socony Vacuum* case that price fixing was illegal regardless of whether or not it served a worthy end, thus overwhelming any conceivable defense.[22] This means that price fixing is a *per se* (meaning "in itself" or "by definition") violation of the Sherman Act, and admits no defense or justification of any kind. Fixing minimum prices among sellers and fixing maximum prices during an inflationary period for the benefit of consumers are both illegal. Also illegal is any agreement among competitors to limit production, although no specific fixed price is agreed upon. Price fixing applies not only to sellers but also to buyers. An agreement among buyers to offer a particular price or to limit purchases is also illegal per se.

Although price fixing, if proven to have occurred, is an automatic violation of the Sherman Act regardless of the reasons for its occurring, proving price fixing is not an easy task. In this day and age, no one can be so naive as to believe that a formally signed and sealed contract or a written resolution would conceivably be adopted at a meeting of price fixing conspirators.[23] A typical price fixing agreement may be achieved through conscious parallel action. **Conscious parallelism** is a legal term meaning that an unlawful conspiracy to fix prices can be inferred in the absence of an explicit agreement if there is evidence that conduct stemmed from a tacit agreement. Although the 1946 decision by the Supreme Court on the American Tobacco Company case represents a widely cited application of the conscious parallelism doctrine, proving price fixing on the basis of conscious parallelism is by no means easy.[24]

Price Discrimination

Another important antitrust policy relates to price discrimination. According to the Robinson-Patman Act, it is illegal for any person to discriminate prices among different buyers of

---

[21]References on merger guidelines include Merger guidelines of the Department of Justice, *Trade Regulation Reporter,* Commerce Clearing House, Paragraph 4510 (1980); Albert A. Foer, The new antitrust guidelines: Full speed ahead for business combinations, *Business and Society Review* 44(Winter 1983):23–28; and Joseph E. Gagnon, The new merger guidelines: Implications for New England banking markets, *New England Economic Review* (July-August 1982):18–26.

[22]*United States* v. *Socony-Vacuum Oil Co.,* 310 U.S. 150 (1940).

[23]*Esco Corp.* v. *United States,* 340 F.2d 1000 (9th Cir. 1965).

[24]For details on the American Tobacco case, see William H. Nicholls, The tobacco case of 1946, *American Economic Review* 39(May 1949):284–296.

commodities of like quality where the effect is to reduce or prevent competition substantially. Some interesting aspects of price discrimination are the following.

First, both the seller who offers and the preferred buyer who knowingly receives discriminatory prices are guilty. Second, suppose that a product is produced in Paducah, Kentucky, and that the price of the product is the same all over the country. Such a uniform delivered price system may be judged illegal if buyers near Paducah are forced to pay *phantom freight,* the costs for freight that does not exist. Third, *basing point prices* may also be illegal if these prices contain phantom freight costs. According to the **basing point pricing system,** a firm selects one or more basing points or delivery points, and the delivered price is quoted as the product price at the nearest basing point, plus transportation cost.

The product price at the basing point is called an *FOB* (free on board) price, and the buyer is responsible for transportation cost. Phantom freights incur when the actual delivery of the product is made from a plant other than the basing point. Suppose a buyer in St. Louis buys a product that has a basing point in Kansas City. If the product is shipped from Kansas City to St. Louis and the delivered price is the FOB Kansas price plus transportation cost, there is no violation of the Robinson-Patman Act. If, however, the product is actually delivered from the company's warehouse in St. Louis, the basing point pricing system enables the firm to charge phantom freight from Kansas City to St. Louis, thus violating the Robinson-Patman Act.

Discriminatory prices do not violate the antitrust law if the differences in prices are based on (1) cost differentials, (2) meeting competition in good faith, or (3) changing conditions affecting the market or the marketability of goods such as deterioration of perishable goods, obsolescence of seasonal goods, or distress sales under court order or due to business closings.

SUMMARY

When price loses the signaling function, economists say that the market has failed. There are two types of market failure: competitive and contrived. Competitive market failures occur even if firms have no intention of monopolizing the market. Examples of competitive market failures are natural monopoly and externalities. Contrived market failures occur when firms intend to and succeed in monopolizing the market. When external economies exist, the market price is higher than it should be and causes underproduction of the product. When external diseconomies exist, the market price is lower than it should be and causes overproduction of the product.

There are two theories that explain why government regulates the private sector of the economy. According to the public interest theory of regulation, government regulates industries to preserve the public interest by responding to the public demand for correction of market failures. According to the capture theory, government regulates industries not to protect the public interest but to protect and promote the interests of the industries that are regulated. The primary objective of deregulating industries is to improve economic efficiency by achieving lower prices and increased quantities of products traded, improved quality of services, and improved managerial efficiency. The major theoretical basis for the deregulation of industries is the theory of contestable markets.

Antitrust laws are concerned mainly with the behavior of firms that relates to contrived market failures. The Sherman Antitrust Act of 1890 was the first nationwide antitrust act in the

United States. Section 1 of the Act declared illegal any contract that restrained interstate trade, while Section 2 of the Act declared any attempt to monopolize a market illegal. The Clayton Act of 1914 was designed to correct the deficiency of the Sherman Act by spelling out some major practices of firms that constituted restraints of trade. Practices which the Clayton Act declared illegal, provided that their effects were to reduce competition substantially, include price discrimination, tying contracts, exclusive contracts, and interlocking directorates. The Clayton Act allowed treble damages, but did not create criminal offenses. The Federal Trade Commission Act of 1914 created the Federal Trade Commission and charged it with the exclusive authority to correct unfair methods of competition.

EXERCISES

1. What are some reasons that make it necessary for the government to regulate the private sector of the economy?

2. What options does government have for dealing with natural monopolies such as public utilities?

3. When externalities exist, price is said not to represent accurately the benefits and costs associated with the production and consumption of a good or service. Explain how externalities may affect market price.

4. What are possible options for handling the pollution problem?

5. Two theories have been proposed to explain why government regulates the private sector of the economy. Explain the two theories.

6. Economists say that specific industries are deregulated in order to improve economic efficiency. Explain economic efficiency in specific terms by listing the practical improvements that can be made through deregulation.

7. When markets are deregulated, market share tends to be concentrated among a smaller number of firms. Are all types of market concentration bad? If not, how do we know which types of concentration to leave alone and which types to discourage?

8. Briefly explain the Sherman Antitrust Act.

9. List the types of business conduct prohibited by the Clayton Act of 1914.

10. What is the difference between Section 7 of the Clayton Act and the Celler-Kefauver Act?

11. Why is it important for a business practice allegedly violative of antitrust laws to involve interstate commerce rather than intrastate commerce?

12. What is meant by the substantial effect doctrine?

13. What are the two requirements for a monopolization to be illegal in the context of antitrust laws?

14. Explain the three types of mergers.

15. Price fixing is called a per se violation of the Sherman Act. What does *per se violation* mean?

SUGGESTED READINGS

Bauer, Paul W. (1986). "Don't panic": A primer on airline deregulation, Federal Reserve Bank of Cleveland *Economic Review,* Quarter 4, pp. 17–24.

A good analysis of the effects of airline deregulation.

Koepp, Stephen. (1987). Rolling back regulation, *Time,* July 6, pp. 50–52.

A brief summary of the effect of deregulation by industry.

Rutter, William A. (1975). *Antitrust.* 5th ed. Gardena, Calif.: Gilbert Law Summaries.

A concise but thorough summary of antitrust laws and issues, prepared for law students.

Weidenbaum, Murray L. (1986). *Business, government, and the public.* 3rd ed. (Englewood Cliffs, N. J.: Prentice Hall).

A reference, written by the former chairman of the Council of Economic Advisors to the President, that presents both obvious and hidden costs of government regulation of businesses.

PART THREE

MACROECONOMICS

Somehow, we human beings always seem stuck with economic problems. We may not experience all of the following problems at the same time, but many of these problems appear to stay with us: inflation, unemployment, trade deficit, budget deficit, a low value of our currency, high rates of interest, and recession. We may wonder whether or not there are coherent policies somewhere that prevent us from falling into economic disasters. Economic policies intended to protect us from economic disasters and guide us to higher standards of living are based mostly on macroeconomics.

Macroeconomics is concerned with the economy as a whole or with aggregates that make up the economy. Subjects that we study in macroeconomics include total output, total employment, and the general level of prices.

The origin of macroeconomics may be traced all the way back to mercantilism, the economic philosophy that prevailed from the close of the sixteenth century to the middle of the eighteenth century. The core of mercantilism is the doctrine that a favorable balance of trade will produce national prosperity. Mercantilists developed neither economic principles beyond the doctrine of the favorable balance of trade nor common analytical tools. Nevertheless, they were still interested in understanding the forces that determined the capacity of an economy to produce goods and services.

Classical economics, which followed mercantilism, was as much macroeconomics as microeconomics. Adam Smith (1723–1791) studied mathematics and science at the University of Glasgow and later became a professor of moral philosophy at the university. The *Wealth of nations*, which Smith published in 1776, became the basis of economics as a science. Smith, like the mercantilists, was concerned with questions of the nature and causes of wealth and the growth of an economy, which are macroeconomic questions. By formulating what is now known as the *laissez faire* doctrine, however, Smith diverted attention from macroeconomics to such microeconomic topics as value theory. In value theory, economists attempt to find out how the price of a product is determined. The idea of laissez faire hypothesizes that the economy, if left alone, will produce full employment of resources through the interaction of the forces of supply and demand.

From the mid-1930s until today, economists in general have paid greater attention to macroeconomics than to microeconomics. There are three related reasons for the emergence of macroeconomics during this period. The first reason was the Great Depression, which lasted from 1929 until the outbreak of World War II in 1940. The self-correcting mechanism of classical economics was not perceived as capable of ending the depression, motivating economists to re-evaluate the usefulness of classical economics for solving the problem. The second reason was the Keynesian revolution. John M. Keynes (1883–1946), through his seminal book entitled the *General theory of employment interest and money,* called for active governmental policies for correction of economic problems. The third reason was the development of national income concepts by Simon Kuznets, for which he won a Nobel Prize in economics in 1971 for his contribution. National income concepts developed under the leadership of Kuznets made it possible to measure the performance of the nation's economy.

We study national income concepts in Chapter 13, then in Chapter 14 meet the twin evils of the modern economy—unemployment and inflation. To understand modern macroeconomic theories, it is necessary to have a firm grip on underlying ideas of classical economics and Keynesian economics. Chapter 15, therefore, presents an overview of macroeconomic theories by summarizing the main ideas of classical economics and Keynesian economics. The Keynesian model for determination of gross national product is presented in Chapter 16. Following studies on money and banking in Chapter 17, we summarize major developments in macroeconomics since Keynes in Chapter 18. These developments include monetarism, rational expectations theory, and supply-side economics.

13

Measuring the National Economy

WE ALL WANT to know how well the national economy is doing. Wage earners want to know whether sales of their employers' products or services will continue to grow or start to decline resulting in layoffs. Managers of businesses want to reduce inventories if the national economy is about to decline. Federal policymakers want to know the status of the national economy in order to develop policy measures that help sustain its growth. The first step toward the study of macroeconomics is to learn how to measure the national economy.

The process of defining, collecting, and classifying aggregate data of an economy is called **national income and product accounting.** National income and product accounts are to the nation's economy what the profit-and-loss statement is to a firm or the monthly budget is to a household. The most important national income concept is gross national product. As a summary of several national income and product accounts, GNP provides a broad overview of a nation's economic activities. Currently, gross national product and other national income accounts are used by various levels of government as well as by the private sector. Because it is so widely accepted as a gauge of an economy, we devote this entire chapter to the study of gross national product and concepts related to it.

GROSS NATIONAL PRODUCT

The U.S. Department of Commerce became involved in measuring national income in response to a Senate resolution of the Seventy-second Congress in 1932. The resolution requested the department of Commerce to provide estimates of the origin and destination of the national income for years 1929, 1930, and 1931. The first estimates of GNP, however, were prepared by the department during World War II to support the war effort and to evaluate the impact of the war effort. Currently, the Commerce Department's Bureau of Economic Analysis prepares estimates of the gross national product quarterly at annual rates, and also annually. The quarterly data at an annual rate refer to statistical observations collected for a quarter but extended for the entire year. For instance, suppose that the U.S. GNP during the first quarter of 1990 was $1.5 trillion. The quarterly GNP at an annual rate is $6 trillion, which is obtained by multiplying $1.5 by 4.

What Is GNP?

Gross national product (GNP) is the total market value of all final goods and services that are produced by the nation during a year. Let us elaborate on this definition in the remaining subsections.

Measures in Market Value

GNP is obtained by adding market values of all final goods and services produced in a year. For most goods and services traded in the marketplace, there are market prices that measure their market value. Defining the market price is, however, not simple.

Suppose that we are interested in buying a car that is newly produced this year. The list price of the car is $10,500. Suppose that we are successful in discounting the price of the car to $10,000.

Incidentally, there is a sales tax of 7 percent, requiring an additional payment of $700. What is the market value of the car that is included in GNP calculations? The answer is $10,700. It is easy to see that the list price is not necessarily the market price. The list price is more a price that car sellers wish to charge or use as a starting price for negotiation. It is not easy to see why the sales tax has to be included in the price. The reason is the following. GNP can be measured in one of two ways: the expenditures approach and the income approach. If the sales tax is not included in the market value of the car, the GNP figure based on the expenditures approach will be greater than the GNP figure based on the income approach. The discrepancy arises because sales tax is an expenditure by a consumer but not an income to any resource owner. The expenditures approach and the income approach to GNP are explained later in this chapter.

Services as Well as Goods

GNP includes not only the market value of goods but the value of services as well. Goods are such tangible products as cars, doughnuts, houses, spacecraft, boats, and more. Services include the work of plumbers, accountants, entertainers, professional athletes, and teachers. The market value of services is measured in terms of the amount that those who produce services earn or are paid. Take an example of the services of a lawyer who is making $150,000 per year. The market value of the lawyer's services for the purpose of calculating GNP is $150,000. Take an example of two professors: one, an excellent teacher, and the other, a very poor teacher. It does not matter whether a professor is a good teacher or a bad teacher. Their market values that are included in GNP are the salaries they earn.

Intermediate Goods or Final Goods

The definition of GNP says that only those goods and services that are produced as final output during a year are counted in estimating GNP. To understand what this statement means, let us consider the process of making the paper used in printing this book. At least 20 steps are needed to transform trees into a reel of paper. To show why only final products are counted in computing GNP, the paper-making process is simplified into five broad steps, as shown in Table 13.1.

The first step in making the paper is taken by tree farmers who grow super pine trees and sell them lumberyard operators. The price charged by tree farmers for a batch of trees is $150. At this point, tree farmers add a $150 value to the production process. The $150 represents a **value added** by tree farmers. Lumberyard operators remove the bark, cut the debarked trees into small chips, and sell wood chips to pulp mill operators at $200. This $200 represents a value of $50 the lumberyard operators add to the $150 that was charged by tree farmers. The adding of value continues until the final product reaches the consumer. The column headed "Selling Price" lists total selling prices charged by producers at each stage of paper making. The column headed "Value Added" lists values added by producers at each stage of paper making.

The value of the newly produced paper product can be obtained either by reading the last selling price, which is the price that consumers finally pay, or by adding all values added at each stage of production. Either way, the answer is $400. Boxes of paper bought by consumers are final products, while trees, wood chips, pulp, and the services of distributors represent intermediate goods. If all dollar values listed in the "Selling Price" column were added, the sum would

TABLE 13.1 Simplified Process of Paper Making

Process	Selling Price	Values Added
1. Trees sold by tree farmers to lumberyard operators	$150.00	$150.00
2. Wood chips sold by lumberyard operators to pulp mill operators	200.00	50.00
3. Pulp sold by pulp mill operators to paper mill operators	240.00	40.00
4. Boxes of paper sold by paper mill operators to distributors	340.00	100.00
5. Boxes of paper sold by distributors to consumers	400.00	60.00
Total values added	$400.00	$400.00

overestimate the value of the final product produced. The overestimation is caused by double-counting the values of intermediate products that are already included in the value of the final product.

Annual Concept

GNP is an annual concept. Whenever GNP figures are cited, appropriate years should be specified. There could still be a problem, however.

Suppose that a home-building firm built a home, and the market price of the home was $100,000. The home was completed in October of last year but sold in March of this year. Should the value of the home be included in last year's GNP or this year's GNP? To answer this question, we again resort to the definition of GNP. Products included in a given year's GNP should have been produced, not necessarily sold, during that year. Since the home was built last year, the price of the house is included in last year's GNP, not in this year's GNP.

Beware of Revisions

The GNP estimates are constructed from so many data series that any initial release of a GNP estimate is subject to several revisions in order to incorporate subsequently available and revised source data. Quarterly GNP estimates are revised at least three times: 15 days, 45 days, and 75 days after the end of the quarter. Quarterly GNP estimates are again revised whenever annual GNP estimates are revised. Annual GNP estimates are released and revised in mid-January, mid-February, and mid-March following the calendar year. The first full set of GNP estimates for the preceding year is published in July. Annual estimates are revised two more times during July of each of the following two years. Because of these revisions, GNP estimates cited in one source may not be the same as GNP estimates cited in another source.[1]

MORE ON GROSS NATIONAL PRODUCT

Transactions that enter GNP are essentially all market transactions, valued at market prices. Not all market transactions, however, are included in GNP. Three types are excluded: financial transactions, transactions of used goods, and transactions in the underground economy.

Market Transactions Excluded from GNP

Purely financial transactions, such as buying and selling of securities, are excluded from GNP. Security transactions are paper transactions, which do not involve current production. Suppose that Mrs. R(ich) buys 500 shares of IBM common stock at $100 per share. To purchase these shares, Mrs. R pays $50,000 for the shares and $250 as a commission to her stockbroker. The dollar value of shares ($50,000) is excluded from GNP, but the commission ($250) is included. The commission represents payment for current services of the broker.

When used goods such as a 1958 Chevrolet or a 1965 Mustang are traded, their values are excluded from this year's GNP because these cars are not newly produced during this year. The value of the 1958 Chevrolet was already included in the 1958 GNP and the value of the 1965 Mustang was included in the 1965 GNP. If used goods are traded through a broker who charges a commission, however, the commission as well as the seller's markup on the used car is included in GNP.

Transactions occurring in the underground economy are not included in GNP. The **underground economy** refers to illegal incomes and legal incomes that are not reported. Illegal activities that generate illegal incomes include gambling, drug trafficking, loan sharking, business theft, and more. Legal incomes not reported as incomes include bartering and other incomes unreported to avoid taxes. Illegal transactions are excluded from GNP mainly because there is no accurate way of measuring the extent of such activities.[2]

Nonmarket Transactions Included in GNP

Economists at the Department of Commerce believe that certain activities must be included in GNP even if these activities are not market transactions. The process of developing estimates for missing or incomplete data in national income accounting is called **imputation.** The values of GNP imputed from nonmarket transactions include the rental value of owner-occupied houses, food and fuel produced and consumed on farms, and services such as free banking that are rendered without charge by financial institutions.

---

[1]U. S. Congress, General Accounting Office, *A primer on gross national product: Concepts and issues,* GGD-81-47, April 8, 1981, pp. 13–15.

[2]For references on the underground economy, see Suggested Readings.

GNP and Social Welfare

Does an increase in GNP mean that a society is better off? Remember that GNP is measured in the market value. If the entire increase in GNP were due to increases in market prices, the society would not be better off. Consumers are simply paying higher prices for the same products, and probably earn a proportionately higher income. Suppose that prices remain constant and any increase in GNP is due to increased production of goods and services. Does this mean that the overall level of happiness of the society has improved? The answer is again no. Whether or not the welfare of a society improves with increased production of goods and services depends on how the increased output and income are shared among the members of the society.

If the increased output and income were shared by a select few, it would be difficult to say that social welfare has improved. If the increased output and income were shared equally by all members of the society, it would also be difficult to say that social welfare has improved. The equal distribution of income might have such an adverse impact on the incentive to produce that there might not be any more increase in output and income. Social welfare is likely to improve when the increased output and income are shared by many through political democracy.

Finally, let us reconsider that GNP is an estimate of current production. Because GNP measures current production rather than output accumulated over the years, we have an interesting problem. Suppose, for instance, that there is a disaster, natural or man-made. Hurricanes in the Gulf, earthquakes in the West, avalanches in the Rockies, chemical explosions in the East, or even automobile accidents in the neighborhood will do. How will the disasters affect GNP? The disasters will obviously reduce the community's assets, and the society will suffer. The recovery efforts of disasters, however, will increase GNP. Recovery efforts represent current production, and expenditures on recovery efforts such as overtime pay for clean-up workers or rebuilding of damaged properties are included in GNP.

EXPENDITURES APPROACH TO GNP

In principle, there are two ways of measuring GNP: the expenditures approach and the income approach. The **expenditures approach** measures GNP by looking at how much an economy spends on goods and services produced as final output in the economy, while the **income approach** measures GNP by looking at the costs of producing and distributing final output. The costs of production and distribution should cover all costs incurred during production and distribution, including associated profits. The costs of production and distribution eventually become the incomes of those who provide productive resources. The income approach, therefore, is concerned with who ultimately receives the amount spent on these goods and services. Since these approaches are two different ways of measuring the same GNP, both approaches should result in an identical measurement. Policy implications of the two approaches are vastly different, however, making it necessary to review the two approaches carefully. This section is concerned with the expenditures approach, while the next section is concerned with the income approach.

Broadly classifying, there are four different groups that demand, and thus spend dollars on, the total final output produced in an economy. The total final output is also called **aggregate output** or **aggregate supply.** The four groups that spend dollars on aggregate output are consumers, businesses, government, and foreign countries. Table 13.2 is adapted from the *Survey of Current*

MEASURING THE SCOPE OF THE UNDERGROUND ECONOMY IN THE UNITED STATES

Perhaps the first question that we want to ask ourselves is why anyone would want to estimate the scope of the underground economy. What good would the estimate do for us? In fact, there are at least two important reasons why we need to know the scope of the underground economy. One reason is to find out the extent of the underpayment of tax liabilities. The Internal Revenue Service may develop plans to increase tax revenues based on the estimate. The other reason is that, if the scope of the underground economy grows relative to the known economy, public policies developed from data of the known economy may not stabilize the economy. Policymakers need to know the scope of the underground economy to develop more effective public policies.

One way of estimating the scope of the underground economy is the monetary-statistic approach. This technique assumes that the ratio of currency to checkable deposits in the known economy is constant over time. This technique then hypothesizes that an increase in the amount of money held as currency relative to money held as checkable deposits is due to an increase in underground economic activity. In simple terms, an increase in the use of cash relative to checking accounts is due to rising underground activity. The idea is that it is much easier to hide income in the form of cash from taxing authorities than income in the form of checks. Using the monetary-statistic approach, Richard D. Porter and Amanda S. Bayer of the Division of Research and Statistics, Board of Governors of the Federal Reserve System, obtained the following ratios of the underground economy relative to the recorded GNP.

Year	Ratio of Underground Economy to Recorded GNP (%)
1950	5.6
1955	3.7
1960	3.4
1965	4.6
1970	6.3
1975	9.7
1980	14.2
1981	14.5
1982	14.6

Source: Richard D. Porter and Amanda S. Bayer, A monetary perspective on underground economic activity in the United States, *Federal Reserve Bulletin* 70(March 1984):177–190.

Business, a monthly publication of the U.S. Department of Commerce that announces official GNP figures. The discussion of the four types of expenditures in this section follows their order of presentation in Table 13.2.

Personal Consumption Expenditures

The group that purchases the largest amount of aggregate output comprises individuals and nonprofit institutions. **Personal consumption expenditures** include expenditures by individuals on (1) durable goods such as automobiles, washers and dryers, and sewing machines, (2) nondurable goods such as groceries and gasoline, and (3) services such as legal, educational, and

TABLE 13.2 Expenditure Categories of 1988 U.S. GNP

Expenditure Category		*Amount ($billions)*	
Personal consumption expenditures			3,226.0
Durable goods		449.9	
Nondurable goods		1,047.2	
Services		1,728.9	
Gross private domestic investment			765.5
Fixed investment		717.4	
Nonresidential	487.7		
Residential	229.7		
Change in business inventories		48.1	
Nonfarm	41.8		
Farm	6.3		
Government purchases of goods and services			963.5
Federal		380.2	
National defense	297.5		
Nondefense	82.7		
State and local		583.4	
Net exports of goods and services			−93.2
Exports		518.7	
Imports		611.9	
Gross national product			4,861.8

Source: Adapted from U.S. Department of Commerce Bureau of Economic Analysis, *Survey of Current Business* 69(January 1989): 8, Table 1.1.

entertainment services. Also included in personal consumption expenditures are operating expenses of nonprofit institutions serving individuals, and the value of food, fuel, clothing, housing, and financial services received *in kind* by individuals. The term *in kind* means noncash.

Gross Private Domestic Investment

Expenditures on final output by private businesses are called **gross private domestic investment.** In ordinary conversation, investment means the purchase of stocks, bonds, land, and precious metals for speculative purposes. In the economic sense, however, **investment** means the production of new machines and durable equipment, the construction of new buildings, including residential homes, and the value of the change in the physical volume of inventories held by private businesses. Investment in machines, equipment, and buildings, excluding changes in inventories, is also called **fixed investment.** Investment in ordinary conversation represents purely financial transactions, whereas investment in the economic sense represents an increased capacity for further production. The term *domestic* in gross private domestic investment means that investment is made within the legal boundaries of a nation. The term *private* in the definition means that the domestic investment is made by private businesses rather than by the public sector.

Gross versus Net Investment
The term *gross* in gross private domestic investment requires a longer explanation. The production of new machines and equipment and the construction of new buildings are investments. Machines, equipment, and buildings are called **capital** or **capital goods.** Thus, capital is accumulated investment. Capital goods do not stay new, because the machines, equipment, and buildings are used repeatedly to produce other final output. The decreasing value of capital goods over time due either to wear from repeated use or to technological obsolescence is called **depreciation.** If depreciation is not subtracted from investment, then the investment is **gross investment.** If depreciation is subtracted from investment, then the investment is **net investment.** If depreciation is greater than gross investment, net investment becomes negative. A negative net investment means that the economy does not even replace capital goods that become obsolete. Depreciation is also referred to as **capital consumption allowance,** since depreciation is an allowance for the use (or consumption) of capital goods.

Flow versus Stock
Another difference between investment and capital is that investment is a flow concept, whereas capital is a stock concept. A **flow** concept can be expressed only in terms of a period of time such as a month or a year. Examples of the flow concept include income (from January 1 to December 31 of this year), saving (during the month of July), and investment (during the previous year). A **stock** concept is expressed at a given point in time. Examples of the stock concept include wealth, savings, and capital, all of which should be expressed as an amount as of a given date. Natural disasters reduce the stock of the community's assets, but recovery efforts increase the flow of production and income.

Changes in Inventory
Businesses selling goods rather than services need to carry inventories in their storage rooms or on their shelves. Changes in inventories create problems in GNP calculations. Consider robots.

Suppose that in 1986 domestic manufacturers made 7,000 robots. The actual number of robots shipped during the year was 6,150, meaning that manufacturers ended the year with an increase in inventory of robots by 850 (the difference between 7,000 and 6,150). An interesting question arises regarding the role of the increased inventory in GNP calculations. The question is where the increased inventory should be placed among the four GNP components of personal consumption expenditures, gross private domestic investment, government expenditures, and net exports. Through the process of elimination, economists have decided to include changes in inventory in investment.

Government Purchases of Goods and Services

Government purchases of goods and services include expenditures by all levels of government: federal, state, and local government. Government purchases include all *direct expenditures* on the economy's final output, including services of governmental employees. Government purchases do not include government *transfer payments* such as welfare payments, unemployment insurance, social security payments, veterans' benefits, interest on public debt, and the like. **Transfer payments** are the payments made in return for which no services are rendered at the time the payments are made. Transfer payments are excluded from GNP calculations because these payments do not represent current production of goods and services. Consider welfare payments. Welfare payments do not reflect current production unless and until these payments are spent by welfare recipients on groceries, haircuts, and other goods and services that are currently produced. These direct expenditures on goods and services, however, are already counted as personal consumption expenditures.

Net Exports of Goods and Services

Net exports refer to total exports from which total imports are subtracted. When foreigners spend money on goods and services produced in the United States, these expenditures cause U.S. output to increase in exactly the same way as expenditures by U.S. citizens on domestically produced goods and services cause U.S. output to increase. Conversely, when U.S. citizens spend money on goods and services produced in, say, Canada, these expenditures cause Canadian output to increase at the expense of U.S. output. If exports are equal to imports, the net impact of foreign trade on the U.S. GNP is zero. In calculating GNP, therefore, only the difference between exports and imports is added. In other words, imports are deducted from exports because imports are not part of national production. If imports exceed exports, net exports become negative. Negative net exports mean that the U.S. GNP will be lower.

Reviewing the Expenditures Approach

To summarize this section, GNP can be calculated by adding expenditures on all goods and services produced in an economy. There are four major categories of expenditures, depending on who spends the money. The four categories are personal consumption expenditures (C), gross private domestic investment (I), government purchases of goods and services (G), and net exports of goods and services $(X - M)$. For instance, if we as consumers buy a new stove, it is consumption; if the owner of Pier 4 in Boston buys a new stove for his restaurant, it is investment; if the U.S. Army buys a new stove for a mess hall, it is government expenditure; and if a Mexican citizen buys a new stove in Corpus Christi, Texas, that will be shipped to Mexico, it is export.

The relation between GNP and its four components is expressed in symbols:

$$GNP = C + I + G + (X - M). \tag{13.1}$$

Symbols C, I, G, and $(X - M)$ are frequently referred to simply as consumption, investment, government spending, and net exports. Actual figures for these components of GNP and the GNP for 1988 in billions of dollars were

$$4,861.8 = 3,226.0 + 765.5 + 963.5 - 93.2. \tag{13.2}$$

For those who wonder where the government finds all the data needed to calculate the GNP, one of the best references on sources of data for GNP calculations is the July 1987 issue of the *Survey of Current Business*.[3] An article in the *Survey* tabulates the principal sources of data and the methods of estimating GNP for each subcomponent of GNP components.

INCOME APPROACH TO GNP

Consider again the car mentioned earlier in this chapter. The price of the car after discounting was $10,000, and $10,700 was paid for the car including sales tax. In the expenditures approach to GNP, we simply counted the total expenditure, $10,700, as GNP. In the income approach to GNP calculation, we take a look at who receives as income the money paid for the car. Keep in mind that expenditures for the car eventually reach individuals as income. When the incomes that individuals receive from the car sale are added, the sum should be equal to GNP. The **income approach** to GNP refers to the process of calculating GNP by adding incomes received by all individuals for their productive services. The difference between the expenditures approach and the income approach is shown in Figure 13.1.

Components of National Income

National income is the sum of all payments for productive services that were used to turn out final product. These payments are made for use of labor and other resources used in production. Unlike transfer payments, these payments are earned by the owners of productive resources. National income is the sum of all earned incomes. There are five components in national income: compensation of employees, proprietors' income, rental income, corporate profits, and net interest. U.S. national income figures for 1988 are summarized in Table 13.3. The discussion below follows the order of presentation of these components in Table 13.3.

---

[3]For more sources of data, see references on GNP listed in Suggested Readings.

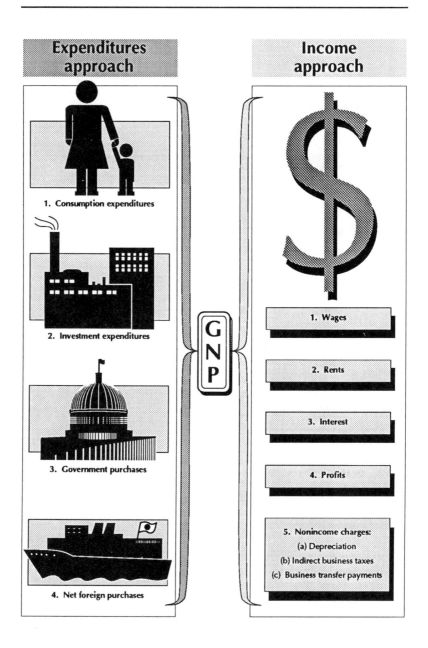

FIGURE 13.1 Expenditures and Income Approaches to GNP. Both the expenditures and the income approach, result in the same GNP. To equate estimates of the two approaches, depreciation and indirect business taxes are added to the income approach.

TABLE 13.3 Components of 1988 U.S. National Income

		Amount ($billions)
Compensation of employees		2,904.9
Wages and salaries	2,437.1	
Supplements to wages and salaries	467.8	
Proprietors' income		324.7
Farm	36.4	
Nonfarm	288.3	
Rental income		19.6
Corporate profits		323.6
Net interest		391.5
National income		3,964.3

Source: U. S. Department of Commerce Bureau of Economic Analysis, *Survey of Current Business* 69(January 1989): 10, Table 1.14.

Compensation of Employees

The compensation of employees is the largest component of national income. The compensation of employees is the sum of (1) all wages and salaries paid to employees including commissions, tips, and bonuses, and (2) supplemental payments to wages and salaries such as payments made by employers for their employees on social security, unemployment insurance, workers' compensation, military medical insurance, private pensions, and health insurance programs.

Proprietors' Income

In calculating national income, the incomes of sole proprietors and owners of partnerships are treated separately from the compensation of employees because proprietors and partners are owners rather than employees.

Rental Income of Persons

Rental income of persons consists of (1) earnings from renting property such as a house,[4] (2) royalty earnings from the ownership of patents and copyrights, and (3) royalty earnings from the ownership of natural resources such as oil wells and timberland. Rental income of persons is different from rental income of firms in the rental business. Rental income of firms in the rental business is included in national income as proprietors' income or corporate profits.

Corporate Profits

Corporate profits are the net income generated from domestic and foreign operations of private corporations. Corporate profits are usually disposed in three ways. First, corporate profits are used

---

[4]The rental value of owner-occupied houses is also included in computing rental income. The rental value of owner-occupied houses is an imputed value since there is no actual transaction in owner-occupied houses.

to pay corporate income tax. Second, corporate profits are used to pay dividends to stockholders. Dividends, their share of the profit, are paid quarterly to stockholders, who are the owners of the corporation. If profits are low, companies may not pay dividends for any or several quarters. If profits are high, companies may increase dividends. Third, corporate profits that remain after corporate income taxes are paid and dividends are deducted are called **undistributed corporate profits.** Undistributed corporate profits are used to replace aging machines and equipment. Corporations may also invest these earnings in new plants, equipment, or buildings for expansion.

Net Interest

Net interest refers to interest payments made to persons and to governments from businesses in the United States and abroad. Interest payments made to businesses are not included in calculating net interest because these payments are part of business income, counted already as corporate profits. Interest payments made by governments are also excluded from calculating net interest because economists have judged that governmental debt does not yield productive assets and thus does not represent current production.

Adding Up GNP

When the compensation of employees, proprietors' income, rental income, corporate profits, and net interest are all added, national income is obtained. The national income, however, is smaller than GNP. To understand why national income is smaller than GNP, let us reconsider the $10,700 that we paid for a new car. This amount is a business income. Not all business income is distributed as earned income to the suppliers of resources used in production.

There are three components of business income that do not reach individuals as earned income. One is the capital consumption allowance set aside by businesses to replace wearing capital goods. Another is the amount of business transfer payments that businesses subtract from total revenue before computing profits. **Business transfer payments** are payments made by businesses to persons who perform no current services. Business transfer payments are not a national income, since national income is the sum of all *earned* incomes only. Business transfer payments include corporate gifts to nonprofit institutions such as charities and colleges, liability payments for personal injury, and defaults by consumers on debts owed to businesses.

The third component is the amount of tax liabilities that businesses collect from consumers for government or can charge as business expenses in the calculation of business profits. These payments to the government are known as **indirect business taxes,** and include sales tax, excise tax, and property tax. These payments are *indirect* because consumers pay to the government indirectly through businesses, and they are *business taxes* because it is businesses that actually submit them to the government.

A concept called the net national product bridges the gap between national income and GNP. The **net national product** is obtained by subtracting capital consumption allowance from gross national product. National income is obtained by subtracting indirect business taxes and business transfer payments from net national product. The relations among GNP, net national product, and national income are shown in Table 13.4.

TABLE 13.4 Relations among GNP,
NNP, and NI

Gross national product

minus	capital consumption allowance
equals	net national product
minus	indirect business taxes business transfer payments
equals	national income.

Additional Income Concepts

National income is the sum of all earned incomes. Not all earned income reaches individuals, however. **Personal income** measures all incomes received by individuals either as payments for productive services or as transfer payments. The process of deriving personal income from national income is illustrated in Table 13.5 on the basis of 1988 data.

The differences between national income and personal income are as follows. First, corporate profits beyond dividend income do not reach individuals. Therefore, total corporate profits (1) are subtracted from national income, but dividend income (4) is added back to national income in order to obtain personal income. Second, net interest has two components: interest income paid to persons and interest income paid to governments. Since only the interest income paid to persons reaches individuals, the entire net interest (2) is subtracted from national income, but personal interest income (5) is added back to national income in order to obtain personal income. Third, social insurance payments paid by employers (3), such as social security tax and pension contributions, do not reach individuals and, therefore, are subtracted from national income in order to obtain personal income. Fourth, transfer payments are not earned by resource owners and, thus, are not included in national income. Both government transfer payments (6) and business transfer payments (7), however, are received by individuals and, therefore, are added to national income in order to obtain personal income. Business transfer payments (7) are the same ones that we subtracted from net national product to obtain national income.

When personal taxes are subtracted from personal income, **disposable (personal) income** is obtained. Disposable income can only be disposed in two ways: spending and saving.

Of all the national income concepts, personal income data are the only data that are available for areas as small as individual counties. The U.S. Department of Commerce Bureau of Economic Analysis has a branch called the Regional Economic Measurement Division. The Division publishes countywide time-series data on (1) earnings and employment for major industry groups, (2) personal income, (3) transfer payments, and (4) population. County estimates of personal income data are widely used in the public and private sectors. For instance, personal income data for small areas are used in preparing environmental impact statements and resource management

TABLE 13.5 Income Categories of 1988 U.S. GNP

		Amount ($billions)	
Gross national product			4,861.8
less	capital consumption allowances	506.0	
equals	net national product		4,355.8
less	indirect business tax	389.0	
	business transfer payments	30.7	
	other adjustments	−28.2	
equals	national income		3,964.3
less	(1) corporate profits	323.6	
	(2) net interest	391.5	
	(3) contributions for social insurance	444.6	
plus	(4) personal dividend income	96.3	
	(5) personal interest income	576.3	
	(6) government transfer payments to persons	555.3	
	(7) business transfer payments	30.7	
equals	personal income		4,063.2
less	personal tax and nontax payments	590.3	
equals	disposable personal income		3,472.9
	Personal outlays	3,325.9	
	Personal saving	147.0	

Source: Adapted from U.S. Department of Commerce Bureau of Economic Analysis, *Survey of Current Business* 69(January 1989): 10, Table 1.9, and 12, Table 2.1.

plans required by the National Environmental Act of 1969 and the Federal Land Policy and Management Act of 1976. Businesses use the data to evaluate the regional market potential for their products and to determine the location of their businesses. Public agencies may use the data in allocating federal funds and in projecting local tax revenues. Economists use the data to forecast state and local economies.

NATIONAL INCOME CONCEPTS: A SUMMARY

Let us summarize all major national income concepts and their relations to one another. Equations for gross national product (GNP), net national product (NNP), and national income (NI) are

$$\text{GNP} = C + I + G + (X - M) \tag{13.1}$$

$$NNP = GNP - CCA \tag{13.3}$$

$$NI = NNP - IBT - BTP \tag{13.4}$$

where

C	=	personal consumption expenditures
I	=	gross private domestic investment
G	=	government expenditures on goods and services
$X - M$ =		net exports
CCA	=	capital consumption allowance
IBT	=	indirect business taxes
BTP	=	business transfer payments

National income (NI) may also be obtained by adding all earned incomes. That is,

$$
\begin{aligned}
NI = \ & \text{compensation of employees} \\
+ \ & \text{proprietors' income} \\
+ \ & \text{rental income of persons} \\
+ \ & \text{corporate profits} \\
+ \ & \text{net interest income}
\end{aligned}
\tag{13.5}
$$

Finally, personal income (PI) and disposable income (DI) are related to national income in the following way:

$$
\begin{aligned}
PI = \ & NI \\
- \ & \text{corporate profits} \\
- \ & \text{net interest income} \\
- \ & \text{contributions for social insurance} \\
+ \ & \text{dividends} \\
+ \ & \text{personal interest income} \\
+ \ & \text{government transfer payments} \\
+ \ & \text{business transfer payments}
\end{aligned}
\tag{13.6}
$$

$$
\begin{aligned}
DI = \ & PI \\
- \ & \text{personal taxes}
\end{aligned}
\tag{13.7}
$$

$$
\begin{aligned}
DI = \ & \text{personal consumption expenditures} \\
+ \ & \text{personal saving}
\end{aligned}
\tag{13.8}
$$

NOMINAL GNP AND REAL GNP

According to estimates made by the Recreation Vehicle Industry Association of Reston, Virginia, approximately 400,000 RVs are sold each year at an average price of about $20,000 per vehicle.

Assume for the sake of simplicity that RVs are the only product the U.S. economy produced last year. Last year's GNP would then be $8 billion, obtained by multiplying 400,000 by $20,000. Assume also that the only product the U.S. economy produces this year is again RVs, and the same number (400,000 RVs) will be produced by the end of this year. Suppose that the price per RV doubles from $20,000 last year to $40,000 this year. This year's GNP then becomes $16 billion, obtained by multiplying 400,000 by $40,000. A doubling of the price of RVs doubles GNP even if the number of RVs produced remains unchanged. GNP figures expressed in prevailing market prices are called by several different names: **nominal GNP, money GNP, GNP in current dollars,** or simply **GNP.** GNP estimates such as $8 billion for last year and $16 billion for this year are nominal GNPs, since these estimates are made in market prices that prevailed in each of the two years. Keep in mind that we are not any better off when the price of RVs doubles: We still have the same number of RVs to drive. When nominal GNP is adjusted for inflation so that the actual number, rather than the total dollar value, of RVs can be counted, a real GNP is obtained. **Real GNP** refers to nominal GNP adjusted for inflation.

The process of adjusting a value for inflation is important because the process has a wide range of business applications. When a person's salary increases by 10 percent, the person is not necessarily better off. Whether he or she is better off with the pay raise depends on whether the pay raise is greater or smaller than the rate of inflation. One would be better off with a 2 percent pay raise and no inflation than with a 10 percent pay raise and 10 percent inflation. To learn how money values can be converted to real values, it is necessary to study the concept of a price index.

Price Index

A **price index** is a weighted average of prices for a given basket of goods and services, expressed as an index. When a price index rises, inflation is said to exist. The most widely known price index is the consumer price index.

Consumer Price Index
The **consumer price index** (CPI) is derived from prices for an "average market basket" of goods and services that an average consumer is likely to buy. There are two types of CPI: CPI-U and CPI-W. The more popular CPI-U represents the spending habits of about 80 percent of the U.S. population, including wage earners, clerical workers, professionals, technical workers, unemployed persons, and retirees. The CPI-W represents the spending habits of only those who derive more than one-half of their income from clerical or wage occupations.

The market basket measured by CPI consists of about 100,000 items from seven categories of consumer expenditure. The seven categories and their weights in the CPI are food and beverages (17.8%), housing (42.6%), apparel and upkeep (6.5%), transportation (18.7%), medical care (4.8%), entertainment (4.4%), and other goods and services (5.1%). Monthly surveys are conducted by the U.S. Department of Labor, Bureau of Labor Statistics (BLS), for 8,300 households and 21,000 retail establishments in 91 urban areas. Results from these surveys determine price indexes for both the United States as a whole and selected local areas.[5]

[5]For more on CPI, see U.S. Department of Labor, Bureau of Labor Statistics, *The Consumer Price Index: 1987 revision,* Report No. 736, January 1987.

ESTIMATING THE VALUE OF A HOUSEWIFE'S WORK

At present, the value of a housewife's work is not included in calculating GNP. One reason for the exclusion is that no one method for obtaining a reliable measure of its value has been supported by many economists. Two ways of estimating the value have been suggested: the opportunity cost approach and the market cost approach. The opportunity cost approach measures the value of a housewife's work by the income the housewife could earn in the labor market, while the market cost approach measures the value of a housewife's work by the cost of hiring someone to do housework.

Based on 516 female clerical employees ages 35 and above employed by the University of Illinois, Urbana-Champaign, Professors Ferber and Birnbaum estimated the lifetime value of a woman's housework. Selected estimates of the value of housework of married women between the ages of 18 and 65 are summarized below in 1989 dollars:

	Market Cost	Opportunity Cost
High school graduate with two children		
Worked all the time	$163,428	$256,856
Worked ages 18–22 only	265,127	299,636
College graduate with two children		
Worked all the time	$231,254	$290,121
Worked ages 22–24 only	339,144	309,892

It is worth noting that the difference in the estimated values is quite small between females working all the time and females who do not work. Ferber and Birnbaum claim that potential market earnings may be important in determining how much time a person will devote to market work and housework, but they do not provide an acceptable estimate of the value of housework. They suggest that the market cost approach is preferable to the opportunity cost approach. Housework may be priceless but not valueless.

Source: Marianne A. Ferber and Bonnie G. Birnbaum, Housework: Priceless or valueless? *The Review of Income and Wealth* 26(December 1980):387–400.

One important use of the CPI is to escalate income payments. In the private sector, more than 3 million workers are covered by collective bargaining agreements that provide for increases in wages based on increases in the CPI. The CPI also affects the income of about 60 million persons through federal programs such as social security, federal civilian retirement, military retirement, the food stamp program, and the school lunch program.

The CPI is known as the cost of living index for its usefulness in adjusting wage increases. Strictly speaking, however, the CPI is not a cost of living index, and for two reasons. One reason is that the CPI is not adjusted by changes in income taxes or social security taxes. The other reason is that the CPI measures price changes of a constant basket of goods and services, but consumers tend to adjust spending habits to avoid items whose prices rise. To the extent that consumers make the adjustment in spending habits, the cost of living rises more slowly than a price change indicated by the CPI.

Base Year

Since a price index is designed to compare the price level of one period with the price level of another period, the price index needs a base period. The price level of the base period is compared with the price level of another period. The base period for annual price indexes is called the **base year.** The price index of the base year is always 100. If the base year of a price index is 1967, it is expressed as 1967=100. This expression does not mean that 1967 equals 100; it simply means that 1967 is the base year of the particular price index. In recent years, 1982 or the period of 1982 through 1984 has also been used as the base year for selected price indexes. This means that the base price is the average of prices that prevailed in 1982 or in 1982 through 1984.

Computing Real Values from Money Values

Real values are money values from which inflationary effects are subtracted. To see how money value can be converted to real value, let us consider U.S. per capita personal income presented in Table 13.6. Per capita personal income is total personal income divided by total population. The U.S. per capita personal incomes for 1984 through 1987 are shown in column (2). Column (3) figures are CPIs for the same period. The expression 1967=100 in column (3) means that 1967 is the base year of the CPI. To convert nominal values of the per capita personal income in column (2) into per capita personal income in 1967 prices in column (5), we divide nominal values by the CPI and multiply the product by 100. Alternatively, we first divide CPIs by 100 in order to convert index numbers into plain ratios, and then divide nominal values by these ratios. The process of converting nominal values into real values in the base year prices is shown in column (4) in Table 13.6. Figures in column (5) are U.S. per capita personal incomes in 1967 prices.

Adjusting Nominal GNP to Real GNP

The CPI measures changes in prices of goods and services that an average consumer is expected to buy. GNP, however, is a market value of goods and services that are purchased not only by consumers but also by businesses, the government, and foreign countries. Obviously, the CPI alone will not be sufficient to derive real GNP from nominal GNP.

Conceivably, there are two ways of obtaining real GNP from nominal GNP. One way is to add the various physical quantities of all goods and services produced each year. The problem with this approach is that it is like adding apples and oranges, with the further problem of adding the quantity of services. The second way is to convert each component of GNP into real value using a price index appropriate to the particular component. Economists use the second alternative to derive real GNP from nominal GNP. When GNP is expressed in the base year prices, such GNP

TABLE 13.6 U.S. Per Capita Personal Income

Year	Income in Current Dollars	CPI (1967=100)	Converting Nominal Value to Real Value	Income (1967 Dollars)
(1)	(2)	(3)	(4)	(5)
1984	$13,114	311.1	13,114/3.111	$4,215
1985	13,908	322.2	13,908/3.222	4,317
1986	14,636	328.4	14,636/3.284	4,457
1987	15,340	340.4	15,340/3.404	4,506

Source: For income in current dollars: U.S. Department of Commerce Bureau of Economic Analysis, *NEWS*, released April 20, 1988, Table 2: Per Capita Personal Income by State and Region, 1984–87.

figures are called **GNP in "constant" dollars.** When GNP is expressed simply as money GNP such as 1951 GNP (in 1951 prices) or 1990 GNP (in 1990 prices), such GNP figures are called **GNP in "current" dollars.**

Since there are numerous components in GNP, there is no single price index that can be used to convert current dollar GNP into constant dollar GNP. Several different price and earnings indexes are used to deflate services, imports and exports, and national defense components of GNP. Two price indexes are used to deflate over 75 percent of GNP, however. The two indexes are the consumer price index (CPI) and the producer price index (PPI). Unlike CPI, which measures a market basket of goods and services purchased by a consumer, the **producer price index** measures changes in the prices of selected raw materials and intermediate goods purchased by producers. PPI is likely to foretell changes in CPI.

The preparation of current dollar GNP and constant dollar GNP yields a by-product called the implicit price deflator. The **implicit price deflator** is obtained when a current dollar GNP is divided by a constant dollar GNP and the product is multiplied by 100. In other words, the GNP price deflator is not used to derive constant dollar GNP from current dollar GNP. Rather, it is the by-product, obtained after constant dollar GNP is already computed. Money GNP, real GNP, and GNP price deflator from 1951 to 1988 are summarized in Table 13.7.

In Table 13.7, the base year of the GNP price deflator is indicated as 1982. In 1982, therefore, money GNP and real GNP are equal to each other at $3,166.0 billion. Real GNP figures in 1982 prices after 1982 are smaller than corresponding money GNP figures, since money GNP figures after 1982 are inflated with actual rates of inflation. Real GNP figures in 1982 prices before 1982 are greater than corresponding money GNP figures, since money GNP figures prior to 1982 are expressed in prices that prevailed in these earlier years. Finally, when the real GNP of a given year declines from the real GNP of the preceding year, the economy is said to be in a **recession** during the year.

TABLE 13.7 Nominal GNP, Real GNP, and GNP Price Deflator

Year	Gross National Product ($billions)	Real GNP (1982=100: $billions)	GNP Price Deflator (1982=100)
1951	$ 333.4	$1,328.2	25.1
1952	351.6	1,380.0	25.5
1953	371.6	1,435.3	25.9
1954	372.5	1,416.2	26.3
1955	405.9	1,494.9	27.1
1956	428.2	1,525.7	28.1
1957	451.0	1,551.1	29.0
1958	456.8	1,539.3	29.7
1959	495.8	1,629.1	30.4
1960	515.3	1,665.2	31.0
1961	533.8	1,708.7	31.3
1962	574.7	1,799.4	31.9
1963	606.9	1,873.3	32.4
1964	649.8	1,973.3	32.9
1965	705.1	2,087.5	33.8
1966	772.0	2,208.4	35.0
1967	816.4	2,271.3	36.0
1968	892.7	2,365.6	37.8
1969	963.9	2,423.3	39.8
1970	1,015.5	2,416.2	42.0
1971	1,102.7	2,484.8	44.4
1972	1,212.8	2,608.5	46.5
1973	1,359.3	2,744.0	49.5
1974	1,472.8	2,729.3	54.0
1975	1,598.4	2,695.0	59.3
1976	1,782.8	2,826.7	63.0
1977	1,990.5	2,958.6	67.3
1978	2,249.7	3,115.1	72.2
1979	2,508.1	3,192.3	78.6
1980	2,732.0	3,187.2	85.7
1981	3,052.6	3,248.7	93.9
1982	3,166.0	3,166.0	100.0
1983	3,405.7	3,279.1	103.8
1984	3,772.2	3,501.4	107.8
1985	4,014.9	3,618.7	110.9
1986	4,240.3	3,721.7	113.9
1987	4,526.7	3,847.0	117.7
1988	4,861.8	3,995.0	121.7

Source: Adapted from *Survey of Current Business.*

SUMMARY

Gross national product (GNP) is the total market value of all final goods and services that are produced during a year. To avoid double counting, GNP is calculated either by adding the values of final products only or by adding all values added at each stage of production. Although GNP measures all market transactions valued at market prices, some market transactions such as purely financial transactions, transactions of used goods, and illegal transactions are excluded. There are two ways of measuring GNP: the expenditures approach and the income approach. The expenditures approach measures GNP by looking at how much an economy spends on goods and services produced newly in an economy, while the income approach measures GNP by looking at who ultimately receives the amount spent on these goods and services. Both approaches result in an identical measurement. The expenditures approach to GNP has four main components: personal consumption expenditures, gross private domestic investment, government expenditures, and net exports. In economics, investment means money spent to purchase new machines, new durable equipment, and new buildings including residential construction. Changes in inventory are also included in investment in national income accounting. The income approach to GNP refers to the process of calculating GNP from the income side.

Real GNP refers to GNP adjusted for inflation. A price index is a weighted average of prices for a basket of goods and services. Inflation or changes in the cost of living are measured by changes in the consumer price index (CPI). The price index of the base year is always 100. Real GNP is obtained by adjusting money GNP for inflation. The GNP price deflator measures changes in prices of all goods and services produced in the economy. When GNP is expressed in the base year prices, such GNP figures are called GNP in "constant" dollars. When GNP is expressed simply as money GNP, such GNP figures are called GNP in "current" dollars. When the real GNP of a given year declines from the real GNP of the preceding year, the economy is in a recession during that year.

EXERCISES

1. Black & Decker, with headquarters in Towson, Maryland, is well known as a major manufacturer of such power tools as jigsaws and drills. Financial highlights of Black & Decker indicated that in 1986 the company's net sales were $1,791.2 million, net earnings were $6.3 million, average shares outstanding were 55.6 million, and dividends per share were 58 cents. What is the amount of Black & Decker's contribution toward the 1986 GNP?

2. As a person moves up the management ladder, he or she will be asked to participate in more and more volunteer services. Assuming that volunteers displace services that had previously been provided by paid workers, what would be the impact of volunteer services on GNP?

3. List at least three uses of personal income data at the local level.

4. On September 12, 1979, Hurricane Frederic passed through the coastal counties of Alabama. According to a study by Semoon Chang that was published in the June 1983

issue of the *Urban Affairs Quarterly,* the coastal counties of Alabama suffered $1.6 billion in damages to property and natural resources. Does this finding mean that the 1979 U.S. GNP was lower by $1.6 billion because of the damage from the hurricane? If not, why not?

5. In 1987, the U.S. GNP per person was $18,556, whereas the GNP per person of Afghanistan was no more than $271. Is it possible for a person to survive with $271 per year?

6. According to the expenditures approach, GNP comprises four expenditure categories: consumption, investment, government spending, and net exports. If investment represents net investment instead of gross investment, how will the sum of the four expenditure categories differ from GNP?

7. When print media state that the economy next year will grow at a 3 percent pace, which of the national income concepts do the media refer to?

8. Suppose that a worker's wages increased by 10 percent this year. Does this mean that the worker's purchasing power has also increased by 10 percent this year? If not, why not?

9. What are the main differences between national income and personal income?

10. GNP figures are released on a quarterly basis in the *Survey of Current Business* and the *Business Conditions Digest.* The quarterly GNP figures for the four quarters of 1987 were $4,391.8, $4,484.2, $4,568.0, and $4,662.8 billion. How can these quarterly GNP figures be converted to the 1987 annual GNP?

SUGGESTED READINGS

Blaug, Mark. (1985). *Economic theory in retrospect.* 4th ed. Cambridge, England: Cambridge University Press.

Blaug's Chapter 16 explains how macroeconomics has progressed. The chapter enables readers to put national income concepts presented in this chapter in proper perspective.

Carson, Carol S. (1984). The underground economy: An introduction. *Survey of Current Business* 64(May):21–37.

Carson, Carol S. (1984). The underground economy: An introduction. *Survey of Current Business* 64(July):106–118.

Gutman, Peter. (1979). Statistical illusions, mistaken policies. *Challenge* (November-December):14–15.

Houston, Joel F. (1987). The underground economy: A troubling issue for policymakers. Federal Reserve Bank of Philadelphia *Business Review* (September-October):3–12.

McDonald, Richard J. (1984). The "underground economy," and BLS statistical data. *Monthly Labor Review* 107(January):4–18.

Porter, Richard D., and Bayer, Amanda S. (1984). A monetary perspective on underground economic activity in the United States. *Federal Reserve Bulletin* 70(March):177–190.

The references above provide interesting data on the underground economy.

U.S. Congress, General Accounting Office. (1981). *A primer on gross national product: Concepts and issues.* GGD-81-47, April 8.

(1987). GNP: An overview of source data and estimating methods. *Survey of Current Business* 67 (July):103–126.

U.S. Department of Commerce Bureau of Economic Analysis. (1987). *GNP: An overview of source data and estimating methods.* Methodology Paper Series MP-4 (Washington, D.C.: U.S. Government Printing Office, September).

Good references on the concept of GNP, sources of data, and the estimation of GNP.

U.S. Department of Commerce Bureau of Economic Analysis. (1988). A user's guide to BEA information. *Survey of Current Business* 68(March):62–74.

Explains how to obtain directly from BEA basic information on such key issues as economic growth, inflation, regional development, and international trade.

14

Fluctuations in the National Economy

Economic Fluctuations

Unemployment

Inflation

Forecasting Economic Fluctuations

IT WOULD BE NICE if the real GNP of our economy, or any economy for that matter, were to grow at a healthy and steady rate to our satisfaction. The economy does not grow that way, not to mention the problem of agreeing on what is meant by *healthy, steady,* and *our satisfaction.* Decisions on production, distribution, and consumption are made by so many different people that an economy inevitably fluctuates, creating in the process two major problems that plague the modern capitalist economy: unemployment and inflation. Economic fluctuations are also called business cycles. To some readers, the term *business cycles* may convey the impression of periodic and regular fluctuations in the economy. Economic fluctuations are periodic in that, sooner or later, they are repeated. Because fluctuations are not regular, however, many economists prefer to use the term *business* or *economic fluctuations* in place of *business cycles.* The terms economic fluctuations and business cycles are used interchangeably in this chapter.

The first learning objective of this chapter is to introduce economic fluctuation. We introduce the concept in the first section and the composite index of leading indicators in the last section. The index of leading indicators is watched widely by business managers as well as economists. The second learning objective of this chapter is to introduce unemployment and inflation that result directly from economic fluctuations. Policy issues relating to the two problems are discussed.

ECONOMIC FLUCTUATIONS

Economic fluctuations mean significant changes in real GNP, and thus are measured by changes in the real GNP. Real GNP may increase for several years, decline for a year or two, and start increasing again. The behavior of real GNP over a full cycle and its variation around the long-term trend line are shown in Figure 14.1.

The period during which real GNP expands is called an **expansion.** The expansion eventually reaches a **peak** before real GNP starts declining. The period during which real GNP declines is called a **recession.** The recessionary period is also called a **contraction.** Nominal GNP tends to increase even during recession years because of inflation. Whether or not there is a recession in a given year is determined by looking at real GNP figures. If real GNP is lower in a given year than in the preceding year, there is a recession during the given year.

Sooner or later, all recessions end. The lowest level of real GNP before it starts increasing again is called the **trough.** Although the period during which real GNP expands is called an expansion, the early stage of an expansion is also known as a **recovery.** If real GNP increases at a rate significantly above the long-term trend line, the economy is said to be in a **boom.**

Economic fluctuations are not unique to post-World War II years of the U.S. economy. All business cycles in the U.S. economy since the middle of the 1850s are summarized in Table 14.1. The longest expansion lasted 106 months (almost 9 years), from February 1961 to December 1969. The longest contraction lasted 65 months (more than 5 years), from October 1873 to March 1879. The 1873–1879 recession lasted longer than the 1930s depression. The longest full cycle measured from peak to peak was 116 months, from April 1960 to December 1969, while the second longest cycle lasted 101 months, from October 1873 to March 1882. The shortest cycle lasted only 17 months, from August 1918 to January 1920.

When there is a recession in an economy, there is a marked slowdown in sales of goods and services. The slowdown in sales causes production and distribution of goods and services to decline. The declining economic activities, in turn, result in falling profits of businesses, falling tax

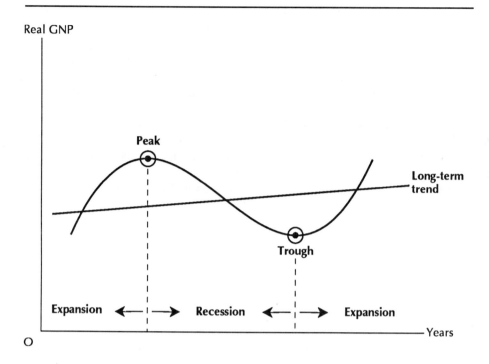

FIGURE 14.1 Different Phases of a Business Cycle. A business cycle passes through expansion, peak, recession, trough, and back to expansion. The early stage of an expansion is also called a recovery.

revenues to government, and an increase in unemployment. Among the several changes that characterize a recession, rising unemployment is the one that attracts the most attention from the public as well as from economists.

UNEMPLOYMENT

Unemployment is one-half of the twin evils of modern economy, the other half being inflation. In this section we study the meaning of unemployment, the ways of measuring it, and the types of unemployment.

What Is Unemployment?

The mere fact that a person does not have a job does not make that person unemployed so far as government statistics are concerned. A full-time housewife or student who considers looking for

TABLE 14.1 Fluctuations of the U.S. Economy

Business Cycles Reference Dates		Duration (months)		Cycle	
		Contraction (Trough from Previous Peak)	Expansion (Trough to Peak)	Trough from Previous Trough	Peak from Previous Peak
Trough	Peak				
December 1854	June 1857	—	30	—	—
December 1858	October 1860	18	22	48	40
June 1861	April 1865	8	46	30	54
December 1867	June 1869	32	18	78	50
December 1870	October 1873	18	34	36	52
March 1879	March 1882	65	36	99	101
May 1885	March 1887	38	22	74	60
April 1888	July 1890	13	27	35	40
May 1891	January 1893	10	20	37	30
June 1894	December 1895	17	18	37	35
June 1897	June 1899	18	24	36	42
December 1900	September 1902	18	21	42	39
August 1904	May 1907	23	33	44	56
June 1908	January 1910	13	19	46	32
January 1912	January 1913	24	12	43	36
December 1914	August 1918	23	44	35	67
March 1919	January 1920	7	10	51	17
July 1921	May 1923	18	22	28	40
July 1924	October 1926	14	27	36	41
November 1927	August 1929	13	21	40	34
March 1933	May 1937	43	50	64	93
June 1938	February 1945	13	80	63	93
October 1945	November 1948	8	37	88	45
October 1949	July 1953	11	45	48	56
May 1954	August 1957	10	39	55	49
April 1958	April 1960	8	24	47	32
February 1961	December 1969	10	106	34	116
November 1970	November 1973	11	36	117	47
March 1975	January 1980	16	58	52	74
July 1980	July 1981	6	12	64	18
November 1982		16	—	28	—

Sources: National Bureau of Economic Research, Inc., as published in U.S. Department of Commerce Bureau of Economic Analysis, *Business Conditions Digest* 23(July 1983):103, and 28(March 1988):10.

a job is not counted as unemployed unless the housewife or the student actively seeks a job. A 12-year-old who is desperately looking for babysitting work is not counted as unemployed until the youngster grows to be at least 16 years old. A discouraged head of a household who has no job and needs to feed his or her family is not counted as unemployed unless he or she continues to actively look for a job.

Civilian Labor Force

To understand how government collects unemployment figures, we need to study several new concepts. To be counted as employed or unemployed, a person must be a member of the labor force. **Labor force** refers to the number of persons who are

1. 16 years of age and older;
2. not in institutions such as prisons and mental hospitals; and
3. either employed or actively seeking jobs.

If military personnel are included, the labor force is the **total labor force.** If military personnel are excluded, the labor force is the **civilian labor force.** Unless stated otherwise, labor force means the civilian labor force. If a person under 16 years of age seeks gainful employment, the youngster needs permission either from the state employment agency or from the school that he or she attends. A person is said to be **gainfully employed** when the person works for pay. Once a person is classified as a member of the labor force, the person is either employed or unemployed.

Unemployment

The official U.S. government statistics on the nation's labor market are compiled by the Bureau of the Census for the U.S. Bureau of Labor Statistics. Monthly surveys are taken of a representative cross section of about 56,000 households in the nation. Labor market data such as labor force and unemployment are released every month by the Bureau of Labor Statistics.

Among the requirements to be included in the labor force is that the unemployed person should *actively seek* a job. Whether a person is seeking a job actively or passively is determined during the household interview. Every individual surveyed is classified as either not in the labor force or in the labor force. If the individual is classified as being in the labor force, the person is classified as either employed or unemployed. **Unemployed persons** are those who did not have a job during the survey week and were available for and actively seeking work. Those workers who are waiting to be called back to a job from which they were laid off are also counted as unemployed.

Rate of Unemployment

Statistics on the U.S. labor force are summarized in Table 14.2. Consider the 1988 data. The total U.S. population was 246,200,000 in column (2), of which 121,700,000 were the civilian labor force in column (3). The civilian labor force is the sum of employed persons (115,000,000) in column (4) and unemployed persons (6,700,000) in (5).

The **rate of unemployment** in column (6) is obtained when the number of unemployed persons in column (5) is divided by the civilian labor force in column (3), and the result is multiplied by 100 to convert decimals into the percentage term. That is,

$$\text{Rate of unemployment}$$
$$= (6{,}700{,}000 \div 121{,}700{,}000) \times 100 \qquad (14.1)$$
$$= 5.5 \text{ percent} \qquad (14.2)$$

TABLE 14.2 U.S. Labor Market Data

Year (1)	Total Population (millions) (2)	Civilian Labor Force (millions) (3)	Employed Persons (millions) (4)	Unemployed Persons (millions) (5)	Unemployment Rate (%) (6)
1952	157.5	62.2	60.3	1.88	3.025
1953	160.1	63.1	61.2	1.85	2.925
1954	163.0	63.7	60.1	3.57	5.592
1955	165.9	65.0	62.1	2.83	4.367
1956	168.9	66.5	63.8	2.74	4.125
1957	171.9	66.9	64.1	2.88	4.300
1958	174.8	67.7	63.0	4.63	6.842
1959	177.9	68.4	64.6	3.73	5.450
1960	180.8	69.7	65.8	3.87	5.542
1961	183.7	70.4	65.7	4.71	6.692
1962	186.6	70.6	66.7	3.92	5.567
1963	189.3	71.8	67.8	4.05	5.642
1964	191.9	73.1	69.3	3.78	5.158
1965	194.4	74.4	71.1	3.35	4.508
1966	196.6	75.7	72.9	2.87	3.792
1967	198.8	77.3	74.4	2.97	3.842
1968	200.7	78.7	75.9	2.80	3.558
1969	202.7	80.7	77.9	2.83	3.492
1970	205.1	82.8	78.7	4.13	4.983
1971	207.7	84.4	79.4	5.02	5.950
1972	209.9	87.0	82.1	4.88	5.600
1973	211.9	89.4	85.1	4.36	4.858
1974	213.9	92.0	86.8	5.17	5.642
1975	216.0	93.8	85.8	7.94	8.475
1976	218.1	96.2	88.8	7.40	7.700
1977	220.3	99.0	92.0	6.97	7.050
1978	222.6	102.2	96.0	6.19	6.067
1979	225.1	105.0	98.8	6.14	5.850
1980	227.7	107.0	99.3	7.67	7.175
1981	230.2	108.7	100.4	8.28	7.617
1982	232.5	110.2	99.5	10.71	9.708
1983	234.8	111.5	100.8	10.69	9.600
1984	237.1	113.5	105.0	8.53	7.508
1985	239.3	115.5	107.2	8.31	7.200
1986	241.6	117.8	109.6	8.25	7.008
1987	243.9	119.8	112.4	7.41	6.192
1988	246.2	121.7	115.0	6.70	5.500

Source: Adapted from U.S. Bureau of Labor Statistics, *Handbook of labor statistics* and *employment and earnings.*

In Table 14.2 recession years are underscored. The rates of unemployment are higher during recession years or in years following a recession year. There tends to be a lag between recession and unemployment rate. The lag is due to the way businesses make employment decisions over a cycle of an economic fluctuation. When a recession actually begins and sales start declining, businesses try to hold on to their employees. There are two reasons for this delayed behavior by businesses. One is that businesses may not even know that a recession has started and may consider the decline in sales to be temporary. The other reason is that it is costly to train new employees, leading businesses to keep their employees, especially good ones, as long as they can. When a recovery starts, there is a lag between increasing sales and new hiring. Businesses tend to be cautious about hiring workers until they are convinced that the recovery is genuine and not temporary.

Types of Unemployment

Economists classify unemployment into several categories: frictional, seasonal, structural, and cyclical. These categories are not mutually exclusive, meaning that one person may be counted as more than one classification. Also discussed in this section is the concept of full employment.

Frictional Unemployment

Frictional unemployment refers to those who are unemployed while entering the job market or changing jobs. When a new college graduate is temporarily unemployed while seeking a job, the college graduate's lack of employment is counted as frictional unemployment. If the labor market were perfectly competitive so that everyone knew who was seeking a job and who was looking for a worker, and if labor were perfectly mobile, there would be no frictional unemployment.

Since information on the labor market is not complete, search is an important issue in labor markets. Information about the availability of jobs is poor because the average worker does not look for a job very often. Unemployed workers have to keep on searching for jobs that they like until they can find them. The search efforts are expected to increase as the cost of being unemployed increases. Conversely, search efforts are expected to decrease as the cost of being unemployed decreases. Since benefits such as unemployment insurance payments given to unemployed persons reduce the cost of search for the unemployed persons, some economists argue that these benefits tend to increase search time and, consequently, unemployment.

Seasonal Unemployment

When workers are unemployed because their jobs are seasonal by nature, their lack of employment is called **seasonal unemployment.** Farming is seasonal and many farmers are seasonally unemployed during the off-season. Construction activities are easily affected by weather conditions that change with seasons. Construction activities in northern states, for instance, tend to be slow during winter months. The Christmas season has a significant impact on retailing and many other industries, creating seasonal employment during the holiday season. The increase in the number of students who seek jobs at the end of the school year leads to seasonal unemployment.

Cyclical Unemployment

Unemployment fluctuates with the general level of economic activities. Our economy often experiences levels of aggregate demand that are insufficient to generate jobs for all workers who wish to work at existing wage rates. When workers are unemployed due to insufficient aggregate demand, **cyclical unemployment** is said to exist. Many unemployed persons during a recession are cyclically unemployed.

Structural Unemployment

As technology improves, a mismatch develops between the requirements of vacant jobs and the skills of the unemployed. When workers lose their jobs because of changing job requirements that these workers are not prepared for, their lack of employment is classified as **structural unemployment.** A person accustomed to using an abacus will be structurally unemployed unless the person is retrained for use of the computer. Structural unemployment is characterized by persistent mismatches between the supply of and the demand for workers with skills.

Full Employment

Ideal full employment is a state in which every worker who wants to work at existing wages is employed. Practical full employment is not quite the same as ideal full employment. Many economists consider that frictional unemployment and structural unemployment are unavoidable. Economists designate an economy whose unemployment is mostly frictional or structural as a full employment economy. The unemployment rate at the full employment level, therefore, represents the sum of frictional and structural unemployment. The unemployment rate at the full employment economy is also known as the **natural rate of unemployment.** It is natural in the sense that there is not much the government or anyone else can do about unemployment in the short run. The natural rate of unemployment is rather subjective and changes over time as underlying economic conditions change. If the actual rate of unemployment is high, the natural rate of unemployment as perceived by economists also tends to be high. If the actual rate of unemployment is low, the natural rate tends to be low. The level of GNP that can be produced with unemployment limited to its natural rate is called the economy's **potential GNP.**

Issues of Unemployment

There are two issues of unemployment that we need to discuss to better understand problems associated with unemployment. One issue relates to the way unemployed persons are counted. The official count of unemployment does not necessarily include everyone who is truly unemployed. The underestimation is due to the exclusion from unemployment figures of those who are not actively seeking jobs. This approach is inevitable. The inclusion in the official unemployment statistics of those who read the help-wanted section of the local newspaper while drinking beer and watching *The Young and the Restless* would certainly exaggerate the problem of unemployment. A disadvantage of the approach is its tendency to exclude the so-called hard-core unemployment. **Hard-core unemployment** refers to those whose qualifications for work are so poor that they do not even search for a job and, thus, are not counted as unemployed in the government unemployment statistics. Many high school dropouts fall into this category.

The other issue relates to the size of the labor force. Suppose that the number of people 16 years and over and not in institutions remains the same this year and the next. This year's labor force may not be the same in size as next year's labor force. When the economy expands, the probability of obtaining the kind of job that one wants improves, prompting some individuals such as full-time housewives and students to join the labor force. When the economy is in a recession, on the other hand, fewer jobs are available, prompting some individuals who are unemployed to decide not to seek jobs. Even though the number of working-age people is constant from one year to the next, the labor force becomes larger when the economy expands and smaller when the economy contracts. A **labor force participation rate,** obtained by dividing the labor force by the working-age population, measures such fluctuations in the labor force. The civilian labor force as a percentage of working age population is lower during recession years or in years immediately following a recession. The labor force participation rate varies directly with the level of economic activities.

INFLATION

Inflation is part of modern economic life. When prices rise rapidly, economists are concerned with how to slow down price increases and minimize the adverse effects of inflation on the economy. When prices fall, economists are also concerned because falling prices may indicate falling economic activities.

BLACK MONDAY

October 16, 1987, is known as Black Monday. By the time the 4 P.M. closing bell rang at the New York Stock Exchange, the Dow Jones Industrial Average had plunged 508 points, or 22.6 percent, in one day to close at 1738.74. Some $500 billion in paper value vanished into thin air.

Some analysts claimed the credit for having predicted the panic selling of stocks on Black Monday. Franco Modigliani, a Nobel Prize winner in economics, stated tongue in cheek during a panel discussion at the 1988 meeting of the Eastern Economic Association in Boston, "I predicted it—*since 1981.*" In an October 5 article in *Time,* Stephen Koepp states,

> *Today's worrisome parallels to the 1920s begin with Wall Street. From 1925 to 1929, stock prices more than doubled. But during the current bull market, the Dow Jones Industrial Average has more than tripled in value since the rise began in August 1982. During the rally's first phase, investors put their money in stocks, which were backed by corporate profits and dividends. But in the later stages, the betting has become almost purely speculative. Investors poured money into the market in fear of missing the free ride.*

That situation, Koepp affirmed prophetically only about 10 days before Black Monday, sets up the market for a crash, when investors suddenly realize that the party is over. What would be a sufficiently frightening financial event to trigger such a crash? No one knows precisely.

There are many explanations for the panic selling of stocks on Black Monday. One explanation is the announcement, made two weeks prior to Black Monday, of the

(continued)

continued

U.S. trade deficit for August that exceeded expectations. Another explanation is the high rate of interest that caused investors to transfer money from stocks to bonds. Another explanation is a statement made by James Baker, then secretary of the U.S. Treasury, that criticized the West German policy of raising interest rates, a policy that would make foreign investment in the United States more difficult. Still another explanation is the computer trading by many firms that had programmed their computers to launch massive automatic trade in order to profit from small price changes. Yet another is that stock prices prior to Black Monday were simply too high. Perhaps the best explanation was given by Robert Solow, another Nobel laureate who shared the table with Frank Modigliani at the economists' meeting in Boston. Solow said, "We did not know what caused Black Monday; we do not know what caused Black Monday; we will never know what caused Black Monday. Our ignorance, however, will not keep hundreds of doctoral students from writing dissertations to find out why there was Black Monday."

The stock market crash on Black Monday attracted wide attention because of the unprecedented magnitude of the fall in stock prices. According to economic theory, how much the public spends depends, at least in part, on the amount of assets the public has. When stock prices fall, the money value of assets held by the public declines. The decline in the value of wealth causes people to reduce the amount of money they spend. When the reduction in spending is significant, it may cause a recession or even a depression. The impact of Black Monday on consumption in the U.S. economy was estimated to be approximately $30 billion. This amount represented only about 1 percent of total annual consumption expenditures at the time. What this means is that by itself the market crash on Black Monday would not cause a recession.

What Is Inflation?

Inflation refers to rising prices of goods and services. This definition does not mean that prices of all goods and services rise during an inflationary period. Even during inflation, prices of selected goods and services may fall. When there is inflation, the prices of many goods and services rise in such a way that the overall level of prices rises. When prices rise, the same dollar commands less purchasing power. If $2.00 was sufficient to buy one Big Mac before inflation, we would need more than $2.00 to buy a Big Mac during and after inflation. Inflation reduces the value of money.

Measuring the Rate of Inflation

Inflation is measured by changes in a price index. One price index accepted widely as the measure of inflation is the consumer price index (CPI) for all urban workers, known as CPI-U, introduced in Chapter 13. Like unemployment statistics, the CPI data are collected and released on a monthly basis, and the annual CPI is simply the average of the 12 monthly CPI figures. The CPIs since 1952 are shown in Table 14.3.

TABLE 14.3 Consumer Price Index,
1982–1984 = 100

Year	Consumer Price Index	Annual Rates of Inflation (%)
(1)	(2)	(3)
1952	26.6	—
1953	26.8	0.77
1954	26.9	0.35
1955	26.8	−0.26
1956	27.2	1.47
1957	28.1	3.40
1958	28.9	2.73
1959	29.1	0.92
1960	29.6	1.51
1961	29.9	1.07
1962	30.3	1.17
1963	30.6	1.25
1964	31.0	1.32
1965	31.5	1.59
1966	32.5	2.99
1967	33.4	2.78
1968	34.8	4.24
1969	36.7	5.46
1970	38.8	5.83
1971	40.5	4.26
1972	41.8	3.31
1973	44.4	6.22
1974	49.3	11.04
1975	53.8	9.13
1976	56.9	5.75
1977	60.6	6.49
1978	65.2	7.63
1979	72.6	11.27
1980	82.4	13.55
1981	90.9	10.31
1982	96.5	6.15
1983	99.6	3.22
1984	103.9	4.30
1985	107.6	3.55
1986	109.6	1.90
1987	113.6	3.66
1988	118.3	4.14

Source: Adapted from U.S. Bureau of Labor Statistics, *Monthly Labor Review*.

Annual rates of inflation can be obtained from the CPI figures presented in Table 14.3. The annual rate of inflation from year 1 to year 2 is obtained, first, by dividing the price index of year 2 by the price index of year 1 and, second, by subtracting 1 from the result, and, finally, by multiplying the result by 100. To illustrate, let us compute the rate of inflation from 1980 to 1981. The CPI for 1980 is 82.4 in Table 14.3. The CPI for 1981 is 90.9, meaning that a typical product that cost $82.40 in 1980 would have cost $90.90 in 1981. The rate of inflation from 1980 to 1981 was 10.3 percent:

Rate of inflation

$$= (\frac{1981 \text{ CPI}}{1980 \text{ CPI}} - 1) \times 100 \tag{14.3}$$

$$= (\frac{90.9}{82.4} - 1) \times 100 \tag{14.4}$$

$$= (1.103 - 1) \times 100 \tag{14.5}$$

$$= 0.103 \times 100 \tag{14.6}$$

$$= 10.3 \text{ percent} \tag{14.7}$$

We subtract 1 from the ratio of the 1981 CPI to the 1980 CPI in equation (14.3) for the following reason. If there were no increase in prices from 1980 to 1981, the ratio of the 1981 CPI to the 1980 CPI would be 1. To obtain changes in the price index, therefore, 1 needs to be subtracted from the ratio of the two price indexes. We multiply 100 in equation (14.3) because the rate of inflation is typically expressed in percentage terms. By multiplying the ratio of price indexes by 100, the ratio is converted into a percentage.

Annual rates of inflation since 1952 are shown in column (3) in Table 14.3. During the almost 40-year period, the general level of prices decreased in only one year, 1955. In all of the remaining years, there was inflation. The rate of inflation was relatively low at less than 4 percent per year through 1967. With the Vietnam War becoming an increasing burden on the nation's economy, inflation accelerated in 1968. Although the Vietnam War ended in the early 1970s, inflation became worse and maintained a rapid rate of increase until 1982. This period was characterized by *stag*nant growth with in*flation*, resulting in so-called **stagflation.** Understandably, traditional macroeconomic theories encountered a serious challenge during this period.

Types of Inflation

Inflation may be classified either by how fast prices rise or by what causes it.

Inflation by Rate

Depending on how rapidly prices rise, inflation is classified as creeping inflation, moderate inflation, and hyper inflation. **Creeping inflation** refers to prices that are rising at a slow rate, whereas **moderate inflation** refers to prices that are rising at a moderate rate. **Hyperinflation** is said to exist if prices are rising at a fast rate. There is no consensus regarding an arbitrary, magic rate of inflation that can serve to classify a given inflation rate as being one of the three types. Whether a given inflation rate is creeping, moderate, or hyper depends on individual nations as well as different periods of time within a nation.

Although we do not know whether the rates of inflation presented in Table 14.4 are perceived as being moderate or hyper in the countries that experienced them, these rates are clearly hyper, at least by the U.S. standards. The rate of inflation in Argentina from 1984 to 1985, for instance, was 672.1 percent, meaning that prices rose almost sevenfold during just one year. Assume that a Big Mac costs $2.00 now. With a 672.1 percent inflation, the same hamburger would cost $13.44 in only 12 months.

Inflation by Cause

According to cause, inflation may be classified as demand pull or cost push. If inflation is caused by surprise occurrences, it may also be classified as supply shock inflation.

DEMAND PULL INFLATION. **Demand pull inflation** refers to rising prices caused by an aggregate demand that is greater than aggregate supply. If, for instance, the demand for Miami Sound cassette tapes is greater than their supply, the price of Miami Sound cassette tapes rises. When excess demand exists throughout the economy, there is demand pull inflation. Demand pull inflation is often described as "too much money chasing too few goods."

COST PUSH INFLATION. **Cost push inflation** is a generic term encompassing price increases originating on the seller's side. For this reason, cost push inflation is also called **seller's inflation.** There are two cases of cost push inflation, wage push and profit push.

Let us consider an industry that is either monopolistic or oligopolistic and exerts considerable market power. Suppose that most workers working in the industry are unionized and labor unions in the industry are powerful. What would happen if labor unions demanded wage increases above and beyond the combined rate of general inflation in the economy and of increases in labor productivity in the industry? Rather than risking a disruption in production, firms in the industry

TABLE 14.4 Annual Rates of Inflation for Selected Countries

	From Preceding Year to						
Country	1981	1982	1983	1984	1985	1986	1987
Argentina	104.5%	164.8%	343.8%	626.7%	672.1%	90.1%	131.3%
Brazil	105.6	98.0	142.1	197.0	226.9	145.2	229.7
Israel	116.8	120.4	145.6	373.8	304.6	48.1	19.8
Mexico	27.9	58.9	101.8	65.5	57.7	86.2	131.8
Peru	75.4	64.4	111.2	110.2	163.4	77.9	85.8
Yugoslavia	39.7	32.9	40.2	54.7	72.3	89.8	120.8

Source: U.S. Department of Commerce Bureau of the Census, *Statistical abstract of the United States,* 109th ed. (Washington, D.C.: U.S. Government Printing Office, January 1989), p. 828.

may agree to wage increases and, in turn, raise prices of their products. *Wage push* inflation, therefore, requires two conditions: strong labor unions and the market power of firms.

Firms may also raise prices beyond increases in prices of productive resources even though there is no pressure from labor unions. In this case, there is *profit push* inflation.

SUPPLY SHOCK INFLATION. Some economists prefer to add supply shocks as another cause of inflation. **Supply shocks** are surprise occurrences that temporarily increase or decrease current output. Examples of supply shocks include hurricanes, earthquakes, and a temporary increase in the price of imports. Supply shocks affect not only current output but also prices.

When the Organization of Petroleum Exporting Countries (OPEC) reduced the production of crude oil in the early 1970s, the supply curve of oil shifted to the left, creating an excess demand for oil at the price that existed before production was reduced. The reduced production of oil caused oil prices to rise by 1,700 percent from 1971 to 1973. The higher price of oil led many industries that heavily depended on oil as a source of energy to raise the prices of their products.

Effects of Inflation

Most effects of inflation vary significantly depending on whether inflation is anticipated or unanticipated. Some effects vary little regardless of whether inflation is anticipated or unanticipated.

Anticipated Inflation

If we expect prices to increase by 4 percent this year and prices do increase by 4 percent during the year, we say that this year's inflation is anticipated inflation. If we expect prices to stay the same but they increase by 4 percent during the year, the inflation is unanticipated inflation. If we expect prices to increase by 4 percent but they actually increase by 6 percent during the year, the unanticipated inflation is 2 percent, the difference between anticipated inflation and actual inflation.

The main effect of anticipated inflation over a long period of time would be on investment. Even if inflation is anticipated inflation, there is no way of anticipating the exact rate of inflation for the future. Even anticipated inflation thus creates uncertainty. Those who make decisions on investment tend to prefer a quick return on their investments, since the success of long-term investment projects becomes subject to greater uncertainty. Consequently, industries that require a large amount of investment tend to grow more slowly when inflation is anticipated.

Unanticipated Inflation

The effects of unanticipated inflation are twofold: the creditor-debtor relation and the rationing function of prices.

Let us first discuss the effect of inflation on the creditor-debtor relation. Suppose that we borrow $10,000 now and promise to pay back the principal in one year with 10 percent interest. One year from now, we are scheduled to pay $11,000. Suppose that immediately after we sign the contract, prices start rising at an annual rate of 5 percent. The purchasing power of the $11,000 that we are to pay one year from now would then decrease by $550, which is 5 percent of $11,000. When inflation is unanticipated, debtors gain since the real burden of the debt falls. Creditors lose since the value of the dollar falls in direct proportion to unanticipated inflation.

Unanticipated inflation is usually unpredictable. When inflation is unpredictable, the rationing function of prices is affected. Suppose that the price of a new home rises because of inflation prevailing throughout the economy. A higher price of a product usually indicates a shortage of the product and induces producers of the product to increase the quantity of the product supplied. When unpredictable inflation causes the price of a new home to rise temporarily, home-builders will find it difficult to understand what the higher price means. If the higher price does not represent a lasting shortage of new homes, building additional homes would not be an efficient allocation of resources.

Either Way

Regardless of whether inflation is anticipated or unanticipated, two groups of individuals tend to lose during inflation. The two groups are (1) wage earners working in a competitive industry, and (2) retirees who depend on private pensions.

Suppose that a worker is barely holding on to his job in a competitive industry. He is not in a position to ask for a pay raise. Without a pay raise, his nominal income remains the same but his real income is reduced as prices rise. In fact, anyone whose income increases but lags behind inflation experiences a decrease in real income and, thus, living standards. The point is that without doing anything wrong and although continuing to work as hard as ever, all workers suffer a reduced real income when there is inflation. Income is arbitrarily redistributed from those working in the competitive sector to those who are capable of raising prices, who enjoy higher revenues.

If the worker does have power to ask for a pay raise through, say, membership in a labor union, how he is affected by inflation depends on his ability to predict inflation. If he anticipates inflation and gets an increase in nominal income in direct proportion to rising prices, his real income and living standards will remain the same. One method used by many labor unions to raise nominal income in direct proportion to inflation is the automatic cost of living adjustment (COLA). COLA allows wages to go up automatically as prices rise. If we do not anticipate inflation but prices go up anyway, there is a lag between inflation and the increase in nominal income. The longer the lag, the larger the amount of loss in real income.

Finally, those who depend on private pensions tend to lose during inflation. Unlike many government and military pensions that are automatically adjusted for inflation, private pensions usually are not subject to COLA.

Keeping Up with Inflation

The best way of controlling inflation is to pursue fiscal and monetary policy that can promote economic growth with little inflation, if any. Two problems exist, however. One problem is that economists do not know, at least do not agree on, what the best policy is to combat inflation. The other problem is that inflation is not likely to be subdued for a long time even with the best policy. Shocks such as the 1973 oil embargo by OPEC are bound to occur occasionally and cause prices to go up. Economists, therefore, have proposed incomes policies as measures to minimize the adverse effects of inflation and to moderate wage and price increases.

Incomes policies encompass a wide range of governmental initiatives that affect wages, prices, and real incomes in the economy. The strongest incomes policy would be a general price and wage control, while the weakest incomes policy would be the government's pressure (jawboning) on individual businesses not to raise prices. In this section, we review three ideas that fall between the two extreme incomes policies: tax-based incomes policy (TIP), indexing, and CPI-minus-2.

Tax-Based Incomes Policy
The tax-based incomes policy was proposed originally by Henry C. Wallich and Sidney Wein-traub.[1] **Tax-based incomes policy** (TIP) involves a system of tax penalties and rebates to provide incentives to businesses and labor unions to encourage them to comply *voluntarily* with wage and price guidelines established by the government.

Under a TIP program, a nationwide wage guideline would be established covering all types of compensation, including fringe benefits. If wage increases in any large corporation exceed wage increases suggested in the guideline, the government would impose a tax surcharge on the portion of wage increases that exceed the guideline. Suppose that the guideline suggests that wage increases be limited to 5 percent per year. If Greedy Company granted a 7 percent average annual increase in compensation, its corporate tax rate would be increased by some amount related to the excess over the guideline. If the tax surcharge were 10 percent for every percentage point by which the guideline was exceeded, the Greedy Company would have to pay an additional tax equal in amount to 10 percent of all wage payments in excess of the 5 percent increase. The government would also allow a rebate to businesses that granted pay raises below the increase suggested in the guideline.[2]

Indexing
Indexing is an arrangement in which wages and other future payments such as pension plans, savings accounts, and life insurance contracts are automatically adjusted in response to increases in the cost of living. Indexing ensures that future payments will retain the same purchasing power as before inflation, and thus minimizes the redistribution of income that is induced by inflation. If carried out adequately, indexing allows changes in relative prices to reflect changing conditions in demand and supply as they are supposed to in markets that experience no inflation.

The principal argument in favor of indexing is equity. Inflation hurts primarily those who are unable to protect themselves during inflation. By indexing future payments, the burden of inflation will be shared by all, not simply by those unable to protect themselves. There are also arguments against indexing. The principal argument against indexing is that indexing itself is inflationary, since it reduces any pressure to reduce inflation. Opponents of indexing also argue that any truly equitable system of indexing would have to be so complex that it would defeat the best efforts of any indexing bureaucracy.[3]

CPI-Minus-2
To understand CPI-minus-2 we need to know about indexing in federal programs. The first indexing in federal programs started in 1870 when increases in military retirement benefits were

---

[1]Henry C. Wallich and Sidney Weintraub, A tax-based incomes policy, *Journal of Economic Issues* 5(June 1971):1–19.

[2]For variations on the original TIP, see Arthur Okun, The great stagflation swamp, *Challenge,* November-December 1977, pp. 6–13; and Laurence S. Seidman, Equity and tradeoffs in a tax-based incomes policy, *American Economic Review* 71(May 1981):295–300. For criticisms of TIP, see Albert Rees, New policies to fight inflation: Sources of skepticism, *Brookings Papers on Economic Activity* II(1978):453–490.

[3]For more on indexing, see Congressional Budget Office, The Congress of the United States, *Indexing with the Consumer Price Index: problems and alternatives* (Washington, D.C.: U.S. Government Printing Office, June 1981), and Ronald Krieger, Inflation and the "Brazilian solution," *Challenge,* September-October 1974, pp. 103–112.

first adjusted to reflect increases in active-duty pay in a procedure known as *recomputation*.[4] This adjustment had been discretionary until the Joint Service Pay Act of 1922 made the procedure automatic. The Congress adopted CPI indexation for civil service retirement benefits in 1962 and for military retirement benefits in 1963. The 1962 indexing of the civil service retirement benefits represented the first major federal program to be formally indexed to a price index, setting a powerful precedent for indexation in the future. The Food Stamp Program was indexed in 1971, and a widespread indexing of federal programs followed the 1972 indexing of Social Security benefits, the largest of all indexed federal programs linked to changes in the CPI.

Indexed federal programs are divided into indexed entitlement programs and other indexed programs. **Entitlements** are benefits prescribed by law for all persons meeting a program's eligibility requirements. The total outlays, therefore, are not determined by an annual appropriations decision of the Congress. There are 26 indexed entitlement programs. Table 14.5 shows a list of these programs and the date of indexation of each. Other indexed programs refer to those federal programs of which indexing is either subject to discretionary review by Congress or applicable with ceilings and other restraints. There are over 60 indexed programs that are not entitlements. These programs include price support loans for farm products, military pay, federal civilian pay, the Food Stamp Program, Head Start, Medicare, Medicaid, the Job Corps, College Work Study, and National Direct Student Loans.

The idea of CPI-minus-2 was introduced in 1983 by congressional representative James R. Jones of Oklahoma, then chairman of the House Budget Committee, out of his concern about the rising deficit in the federal budget.[5] **CPI-minus-2** would reduce annual cost of living adjustments on indexed entitlement programs by 2 percentage points below the increase in the CPI. For instance, if inflation were to run at a 5 percent annual rate, the cost of living adjustment for these programs would be adjusted by 3 percent instead of the full 5 percent. CPI-minus-2 would reduce the budget deficit but still allow protection against high inflation.

FORECASTING ECONOMIC FLUCTUATIONS

In a market economy, where decisions on production of goods and services are made by individual producers, aggregate demand will not always match aggregate supply. Fluctuations in business activities are unavoidable. As the economy fluctuates, the rate of unemployment and the rate of inflation are also expected to fluctuate. In this section, we discuss why economic forecasts are necessary and then study the use of the composite index of leading indicators, watched widely by the business community.

Uses of Economic Forecasts

In economic forecasting, we try to predict likely future values of major economic variables. Major economic variables that are regularly forecast by professional forecasters include nominal GNP,

---

[4]For a history of indexing federal programs, see Congressional Budget Office, The Congress of the United States, *Indexing with the Consumer Price Index: Problems and alternatives* (Washington, D.C.: U.S. Government Printing Office, June 1981), p. 21.

[5]The Honorable James R. Jones, CPI-minus-2: A partial solution to a deficit reduction program, *Fiscal Policy Forum* 1(Fall 1983):1–8; and Robert C. Brown, CPI-minus-2 revisited, Tax Foundation, *Tax Features* 30(May 1986):3.

TABLE 14.5 Indexed Entitlement Programs

Program	Date of Indexation
1. Federal Judiciary Survivors' Benefits	1956
2. U.S. Coast Guard Retirement Pay	1958
3. Civil Service Retirement System	1962
4. Military Retirement Pay	1963
5. U.S. Presidents' Pensions (effective 1964)	1963
6. Public Health Service Commissioned Officers Retirement	1965
7. Federal Reserve Board Employees Retirement	1965
8. CIA Retirement and Disability System (effective 1966)	1964
9. Federal Employment Compensation Act	1966
10. Special Benefits for Disabled Coal Miners (HHS)	1969
11. Guaranteed Student Loan Program (Special Allowances)	1976
12. Federal Old Age Survivors and Disability Insurance (OASDI) (effective 1975)	1972
13–18. Child Nutrition Programs	1973–1978
National School Lunch Program (Commodity Subsidy)	
National School Lunch Program (Cash Subsidy)	
School Breakfast Program (Cash Subsidy)	
Summer Food Service (Cash Subsidy)	
Child Care Feeding (Commodity Subsidy)	
Child Care Feeding (Cash Subsidy)	
19. Special Benefits for Disabled Coal Miners	1974
20. Railroad Retirement Benefits (effective 1975)	1974
21. Supplemental Security Income (effective 1975)	1974
22. Foreign Service Retirement and Disability Fund	1976
23–25. Department of Defense	1972–1978
Survivor Benefit Plan	
Retired Servicemen's Family Protection Plan	
Guaranteed Minimum Incorporated	
26. Veterans' Pensions	1979

Source: Congressional Budget Office, The Congress of the United States, *Indexing with the consumer price index: Problems and alternatives* (Washington, D.C.: U.S. Government Printing Office, June 1981), pp. 23–24.

real GNP, components of nominal and real GNP, consumer price index, labor force, employment, unemployment, the rate of unemployment, and sales of major manufactured products such as automobiles. Since most economic variables tend to move together with fluctuations in real GNP, greater attention is paid to forecasting real GNP.

If we can accurately forecast future fluctuations in the economy subject to existing policy constraints, we will be able to minimize the magnitude of the fluctuation and, thus, minimize economic losses. If we know, for instance, that the economy for the next two years is not likely to grow so long as current policies continue, the government may undertake expansionary economic policies to promote additional business activities. If we know that the economy is not expected to grow, private businesses may prepare for the slowdown by reducing their production and tightening inventories. Carrying a large stock of merchandise is not merely costly; it is a quick step toward

---

HOW TO FORECAST REVENUE

To find a value good and true,
Here are three things for you to do:
Consider your replacement cost,
Determine value that is lost,
Analyze your sales to see
What market value really should be
Now if these suggestions are not clear,
Copy the figures you used last year.

Source: Anonymous, quoted from *Property taxation: Effects on land uses and local government revenues,* A study prepared for the Subcommittee on Intergovernmental Relations of the Senate Committee on Government Operations, 92nd Congress, 1st Session, 1971, p. 29.

---

bankruptcy in times of recession. In this situation, the actions of private businesses may worsen, or even cause, the downturn even though the forecast would otherwise have been erroneous. If the economy is not expected to grow, public officials of the local government may expect a slow increase in, if not a decrease in, tax revenues and become cautious about hiring additional police officers or garbagemen.

There are many firms that specialize in forecasting business and economic variables. Well known among these firms are Data Resources Incorporated in Lexington, Massachusetts, which enjoys hundreds of corporate customers, Wharton Econometric Associates in Philadelphia, and Chase Econometrics in New York. Most business magazines routinely carry forecasts of major economic variables made by leading forecasters, although forecasts of specific variables are available only to their paid subscribers.

These days, all professional forecasters employ econometric methods. **Econometric methods** are statistical methods applied to theoretical models of economic reality. The most powerful statistical method applied to economic forecasting is the regression equation, which postulates a causal relation between a dependent variable such as real GNP and one or more independent variables such as business investment and interest rates. Regardless of which specific econometric equations individual forecasting firms use, professional forecasters all watch changes in the composite index of leading indicators.

Composite Index of Leading Indicators

It is an exaggeration, but someone once said, "We probably wouldn't be any worse off if we let the economists predict the weather and the meteorologists predict the economy."[6] Many economists use economic "barometers" to forecast a change in business conditions. One barometer that is watched widely by economic forecasters and the business community is the composite index of leading indicators.

---

[6]James Dent, West Virginia's *Charleston Gazette,* as quoted in *Reader's Digest,* November 1983, p. 36.

Cyclical Indicators

The recurring pattern of expansion and contraction of the overall activity of an economy is called the **business cycle.** Economists have long searched for an economic series that would give a signal of changes in economic activity that can be used to forecast business cycles.

The first serious attempt to select economic series as indicators to predict business cycles was made in the 1920s. The business cycle indicators were published by the Harvard Economic Service. This early system of indicators, called the Harvard ABC curves, was popular but was discontinued when it failed to predict the Great Depression.[7] During the 1937–38 recession, U.S. Treasury Secretary Henry Morgenthau, Jr., asked the National Bureau of Economic Research (NBER) to develop a system of economic indicators that would signal the end of the recession. The NBER was, and still is, a private nonprofit research organization.

Under the leadership of Wesley C. Mitchell and Arthur F. Burns, the NBER had collected and analyzed hundreds of economic series. Based on their analysis, Mitchell and Burns selected a number of series that appeared reliable in predicting past business recoveries. There have been many modifications and refinements in the original list, published in May 1938 by the Treasury Department. A comprehensive review of cyclical indicators was conducted from 1972 to 1975 by the Bureau of Economic Analysis (BEA) of the U.S. Department of Commerce, with the cooperation of the NBER research staff. Data on cyclical indicators and indexes of cyclical indicators are published every month in *Business Conditions Digest* by the U.S. Department of Commerce.

Economic series can be classified with respect to the reference dates of business cycle chronology of peaks and troughs. Series that historically reached their own cyclical peaks and troughs earlier than the corresponding turns in the business cycle are called **leading indicators.** Series that historically reached their own cyclical peaks and troughs at about the same time as the corresponding turns in the business cycle are called **coincident indicators.** Series that historically reached their cyclical peaks and troughs later than corresponding turns in the business cycle are called **lagging indicators.** There are 108 cyclical indicators that are classified as leading indicators, 47 indicators that are classified as coincident indicators, and 60 indicators that are classified as lagging indicators. When news media mention leading, coincident, or lagging indicators, however, these indicators are usually composite indexes of indicators. The composite index of leading indicators comprises only 11 leading indicators; four coincident indicators make up the composite index of coincident indicators; and six lagging indicators make up the composite index of lagging indicators. The components of the three composite indexes are listed in Table 14.6.

Reading the Index of Leading Indicators

Of the three composite indexes, the one that attracts the most attention each month is the composite index of 11 leading indicators, which is often abbreviated as the index of leading indicators. Figure 14.2 is adapted from the Composite Indexes that appear in each issue of the *Business Conditions Digest.* The base year for the index is 1967. The peak and trough months of all recessions since World War II are indicated vertically in the figure. The numbers shown above the index curve are the lead time in months between the beginning of the decline in the index and the beginning of the recession. The numbers shown below the index curve, on the other hand, are the lead time in months between the beginning of the increase in the index and the end of the recession.

[7]For more on the Harvard ABC curves, see Oskar Lange, *Introduction to econometrics,* 2nd ed. (Oxford: Pergamon Press, 1962), pp. 85–95. See also Gary Gorton, Forecasting with the Index of Leading Indicators, Federal Reserve Bank of Philadelphia's *Business Review,* November-December 1982, pp. 15–27.

TABLE 14.6 Composite Index Components

Leading indicators

Average weekly hours of production for nonsupervisory workers, manufacturing
Average weekly initial claims for unemployment insurance, state programs
Manufacturers' new orders in 1982 dollars, consumer goods and materials industries
Vendor performance, percentage of companies receiving slower deliveries
Contracts and orders for plant and equipment in 1982 dollars
Index of new private housing units authorized by local building permits
Change in manufacturing and trade inventories on hand and on order in 1982 dollars, smoothed
Change in sensitive materials prices, smoothed
Index of stock prices, 500 common stocks
Money supply M2 in 1982 dollars
Change in business and consumer credit outstanding

Coincident indicators

Employees on nonagricultural payrolls
Personal income less transfer payments in 1982 dollars
Manufacturing and trade sales in 1982 dollars
Index of industrial production

Lagging indicators

Average duration of unemployment in weeks, inverted scale
Ratio, manufacturing and trade inventories to sales in 1982 dollars
Labor cost per unit of output, manufacturing
Average prime rate charged by banks
Commercial and industrial loans outstanding in 1982 dollars
Ratio, consumer installment credit outstanding to personal income

---

Source: U.S. Department of Commerce Bureau of Economic Analysis, *Business Conditions Digest* 28(October 1988):12–15.

The index of leading indicators does lead turning points of economic fluctuations. The lead time, however, varies widely. The lead months for recessions range from three months for the 1980 recession to as long as 23 months for the 1957–58 recession. In other words, the 1980 recession began only three months after the index of leading indicators started declining, whereas the 1957–58 recession began almost two years after the index started declining. The lead time for recovery is considerably shorter and ranges from one to eight months. The number in the box located at the upper right-hand corner is the latest month for which the data are included in the graph. The latest month included in Figure 14.2 is December 1988.

The index of leading indicators does show the overall strength of the economy. Some have suggested a rule of thumb: If the index falls for three consecutive months, the fall indicates that a recession is coming. The relation between fluctuations in the index and fluctuations in real GNP, however, is too loose to forecast turning points of the economy using the index. It is not unusual for no recession to occur even after the index falls for several consecutive months.

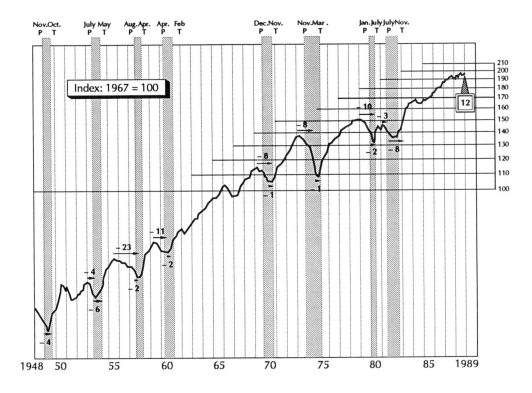

FIGURE 14.2 Index of Leading Indicators. The index of leading indicators leads turning points of a business cycle, but the lead time varies from one cycle to the next.

SUMMARY

The ups and downs of real GNP are called a business cycle or an economic fluctuation. Business cycles are periodic but not regular. When a person has the ability and the willingness to work, then the person is counted as part of the labor force. Those who are 16 years old and over are judged to have the ability to work. Among those, only those who are already working or actively seeking work (applying and interviewing for jobs) are judged to have the willingness to work. Persons who belong to the labor force are either employed or unemployed. If the number of unemployed persons is divided by the civilian labor force, we obtain the rate of unemployment. Unemployment is typically classified into several categories such as frictional, seasonal, structural, and cyclical. When unemployment is mostly frictional or structural, economists say that the economy is a full employment economy. The unemployment rate at full employment is also called the natural rate of unemployment. A labor force participation rate is obtained by dividing the labor force by the working age population.

Inflation is measured by changes in the consumer price index. Inflation is classified into creeping, moderate, and hyperinflation; or into demand pull, cost push, and supply shock. Cost push inflation is wage push or profit push, depending on who is blaming whom between management and labor union. Inflation arbitrarily redistributes income from one group to another. Those who tend to lose from inflation include wage earners working in a competitive industry, and retirees who depend on retirement pensions not structured to increase with inflation. Those who gain from unanticipated inflation include debtors. Incomes policies are designed to distribute the burden of inflation equally among different people as well as to slow inflation. Three ideas discussed in the text are tax-based incomes policy, indexing, and CPI-minus-2. CPI-minus-2 was intended to apply to federal entitlement programs. One of the most widely watched barometers in economic forecasting is the composite index of leading indicators. Although the index of leading indicators does lead turning points of economic fluctuations, the lead time varies widely.

EXERCISES

1. The rate of unemployment is usually higher near the end of a recession and immediately after a recession than at the beginning or middle of a recession. What would explain this tendency?

2. List types of unemployment, and briefly explain each one.

3. Suppose that there are 100 working age people of whom 60 are labor force. Of these, 54 are employed and 6 are unemployed. (a) What is the rate of unemployment? (b) What is the labor force participation rate? (c) Assuming that the economy improves so that employment increases from 54 to 60, will the number of unemployed persons fall to zero? If not, why not?

4. If a person does not have a job and gives up looking for a job because no one seems willing to give that person a job, will the person be counted as an unemployed person in the government unemployment data? If not, why not?

5. Suppose that the CPI in year 1 is 350 and the CPI in year 2 is 385. What is the rate of inflation between the two years?

6. Who are likely losers during unanticipated inflation?

7. Briefly explain the following incomes policies:

   Tax-based incomes policy
   Indexing
   CPI-minus-2

8. Consider the data in Table 14.7 on duration of unemployment and help wanted advertising in commercial newspapers. Recession years are underlined. What conclusion should be drawn regarding the relation between the duration of unemployment and recession?

TABLE 14.7 Help Wanted and
Unemployment

Year	Duration of Unem- ployment (weeks)	Help Wanted Advertising in Newspaper (1967=100)
(1)	(2)	(3)
1952	8.43	68.5
1953	8.02	65.4
1954	11.81	41.5
1955	12.98	59.1
1956	11.29	68.2
1957	10.45	58.2
1958	13.98	41.7
1959	14.37	59.2
1960	12.79	55.6
1961	15.65	51.5
1962	14.67	59.3
1963	14.00	58.6
1964	13.29	66.8
1965	11.79	84.1
1966	10.33	103.9
1967	8.75	100.0
1968	8.42	109.6
1969	7.89	120.9
1970	8.67	92.9
1971	11.35	82.5
1972	12.01	102.6
1973	10.02	125.9
1974	9.73	110.2
1975	14.25	80.2
1976	15.78	95.0
1977	14.27	117.8
1978	11.88	148.9
1979	10.82	157.0
1980	11.93	128.4
1981	13.76	118.2
1982	15.61	86.1
1983	19.94	94.9
1984	18.10	130.3
1985	15.62	138.2
1986	15.06	138.5
1987	14.50	152.6
1988	13.73	157.4

Source: DATADISK from Cambridge Planning.

9. Based on the same table considered in answering question 8, what conclusion should be drawn regarding the relation between help wanted advertising and recession?

10. The index of leading indicators is not just one index, but a composite index of 11 leading indicators. Name as many of the 11 leading indicators as you can.

SUGGESTED READINGS

Hurwood, David L., Grossman, Elliott S., and Bailey, Earl. (1978). *Sales forecasting.* New York: The Conference Board.

Explains various methods of forecasting a company's future sales. Prepared for practitioners of sales forecasting.

Kennedy, Paul. (1987). *The rise and fall of the great powers: Economic change and military conflict from 1500 to 2000.* New York: Random House.

Suggests that if a nation spends too much on the military rather than on production of more wealth, its national power will eventually decline.

Lekachman, Robert. (1974). The inevitability of controls. *Challenge,* November-December:6–8.

Claiming that (1) many American industries are highly concentrated, (2) antitrust laws are a faded dream of American reform, and (3) the American public no longer accepts economic depression, Lekachman suggests permanent control of prices and wages.

Mills, Leonard. (1988). Can stock prices reliably predict recessions? Federal Reserve Bank of Philadelphia *Business Review,* September-October, pp. 3–14.

Movements in stock prices offer some information about the economy's future, but stock prices alone are unreliable as a leading indicator of economic fluctuations.

Temin, Peter. (1976). *Did monetary forces cause the Great Depression?* New York: W. W. Norton.

Temin claims that, contrary to the popular belief among economists, the proposition that monetary forces caused the Great Depression must be rejected.

Wallich, Henry C., and Weintraub, Sidney. (1971). A tax-based incomes policy. *Journal of Economic Issues* 5(June):1–19.

Authors suggest that, in order to control inflation, a surcharge be levied on the corporate profits tax for firms granting wage increases in excess of some guidepost figure.

15

Introduction to Macroeconomic Theories

IN CHAPTER 13 we studied how the GNP is measured. In Chapter 14 we studied two major problems that arise when GNP fluctuates, notably unemployment and inflation. This chapter introduces key ideas that explain how the level of GNP is *determined*. Economists and policymakers need to know how GNP is determined in order to develop economic policies that can stabilize the economy and promote its growth. An economy is stable when the number of unemployed persons is few and price increases are mild. To study macroeconomic theories, we need to group historical developments of economic ideas into different periods. The process of grouping historical ideas into different periods is known as *periodizing*. According to Joseph A. Schumpeter, periodizing economic ideas is an evil. Historical developments of economic ideas are always continuous, and they can never be cut into pieces without arbitrariness and loss. Periodizing, however, is a necessary evil, since it improves our ability to understand problems and search for their solutions—be they economic, social, or political.

There are three learning objectives in this chapter. The first is to study the basic ideas of classical economics that dominated economic thinking at least until the Great Depression. The predominant interpretation in contemporary economics treats works by Adam Smith as the beginning of classical economics. Not all economists agree with this interpretation. Schumpeter, for instance, had little trouble in treating Adam Smith as the end of the preceding period rather than as the beginning of classical economics.[1] In any case, we need to study classical economics because it still exerts a significant influence on contemporary economic policies. Modern monetarism, for instance, was developed from classical economics. Monetarism and supply-side economics are presented in Chapter 18. The second learning objective of this chapter is to study the basic ideas of Keynesian economics that emerged as an alternative to classical economics during the Great Depression. The third learning objective is to generalize the broad picture of macroeconomic theories by presenting the aggregate demand and aggregate supply model. The specific tools and techniques of the Keynesian model of GNP determination are presented in the next chapter.

CLASSICAL ECONOMICS

Classical economics is a loose term encompassing economic ideas that prevailed during the eighteenth and the nineteenth centuries. There is no consensus on either the exact period the classical school covers or even which economists should be classified as classical economists.

Classical School

The classical school refers to either economic ideas that are collectively called classical economics, or economists who developed these ideas. There is a general consensus regarding the beginning of the classical school, which is dated as 1776, when Adam Smith (1723–1791) published the *Wealth of nations*. There is no consensus regarding the end of the classical school, however. Many economists prefer to cite 1871 as the end of the classical school. That was the year when William Stanley Jevons (1835–1882) and Carl Menger (1840–1921) published their works on marginal revenue, marginal cost, and other concepts known as marginalism. Karl Marx, who coined the term

---

[1]Joseph A. Schumpeter, *History of economic analysis* (New York: Oxford University Press, 1966), p. 379.

classical economists, considered only David Ricardo (1772–1823) and his predecessors as classical economists. John Maynard Keynes, on the other hand, considers as classical economists not only David Ricardo and his predecessors but also the followers of Ricardo such as Alfred Marshall (1842–1924) and Arthur Cecil Pigou (1877–1959), effectively extending the period of the classical school from the more widely accepted 100 years to about 150 years.

For the purpose of our presentation, let us define the classical school as the collection of economic ideas that were developed between 1776 and 1870 by such economists as Adam Smith, Thomas R. Malthus (1766–1834), Jean Baptiste Say (1767–1832), David Ricardo, and John Stuart Mill (1806–1873). This definition does not mean that these economists agreed on all economic ideas that were developed during the period. In any era there are always thinkers who deviate from the accepted or prevailing economic ideas. What the definition means is that there were ideas common to these economists that were sufficiently similar to be classified collectively as one school of thought. Also, the definition does not mean that classical economics ended with Ricardo and Mill. Emphasis after Ricardo and Mill was placed on microeconomics until the 1930s. The main features of classical economics, however, were not seriously challenged until 1936, when John Maynard Keynes published his *General theory.* The classical economic ideas are very much alive today, and will be for many years to come.

Social Background

Economic ideas do not simply spring into the mind of someone who is intellectually brilliant. Economic ideas are usually the product of thinking economists who are deeply concerned with the economic problems of the times. To properly understand classical economics, we must delve into the social background that led to the emergence of classical economics.

Industrial Revolution

The period from 1750 to 1850 is often used to date the *industrial revolution* in Europe, and England was the first nation that experienced an industrial revolution. Between 1500 and 1750, the British economy, especially the manufacturing sector, was behind other European countries such as France. By 1750, however, England was ahead of other countries. The rapid industrial development in England was aided by inventions of machines in the cotton textile industry, inventions in metals and machine tools, and inventions to provide power to drive the machines. Recent estimates of the British real output, for instance, indicate that the British GNP rose little until 1740, but more than doubled between 1740 and 1800.[2]

By 1776 England became one of the most efficient and powerful countries in the world. As English entrepreneurs became stronger, they wanted free trade without fear of foreign competition. British businesses needed a mobile, poorly paid, and hard-working labor force. Wages in England had been regulated for centuries until as late as 1762 by local justices of the peace. These justices usually imposed wage *ceilings* rather than wage *floors.* Tenant farmers who lost work as farmland was enclosed, bankrupt Irish peasants, and the fact of a high birth rate with a falling death rate increased the number of workers who were willing to work as wage earners in the industrial sector.

---

[2]P. Dean and W. A. Cole, *British economic growth, 1688–1959* (New York: Cambridge University Press, 1967), p. 78.

Laissez Faire

Government policies to keep wages down were no longer necessary, and laissez faire became the gospel of commerce. The spirit of laissez faire is based on the hypothesis that the best way to promote economic development and the general welfare of a nation is to leave the private enterprise economy alone. The British government strongly supported the economic interests of manufacturers and merchants. The laissez faire doctrine of classical economics was known as **economic liberalism.** It is not difficult to see that personal liberty and private ownership of properties rested on the laissez faire doctrine. Both personal liberty and private ownership presuppose decision-making by individuals.

The term *economic liberalism* should be considered in the historical context. The laissez faire doctrine *was* known as economic liberalism. Since about 1930, however, the same term has acquired almost the opposite meaning.[3] These days, those economists who advocate a *greater* role of government in the administration of economic affairs are called **liberal economists.** Those who advocate a *smaller* role of government are known as **conservative economists.** The flip-flop in the use of the term *liberal* is not difficult to understand. One of the meanings of *liberal* is the act of favoring reform. In the beginning of classical economics, advocating a reduced role of government was against the historical tradition of a strong government, thus constituting a reform. These days, advocating a greater role of government is against the classical trend of minimal government, thus constituting a reform.

Classical Economic Ideas

So far in this chapter, we have discussed classical economics without introducing what classical economics is all about. Let us now define the main features of classical economics. The classical economic ideas are introduced in five broad areas: economic philosophy; labor market; saving, investment, and the rate of interest; output market; and money and prices.

Economic Philosophy

The economic philosophy of classical economics was laissez faire. According to this view, the best government is one that governs least. The forces of the free, competitive market guide production, exchange, and distribution. Each person, if left alone, will seek to maximize his or her own wealth. By seeking his or her own interests, each individual serves the best interests of society. There exists an *invisible hand* that harmonizes the self-interests of individual producers and consumers for the benefit of society. Through the invisible hand, the attempt by each person to maximize his or her own wealth also maximizes the nation's wealth. The invisible hand is equivalent, in modern terms, to the demand and supply mechanism of the competitive market.

Labor Market

Money wages are flexible; they can rise or fall. Wages rise when the demand for workers is greater than the supply of workers. Wages fall when the supply of workers is greater than the demand for workers. More precisely, wages rise when there is a shortage of workers until the shortage no longer exists; and wages fall when there is unemployment until all unemployed persons find work at

---

[3]Joseph A. Schumpeter, *History of economic analysis* (New York: Oxford University Press, 1966), p. 394.

prevailing wages. Because wages are flexible, unemployed workers are all **voluntarily unemployed.** Workers are unemployed because they refuse to work at prevailing wages. There is no involuntary unemployment. Involuntary unemployment, if it exists, is only temporary or frictional in nature.

Not even structural unemployment is permitted under classical economics, since those who are structurally unemployed can find work if they are willing to work at prevailing wages. If persons are not employed because they do not want to work at prevailing wages, the economy is still a full employment economy since the unemployment is voluntary in nature. Under the classical assumption of flexible wages, wages are always at the equilibrium level. This is because changes in wages will make sure that the number of workers demanded always equals the number of workers supplied. The economy envisioned by the classical economists, therefore, is a full employment economy.

Saving, Investment, and the Rate of Interest
Saving is the portion of household income that is left over after part of the income is spent for consumption. Decisions on saving are made by individual households. When households save part of their income, they earn interest on their saving. Saving increases as the interest rate increases, since the interest rate represents a return on saving. Saving decreases as the interest rate decreases.

Decisions on investment are made by individual businesses. When businesses borrow money for investment, they have to pay interest. To businesses, the interest rate represents a cost of investment. Investment decreases as the interest rate increases, since it costs more to borrow money for investment. Conversely, investment increases as the interest rate decreases. The interest rate is a price for borrowing money, and saving is made equal to investment through changes of this price. If saving is greater than investment, the interest rate falls. As the interest rate decreases, saving falls and investment rises until saving is equal to investment. If investment is greater than saving, the interest rate rises. As the interest rate increases, saving rises and investment falls until saving is equal to investment. The equilibrium rate of interest is determined by saving and investment.

The equality between saving and investment is important because, when the two are not equal to each other, the economy fluctuates. If saving is greater than investment, part of the total money supply is taken out of circulation. In this case, economic activities tend to decrease, causing the quantity of output and prices to increase more slowly or decrease. If investment is greater than saving, the economy tries to spend more than is available for spending. In this case, economic activities tend to increase, causing prices and the quantity of output to increase more rapidly. If the economy is already at the full-employment level, the quantity of output may not increase and the impact of an investment greater than saving may be felt on prices only. When saving and investment are equal to each other, the economy is in equilibrium.

Output Market
According to classical economics, prices are flexible, rising and falling. If there is a shortage of a product, the price of the product rises, causing the quantity of the product supplied to increase and the quantity of the product demanded to decrease. If there is a surplus of a product, the price of the product falls, causing the quantity of the product supplied to decrease and the quantity of the product demanded to increase. In either case, the flexibility of prices assures that shortages and surpluses are only temporary phenomena.

To generalize, the supply of a product creates its own demand through changes in prices. Since the quantity of output supplied equals the quantity of output demanded, the economy is in equilibrium. The equality between saving and investment only reinforces this process toward equilibrium. A secular stagnation with significant *gluts* (surpluses) is not possible under the classical assumptions of flexible prices, flexible interest rates, and flexible wages. With flexible prices, interest rates, and wages, the economy does tend toward full-capacity equilibrium. The hypothesis that supply creates its own demand is known as **Say's law,** named after Jean Baptiste Say (1767–1832), a French economist who popularized Adam Smith's ideas on the European continent.

Money and Prices

Consider a small economy in which everybody is working to the best of his or her ability. The quantity of output produced in this economy is the maximum that can be produced in the economy. Any added incentive will not increase the quantity of output so long as the amount of resources, including the number of workers, remains unchanged.

Suppose that the money supply is increased in this economy. Money supply means the amount of money circulating in the economy. When money supply increases, people have more money, but the quantity of output is fixed. When people spend increased money on a constant quantity of output, all they are doing is bidding the prices up. The hypothetical small economy happens to be one envisioned by classical economists. According to classical economics, the general level of prices in the economy depends directly on the quantity of money circulating in the economy. Put differently, the quantity of money circulating in the economy determines the general level of prices. The greater the money supply, the faster prices increase. The causal hypothesis between the supply of money and the general level of prices is known as the **quantity theory of money.** There was a general acceptance of the quantity theory of money by classical economists. Additional discussion of the quantity theory of money is presented in Chapter 17.

FROM CLASSICAL TO KEYNESIAN ECONOMICS

As noted economic historian Mark Blaug states, no assumptions about economic behavior are absolutely true and no theoretical conclusions are valid for all times and places.[4] Some economists came to consider the doctrine of laissez faire to be too simplistic to solve all economic problems as business fluctuations became wilder and competition gave way to changing market structures characterized by monopoly, oligopoly, and regulated industries. The harmony-of-interests hypothesis could no longer be defended when the concentration of wealth called for the government to improve social conditions by helping the poor. Sometimes laissez faire was carried to absurd extremes by the advocates of classical economics. To cite one example, the July 13, 1850, issue of the London *Economist* criticized the "sanitary movement," which urged that the government require a pure water supply and proper sewage disposal. Even after sewage lines were built, owners of houses were not required to hook up to them at first. Personal freedom was more important than requiring home owners to hook up to sewage lines.[5]

---

[4]Mark Blaug, *Economic theory in retrospect,* 4th ed. (Cambridge, England: Cambridge University Press, 1986), p. 3.

[5]Jacob Oser, *The evolution of economic thought* (New York: Harcourt, Brace and World, 1970), p. 43.

On Black Thursday, October 24, 1929, the stock market collapsed, signaling the beginning of the Great Depression. The magnitude of the depression was overwhelming. The U.S. GNP in 1929 dollars was $104.4 billion in 1929, but decreased to $74.2 billion in 1933 and did not return to the 1929 level until 1937. The CPI with 1947–1949 as the base period was 73.3 in 1929, but decreased to 55.3 in 1933 and did not return to the 1929 level until the outbreak of World War II. In 1933 the rate of unemployment reached 25 percent of the labor force, with over half of the labor force having been laid off at least once during the year. There was no social security, no food stamps, no Medicaid, and no aid to families with dependent children in 1933. The Dow Jones Industrial Average fell from 381 in 1929 to 41 in June 1932. It was obvious that the depression shook the capitalistic economic system to its core. The laissez faire policy of classical economics was unable to correct the problem. It was about time for someone to come up with new ideas.

KEYNESIAN ECONOMICS

John Maynard Keynes is considered to be one of the greatest economists of all times. Keynesian economics is often referred to as the Keynesian revolution. Followers admire him; opponents belittle him.[6] In this section, we review the basic ideas of Keynesian economics in the same order as classical economics.

Economic Philosophy

Keynes advocated changes in economic thinking, but the changes he advocated were intended to preserve the essential elements of capitalism rather than replace them. Keynes felt that the classical laissez faire policy would not bring about a full employment economy. Keynes thus advocated government intervention in the private enterprise system. Keynes's economic philosophy was attacked from the left (liberal economists) and the right (conservative economists). Critics on the left accused him of being an apologist for capitalism, while critics on the right accused him of being a socialist who wanted to attack the capitalistic economic system. The truth is that Keynes supported capitalism and opposed totalitarian governments. He supported the individualism and freedom that were inherent in capitalism. He simply foresaw the need for an increased role of government in the capitalistic system.

According to Schumpeter, a visionary glimpse of facts and meanings precedes analytic work. The Keynesian vision of England's aging capitalism was based on his diagnosis of the economy as "the arteriosclerotic economy whose opportunities for rejuvenating venture decline while the old habits of saving formed in times of plentiful opportunity persist."[7] In simpler terms, Keynes, like

[6]A. G. Hines, for instance, states that "so far as pure theory was concerned Keynes would have been well advised not to have written the General Theory at all," and it would have been helped "if he had not clouded the issue . . . by introducing funny mechanical toys such as the multiplier." See A. G. Hines, The (neo)-classical resurgence and the reappraisal of Keynes' theory of employment, in Thomas M. Havrilesky and John T. Boorman, (eds.), *Current issues in monetary theory and policy* (Arlington Heights, Ill.: AHM Publishing, 1980), pp. 29–30.

[7]Joseph A. Schumpeter, *History of economic analysis* (New York: Oxford University Press, 1966), p. 1171.

JOHN MAYNARD KEYNES

Keynes was born on June 5, 1883, the eldest son of Florence Ada Keynes and John Neville Keynes. His mother was once mayor of Cambridge, England, and his father was the author of a good book on economic methodology, *Scope and method of political economy* (1891). In 1897 Keynes won a scholarship to attend Eaton; he enrolled at King's College of Cambridge University in 1902. Upon graduation from King's College, Keynes passed a civil service test and accepted a position in the India Office. In 1908 he became an economics lecturer at Cambridge and in 1915 went to work for the British Treasury until the end of World War I. Following the war, Keynes taught at King's College. Keynes was a member of the Bloomsbury literary group and founded the Cambridge Arts Theatre. He married a Russian ballerina and made a large amount of money by speculating in foreign exchange. Keynes died in 1946.

Books written by Keynes include *Indian currency and finance* (1913), *A treatise on probability* (1921), *A revision of the treaty* (1922), *A tract on monetary reform* (1923), *Treatise on money* (1930), and the *General theory of employment interest and money* (1936).

other great thinkers, conceived a vision before he developed analytical tools to convert the vision into reality. The vision was that the emphasis on saving in classical economics had outlived its usefulness in an environment that needed spending more than saving. The idea of stressing spending not only by consumers but especially by the government became the core of his new macroeconomic theory.

Labor Market

According to Keynes, money wages are flexible upward but not downward. Wages rise when the demand for workers is greater than the supply of workers. However, wages do not fall when the supply of workers is greater than the demand for workers. Wages increase when there is a shortage of workers, but stay the same when there is unemployment. The downward rigidity of wages is due to several factors, such as labor unions, minimum wage regulations, and tradition. Because wages do not fall when unemployment exists, unemployed persons who are willing to work at prevailing wages or wages below the prevailing level cannot find work. In other words, unemployment that exists under the assumption of downwardly rigid wages is **involuntary unemployment.** Unemployed persons cannot find work at prevailing wages even if they want to work. Unemployment is no longer temporary, as classical economists believed it to be.

Saving, Investment, and the Rate of Interest

Keynes agrees with classical economists that saving must equal investment for an economy to be in equilibrium. Like classical economists, Keynes also assumes that investment depends on the interest rate. Business investment increases as the interest rate falls and decreases as the interest rate rises. Unlike classical economists, however, Keynes assumes that saving does not depend on the interest rate. A higher interest rate does not result in increased saving.

According to Keynes, saving depends on consumers' income. When both saving and investment depend on the interest rate, as was assumed in the classical economics, changes in the interest rate make sure that saving equals investment. If saving is greater than investment, the interest rate falls, causing saving to decrease and investment to increase. If investment is greater than saving, the interest rate rises, causing saving to increase and investment to decrease.

If the determinants of saving and investment are different, Keynesian economics assumes the automatic mechanism that equates saving to investment no longer exists. There is no reason why saving and investment must be equal. If saving is not equal to investment, aggregate demand is not necessarily equal to aggregate supply. The imbalance between aggregate demand and aggregate supply causes the level of output and income to change.

Unlike classical economists, who hypothesized that the interest rate was determined by saving and investment, Keynes hypothesizes that the interest rate is determined by the supply of money and the demand for money. Given the demand for money, an increase in money supply lowers the interest rate, and a decrease in money supply raises the interest rate.

Output Market

Keynes assumes that, like wages, prices are also flexible upward but not downward. If there is a shortage of a product, the price of the product rises, causing the quantity of the product supplied to increase and the quantity of the product demanded to decrease. If there is a surplus of a product, however, the price of the product does not necessarily fall and the surplus continues. Because of the downward rigidity of prices and the possibility that saving is not equal to investment, supply does not create its own demand through changes in prices. Keynes thus rejects Say's law, and claims that surplus output and unemployment may persist without government intervention. Even if Say's law is valid, the process of clearing the market is so time-consuming that full employment equilibrium may be forever pursued but never attained.

It is rather odd that because of Keynes's criticism, Say's law has been given an importance out of proportion to its actual role in classical economics.

Money and Prices

Contrary to the classical economists' claim that changes in money supply affect prices but not the interest rate, Keynes claims that the major impact of changes in money supply is on the interest rate. An increase in money supply lowers the interest rate; a decrease in money supply raises the interest rate. Only if the money supply is increased in large amounts is the increase in money supply inflationary. Keynes does not support the quantity theory of money, at least in the short run. The long-run impact of changes in money supply was not the main concern in Keynesian economics.

HOW LONG WILL THE AMERICAN ECONOMY LAST?

Economics hasn't really lived up to its pessimistic reputation engendered by the melancholy age of Malthus, who predicted that population increase would eventually outstrip increases in food production, and perpetuated by Marx, who predicted the collapse of capitalism. For the past 100 years or so optimism has prevailed even in the worst of times. In the depths of the Great Depression, Keynes predicted that the market economy would solve economic ills with a little help from the government. In 1979, when raging inflation and long gasoline lines prompted *Time* magazine to query Nobel laureate Paul Samuelson about the possible bankruptcy of the American economic system, Samuelson retorted that the system was fundamentally sound.

Few economists argue that the sky *couldn't* fall, however. The nightmare may begin with cataclysm: a sudden collapse of the world economy brought on by a banking panic or trade war. Another bad dream is decadence and drift in the United States—the so-called British disease, which could consign the country to a third-rate future. One of the things that go with decline and decay is that society starts fighting for redistribution rather than growth. Tangible manifestations of decline, such as inadequate investment and lagging productivity gains, are not necessarily the most important. More disquieting to many economists are indications of cultural, political, and moral decadence. Among these are the inability of the United States to forge a policy consensus, the erosion of values that stress the future, the absence of vision, and the loss of confidence. The things that disturb some economists most are beyond the control of economic policymakers. Pervasive aimlessness on the part of U.S. businesses, thinks Nobel laureate Wassily Leontief, is a clearer danger: "I am worried that the efficiency of the whole American economy has gone down as compared with that of other countries." Leontief worries that the United States lacks the necessary unity and will to defend its industrial leadership. "I never heard a Japanese remark, 'Ah yes, but it is politically impossible.' In the U.S. very few good things are politically possible. And very many things that are politically possible are not good." James Buchanan, another Nobel laureate economist, fears for the future of a society addicted to instant gratification and short horizons. Weakening moral fiber, he argues, goes hand in hand with a gradual erosion of the values needed to create capital. "The Victorians behaved as if they would live forever," he says. "They were prudent. We are not, in part because we find hedonism morally acceptable. And ever since Keynes, politicians have believed hedonism to be economically acceptable."

Civilizations with all the advantages have nonetheless disappeared when their leaders and citizens became complacent. If nothing else, economists' nightmares serve as a prod against complacency; a reminder that no one can take for granted the durability of a culture or the complex institutions that serve it.

Source: Sylvia Nasar, Worries from the dismal scene, *Fortune,* December 22, 1986, pp. 58–60.

AGGREGATE DEMAND AND AGGREGATE SUPPLY

Equipped with the knowledge of classical economics and Keynesian economics, we are a step closer to generalizing the macroeconomic model. In markets of individual products, the price and the quantity of output produced and traded are determined by demand for and supply of these individual products. In the aggregate economy, the general level of prices and the quantity of output produced are also determined by demand and supply. The meanings of demand and supply for the entire economy, however, are not exactly the same as the meanings of demand and supply for individual products. Let us develop the aggregate demand and aggregate supply model.

Aggregate Demand Curve

Like the demand curve of a product for individual markets, the aggregate demand curve shows the inverse relation between price level and the quantity of output demanded for the entire economy. The demand curve for individual products has a downward slope to the right because of the substitution effect and, to a lesser extent, the income effect. When the price of a product decreases, consumers substitute cheaper products for other more expensive equivalents. In the aggregate economy, there is no substitution effect. Let us see why.

Absolute Prices versus Relative Prices
When we deal with the entire economy, a lower price level does not mean that the price of one product is lower. A lower price level means that prices of all products are lower. Since prices of all products are lower more or less in direct proportion, the *absolute prices* of individual products may decrease, but the *relative prices* of these products remain the same. An **absolute price** is the price of a given good or service. The price of a pineapple at $2.00 is an absolute price. The price of a coconut at $1.00 is also an absolute price. A **relative price,** on the other hand, is the price of a good or service in relation to the price of another good or service. The ratio of the price of a pineapple to that of a coconut is 2 to 1. If the price of a pineapple falls to $1.00 and the price of a coconut falls to $.50, the absolute prices of pineapples and coconuts decrease, but the relative prices remain the same. The price of a pineapple is still twice the price of a coconut. When the prices of both pineapples and coconuts fall, consumers have no incentive to substitute one for the other. When prices of all products fall or rise together, there is no substitution effect.

The downward slope of the aggregate demand curve, shown in Figure 15.1, requires an explanation other than the income and the substitution effects. Remember that the real economy is quite complex. Likewise, macroeconomic theories are also complicated. Although we meet only the mainstream macroeconomic theories in this book, we still need patience and careful reasoning to follow and understand these theories.

Economists believe that there are three reasons why the aggregate demand curve has a downward slope to the right: the real balance effect, the interest rate effect, and the foreign purchases effect. Let us study the three effects in order.

Real Balance Effect
Suppose that we have a savings account of $10,000. If prices of goods and services rise by 10 percent, the price increase will reduce by about 10 percent the amount of goods and services that we can buy with $10,000. As prices rise, the real value of assets held by the public is eroded, making

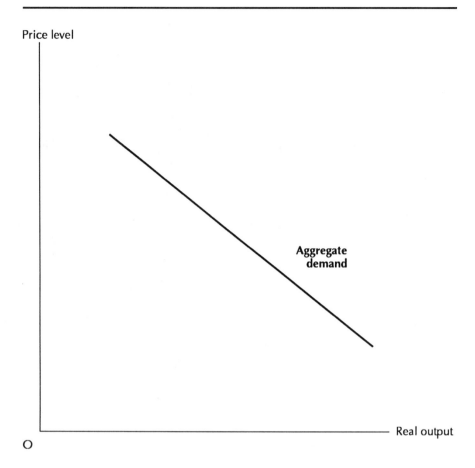

FIGURE 15.1 Aggregate Demand Curve. The aggregate demand curve shows the inverse relation between the general level of prices and the level of real output.

the public feel poorer than before. As the consumers feel poorer, they cut back spending on goods and services. The relation between prices and aggregate demand, therefore, is inverse. The hypothesis that higher prices reduce the purchasing power of accumulated assets and the reduced value of accumulated assets decreases consumer spending is known as the **real balance effect.**

Interest Rate Effect
To explain the negative slope of the aggregate demand using the interest rate effect, we need to assume that the money supply remains constant. If the prices of all products decrease, the public do not need as much money as they needed before for buying and selling of goods and services. If the price of a pineapple decreases from $2.00 to $1.00, for instance, we need to carry only $1.00

instead of $2.00 to buy one pineapple. A decrease in the general level of prices reduces the demand for money.

If the money supply remains the same and the demand for money decreases, the interest rate falls since the reduced demand for money leads to an excess supply of money that is available for loan. As the interest rate decreases, the demand for goods and services that are sensitive to changes in the interest rate will increase. As the interest rate falls, for instance, the consumer demand for washing machines, microwave ovens, and automobiles is expected to increase. At lower interest rates, businesses will find it cheaper to borrow money and, thus, are expected to increase investment. As the interest rate falls, for instance, the investment demand for new machines, equipment, and new plants is expected to increase. As prices fall, therefore, the demand for real output is expected to increase. The interest rate effect of price changes on real output is summarized in Table 15.1.

Two comments are in order regarding the interest rate effect. First of all, in discussing the aggregate demand curve, we stated as if it were a fact that an excess supply of money would lower interest rates and that the lower interest rate would increase the investment demand for output. These statements are all part of Keynesian economics. According to classical economics, interest rates are not affected by changes in the money supply; they are determined by saving and investment. The explanation of the aggregate demand curve by Keynesian terms is not surprising at all, considering that the concept of the aggregate demand itself was the creation of Keynes.

Second, the interest rate effect is presented all in nominal rates of interest. Suppose that prices fall, causing interest rates to fall also. If the decrease in interest rates equals the decrease in prices, the real rate of interest remains the same. To the extent that investment depends on the real, rather than nominal, rate of interest, the interest rate effect is not a good explanation of the negative slope of the aggregate demand curve.

Increased Exports Effect

Suppose that prices of U.S. products decrease in relation to those of foreign products. The lower prices of U.S. products mean that U.S. products are now cheaper for foreign buyers. The lower prices of U.S. products lead to an increase in exports. As exports increase, the quantity of real output produced will have to increase. The relation between prices and real output, therefore, is inverse.

TABLE 15.1 Interest Rate Effect of Price Changes on Real Output

Price Level (1)	Demand for Money (2)	Supply of Money (3)	Interest Rate (4)	Consumption and Investment (5)
Up	Up	Constant	Up	Down
Down	Down	Constant	Down	Up

Aggregate Supply Curve

Like the supply curve of a particular good or service, the aggregate supply curve also has an upward slope to the right. The supply curve of a particular product has an upward slope to the right because a higher price of one product, ceteris paribus, increases the profit margin of the product and induces the producer to increase the quantity of the product produced. The aggregate supply curve, however, represents all products, not simply one particular product. If prices of all products, including productive resources, increase simultaneously, the profit margin of one product is more likely to remain unchanged, and the quantity of the product is not expected to increase. For the entire economy, therefore, the relation between price level and the quantity of output produced cannot be explained by the higher profit margin that results from the higher price of the product. In fact, we need to make two assumptions in order to explain the relation between price level and the quantity of output produced for the entire economy: one concerning the use of labor and the other concerning the effect of wages on the use of labor.

Let us discuss the first assumption. Production requires the use of many different productive resources, such as labor, capital, technology, land, and entrepreneurship. We concentrate on labor by assuming that the quantities of all productive resources are constant with the exception of labor. Since all other productive resources remain constant, the quantity of output produced varies directly with the quantity of labor used in production. The larger the amount of labor used in production, the greater the quantity of output.

The second assumption is that the demand for and the supply of labor depend on wage rate. At a higher wage rate, the quantity of labor demanded falls and the quantity of labor supplied rises. At a lower wage rate, the quantity of labor demanded rises and the quantity of labor supplied falls. Consider that there are two types of wages: money wages and real wages. **Real wages** are money wages from which the inflationary effect is subtracted. If the price level does not change, money wages and real wages are identical. If prices rise, however, real wages may lag behind money wages unless money wages also rise in direct proportion to rising prices. Let us assume that the demand for and the supply of labor depend on real wages, not money wages. In other words, we are assuming that workers are smart enough to know the impact of changing prices on their wages.

To derive the aggregate supply curve, we thus made two assumptions: the quantities of all productive resources are constant except labor, and the supply of and the demand for workers depend on changes in real wages. We are now ready to derive the aggregate supply curve.

The Case of Flexible Money Wages

Flexible wages are part of classical economic ideas. The aggregate supply curve based on the assumption of flexible wages, therefore, is the aggregate supply curve for classical economics.

The aggregate supply curve shows the relation between price and the level of output supplied. To derive the aggregate supply curve under classical economics, let us suppose that the economy is at the full employment level at the existing price level, as was assumed by the classical economists. We then allow prices to vary in order to determine how changing prices affect the level of output.

Suppose that there is a decrease in the general price level in the economy, but not in wages. As prices decrease while money wages remain the same, there is an increase in real wages. As real wages increase, more people join the labor force, but businesses are inclined to hire less workers. The supply of labor becomes greater than the demand for labor at the existing wages, resulting in an excess supply of labor. Since money wages are assumed to be flexible, the excess supply of labor forces money wages to fall until the excess supply disappears. So long as money wages are flexible, the labor market always returns to the equilibrium in which the demand for labor is equal to the supply of labor.

Full employment is defined as the level of employment at which anyone who wants to work at the prevailing wage has a job. That is, full employment is the level of employment at which the supply of labor is equal to the demand for labor. When money wages are flexible, there is full employment in the economy. When money wages are flexible, any deviation of the level of output from the full employment level is only temporary and the level of output always returns to the full employment level. The aggregate supply curve, therefore, is vertical at the full employment level, as shown in Figure 15.2. In Figure 15.2, Y_f is the full employment level of output.

An increase in the general price level works in the opposite way but has the same result. Suppose that there is an increase in the general price level in the economy. As prices increase while money wages remain the same, there is a decrease in real wages. At lower real wages, the supply of labor becomes smaller than the demand for labor, resulting in an excess demand for labor. The excess demand for labor forces money wages to increase until the excess demand disappears. The assumption of flexible money wages led the demand for and the supply of labor to be equal to each other. At this point, the output level is again at the full employment level, since by definition full employment is the level of employment at which the demand for and the supply of labor are equal to each other.

To summarize, the effects of changing prices on the level of output in an economy where money wages are flexible are the following. Regardless of whether prices rise or fall, the assumption of flexible money wages equalizes the demand for labor and the supply of labor, ensuring full employment in the economy. When resources are fully employed, there can be only one level of output at the full employment level. The aggregate supply curve, therefore, is vertical. The process of adjustment from changing prices to equilibrium under the assumption of flexible wages is summarized in Table 15.2.

The Case of Downwardly Rigid Money Wages

Downwardly rigid wages mean that wages are unlikely to decrease even if there is unemployment. Downwardly rigid wages are a part of Keynesian thinking. The aggregate supply curve based on this assumption, therefore, is the aggregate supply curve for Keynesian economics.

TABLE 15.2 Changes in Price Level and Employment: The Case of Flexible Money Wages

Price Level	Money Wage	Real Wage	Demand for Labor	Supply of Labor	Money Wage	Real Wage	Employment
(1)	(2)	(3)	(4)	(5)	(6)	(7)	(8)
Down	Constant	Up	Down	Up	Down	Down	Equilibrium
Up	Constant	Down	Up	Down	Up	Up	Equilibrium

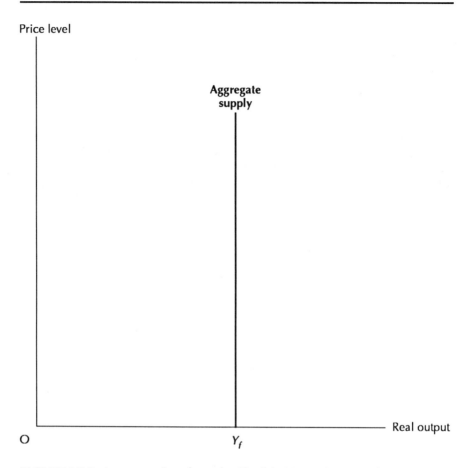

FIGURE 15.2 Aggregate Supply under Flexible Money Wages. If wages are flexible upward and downward, the aggregate supply curve is vertical at the full employment level.

When wages are rigid downward, the aggregate supply curve is no longer vertical. Let us see why. Suppose that the price level falls from P_2 to P_1 in Figure 15.3. As the price level falls while money wages remain constant, real wages increase. As real wages increase, there will be a decrease in the quantity of labor demanded and an increase in the quantity of labor supplied, resulting in an excess supply of labor. If money wages are flexible downward, money wages will decrease. Since money wages are assumed to be rigid downward, real wages remain high and the decreased quantity of labor demanded is permanent. With the decreased use of labor, the level of output also decreases from Y_2 to Y_1. The aggregate supply curve for the portion of rigid wages, therefore, has an upward slope to the right, as indicated as AB in Figure 15.3. As prices fall, the supply of real output also falls. The process of adjustment is summarized in Table 15.3.

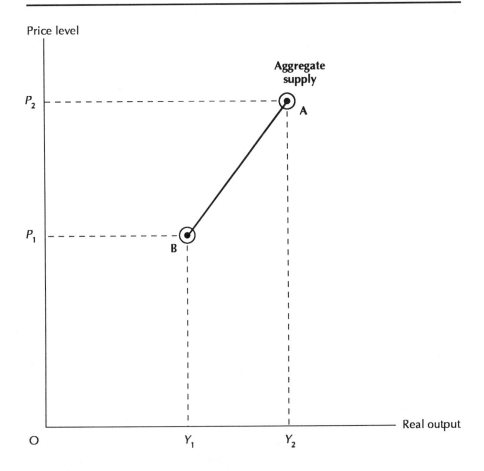

Price level

FIGURE 15.3 Aggregate Supply Curve under Downwardly Rigid Money Wages. The aggregate supply curve when wages are downwardly rigid has an upward slope to the right.

An Extreme Case

How will the process work if there is a high rate of unemployment like that which the U.S. economy experienced during the Great Depression? A high rate of unemployment means that there are large amounts of unemployed resources. In this extreme case, the level of output can be increased without putting any pressure on prices. The availability of large amounts of unemployed resources means that there is an excess supply of resources that can be employed without any increase in their prices. If output can be increased without increases in prices, the aggregate supply curve becomes horizontal.

TABLE 15.3 Changes in Price Level and Employment: The Case of Downwardly Rigid Money Wages

Price Level	Money Wage	Real Wage	Demand for Labor	Supply of Labor	Money Wage	Real Wage	Employment
(1)	(2)	(3)	(4)	(5)	(6)	(7)	(8)
Down	Constant	Up	Down	Up	Constant	Up	Unemployment

AD-AS Model

Like markets for individual goods and services, the general level of prices and the level of real output in the economy are also determined by the intersection between demand and supply. Let us first derive the aggregate supply curve.

Deriving the AS Curve

The aggregate supply curve shown in Figure 15.4 has three distinctive components: vertical, upwardly rising, and horizontal. As we already know, the vertical portion of the aggregate supply curve is drawn based on the assumption of flexible money wages and prices. This assumption is part of classical economics. The vertical portion of the aggregate supply curve in Figure 15.4, therefore, is called the **classical range.** The horizontal portion of the aggregate supply curve is drawn to describe the relation between price and the level of output when there exist large amounts of unemployed resources. Keynesian economics was born out of Keynes's concern with large amounts of unemployed resources during the Great Depression years. We thus call the horizontal portion of the aggregate supply curve the **Keynesian range.** The upward rising portion of the aggregate supply curve is drawn based on the assumption that wages are downwardly rigid. This assumption is also part of Keynesian economics. The upward rising portion, however, is called the **intermediate range** rather than the Keynesian range. The three ranges are identified in Figure 15.4.

The Equilibrium

The aggregate demand curve and the aggregate supply curve are superimposed in Figure 15.5. If the aggregate demand curve crosses the aggregate supply curve in the classical range, the price level is P_1 and the level of output is Y_1, as indicated in panel (a). A small increase in the aggregate demand curve causes prices to increase from P_1 to P_2, but the level of output remains the same at Y_1. The level of output remains constant at the full employment level.

Panel (b) of Figure 15.5 indicates that if the aggregate demand curve crosses the aggregate supply curve in the intermediate range, the price level is P_1 and the level of output is Y_1. A small increase in the aggregate demand curve causes prices to increase from P_1 to P_2 and the level of output to increase from Y_1 to Y_2.

If the aggregate demand curve crosses the aggregate supply curve in the Keynesian range, as shown in panel (c), the price level is P_1 and the level of output is Y_1. A small increase in the aggregate demand curve causes the level of output to increase from Y_1 to Y_2, but prices remain the same at P_1.

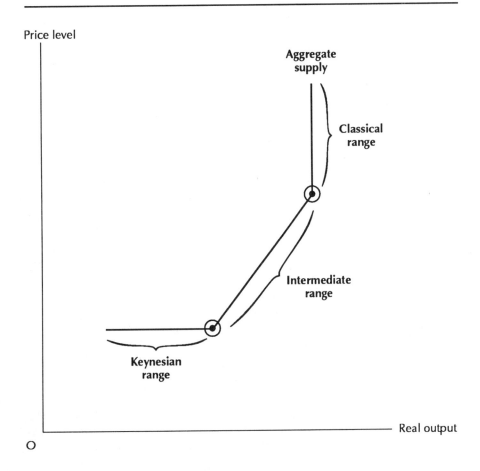

FIGURE 15.4 Aggregate Supply Curve. The vertical portion, the rising portion, and the horizontal portion of the aggregate supply curve are called the classical region, the intermediate region, and the Keynesian region, respectively.

When the aggregate supply curve is horizontal, the quantity of output can be increased without any increase in prices.

Both Keynesian economics (Chapter 16) and monetarism (Chapter 18) stress the control of aggregate demand, whereas supply-side economics (Chapter 18) stresses the control of the aggregate supply. Keynesian economics and monetarism are sometimes called demand-side economics. Aggregate demand and aggregate supply curves are shifted when government undertakes fiscal and monetary policy. Specific tools of fiscal policy are presented in the next chapter, while tools of monetary policy are presented in Chapter 17.

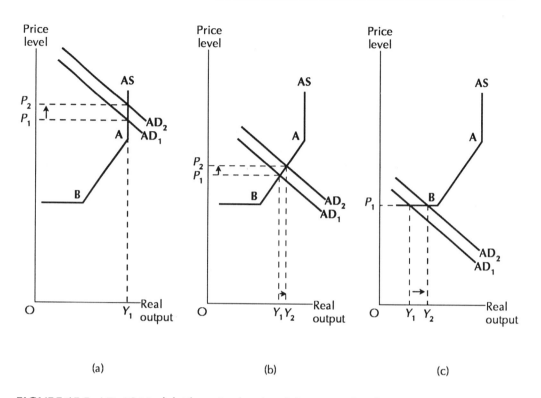

(a)   (b)   (c)

FIGURE 15.5 AD-AS Model. The price level and the output level are determined by both aggregate demand and aggregate supply curves. Depending on where the two curves cross each other, economic policies have different effects on price and output.

SUMMARY

Classical economics dominated economic thinking at least until the Great Depression and became the basis for the development of modern monetarism. The classical school refers to economic ideas that prevailed between 1776 and 1870. Laissez faire is the philosophy that the best government is one that leaves the private sector alone. Classical economic ideas include (1) laissez faire, (2) an invisible hand that harmonizes self-interests of individual producers and consumers for the benefit of the society; (3) flexible money wages that ensure full employment in the economy; (4) the hypothesis that all unemployed persons are voluntarily unemployed; (5) saving and investment, both of which depend on the interest rate; (6) the hypothesis that changes in the interest rate always equate saving and investment; (7) Say's law, stating that supply creates its own demand; (8) price flexibility, which makes Say's law work; and (9) the quantity theory of money, claiming that the general level of prices depends on money supply. Keynesian economics provided justifications for a more active role of government. Keynesian economic ideas include (1) the need for government intervention in the private sector; (2) the hypothesis that downwardly rigid wages cause unemployment to last for a long time; (3) the hypothesis that saving may not be equal to investment; and (4) the rejection of Say's law and the quantity theory of money.

The price level and the level of real output are determined by the intersection between aggregate demand and aggregate supply. The aggregate demand curve has a downward slope to the right because of the real balance effect, the interest rate effect, and the increased exports effect. The aggregate supply curve has three components: vertical, upward rising, and horizontal. The vertical portion of the aggregate supply curve is called the classical range. The vertical aggregate supply curve is located at the full employment level. When an economy operates at a full employment level, shifts in aggregate demand affect prices but not real output. The upward-rising portion is based on the assumption that money wages are downwardly rigid. The upward-rising portion of the aggregate supply curve is called the intermediate range. The horizontal portion of the aggregate supply curve is based on the assumption that there exist large amounts of unemployed resources such that increases in real output have no effect on prices. The horizontal portion is called the Keynesian range.

EXERCISES

1. Suppose that leaders of a political party are mostly in favor of laissez faire so far as the role of government is concerned. In practical terms how will this philosophy translate into some specific policy actions?

2. In the mid-1870s those who advocated a lesser role of government in the private enterprise system were called liberal economists. Since the 1930s those who advocate a greater role of government have been called liberal economists. What could be the reason for this change in definition?

3. When money wages are flexible both upward and downward, as was assumed by classical economists, the rate of unemployment is likely to be low. Why?

4. If both saving and investment depend on the interest rate, and if the interest rate changes freely depending on the supply of and the demand for loanable funds, saving and investment are always equal to each other. Why?

5. What does Say's law mean? How can supply create its own demand?

6. If we had to summarize the main contribution of Keynesian economics from the public policy viewpoint, what would the summary be?

7. The main reason for the downward slope of the demand curve for a product is the substitution effect. Can the downward slope of the aggregate demand curve also be explained by the substitution effect? Why not?

8. When we explain the inverse relation in an aggregate demand curve between price level and real output on the basis of the interest rate effect, what assumptions do we need to make?

9. Consider the three ranges of the aggregate supply curve. Determine for each of the three ranges what would happen to price and real output when (a) aggregate demand shifts to the right, and (b) the aggregate supply curve shifts to the right.

10. David Mermelstein once stated that classical economics had become irrelevant because it theoretically ruled out the possibility of economic depression, and did so at a time when a quarter of the work force was unemployed. This historical analogy suggests the possibility that the orthodoxy of Keynesian economics may suffer the same fate. Please comment on this statement. [Statement adapted from David Mermelstein, (ed.), *Economics: Mainstream readings and radical critiques* (New York: Random House, 1976), p. 249.]

SUGGESTED READINGS

Hansen, Alvin H. (1953). *A guide to Keynes*. New York: McGraw-Hill.

Introduces the student to the *General theory*. This author, along with Paul Samuelson, is credited with popularizing Keynesian economics.

Heilbroner, Robert L. (1967). The heresies of John Maynard Keynes. *The worldly philosophers*. New York: Simon & Schuster, pp. 225–261.

Explains the life and contribution of John M. Keynes to our understanding of macroeconomic relations.

Wolfson, Murray, and Buranelli. Vincent. (1984). *In the long run we are all dead*. New York: St. Martin's Press.

The book explains the main ideas of macroeconomics in mystery story form. The title of the book is a quote from *A tract on monetary reform* (1923) written by Keynes.

16

The Keynesian Model of GNP Determination

ABOUT 10 YEARS after the publication of John Maynard Keynes's *General theory of employment interest and money,* Alvin H. Hansen, then professor of economics at Harvard University, stated that Keynes would in the end rival Adam Smith in his influence on economic thinking and governmental policy. Hansen further stated that both Smith and Keynes were products of their times.[1] Studying Keynesian economics is not an easy task. Mark Blaug once commented, "What soon happened to Keynes is precisely what happened to Ricardo and Marx and Walras and Marshall: he was dissected, interpreted, reinterpreted, standardized, simplified, reduced to graphs and alternative mathematical models of Keynes I, Keynes II, et cetera, becoming in the process someone that everybody quotes but no one actually reads."[2] Our presentation of the Keynesian model of GNP determination is a simplified version of the model, and is thus subject to Blaug's comment. The simplification is inevitable since, as Keynes stated in the very first sentence of the preface, the book was written chiefly for other professional economists. Consider, for instance, that although we use many graphs to explain the Keynesian model, there is only one graph in the entire *General theory.*[3]

The first learning objective of this chapter is to study how GNP is determined using the tools and techniques of Keynesian economics. The second learning objective of this chapter is to study how governmental policies affect economic activities of a nation.

INTRODUCING THE KEYNESIAN MODEL

As the equilibrium quantity of any product is determined by supply and demand in the product's market, so is the equilibrium level of GNP determined by the aggregate supply and the aggregate demand in a given economy. **Aggregate supply** (AS) refers to total goods and services produced and thus made available for purchase in an economy during a period. Aggregate supply of a given year is equivalent to the year's GNP. **Aggregate demand** (AD), on the other hand, refers to total demand for goods and services produced in an economy during a period. In equilibrium,

$$AS = AD. \tag{16.1}$$

Essence of the Keynesian Model

Reconsider the expenditures approach to estimating GNP that we studied in Chapter 13. According to the expenditures approach, GNP can be calculated by adding expenditures on all goods and services produced in an economy. There are four major categories of expenditures, depending on

---

[1]Alvin H. Hansen, The general theory, in Seymour E. Harris (ed.), *The new economics* (New York: Alfred A. Knopf, 1947), pp. 133–144.

[2]Mark Blaug, *Economic theory in retrospect,* 4th ed. (Cambridge, England: Cambridge University Press, 1986), pp. 654–655.

[3]John Maynard Keynes, *The general theory of employment interest and money* (London: Macmillan, 1960). The lone graph is on p. 180 and explains the relation between investment and interest rates.

who spends the money. The four categories are personal consumption expenditures, gross private domestic investment, government purchases of goods and services, and net exports of goods and services. Expenditures on goods and services are, in fact, the demand for these goods and services. The aggregate demand, therefore, has the same four components: consumption demand (C), investment demand by private domestic businesses (I), government demand (G), and demand by the foreign sector called net exports ($X - M$). Aggregate demand (AD) is the sum of these four components. That is,

$$AD = C + I + G + (X - M). \tag{16.2}$$

In equation (16.1), AS is the GNP, and economists prefer to use the symbol Y to represent GNP or incomes in general. The equilibrium condition in (16.1) is restated

$$Y = C + I + G + (X - M). \tag{16.3}$$

Equation (16.3) is the essence of the Keynesian model of GNP determination. The equation states that GNP is determined by the level of aggregate demand, whereas aggregate demand has four components. The four components are referred to simply as consumption, investment, government expenditure, and net exports. In 1987, for instance, figures for consumption, investment, government expenditure, and net exports were, respectively,

$$
\begin{aligned}
C &= \$3{,}012.1 \text{ billion,} \\
I &= 712.9 \text{ billion,} \\
G &= 924.7 \text{ billion,} \\
X - M &= -123.0 \text{ billion.}
\end{aligned}
$$

When these four figures are added, the 1987 GNP is obtained as $4,526.7 billion.

The Problem

Our problem is that we want to use the Keynesian model to predict future GNP, not simply to recite past GNP figures. Suppose that we are interested in predicting GNP for the year 2000. If we knew the figures of the four components in equation (16.3) for the year 2000, all we would have to do would be to add these four figures. The problem is that we do not know these figures. In addition, at least some of these figures in the year 2000 may depend on the level of GNP in the year 2000. For instance, one of the four components of aggregate demand is consumption. To estimate GNP for the year 2000, we need to know how much consumers spend on goods and services (C) produced in the year 2000. How much consumers spend on goods and services in the year 2000 depends on how much consumers *earn* in the year 2000, whereas how much consumers earn depends on the level of production (GNP).

To summarize, the estimation of GNP requires the value of C, which in turn depends on the very GNP that this C is being used to help estimate. Estimating GNP is like the chicken-and-egg problem: We do not know which came first. Unlike the chicken-and-egg paradox, however, the Keynesian model helps us break out of the trap and estimate future GNPs. Let us return to the very beginning of the Keynesian model.

KEYNESIAN MODEL WITHOUT GOVERNMENT AND FOREIGN TRADE

To simplify the process of learning the Keynesian model, let us make three assumptions: no government, no foreign trade, and no price change. If there were no government, we would not have to worry about government expenditure (G) or taxes. In the absence of foreign trade, we would not have to worry about net exports ($X - M$). Without price changes, there would be no need to be concerned with money GNP or real GNP. Nominal values would be exactly the same as real values. Under these assumptions, equation (16.3) becomes

$$Y = C + I. \tag{16.4}$$

Equation (16.4) indicates that if we know the values of consumption (C) and investment (I) for any given year, we can easily determine the value of the year's GNP. If consumption is $5,000 and investment is $1,000 for the next year, the next year's GNP is $6,000.

The problem with equation (16.4) in predicting future GNPs is that the amount of consumption itself depends on the value of GNP for the same year. GNP cannot be predicted without knowing the amount of consumption, whereas consumption cannot be predicted without knowing the value of GNP. The Keynesian solution to this chicken-and-egg dilemma is to determine a relation between consumption and income on the basis of past experience, and to use the relation in place of consumption in equation (16.4).

In the following sections, we study consumption demand (C) and investment demand (I), and then combine C and I to determine the equilibrium level of GNP as indicated by equation (16.4).

Consumption Demand

How much all consumers in an economy spend on goods and services produced in any given year depends on several factors. The consumption expenditure is expected to be greater (1) the larger the amount of income consumers have; (2) the larger the amount of wealth consumers have; (3) the lower the market rates of interest are; (4) the more strongly consumers expect prices to increase; and many more factors. Following Keynes, however, let us assume that in the short run consumption depends on the level of income alone. The causal relation between consumption (C) and income (Y) is called the **consumption function:**

$$C = f(Y), \tag{16.5}$$

which reads that consumption is a function of income, meaning that consumption depends on income.

Let us study the consumption function first using tables and next using graphs.

Consumption and Saving Functions in Tables
A hypothetical aggregate consumption function is presented in Table 16.1. If figures look rather too small for an aggregate consumption function, all we need to do is to add nine more zeroes to make them more realistic for the U.S. economy. Column (1) shows different levels of income

TABLE 16.1 Consumption and Saving Schedule

Level of Income (1)	Consump- tion (2)	Saving (3)	APC (4)	APS (5)	APC+APS (6)	MPC (7)	MPS (8)	MPC+MPS (9)
$ 0	$ 500	$ -500	—	—	—	—	—	—
1,000	1,250	-250	1.25	-0.25	1	0.75	0.25	1
2,000	2,000	0	1.00	0	1	0.75	0.25	1
3,000	2,750	250	0.92	0.08	1	0.75	0.25	1
4,000	3,500	500	0.875	0.125	1	0.75	0.25	1

ranging from zero to $4,000. Column (2) shows consumption at each income level. When income is zero, consumption is $500. The amount of $500 is called the **autonomous consumption,** since this amount does not depend on the level of income. When income increases to $1,000, consumption also increases, but only by $750, which is smaller than the increased income. The amount of $750 is called the **induced consumption,** since this amount is induced by how much consumers earn. According to Keynes, consumers behave in such a way that an increase in income is divided between increased consumption and increased saving. When income increases from zero to $1,000, for instance, consumption is increased by $750 and saving is increased by $250. As income increases from $1,000 to $2,000, consumption increases again by $750 from $1,250 to $2,000.

Column (3) shows saving. Saving is obtained by subtracting consumption in column (2) from income in column (1). When income is zero, saving is negative $500 since the entire consumption has to be borrowed or come out of saving. When income is $1,000, saving is negative $250 since $1,000 minus $1,250 is negative $250. When income is $2,000, consumption is equal to income, and thus there is no saving. As income level exceeds $2,000, income exceeds consumption and saving becomes positive.

At this point, we need to introduce four new terms: the average propensity to consume, the average propensity to save, the marginal propensity to consume, and the marginal propensity to save.

AVERAGE PROPENSITY TO CONSUME. The **average propensity to consume** (APC) is the ratio of consumption to income at a given level of income. APC figures in column (4) are obtained by dividing consumption for a given level of income by the income. At $Y = \$1,000$, for instance,

$$APC = \frac{1,250}{1,000} = 1.25. \qquad (16.6)$$

At $Y = \$3,000$,

$$APC = \frac{2,750}{3,000} = 0.92. \qquad (16.7)$$

Propensity means a tendency or an inclination. An APC of 0.92 means that consumers tend to spend 92 percent of their income when income is $3,000.

AVERAGE PROPENSITY TO SAVE. The **average propensity to save** (APS) is the ratio of saving to income. The APS figures in column (5) are obtained by dividing saving for a given level of income by the income. At $Y = \$1,000$, for instance,

$$APS = \frac{-250}{1,000} = -0.25. \tag{16.8}$$

At $Y = \$3,000$,

$$APS = \frac{250}{3,000} = 0.08. \tag{16.9}$$

An APS of 0.08 means that consumers tend to save an average of 8 percent of their income when income is $3,000. Since consumption plus saving is equal to total income, the sum of APC and APS is always unity, as indicated in column (6). This property of APC and APS also means that APS can be obtained simply by subtracting APC from one.

MARGINAL PROPENSITY TO CONSUME. The **marginal propensity to consume** (MPC) is the ratio of change in consumption to change in income. The MPC at $Y = \$1,000$ in column (7), for instance, is obtained as follows. An increase in income from zero to $1,000 represents a change in income by $1,000. An increase in consumption from $500 at zero income to $1,250 at $Y = \$1,000$ represents a change in consumption by $750. At $Y = \$1,000$, therefore,

$$MPC = \frac{750}{1,000} = 0.75. \tag{16.10}$$

Every time income increases by $1,000 in column (1), consumption increases by $750 in column (2). This constant relation between change in income and change in consumption means that the MPC remains constant at 0.75, as indicated in column (7).

MARGINAL PROPENSITY TO SAVE. The **marginal propensity to save** (MPS) is the ratio of change in saving to change in income. The MPS at $Y = \$1,000$ in column (8), for instance, is obtained as follows. An increase in income from zero to $1,000 represents a change in income by $1,000. An increase in saving from negative $500 at zero income to negative $250 at $Y = \$1,000$ represents a change in saving by $250. At $Y = \$1,000$, therefore,

$$MPS = \frac{250}{1,000} = 0.25. \tag{16.11}$$

Every time income increases by $1,000 in column (1), saving increases by $250 in column (3). This constant relation between change in income and change in saving means that the MPS remains constant at 0.25, as indicated in column (8). Since any additional income will have to be either spent or saved, the sum of MPC and MPS is always equal to one, as shown in column (9).

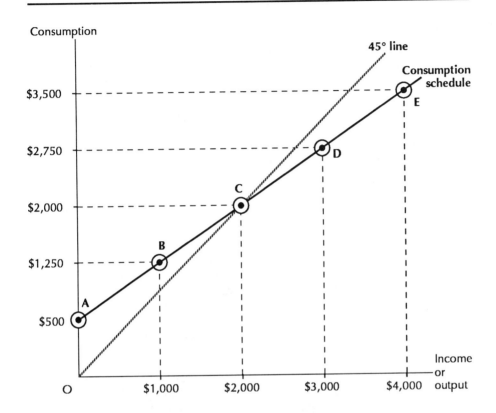

FIGURE 16.1 Consumption Function. A consumption function shows the relation between consumption and disposable income. The vertical intercept, 500, represents autonomous consumption. Consumption increases with income but not as much as the increase in income because MPC is less than 1.

SECTION SUMMARY. Let us summarize our findings in Table 16.1. First, there is an autonomous consumption expenditure when there is no income at all. In Table 16.1 the autonomous consumption is $500. Second, as income increases, consumption also increases, but by an amount less than the increase in income. This second property of the consumption function is the key assumption that we use in determining GNP. In Table 16.1 this relation between changing income and changing consumption is indicated as MPC 0.75. Third, as income increases, saving also increases, but by an amount significantly less than the increase in income. In Table 16.1 this relation between changing income and changing saving is indicated as MPS 0.25.

Graphic Analysis of Consumption Function
The graphic analysis of the consumption function means that a graph can be drawn that conveys the same information as Table 16.1, as shown in Figure 16.1. A consumption function can be drawn from the income and consumption figures presented in Table 16.1. To draw the consumption

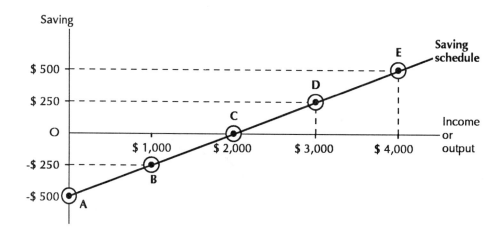

FIGURE 16.2 Saving Function. The saving function shows the relation between saving and income. The saving schedule is drawn based on income and saving data in Table 16.1.

function, we draw two lines: one vertical and the other horizontal. Since consumption depends on income, consumption is the dependent variable and income is the independent variable. We thus write consumption on the vertical line and income on the horizontal line.

Let us draw a line at a 45 degree (45°) angle to understand the graph better. We then plot the five relations between income and consumption shown in Table 16.1. When income is zero, consumption is $500, indicated as point A. When income is $1,000, consumption is $1,250, indicated as point B. When income is $2,000, consumption is $2,000, indicated as point C. Likewise points D and E are obtained. Connect these five points to obtain the consumption function. The consumption function crosses the 45° line at point C, since at point C consumption ($2,000) equals income ($2,000).

Consider point A in Figure 16.1. Point A is crossed by zero income and consumption of $500. In other words, point A indicates that consumption is $500 when income is zero. Point A thus tells us exactly the same information that the first set of income and consumption figures tells us in Table 16.1. Similarly, points B through E reveal exactly the same relations between income and consumption that the remaining sets of income and consumption figures reveal in Table 16.1. The consumption function can be explained either in table form or in graphic form. In Figure 16.1, the consumption function has a smaller slope, and is thus flatter, than the 45° line. If APC happens to be unity, meaning that all incomes are spent and no money is borrowed or saved, the consumption function will be identical to the 45° line.

Graphic Analysis of Saving Function
The graphic analysis of saving function means that a graph can be drawn that conveys the same information as Table 16.1. Saving function is a mirror image of the consumption function. The

PAUL A. SAMUELSON

Paul Samuelson, born in 1915 and trained at the University of Chicago and Harvard, is the first American economist to win the Nobel Prize in economics. Samuelson received the award in 1970 for "raising the level of analysis in economic science." His *Economics*, an introductory textbook, has been one of the most popular introductory texts since its first publication in 1948. The book has gone through 12 editions. A professor of economics at Massachusetts Institute of Technology for more than 30 years, Samuelson has contributed to many different areas of economics. His *Collected scientific papers* encompasses three volumes. Like other great economists such as Schumpeter and Marshall, Samuelson views economic problems as complex and suggests that precise and generalized solutions to these problems can seldom be drawn. There is a story that when Samuelson took an oral examination for his doctoral degree in economics, members of the examining committee were heard to ask among themselves, "Did *we* pass?"

saving function is drawn in Figure 16.2 on the basis of the income data in column (1) and saving data in column (3) of Table 16.1. The relation between zero income and saving of –$500 is indicated as point A in Figure 16.2. When income is $2,000, consumption is also $2,000. The same amount of income and consumption means that there is no saving. The saving function, therefore, crosses the horizontal line at point C, which represents the income level of $2,000. All five relations between income and saving data in Table 16.1 are plotted in Figure 16.2, as points A, B, C, D, and E.

Consider point A in Figure 16.2. Point A is crossed by zero income and saving of -$500. In other words, point A indicates that saving is –$500 when income is zero. Point A thus tells us exactly the same information that the first set of income and saving figures tells us in Table 16.1. Similarly, points B through E in Figure 16.2 reveal exactly the same relations between income and saving that the remaining sets of income and saving figures reveal in Table 16.1. Like the consumption function, the saving function can also be explained either with a table or a graph.

Investment Demand

We move on to the second component of equation (16.4), investment (I). When consumers buy bread and butter for consumption, these products have to be produced. The production of these products adds to the GNP. When businesses want to buy machines, equipment, and new buildings, these products will have to be produced. The production of these investment goods also adds to the GNP. Income is the dominant determinant of consumption. Economists do not believe that such a dominant determinant exists for investment. To simplify our presentation, therefore, let us assume that an investment decision is made independently of the level of GNP and is constant at $1,000. The investment function, then, is

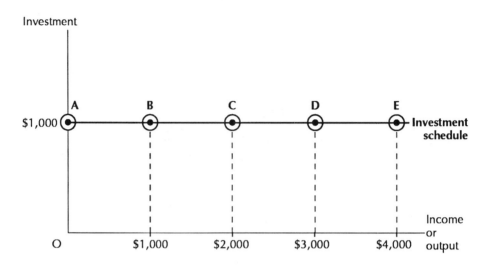

FIGURE 16.3 Investment Function. Investment is assumed constant at $1,000 at all levels of income in our simple Keynesian model.

$$I = \$1,000. \tag{16.12}$$

The investment function is graphed in Figure 16.3. Since investment remains constant for all levels of income, the investment function is horizontal.

In reality, many economists, including Keynes, believe that changes in the interest rate affect business borrowing, thus influencing business investment. The effect of changes in interest on investment is more evident in the home-building industry than in other industry. Demand for new homes is believed to be quite sensitive to changes in, and expected changes in, mortgage rates.

DETERMINATION OF GNP WITHOUT GOVERNMENT AND FOREIGN TRADE

In this section, we combine consumption demand and investment demand so that we can determine the level of GNP. There are two ways of determining the equilibrium GNP: the AD = AS approach and the $S = I$ approach. First, we study the AD = AS approach.

AD = AS Approach

The **equilibrium GNP** is defined as the level of GNP that is obtained when aggregate supply is equal to aggregate demand. The equilibrium GNP in the Keynesian model is thus determined when

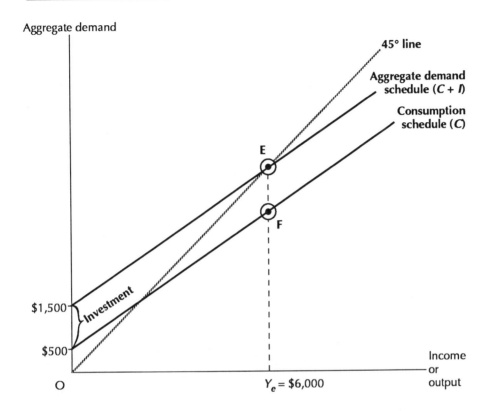

FIGURE 16.4 Determination of GNP. The equilibrium GNP (Y_e) is determined when aggregate supply (Y) equals aggregate demand. Aggregate demand is the sum of consumption demand (C) and investment demand (I).

aggregate supply (Y) is equal to aggregate demand. Aggregate demand in our simplified model has only two components: consumption demand (C) and investment demand (I). This relation was stated as equation (16.4)

$$Y = C + I. \tag{16.4}$$

To determine the equilibrium GNP, it is necessary to add consumption and investment. The consumption schedule is drawn in Figure 16.1, and the investment schedule is drawn in Figure 16.3. The investment schedule is superimposed onto the consumption schedule in Figure 16.4. The consumption schedule in Figure 16.4 is the same as the consumption schedule in Figure 16.1. To superimpose the two schedules, add the amount of investment ($1,000) to the consumption schedule at every income level. The combined schedule of consumption and investment is parallel to the consumption schedule, but higher than the consumption schedule by $1,000.

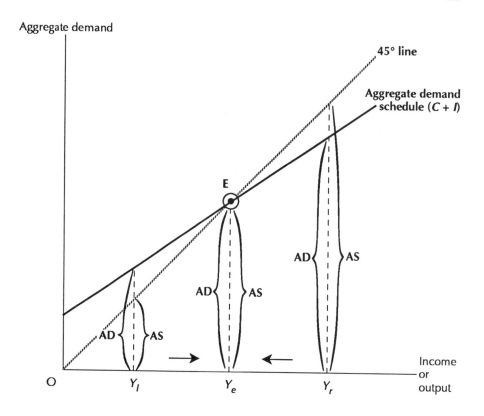

FIGURE 16.5 Generalizing the Determination of GNP. To the left of the equilibrium GNP, AD is greater than AS, causing GNP to increase. To the right of the equilibrium GNP, AS is greater than AD, causing GNP to decrease.

The process of reading the equilibrium GNP in Figure 16.4 is the following. First, locate the point (E) at which the aggregate demand schedule crosses the 45° line. Second, draw a vertical line from point E until it crosses the horizontal line at Y_e. Point Y_e represents the equilibrium GNP.

Keep in mind that the equilibrium GNP is obtained when aggregate demand is equal to aggregate supply. At point Y_e, the aggregate demand is the vertical distance EY_e, which is the sum of consumption demand (FY_e) and investment demand (EF). Consider the triangle OEY_e. The triangle is a right triangle, since EY_e is perpendicular to OY_e. Line OE is a 45° line. In the triangle, therefore, distance OY_e is equal to distance EY_e. Since distance EY_e represents aggregate demand, OY_e is the only GNP that equals aggregate demand. So long as the aggregate demand curve crosses the 45° line at E, Y_e is the only point on the horizontal line at which GNP is equal to aggregate demand. The level of output represented by Y_e, therefore, is the equilibrium level of GNP.

The process of determining the equilibrium GNP is generalized in Figure 16.5. If the current level of output is Y_l, aggregate demand is greater than aggregate output. There is a shortage of goods and services. The shortage will induce businesses to increase production. The output level Y_l is unstable. GNP increases as production is increased. If the current level of output is Y_r, on the other hand, aggregate output is greater than aggregate demand. There is a surplus of goods and services in the economy. The surplus will induce businesses to reduce production. Like Y_l, Y_r is also unstable. GNP decreases as production is reduced. The economy tends to move toward the equilibrium level of GNP Y_e.

$S = I$ Approach

The equilibrium GNP can also be determined by equalizing saving and investment. Reconsider the simple economic circular flow drawn as Figure 2.1 in Chapter 2. The household sector earns income by providing productive resources to the business sector. In reality, not all incomes the household sector earns are spent on goods and services. Part of the income is leaked out of the circular flow as saving. If an equal amount were not injected into the circular flow, aggregate demand would be smaller than aggregate output. The level of GNP is expected to decrease without an injection equal in amount to the leakage.

Leakage and Injection

The relation between saving as a leakage and investment as an injection is illustrated in Figure 16.6, which is an extension of Figure 2.1. In Figure 16.6, saving is the portion of income that flows back to the household sector. The leakage needs to be balanced out by investment. The circular flow becomes smooth only when the amount of saving is exactly the same as the amount of investment.

The graphic illustration of the $S = I$ approach toward GNP determination is shown in Figure 16.7. In this figure the saving schedule from Figure 16.2 and the investment schedule from Figure 16.3 are superimposed onto each other. The equilibrium level of GNP, Y_e, is obtained by the intersection between the saving schedule and the investment schedule. The amount thus obtained is $6,000, which is equal to the GNP obtained by the AS = AD method in Figure 16.4.

An Illustration

Let us illustrate how saving and investment interact to equalize aggregate supply and aggregate demand. Suppose that this year our economy is producing automobiles at a rate that will give us 100 cars at the end of the year. Let us also suppose that the economy produces nothing but automobiles. If the income generated during the production is all spent to purchase automobiles, the aggregate supply (100 cars available) is equal to the aggregate demand (100 cars demanded). In reality, part of the income will be saved. If 10 percent of total income were saved so that only 90 cars were bought by consumers, the remaining 10 cars need to be purchased by businesses as investment. Depending on how businesses purchase the remaining 10 cars, the course of the economy will be different.

PLANNED INVESTMENT MORE THAN SAVING. Suppose that businesses *plan* to buy 13 cars. When businesses purchase new cars for their use, the purchase is an investment. The planned purchase of 13 cars by businesses means that aggregate demand is 103 (90 by consumers and 13 by businesses) but aggregate supply is only 100. Since aggregate demand is greater than aggregate supply, economic activities rise. The economy may end up producing 103 cars instead of 100 cars if resources are available for increased production.

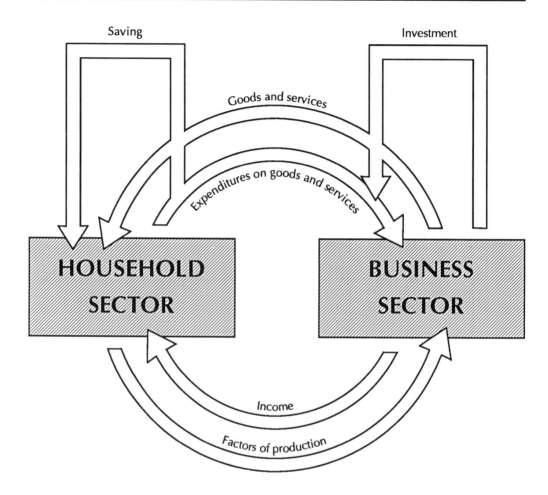

FIGURE 16.6 Saving and Investment in the Economic Circular Flow. Saving is a leakage and investment is an injection in the economic circular flow. For the economy to be in equilibrium, saving must be equal to investment.

PLANNED INVESTMENT LESS THAN SAVING. Suppose that businesses *plan* to buy only 7 cars. Aggregate demand, then, is 97 (90 by consumers and 7 by businesses). Since aggregate demand (97) is smaller than aggregate supply (100), economic activities fall. In fact, one of two things will happen. One is that the economy will cut back its production to 97 cars. In this case, saving is 7, obtained as the difference between 97 and 90, and the saving is equal to planned investment. The other development is that the economy may go ahead and produce 100 cars. In this case, saving is 10, obtained as the difference between 100 and 90. Saving (10) is greater than planned investment (7). To be

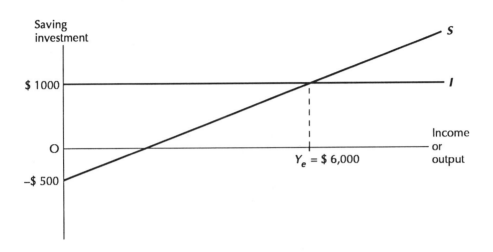

FIGURE 16.7 *S* = *I* Approach to GNP Determination. The equilibrium GNP is determined when saving is equal to investment. The GNP thus determined is the same as that determined by the AS = AD approach.

exact, saving (10) is equal to planned investment (7) plus increased inventory (3). When unintended changes in inventory are added to planned investment, the result is known as **realized investment.** **Planned investment** does not include unintended changes in inventory.

KEYNESIAN MODEL IN A REAL ECONOMY

Remember the three assumptions that we made earlier in this chapter? The three assumptions were no government, no foreign trade, and no inflation. Let us now relax these assumptions and make the Keynesian model more practical. We assume that there are governments as well as foreign trade. We incorporate inflation into our model by converting all nominal values into real values.

AD = AS Approach in a Real Economy

When the government and foreign trade sectors are added to the Keynesian model, the equilibrium condition does not change. In equilibrium, aggregate supply still equals aggregate demand. The components of the aggregate demand are expanded, however, to include not only consumption demand and investment demand, but also government demand and demand by the foreign trade sector. The equilibrium condition for the real economy is

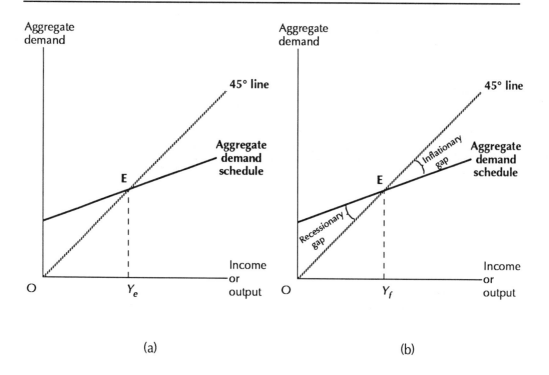

(a)   (b)

FIGURE 16.8 Keynesian Model of GNP Determination. The equilibrium GNP is determined, in panel (a), when aggregate supply equals aggregate demand. If the equilibrium GNP is at the full employment level, in panel (b), the right and the left sides of the equilibrium point E are called inflationary gap and recessionary gap.

$$Y = C + I + G + (X - M), \tag{16.3}$$

where G represents government expenditure on goods and services and $(X - M)$ represents net foreign expenditures on goods and services.

The graphic explanation of the Keynesian model of GNP determination for the real economy is an easy extension of Figure 16.5. The aggregate demand schedule in Figure 16.5 was the sum of consumption demand and investment demand. The aggregate demand schedule in Figure 16.8 is the sum of consumption demand, investment demand, government expenditure, and net foreign demand. The equilibrium level of GNP in panel (a) is determined by the intersection E between aggregate demand and the 45° line. If, for some reason, consumption, investment, government expenditure, or exports fall, the aggregate demand schedule shifts downward, and the equilibrium level of GNP also falls. If, on the other hand, consumption, investment, government expenditures, or exports rise, the aggregate demand schedule shifts upward, and the equilibrium level of GNP also rises.

Suppose that the equilibrium GNP, Y_e, happens to be the full employment level, as shown in Figure 16.8(b). If the aggregate demand schedule shifts upward, output and employment cannot increase because the economy is already at the full employment level. The increase in aggregate demand above the full employment level will simply raise prices. The right-side gap between the 45° line and the aggregate demand schedule is called the *inflationary gap*. If the aggregate demand shifts downward, output and employment are expected to fall. The left-side gap between the 45° line and the aggregate demand schedule is called the *recessionary gap*.

$S = I$ Approach in a Real Economy

As we know, there are two ways of determining the equilibrium GNP. One is the AD = AS approach, presented in the preceding section, and the other is the $S = I$ approach. When we excluded government and foreign trade from our discussion, saving represented the entire leakage from the economic circular flow, and investment represented the entire injection to the economic circular flow. We thus claimed that saving should be equal to investment in order to determine the equilibrium level of GNP. In a real economy with foreign trade as well as government, it is a little more complicated.

In a real economy, there are three leakages that will keep incomes from being spent on domestically produced goods and services. The three leakages are saving (S), taxes (T), and imports (M). When we save, no purchases are made; when we pay taxes, no purchases are made on the amount of taxes we pay; and when we buy foreign goods, no purchases are made on domestically produced goods and services. In a real economy, on the other hand, there are three injections that will make up for leakages due to saving, taxes, and imports. The three injections are investment (I), government expenditure (G), and exports (X). Investment, government expenditure, and exports all represent purchases of currently produced goods and services in the economy. To have an equilibrium in a real economy, total leakages must be equal to total injections. In reality, therefore, the $S = I$ approach becomes

$$S + T + M = I + G + X. \qquad (16.13)$$

Multiplier

One analytical tool developed by Keynes that attracted wide attention from economists and policymakers is the multiplier. To explain the multiplier, let us suppose that a group of business-persons decides to build a new convention center in our city in an attempt to attract more visitors to the city. The convention center is expected to cost $10 million. What would be the impact of the construction of the new convention center on GNP? Will GNP increase? If it does, by how much? The multiplier concept helps us answer these questions.

Concept of the Multiplier

The construction of the convention center is counted as an investment in national income accounting. Since the convention center is new, GNP increases as the construction progresses. To determine the exact impact on GNP, we need to track where the $10 million is spent. Some of this amount will be spent to pay economists to conduct a feasibility study. Some of the money will be spent to pay an architectural firm to design its physical structure. Some of the money will be spent to purchase the land on which the convention center is to be built. The remaining amount will be spent for actual construction on such items as bricks, cement, glass, tile, carpet, water sprinklers, kitchen equipment, furniture, and wages. As soon as the convention center is completed, GNP increases by $10 million since a new building is added to the economy. Total increase in GNP, however, is greater than $10 million.

Consider bricklayers. When they get paid for their work on the convention center, they pay taxes and spend the disposable income on groceries, videotapes, and automobiles. The purchase of these products by bricklayers means that these products will have to be produced. The dollar value of these additional groceries, videotapes, and automobiles is added to GNP. The impact of the new convention center on GNP, therefore, exceeds $10 million. The **investment multiplier** is the ratio of a change in GNP to the initial change in investment that causes the change in GNP. That is,

$$\text{Investment multiplier} = \frac{\text{change in GNP}}{\text{change in investment}}. \tag{16.14}$$

Mechanics of the Multiplier

The $10 million spent on the construction of the convention center eventually reaches owners of all productive resources employed for the construction as income. The owners of productive resources spend the income on a wide range of goods and services, generating additional GNP. By the time the owners of productive resources spend their income, the amount of spending will be significantly smaller than $10 million. Although exact figures vary from year to year and also with the type of the initial spending, on the average, only about half of the initial spending is spent again during the second round.

The sources of leakages from the initial spending ($10 million) to the second round spending ($5 million) are (1) capital consumption allowance by the firms that employ resource owners, (2) corporate income tax paid by these firms, (3) indirect business taxes paid by these firms, (4) business transfer payments paid by these firms, (5) personal income taxes paid by individual resource owners, and finally (6) savings made by individual resource owners. Savings made by individual resource owners depend on their marginal propensities to consume. The greater the MPC is, the smaller the saving will be.

Because of the leakages listed above, by the time the initial $10 million investment is spent for the second round expenditure, the actual expenditure becomes approximately half the initial investment. The $5 million spent during the second round will go through the same procedure and be spent again, generating a third round expenditure. The procedure of respending through the third round is summarized in Table 16.2.

The total impact on GNP of the initial investment in the convention center is obtained when the initial investment of $10 million is added to the sum of the last row figures in Table 16.2, called additional expenditures. Total impact through the third round is already $18.75 million, obtained by adding $5 million, $2.5 million, $1.25 million, and the initial investment of $10 million. The ratio of additional expenditure, shown in the last row, in any given round to the initial spending, shown in the first row of the same round, is called the **respending ratio.** Since the additional expenditure is 50 percent of the initial spending, the respending ratio is 0.5. When a number, say 1, decreases at a constant rate such as 0.5, the final total (MULT) of all these numbers is obtained by a simple formula,

$$\text{MULT} = \frac{1}{1 - \text{respending ratio}}. \tag{16.15}$$

The figure obtained through equation (16.15) is called the multiplier. When the respending ratio is 0.5, the multiplier is

$$\text{MULT} = \frac{1}{1 - 0.5}, \tag{16.16}$$

$$= \frac{1}{0.5}, \tag{16.17}$$

$$= 2. \tag{16.18}$$

In our convention center example, the total increase in GNP from the initial spending of $10 million is $20 million. Returning to equation (16.14), the investment multiplier is obtained as

$$\text{Investment multiplier} = \frac{\text{change in GNP}}{\text{change in investment}}, \tag{16.14}$$

$$= \frac{\$20 \text{ million}}{\$10 \text{ million}}, \tag{16.19}$$

$$= 2. \tag{16.20}$$

Properties of the Multiplier
There are three properties of the multiplier that we need to pay attention to. First of all, the exact size of the multiplier for any given expenditure depends on the amount of leakage and the value of the MPC. The larger the leakage, the smaller the size of the multiplier. A larger leakage means that consumers have that much less money to spend. Also, the larger the value of the MPC, the larger

TABLE 16.2 Multiplier Effect

	First Round	Second Round	Third Round
Initial spending	$10,000,000		
		→ $5,000,000	→ $2,500,000
Leakages:	5,000,000	2,500,000	1,250,000
Depreciation			
Income taxes			
Personal saving			
Etc.			
Additional expenditure	$ 5,000,000 →	$2,500,000 →	$1,250,000

the size of the multiplier. A larger value of MPC means that consumers spend that much more out of additional income. The whole idea of the multiplier concept is based on respending.

Consider two different government programs. One program is to give cash to transients served by a charitable agency. The money given to these transients will be spent in its entirety during the first round of spending. Expenditures of this type have a larger multiplier. The other program is to give a subsidy to large businesses through congressional pork barrel projects. Expenditures of this second type have a smaller multiplier, since a sizable portion of the subsidy is saved by recipients rather than spent.

The second property of the multiplier is that it works in both expansionary and contractionary ways. If an investment increases by, say, $10 billion, GNP is expected to increase by $20 billion because of the multiplier. If an investment decreases by $10 billion, GNP is expected to decrease by $20 billion. The multiplier magnifies the effect of changes in autonomous spending on GNP.

The third property is that the multiplier effect is not limited to investment. The multiplier works by means of the process of initial spending being respent through induced consumption. There is a multiplier effect not only when investment is increased (investment multiplier), but also when there are increases in other components of aggregate demand such as autonomous consumption (autonomous consumption multiplier), taxes (tax multiplier), government expenditure (government expenditure multiplier), exports (export multiplier), and imports (import multiplier). Since taxes and imports are leakages from the economic circular flow, GNP falls as taxes or imports increase. The tax multiplier and the import multiplier are negative.

FISCAL POLICY

Fiscal policy refers to deliberate changes in government expenditure and taxes in order to stabilize the economy and promote economic growth. One of the main contributions that Keynes made toward macroeconomics was to recognize the importance of fiscal policy and of the government itself in a nation's economic affairs.

There are four main components in aggregate demand: consumption, investment, government expenditure, and net exports. Government is capable of influencing the level of expenditure on each of these components. If the government deliberately changes tax rates on individual incomes, it affects consumption. If it deliberately changes tax rates on corporate incomes, it affects investment. Government can directly alter the level of government expenditure. Finally, government can raise export subsidies, thus affecting exports, or change import duties, thereby affecting imports.

All these tax and expenditure policies affect aggregate demand and, thus, the level of GNP. The acts of changing tax rates and government expenditure are *discretionary* in the sense that the government deliberately undertakes these actions for promotion of steady economic growth. For this reason, tax and expenditure policies of the government are sometimes called the **discretionary fiscal policy.**

Impact of Government Expenditure

Changes in government expenditure are a powerful tool of fiscal policy. To understand how changes in government expenditure affect the economy, let us assume that changes in government

CONSUMPTION FUNCTION AND INCOME TAX SURCHARGE

The consumption function is not simply an academician's useless jargon. Suppose that the economy is inflationary, and we all agree that something has to be done to control aggregate demand. Suppose also that the policy option under consideration is a temporary increase in tax rates on personal income. According to the Keynesian consumption function, the higher income tax rates will reduce consumption and, thus, aggregate demand. According to the permanent income hypothesis and the life-cycle income hypothesis, consumers change their spending behavior only if they believe that higher tax rates will affect their long-term expected income. A temporary increase will have little effect on consumption, if any, since consumers perceive these higher tax rates to be temporary. If the Keynesian consumption function were valid, the surcharge on income tax would be effective in controlling inflationary pressure. If the permanent income and the life-cycle income hypotheses were valid, the surcharge would not be effective in controlling inflationary pressure.

The Revenue and Expenditure Control Act of 1968 levied an income tax surcharge that raised $17.0 billion in 1969 and $4.7 billion in 1970. Was the surcharge effective in reducing consumption? Arthur M. Okun, a Keynesian, concludes that the evidence indicates that the surcharge curbed consumption nearly as much as was expected, and provides "further confirmation of the general efficacy and continued desirability of flexible changes in personal income tax rates—upward or downward, permanent or temporary" (Okun, 1971, p. 200). William L. Springer, a monetarist, concludes that the actual impact of the 1968 surcharge on consumer expenditures was at best about one-fourth of what could be expected from a permanent tax change. Springer further suggests that "in order to have a significant effect on consumption expenditures, an income tax change must be permanent" (Springer, 1975, p. 658).

Sources: Arthur M. Okun, The personal tax surcharge and consumer demand, 1968–70, *Brookings Papers* (Washington, D.C.: The Brookings Institution, 1971), pp. 167–212; W. L. Springer, Did the 1968 surcharge really work?, *American Economic Review* 65(September 1975):644–658; and Arthur M. Okun, Did the 1968 surcharge really work?: Comment, *American Economic Review* 67(March 1977):166–169.

expenditure are not accompanied by changes in tax rates or in the money supply. For instance, government may use a budget surplus for the increase in expenditure, or save revenue when expenditure is reduced. This assumption would be valid only in the short run. In the long run, a budget surplus, if it existed in the first place, will run out, and government expenditure cannot be increased without an increase in taxation, borrowing, or printing of currency. Also, it is highly unlikely that revenues will be saved year after year. Our assumption, however, permits us to see clearly the impact of an increase in government expenditure.

An increase in government expenditure on such products as new naval destroyers, space shuttles, AIDS research, and highway programs will increase the demand for these goods and services. The increased demand, in turn, causes jobs and wage payments to increase. Overall, an increase in government expenditure raises aggregate demand and is *expansionary*. An expansionary policy is usually intended to increase output and employment. A decrease in government expenditure, on the other hand, may cause businesses to lay off workers and individuals to cut back their spending. A decrease in government expenditure lowers aggregate demand and is *contractionary*. A contractionary policy is usually intended to reduce an inflationary pressure in the economy.

The effects of changes in government expenditure are illustrated in Figure 16.9. An increase in government expenditure raises the aggregate demand schedule, is expansionary, and, thus, increases nominal GNP. A decrease in government expenditure lowers the aggregate demand schedule, is contractionary, and, thus, decreases GNP.

Impact of Changes in Tax Rates

Changes in tax rates, ceteris paribus, have the opposite effect. If tax rates are raised on individual incomes, for instance, consumers will have to pay more taxes and will thus have less disposable income to spend. Consumption will fall. An increase in tax rates is contractionary. A decrease in tax rates on individual incomes is expansionary, since consumers have more disposable income to spend.

An increase in tax rates on corporate incomes is contractionary, since corporations will have less money to spend with the tax hike. A decrease in tax rates on corporate incomes is expansionary, since corporations will have more money to spend for investment with the tax cut. The effects of changes in government expenditure and tax rates are summarized in Table 16.3.

Different Impact with Different Ways of Financing

Government expenditure cannot be increased for long unless it is financed somehow. Broadly speaking, there are two ways of financing government expenditure. One is tax financing and the other is deficit financing. The impact of government expenditure varies with the way it is financed.

TABLE 16.3 Effects of Changes in Government Expenditure and Tax Rates

Tools of Fiscal Policy	Effects
Government expenditure	
Increase	Expansionary
Decrease	Contractionary
Tax rates on individual and corporate incomes	
Increase	Contractionary
Decrease	Expansionary

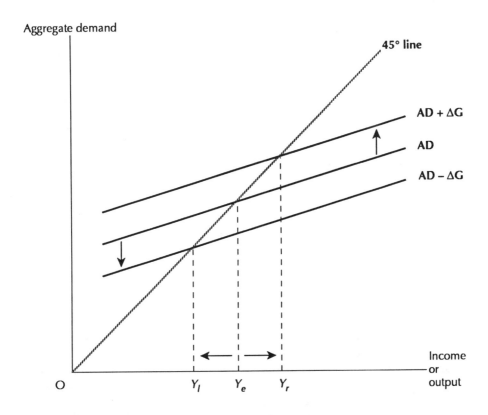

FIGURE 16.9 Effects of Changes in Government Expenditure. An increase in government expenditure raises the aggregate demand schedule and is expansionary. A decrease in government expenditure lowers aggregate demand and is contractionary.

Tax Financing

Consider a new government program that costs $10 billion. The total impact of this program on GNP will be an increase in GNP by $20 billion so long as the multiplier remains at 2. Suppose that the program is financed by an increase in tax by the same amount. An increase in tax, ceteris paribus, will reduce GNP. The decrease in GNP owing to the tax increase by $10 billion, however, will be less than $20 billion. In other words, if the government increases expenditures and taxes simultaneously by the same amount, the net impact is expansionary. To understand why this is true, we need to understand why an increase in tax by $10 billion will reduce GNP by an amount less than $20 billion.

Consider that consumers in general do not spend every penny they earn. Consumers save part of their income, meaning that the marginal propensity to consume is less than 1. Suppose that MPC is 0.75. When taxes are increased by $10 billion, consumption does not decrease by $10 billion. Consumption is expected to decrease by $7.5 billion, which is 75 percent of $10 billion. The remaining $2.5 billion tax increase will be paid out of savings. The multiplier affects consumption but not saving. When tax is increased by $10 billion, therefore, GNP decreases by $15 billion, obtained by multiplying the $7.5 billion decrease in consumption by the multiplier 2.

The preceding analysis has an interesting policy implication. If expenditures and taxes are raised by an equal amount, the effect of the increase in government expenditure is greater in absolute value than that of the increase in tax. This finding means that if government expenditure and taxes increase simultaneously by the same amount, the net impact of the balanced budget is expansionary, not neutral. Similarly, if government expenditure and taxes decrease simultaneously by the same amount, the net impact is contractionary, not neutral.

The expansionary effect of an increase in the balanced budget or the contractionary effect of a decrease in the balanced budget is called the **balanced budget multiplier effect.** In our example, the positive impact on GNP of a $10 billion increase in government expenditure is $20 billion, whereas the negative impact on GNP of a $10 billion increase in taxes is $15 billion. There is a net increase in aggregate demand by $5 billion.

Deficit Financing

Government expenditure can be increased without an increase in taxes. In fact, there are two ways of financing government expenditure when there is no tax revenue to support it: to print money, and to borrow from the public.

Let us speculate, for a moment, what would happen if government prints money to pay for all the programs that it wants to carry out such as homes for the homeless, day care centers for the children of working parents, and the like. For a short period of time, the impact of the increased money supply on the economy might be expansionary. Very soon, however, the continuous increase in money supply will cause inflation. Eventually, the policy of financing most government programs through increases in money supply becomes self-destructive. No one will accept paper currency as a medium of exchange, and most, if not all, economic activities will cease to function.

The other way of financing government expenditure in the absence of tax increases is to borrow money in the money market. When deficit spending is financed by borrowing in the money market, government competes against the private sector for the available loanable funds. If government borrows a large amount of money in the money market, the borrowing tends to raise interest rates and thus forces private firms to reduce their borrowing. Because government borrowing thus crowds out private investment, this negative effect is called the **crowding-out effect.**

Economists do not agree on the extent of the crowding-out effect of deficit financing. Some argue that, at least in the short run, the role of federal debt is insignificant in the determination of interest rates. Other factors such as expected inflation and money supply are more important determinants of interest rates than federal debt. Others claim that federal deficits cause long-term interest rates to rise. Since long-term rates are more closely related to many consumer and business spending decisions than are short-term rates, these economists claim that the crowding-out effects of deficit spending are potentially significant.[4]

---

[4]Studies that support or reject the crowding-out hypothesis of federal debt are listed in Suggested Readings.

Built-in Stabilizers

There are many programs that reduce the severity of business cycles by raising expenditure during a recession and reducing expenditure during an inflationary period. When these programs do not require explicit action by policymakers, they are called **automatic stabilizers** or **built-in stabilizers.**

One example of built-in stabilizers is the federal income tax revenue. During a recession, it is desirable to increase aggregate demand through additional expenditure. During a recession, income levels of many individuals stay at, or move back to, lower income tax brackets. This tendency automatically reduces government revenue and encourages the private sector to increase expenditure. Other examples relate to government income security programs such as social security, unemployment insurance, food stamps, and Aid to Families with Dependent Children (AFDC). Consider, for instance, the unemployment insurance program. In certain industries, workers and their employees pay premiums on the insurance program so that when workers are laid off, say, during a recession, they receive payments. During an expansion, when there is no strong need to raise aggregate demand, workers return to work and no payments are made to them from the unemployment insurance program.

Expenditures from built-in stabilizers rise during a recession and fall during an inflationary period without any discretionary action by policymakers. Built-in stabilizers tend to reduce the magnitude of economic fluctuations.

SUMMARY

This chapter summarizes the tools and techniques of the Keynesian model of GNP determination as well as policy implications of the model. The equilibrium GNP is determined when aggregate supply equals aggregate demand. Aggregate supply is GNP, whereas aggregate demand has four components: consumption, investment, government expenditure, and net exports. Keynes assumes that as income increases, consumption also increases but by an amount less than the increase in income. This assumption makes it possible to estimate future GNP without knowing the actual value of future consumption. The equilibrium GNP is determined graphically when the aggregate demand curve crosses the 45° line. An increase in autonomous spending raises GNP by its multiple due to the multiplier effect. Changes in autonomous spending may originate from autonomous consumption, taxes, business investment, government expenditure, exports, or imports. Fiscal policy refers to deliberate changes in government expenditure and taxes in order to stabilize the economy and promote its growth. Through fiscal policy government may influence the level of expenditure on each of the four components of aggregate demand. Policy actions that increase the level of spending are expansionary. Policy actions that decrease the level of spending are contractionary. Increased government expenditures may be financed by increased tax revenues, increased money supply, or by borrowing. When expenditures are financed by an increase in the equal amount of tax, the policy is expansionary. When deficit spending is financed by issuing new money, the net effect is inflationary. When deficit spending is financed by borrowing in the money market, government needs to compete against the private sector for the available loanable funds, resulting in the crowding-out effect. Built-in stabilizers tend to reduce economic fluctuations without discretionary actions by policymakers.

EXERCISES

1. Assuming that we know the values of consumption, investment, government expenditure, and net exports for any future year, we can predict the year's GNP simply by adding these four figures. One major problem is that the future value of consumption depends on the year's GNP, creating the chicken-and-egg dilemma. How does the Keynesian model solve the dilemma?

2. What is meant by a consumption function? Assuming that investment also depends on the level of output (Y), what will be the general description of such an investment function?

3. Suppose that a consumer has an income of $10,000. Suppose also that the consumer's APC is 0.95. What are the consumer's expected amounts of consumption and saving? If the consumer wins $1,000 in a lottery and has an MPC of 0.75, what are the consumer's expected amounts of consumption and saving from the lottery income?

4. Consider a closed economy without the government. Can saving be greater than planned investment? If saving is greater than planned investment, what would be its impact on the economy?

5. How does MPC affect the size of the investment multiplier?

6. Determine for each of the following policy actions whether it is expansionary (E) or contractionary (C). Assume that other factors remain the same while you answer the questions.

   Government expenditure on two more space shuttles
   Increase in tax rates on individual incomes
   Increase in business licenses
   Increase in property tax
   Surcharge on income tax
   Decrease in tax rates on corporate profits

7. Suppose that the government decides to expand the provision of public services and finance the program through increased taxes. Is this program expansionary, neutral, or contractionary?

8. How will a federal budget deficit affect the economy, assuming that the deficit is financed by borrowing from the money market?

9. During a press interview, President Gerald Ford once commented that there would be no more depressions because there are built-in stabilizers. Comment.

10. Let us first explain how the U.S. Treasury sells Treasury bills. Each week the U.S. Treasury holds an auction to sell Treasury bills to major buyers. On Tuesday the Treasury announces the amount of 91-day and 182-day bills it wishes to sell on the following Monday and invites bids for specified amounts of these bills. Bids are due by 1:00 P.M. Eastern time on the Monday after the announcement, and the Treasury usually publicizes the results later that afternoon. The bills are issued to the successful bidders on Thursday. Two different types of bids can be submitted in the T-bill

auction: competitive and noncompetitive. Competitive bidders include money market banks, dealers, and other institutional investors who buy large quantities of T-bills. The bids they submit indicate the amount of bills they wish to purchase and the price they are willing to pay. Noncompetitive bidders are usually small or inexperienced bidders who indicate the amount of bills they want to purchase (up to $1,000,000) and agree to pay the average of the accepted competitive bids. After all bids are in, first the Treasury sets aside the amount of bills requested by the noncompetitive bidders. The remainder is allocated among the competitive bidders, beginning with those who bid the higher price, until the total amount is issued. The price paid by the noncompetitive bidders can then be calculated based on the competitive bids that were accepted. The question is, Which of the concepts presented in the text relates most closely to this story?

SUGGESTED READINGS

Canto, Victor A., and Rapp, Donald. (1982). The "crowding out" controversy: Arguments and evidence. Federal Reserve Bank of Atlanta *Economic Review*, August, pp. 33–37.

Dewald, William G. (1983). Federal deficits and real interest rates: Theory and evidence. Federal Reserve Bank of Atlanta *Economic Review*, January, pp. 20–29.

Hoelscher, Gregory. (1983). Federal borrowing and short-term interest rates. *Southern Economic Journal* 50(October):319–333.

Makin, John H. (1983). Real interest, money surprises, anticipated inflation, and fiscal deficits. *Review of Economics and Statistics* 65(August):374–384.

Mascaro, Angelo, and Meltzer, Allan H. (1983). Long and short term interest rates in a risky world. *Journal of Monetary Economics* 12(November):485–518.

The studies above claim no significant relation between federal debt and interest rates.

Greider, William. (1981). The education of David Stockman. *The Atlantic Monthly*, December, pp. 27–54.

An article describing the concern over the large federal deficit by, and the budget-making experience of, David Stockman, who was the director of the Office of Management and Budget. Stockman was quoted as saying "None of us really understands what's going on with all these numbers."

Hoelscher, Gregory. (1986). New evidence on deficits and interest rates. *Journal of Money, Credit and Banking* 18(February):1–17.

A good study supporting the crowding-out hypothesis.

17

Money, Banking, and Monetary Policy

ALL ECONOMIC SOCIETIES, including the most primitive ones, require the exchange of goods and services. At first, the exchange took the form of **barter.** Person A exchanged his good or service that person B wanted for person B's good or service that person A wanted. Person A, who wanted what person B had, however, did not necessarily have what person B wanted. This inconvenience of bartering induced people to choose one or more commodities as a medium of exchange. The commodity or commodities thus selected as a medium of exchange are known as money. When societies were rather small and unsophisticated, the selection of a medium of exchange was tacit. As societies grew large and sophisticated, legislative action replaced a tacit agreement among members of a society in selecting a medium of exchange. When we study money in the context of macroeconomics in this chapter, we are interested in understanding two aspects of money: what money is and what money does. As economic theories progress, our understanding of what money is and what money does changes also.

WHAT IS MONEY?

What constitutes money is not an easy question to answer. Consider the dollar bill in your wallet. Is the dollar bill money? Consider two dimes and one nickel in your pocket. Are they money? We know that the dollar bill and coins of different denominations in our pockets are all money. Why are they money? They are money because they are used as media of exchanging goods and services.

What about the amounts we maintain in our checking accounts, the amounts in our savings accounts, the amounts that we are allowed to spend in credit cards, and the values of stocks and bonds we own: Are all these money? Why and why not? We may feel better to know that economists are having almost as much trouble as we are in defining money. Currently, at least four different measures of monetary aggregates are published regularly by the Federal Reserve Bank. The reason for having several definitions of money measures is that economists want to know how the money supply affects the economy, but no one definition of money measure works to the satisfaction of all economists. The four measures are M1, M2, M3, and L. The actual dollar values of these money measures are shown in Table 17.1.

M1

M1 is the narrowest and the most widely used definition of money. The **M1** definition of money has the following four components: currency, traveler's checks, demand deposits, and other checkable deposits.[1] **Currency** refers to dollar bills and coins that are held outside the Treasury, Federal Reserve Banks, and the vaults of commercial banks. So long as currency is stored in the vaults of commercial banks, it is not readily available for its role as a medium of exchange and it loses its purchasing power. Currency held in the vaults of commercial banks, the Treasury, and

---

[1]When monetary aggregates were newly defined in 1980, two M1 measures, M1A and M1B, were adopted primarily because of uncertainties that would arise during a transition period when NOW accounts were permitted nationwide. NOW accounts have properties of both a transaction account (for writing checks) and a savings account (for earning interest on balances). M1A consisted of currency and demand deposits, while M1B was defined as M1A plus other checkable deposits.

Federal Reserve Banks, therefore, is not counted as money. Paper money circulated in the United States today is in the form of Federal Reserve notes. Federal Reserve notes are issued in denominations of $1, $2, $5, $10, $20, $50, and $100. The $2 note is the most recent addition, appearing in April 1976, while notes in denominations of $500, $1,000, $5,000, and $10,000 were discontinued in 1945.

Demand Deposits

Demand deposits refer to checkable accounts at depository institutions. A widely used demand deposit is a checking account that does not pay interest on balances. Demand deposits owned by commercial banks, foreign banks, and the U.S. government are not counted as money. The term *depository institutions* is often used in studies of money and banking. **Depository institutions** refer to institutions at which deposits can be made. Depository institutions include commercial banks, savings and loan associations, and credit unions. The number of depository institutions is summarized in Table 17.2.

Other Checkable Deposits

Other checkable deposits include negotiable orders of withdrawal (NOW), automatic transfer service (ATS) accounts at depository institutions, credit union share drafts, and demand deposits at savings and loan associations.

    NOW accounts are checking accounts that pay interest on account balances. ATS is an arrangement by which balance in a checking account, if it falls below a minimum required level, is automatically transferred from the person's savings account to the checking account. ATS allows depositors to keep as much as possible in interest-paying savings accounts rather than in checking accounts that pay no interest. Credit union share drafts are checking accounts made available by credit unions.

TABLE 17.1 Four Measures of Money as of April 1989

Aggregate and Component	Amount ($billions)
M1	783.2
Currency	215.9
Traveler's checks	7.3
Demand deposits	281.5
Other checkable deposits	278.5
M2	3,081.3
M3	3,957.6
L	4,739.2

Source: Federal Reserve Bulletin 75(August 1989):A13.

Dollar bills and coins constitute about one-fourth of M1, with the remaining being the amount that the public maintains in the form of checkable deposits.

Other Measures of Money

The remaining measures of money are M2, M3, and L. These money measures are reviewed in order.

M2

M2 is M1 plus overnight repurchase agreements issued by commercial banks, certain overnight Eurodollars held by U.S. residents other than banks, money market mutual fund shares, savings deposits, and small-denomination time deposits at all depository institutions.

The **overnight repurchase agreement** (RP) is an arrangement in which a bank borrows money from a nonbank source such as a large corporation for a short period, usually overnight. Overnight Eurodollars counted in M2 are those issued by Caribbean branches of commercial banks. Other overnight Eurodollars and longer term Eurodollars of U.S. residents are included in the broader measure of money, L. **Eurodollars** are deposits denominated in U.S. dollars held by individuals and nonbank businesses in banks located outside the United States.

Money market mutual funds refer to investment funds managed by banks or investment companies that pool investors' money and buy or sell interest-bearing securities that can be bought with a large amount of money only. **Savings deposits** are savings accounts that pay interest on balances but do not permit account holders to write checks against them. The only difference between a savings deposit and a time deposit is that money can be withdrawn any time from a savings deposit, but not from a time deposit. A **time deposit** has a maturity date prior to which money cannot be withdrawn without a penalty. Time deposits are also called **certificates of deposit** (CDs). Small-denomination time deposits are those issued in denominations of less than $100,000.

TABLE 17.2 Numbers of Depository Institutions

Depository Institutions	1987
Commercial Banks	13,699
Savings and Loan Associations	3,147
Credit Unions	14,335
Savings Banks	484

Source: U.S. Department of Commerce, Bureau of the Census, *Statistical abstract of the United States,* 109th ed., (Washington, D.C.: U.S. Government Printing Office, January 1989), p. 489.

M3

M3 is equal to M2 plus large-denomination time deposits at all depository institutions. **Large-denomination time deposits** are certificates of deposit issued in denominations of $100,000 or more.

L

The very broad measure of liquid assets, **L,** equals M3 plus other liquid assets such as other Eurodollar holdings of U.S. residents other than banks, bankers' acceptances, commercial paper, U.S. savings bonds, and short-term Treasury securities.

     Bankers' acceptances are promissory notes issued by businesses and accepted by banks and other financial institutions to obtain short-term credit. Acceptance by the bank indicates that the bank stands ready to pay the principal of the note to the holder at the note's maturity. Bankers' acceptances are used frequently by importers of goods from other countries. **Commercial papers** are financial obligations of large corporations and are publicly bought and sold. Commercial papers are issued typically in large denominations such as millions of dollars.

Stocks, Bonds, and Credit Cards

By now it is clear that stocks, bonds, and credit cards are all excluded from money measures. It is relatively easy to see why stocks and bonds are excluded. Stocks and bonds are assets that the owners may convert into money by selling them. The case of credit cards is less clear. Credit cards such as Visa, MasterCard, Exxon card, and Macy's card are simply a means of obtaining a short-term loan from banks and stores that issue these cards. When we use credit cards, we simply postpone payments for a short period of time rather than add any more purchasing power to the economy. To the extent that credit cards change our spending habits, their availability and the amount of credit allowed in credit cards may affect the total purchasing power at least for short periods of time. Regardless, economists have decided to exclude credit cards from money measures.

FEDERAL RESERVE BANKS

In most countries there is one central bank, closely controlled by the government, with a small number of commercial banks, each of which has many branches throughout the country. In this country there are about 14,000 commercial banks, each of which has either a small number of branches or no branches at all. The average number of branches of the U.S. commercial bank is about four. These commercial banks are accompanied by approximately 3,000 savings and loan associations and 14,000 credit unions that perform essentially the same functions as commercial banks. The numbers of depository institutions by type are shown in Table 17.2. Until the establishment of the Federal Reserve System in 1913, there had not been a formal central bank in the United States. Because the Federal Reserve System plays an important role in determining the nation's money supply and credit market conditions, it is necessary to learn more about the Federal Reserve.

Development of the Federal Reserve System

In 1811 there were 88 banks chartered by states. One of them was the Manhattan Company. The company had been chartered in 1799 as a water supply company but was allowed to invest its surplus funds in other ventures. This provision made it possible for its owner, Aaron Burr (1756–1836), to establish the bank that eventually became the Chase Manhattan Bank.[2] The number of banks increased to 901 in 1840, and 1,601 by 1861. In 1863 the National Currency Act was passed and the first nationally chartered bank was opened in June 1863. During the same year, the number of state-chartered banks decreased to 1,466. The National Banking Act of 1864 replaced the National Currency Act, and the establishment of national banks accelerated. By 1870 there were 1,612 national banks but only 325 state banks.[3] National banks were different from state banks in that (1) the former were chartered from the federal government while the latter by state governments, and (2) national banks secured their currency by the pledge of U.S. government securities only. The establishment of national banks was intended to provide a safe and uniform currency as well as provide a source of loans to the federal government.

Restrictions placed on national banks were more severe than those placed on state banks. For instance, national banks were forbidden to make real estate loans and were required to report their financial condition periodically. The disadvantages of being chartered as national banks encouraged the resurgence of state banks. By 1900 there were 3,731 national banks and 9,322 state banks.

Banks make profits by accepting deposits from those who use depository accounts and lending money based on these deposits to those who need money. Those who deposit may withdraw money any time. To guard against the sudden withdrawal of deposits, banks are required to keep a certain portion of deposits. In recent years the practice of requiring banks to keep a portion of deposits has been based more on its use as an instrument of monetary policy than a safeguard against sudden withdrawals. Before the establishment of the Federal Reserve System, banks were allowed to earn interest on required reserves. Banks therefore kept part of their reserves in the large city banks. When money shortages developed occasionally, the city banks were not able to provide currency on short notice, creating a banking crisis. Severe shortages of money were experienced in 1873, 1884, 1893, and 1907. Following the Panic of 1907, a national Monetary Commission was appointed to study banking practice and make recommendations that led to the signing of the Federal Reserve Act in December 1913.

The Federal Reserve System

The Federal Reserve System divides the nation into 12 districts. There is one Federal Reserve bank in each of the districts. The names of cities in which the Federal Reserve banks are located and cities in which the branch offices of the Federal Reserve banks are located are listed in Table 17.3. The Federal Reserve System is run by the Board of Governors. There are seven members on the Board, with one of the seven serving as the chairman. The governors are appointed by the president of the

[2]David Kamerschen, *Money and banking*, 8th ed. (Cincinnati: South-Western, 1984), p. 142.

[3]For the early statistics on banks, see Board of Governors of the Federal Reserve System, *Banking studies*, 1948, and U.S. Department of Commerce, *Historical statistics of the United States* (Washington, D.C.: U.S. Government Printing Office, 1960).

United States for a 14-year term subject to confirmation by the U.S. Senate. In addition to 11 divisions and 6 offices that carry on routine business of the Federal Reserve System, there are one committee and three advisory councils to assist the decision-making by the Board of Governors: the Federal Open Market Committee, Federal Advisory Council, Consumer Advisory Council, and

TABLE 17.3 Federal Reserve Banks and Branches

District Number	Cities with Federal Reserve Bank	Cities with Branches
1	Boston	
2	New York	Buffalo
3	Philadelphia	
4	Cleveland	Cincinnati Pittsburgh
5	Richmond	Baltimore Charlotte
6	Atlanta	Birmingham Jacksonville Miami Nashville New Orleans
7	Chicago	Detroit
8	St. Louis	Little Rock Louisville Memphis
9	Minneapolis	Helena
10	Kansas City	Denver Oklahoma City Omaha
11	Dallas	El Paso Houston San Antonio
12	San Francisco	Los Angeles Portland Salt Lake City Seattle

Source: Federal Reserve Bulletin 75(August 1989):A96.

Thrift Institutions Advisory Council. Of these four the Federal Open Market Committee is most important.

The Federal Open Market Committee has 12 members—the seven governors and five of the 12 presidents from the 12 Federal Reserve banks. The five presidents are selected separately from the Federal Reserve banks of (1) New York; (2) Boston, Philadelphia, and Richmond; (3) Cleveland and Chicago; (4) Atlanta, Dallas, and St. Louis; and (5) Minneapolis, Kansas City, and San Francisco. Members of the Committee make decisions on money supply, thus influencing the nation's credit conditions. The Federal Reserve System changes the nation's money supply using a procedure known as open market operations, explained later in this chapter.

MONEY CREATION

One of the remarkable by-products of modern depository institutions is the ability of these institutions to create money. Understanding the process of money creation by depository institutions is important because policy decisions made by the Federal Open Market Committee cannot be carried out unless depository institutions are in a position to support these decisions. Before we can understand how money is created by depository institutions, we need to understand how these institutions handle the money that we deposit.

Reserve Requirements Ratio

Suppose that we own a home in Monterey, California, the market value of which is $1 million. We sell the home to a Japanese firm and receive a check from the buyer that is written on its account at the Bank of Tokyo. The selection of a Japanese firm as an illustration here is intended to make sure that the home is not sold to a U.S. citizen. If the home were sold to a U.S. citizen, there would not be an increase in money supply. As soon as we receive the check, we deposit the check at First California Bank, where we maintain a checking account, and the check is cleared immediately so that we can spend the money without any delay. Suppose also that the $1 million happens to be the entire deposit at the bank. What will First California do with the money? The answer to this question, presented in the next section, requires us to learn new terms on bank reserves.

The main source of revenue for depository institutions is to lend money at an interest rate higher than one that these institutions pay on deposits. Obviously, the larger the amount of the loan, the greater the profit. First California cannot lend the entire $1 million, since the Depository Institutions Deregulation and Monetary Control Act of 1980 requires all depository institutions to keep a certain percentage of deposits. The portion of deposits that depository institutions must keep by law is called **required reserves**. Required reserves are held in the form of deposits with Federal Reserve banks or vault cash. Depository institutions may also hold reserves in excess of required reserves. Reserves that exceed required reserves are called **excess reserves**; depository institutions are free to lend these. The ratio of required reserves to total deposits is the **required reserve ratio** or **reserve requirements ratio.**

The reserve requirements ratio varies with type of deposit, as shown in Table 17.4. As a rule, the reserve requirements ratio is higher the larger the amount of deposit and the shorter the period until maturity of the deposit.

THE DEPOSITORY INSTITUTIONS DEREGULATION AND MONETARY CONTROL ACT OF 1980

The Depository Institutions Deregulation and Monetary Control Act of 1980 was approved by President Carter on March 31, 1980, as Public Law 96-221. This legislation was described by Senator William A. Proxmire, then chairman of the Senate Committee on Banking, Housing, and Urban Affairs, as the most significant banking legislation since the passage of the Federal Reserve Act of 1913. The Act consists of nine *titles*. The most important titles in the Act are Title I Monetary Control Act of 1980, Title II Depository Institutions Deregulation Act, Title III Consumer Checking Account Equity Act of 1980, and Title V State Usury Laws.

Title I imposed universal reserve requirements on all depository institutions. Depository institutions are required to maintain a reserve of 3 percent against transaction accounts of $25 million or less, and a reserve ranging between 8 and 14 percent for transaction accounts in excess of $25 million. In addition, each depository institution is required to maintain reserves against nonpersonal time deposits in an amount ranging from zero to 9 percent. Depository institutions, for the purposes of the act, include commercial banks, mutual savings banks, savings banks, savings and loan associations, and credit unions, if they are federally insured or eligible for federal insurance. Title II phased out maximum rates of interest paid on deposits and accounts by depository institutions. As of March 31, 1986, the various authorities to impose interest rate ceilings on deposits were repealed, and the Deregulation Committee ceased to exist. Title III extended nationwide the authority of depository institutions to offer NOW accounts, and increased the insurance of accounts of federally insured banks, savings and loan associations, and credit unions from $40,000 to $100,000. Finally, Title V made illegal all state usury laws in loan amounts of $25,000 or more. Usury laws set ceiling interest rates that lenders could charge.

Creating Money

Reconsider that the most common definition of money is M1, which consists of coins, currency, and checkable deposits. When we deposit the $1 million check to our checking account at First California Bank, the money supply in the United States is increased by $1 million. Let us make two assumptions. One is that depository institutions maintain no excess reserves and thus lend every penny that they can, and the other is that the reserve requirements ratio is 10 percent.

Loan to Tara Seafood
Suppose that Tara Seafood Company in San Diego needs to borrow $900,000 to buy a new tuna boat and contacts First California Bank. When Tara Seafood borrows $900,000, Tara Seafood writes a promissory note to the bank and promises to pay the loan with interest at a certain date in the future. When the transaction is completed, Tara Seafood is not likely to carry out bags of coins and currency. Instead, it will transfer the loan to the checking account that it maintains at First

California. When the loan transaction is completed, the status of our $1 million at First California is as follows:

Deposit	$1,000,000
Loan to Tara	900,000
Total reserves	100,000
Required reserves	100,000
Excess reserves	0

As soon as the loan transaction to Tara Seafood is completed, however, something dramatic happens to the nation's money supply. The loan increases the balance of Tara Seafood's checking account by $900,000, without reducing the $1 million balance that we maintain in our checking account. Money, by definition, includes amounts maintained in checkable deposits. The loan to Tara Seafood, therefore, increased the nation's money supply by $900,000. First California literally created money.

When Tara Seafood borrows $900,000, it does not intend to keep the money in its checking account for long. The next morning, Tara Seafood contracts with Ingalls Shipbuilding Company in Pascagoula, Mississippi, for the construction of a tuna boat at $900,000. When Ingalls receives the $900,000 check from Tara Seafood, Ingalls deposits the check at Second Mississippi Bank and adds the amount to its checking account. At this point no additional money is created. There is simply a transfer of $900,000 from Tara Seafood's checking account at First California to Ingalls's checking account at Second Mississippi. When Tara Seafood's check clears, an amount of $900,000 is subtracted from reserves of First California and added to reserves of Second Mississippi.

TABLE 17.4 Reserve Requirements of Depository Institutions

Type of Deposit, and Deposit Interval	Percent of Deposits	Effective Date
Checkable deposits		
$0 million–$41.5 million	3%	12/20/88
More than $41.5 million	12	12/20/88
and time deposits by maturity		
Less than 1 1/2 years	3	10/6/83
1 1/2 years or more	0	10/6/83

Source: Federal Reserve Bulletin 75(August 1989):A8.

Loan to Paducah River Services

The additional $900,000 reserves at Second Mississippi make it possible for the bank to lend money to Paducah River Services. Since the reserve requirements ratio is 10 percent, Second Mississippi needs to keep $90,000 as required reserves and thus lends $810,000 to Paducah River on the basis of the $900,000 reserves. As soon as Paducah River deposits the $810,000 check at Third Kentucky Bank, the nation's money supply is increased further by $810,000. This time, Second Mississippi created $810,000.

Loan to Struggling Steel

Third Kentucky needs to keep 10 percent of the $810,000 as required reserves. The additional reserve of $810,000, therefore, allows Third Kentucky to lend $729,000 to the Struggling Steel Company in Pittsburgh. As soon as Struggling Steel deposits the $729,000 check at Fourth Pennsylvania Bank, additional money is created.

Deposit Multiplier

The procedure of money creation by depository institutions is summarized in Table 17.5. The question is, what would be the total increase in deposit when the money creation process is completed? The answer can be found by a simple formula

$$TD = ID \times \frac{1}{R}, \tag{17.1}$$

where

TD = total increase in deposit,
ID = initial deposit,
R = reserve requirements ratio.

Since the initial deposit is $1 million and the reserve requirements ratio is 0.10, the total increase in deposit is

$$TD = \$1,000,000 \times \frac{1}{0.10}, \tag{17.2}$$

$$= \$1,000,000 \times 10, \tag{17.3}$$

$$= \$10,000,000. \tag{17.4}$$

The term $1/R$ is called the **deposit multiplier** or the **monetary multiplier.** If the reserve requirements ratio is 10 percent, the deposit multiplier is 10. If the reserve requirements ratio is 20 percent, the deposit multiplier is reduced to 5. As indicated in Table 17.5, almost 70 percent of the multiplier effect is completed by the time the deposit passes through the tenth bank.

Qualifications of the Money Creation Effect

The assumption of 10 percent reserve requirements ratio is realistic. The size of the deposit multiplier, however, is not believed to be near 10. There are two reasons why the actual size of the deposit multiplier is closer to 4 than to 10. One reason is that practically all depository institutions maintain excess reserves. If all banks in our example maintained 10 percent reserves in excess of required reserves, so that total reserves were 20 percent, the size of the multiplier would be reduced to 5. The other reason is that not all transactions are handled with checks. When a borrower requests and accepts cash, the money creation process stops with the borrower. If, for instance, Tara Seafood accepts cash and all subsequent transactions are paid in cash, the total increase in the money supply is limited to $1,900,000, the sum obtained by adding the $1,000,000 of our checking account and the $900,000 loan made in cash.

Finally, the money creation effect works both ways. Suppose in Table 17.5 that, one day following a full moon, we decide to withdraw $1 million deposit in cash. The cash withdrawal will reverse the entire process of money creation, reducing the nation's money supply by $9 million.

TOOLS OF MONETARY POLICY

Equipped with the knowledge of money, the Federal Reserve System, and money creation, we are nearly ready to study the first step of how money supply affects the economy. In reality, the Japanese do not control our money supply; the Federal Reserve System does. The Federal Reserve System undertakes a discrete act to change the nation's money supply. These discretionary changes in money supply intended to stabilize the economy and promote its growth without inflation are called **monetary policy.** There are three major tools of monetary policy: federal open market operations, changes in the reserve requirements ratio, and changes in the discount rate. We study the three tools in order.

TABLE 17.5 Creation of Money by Depository Institutions

Process	Amount
Initial deposit	$ 1,000,000
Money creation by	
First California Bank	900,000
Second Mississippi Bank	810,000
Third Kentucky Bank	729,000
Fourth Pennsylvania	656,100
Fifth	590,490
Sixth	531,441
Seventh	478,297
Eighth	430,467
Ninth	387,420
Tenth	348,678
Other banks	3,138,107
Total	$10,000,000

Federal Open Market Operation

Open market operations refer to the buying and selling of Treasury securities by the Federal Reserve banks. After the Federal Open Market Committee determines the objectives for monetary growth, the task of implementing the policy is delegated to the staff of the Open Market Desk at the Federal Reserve Bank of New York. The Open Market Desk implements the policy by buying and selling federal government securities for the Federal Reserve System. Those in charge of the open market account at the Open Market Desk deal with a small number of banks and security dealers. The banks are typically large money market banks whose departments routinely deal in government securities, while the security dealers are either private citizens or brokerage houses, numbering about 75, who buy and sell government securities in large amounts. These dealers participate in open market transactions by being listed on the *reporting list* of the Federal Reserve. Only those dealers who have bought and sold a large volume of Treasury securities are qualified for the reporting list. Once dealers are on the reporting list, these dealers are called and offered an opportunity to bid on purchases and sales of Treasury securities.

Although managers of the open market account have considerable latitude in the types of securities to buy and sell, the instruments used in most cases are Treasury securities. The use of Treasury securities is based on the fact that purchases and sales of Treasury securities are completed in a single day, whereas purchases and sales of other securities such as state and local government securities and bankers' acceptances may take several days to clear. By clearing in a single day, the effect of a sale or purchase of a Treasury bill on bank reserves is immediate.

A purchase of Treasury securities by Federal Reserve banks creates reserves for the selling or clearing bank. Since reserves that banks maintain with Federal Reserve banks do not earn interest, commercial banks increase loans to reduce the excess reserves. When loans are increased, there will be a money creation effect leading to an additional increase in money supply. A sale of Treasury securities by Federal Reserve banks, on the other hand, reduces the reserves of the buying or clearing bank. Since banks need to maintain required reserves with Federal Reserve banks, commercial banks reduce loans or recall loans made previously. When loans are reduced, there will be a *reverse* money creation effect leading to a decrease in money supply. Federal open market operations are the most important tool of monetary policy.

Changes in Reserve Requirements Ratio

The Federal Reserve System can also change the reserve requirements ratio to influence money supply. Until 1980 only the member banks of the Federal Reserve System were subject to the reserve requirements regulation by Federal Reserve banks. Since the Depository Institutions Deregulation and Monetary Control Act of 1980, however, all depository institutions, including savings and loan associations, credit unions, and savings banks, became subject to reserve requirements regulation by the Federal Reserve System. Under the terms of the International Banking Act of 1978, branches of foreign banks are also subject to reserve requirements regulation.

Member banks of the Federal Reserve System must hold required reserves in the form of deposits with Federal Reserve banks or vault cash. Nonmember depository institutions may deposit their required reserves directly with Federal Reserve banks or pass the required reserves through certain approved institutions such as a Federal Home Loan Bank or a depository institution that holds a reserve balance with a Federal Reserve bank.

A decrease in the reserve requirements ratio has a twofold impact on the money supply. First, the decrease creates excess reserves for depository institutions. Since reserves that depository institutions maintain with Federal Reserve banks do not earn interest, these institutions increase loans to reduce the excess reserves. When loans are increased, there will be a money creation effect leading to an additional increase in money supply. Second, the decrease in the reserve requirements ratio increases the size of the deposit multiplier, causing money supply to increase even further.

An increase in the reserve requirements ratio, on the other hand, reduces the reserves of depository institutions. Since depository institutions need to maintain required reserves with Federal Reserve banks, these institutions reduce loans or recall loans made previously. When loans are reduced, there will be a *reverse* of the money creation effect leading to a decrease in money supply. The increase in the reserve requirements ratio also reduces the size of the deposit multiplier, causing money supply to decrease further.

Changes in Discount Rate

All depository institutions may occasionally experience an unexpected need for additional funds. When they do, they borrow among themselves or from Federal Reserve banks. Funds borrowed among depository institutions on an overnight basis are known as **federal funds,** and the interest charged on federal funds is called the **federal funds rate.**

Regardless of whether they are members of the Federal Reserve System or not, depository institutions that maintain required reserves can use Federal Reserve banks as a last-resort provider of additional funds. These loans from Federal Reserve banks are not free, however. The interest rate that Federal Reserve banks charge on short-term loans made to depository institutions is called the **discount rate.**

Changes in discount rate can be used as a tool of monetary policy. Changes in discount rate are not an effective tool in determining the amount of money supply, however. The amount of borrowing at any given moment from Federal Reserve banks by all depository institutions is rather small. In the mid-1980s, the amount averaged, at the most, $3 billion to $4 billion, and usually less than $1 billion. However, changes in discount rate are important in signaling the direction of the monetary policy. A lowering of the discount rate may signal an **easy money policy,** meaning that the Federal Reserve intends to accelerate money growth, lower interest rates, and make credit more easily available. A raising of the discount rate, on the other hand, may signal a **tight money policy,** meaning that the Federal Reserve intends to slow down money growth, raise interest rates, and make credit less easily available.

MONEY AND MACROECONOMY

The question that we wanted to ask all along was, how do changes in the money supply affect the economy? The answer, again, is different, depending on who answers the question. This section examines the pre-Keynesian view of the issue, known as the quantity theory of money, which was briefly introduced in Chapter 15. Views after Keynes are presented in Chapter 18.

Like other theories in economics, the quantity theory of money has also gone through an evolutionary process. Jean Bodin, a sixteenth-century French philosopher and royal official, is

---

PRIME RATE

One of the most widely quoted interest rates is the prime rate. The **prime rate** is an interest rate that a bank charges on loans made, allegedly, to its most creditworthy business customers. The prime rate is set by each commercial bank.

The concept of a prime rate was born in 1934 during the Great Depression. Many banks failed during the 1930s. Those that managed to survive had plenty of loanable funds but not many borrowers. The idea of the prime rate was designed to avoid cutthroat competition. An interest rate of 1 1/2 percent then won acceptance as a floor rate below which banks would incur losses at a time when they could ill afford them. This minimum became known as the prime rate. The prime rate remained at 1 1/2 percent for 13 years; it was raised to 1 3/4 percent in December 1947.

These days, the prime rate is no longer a protective device. There is a significant uniformity among banks in their prime rates because competition among banks for prime customers and for sources of funds, as well as competition between banks and other credit instruments, limit differences in prime rates. Adjustment of the prime rate may be viewed as a lagged indicator of credit conditions as well as a leading indicator of the lending policies of the commercial banks in general.

---

generally considered as the originator of the quantity theory of money. In his 1568 book titled *Response to the paradoxes of Monsieur de Malestroict,* Bodin claimed that the abundance of gold and silver, used as money at the time, caused the prices of these metals to fall and prices of goods and services to rise. Although a number of scholars have since developed and refined the theory, it was Irving Fisher (1867–1947) who presented the familiar version of the quantity theory in his 1911 publication, *The purchasing power of money.*[4]

The Equation of Exchange

Consider the exchange of goods and services between buyers and sellers:

$$M \times V_t = P \times T, \tag{17.5}$$

where

M = average money supply for a given period,
V_t = the number of times money changes hands for transaction of goods and services, also called the transactions velocity of money,

---

[4]For more on the quantity theory, see Edwin Dean (ed.), *The controversy over the quantity theory of money* (Boston: D. C. Heath, 1965).

P = average price of goods and services traded,
T = total goods and services traded.

Suppose that the average money supply is $100, the price of the product is $10 per unit, and the total number of units of the product traded is 40. That is,

$$100 \times V_t = 10 \times 40. \tag{17.6}$$

The transactions velocity of money V_t, then, has to be 4 in order to make both sides equal:

$$100 \times 4 = 10 \times 40, \tag{17.7}$$
$$400 = 400. \tag{17.8}$$

All that equation (17.5) says is that money supply times the number of times this money changes hands is equal to total expenditures on all goods and services traded. Equation (17.5) is an identity with the right-hand side, repeating what the left-hand side indicates in a different form. Identities are not very useful since they do not say much.

The Quantity Theory of Money

In order to derive a theory that can tell us something about the role of money in the economy, let us replace T in equation (17.5) with Y so that

$$M \times V = P \times Y, \tag{17.9}$$

where Y refers to total goods and services newly *produced* during the year, not *traded* during the year. The term P then changes to represent the average price of goods and services produced instead of traded. Goods and services produced are smaller than goods and services traded, since goods and services traded include transactions of all intermediate and used goods as well as final goods produced. In equation (17.9), V is called the income velocity of money in order to differentiate the velocity for goods and services produced, in equation (17.9), from the velocity for goods and services traded, in equation (17.5).

Equation (17.9) is still an identity. All the equation says is that money supply times the number of times this money changes hands is equal to the total expenditures on all goods and services produced. At this point, let us make two assumptions. One is that total goods and services produced in any given year (Y) are constant, and the other is that the velocity (V) remains constant. Mathematically,

$$M\bar{V} = P\bar{Y}. \tag{17.10}$$

The two assumptions merit comments. First, total goods and services newly produced during a year (Y) are the real GNP. The real GNP on the whole is determined by real factors such as the size of the labor force, amount of other resources available, and the general level of technology. According to pre-Keynesian economics, these factors change over time but very slowly. More importantly, pre-Keynesian economics assumes that the level of real GNP would not be affected by changes in the quantity of money in any significant way. Second, pre-Keynesian economics also assumes that the income velocity (V) is determined by institutional factors and is thus unaffected by changes in the quantity of money. The velocity is determined by such factors as the state of banking practice and the ways in which payments are made in the economy.

What happens when money supply is changed? Since V and Y are assumed to remain constant, the only variable in equation (17.10) left to be affected by changes in the money supply is P. According to equation (17.10), there is a one-to-one relation between money supply (M) and price level (P). If money supply increases, prices are expected to increase in direct proportion. If money supply decreases, prices are expected to decrease in direct proportion. This direct relation between money supply and price level is known as the **quantity theory of money.** According to the quantity theory of money, therefore, "money does not matter" so far as real output and employment are concerned, but "money alone matters" so far as prices are concerned.

We may recall that unlike the quantity theory of money, Keynesian economics assumes that an increase in money supply would lower interest rates, instead of raising prices. Keynes claims that the lower interest rate stimulates investment. The increased investment in turn stimulates income, consumption, and finally, employment.

The Impact Lag of Monetary Policy

One key question that needs to be answered before monetary policy is employed as a tool of stabilization policy is, how long does it take for changes in money supply to have an impact on the economy? The time lag between the initiation of an economic policy such as changes in money supply and the time that these changes have an impact on the economy is called the **impact lag.**

Suppose that the Federal Reserve takes an action to increase money supply by $50 billion. How many months will it take before businesses feel the impact and increase their production and sales activities? Unlike fiscal policy in which most economists agree that the impact lag is short, there is a wide range of opinions regarding the impact lag of monetary policy. The knowledge of the impact lag is crucial since a long impact lag that lasts, say, two or three years will make monetary policy practically useless. By the time monetary policy takes effect, the economy may be in a situation that does not need the policy that was initiated two or three years earlier. A relatively short impact lag is essential if monetary policy is to be utilized as an effective tool of stabilization policy.

Prior to 1960, many economists accepted the proposition that monetary policy created sufficient impact on the economy in a reasonably short period of time. The main challenge to the conventional thinking came from economist Milton Friedman. Friedman argues that monetary policy acts with such a long and variable lag that attempts to pursue a countercyclical monetary policy might aggravate, rather than stabilize, economic fluctuations. Friedman points out that, on the average of 18 cycles, peaks in the rate of change in the stock of money preceded peaks in general business by about 16 months, and troughs in the rate of change in the stock of money preceded troughs in general business by about 12 months. Furthermore, the recorded lead for individual cycles has varied between 6 and 29 months at peaks and between 4 and 22 months at troughs.[5]

Many economists do not agree with Friedman's estimates of the length and the variability of the impact lag. For instance, J. M. Culbertson suggests that the broad record of experience supports the view that monetary policy as well as fiscal policy can be counted on to have their predominant

[5]Milton Friedman, *A program for monetary stability* (New York: Fordham University Press, 1960), p. 87.

direct effects within 3 to 6 months. A. Ando and others suggest that substantial effects of monetary policy come after about 6 to 9 months, although the full effects may be spread over a wide interval. Arthur Laffer and R. David Ranson claim an even shorter impact lag by stating that monetary policy, as represented by changes in the conventionally defined money supply, has an immediate and permanent impact on the level of GNP. Laffer and Ranson claim that for every dollar increase in the money supply, GNP will rise by about $4.00 or $5.00 in the current quarter, and not fall back or rise any further in the future.[6] The different opinions on the impact lag of monetary policy result in vastly different policy recommendations, as Chapter 18 will demonstrate.

SUMMARY

There are at least four measures of monetary aggregates that the Federal Reserve System announces regularly. The four measures are M1, M2, M3, and L. The M1 definition of money consists of currency, traveler's checks, demand deposits, and other checkable deposits. Checkable deposits are the accounts at all depository institutions against which checks can be drawn. Checkable deposits include demand deposits at commercial banks, negotiable orders of withdrawal, automatic transfer service accounts, credit union share drafts, and demand deposits at savings and loan associations. M2 is M1 plus overnight repurchase agreements issued by commercial banks, certain overnight Eurodollars held by U.S. residents other than banks, money market mutual fund shares, savings deposits, and small-denomination time deposits at all depository institutions. M3 is equal to M2 plus large-denomination time deposits at all depository institutions. L equals M3 plus other liquid assets such as other Eurodollar holdings of U.S. residents other than banks, bankers' acceptances, commercial paper, U.S. savings bonds, and short-term Treasury securities.

The Federal Reserve System was established according to the Federal Reserve Act in December 1913. There are 12 Federal Reserve banks. Decisions on money supply are made by the Federal Open Market Committee. In a multibank system, the practice whereby banks make loans beyond required reserves creates money. The ratio of total increase in deposit to the initial deposit is the deposit multiplier. The money creation effect works both ways: expansionary when new deposits are made, and contractionary when deposits are withdrawn. The Federal Reserve System makes discretionary changes in money supply intended to stabilize the economy and promote the growth of the economy without inflation. The discretionary changes are monetary policy. Three tools of monetary policy are federal open market operations, changes in reserve requirements ratio, and changes in discount rate. Of the three, open market operations are most important. The purchase of Treasury securities by the Fed tends to increase money supply and thus is expansionary, whereas the selling of Treasury securities by the Fed tends to decrease money supply and thus is contractionary. A decrease in the reserve requirements ratio is expansionary, and an increase in the

[6]J. M. Culbertson, Friedman on the lag in effect of monetary policy, *Journal of Political Economy* (December 1960):617–621; A. Ando, E. C. Brown, R. Solow, and J. Kareken, Lags in fiscal and monetary policy, in Commission on Money and Credit, *Stabilization policies* (Englewood Cliffs, N.J.: Prentice-Hall, 1963), pp. 1–163; and A. B. Laffer and R. D. Ranson, A formal model of the economy, *Journal of Business* (July 1971):247–270. For summaries see also Michael J. Hamburger, The lag in the effect of monetary policy: A survey of recent literature, in Thomas M. Havrilesky and John T. Boorman (eds.), *Current issues in monetary theory and policy,* 2nd ed. (Arlington Heights, Ill.: AHM, 1980), pp. 238–254.

ratio is contractionary. A decrease in the discount rate signals an easy money policy, while an increase in the discount rate signals a tight money policy.

According to the quantity theory of money, changes in money supply determine the general price level. This hypothesis is in contrast with Keynesian economics, which assumes that an increase in money supply lowers interest rates instead of raising prices. Estimates of the impact lag in monetary policy vary widely from three months or less to as long as two years. A short time lag is important if monetary policy is to be used as an effective tool of economic policy.

EXERCISES

1. There are at least four different measures of monetary aggregates. Why can't economists agree at least on what money is?

2. What is the difference between a demand deposit and a checkable deposit?

3. What is the difference between a savings deposit and a time deposit?

4. When was the Federal Reserve System established? Summarize the structure of the Federal Reserve System.

5. Assuming that depository institutions maintain no excess reserves and that all transactions are handled in checks, indicate the total increase in deposit for each of the following cases. Note that the total increase includes the initial deposit.

Initial deposit	Required reserve ratio
$ 1,000,000	.10
$ 1,000,000	.20
$ 1,000,000	.25
$ 5,000,000	.10
$10,000,000	.10

6. The actual reserve requirements ratio is near 10 percent. According to the deposit multiplier formula, the size of the deposit multiplier should be 10. In reality, the size is more like 4 than 10. Why?

7. An expansionary monetary policy tends to increase or speed up the rate of increase of money supply, lower interest rates, and increase nominal GNP, whereas a contractionary monetary policy tends to decrease or slow down the rate of increase of money supply, raise interest rates, and decrease nominal GNP. For each of the following policy actions, indicate whether the action is expansionary or contractionary.

    a. Sales of Treasury securities by the Federal Reserve

    b. An increase in the reserve requirements ratio

    c. An increase in the discount rate

    d. Purchase of Treasury securities by the Federal Reserve in the range of $50 billion

    e. A change in the reserve requirements ratio from 12 to11 percent

    f. A change in the discount rate from 9 to 8 percent

8. What is meant by an easy money policy? A tight money policy?

9. The time lag between the initiation of an economic policy such as changes in money supply and the time of the impact that these changes have on the economy is called the impact lag. Some economists, such as Milton Friedman, argue that monetary policy acts with a long and variable lag. Friedman points out that, on the average of 18 cycles, peaks in the rate of change in the stock of money preceded peaks in general business by about 16 months, and troughs in the rate of change in the stock of money preceded troughs in general business by about 12 months. Assuming that Friedman's assessment of the impact lag in monetary policy is accurate, how will the long impact lag affect the way monetary policy is carried out?

10. Summarize the difference between the quantity theory of money and Keynesian economics regarding the effect of an increase in money supply.

SUGGESTED READINGS

Axilrod, Stephen H. (1985). U.S. monetary policy in recent years: An overview. *Federal Reserve Bulletin* 71(January):14–24.

> A summary of the Federal Reserve's monetary policy during the mid-1970s to the early 1980s. Explains the October 6, 1979 change in emphasis from control of interest rates to monetary aggregates.

Friedman, Milton, and Jacobson Schwartz, Anna. (1963). *A monetary history of the United States 1867–1960*, Princeton: Princeton University Press, pp. 299–301.

> Considered as the book that laid the foundation for modern monetarism. Suggests that the Great Depression of the 1930s is a tragic testimonial to the importance of monetary forces.

Geider, William. (1987). *Secrets of the temple: How the Federal Reserve runs the country.* New York: Simon & Schuster.

> Claims that the Federal Reserve wields too much power and should cease to exist in its present, independent form.

Mackara, W. F. (1974). The ABC's of the prime rate. Federal Reserve Bank of Atlanta *Monthly Review* 59(July 1974):100–104.

> A good summary of the meaning and the history of the prime rate.

McNeill, Charles R. (1980). The Depository Institutions Deregulation and Monetary Control Act of 1980. *Federal Reserve Bulletin* 66(June):444–453.

> A good summary of the Depository Institutions Deregulation and Monetary Control Act of 1980.

Simpson, Thomas D. (1980). The redefined monetary aggregates. *Federal Reserve Bulletin* 66(February):97–112.

> Explains the definitions of money.

18

Macroeconomics Since Keynes

A Visit to the Keynesian Model

Monetarism

Natural Rate of Unemployment

Variations of Mainstream
  Macroeconomic Theories

Alternative Policy Prescriptions

KEYNESIAN ECONOMICS was born during the Great Depression, when inflation was not a problem. The issue of inflation was not significant in the Keynesian model, and the role of money supply in the Keynesian model was limited mostly to its influence on changes in interest rates, which in turn affected the level of investment. This statement does not mean that Keynes totally ignored the possibility of inflation. In his 1940 pamphlet, *How to pay for the war,* for instance, Keynes discussed the possibility of inflation as the equilibrium level of GNP passes the full employment level, and as excess demand beyond the full employment level causes wages to go up. The role of inflation, however, was not a significant variable in the Keynesian model of GNP determination that stressed demand management as a means of increasing the level of output.

As World War II ended and world economies entered postwar prosperity, economists' concern grew over the relatively insignificant role that inflation played in the Keynesian model. Modern economic theories are concerned with the interaction among real output, money supply, and prices as well as with the role of the government. The heading of this chapter was borrowed from a subheading of the book, *Economic theory in retrospect,* written by an excellent economic historian, Mark Blaug.

A VISIT TO THE KEYNESIAN MODEL

Before we embark on our survey of modern macroeconomic theories, let us pay another visit to the Keynesian model and review its major policy recommendations. This brief detour is necessary because modern macroeconomic controversies are based not only on an extension of Keynesian economics but on a criticism of it as well.

Keynesian Approach to Macroeconomic Policies

According to Keynes, the equilibrium level of GNP is determined by aggregate supply and aggregate demand. Aggregate demand has four components: consumption (C), investment (I), government expenditure (G), and net exports ($X - M$). Due to the downward inflexibility of prices and wages, Keynes hypothesizes that the equilibrium level of GNP does not necessarily coincide with the full employment level of GNP. This hypothesis is a major departure from classical economics, which claimed that any deviation of GNP from the full employment level was temporary. If policymakers judge the equilibrium level of GNP to be too low, Keynes suggests that the government undertake expansionary fiscal policies such as increasing government expenditures or decreasing tax rates. Such expansionary fiscal policies will inject more spending into the economy, raise the level of aggregate demand, and increase the equilibrium level of GNP closer to the full employment level. Government may also undertake an expansionary monetary policy through an increase in money supply that, according to Keynes, lowers interest rates and eventually increases business investment.

One question that was not addressed adequately by the Keynesian model was what the government should do if prices were to rise when expansionary fiscal and monetary policies were undertaken. Worse yet, what should the government do if the economy slides into stagflation, in which the economy suffers from unemployment and rising prices at the same time? These questions were not simply hypothetical. They were real problems. Keynes did not have to worry about these problems because inflation was not a problem during the Great Depression. Only the low level of output was. It was obvious that answers to these questions were necessary within the Keynesian model if the model were to continue to play a guiding role for policymakers. Answers to these questions appeared in 1958 when A. W. Phillips published an article studying the relation between unemployment and inflation.

Phillips Curve Hypothesis

A. W. Phillips, formerly a professor at the London School of Economics and the Australian National University, made a pioneering study on the trade-off between unemployment and inflation.[1] The result was later named the **Phillips curve** by Paul Samuelson when he introduced the curve in 1964 in the sixth edition of his *Economics*. Phillips was not the first economist who recognized the potential inverse relation between unemployment and inflation. As early as 1926, a Yale University professor, Irving Fisher, had investigated the subject.[2] Other studies also appeared in 1959.[3] It was the study by Phillips that caught the economists' attention, presumably because of the simple graphic presentation of the inverse relation in what is now known as the Phillips curve.

Importance of the Phillips Curve
Before we present the Phillips curve itself, let us point out why the Phillips curve is important within the framework of Keynesian economics. The Phillips curve is important because it is an analysis that still permits the effectiveness of Keynesian macroeconomic policies in post-World War II economies threatened by inflation. The one constraint added by the Phillips curve analysis to the mainstream Keynesian model is that we now need a trade-off between unemployment and inflation. The trade-off was not necessary in the mainstream Keynesian model. Expansionary economic policies would have reduced unemployment without causing inflation.

Presenting the Phillips Curve
Although the Phillips curve is now known to show an inverse relation between unemployment and inflation, the original curve in the Phillips study related the unemployment rate to changes in nominal wage rates. Based on the assumption that the overall wage rate changes more or less in direct proportion to inflation, the Phillips curve is now interpreted to show an inverse relation between unemployment and inflation. The curve was estimated with British data for years 1861 through 1913. Phillips concluded that if demand were kept at a level that would maintain stable wage rates, the associated rate of unemployment would be about 5 1/2 percent.

The Phillips curve is presented in Figure 18.1. The figure indicates that as the rate of unemployment falls, inflation rises; and as the rate of unemployment rises, inflation falls. It is not possible to have low rates of both unemployment and inflation at the same time. A trade-off is necessary.

[1]A. W. Phillips, The relation between unemployment and the rate of change of money wage rates in the United Kingdom, 1861–1957, *Economica,* New Series 25(November 1958):283–299.

[2]Irving Fisher, A statistical relation between unemployment and price changes, *International Labor Review* 13(June 1926):185–192; reprinted in *Journal of Political Economy* 8(March-April 1973): Part I, 496–502.

[3]Lawrence R. Klein and Robert J. Ball, Some econometrics of the determination of absolute prices and wages, *Economic Journal* 69(September 1959):465–482.

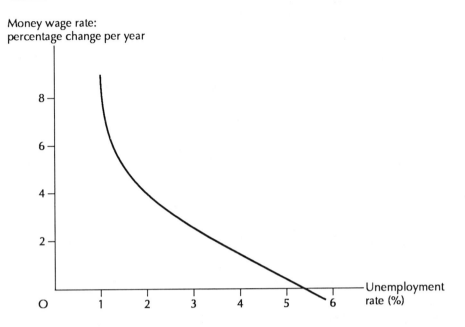

FIGURE 18.1 The Hypothetical Phillips Curve. The hypothetical Phillips curve shows an inverse relation between unemployment and inflation. Inflation is represented by percentage changes in money wage rate.

The policy implication of the Phillips curve is interesting. Suppose that the Phillips curve hypothesis is correct in that a trade-off between unemployment and inflation is inevitable. Suppose also that the curve can be estimated accurately for any given economy. Consider two possible combinations between unemployment and inflation. One combination represents 4 percent inflation and 1 percent unemployment, whereas the other combination represents 1 percent inflation and 4 percent unemployment. Suppose that the economy is operating at the second combination, with lower inflation and a higher unemployment rate, but prefers the first combination representing higher inflation and lower unemployment. Expansionary fiscal and monetary policies may then be undertaken to reduce the unemployment rate at the expense of higher inflation. Assuming that the society knows its preference among different combinations between unemployment and inflation, the Phillips curve allows the society to achieve the objective. The society's preference among different combinations of unemployment and inflation is sometimes called the society's *welfare function*.

Phillips Curve and the U.S. Economy

Is the Phillips curve hypothesis applicable to the U.S. economy? To answer this question, let us consider the unemployment rate and the inflation rate data for the U.S. economy since 1956,

TABLE 18.1 Unemployment and Inflation
Rates of the United States

Year	Unemployment Rate (%)	Inflation Rate (%)
1956	4.13	1.47
1957	4.30	3.40
1958	6.84	2.73
1959	5.45	0.92
1960	5.54	1.51
1961	6.69	1.07
1962	5.57	1.17
1963	5.64	1.25
1964	5.16	1.32
1965	4.51	1.59
1966	3.79	2.99
1967	3.84	2.78
1968	3.56	4.24
1969	3.49	5.46
1970	4.98	5.83
1971	5.95	4.26
1972	5.60	3.31
1973	4.86	6.22
1974	5.64	11.04
1975	8.48	9.13
1976	7.70	5.75
1977	7.05	6.49
1978	6.07	7.63
1979	5.85	11.27
1980	7.18	13.55
1981	7.62	10.31
1982	9.71	6.15
1983	9.60	3.22
1984	7.51	4.30
1985	7.20	3.55
1986	7.01	1.90
1987	6.19	3.66
1988	5.50	4.14

Source: Tables 14.2 and 14.3.

presented in Table 18.1. A casual observation of Table 18.1 indicates that inflation and unemployment rates were relatively higher in the 1970s. Let us, therefore, divide data into two groups: those for 1956 through 1969 and those for 1970 and after. Inflation and unemployment rates for 1956 through 1969 are plotted in Figure 18.2, while inflation and unemployment rates for 1970 through 1988 are plotted in Figure 18.3.

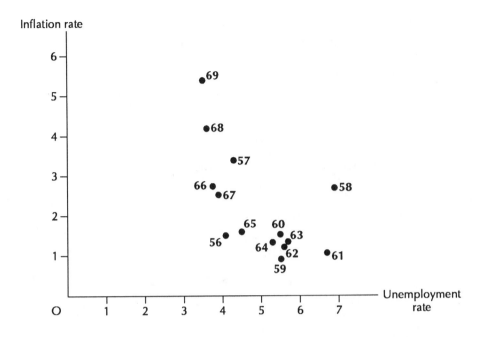

FIGURE 18.2 The Phillips Curve for 1956 through 1969. The Phillips curve for years 1956 to 1969 of the U.S. economy exhibits an inverse relation between unemployment and inflation.

In Figure 18.2, excluding the 1958 combination of a 6.84 percent unemployment rate and a 2.73 percent inflation rate, combinations of unemployment and inflation rates for other early years clearly indicate an inverse relation between inflation and unemployment. The inverse relation can be seen clearly by the scatter of combinations that indicates a down-to-the-right tendency. If we have to answer the question we raised earlier on the basis of the 1956 to 1969 data, our answer is that the Phillips curve hypothesis appears to be applicable to the U.S. economy.

In Figure 18.3, combinations of inflation and unemployment rates for 1970 through 1988 do not exhibit any inverse relation between unemployment and inflation. Some economists claimed that the Phillips curve shifted away from the origin. This shift, if true, means that the U.S. economy will have to suffer a combination of inflation and unemployment rates both higher than prevailed before 1970. Others claimed that there was no such thing as the Phillips curve. The seeming absence of an inverse relation for unemployment and inflation rates for 1970 and thereafter has been the focus of a great controversy between Keynesian economists and monetarists. The absence of an inverse relation led to the revival of the natural rate of unemployment hypothesis by monetarists, as we discuss later in this chapter.

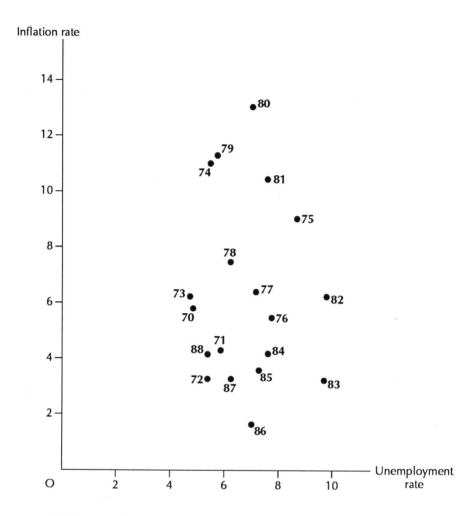

FIGURE 18.3 The Phillips Curve for 1970 through 1987. The Phillips curve for years 1970 to 1987 of the U.S. economy shows no inverse relation between unemployment and inflation.

MONETARISM

Significant advances in macroeconomic theory were made during the 1960s by Milton Friedman and other economists who shared Friedman's view regarding the important role that money supply plays in the economy. Ideas by these economists are collectively called **monetarism,** and these economists are known as **monetarists.** Since the origin of monetarism is the quantity theory of money, let us visit the quantity theory of money for the introduction of monetarism.

MILTON FRIEDMAN

Milton Friedman, born in 1912, is known as the founder of modern monetarism. He is one of the most creative economists, and his style of writing and lecture is provocative. Friedman is known as a staunch defender of free markets, and his main contribution to economic science lies in his ability to convince the public of the importance of his contention that money matters.

The most influential work of Friedman is the 850-page book that he co-authored with Anna Jacobson Schwartz, *A monetary history of the United States.* Based on this analysis, Friedman argues that business fluctuations are the result of short-run changes in the supply of money, and suggests a steady rate of growth in the supply of money as the key to a stable economy. Friedman retired from his professorship at the University of Chicago and won the Nobel Prize in economics in 1976.

A Visit to the Quantity Theory of Money

The quantity theory of money was presented in equation (17.10), which is repeated here:

$$M\bar{V} = P\bar{Y}, \tag{17.10}$$

where

M = average money supply for a given period,
V = income velocity,
P = average price of goods and services produced,
Y = total goods and services newly-produced during a given period.

Two Assumptions

In equation (17.10) it is assumed that the income velocity remains constant, and the quantity of goods and services newly produced in any given year also remains constant. The assumption of the constant income velocity means that the ratio of money supply to the total dollar value of goods and services produced remains stable over time. If the dollar value of goods and services doubles, the assumption of the constant income velocity suggests that the need for money supply also doubles. The assumption of the constant quantity of goods and services produced in equation (17.10) means that the quantity of goods and services produced is unaffected by changes in the money supply. The quantity theory of money hypothesizes that these two assumptions are valid assumptions and, thus, price level (P) depends directly on changes in the money supply (M).

Changes in Money Supply and Changes in Nominal GNP

Equation (17.10) can be converted into one familiar to us. When the average price of all goods and services produced (P) is multiplied by total goods and services newly produced in the economy, we obtain the gross national product. In other words, the right-side term of equation (17.10) is GNP:

$$M\overline{V} = \text{GNP}. \tag{18.1}$$

So long as velocity remains constant, any increase in money supply is expected to increase nominal GNP in direct proportion, and any decrease in money supply is expected to decrease nominal GNP in direct proportion. The idea underlying modern monetarism is that there is a direct relation between changes in the money supply and changes in the nominal GNP. The main contribution made by monetarists, however, lies more in making recommendations on how monetary policy should be conducted than in revealing the one-to-one relation between changes in the money supply and changes in the nominal GNP. Let us clarify.

Reconsider equation (18.1). We continue to accept the monetarists' assumption that the income velocity (V) remains constant. If an increase in money supply is expected to increase GNP in direct proportion, why not increase money supply indefinitely? Isn't a larger GNP preferable to a smaller GNP? The answer, of course, is, not necessarily. Remember that GNP in equation (18.1) is nominal GNP obtained as PY, not real GNP which is represented as Y in the equation. If the GNP is already at the full employment level, real GNP cannot be increased. An increase in money supply will increase nominal GNP, but this increase in nominal GNP merely reflects increased prices of goods and services.

If the real GNP is at a level below full employment, an increase in money supply will increase nominal GNP. This increase in nominal GNP, however, represents both an increase in real output (Y) and an increase in prices (P). Monetarists as well as other economists hope that an increase in money supply will increase real output rather than prices. The economy would be better off the greater the portion of the increase in nominal GNP that represents an increase in real output. How the effects of an increase in money supply are divided between increases in real output and increases in prices is one of those questions to which economists do not yet know the answers. In the absence of government regulation, economists do not know how to increase money supply and limit the effect of increased money supply to increases in real output while holding prices constant.

The hypothesis that changes in the money supply directly influence nominal GNP is only the foundation of monetarism onto which the structure and decorations of monetarism have subsequently been added. The structure of mainstream monetarism was developed by Milton Friedman, while subsequent decorations were added by other monetarists. Let us introduce Friedman's view of monetarism in the following section.

Friedman's View of Monetarism

Milton Friedman is best known for his contribution to the development of modern monetarism. Walter W. Heller, a noted Keynesian economist, once stated, "My intent today is neither to praise nor to bury that towering iconoclast Milton Friedman, for to praise him and his works would absorb far too much of my limited time, and to bury him is, in a word, impossible."[4]

Foundation of Monetarism

A firm foundation of modern monetarism was laid when Milton Friedman and Anna Jacobson Schwartz published *A monetary history of the United States, 1867–1960*.[5] After examining the

---

[4]Monetary vs. fiscal policy: Milton Friedman and Walter W. Heller (New York: W. W. Norton, 1969), p. 15.

[5]Milton Friedman and Anna Jacobson Schwartz, *A monetary history of the United States, 1867–1960* (Princeton: Princeton University Press, 1963).

monetary history of the United States for the 93-year period, Friedman and Schwartz concluded (1) that changes in the behavior of the money stock have been closely associated with changes in economic activity, money income, and prices; (2) that the interaction between monetary and economic changes has been highly stable; and (3) that monetary changes have not simply been a reflection of changes in economic activity but have an independent origin. Money does not simply react to changes in economic activity; money determines the course of economic activity. In other words, money matters.

Friedman and Schwartz pointed out that on three occasions the Federal Reserve System took policy steps of major magnitude that could not be regarded as inevitable responses to changes in money income and prices.[6] The three occasions were (1) January to June 1920, (2) October 1931, and (3) July 1936 to May 1937. Policy steps undertaken during these periods were sharply restrictive and resulted in contractions in the economy.

The first occasion was when the Federal Reserve System raised the discount rate from 4 3/4 percent to 6 percent in January 1920 and raised it again to 7 percent in June 1920. During the same period, member banks were borrowing heavily from Federal Reserve banks. During the next 12 months, the money supply declined by 9 percent. After a lag of several months, industrial production declined by 30 percent within a 12-month period. The second occasion was when the Federal Reserve System raised the discount rate from 1 1/2 percent to 3 1/2 percent within a two-week period in October 1931 during which bank failures were rapidly spreading in the economy. For the next 12 months following this action, the money supply declined by 14 percent. After a lag of several months, industrial production declined by 24 percent within a 12-month period. The third occasion was when the Federal Reserve System doubled reserve requirements between July 1936 and May 1937 at a time when the Treasury was undertaking what was equivalent to a large-scale restrictive open market operation policy. During the following 12 months, the money supply declined by 3 percent. Immediately following the doubling of reserve requirements, industrial production declined by 34 percent within a 12-month period.

A stronger indictment against the Federal Reserve for mismanaging money supply was made by Friedman and Schwartz. They pointed out that during the beginning years of the Great Depression (1929–1931) the stock of money circulating in the economy declined by one-third. The deadlock between the Federal Reserve Bank of New York, which advocated an expansionary monetary policy, and the Federal Reserve Board, which was more resigned to the admission of the impotence of monetary policy, made the depression last many more years than necessary. Friedman and Schwartz shared the view that the depression might have ended in 1930 if Benjamin Strong had been healthy for 12 more months.[7] Benjamin Strong was president of the Federal Reserve Bank of New York and was strongly in favor of an expansionary monetary policy. Strong died in 1928.

Key Propositions of Monetarism
Reinforcing the findings from the historical analysis of U.S. monetary policy, Friedman suggested key propositions of monetarism as summarized in the following.[8]

---

[6]Ibid., pp. 688–689.

[7]Ibid., p. 692.

[8]Adapted from Milton Friedman, The key propositions of monetarism, *Money and economic development: The Horowitz lectures of 1972* (New York: Praeger Publishers, 1973), as printed in Richard T. Gill, *Great debates in economics*, Vol. 2 (Pacific Palisades, Calif.: Goodyear Publishing Company, 1973), pp. 125–127; and the seminal AEA presidential address by Friedman, The role of monetary policy, *American Economic Review* 58(March 1968):1–17.

There is a consistent relation between the rate of growth of the quantity of money (*M*) and the rate of growth of nominal GNP. If the quantity of money grows rapidly, so will nominal GNP. Because it takes time for changes in monetary growth to affect GNP and how long it takes is not a constant number, the rate of monetary growth today is not very closely related to the rate of GNP growth today. Today's GNP growth depends rather on what has been happening to money before now. On the average, a change in the rate of monetary growth produces a change in the rate of growth of nominal income about six to nine months later.

When GNP changes due to changes in the money supply, the change in nominal GNP typically shows up first in output and later in prices. On the average, the effect on prices comes some 9 to 15 months after the effect on income and output, so the total delay between a change in monetary growth and a change in the rate of inflation averages 15 to 24 months. The lag works both ways. When the rate of change of monetary growth accelerates, the effect on inflation of this acceleration is felt about 15 to 24 months after the change in the money supply. When monetary growth slows down, the effect on inflation of this slowdown is felt about 15 to 24 months after the slowdown of monetary growth started. Inflation cannot be stopped overnight.

Inflation is always and everywhere a monetary phenomenon in the sense that it is, and can be, produced only by a more rapid increase in the quantity of money than in output. When aggregate demand increases through increased government expenditure or a cut in income tax rates, this fiscal action is not inflationary unless it is accompanied by an increase in money supply. Money supply is the only determinant of inflation. This means that government spending is inflationary if it is financed by creating money. If it is financed by taxes or by borrowing from the public, it is not inflationary. Fiscal policy is important in determining what fraction of total national income is spent by government and who bears the burden of that expenditure. By itself, fiscal policy has little bearing on inflation.

A change in monetary growth affects interest rates in one direction at first but in the opposite direction later on. More rapid monetary growth at first tends to lower interest rates. But later on, as it raises spending and stimulates price increases, it also produces a rise in the demand for loans, which will tend to raise interest rates. In the opposite direction, a slower rate of monetary growth at first raises interest rates, but later on, as it reduces spending and inflation, it lowers interest rates. The two-edged relation between money and interest rates explains why monetarists insist that interest rates are a highly misleading guide to monetary policy.

The policy implication of these propositions is that we must carry out monetary policy in such a way as to keep it from making economic fluctuations worse. To achieve this objective, the monetary authority should guide itself by magnitudes such as M1, M2, and M3, which it can control, not by ones such as interest rates, which it cannot control. The monetary authority should also avoid sharp swings in policy by pursuing a steady monetary growth.

Importance of a Stable Velocity

Reconsider equations (17.10) and (18.1). If velocity (*V*) is not stable, the relation between money supply and prices in equation (17.10) or the relation between money supply and nominal GNP in equation (18.1) would not be predictable. Monetarists, therefore, claim that the velocity of money is stable in the short run. The income velocities (GNP divided by M1) for 1952 and thereafter are presented in Table 18.2. The velocity does change over the long run. Whether or not velocity

SPECIFIC GUIDELINES OF MONETARY POLICY

The Federal Reserve changes money supply to stabilize the economy while promoting its growth. How does the Fed determine when and how much to increase money supply? In other words, what guidelines does the Fed use?

During the 1970s, the Federal Reserve attempted to control the amount of money available in the economy by confining the federal funds rate to narrow ranges as specified at each Federal Open Market Committee meeting. The federal funds rate is the interest paid on short-term loans made among member banks. The major problem with the procedure of controlling the federal funds rate was that, in its attempt to stabilize the federal funds rate, the Federal Reserve could miss its targets for the money stock for periods long enough to affect total spending in the economy. On October 6, 1979, therefore, it abandoned the procedure of targeting on the federal funds rate. The Fed adopted, instead, a procedure in which the objective of open market operations was to supply the amount of reserves consistent with the objectives for money-growth, while permitting larger fluctuations in the federal funds rate. In other words, the primary emphasis since 1979 had been on controlling the so-called monetary aggregates such as M1, M2, etc. In October 1982 the Federal Reserve again changed its guidelines. Since that time, the Fed has targeted open market operations on average levels of reserves borrowed from Federal Reserve Banks. A comment by *Fortune* indicates that the Fed now watches many different economic indicators including commodity prices, the foreign exchange of the dollar, and the difference between the federal funds rate and the long-term Treasury bonds rate.

Stated bluntly, the Federal Reserve System is still searching for new indicators to help determine America's monetary policy.

Sources: R. Alton Gilbert, Operating procedures for conducting monetary policy, Federal Reserve Bank of St. Louis *Review,* February 1985, pp. 13–21; and Robert E. Norton, The Fed heads into no man's land, *Fortune* April 25, 1988, pp. 121–136.

changes in the short run appears subject to opinion. Monetarists acknowledge that velocity changes as the financial institutions of an economy improve over a long period of time.

The main threat to the monetarists' position does not lie in long-term changes in the financial institutions. The threat lies in the possibility that the velocity may change without any change in money supply if the general public decides to transfer a large amount of money back and forth between transactions funds and speculative funds. **Transactions funds** refer to funds that are used for buying and selling of goods and services, whereas **speculative funds** are funds that the public use for investment purposes. Suppose, for instance, that the money supply is doubled and all of that extra money is added to speculative funds. The increase in money supply in this case will not raise prices, as the monetarists claim it should. Monetarists, therefore, usually assume that the proportion of cash balances that people desire to hold for transactions purposes relative to total money supply

TABLE 18.2 Velocity of Money Circulation

Year	GNP ($billions)	M1 ($billions)	Velocity
1952	351.6	122.3	2.875
1953	371.6	125.3	2.966
1954	372.5	127.3	2.926
1955	405.9	131.4	3.089
1956	428.2	132.9	3.222
1957	451.0	133.6	3.376
1958	456.8	135.1	3.381
1959	495.8	140.4	3.531
1960	515.3	140.3	3.673
1961	533.8	143.1	3.730
1962	574.7	146.5	3.923
1963	606.9	151.0	4.019
1964	649.8	156.8	4.144
1965	705.1	163.5	4.313
1966	772.0	171.0	4.515
1967	816.4	177.8	4.592
1968	892.7	190.2	4.693
1969	963.9	201.5	4.784
1970	1015.5	209.2	4.854
1971	1102.7	223.2	4.940
1972	1212.8	239.1	5.072
1973	1359.3	256.4	5.301
1974	1472.8	269.3	5.469
1975	1598.4	281.5	5.678
1976	1782.8	297.3	5.997
1977	1990.5	320.1	6.218
1978	2249.7	346.4	6.495
1979	2508.1	372.7	6.730
1980	2732.0	396.0	6.899
1981	3052.6	425.1	7.181
1982	3166.0	453.1	6.987
1983	3405.7	503.2	6.768
1984	3772.2	538.6	7.004
1985	4014.9	586.9	6.841
1986	4240.3	666.7	6.360
1987	4526.7	744.0	6.084
1988	4861.8	775.0	6.273

Source: *Federal Reserve Bulletin* and *Business Conditions Digest.*

is very stable. If this assumption does not hold true, an increase in money supply may not lead to proportionate increases in prices or nominal GNP even in the short run.

Keynesians challenge this conclusion by claiming that the amount of money people want to hold for speculative purposes does change significantly in the short run. They point out that the interest rate is unstable in both the short run and the long run. Keynesians then argue that V is unstable because the speculative demand for money changes inversely with changes in the interest rate. The higher the market rate of interest, the lower the speculative demand for money, since the opportunity cost of holding money becomes that much greater at a higher interest rate.

NATURAL RATE OF UNEMPLOYMENT

Earlier it was stated that the origin of monetarism was classical economics. Like classical economists, monetarists claim that natural market forces will eliminate unemployment. Reduction in unemployment will have occurred sooner or later through the forces of supply and demand. The key phrase is *sooner or later*. Monetarists claim that unemployment will be reduced sooner than later. Keynesians disagree, stating that the process through which market forces reduce unemployment is very slow. Keynesians claim that the process through which market forces work in reducing unemployment is so slow that government intervention is necessary through fiscal and monetary policy. If we agree with the natural rate of unemployment hypothesis that monetarists hold dear, the Phillips curve hypothesis of a trade-off between unemployment and inflation becomes totally irrelevant. We will study step by step what this statement is all about.[9]

What Is the Natural Rate?

Reconsider the concept of full employment, presented in Chapter 14. Full employment does not mean that everyone who wants to work has a job. Even when an economy experiences a boom, there are unemployed persons. Some are unemployed because they are in the process of changing jobs, while others are unemployed because new technologies make their skills obsolete. The former condition is known as frictional unemployment and the latter, structural unemployment. The **natural rate of unemployment** is the rate of unemployment that exists when there is full employment in an economy. In other words, unemployment at the natural rate of unemployment is the sum of frictional unemployment and structural unemployment.

According to monetarists, the natural rate of unemployment is determined by real economic conditions such as the level of competition, tax rates, and government programs. The natural rate of unemployment would be lower, the more competitive the markets are and the more work incentive the tax rate structure provides. Government programs such as unemployment compensation and welfare programs may also raise the natural rate of unemployment.

Alternatively, the **natural rate of unemployment** is defined as that rate of unemployment at which there is no tendency for the rate of inflation to rise or fall. Is it puzzling that the natural

[9]For a good summary of the natural rate of unemployment, see Stuart E. Weiner, The natural rate of unemployment: Concepts and issues, Federal Reserve Bank of Kansas City *Economic Review* (January 1986):11–24.

rate of unemployment is defined in terms of inflation? The basis is the following. The **natural rate of unemployment hypothesis** claims that fiscal and monetary policies cannot change the rate of unemployment over a long period of time; the rate of unemployment always returns to the natural rate. Economists who believe in the natural rate of unemployment hypothesis explain that when government undertakes expansionary policies, prices of goods and services may increase, but wage increases may lag behind inflation. The unemployment rate may be reduced below the natural level in the short run until wage increases catch up with inflation. As will be shown shortly, the monetarists' explanation of the Phillips curve is based on the practice of defining the natural rate of unemployment in terms of inflation.

When the economy is at the natural rate, the rate of inflation is constant from one year to the next. Both workers and firms expect this inflation rate to continue, and they base their decisions on wage contracts on this expected rate. For this reason, the natural rate of unemployment is sometimes called the constant inflation rate of unemployment.

The Natural Rate and the Phillips Curve

Consider the hypothetical example depicted in Figure 18.4. The inflation rate is measured along the vertical axis and the unemployment rate is measured along the horizontal axis. Suppose the economy is initially at point A. At that point, the inflation rate is 3 percent and the unemployment rate is 6 percent. Suppose that the 6 percent unemployment rate is the natural rate. For the sake of simplicity, let us assume that there is no increase in labor productivity, and thus all wage increases are based on expected inflation. All unemployed persons are either frictionally or structurally unemployed. There is no cyclical unemployment. Because the unemployment rate is at its natural rate, workers expect and receive a 3 percent increase in wages, and firms expect and receive a 3 percent increase in prices. There is no pressure for changes in wage contracts. The economy is stable at point A.

Now suppose that election time comes and policymakers decide to lower the unemployment rate below 6 percent. To reduce unemployment it is necessary to increase aggregate demand. Aggregate demand can be increased through an expansionary fiscal policy such as deficit-financed government spending or an increase in money supply or both. An increase in aggregate demand means that there is an increase in spending in the economy. Sales increase and firms hire more workers. A higher level of employment means that firms will have to bid up wages. Higher wages, on the other hand, will be passed on to consumers through higher prices of products. The initial effect of the expansionary policy, therefore, is a decline in the unemployment rate and a rise in prices. The economy moves to a position such as point B.

At point B, inflation is higher at 5 percent than the 3 percent represented by point A, and unemployment is lower at 4 percent than the 6 percent represented by point A. The natural rate of unemployment hypothesis claims that point B is not sustainable. The economy will not stay at point B but will move to point C. Why?

At point A, there was 3 percent annual inflation, and workers were expecting 3 percent inflation and receiving a 3 percent increase in wages. With an expansionary policy, there is a decrease in the unemployment rate from 6 percent to 4 percent, but the rate of inflation changes from 3 percent to 5 percent. A higher rate of inflation means that real wages of workers decline. As existing labor contracts expire and new contracts are negotiated, workers demand and receive higher wages at a rate of 5 percent per year. As wages increase, firms reduce employment. As

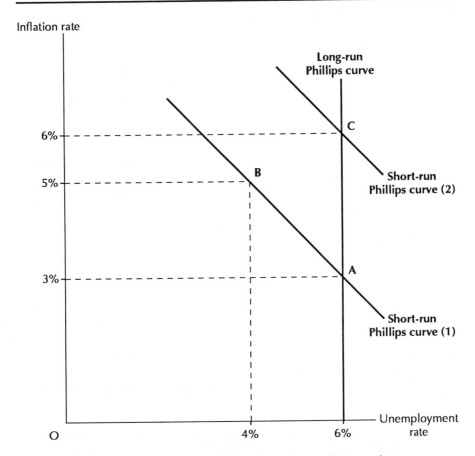

FIGURE 18.4 The Phillips Curve and the Natural Rate of Unemployment. According to the natural rate of unemployment hypothesis, the long-term Phillips curve is vertical at the natural rate of unemployment. Expansionary policies simply cause the short-run Phillips curve to shift from (1) to (2).

employment is reduced, the unemployment rate increases. Eventually, the economy settles at point C, with an unemployment rate of 6 percent and an inflation rate of 6 percent. Point C is a sustainable position for the economy, since the unemployment rate is once again at its natural rate. Workers and firms both are expecting an inflation rate of 6 percent. There is no pressure for changes in wage contracts. The only long-term impact of the expansionary macroeconomic policy has been a doubling of the inflation rate.

According to the natural rate of unemployment hypothesis, the trade-off between unemployment and inflation was only temporary. There is no trade-off in the long run. The rate of unemployment always returns to the natural rate regardless of whether government undertakes expansionary economic policies or contractionary economic policies. The long-run Phillips curve, therefore, is vertical at the natural rate of unemployment.

LEFT AND RIGHT SIDES OF THE BRAIN

Whether the brain is equipotential, so that all parts of the brain work together, or whether it is divided into two hemispheres, each of which has its own specialized functions, has been a subject of interest for more than 100 years. According to those who believe in a dichotomy of brain function, the left side of the brain is verbal and analytic, and is dominant for speech and language functions. The right side of the brain specializes in creative activities such as recognizing melodies or spatial findings. Studies based on split-brain patients (whose brains were surgically split to cure profound epilepsy, for example) indicate the two halves perform different tasks. The left hemisphere looks for special features such as glasses or a long nose, while the right hemisphere tends to view the face as a whole. Our knowledge of the differences in function between the left and right sides of the brain came from clinical work in which the effects of injury to different parts of the brain were studied. One of the earliest findings on the asymmetric nature of the brain was one by a French surgeon named Paul Broca, who observed a significant relationship between injury to part of the left hemisphere of the brain and the loss of speech.

Some claim that our educational system pays more attention to the left side of the brain for verbal and analytic education than to the right side of the brain, the side that specializes in creativity. This claim suggests that by paying more attention to educating the right side of the brain, we may be able to educate the young better, and society may be able to enjoy increased productivity.

Upon reviewing alternative macroeconomic theories, it appears that economists need a greater use of the creative right side of the brain than the analytical left side.

Source: Adapted from Sally P. Springer, Educating the left and right sides of the brain, *National Forum,* the Phi Kappa Phi journal 67(Spring 1987):25–28.

VARIATIONS OF MAINSTREAM MACROECONOMIC THEORIES

Let us designate Keynesian economics inclusive of the Phillips curve, and monetarism as summarized by Milton Friedman, as mainstream macroeconomic theories. In this section we study two more ideas that have surfaced in the 1970s and thereafter: rational expectations and supply-side economics. These ideas are variations of mainstream macroeconomic theories.

Rational Expectations

The idea of rational expectations first appeared in 1961 at about the same time that Friedman began his presentation of mainstream monetarism. In a 1961 article, John F. Muth asked why no single approach had been consistently successful in predicting prices in financial markets.[10] The answer, according to Muth, is that speculators of security prices were incorporating all available information needed to maximize the accuracy of price forecasts almost instantaneously. This behavior by speculators of incorporating all information into decision making is *rational*.

When speculators behave rationally, identical information will have a different impact on speculators at different times. For instance, when the information is offered for the first time and, thus, is new, decision makers make decisions without knowing what to expect from the information. When the same information is available the second time, however, it is no longer new, and the reaction by speculators to the same information is different, since they now know what to expect. As mainstream Keynesian economics became relatively ineffective in managing the economy in the 1970s, several economists revived the idea of rational expectations and developed the theory of rational expectations as an alternative to mainstream economic theories.[11]

The Theory

Those who advocate rational expectations reach the same conclusion as mainstream monetarists, that the Federal Reserve should expand the money supply at a steady rate of, say, 4 percent per year. The conclusion, however, is reached in a different way.[12]

Like classical economics and mainstream monetarism, rational expectationists assume that prices and wages are flexible and are determined competitively. This assumption means that all markets are cleared, and supply equals demand in all markets. To this key assumption, **rational expectationists** add the second assumption that individual agents such as consumers, workers, and businesses are rational. Individuals are *rational* in the sense that they use all the available information when they make decisions on, say, investment, consumption, employment, wage negotiation, and other economic matters. These two assumptions make sure that the economy operates efficiently.

Suppose that the Federal Reserve undertakes an expansionary monetary policy by increasing the money supply. With increased money supply, there is more money relative to the amount of goods being produced. Money is plentiful and the price level rises. At this point, individual firms experience rising prices of their products. They do not realize, however, that prices of products produced by other firms are also rising. These firms, therefore, increase output and hire more workers. If everyone knew that all prices were rising, firms would have no incentive to change output or employment. This process is reversed when the money supply is decreased. Suppose that the Federal Reserve undertakes a contractionary monetary policy by decreasing money supply. With decreased money supply, there is less money relative to the amount of goods being produced. Money is scarce and the price level falls. At this point individual firms experience falling prices of

---

[10]John F. Muth, Rational expectations and the theory of price movements, *Econometrica* 29(July 1961):315–335.

[11]Robert E. Lucas, Jr., Testing the natural rate hypothesis, in Otto Eckstein (ed.), *The econometrics of price determination conference* (Washington, D.C.: Federal Reserve Board, 1972), pp. 50/59; Robert E. Lucas, Jr., Some international evidence on output-inflation tradeoffs, *American Economic Review* 63(June 1973):326–334; and Thomas Sargent and Neil Wallace, "Rational" expectations, the optimal monetary instrument, and the optimal money supply rule, *Journal of Political Economy* 83(April 1975):241–254.

[12]For a commonsense summary of the theory of rational expectations, see Martin Neil Bailey, Are the new economic models the answer? in Peter D. McClelland, *Introductory macroeconomics, 1985–86* (Ithaca: Cornell University Press, 1985), pp. 92–95; A. Steven Holland, Rational expectations and the effects of monetary policy: A guide for the unlimited, Federal Reserve Bank of St. Louis's *Review* (May 1985):5–11; and Bennett T. McCallum, The significance of rational expectations theory, *Challenge* (January-February 1980):37–43.

their products, but they do not realize that prices of products produced by other firms are also falling. These firms, therefore, reduce output and lay off workers. If everyone knew that all prices were falling, firms would have no incentive to change output or employment.

So long as policy changes are unexpected by firms, these policies affect the level of real output and employment as described in the preceding paragraph. The ability of policy changes to affect real output and employment is limited, however, since individual firms soon find out that the general price level, not simply the prices of their separate products, is changed by government policies. As soon as firms realize that the prices of products produced by other firms have also changed in direct proportion to changes in prices of their own products, the level of real output and employment returns to the natural rate. In addition, if the same policy is repeated, individuals come to learn how this policy affects the economy and act accordingly. For instance, when the Federal Reserve increases money supply for the second time, rational expectationists claim that firms know that the increased money supply raises prices of all products in the economy. Firms neither increase real output nor hire more workers. Only unanticipated policy changes, rational expectationists claim, can affect real output and employment.

Rational expectationists conclude that government policies are not effective in changing real output and employment in both the short run and the long run, since there are not that many unanticipated policy changes that the government can try. All policy changes will eventually have to be repeated and will thus be anticipated. The policy suggestion of rational expectationists, therefore, is to adopt a fixed policy rule such as an increase in money supply at a steady rate each year.

An Evaluation

The most important contribution that the rational expectations movement has made to macroeconomic theories is that expectations adjust to the way policy is conducted, thereby altering the results of the policy. Thus, the effects of a given policy will not necessarily be the same every time it is used. Unlike Keynesians, who claim that an increased money supply affects aggregate demand through lower interest rates and increased investment, rational expectationists claim that an increased money supply affects aggregate demand directly. In this regard, there is no difference between rational expectationists and mainstream monetarists. Unlike mainstream monetarists, who claim that monetary policy is effective in the short run but not in the long run, rational expectationists claim that monetary policy is ineffective both in the short run and in the long run.

Martin Bailey suggests two difficulties that the theory has with factual observations.[13] The first difficulty relates to the persistence problem. If the rational expectations theory were correct, recessions should not last long since any deviation from the natural rate should last only until the unanticipated element is in effect. Recessions can last a long time, however. Business was clearly depressed from 1929 to 1941, from 1958 to 1962, and from 1974 to 1977. The theory of rational expectations makes excess unemployment purely a result of unexpected events. This hypothesis means that unemployment fluctuates at random around its natural rate. It did not.

The second difficulty relates to the assumption of the rational expectations theory that firms and workers make decisions on production and work based only on wages or prices that are determined competitively in the marketplace. Their choices are never constrained by a shortage of jobs or customers. A typical business cycle is characterized by large changes in output and

---

[13]Martin Neil Bailey, Are the new economic models the answer? in Peter D. McClelland, *Introductory macroeconomics 1985–86* (Ithaca: Cornell University Press, 1985), p. 94.

employment but by only small changes in wages and prices. This relation between large changes in output and small changes in price means that the price elasticity of supply must be very large so that a small increase in price should lead to a very large increase in the quantity of the product supplied. When prices or wages have changed for reasons unrelated to the business cycle, we do not find such large responses in real output.

Supply-Side Economics

If the 1960s were characterized by the resurgence of classical economics through monetarism, and if the 1970s were characterized by a variation of monetarism through rational expectations, the 1980s may be characterized by supply-side economics and its political implications.

Keynesian economics is demand-side economics in that the theory stresses aggregate demand as the determinant of the nation's real output and employment. Aggregate demand can be stimulated by an easy money policy and increased government expenditure. Monetarism is also demand-side economics in that the theory stresses the effect of money supply on aggregate demand. Supply-siders stress policy measures that can increase the aggregate supply more than the aggregate demand. Supply-side economics is known more for its policy design than for its theoretical substance. In fact, there may have been more supply-side politicians, such as Ronald Reagan, who was president of the United States from 1981 through 1989, than supply-side economists.

Key Propositions
The key propositions of **supply-side economics** are the following.[14] First, a cut in marginal tax rates on individual incomes improves work incentives, increases real output, and thus leads to increased tax revenue. Supply-siders claim that reductions in tax rates will induce individuals to shift from leisure to work, since the opportunity cost of leisure becomes greater with tax cuts. Unlike Keynesians, who view tax cuts as increased income, supply-siders view tax cuts as an increase in work incentive.

Second, tax cuts may or may not result in an increased budget deficit. Even if tax cuts result in an increased budget deficit, there will not be a crowding-out effect. The increased budget deficit will not reduce the funds available for investment in plant and equipment because tax changes will raise the saving rate by enough to finance the increased deficit.

Finally, the rapid increase in real output that results from the increased incentive to work will increase aggregate supply. The increased aggregate supply will slow the rate of inflation without the need for a rise in unemployment. This view is different from the Phillips curve hypothesis, which requires a higher rate of unemployment as the cost for slowing the rate of inflation.

The Laffer Curve
The most widely known graph relating to supply-side economics is the Laffer curve, shown in Figure 18.5. Figure 18.5 shows the relation between tax rates and tax revenue. As the tax rate rises from O to A, tax revenues also rise from O to M. When tax rate is OA, tax revenues are maximized at OM. If tax rates are too high, the high tax rate will reduce workers' incentive to work, resulting in a reduction in working hours and, subsequently, tax revenues.

[14]Arthur B. Laffer, Supply-side economics, *Financial Analysts Journal* (September-October 1981):29–43.

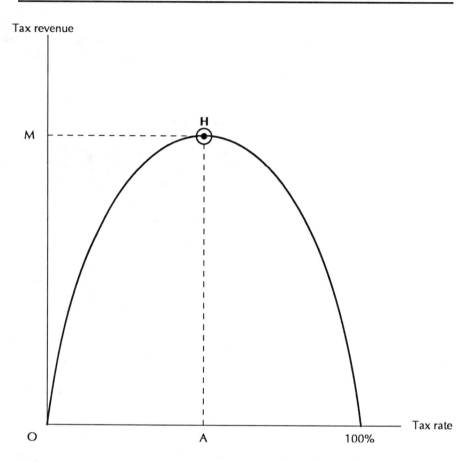

FIGURE 18.5 The Laffer Curve. According to the Laffer curve hypothesis, tax rates higher than OA reduce tax revenue below the maximum level, indicated as OM.

By itself, the Laffer curve does not say that tax rates in the early 1980s were above the OA level. Those who supported supply-side economics, however, left little doubt that tax rates in the early 1980s were above the OA level. They all supported reductions in income tax rates by citing advantages that included increased tax revenue. Arthur Laffer himself lists at least five advantages of a tax rate reduction, which include (1) lessening the amount of revenue collected per unit of the lower taxed input; (2) increasing the employment of the lower taxed input; (3) increasing the employment of other inputs, hence increasing their tax payments; (4) reducing total spending as the number of unemployed persons and the number of welfare recipients decline; and (5) reducing tax evasion and avoidance.[15]

[15] Arthur B. Laffer, Supply-side economics, *Financial Analysts Journal* (September-October 1981):42.

An Evaluation

Supply-side economics provided an intellectual basis for actions of conservative politicians in the early 1980s. Supply-siders and their political allies believed that government in general was too big and thus inefficient, and that free markets were a more efficient way of allocating resources than government controls. Aided by supply-side economics, Congress passed two important tax laws during the 1980s. One was the Economic Recovery Tax Act of 1981, which reduced Federal tax revenue by more than 2 percent of GNP by cutting income tax rates significantly. The other was the Tax Reform Act of 1986, which reduced the 14 income tax brackets to only three, thus effectively reducing the marginal tax rate of higher income individuals. The Tax Reform Act of 1986 also shifted the tax burden from individuals to corporations.

Martin Feldstein states that much of supply-side economics was a return to the 200-year-old ideas of Adam Smith that long-term economic growth requires creating capacity and removing government impediments to individual initiatives.[16] In this sense, there is no difference between the *new* supply-side economics of the 1980s and the *traditional* supply-side emphasis shared by most, if not all, mainstream economists. The difference between the two groups is that the new supply-siders were extravagant in their claims. New supply-siders, according to Feldstein, overestimated advantages of tax cuts by projecting rapid growth, dramatic increases in tax revenue, significant increases in saving, and painless reduction of inflation.

ALTERNATIVE POLICY PRESCRIPTIONS

Different macroeconomic theories suggest different policy prescriptions for modern economic problems. Before we leave this chapter behind, let us go over two issues, inflation and the trade-off between unemployment and inflation, and inquire how different macroeconomic theories attempt to deal with these issues.

Inflation

Causes and solutions of the inflation problem by Keynesian economics, mainstream monetarism, rational expectationism, and supply-side economics are summarized in this section.

Keynesian Economics

At least in the short run, Keynesians view the cause of inflation as an aggregate demand that is greater than aggregate supply. In the long run, Keynesians agree that inflation cannot be sustained for long unless the excessive aggregate demand is accompanied by a rapid increase in money supply. Keynesian solutions to the inflationary problem include contractionary fiscal policies such as an increase in tax rate or reduced government expenditure in the short run, and a contractionary monetary policy in the long run.

---

[16]Martin Feldstein, Supply-side economics: Old truths and new claims, *AEA Papers and Proceedings* 76(May 1986):26–30.

Mainstream Monetarism

Mainstream monetarists believe that inflation is caused by a rapid increase in money supply. The suggested solution to an inflationary problem is a contractionary monetary policy.

Rational Expectationism

Those who advocate rational expectations have the same view of inflation as mainstream monetarists do. Inflation is caused by a rapid increase in money supply, they believe, and the solution is to reduce the rate of growth of the money supply.

Supply-Side Economics

Like mainstream monetarists and rational expectationists, supply-side economists believe that the cause of inflation is a rapid increase in money supply. Suggested solutions, however, include an increase in aggregate supply through reduced income tax rates as well as a reduced rate of growth of money supply.

The views of four macroeconomic theories on inflation and the trade-off between unemployment and inflation are summarized in Table 18.3.

Trade-off between Unemployment and Inflation

The following paragraphs summarize the different views on the trade-off between unemployment and inflation among Keynesian economics, mainstream monetarism, rational expectationism, and supply-side economics.

TABLE 18.3 Policy Prescriptions of Alternative Macroeconomic Theories

| | *What Should the Government Do about* | |
Alternative Theories	*Inflation*	*Trade-off between Unemployment and Inflation*
Keynesian economics	Raise tax or reduce government spending in the short run; reduce money supply in the long run	There is a trade-off in the short run and in the long run
Mainstream monetarism	Reduce money supply in the short run and in the long run	There is a trade-off in the short run, not in the long run
Rational expectationism	Reduce money supply in the short run and in the long run	No trade-off in the short run nor in the long run
Supply-side economics	Cut taxes to increase aggregate supply and reduce money supply in the short run and in the long run	No trade-off in the short run nor in the long run

Keynesian Economics

Keynesian economists believe that there is a trade-off between unemployment and inflation both in the short run and in the long run. To reduce unemployment, therefore, the economy may have to tolerate a higher rate of inflation. To reduce inflation, on the other hand, the economy may have to tolerate a higher rate of unemployment.

Mainstream Monetarism

Mainstream monetarists believe that there is a trade-off between unemployment and inflation in the short run, but not in the long run. The best way of reducing both unemployment and inflation, therefore, is to gradually decrease the rate of growth of money supply, which will minimize the trade-off between unemployment and inflation in the short run.

Rational Expectationism

Rational expectationists believe that there is no trade-off between unemployment and inflation either in the short run or in the long run. Inflation thus can be reduced by reducing the rate of growth of money supply without increasing the rate of unemployment.

Supply-Side Economics

Like rational expectationists, supply-side economists do not believe in the existence of a trade-off between unemployment and inflation in the short run or in the long run. To reduce inflation and increase employment, supply-siders suggest reducing income tax rates as an incentive to more work as well as reducing rate of growth of the money supply.

SUMMARY

This chapter summarizes major developments in macroeconomic theories after Keynes. Keynesian economics was not concerned with inflation. When inflation as well as unemployment became problems in post-World War II economies, a trade-off between unemployment and inflation was injected into the Keynesian model. The inverse relation between unemployment and inflation was represented by the Phillips curve.

The 1960s is characterized by the resurgence of classical economics through monetarism. Monetarists recognize the important role that money plays in the economy. Due to the time lag of monetary policy, monetarists recommend a fixed rule approach toward increases in money supply in place of discretionary stabilization policies. A fixed rule approach is claimed to keep changes in the money supply from destabilizing the economy. Like classical economists, monetarists claim that natural market forces will eliminate unemployment. The rate of unemployment that is determined by natural market forces is called the natural rate of unemployment. Mainstream monetarists such as Milton Friedman claim that expansionary economic policy is effective in increasing real output and reducing unemployment only in the short run, but not in the long run. Mainstream monetarists, therefore, claim that the long-run Phillips curve is vertical at the natural rate of unemployment. Mainstream monetarists believe that the trade-off between unemployment and inflation is possible only in the short run, but not in the long run.

Rational expectationists agree with mainstream monetarists in that prices and wages are flexible and are determined competitively. Rational expectationists, however, add the assumption that individuals are rational in the sense that they use all the available information when they make decisions. This added assumption leads to the conclusion that the Phillips curve is vertical at the natural rate of unemployment in both the short run and the long run. A vertical Phillips curve means that there is no trade-off between unemployment and inflation even in the short run. The most important contribution that the rational expectations movement made to macroeconomic theories is the idea that expectations adjust to the way policy is conducted, and thus the effects of a given policy will not necessarily be the same every time it is used. Supply-side economists claim that a cut in income taxes improves work incentives and thus leads to increased tax revenues as well as increased real output.

EXERCISES

1. In the text it was stated that "It was obvious that answers to these questions were necessary within the Keynesian model if the model were to continue to play a guiding role for policymakers." What are the questions and what was the suggested solution?

2. Based on the unemployment and inflation data of the U.S. economy for 1956 through 1987, what might one conclude regarding whether or not the Phillips curve applies to the U.S. economy?

3. The equation

   $$M\bar{V} = GNP$$

   represents the underlying idea of modern monetarism. The equation indicates that, so far as velocity remains constant, changes in the money supply directly affect GNP. Does this interpretation mean that whenever we need to increase real output and employment, all we need to do is to increase money supply?

4. Summarize the two policy recommendations of mainstream monetarists.

5. Monetarists, including rational expectationists, claim that there is no trade-off between unemployment and inflation. How do monetarists explain their claim that there is no trade-off between unemployment and inflation? Assuming that there is no trade-off as monetarists claim, how will the Phillips curve change?

6. Suppose that the Federal Reserve increases money supply by a significant amount. What would be a reaction to the increase by (1) labor unions, and (2) lending institutions? Answer this question from the view of rational expectationists.

7. In short, what is the policy recommendation of rational expectationism?

8. What are some key policy suggestions made by supply-side economists?

9. The rates of unemployment and inflation of the U.S. economy for 1960 to 1969 were as follows:

Year	Unemployment Rate (%)	Inflation Rate (%)	Total
1960	5.54	1.51	
1961	6.69	1.07	
1962	5.57	1.17	
1963	5.64	1.25	
1964	5.16	1.32	
1965	4.51	1.59	
1966	3.79	2.99	
1967	3.84	2.78	
1968	3.56	4.21	
1969	3.49	5.42	

Add the rate of unemployment and the rate of inflation in the last column of the table. Is it possible to tell by looking at the last column whether the figures indicate any inverse relation between unemployment and inflation as suggested by the Phillips curve?

10. Summarize the views on the trade-off between unemployment and inflation by all four macroeconomic theories explained in the text.

SUGGESTED READINGS

Humphrey, Thomas M. (1978). Some recent developments in Phillips curve analysis. Federal Reserve Bank of Richmond *Economic Review,* January-February, pp. 15–23.

An easy-to-read article that explains the issue of a trade-off between unemployment and inflation as well as the natural rate of unemployment hypothesis.

Maddock, Rodney, and Carter, Michael. (1982). A child's guide to rational expectations. *Journal of Economic Literature* 20(March):39–51.

Not quite a "child's guide," this article nonetheless presents rational expectationism in an engaging dialogue.

Modigliani, Franco. (1977). The monetarist controversy or, should we forsake stabilization policies? *American Economic Review* 67(March):1–19.

The presidential address delivered at the eighty-ninth meeting of the American Economic Association in Atlantic City; a good summary of the controversy between monetarists and Keynesians.

Tax Foundation. (1988). *Tax Features* 32(January):2, Table 1, titled Federal Revenue Impact of Major Enacted Tax Legislation, Fiscal Years 1964–1990.

Presents in tabular form the revenue impact of all revenue acts since the Revenue Act of 1964.

PART FOUR

GLOBAL ECONOMY

Deep Springs College is located 30 miles from the nearest town, in a high mountain desert in California. The college is so isolated that even its mail comes via Dyer, Nevada. Deep Springs College was founded in 1917 by L. L. Nunn, a pioneer in the electric power industry. Nunn felt that he could not rely on engineers trained in eastern schools to staff power plants in Colorado, Utah, Idaho, and Montana. He thus developed Deep Springs College to hire untrained young men from the West and provide them with a basic college education. The college is a two-year, private, nondenominational, and fully accredited college. The total enrollment of the college is 24, and every student receives a full scholarship. There are seven professors. There are no majors. The sum of SAT math and verbal scores of Deep Springs students has averaged over 1400. Most graduates of the college transfer to other quality institutions such as Harvard, Cornell, Yale, or Berkeley.

Deep Springs College may have achieved Nunn's dream by operating in isolation. If all nations operated in isolation like Deep Springs, practically all goods and services that nations need would have to be produced within their own boundaries. Economists have long contended that self-sufficiency of nations is not necessarily a virtue. Nations can enjoy greater quantities of output by specializing in production of certain products. According to the comparative advantage doctrine, a nation does not have to be more productive than other nations in producing any single product in order to benefit from specialization and trade.

The opposite case of Deep Springs may be Queensland's Gold Coast in Australia, a 25-mile strip of clean beach. According to the August 1, 1988, issue of *Time,* about 70 percent of the land earmarked for development on the Gold Coast was controlled by Japanese interests in 1988. Many young Australians living in Queensland voice fears that they might

417

become waiters and cabdrivers for wealthy Japanese. A free flow of capital becomes more than an economic problem. In modern society it is simply not possible to live without financial transactions with other nations. Even Deep Springs does not operate in total isolation. Many of the daily necessities have to be brought in.

It is dangerous for nations to simply take what is forced upon them by other nations. Each nation should be able to chart the course that it wishes to take. To chart proper courses, policymakers should understand that the behavior of individual nations to maximize their own benefit may actually reduce the collective benefit of all nations when combined. A coordination of economic policies among nations is vitally important in today's global economy. We need to study essentials of foreign trade and their relations to domestic economic policies. We thus introduce basic concepts of foreign trade in Chapter 19, followed by the discussion in Chapter 20 of macroeconomic policies in the context of the global economy.

19

Economics of Trade among Nations

Measuring Trade among Nations

Economic Basis for Trade

Protectionism

Foreign Exchange Rates

LIVING IN A BIG COUNTRY, we are seldom concerned with how much we really depend on other nations for our daily needs. Our dependency on foreign products has increased so much in recent years that we buy many imported goods thinking it is only natural that they came from other nations. We dress in shirts made in Taiwan, wear shoes made in Italy, live in homes built with lumber imported from Canada, and drive cars made in Japan. In the United States it is at least conceivable that the economy might be able to survive without foreign trade. For other nations such as Japan and newly industrialized countries (NICs) such as Korea and Taiwan, it would be almost impossible to survive without a dramatic decrease in living standards. Studying economics of trade among nations enhances our understanding of many important issues that relate to trade among nations. These issues include why we use so many imported goods, why other nations build plants in our neighborhood, why the cost of traveling overseas fluctuates with changing values of the dollar, why nations maintain trade barriers, how changing values of the dollar affect national security, and more.

The learning objective of this chapter is to study basic concepts of trade among nations. These concepts include imports, exports, the balance of trade, the balance of payments, free trade, trade barriers, protectionism, and foreign exchange rates. Policy issues of foreign trade are presented in the next chapter.

MEASURING TRADE AMONG NATIONS

When we study trade among nations, we are more interested in the overall picture of the exchange of goods and services than in counting the number of shirts and computer chips that we sell to or buy from other nations. Information on the number of shirts and computer chips traded would be of more interest to the garment industry and the computer industry. The overall picture of the exchange of goods and services among nations is presented in terms of imports and exports.

Imports and Exports

We buy all kinds of products made in other nations and sell numerous products of our own to other nations. When we buy products from other nations, these products or the dollar values of these products are called **imports**. When we sell products to other nations, these products as well as their dollar values are called **exports**. As we studied in Chapter 13, an increase in exports, ceteris paribus, increases the GNP of the exporting nation, thus exerting an expansionary effect on the nation's economy, while an increase in imports, ceteris paribus, lowers the GNP of the importing nation and thus exerts a contractionary effect on the nation's economy. It is important to know the trends of imports and exports. The trends of merchandise exports and imports of the United States since 1952 are presented in Table 19.1. Presented also in the table are the U.S. GNP figures as well as exports and imports as percentages of the GNP.

The percentages of merchandise exports and imports relative to GNP remained at less than 5 percent until 1972. In 1973 both percentages exceeded 5 percent and started increasing. In the 1980s, the percentage of exports relative to GNP started declining again, but imports stayed at a high level, approaching almost 10 percent of GNP. More significantly, 1971 marked the first year since World War II during which imports exceeded exports. In 1984 and several years after that, imports

TABLE 19.1 Merchandise Exports and Imports, excluding Military Shipments ($billions)

Year	Exports	Imports	Surplus or Deficit (−)	GNP	As Percentage of GNP Exports	Imports
1952	$ 13.2	$ 10.7	$ 2.5	$ 351.6	3.57%	3.04%
1953	12.3	10.9	1.4	371.6	3.31	2.93
1954	12.8	10.2	2.6	372.5	3.44	2.74
1955	14.3	11.4	2.9	405.9	3.52	2.81
1956	17.3	12.6	4.7	428.2	4.04	2.94
1957	19.5	13.0	6.5	451.0	4.32	2.88
1958	16.4	12.8	3.6	456.8	3.59	2.80
1959	16.4	15.2	1.2	495.8	3.31	3.07
1960	19.6	15.0	4.6	515.3	3.80	2.91
1961	20.2	14.8	5.4	533.8	3.78	2.77
1962	21.0	16.4	4.6	574.7	3.65	2.85
1963	22.4	17.2	5.2	606.9	3.69	2.83
1964	25.6	18.6	7.0	649.8	3.94	2.86
1965	26.5	21.3	5.2	705.1	3.76	3.02
1966	29.4	25.6	3.8	772.0	3.81	3.32
1967	31.0	26.9	4.1	816.4	3.80	3.29
1968	34.1	33.1	1.0	892.7	3.82	3.71
1969	37.3	36.0	1.3	963.9	3.87	3.73
1970	42.7	39.9	2.8	1,015.5	4.20	3.93
1971	43.6	45.5	−1.9	1,102.7	3.95	4.13
1972	49.2	55.6	−6.4	1,212.8	4.06	4.58
1973	70.9	69.4	1.5	1,359.3	5.22	5.11
1974	98.2	103.4	−5.2	1,472.8	6.67	7.02
1975	107.8	99.3	8.5	1,598.4	6.74	6.21
1976	115.3	124.5	−9.2	1,782.8	6.47	6.98
1977	121.3	151.5	−30.2	1,990.5	6.09	7.61
1978	143.6	176.1	−32.5	2,249.7	6.38	7.83
1979	181.8	210.3	−28.5	2,508.1	7.25	8.38
1980	220.7	245.4	−24.7	2,732.0	8.08	8.98
1981	233.5	261.0	−27.5	3,052.6	7.65	8.55
1982	212.3	244.0	−31.7	3,166.0	6.71	7.71
1983	200.7	258.2	−57.5	3,405.7	5.89	7.58
1984	217.6	325.6	−108.0	3,772.2	5.77	8.63
1985	213.3	346.2	−132.9	4,014.9	5.31	8.62
1986	227.2	365.4	−138.2	4,240.3	5.36	8.62
1987	254.1	406.2	−152.1	4,526.7	5.61	9.87
1988	319.3	438.2	−118.9	4,861.8	6.57	9.01

Source: Adapted from DATADISK of Cambridge Planning (Cambridge, Mass.).

exceeded exports by more than $100 billion each year. The large amount of imports in excess of exports that prevailed during the second half of the 1980s was a concern of many economists as well as politicians. Many policy issues that we discuss in Chapter 20 arose due to the imbalance in foreign trade during this period.

Balance of Payments

There are two aspects of trade among nations that we need to study. One is the flow of goods and services and the other is the flow of a nation's currency. The **balance of payments** is the record of all transactions that affect the flow of a nation's currency. The balance of payments has three components: the balance of trade, the current account, and the capital account. These components are illustrated in Table 19.2.

TABLE 19.2 U.S. Balance of Payments in 1988 ($billions)

Balance of trade		
Exports of goods		320.7
Imports of goods		446.8
Surplus (+) or deficit (−)		−126.1
Balance on goods and services		
Balance of merchandise trade		−126.1
Trade of services		33.0
Exports of services	198.0	
Imports of services	165.0	
Surplus (+) or deficit (−)		−93.1
Current account		
Balance on goods and services		−93.1
Unilateral transfers		−41.3
Transfer payments (net)	13.9	
Interest paid by U.S. government to foreigners	27.4	
Surplus (+) or deficit (−)		−134.4
Capital account		
Net foreign investment and loans, capital outflow (+) or inflow (−)		−134.4

Source: Adapted from U.S. Department of Commerce Bureau of Economic Analysis, *Survey of Current Business* 69(January 1989):14, Table 4.1.

Balance of Trade

The narrowest component of the three is the balance of trade. The **balance of trade** refers to a nation's record of transactions of goods with other nations. If imports are greater than exports, there is a deficit in the balance of trade. If exports are greater than imports, there is a surplus in the balance of trade. It is easy to understand that an export of merchandise such as an IBM PC to another nation brings that nation's currency to us. Transactions of services have the same effect on the flow of foreign currency as transactions of merchandise. If businesses in other nations purchase insurance from our insurance companies, ship their products on our ships, and maintain deposits at our banks, foreign currency will flow to the United States in the same way it does when an IBM PC is sold to other nations. Services also include income earned by U.S. investments abroad, since this income also causes foreign currencies to flow to the United States. Although transactions of both goods and services have the same effect on the flow of foreign currency, the term *balance of trade* has traditionally been used to represent transactions of goods only.

Current Account

The **current account** is the summary of transactions of a nation's exports and imports of goods and services plus unilateral transfers. There are two components in unilateral transfers: transfer payments and interest paid by the U.S. government to foreign owners of U.S. government securities. Transfer payments in the current account refer to private gifts from U.S. residents to their relatives or other individuals in other nations as well as to foreign aid between governments.

Capital Account

The deficit or surplus in the current account must somehow be paid by the nation that owes money to another nation. To be specific, when businesses in other nations earn dollars from the United States because they sell more to U.S. consumers than they buy from U.S. businesses, there are two ways through which these foreign businesses can help the United States close the U.S. trade deficit. One is to send the dollars back to the United States for purchase of existing businesses or formation of new businesses such as new plants. The other alternative is to lend money to U.S. consumers. The first option is called **foreign direct investment,** whereas the latter is simply a loan transaction between two nations.

The **capital account** is the summary of capital flows through such means as foreign direct investment and loans among nations. When dollars flow into the United States because of the deficit in the U.S. current account, the flow of dollars is called a **capital inflow.** When the United States has a trade surplus so that we send dollars back to other nations, there is a **capital outflow.** In Table 19.2, there is a capital inflow into the United States because there was a deficit in the U.S. current account in 1988. In Chapter 13, the difference $(X-M)$ between exports and imports was called net foreign investment. In 1988 net foreign investment was $134.4 billion.

ECONOMIC BASIS FOR TRADE

Just as two persons exchange goods and services because the trade benefits both persons, two nations also exchange goods and services because both nations benefit from the trade. We introduce two new concepts, absolute advantage and comparative advantage, to illustrate the basis for mutual benefits from a trade.

Absolute Advantage

Consider two countries, the United States and Korea. Also consider two products, rice and oriental silk. Rice is measured in bushels and silk is measured in yards. Let us suppose that only two persons live in each country: one growing rice and the other making silk. Let us suppose that the U.S. farmer grows 10 bushels of rice per year and the U.S. silk maker makes 1 yard of silk per year, whereas the Korean farmer grows 1 bushel of rice per year and the Korean silk maker makes 2 yards of silk per year. We also suppose that the farmer and the silk maker can exchange their occupations without being less productive in the other occupation. These assumptions are summarized in Table 19.3. The U.S. farmer is more productive than the Korean farmer in growing rice, while the Korean silk maker is more productive than the U.S. silk maker in making silk. In this case, the United States is said to have an *absolute advantage* in growing rice, and Korea is said to have an absolute advantage in making silk.

Specialization under an Absolute Advantage

Since the United States has an absolute advantage in growing rice, it would be to the advantage of the United States to specialize in growing rice and exporting it to Korea in exchange for silk that can be produced more cheaply in Korea. The production of 1 yard of silk requires the sacrifice of 10 bushels of rice in the United States, but only 0.5 bushels in Korea. Put differently, the opportunity cost of making 1 yard of silk is 10 bushels of rice in the United States but only 0.5 bushels in Korea. Korea, therefore, may specialize in making silk and export it to the United States for rice that the United States can grow more cheaply. When both workers grow rice in the United States, the total number of bushels of rice becomes 20. When both workers make silk in Korea, the total yards of silk becomes 4. After specialization, therefore, the total production of grain increases from 11 to 20 bushels, and the total production of silk increases from 3 to 4 yards. This increased output with specialization is shown in Table 19.4.

Benefits from Specialization

When nations specialize in production of products in which they have an absolute advantage, the total quantity of output produced by all nations increases. Does the increased total output necessarily mean that all nations benefit from specialization and trade? The answer depends on the prices of the two products during trade. Look again at Table 19.3. The opportunity cost of making 1 yard of silk in the United States before specialization was 10 bushels of rice, obtained by dividing 10 bushels by 1 yard. If the United States can buy silk at a price below 10 bushels of rice for each

TABLE 19.3 Per Capita Output in the United States and Korea before Specialization

Nation	Rice (bushels)	Silk (yards)
United States	10	1
Korea	1	2
Total	11	3

TABLE 19.4 Per Capita Output in the United States and Korea after Specialization

Nation	Rice (bushels)	Silk (yards)
United States	20	0
Korea	0	4
Total	20	4

yard of silk, the United States would benefit from the trade. The price of silk in Korea before specialization was 0.5 bushels of rice, obtained by dividing 1 bushel by 2 yards. If Korea can sell silk at a price higher than 0.5 bushels of rice for each yard of silk, Korea would benefit from trade. After specialization, therefore, the price of silk will range from 0.5 bushels to 10 bushels of rice per yard. The higher the price of silk, the greater the benefit that accrues to Korea.

In the case of rice, the price per bushel of rice in the United States before specialization was 0.1 yard of silk, obtained by dividing 1 yard by 10 bushels, and the price per bushel of rice in Korea before specialization was 2 yards of silk, obtained by dividing 2 yards by 1 bushel. The price per bushel of rice after specialization will range between 0.1 and 2 yards of silk. The higher the price per bushel of rice, the greater the benefit that accrues to the United States. Both countries benefit from trade so long as the prices of the two products remain within the ranges indicated as follows:

Price per yard of silk
    minimum   0.5 bushels
    maximum   10 bushels

Price per bushel of grain
    minimum   0.1 yards
    maximum   2 yards

Comparative Advantage

Based on figures given in Table 19.3, it is easy to understand why specialization and trade will benefit both the United States and Korea. The reality may be a little more complicated, however. Consider Table 19.5. Let us suppose that the increasing number of Koreans who migrate to the United States has increased the productivity of the U.S. silk maker from 1 to 4 yards. The United States now has an absolute advantage over Korea not only in rice growing but in silk making as well. Will specialization and trade still benefit both the United States and Korea? According to the theory of comparative advantage, the answer is *yes,* so long as the cost of growing rice relative to the cost of making silk is different between the two countries.

Specialization under Comparative Advantages
In Table 19.5, the cost of making 1 yard of silk in the United States is 2.5 bushels of rice, obtained by dividing 10 bushels by 4 yards. The cost of making 1 yard of silk in Korea is 0.5 bushels of rice,

TABLE 19.5 Per Capita Output in the United States and Korea before Specialization

Nation	Rice (bushels)	Silk (yards)
United States	10	4
Korea	1	2

obtained by dividing 1 bushel by 2 yards. The cost of making silk is still cheaper in Korea than in the United States. The cost of growing 1 bushel of rice in the United States is 0.4 yards of silk, obtained by dividing 4 yards by 10 bushels. The cost of growing 1 bushel of rice in Korea is 2 yards of silk, obtained by dividing 2 yards by 1 bushel. The cost of growing rice is still cheaper in the United States than in Korea. In Table 19.5, the United States is said to have a *comparative advantage in growing rice,* and Korea is said to have a *comparative advantage in making silk.* So long as nations have comparative advantages in production of certain products, these nations benefit from specialization and trade. The comparative advantage doctrine encourages the United States to specialize in growing rice and trade it for the silk that Korea has a comparative advantage in.

Comparative advantage may also be explained intuitively as follows. Suppose that Marvin Mitchelson, an attorney who became famous for his involvement in palimony suits, can type faster than his secretary. Mitchelson has an absolute advantage in both legal defense and typing. One hour of typing by Mitchelson, however, may require him to sacrifice as much as several thousand dollars of income from his legal profession. In other words, the opportunity cost of typing is much greater for Mitchelson than for his secretary. Mitchelson has a comparative advantage in legal defense, and his secretary has a comparative advantage in typing. Total income for both Mitchelson and his secretary can be maximized when Mitchelson limits his use of time to legal matters, while his secretary handles all his typing needs.

The Basis for Comparative Advantages

The credit for originating the comparative advantage doctrine has been attributed to several economists, including James Mill (1773–1836) and Robert Torrens (1780–1864). Modern economists nominate David Ricardo (1772–1823) as the one who developed, if not originated, the doctrine.

An interesting question relates to why there are comparative advantages. What is the basis for the existence of comparative advantage? The answer is given by Swedish economists Eli Hecksher (1879–1952) and Bertil Ohlin (1899–1979). According to Hecksher and Ohlin, a comparative advantage exists because there are differences among nations in their endowments of productive resources. Countries such as the United States that are endowed with a large amount of capital may export capital-intensive goods such as automobiles and computers, whereas countries such as Korea, Taiwan, and China that are endowed with relatively inexpensive labor may export labor-intensive goods such as silk and other textile products.

Another interesting question relates to whether a comparative advantage of a given nation will last year after year or have a tendency to diminish over time. According to Ohlin, a free migration of productive resources such as labor across nations will equalize wages and prices of other productive resources among these nations. Even if there is no movement of productive factors across national boundaries, Ohlin hypothesizes that free trade among nations has a tendency to equalize wages and prices of other productive resources.

Institutional Arrangements for Free Trade

The theory of comparative advantage provided a theoretical basis for promoting free trade among nations. Since the mid-1940s, several important arrangements were made for the promotion of free trade among all as well as groups of nations. The International Monetary Fund (IMF), the General Agreement on Tariffs and Trade (GATT), the European Economic Community (EEC), and the U.S.-Canada Trade Agreement are four examples.

International Monetary Fund

On July 22, 1944, the Articles of Agreement of the International Monetary Fund was adopted at the United Nations Monetary and Financial Conference in Bretton Woods, New Hampshire. The Articles took effect on December 27, 1945. The International Monetary Fund was established to promote international monetary cooperation through a permanent institution that provides the machinery for consultation and collaboration on international monetary problems: to facilitate the expansion and balanced growth of international trade and to promote exchange stability.[1]

The primary objective of IMF was to preserve stable exchange rates and to avoid competitive depreciations and devaluations. IMF thus developed a schedule of fixed exchange rates, established a fund on the basis of contributions in gold and money from the major trading nations, and made loans from the fund to individual countries so that these countries could maintain fixed exchange rates. According to the schedule, the U.S. dollar was established as a joint monetary standard and the price per ounce of gold was set at 35 U.S. dollars.

The fixed exchange rate system operated rather well for about 25 years. There were two problems, however. One was that the Soviet Union and other Eastern European countries never joined IMF. More important, as the value of the U.S. dollar declined in the late 1960s, nations preferred gold to the U.S. dollar. In August 1971 President Nixon announced a new policy that discontinued the exchange of gold for dollars, thus effectively ending the fixed exchange rate system. Many developing countries still pegged their currencies to the U.S. dollar. Industrialized nations, however, floated their currencies by adopting the flexible exchange rate system. Both fixed and flexible exchange rate systems are explained later in this chapter.

General Agreement on Tariffs and Trade

The upward trend of tariffs that culminated in the Hawley-Smoot Tariff Act of 1930 was reversed when Congress passed the Reciprocal Trade Agreements Act of 1934. This Act authorized the president to negotiate agreements with foreign nations for reduction of American tariffs up to 50 percent of the existing rates. The reduction of American tariffs depended on the willingness of other nations to reciprocate by lowering their tariffs on American exports. The Reciprocal Trade Agreements Act, however, encouraged tariff reductions between the United States and one other

---

[1]Margaret Garritsen de Vries, *The International Monetary Fund, 1966–1971: The system under stress,* Vol. 2 (Washington, D.C.: International Monetary Fund, 1976), pp. 97–98.

nation whenever tariff reductions were negotiated. This approach was broadened to include many nations when the General Agreement on Tariffs and Trade (GATT) was adopted on October 30, 1947.[2] GATT has provided a forum for the negotiation of tariff reductions on a multinational basis.[3]

Perhaps the most important component of GATT is the General Most-Favored Nation Treatment, spelled out in Article I in Part I of the Agreement. Article I states in part that "any advantage, favor, privilege or immunity granted by any contracting party to any product originating in or destined for any other country shall be accorded immediately and unconditionally to the like product originating in or destined for the territories of all other contracting parties."[4] This agreement is commonly known as the most-favored nation (MFN) treatment. Stated plainly, the MFN agreement requires a nation to levy the same amount of tariff on all like products that are imported from or exported to all nations that agreed to uphold GATT.

Another important component of GATT is Article XI, which requires contracting nations to eliminate quantitative restrictions such as quotas. Paragraph 1 of Article XI states in its entirety that "No prohibitions or restrictions other than duties, taxes or other charges, whether made effective through quotas, import or export licenses or other measures, shall be instituted or maintained by any contracting party on the importation of any product of the territory of any other contracting party or on the exportation or sale for export of any product destined for the territory of any other contracting party."[5]

European Economic Community

In 1946 Winston Churchill called upon European states to create "a kind of United States of Europe." This call for a united Europe was followed in 1947 by the Marshall Plan. George C. Marshall, then secretary of state, declared at the June 5, 1947 commencement at Harvard University:

> *Our policy is directed not against any country or doctrine but against hunger, poverty, desperation and chaos. Its purpose should be the revival of a working economy in the world so much as to permit the emergence of political and social conditions in which free institutions can exist. Such assistance, I am convinced, must not be on a piecemeal basis as various crises develop. Any assistance that this Government may render in the future should provide a cure rather than a mere palliative.[6]*

The Marshall Plan asked the European nations to draw up a joint program for the reconstruction of the continent devastated by World War II. The Organization for European Economic Cooperation (OEEC) was established in 1948 as a result of the Marshall Plan. It had two objectives: reconstruction of Europe with American aid and liberalization of trade among the European countries.

---

[2] For details on GATT see *United States statutes at large,* Vol. 61, Part 5, titled International Agreements Other Than Treaties (Washington, D.C.: U.S. Government Printing Office, 1948), pp. A11–A90.

[3] Countries that provided signatures to GATT at the time of its adoption in 1947 were Australia, Belgium, Brazil, Burma, Canada, Ceylon, Chile, China, Cuba, the Czechoslovak Republic, the French Republic, India, Lebanon, Luxembourg, Netherlands, New Zealand, Norway, Pakistan, Southern Rhodesia, Syria, South Africa, Great Britain, Northern Ireland, and the United States.

[4] *United States statutes at large,* Vol. 61, Part 5, p. A12.

[5] Ibid., pp. A32–A33.

[6] Gordon L. Weil, *A handbook on the European Economic Community* (New York: Frederick A. Praeger, 1965), pp. 4–5.

Many leaders in Europe felt that cooperation and discussion alone were not sufficient. In 1950, therefore, French Foreign Minister Robert Schuman proposed the European Coal and Steel Community (ECSC), designed to merge the coal, iron, and steel industries of those European countries willing to accept and execute decisions made by a group of officials completely independent of national control. The ECSC began functioning in 1952. The European unity movement took a new direction when the six members of the ECSC—Belgium, France, the Federal Republic of Germany, Italy, Luxembourg, and the Netherlands—agreed in 1955 at Messina, Italy, to create a full economic union. Negotiations on the new European Economic Community were carried on during the last half of 1956 and were signed by these nations on March 25, 1957. The EEC was officially created on January 1, 1958.[7] The EEC membership has been expanded to 12. The names of EEC countries and their years of entry are presented in Table 19.6.

The main functions of the EEC are described in the first chapter of the document that drafted the European Economic Community Treaty. There were two main objectives. The first objective was to eliminate customs duties within the common market. The starting point for the reduction was the average duty levied during the years 1953, 1954, and 1955, or the scheduled duty if it was lower. The other objective was to establish a common external tariff. Again the starting point for the calculation of the tariff was based either on the average of the duties levied during the years 1953, 1954, and 1955, or on the scheduled duty rate if it was lower. EEC has been a highly successful trade organization. Its latest objective is to establish a unified, open European market by December 31, 1992, by eliminating all trade barriers among all EEC countries. The establishment of one free trade zone within the EEC will encourage multinational companies outside the EEC to invest in joint ventures with EEC countries. Without a foothold within EEC countries, external tariffs by these countries would make it difficult for companies from other nations to maintain a significant trade with EEC countries.

U.S.-Canada Free Trade Agreement

In March 1985 at the Shamrock Summit, President Ronald Reagan of the United States and Prime Minister Brian Mulroney of Canada asked their trade officials to explore ways to reduce and eliminate existing barriers to trade between the United States and Canada. On January 2, 1988, President Reagan and Prime Minister Mulroney signed the final text of the U.S.-Canada Free Trade Agreement. The Agreement was subsequently approved by both the Canadian Parliament and the U.S. Congress, and took effect on January 2, 1989. The Agreement will eliminate all tariffs and most other restrictions on the flow of goods and services between the two countries by 1999.[8]

The Agreement in fact will create a free trade zone covering the entire territory of the United States and Canada. The free-trade zone established under the agreement, however, would differ from a common market. The European Economic Community, for example, maintains a unified trade policy toward the rest of the world. The U.S.-Canada free-trade zone would merely remove barriers to trade between the two countries. Canada and the United States will continue to have separate sets of tariffs and quotas on imports from the rest of the world. Until the U.S.-Canada Free Trade Agreement took effect, Israel was the only country that maintained a free-trade agreement with the United States.

---

[7]For early history of EEC, see Gordon L. Weil, *A handbook on the European Economic Community* (New York: Frederick A. Praeger, 1965), pp. 1–2.

[8]A facsimile report, reproduced by the United States Department of Energy, Office of Scientific and Technical Information, Tenn., DOE 15-0060 (no page numbers).

TABLE 19.6 Members of the EEC

Country	Year of Entry
France	1958
West Germany	1958
Italy	1958
Netherlands	1958
Belgium	1958
Luxembourg	1958
Britain	1973
Denmark	1973
Ireland	1973
Greece	1981
Portugal	1986
Spain	1986

PROTECTIONISM

Given a choice, we would prefer to have markets in which goods and services flow freely according to supply and demand. In reality, many domestic markets have imperfections and barriers that prevent them from functioning as they should. In trade among nations, we would also prefer an arrangement in which goods and services flow freely according to the comparative advantage doctrine. In reality, international markets are also subject to many barriers to free competition and trade. In this section we first study trade barriers and then study why nations pursue protectionism that keeps imports from flowing into these nations.

Trade Barriers

Trade barriers refer to government laws, regulations, policies, or practices that are intended either to protect domestic producers from foreign competition or to artificially stimulate exports of particular domestic products. According to this definition, practices by private businesses that have a similar effect on foreign trade and governmental measures that protect public health and national security are not considered trade barriers. When we think of trade barriers, we think of import duties and quotas. Actual trade barriers practiced in most countries are much more diverse and complicated than duties and quotas.[9] The following paragraphs introduce major trade barriers practiced by nations.

[9]Office of the United States Trade Representative, *Foreign trade barriers,* National Trade Estimate, 1986 Report (Washington, D.C.: U.S. Government Printing Office, 1986), pp. 281–291.

Tariffs and Other Import Charges

Tariffs are taxes on imports or the rates at which imported goods are taxed. Tariffs are used either to raise government revenues or to shield domestic industry from foreign competition, or both. Tariffs are also called customs duties or customs tariffs.

Tariffs distort the manner in which resources are allocated. When significant tariffs are imposed on, say, video recorders, the imports of video recorders decrease and additional domestic resources are employed to produce video recorders at a higher cost and most likely at a higher price as well. As a general rule, countries that adhere to the General Agreement on Tariffs and Trade (GATT) are bound to uphold the most-favored nation (MFN) principle. Exceptions to the MFN principle are permitted in the form of regional trading arrangements such as the European Economic Community, when a group of countries agrees to abolish barriers against imports from one another. Exceptions to MFN may also be allowed when developed nations extend nonreciprocal tariff preferences to developing nations. Developed nations may admit goods from developing nations at tariff rates below those imposed on competing imports from other developed nations.

Quantitative Restrictions

Quantitative restrictions refer to a wide range of nontariff measures restricting trade. These restrictions include complete bans on the import or export of specific commodities as well as import and export quotas that limit the import volume of specified commodities on either a global or country-specific basis. GATT generally prohibits the use of quantitative restrictions.

Additional Trade Barriers

Trade barriers other than tariffs and quantitative restrictions include import licensing, customs valuation, standards, and service barriers. **Import licensing** means requiring a permit as a prior condition for importing goods. Although quotas are often administered through licensing, import licensing is broader than import quotas and curtails trade by creating uncertainty, delays, and discrimination in license issuance as well as additional documentation costs. **Customs valuation** refers to the process of determining the value of imported goods by customs officers. Nations may arbitrarily overvalue imports to reduce the amount of imports. As part of arbitrary customs valuation, nations may also require unnecessary documents to discourage imports.

A **standard** is a technical specification approved by a recognized agency. Standards, testing, labeling, and certification are regulations that governments often use to protect the domestic economy by specifying minimal acceptable quality, performance, or safety. Trade problems arise when governments use unnecessary or discriminatory standards to restrict trade. Finally, GATT is primarily designed to deal with merchandise trade. Trade barriers relating to service industries have not attracted sufficient attention from trading nations. Governments may impose trade barriers in service industries such as banking, insurance, telecommunications, transportation, data processing, construction, and engineering.

Cases for Protectionism

Protectionism in foreign trade refers to the governmental adoption of trade barriers in order to restrict imports that may compete against domestically produced products. Protectionism is intended to protect domestic industries against foreign competition. All nations use protective measures, although the extent of use varies from one nation to another. Several arguments have been suggested to promote or justify protectionism. Most popular among these arguments are the infant industry argument, the high wages argument, and the national defense argument.

The Infant Industry Argument

One of the early applications of the infant industry argument was by Germany during the eighteenth century to protect its inefficient agricultural industry. Those who promote the infant industry argument argue that certain domestic industries are not mature enough to compete against foreign competition and, thus, need to be protected. If the domestic agricultural industry is not capable of competing in the world grain market, the infant industry argument claims that imports of agricultural products should be restricted until the domestic agricultural sector grows strong enough to compete against farmers in other nations.

One problem with the infant industry argument is that the argument can easily be extended to an old industry argument. The old industry argument may claim that domestic industries that have been declining need to be protected until these industries are reborn and grow strong enough to compete against foreign competition. The infant industry argument may also be abused by treating every emerging technology as an infant industry, as has been practiced by Japan and other newly industrialized countries (NICs).

The High Wages Argument

The high wages argument claims that certain domestic industries that pay high wages need to be protected from foreign competition, since these industries cannot compete against similar industries in other countries that pay low wages to their workers.

There are at least two problems with the high wages argument. One problem is that those in favor of the argument may claim that all industries in developed nations need to be protected, since average wages of an industry in developed nations are higher than average wages of a comparable industry in developing nations. The other problem is that a similar argument could be proposed in NICs to protect their industries against competition from developed nations. For instance, machines are cheaper in developed nations than in developing nations. Developing nations, therefore, could argue that their industries need to be protected against competition from developed nations that pay low prices for their machines. The high wages argument represents a direct rejection of the theory of comparative advantage. The comparative advantage doctrine suggests that developing nations specialize in producing and exporting products that can be produced with relatively inexpensive labor, while developed nations specialize in producing and exporting products that can be produced with relatively inexpensive machines.

The National Defense Argument

Like the infant industry argument, the national defense argument also has historical roots. During the seventeenth and eighteenth centuries, the Navigation Acts required Britain to use British ships and crews for coastal shipment along Britain and its colonies. Adam Smith used the national defense argument in defending the Navigation Acts. The modern version of the national defense argument is similar to Adam Smith's. Those who use the argument for promotion of protectionism claim that industries such as steel and shipbuilding need to be protected from foreign competition because these industries are vital to national defense. In international crises, steel products and merchant ships may not be available to the nation. Industries producing these products, therefore, should be preserved even if they are not as efficient as their counterparts in other countries.

An Evaluation of Protectionism

In 1981 the U.S. automobile industry succeeded in forcing Japan to *voluntarily* restrict its car exports to the United States to 1.7 million. The number was later expanded to 2.3 million. According to one estimate, the restriction added $2,500 to the price of a Japanese vehicle, and $750 to an American car. At the same time, Japan exported the more expensive luxury cars, further increasing profits of Japanese automobile manufacturers. In fact, the *voluntary* restriction of Japanese automobiles to the United States was so profitable to Japan that Japanese automobile manufacturers have voluntarily extended the involuntary restriction at least through the end of the 1980s.[10]

It is rather rare that a country forced to limit its exports actually benefits from the export restriction. More likely, the impact of a nation's protective measures in favor of certain domestic industries is the following. First, there are fewer imports of the protected product and thus sales of the domestically produced product increase. Owners and workers of protected industries, therefore, benefit in terms of jobs and higher wages. Second, the prices of products produced in protected industries are higher than they would be without protective trade barriers. All consumers of these products in the country that practices trade barriers, therefore, are forced to pay higher prices. Third, if these trade barriers are excessive, they may trigger retaliation from exporting countries. The retaliation will lead to decreased exports of products produced in the country that first adopted protective measures.

Overall, protectionism hurts practically everyone except those few associated with protected industries. Why, then, do all nations use protective trade barriers? The answer depends on whether the nation practicing protectionism is a developed nation or a developing nation.

In the case of developed nations, there are two reasons why governments adopt protective measures in favor of certain domestic industries. First, governments adopt protective measures mainly because of the pressure that special interest groups have exerted on elected officials. Elected officials make decisions in such a way that they maximize the probability of getting votes. When these politicians make decisions in favor of special interest groups, they win votes of these groups but are not likely to lose votes of the general public. Second, governments in developed nations adopt protective measures as a defensive strategy against trading partners that establish significant trade barriers.

Developing nations, on the other hand, need foreign exchange to purchase machines and other intermediate goods that they need for economic development. These nations, however, have a limited amount of exports. The comparative advantage doctrine does not work fast enough when the nation's level of education is low, resulting in inadequate managerial skills for its industrial sector. The comparative advantage doctrine suggests that developing nations should take advantage of the availability of low-wage workers and produce products most suitable for low-wage workers. These nations are rarely endowed with managerial skills that can utilize low wages for their comparative advantage. Consequently, developing nations raise protective walls to keep imports from depleting the nations' precious foreign exchange.

---

[10]For more on the story, see Robert W. Crandall, What have auto-import quotas wrought? *Challenge,* January-February 1985, pp. 40–47; and Robert J. Shapiro, A hidden tax on all our houses, *U.S. News & World Report,* March 21, 1988, p. 51.

FOREIGN EXCHANGE RATES

When we shop at Wal-Mart, we pay in dollars. When we buy German goods from Germany, we also pay in dollars. German businesses who sell goods to us, however, do not want dollars. They want payment in German marks that they can use in Germany. Dollars that we pay for German goods must somehow be converted to German marks. We study foreign exchange rates because different nations use different currencies.

Exchange Rates

Foreign exchange simply means the currency of other nations. The **foreign exchange rate** is the price of one currency in terms of another. Since an exchange rate involves two currencies, it can be expressed in two ways. Consider an exchange rate between the U.S. dollar and French franc. One expression of the exchange rate is the price of the dollar in terms of francs, which is 6 francs. In other words, $1.00 is worth 6 francs. The other expression is the price of the franc in terms of the dollar. The price of the franc in dollars is obtained by dividing $1.00 by 6 francs. One franc is worth 17 cents. Exchange rates as of June 1989 between the U.S. dollar and currencies of 30 selected nations are presented in Table 19.7. All exchange rates are expressed as the price of the dollar in terms of other currencies, with the exceptions of (1) the Australian dollar, (13) Ireland's punt, (18) New Zealand's dollar, and (30) the British pound, which are all expressed in terms of U.S. cents. Keep in mind that these exchange rates fluctuate daily.

Fluctuations in exchange rates have a direct effect on individuals as well as the entire economy of a nation. Consider an American GI stationed in Germany. (GI stands for "government issue" and is slang meaning a member of the U.S. armed forces.) Suppose that the exchange rate between the U.S. dollar and German mark is 1 to 2. In other words, the price of the dollar in terms of the mark is 2 marks. Suppose that the GI rents a room from a German who charges 400 marks. Since one dollar is 2 marks, 400 marks are equivalent to 200 dollars. The GI thus pays $200 to the German landlord. Suppose that the German mark becomes scarcer and the exchange rate doubles, so that the price of the dollar is reduced from 2 marks to 1 mark. The German landlord still charges the same 400 marks, but the poor GI now has to pay $400.

Consider another example. Suppose that the value of the dollar falls by half against most foreign currencies. The price of the dollar in terms of Austrian schillings falls from 12 schillings to 6 schillings; the price of the dollar in terms of Indian rupees falls from 16 rupees to 8 rupees; the price of the dollar in terms of Sweden's krona falls from 6 kronas to 3 kronas; and so on. When the value of the dollar falls, foreign exporters to the United States will demand more dollars for their products, since the dollar is now worth half its previous value. Suppose, for instance, that the price of the dollar in terms of francs was 6 francs and a French brandy exporter previously charged 180 francs for a bottle of Cognac. Since the exchange rate was one dollar to 6 francs, we paid $30 for the bottle of Cognac. Suppose that the value of the dollar falls so that the exchange rate changes from $1.00 = 6 francs to $1.00 = 3 francs. The new exchange rate means that $30 are now worth only 90 francs. If the French exporter still wants 180 francs, as is likely, we now have to pay $60 for the same bottle of Cognac. In other words, the falling value of the dollar against most foreign currencies is inflationary in the United States because it raises the dollar prices of imports.

TABLE 19.7 Selected Foreign Exchange Rates
(Currency units per dollar unless noted otherwise)

Country/currency	June 1989
1. Australia/dollar, value in U.S. cents	75.61
2. Austria/schilling	13.912
3. Belgium/franc	41.414
4. Canada/dollar	1.1986
5. China, P.R./yuan	3.7314
6. Denmark/krone	7.7087
7. Finland/markka	4.4302
8. France/franc	6.7135
9. Germany/deutsche mark	1.9789
10. Greece/drachma	170.42
11. Hong Kong/dollar	7.7934
12. India/rupee	16.420
13. Ireland/punt, value in U.S. cents	134.92
14. Italy/lira	1434.40
15. Japan/yen	143.98
16. Malaysia/ringgit	2.7086
17. Netherlands/guilder	2.2292
18. New Zealand/dollar, value in U.S. cents	57.376
19. Norway/krone	7.1852
20. Portugal/escudo	164.92
21. Singapore/dollar	1.9572
22. South Africa/rand	2.7828
23. South Korea/won	669.43
24. Spain/peseta	126.55
25. Sri Lanka/rupee	33.475
26. Sweden/krona	6.6872
27. Switzerland/franc	1.7089
28. Taiwan/dollar	26.023
29. Thailand/baht	25.909
30. United Kingdom/pound, value in U.S. cents	155.30

Source: Federal Reserve Bulletin 75(August 1989):A70.

Determinants of Exchange Rates

An exchange rate is defined as the price of one nation's currency in terms of the currency of another nation. Like prices of other goods and services, the exchange rate is also determined by supply and demand. The price of the dollar in terms of other currencies goes up when the demand for dollars is greater than their supply. In this case the dollar is said to have *appreciated*. The price of the dollar in terms of other currencies falls when the supply of dollars is greater than their demand. In this case the dollar is said to have *depreciated*. The term **devaluation** may be used synonymously with depreciation. Devaluation, however, frequently means the depreciation of a currency that results from a government's policy to lower the value of the nation's currency. Numerous variables affect the demand and supply of dollars. Let us illustrate some of these variables.

The demand for the dollar increases and thus the price of the dollar in terms of other currencies increases if

1. the quality of U.S. products improves relative to the quality of foreign products so that foreign consumers demand more of the U.S. products;
2. foreign businesses purchase more U.S. services such as shipping, insurance, and satellite communication;
3. more foreigners visit the United States for sightseeing, study, and business meetings;
4. other nations become politically unstable relative to the United States;
5. the rate of inflation in other nations accelerates relative to that in the United States so that the value of currencies of these nations falls; and
6. governments of other nations purchase dollars.

The supply of the dollar increases and thus the price of the dollar in terms of other currencies decreases if

1. the quality of U.S. products falls relative to the quality of foreign products so that U.S. consumers demand more foreign products;
2. U.S. businesses utilize more foreign services such as shipping, insurance, and satellite communication;
3. more U.S. citizens visit other nations for sightseeing, study, and business meetings;
4. the rate of inflation in the United States accelerates relative to price changes in other nations so that the value of the dollar within the United States falls; and
5. governments of other nations sell dollars.

Exchange Rate Systems

Exchange rates may be fixed by governments or allowed to vary according to supply and demand. If they are fixed by governments, there is a fixed exchange rate system. If they are allowed to vary, there is a flexible exchange rate system. If they are allowed to vary according to changes in the value of another currency, there is a pegged exchange rate system.

Fixed Exchange Rate System
The **fixed exchange rate** system is an arrangement among countries in which the value of a currency is fixed to the value of another currency or to gold. One of the fixed exchange rate systems is the gold standard system. Under the gold standard system, the value of a currency is stated in terms of a certain amount of gold, and the government promises to buy and sell its own currency in

EXCHANGE RATE ARRANGEMENTS IN REALITY

It is easy to say that some countries practice the freely flexible exchange rate system and others practice the pegged exchange rate system. When we are asked to name countries that practice the flexible exchange rate system, we usually name the United States, Britain, Japan, Canada, and perhaps one or two more. When we are asked to name countries that practice the pegged exchange rate system, however, few of us can name them. This box lists the types of exchange rate systems and countries that practice these systems as of March 31, 1988.

The following nations practice the freely flexible exchange rate system, known also as the floating or independently floating exchange rate system:

Australia	Japan	South Africa
Bolivia	Lebanon	Spain
Canada	Maldives	United Kingdom
The Gambia	New Zealand	United States
Ghana	Nigeria	Uruguay
Guinea	Philippines	Zaire

Currencies of the following nations are floating, but the flexibility is limited either through adjustments by the government or through participation of the European Monetary System:

Argentina	Egypt	Jamaica	Qatar
Bahrain	France	Korea	Singapore
Belgium	Germany, FR	Luxembourg	Saudi Arabia
Brazil	Greece	Madagascar	Sri Lanka
Chile	Guinea-Bissau	Mauritania	Tunisia
China, People's R.	Iceland	Mexico	Turkey
Colombia	India	Morocco	U. Arab Emirates
Costa Rica	Indonesia	Netherlands	Yugoslavia
Denmark	Ireland	Pakistan	
Dominican Rep.	Italy	Portugal	

Finally, no fewer than 96 nations maintained pegged exchange rate systems in which the value of a nation's currency was pegged either to another currency or to a currency composite. These nations include Afghanistan, Austria, The Bahamas, El Salvador, Grenada, Hungary, Iran, Iraq, Israel, Liberia, Malaysia, Mozambique, Nicaragua, Norway, Peru, Poland, Sweden, Suriname, Thailand, and Vietnam.

Source: International Monetary Fund, *Exchange arrangements and exchange restrictions, annual report 1988* (Washington, D.C.: International Monetary Fund, 1988), p. 11.

exchange for the stated amount of gold. Suppose that the United States maintains the gold standard system and fixes the value of one ounce of gold at $500. Under the gold standard system, the U.S. government accepts $500 dollars in exchange for one ounce of gold from anyone who demands it. All nations abandoned the gold standard system during the Great Depression years, including Great Britain in 1931 and the United States in 1933.

After World War II, nations adopted the Bretton Woods system in which the U.S. dollar and gold were established as international monetary standards. The values of all other currencies were fixed in relation to the dollar and thus to one another. Under this system exchange rates of individual nations were allowed to change subject to the approval from the International Monetary Fund.

Flexible Exchange Rate System

The Bretton Woods system ended in August 1971, when President Nixon no longer allowed any exchange of gold for dollars even with foreign governments and central banks. Since 1971 some nations, including Canada, Japan, the United Kingdom, and the United States, adopted a flexible exchange rate system in which exchange rates were allowed to fluctuate with no governmental interference. The **flexible exchange rate system** is an arrangement in which exchange rates are allowed to float according to the forces of supply and demand in the foreign exchange market. For this reason, the flexible exchange rate system is also called the **freely flexible** or **floating exchange rate system.** When the floating is controlled through occasional government interference, the exchange rate system is called the **managed floating exchange rate system.**

There is one main advantage of the flexible exchange rate system, in that the system is capable of correcting a deficit in the balance of trade without government interference. To understand how the self-correcting mechanism works, let us consider two nations, the United States and Mexico. Suppose that the two nations maintain a balanced trade and the current exchange rate is $1.00 = 200 pesos. Suppose that a significant increase in oil drilling activities among OPEC nations causes the export of Mexican oil to the United States to decrease, while Mexican imports of U.S. products remain the same. Imports from the United States to Mexico are now greater than exports from Mexico to the United States, causing a deficit in the balance of trade in Mexico. The deficit means that the dollar becomes scarce in Mexico. As the demand for dollars increases in Mexico, the value of the dollar rises and the value of the peso falls. Under the flexible exchange rate system, the exchange rate may change from the previous $1.00 = 200 pesos to $1.00 = 400 pesos. One dollar is now worth 400 pesos instead of 200 pesos.

As the value of the dollar rises, U.S. consumers find the prices of Mexican products to be only half the previous level, and trips to Mexico become significantly less expensive. At the same time, Mexicans find that prices of U.S. products have doubled, and trips to the United States are significantly more expensive. Exports from Mexico to the United States rise, while exports from the United States to Mexico fall. If the process is allowed to work itself out, the exchange rate will eventually return to a level such as $1.00 = 200 pesos at which the trade between the two nations is again balanced. The sequence is summarized in Table 19.8.

Pegged Exchange Rate System

Most nations do not float their currencies. Instead, these nations *peg* their currencies to changes in the value of the U.S. dollar, French franc, or a combination of selected currencies. When a nation's currency is pegged to changes in the value of another currency, the exchange rate system is known as the **pegged exchange rate system.** In 1988 more than 90 nations that were members of the International Monetary Fund had pegged exchange arrangements of one form or another.

TABLE 19.8 Self-Correction of Deficit under the Flexible Exchange Rate System

Sequence	Adjustment
1.	Initial equilibrium exchange rate
	$1.00 = 200 pesos
2.	Changes in trade
	Imports greater than exports in Mexico
3.	Changes in exchange rate
	Demand for dollar in Mexico rises
	Value of dollar rises
	Value of peso falls
4.	Hypothetical interim exchange rate
	$1.00 = 400 pesos
5.	Self-correction
	Mexican goods cheaper to the United States
	U.S. goods more expensive to Mexicans
	Exports from Mexico to the United States increase
	Imports from the United States to Mexico decrease
6.	Return to the new equilibrium exchange rate such as
	$1.00 = 200 pesos

SUMMARY

The balance of payments is the record of all transactions that affect the flow of a nation's currency. Two nations benefit from specialization and trade so long as the cost of producing one product relative to another is different between the two nations. Several important institutional arrangements were made to promote free trade among all or groups of nations. The International Monetary Fund (IMF) was established in 1945 to preserve stable exchange rates and to avoid competitive depreciations and devaluations. The General Agreement on Tariffs and Trade (GATT) was adopted in 1947 to reduce trade barriers on a multinational basis. The most-favored nation agreement was made in GATT and requires a nation to levy the same amount of tariff on all like products that are imported from or exported to nations that agreed to uphold GATT. The European Economic Community was created in 1958 to eliminate customs duties and thus promote free trade within the common market. In 1988, the U.S.-Canada Free Trade Agreement was signed to eliminate all tariffs and most other restrictions on the flow of goods and services between the two countries by 1999. Trading nations have adopted various forms of trade barriers to keep imports from flowing into these nations. Protectionism has been justified by the infant industry argument, the high wages argument, and the national defense argument. Protectionism tends to benefit owners and workers of protected industries in terms of jobs and higher wages. It also tends to raise the prices of products produced in protected industries and triggers retaliation. A foreign exchange rate is the price of one currency in terms of another. If the value of the dollar rises in terms of foreign currencies, there is an appreciation of the dollar. The higher value of the dollar makes imports cheaper to U.S. consumers and exports from the United States more expensive to foreign buyers. The higher value of the dollar also makes foreign travel by U.S. residents cheaper since the same dollar now commands a greater quantity of foreign currencies. Markets for foreign exchange rates are of three types: the fixed exchange rate system, the flexible exchange rate system, and the pegged exchange rate system.

EXERCISES

1. Explain the difference between the balance of trade and the balance of payments.

2. Suppose that the United States can produce both personal computers and wheat more cheaply than the Soviet Union. Assuming that these are the only products both nations produce, can specialization and trade between the two nations benefit both nations?

3. Suppose that a dentist can type faster than her typist. Should the dentist fire her typist and type all bills for herself, or should the dentist specialize in treating patients and leave the typing to her typist? Why?

4. Shortly after World War II, the German and the Japanese economies were in shambles, and wages were very low. As postwar prosperity swept both nations with a relatively free trade with the United States, both Germany and Japan made rapid economic progress. What would have been Ohlin's prediction regarding the difference between U.S. wages and wages in Germany and Japan?

5. What are the primary objectives of IMF, GATT, and EEC?

6. What would be the impact of a significant tariff on imports of shoes?

7. Protectionism is not likely to benefit many nations, including the one that adopts trade barriers. Why are nations practicing protectionism?

8. Determine whether each of the following represents an appreciation of the dollar or a depreciation of the dollar:

From	To	Appreciation or Depreciation
$1.00 = 200 pesos	$1.00 = 300 pesos	
$1.00 = 140 yen	$1.00 = 180 yen	
$1.00 = 6 krona	$1.00 = 5 krona	
$1.00 = 1,300 lira	$1.00 = 1,500 lira	
$1.90 = 1 pound	$1.50 = 1 pound	

9. Suppose that the exchange rate between the U.S. dollar and the Japanese yen changes from $1.00 = 125 yen to $1.00 = 150 yen. Determine if each of the following will either increase or decrease:

   a. imports from Japan
   b. exports to Japan
   c. Japanese tourists in California
   d. Japanese tourists in Georgia
   e. U.S. tourists in Tokyo
   f. dollar value of apartment rents for U.S. soldiers stationed in Yokohama
   g. use of Japanese ships by U.S. businesses

10. Determine for the following cases whether the price of the dollar in terms of other currencies increases or decreases:

   a. The relative quality of U.S. products improves so that foreigners demand more U.S. products.
   b. More foreigners visit the U.S. for sightseeing.
   c. Other nations become politically unstable relative to the United States.
   d. U.S. businesses use more foreign services such as shipping, insurance, and satellite communication.
   e. The rate of inflation in the United States accelerates in relation to other countries so that the value of the dollar within the U.S. falls.

SUGGESTED READINGS

Crandall, Robert W. (1985). What have auto-import quotas wrought? *Challenge,* January-February, pp. 40–47.

Explains that the voluntary export restriction of Japanese cars to the United States helped Japan and hurt the United States.

Culbertson, John M. (1986). The folly of free trade. *Harvard Business Review,* September-October, pp. 122–128.

Explains why the U.S. trade policy that tries to force free trade on other nations is doomed to failure.

Office of the United States Trade Representative. (1986). *Foreign trade barriers.* National Trade Estimate, 1986 Report. Washington, D.C.: U.S. Government Printing Office.

An excellent source for description of specific trade barriers by country.

Ohlin, Bertil. (1933). *Interregional and international trade.* Cambridge, Mass.: Harvard University.

A seminal study that extended the comparative advantage doctrine.

Rosensweig, Jeffery A., and Koch, Paul D. (1988). The U.S. dollar and the "delayed J-curve." Federal Reserve Bank of Atlanta *Economic Review,* July-August, pp. 2–15.

Explains that the J-curve works only after a delay. According to the J-curve hypothesis, the trade deficit initially worsens after a currency depreciation, bottoms out, and eventually improves to a point above its original level.

20

The United States in the Global Economy

Imbalance in the U.S. Balance of Trade

Trade Deficit and Floating Exchange Rate System

Macroeconomic Policies and Foreign Trade

Foreign Direct Investment

SOME OF US have a tendency to propose solutions that are too simplistic for the problems at hand. When the U.S. imports of lumber products from Canada exceed our exports of similar products to Canada, we propose a quota on imports of Canadian lumber products. When the U.S. steel industry has difficulty competing with imported steel from Japan, we propose restrictions on imports of Japanese steel. When the U.S. automobile industry loses part of its market share to Japan, we force Japanese automobile manufacturers to restrict their exports of automobiles to the United States. When Australia and Canada become more successful than we are in selling wheat in the world market, we propose that the government subsidize wheat farmers. These proposed solutions are microeconomic in nature and are focused on one industry or one country at a time. As pointed out in Chapter 19, these solutions may not solve the problems in the long run. There is another approach to solving the problems that arise from trade among nations. The approach is macroeconomic and involves fiscal as well as monetary policy. Because of the interrelations among nations, fiscal and monetary policies in one nation have a direct effect on trade among nations.

The learning objective of this chapter is to combine the issues of foreign trade and domestic macroeconomic policies so that we can study (1) the mutual interdependence between trade policies and domestic economic policies, and (2) policy options available to us and, for that matter, to the rest of the world.

IMBALANCE IN THE U.S. BALANCE OF TRADE

The 1980s was not the first time the U.S. economy had to deal with trade deficits. The United States had to endure deficit in foreign trade during most of its first 100 years.[1] Still, the large trade deficit that the U.S. economy experienced in the late 1980s was disturbing news to many.

Seeds of the 1980s' Trade Deficit

In retrospect, the seeds of the large trade deficit in the United States were sown by two changes in fiscal policy that were the bases of President Reagan's economic policies, known in the popular press as **Reaganomics.** One change was the Economic Recovery Tax Act of 1981. The Act substantially increased businesses' incentives to invest, especially in equipment and in commercial buildings. The after-tax profitability of investment was raised by increasing the size of depreciation write-offs and by making the investment tax credit more widely available. **Depreciation write-offs** are the amounts that firms can deduct from their taxable income for depreciation allowance. The **investment tax credit** is the amount, usually a fraction of capital investment, that firms are allowed to subtract from tax liability for the encouragement of business investment.

Owing to the Economic Recovery Tax Act, investment spending grew at an average annual rate of 8.9 percent from 1981 through 1985, significantly faster than the growth rate of GNP. The Act also cut personal income taxes, although much of the cut was offset by increases in social security taxes. Consumption spending rose at an average annual rate of 8.3 percent during 1981

---

[1]For the history of U.S. foreign investment, see Robert E. Lipsey, Changing patterns of international investment in and by the United States, in Martin Feldstein (ed.), *The United States in the world economy* (Chicago: The University of Chicago Press, 1988), pp. 475–544.

through 1985, also faster than the growth rate of GNP. The other change embodied in the economic policies of the Reagan administration was the increase in military expenditures to modernize defense capabilities. Largely as a result of the defense build-up, federal government purchases rose at an annual average rate of 11.3 percent during 1981 through 1985. By comparison, GNP grew at a 7.9 percent annual rate during the same period.[2]

Overall, total domestic spending increased at an annual rate of 8.5 percent during 1981 through 1985. Total output measured in nominal GNP, however, increased at an annual rate of 7.9 percent. The difference in growth rates between total spending and total output raised total domestic spending on goods and services in the United States from slightly less than 99 percent of U.S. GNP in 1980 to 102 percent of U.S. GNP in 1985. That 3 percent swing corresponds to the deterioration in the U.S. trade balance from a surplus of a little more than 1 percent of GNP in 1980 to a deficit of 2 percent of GNP in 1985.

Why did the U.S. GNP not increase to satisfy the growing demands for goods and services? According to Keynesian economics, output should increase as demand increases so long as there exists a large amount of unemployed resources. Unemployment rates were high and excess capacity did exist in the U.S. economy during the period. The increase in output, however, was not sufficient to meet the increasing demand, causing rising imports to fill the gap between aggregate demand and aggregate supply. We need to explain why the U.S. output did not increase fast enough to curb rising imports.

Causes of the 1980s' Trade Deficit

During the first half of the 1980s, the dollar appreciated and the high value of the dollar made imported goods relatively cheaper in the United States compared to domestically produced goods. The high value of the dollar also made U.S. products relatively more expensive in the world market. The question that we wish to answer then becomes why the value of the dollar increased in the early 1980s.

To find the answer we need to look at both fiscal and monetary policies. In fiscal policy, the 1981 Tax Act increased domestic spending, which led to an increase in demand for loanable funds. The increased domestic spending also means a decrease in saving, which led to a decrease in the supply of loanable funds. In monetary policy, the Federal Reserve tightened money supply to reduce the rate of inflation that was at a double-digit level in the late 1970s. The reduced rate of growth of money supply led to a further decrease in the supply of loanable funds. Combining fiscal policy that increased the demand for loanable funds and monetary policy that decreased the supply of loanable funds resulted in higher rates of interest, both nominal and real. The higher interest rates in the United States relative to those in other countries made U.S. financial securities more attractive to foreign investors. To purchase U.S. financial securities, foreign investors needed dollars. These investors, therefore, sold foreign currencies to buy dollars in the foreign exchange market. The increased demand for dollars pushed up the value of the dollar.

As the value of the dollar increased, imports to the United States became cheaper to U.S. consumers, while U.S. exports to other nations became more expensive to consumers in these

---

[2]Stephen A. Meyer, Trade deficits and the dollar: A macroeconomic perspective, Federal Reserve Bank of Philadelphia *Business Review*, September-October 1986, pp. 15–25.

nations. Consequently, imports to the United States from other nations rose, but exports from the United States to other nations fell. The deficit in the U.S. balance of trade became greater.

Trade Deficit and Capital Flows

A deficit in the U.S. balance of trade means that we buy more from other nations than we sell to these nations. To see what happens when a nation experiences a continuing trade deficit, let us suppose that there are only two nations in the world: the United States and Japan. Let us also suppose that for several years in a row the United States buys from Japan more than it sells to Japan. There is a deficit in the U.S. balance of trade. Dollars flow to Japan as payments for imports. What will the Japanese do with dollars? The Japanese need yen in Japan, not dollars, for daily transactions. Somehow, these surplus dollars in Japanese possession will have to return to the United States. In other words, capital must be transferred from Japan to the United States. The Japanese have three choices in disposing of the surplus dollars: short-term capital transfers, portfolio investment, and foreign direct investment.[3]

Short-Term Capital Transfers
The first type of capital transfer is short-term capital transfers. **Short-term capital transfers** are defined as financial transactions that involve financial instruments having maturities of less than one year. The primary characteristic of short-term capital transfers is that those who transfer financial assets seek interest income on securities that expire in less than a year. If a Japanese investor buys a six-month certificate of deposit from a U.S. bank, the transaction is considered a short-term capital transfer into the United States. If a Japanese corporation opens a bank account in Atlanta, it is a short-term capital transfer out of Japan into the United States. The amount involved in short-term capital transfers between countries is large.

One problem with short-term capital transfers is that these transactions involve highly liquid financial instruments with short-term maturities. Short-term capital transfers are highly responsive to minor changes in yields or exchange rates. These funds can be moved around quickly and easily among nations.

Portfolio Investment
The second type of capital transfer is portfolio investment. **Portfolio investment** is defined as financial transactions that involve stocks and bonds with no intention of controlling the firms that issue these stocks and bonds. Portfolio investment has two characteristics. One characteristic is that those who transfer financial assets seek interest or dividend income on securities such as stocks and bonds that either do not have any expiration date or expire in more than a year. The other characteristic is that portfolio investors do not seek control of the company that issues these stocks and bonds. If Japanese investors purchase shares of IBM common stock on the New York Stock Exchange and this purchase does not result in the effective control of IBM by Japanese, it is a portfolio investment.

---

[3]Niles C. Schoening, A slow leak: Effects on the United States of shifts in international investment, The University of Tennessee *Survey of Business* 23(Spring 1988):21–26.

Foreign Direct Investment

The third type of capital transfer is foreign direct investment. **Foreign direct investment** refers to the acquisition of assets in another nation through purchase or new construction with the intention of seeking control over firms. Foreign direct investment usually involves investment in branches and subsidiaries abroad by domestic parent companies. When Toyota built a new automobile assembly plant in Tennessee, Toyota made a direct investment. When Hyundai built a new automobile manufacturing plant in Canada, Hyundai made a foreign direct investment. If Shell Oil of Great Britain purchases an operating chemical plant in California, Shell Oil is making a foreign direct investment.

Interim Summary

Before we proceed, let us summarize our findings thus far. In the first half of the 1980s, aggregate demand increased rapidly due to Reaganomics, but aggregate supply did not increase as rapidly as aggregate demand. High interest rates in the United States attracted foreign investors and pushed up the value of the dollar in the foreign exchange market. The high value of the dollar made foreign products cheaper to U.S. consumers but U.S. products more expensive to consumers in other nations. Consequently, imports of foreign goods into the United States rose, but exports of U.S. goods to other nations fell. What this sequence of events means is that the excess aggregate demand in the United States was met through increased imports rather than increased domestic production. The result was a large deficit in the balance of trade. A significant amount of dollars that were used to pay for imports returned to the United States through capital transfers from trading nations that enjoyed trade surplus against the United States.

Effects of the U.S. Trade Deficit

What would happen if the large amount of the trade deficit in the United States were allowed to continue? If the effects of such long-term U.S. trade deficit were not harmful to anyone, there would be no need to be concerned about the deficit. If the effects were harmful to the health of the United States as well as other nations, we would need to know more about the effects of the deficit. Let us discuss the effects from two different perspectives: global and domestic.

To understand the effects of the U.S. trade deficit on other trading nations in the world, we need to understand the special role that the U.S. economy has played in the global economy since World War II.

The U.S. Dollar in the Global Economy

Like most developing countries today, the United States was a debtor nation during most of the early years of its history. Until 1914, we were buying more from European countries than we were selling to these countries. With the money that they received for their exports to the United States, European nations invested heavily in the United States. When World War I broke out in 1914, the U.S. trade balance turned in favor of the United States. Major European nations that were creditors of the United States were forced to sell their U.S. investments to pay for arms that they needed. The position of the United States as the world's major creditor nation strengthened during World War II. At the end of the war the U.S. dollar was the strongest currency in the world, and the United States possessed more than one-half of the world's gold reserves.

The position of the United States in the global economy was accepted as being pivotal at the World Monetary Conference held in Bretton Woods, New Hampshire, in 1944. The Bretton Woods Agreement selected the U.S. dollar as the only currency that could be exchanged for gold. The Bretton Woods Agreement led governments to fix exchange rates between any two currencies by making these currencies convertible into dollars at a fixed exchange rate. If, for instance, the German mark and Japanese yen were fixed at $1.00 = 2 marks and $1.00 = 200 yen, the exchange rate between mark and yen would be 1 mark = 100 yen.

Since the U.S. dollar was the only currency exchangeable for gold, the dollar became the reserve currency that other trading nations were willing to hold in lieu of gold. In order for the Bretton Woods system to work, there had to be a significant supply of dollars outside the United States for other countries to hold. A massive increase in dollars available in other nations was achieved in three ways: the Marshall Plan to European nations, growing foreign aid to developing nations, and an increase in foreign direct investment mostly by American multinational corporations.

By 1960 the outflow of the U.S. dollar had become so substantial that the value of dollar holdings of other nations exceeded the value of U.S. gold holdings. If all nations holding dollars were to ask for gold in exchange for dollars, the United States would not be able to support the exchange as mandated in the Bretton Woods Agreement. The Bretton Woods system ended in 1971 when President Nixon made the announcement that the dollar could no longer be converted into gold. With the end of the Bretton Woods system, exchange rates have since been allowed to float or be pegged to other currencies.

Global Effects of the U.S. Trade Deficit

In the short run, nations that export to the United States will enjoy increased output and employment from the U.S. trade deficit. These exporting nations will also be able to increase their direct investment in the United States and thus enjoy the ownership of U.S. businesses along with the additional income that the ownership generates. In the long run, however, the continuing trade deficit in the United States would not be beneficial to exporting nations.

Although the U.S. dollar has lost much of the glitter that it enjoyed in the 1950s and the 1960s, it still plays the role of a leading currency in the world. A large trade deficit in the United States tends to create uncertainty in the global financial market and encourage speculation by transferring assets in search of a higher return based on fluctuating exchange rates rather than on productivity differences.

If the trade deficit in the United States continues indefinitely, other nations may eventually lose confidence in the U.S. dollar. The loss in confidence in the U.S. dollar will encourage all trading nations to search for a substitute currency that these nations can use as reserve currency in foreign trade. The absence of a dominant currency that nations can use as a reserve currency may result in confusion among importers and exporters, and finally a reduced level of world trade.

Domestic Effects of the U.S. Trade Deficit

Suppose that the deficit in the U.S. balance of trade continues year after year. How will the deficit affect the domestic economy?

In the short run, no one will notice any difference. A Big Mac and a bucket of fried chicken will still be affordable, and the same number of greenbacks will pay the rent. In fact, a cheaper dollar will make U.S. goods cheaper to consumers in other nations, exports will increase, and more jobs will be created to produce rising exports.

But the cheaper dollar will eventually erode our standard of living. Imports will become so expensive that they will be luxury goods. In the extreme, Hyundais and Yugos may become as expensive to a middle class family as BMWs and Volvos are these days. As prices of imports increase, the prices of domestically produced products will also rise. There will be inflation.

As the deficit persists, however, the United States will gradually lose control of U.S. businesses to foreign investors. A significant amount of financial assets, plants, and other businesses will be bought and thus controlled by foreign investors. An increasing quantity of the output that Americans produce may have to be shipped to other nations as payments for excessive imports. Long-term investment decisions of firms located in the United States but controlled by foreign investors may be made more for the interests of nations that own these firms than for the interest of the United States.

A falling currency affects interest rates. Foreign investors will have to be bribed through high interest rates so that they do not dump their investments. If they dump their investments and no longer accept dollars, there will be a recession in the United States and eventually in the rest of the world.

The falling value of the dollar may also have an important impact on national security decisions. The trade deficit will cause the value of the dollar to decline. The decline in the value of the dollar will make it more expensive for the United States to maintain troops abroad. The U.S. government may respond to this higher financial burden of maintaining troops overseas by cutting back such overseas commitment. Alternatively, other nations that own a large amount of U.S. assets may demand a stronger defense commitment from the United States, making the U.S. deficit in the balance of payments a hostage in world politics. The large trade deficit in the U.S. balance of payments should be corrected or at least be reduced.

TRADE DEFICIT AND FLOATING EXCHANGE RATE SYSTEM

We studied in Chapter 19 that one of the main advantages of the floating exchange rate system was that the deficit in a nation's balance of trade would be self-correcting. The deficit lowers the value of the currency of the nation that experiences the deficit. The lower value of the currency, in turn, encourages exports and discourages imports so that the deficit is reduced. The value of the dollar stopped rising in 1985 and fell significantly against most foreign currencies during the late 1980s. As the value of the dollar fell, imports to the United States were expected to fall and exports from the United States were expected to rise. In theory, the floating exchange rate system tends to correct a nation's trade deficit without government interference.

In this section we study practical aspects of the procedure through which the self-correcting mechanism of the floating exchange rate system reduces the trade deficit.

A Slow Response

The market mechanism tends to work rather slowly in correcting a trade deficit. Sure enough, the U.S. trade deficit was slow to respond to the falling value of the dollar. There were three reasons for the slow response of the U.S. trade deficit to the falling value of the dollar.[4] First, some foreign

---

[4]Charles B. Garrison, Eliminating the trade deficit: What are the options?, The University of Tennessee *Survey of Business* 23(Spring 1988):15–20.

producers apparently cut profit margins in an effort to prevent a major rise in the dollar price of their goods. Because they had been able to raise profit margins when the value of the dollar was high, this course of action was not too difficult for foreign producers. Second, the value of the dollar declined relatively little against the currencies of some major trading partners, especially Canada, Korea, and Taiwan. Third, in terms of the real volume of physical goods, exports increased faster than imports, but the dollar price of imports rose sharply due to the falling value of the dollar. As a result, the dollar value of imports continued to rise even when the physical volume of imports fell.

Feldstein's Hypothesis

Another hypothesis was proposed by Martin Feldstein to explain how the market would react to the U.S. trade deficit.[5] The theory of flexible exchange rate suggests that the value of the dollar will continue to fall so long as the U.S. trade deficit continues. Eventually, the decline in the value of the dollar will be sufficient to eliminate the trade deficit. According to Feldstein, however, it is not the falling value of the dollar that will reverse the U.S. trade deficit; the U.S. trade deficit will be eliminated because the world financial markets will not indefinitely finance the flow of capital to the United States. Without the continuous flow of foreign capital to the United States, the U.S. trade deficit would not be able to continue.

Feldstein explains that if the dollar remained at its level of early 1987, the U.S. trade deficit would shrink from $170 billion to about $90 billion but would then stop declining. To finance the $90 billion deficit, it would be necessary for the rest of the world to send to the United States $90 billion each year as a capital transfer. In addition to this capital inflow, the United States would also require additional credit from the rest of the world to finance the interest and dividends that accrued on cumulative foreign investments in the United States. Feldstein hypothesizes that foreign investors would be unwilling to continue to devote so much of their own savings to investments in U.S. assets. If they did, the capital inflow to the United States would be equivalent to the U.S. economy receiving that much money from the rest of the world without ever giving anything in return.

In the framework of the Feldstein hypothesis, the interesting question is, what would happen if the rest of the world stops sending capital to the United States? Will U.S. trade become balanced without causing any problems both in the United States and the rest of the world? Will there be a recession in the United States, the world, or both? We need to examine macroeconomic policies to answer these important questions.

Foreign Response to the Falling Value of the Dollar

Let us continue our discussion of the market solution of the trade deficit in the United States. According to the market solution, the U.S. trade deficit leads to a decline in the value of the dollar. The falling value of the dollar in turn leads to a decrease in U.S. imports from, and an increase in U.S. exports to, other countries. In presenting the market solution, we made the one crucial assumption that other nations would do nothing that interfered with the market process. Clearly, any significant increase in U.S. exports to other nations depends on how other nations respond to

---

[5]Martin Feldstein, The United States in the world economy: Introduction, in Martin Feldstein (ed.), *The United States in the world economy* (Chicago: The University of Chicago Press, 1988), pp. 1–3.

the falling value of the dollar. To protect domestic income and jobs, other nations may impose trade barriers and thus close their markets to U.S. firms.

If foreign markets were closed to U.S. firms and if foreign investors were unwilling to send any more capital to the United States, the United States might still have a trade balance. The trade balance, however, would be achieved by reducing imports into the United States. This reduction in imports could be obtained either by a greater fall in the value of the dollar or by protectionist policies of the U.S. government through imposition of additional trade barriers such as quotas and tariffs. In either case, U.S. firms would be unable to produce and sell products in which they have a comparative advantage; U.S. consumers would be unable to buy the foreign goods that they would have been able to buy if other nations imported more U.S. products; and there would be a risk of escalating retaliation among trading partners by becoming more protectionistic, resulting in a slowdown in the global economy.

MACROECONOMIC POLICIES AND FOREIGN TRADE

Our discussion so far in this chapter has focused on the market solution to the trade deficit problem. This section introduces the last element of our discussion: domestic macroeconomic policies and their effects on foreign trade.

Policies without Budget Deficit

Let us suppose that there is no deficit in the U.S. government budget and that the only objective of macroeconomic policies is to reduce the trade deficit. We then need a mixture of policies. One such policy is to reduce the level of aggregate spending so that expenditures on imported goods can be decreased. Another policy would be to lower the rate of interest so that foreign investors have less incentive to acquire U.S. financial assets. As the purchase of U.S. financial assets by foreign investors falls, the value of the dollar will continue to decline, and the market solution to the U.S. trade deficit may work without major damage. These objectives can be achieved through fiscal and monetary policies.

In terms of fiscal policy, the government may raise taxes and cut government expenditures. These actions by the U.S. government will lower aggregate demand in the United States and force U.S. consumers to buy fewer imported goods. The reduced aggregate demand will also lower the rate of interest, since there is less need to borrow money. These very actions are contractionary, however, and may cause the U.S. economy to grow slowly, if not lead it into a recession.

In terms of monetary policy, the Federal Reserve may consider increasing the money supply. The increase in money supply will lower interest rates and make the United States a less attractive place for foreign investors. The lower interest rate, therefore, decreases the demand for the dollar. The decreased demand for the dollar will lower the value of the dollar against foreign currencies. As the value of the dollar falls, U.S. exports to other countries rise and U.S. imports from other countries fall. The U.S. trade deficit is reduced. The problem with an expansionary monetary policy is that the increased supply of money may cause inflation in the United States. If inflation develops in the United States, the interest rate may go back up and U.S. exports to other nations become proportionately more expensive, making the trade deficit worse.

THE HAWLEY-SMOOT TARIFF ACT OF 1930

The origin of the Hawley-Smoot Tariff Act of 1930 is the Fordney-McCumber Tariff Act of 1922, since the latter marked the return to the protective mood of the Congress. On the basis of the 1928 platform of the Republican party, President Hoover asked Congress for a limited revision of the Fordney-McCumber Tariff Act of 1922. As Professor Dewey remarked, however, it is practically impossible to limit changes once the tariff is opened up for revision. There were 809 increases and 235 decreases in tariffs. The legislation took over a year. The testimony at public hearings covered almost 20,000 pages, and the potential number of items under discussion came to 25,000. Senators were aware of the foreign reaction to proposed changes in tariffs, since for three months prior to July 26, 1929, 24 nations sent to Congress more than 200 pages of written expressions of deep concern over the bill.

The protests and warnings were not confined to foreign countries. On May 5, 1930, 1,028 American economists from 46 states and 179 colleges asked President Hoover to veto the Hawley-Smoot bill. Economists stated in their petition that increased restrictive duties would be a mistake; that the bill would raise the cost of living and injure the great majority of our citizens; that our export trade, in general, would suffer, since countries cannot permanently buy from us unless they are permitted to sell to us; and that a policy of higher tariffs would inevitably inject bitterness into our international relations.

Retaliation came soon after the passage of the Act, and from many nations. Let us illustrate the tariff retaliation from only one such nation, Italy. The Italian reaction took the form of indignant editorials charging that the United States was attempting to corner the gold supply and ruin the entire world, especially Italy. The campaign against American automobiles was especially bitter. Italian drivers of American automobiles were embarrassed and annoyed by having their tires punctured, their windows spat upon or broken, and by being further harassed by the Royal Automobile Club of Italy, which wanted to publicize the names of all Italians buying American automobiles and to demand an official statement of reasons for their choice. The importation of new cars was stopped by unheard-of duties. For example, a new duty of $815.50 was imposed on each Ford car; $950 on a Plymouth; $1,385 on a Chrysler 77; and $1,660 on each Chrysler Imperial. American agencies closed up by November, 1930, and Ford closed its assembly plant. In general, an increase of 15 percent was placed on practically everything that was not assessed at a higher rate. Mussolini's dictum was unmistakable: "We will make purchases only in those countries which will buy our agricultural products, our marble, our cars, our ships, our silk, our wool and cotton manufactures. We will buy in the United States only the amount of goods equivalent to the amount of goods the United States will buy in Italy. We will purchase the rest elsewhere."

Source: Asher Isaacs, *International trade: Tariff and commercial policies* (Chicago: Richard D. Irwin, 1948), pp. 226–237. Quotation from p. 237.

To summarize, a contractionary fiscal policy will reduce the trade deficit but may cause the U.S. economy to slow down or may even cause a recession. An expansionary monetary policy will help reduce the trade deficit so long as the policy is not too expansionary. If the money supply is too expansionary, it will speed up price increases that widen the trade deficit.

Policies with Budget Deficit

During the late 1980s, the U.S. government incurred budget deficits in excess of $100 billion a year. The budget deficit can be financed in one of two ways: borrowing from the public or increasing the money supply by forcing the Federal Reserve to purchase Treasury securities. An increase in the money supply of the amount necessary to finance such a large budget deficit would be inflationary. The U.S. government, therefore, pursued the other route to finance its deficit: government borrowing in the same money market from which private businesses borrowed money for their capital investment. An increase in government borrowing shifts the demand curve for loanable funds to the right, causing interest rates to rise, unless the supply of loanable funds also increases in direct proportion. In the absence of an increase in the money supply by the Federal Reserve, the supply of loanable funds can be increased either by an increase in domestic saving or through loans from investors in other nations. It was simply not possible to increase domestic saving by almost 50 percent, the amount needed to finance the budget deficit in the late 1980s. The government financed the budget deficit through loans from other nations. These loans were the money that U.S. consumers sent to other nations as payments for imports in the first place.[6]

What would happen to the U.S. economy if trade were balanced without any significant reduction in the federal budget deficit? There would be no more capital inflow that could finance the U.S. budget deficit. If the capital inflow from the rest of the world declines without a corresponding fall in government borrowing, real interest rates in the United States will have to rise. The increase in real interest rates will induce a substantial fall in net investment in plants and equipment and in housing. The fact that real long-term interest rates throughout the 1980s (averaged between 5 to 6 percent) had been nearly twice their historic average (which is no more than 2 to 3 percent) reflected the market's concern that this clash between the government's borrowing needs and private investment demand would soon take place because of a decline in the inflow of foreign capital.

Clearly, a reduction in budget deficit needs to be carried out at the same time that the trade deficit is reduced. Otherwise, the U.S. economy will experience a slowdown, an alternative that many would rather not have.

Needs for Global Coordination

By now it should be clear that all nations, including the United States, are single parts of a larger entity called the global economy. There are small nations and large nations, but no one nation

---

[6]Some economists do not perceive budget deficits as being a serious problem. See Paul Davidson, The conventional wisdom on deficits is wrong, in Peter D. McClelland, *Introductory macroeconomics, 1985–86* (Ithaca, N.Y.: Cornell University Press, 1985), pp. 114–115; Paul Craig Roberts, It's time to stop misreading the deficit, *Business Week,* September 1, 1986, p. 16; Paul Craig Roberts, Read my lips, George: Don't raise taxes, *Business Week,* December 5, 1988, p. 16; and Laurence J. Kotlikoff, Forget about the deficits, *The New York Times,* November 2, 1987.

dominates the global economy as the United States did during the 1950s and the 1960s. There is increasing need for a global coordination of economic policies and a global strategy of individual firms.

Reduced Trade Barriers

Trade barriers need to be lowered for the benefit of all trading nations. If U.S. trade were balanced through reduced imports to the United States from other nations, the trade balance would be achieved at the expense of a slowdown in the global economy. A sudden elimination of all trade barriers, on the other hand, might disrupt domestic economies. The elimination of trade barriers needs to be gradually introduced and coordinated to minimize disruptions and losses in importing nations.

Tax Impact on Capital Flows

One of the long-lasting impacts of the oil crisis in the early 1970s was a gradual integration of the world capital market. The integration accelerated when the United States incurred a significant trade deficit in the 1980s. One important implication of the integrated capital market is that it would no longer be possible to change tax laws without taking capital transfers into account. A country that enacts higher tax rates will drive away businesses. A country that lowers taxes on investment will attract more investments in plant and equipment from other nations.

A Global Strategy of Firms

Many of the nations that were able to sell more to the United States than they bought from it in the 1980s tend to have a closeknit culture difficult for U.S. firms to penetrate. To maximize exports to these nations, U.S. firms need to adapt their marketing and other business practices to different cultures. American business leaders must become increasingly global in their vision of the market environment within which they operate.

Mutual Dependence in Policies

Trade policies undertaken by one nation can easily be negated by its trading partners. When a nation changes its trade policy, it would be simplistic to assume that its trading partners will do nothing that will negate the effects of the nation's trade policy. If U.S. trading partners undertake expansionary policies such as a cut in taxes, increased government expenditure, or an increase in the money supply, these economies will grow faster and increase their imports from the United States. All trading nations in the modern global economy are mutually dependent. Coordinated changes in macroeconomic policies are not only desirable but critical as well for the improved welfare of all nations.

FOREIGN DIRECT INVESTMENT

There are three types of capital transfers: short-term capital transfers, portfolio investments, and foreign direct investments. Of the three, the type that has the most visible effect on the general public is the third type, foreign direct investments. We thus study foreign direct investment in the remainder of this chapter.

The United States in Global Direct Investment

Foreign direct investment refers to the obtaining of ownership of firms in other nations through the purchase of stocks or the investment in new productive facilities. Foreign direct investment and investment by multinational corporations are synonymous, since foreign direct investment is carried out typically by existing multinational corporations. Conversely, if a domestic corporation builds a productive facility in another nation, by definition the corporation becomes a multinational corporation. **Multinational corporations** (MNCs) are firms that control and manage production establishments in two or more countries.

Multinational corporations were of little concern to U.S. consumers until recently when many American jobs were threatened by imports and many states began courting foreign investment in productive facilities. Although the U.S. public was not aware of its extent, U.S. involvement in foreign direct investment has been quite extensive. Table 20.1 shows the dollar value of U.S. direct investment abroad in the period 1983 through 1987, whereas Table 20.2 shows the dollar value of foreign direct investment in the United States in the same period. Nations involved in investments of less than $1 billion in either direction are excluded from the two tables.

The United States is involved in foreign direct investment with practically all nations on the globe. As of 1987 the United States maintained an overall surplus in cumulative foreign direct investment. The total U.S. direct investment abroad in 1987 was $309 billion, while the total foreign direct investment in the United States for the same year was $262 billion. In 1987 the United States maintained a significant deficit in cumulative foreign direct investment against three nations: the Netherlands ($32.9 billion), the United Kingdom ($30.3 billion), and Japan ($19.1 billion).

Why Foreign Direct Investment?

Why do nations invest in other nations? Until 1960 foreign direct investment was explained mainly on the basis of the neoclassical theory of competitive markets. According to this theory, capital flows to those countries in which the capital can earn a maximum return. This theory claims that capital is transferred in response to interest rate differentials after transaction costs and risk premiums have been adjusted. The flow of capital thus was believed to contribute to an efficient allocation of world resources.[7]

Since 1960 economists have broadened their views on foreign direct investment. According to the modern view, developed by Stephen Hymer, the neoclassical theory is too simplistic and applies to individuals whose investment decisions are based mainly on the expected rate of return and the investment risk.[8] Multinational corporations are more likely to concentrate on the profitability or return on investment over the long term. The modern view thus claims that multinational corporations make decisions on foreign direct investment on the basis of many factors, of which interest rate differentials are only one.

---

[7]William J. Kahley, Direct investment activity of foreign firms, Federal Reserve Bank of Atlanta *Economic Review*, Summer 1987, pp. 36–51.

[8]Stephen H. Hymer, *International operations of national firms—A study of direct foreign investment*, Ph.D. thesis at Massachusetts Institute of Technology, 1960. (Cambridge, Mass.: MIT Press, 1976).

TABLE 20.1 U.S. Direct Investment Abroad by Country ($millions)

Countries Involved	Year				
	1983	1984	1985	1986	1987
All countries	207,203	211,480	230,250	259,562	308,793
North America					
Canada	44,339	46,730	46,909	49,994	56,879
Europe					
Belgium	4,438	4,584	5,038	5,229	7,078
Denmark	1,136	1,144	1,281	1,113	1,114
France	6,614	6,406	7,643	8,857	11,478
Germany	15,319	14,823	16,764	20,846	24,450
Ireland	2,460	2,869	3,693	4,395	5,484
Italy	4,461	4,594	5,906	6,935	8,449
Netherlands	6,613	5,839	7,129	11,618	14,164
Norway	3,094	2,841	3,215	3,626	4,142
Spain	2,287	2,139	2,281	2,612	4,037
Sweden	894	844	933	1,002	1,188
Switzerland	14,099	14,725	15,766	17,842	19,973
United Kingdom	27,637	28,553	33,024	35,692	44,673
Asia					
Hong Kong	3,068	3,253	3,295	3,980	5,453
Indonesia	2,770	4,093	4,475	4,395	3,929
Japan	7,661	7,936	9,235	11,332	14,270
Malaysia	1,157	1,101	1,140	1,109	1,111
Philippines	1,331	1,263	1,032	1,135	1,211
Singapore	1,821	1,932	1,874	2,238	2,521
South Korea	589	716	743	800	1,018
Taiwan	613	736	750	870	1,312
Thailand	892	1,081	1,074	1,079	1,282
South Pacific					
Australia	9,005	8,918	8,772	9,120	10,988
South America					
Argentina	2,702	2,753	2,705	2,919	2,854
Brazil	9,068	9,237	8,893	9,187	9,955
Colombia	2,123	2,111	2,148	2,033	2,037
Peru	2,042	1,902	1,243	1,131	1,102
Venezuela	1,711	1,761	1,588	2,139	2,124
Central America					
Mexico	4,381	4,597	5,088	4,750	4,997
Panama	4,837	4,474	3,959	4,293	4,780
Caribbean					
Bahamas	3,762	3,331	3,795	2,762	2,566
Bermuda	11,056	13,019	13,116	14,765	18,229
Netherlands Antilles	−22,956	−24,664	−20,499	−15,817	−13,208
United Kingdom Islands—Caribbean	1,960	2,992	3,490	3,771	3,970
Africa					
Egypt	1,421	1,538	1,926	1,814	1,663
Nigeria	216	327	44	575	1,267
South Africa	1,987	1,440	1,394	1,567	1,590
Middle East					
Kuwait	44	45	41	54	−7
Saudi Arabia	2,156	2,352	2,442	1,972	2,385

Source: Adapted from U.S. Department of Commerce, *Survey of Current Business* 68(August 1988):65, Table 29, U.S. Direct Investment Abroad: Country Detail for Selected Items. Only countries with foreign direct investment in the United States or U.S. direct investment of $1 billion or more are included.

TABLE 20.2 Foreign Direct Investment in the United States by Country ($millions)

Countries Involved	Year				
	1983	1984	1985	1986	1987
All countries	137,061	164,583	184,615	220,414	261,927
North America					
Canada	11,434	15,286	17,131	20,318	21,732
Europe					
Belgium	2,261	2,548	2,291	2,487	2,598
Denmark	308	404	577	552	728
France	5,726	6,591	6,670	7,709	10,195
Germany	10,845	12,330	14,816	17,250	19,637
Ireland	219	285	(D)	360	467
Italy	1,238	1,438	1,237	1,323	1,230
Netherlands	29,182	33,728	37,056	40,717	47,048
Norway	311	311	396	241	498
Spain	194	231	273	350	421
Sweden	2,124	2,258	2,357	3,963	4,699
Switzerland	7,464	8,146	10,568	12,058	14,343
United Kingdom	32,152	38,387	43,555	55,935	74,941
Asia					
Hong Kong	324	659	640	605	699
Indonesia	–2	15	49	37	40
Japan	11,336	16,044	19,313	26,824	33,361
Malaysia	22	22	16	39	6
Philippines	116	121	118	113	122
Singapore	186	208	242	169	358
South Korea	–57	–81	–101	383	210
Taiwan	69	70	107	177	138
Thailand	6	18	13	14	56
South Pacific					
Australia	930	2,125	3,264	5,466	6,373
South America					
Argentina	194	237	280	292	312
Brazil	84	160	201	182	195
Colombia	63	69	75	78	82
Peru	3	3	4	(D)	6
Venezuela	24	48	103	476	451
Central America					
Mexico	244	308	533	847	880
Panama	2,073	1,924	2,204	2,202	2,223
Caribbean					
Bahamas	175	158	154	309	209
Bermuda	1,168	1,370	1,691	2,002	2,188
Netherlands Antilles	9,948	10,935	10,443	9,685	8,895
United Kingdom Islands—Caribbean	985	866	1,028	560	–275
Africa					
Egypt	3	3	4	9	8
Nigeria	–7	–8	–8	6	5
South Africa	–28	–25	–12	72	68
Middle East					
Kuwait	3,606	4,333	3,968	3,771	4,002
Saudi Arabia	353	425	420	436	415

Source: Adapted from U.S. Department of Commerce, *Survey of Current Business* 68(August 1988):80, Table 22, Foreign Direct Investment in the United States: Country Detail for Selected Items. D represents an amount suppressed to avoid disclosure of data of individual companies. Only countries with foreign direct investment in the United States or U.S. direct investment of $1 billion or more are included.

Let us suppose that a parent firm decides to build a new plant in another nation.[9] To be successful, the firm must overcome several disadvantages that an investment in its own country does not create. These disadvantages include higher transportation and communications costs associated with managing from a distance, less knowledge of the prevailing language and customs, and problems in dealing with another currency. A firm that penetrates such a market with production facilities is not expected to make a decision based solely on risk-adjusted interest rate differentials. The firm must possess some production or marketing edge that will enable it to survive.

A study by the U.S. Department of Commerce supports the modern view by spelling out several factors behind foreign investment in the United States.[10] These factors include (1) a greater recognition among foreign companies of the size and growth of the U.S. market and a growing perception of this country as an economically and politically safe haven; (2) an increasing number of large foreign MNCs whose experience with American firms abroad convinced them that they could compete successfully in the U.S. domestic market; (3) a narrowing spread between American and foreign production costs, which renders production here relatively more attractive to foreign firms than exporting to the United States; (4) concern about increasing U.S. protectionism and a feeling that investment in this country offers an effective way to hurdle trade barriers; and (5) the wooing of foreign investors by state development agencies, particularly in the South.

Debts of Developing Nations

Developing nations have always had to borrow money from developed nations in order to finance various projects for economic development. The debt problems of developing nations became greater in magnitude since the oil crisis in the early 1970s. When the Organization of Petroleum Exporting Countries (OPEC) was able to establish a near monopoly of the world's oil supply and increased oil prices by more than 15 times between 1971 and 1973, developed nations that depended heavily on petroleum as a source of energy paid the price, resulting in one of the largest transfers of wealth in history from one group of nations to another. OPEC nations that received these several hundred billions of petrodollars did not know what to do with all the money. If these nations simply accepted this large amount of money and let it circulate in their economies, there would have been runaway inflation. OPEC nations, therefore, simply deposited the money back into the banks of the industrialized world from which the money originated.

Commercial banks in developed nations, in turn, loaned the money to developing nations that, as usual, needed investment capital. When commercial banks made the loans, the premise was that governments of both developed and developing nations could not go bankrupt. The loan of petrodollars to developing nations was also supported by the International Monetary Fund. Commercial banks in developed nations would collect interest on loans from developing nations and make interest payments to OPEC nations, completing the petrodollar cycle.

If the borrowing nations were able to invest the funds in such a way as to earn a rate of return that was higher than the rate of interest on the loans, there would not have been a problem. As is

[9]William J. Kahley, Direct investment activity of foreign firms, Federal Reserve Bank of Atlanta *Economic Review,* Summer 1987, p. 40.

[10]William J. Kahley, Direct investment activity of foreign firms, Federal Reserve Bank of Atlanta *Economic Review,* Summer 1987, p. 38.

typical with many developing nations, the loans were not invested productively. By the late 1970s, many debtor nations realized that their exports were not sufficient to make interest payments, let alone payments of the principal.

In August 1982 the Mexican government announced that it could no longer service its debt. At the time Mexico was a major oil producer and was regarded as one of the more creditworthy nations. This announcement sent a shock wave through the international financial system. There is a saying that when the amount of a loan is small, the borrower is the one who worries about it; when the amount of a loan is large, however, the bank is the one who worries about it. In a near panic atmosphere, the banking authorities quickly arranged a temporary bailout, rescheduling the Mexican debt. The rescheduling of the Mexican debt was followed by similar arrangements in Argentina, Brazil, and other debtor nations.[11]

Some intriguing questions arise concerning the debt problem of developing nations. What would happen to the world banking system if one of the debtor countries with a significant amount of debt simply refused to repay the loan? Would the default lead to a worldwide depression? Would governments in developed nations bail commercial banks out of their bad debt problems? If they did, what would be the effect of the government bail-out on income distribution in these nations? Wouldn't the government bail-out be equivalent to taking money away from middle and low income households and giving it to the wealthier stockholders of large commercial banks? There are no easy answers.

SUMMARY

The United States' trade deficit during the second half of the 1980s was caused by the policies of the Reagan administration, which increased aggregate demand, and by the rising value of the dollar in the first half of the 1980s. The high value of the dollar was caused by economic policies that led to an increase in interest rates. A large trade deficit causes capital to flow into the nation. The capital transfer may take the form of short-term capital transfers, portfolio investment, or foreign direct investment. Short-term capital transfers are different from the other two in that these transfers seek interest income on securities that expire in less than a year. Foreign direct investments are different from the other two in that these investments seek control of firms in another nation.

A chronic trade deficit in the United States tends to undermine the stability of the international capital market by creating uncertainty and encouraging speculation. The floating exchange rate system is capable of correcting a nation's trade deficit without government interference by depreciating the currency that makes domestic products cheaper to overseas buyers. The floating exchange rate system, however, works slowly. Trade deficits can be corrected by a contractionary fiscal policy and expansionary monetary policy. Nations may not favor these policies because these policies may lead to a slowdown in the economy or inflation.

---

[11]For more on the debt problem of developing nations, see John Charles Pool and Steve Stamos, *The ABCs of international finance* (Lexington, Mass.: D. C. Heath, 1987), pp. 3–4.

In the late 1980s the U.S. government ran a large budget deficit in addition to the trade deficit. The budget deficit was financed substantially by the inflow of capital that was generated by the trade deficit. A global coordination of economic and trade policies is important for the improvement of the welfare of all nations. Nations need to reduce trade barriers, consider international impact when tax cuts are considered, and clearly understand that policies undertaken by one nation may easily be negated by its trading partners.

EXERCISES

1. In the 1980s the U.S. economy experienced a large trade deficit. One major reason for the trade deficit was the strong dollar in the early 1980s. Why did the value of the dollar increase in the early 1980s?

2. When a nation experiences a trade deficit, capital is transferred to the nation. What are the three ways in which capital can be transferred from one nation to another?

3. How is foreign direct investment different from the other two types of capital transfer?

4. Determine whether each of the following international financial transactions represents short-term capital transfers (SHORT), portfolio investment (PORT), or foreign direct investment (INVEST).

   opening a NOW account
   purchase of a 3-month CD
   purchase of a 6-month Treasury security
   purchase of AT&T bonds
   purchase of over 50 percent of stocks of McDonald's
   construction of a new chemical plant
   purchase of farmland in Kansas

5. The position of the U.S. dollar in the global economy was accepted as being pivotal at the World Monetary Conference held in Bretton Woods, New Hampshire, in 1944. What was the arrangement regarding the use of the dollar in global trade?

6. If the German mark and Japanese yen were fixed at $1.00 = 3 marks and $1.00 = 150 yen, what would be the exchange rate between the mark and yen?

7. What are the likely short-term effects of the U.S. trade deficit on other nations?

8. What are the likely long-term effects of the U.S. trade deficit on national security issues?

9. Suppose that Mexico raises taxes and reduces government spending in order to reduce trade deficit. What are likely effects of these policies on Mexico's balance of trade and its domestic economy?

10. What are some likely effects of balanced trade when the federal budget deficit remains at a significant level?

SUGGESTED READINGS

Feldstein, Martin (ed.). (1988). *The United States in the world economy*. Chicago: The University of Chicago Press.

Collection of timely and excellent articles on the trade deficit problems of the United States.

Grayson, Jackson, Jr., and O'Dell, Carla. (1988). *American business: A two-minute warning*. New York: The Free Press.

Warns that unless U.S. companies quickly improve productivity and quality, Japan will take over as the economic leader of the world within two decades; and urges a national commitment to improved education.

Herr, Ellen M. (1987). U.S. business enterprises acquired or established by foreign direct investors in 1986. *Survey of Current Business* 67(May):27–35.

A good introduction to statistical research on foreign direct investment in the United States.

Kahley, William J. (1987). Direct investment activity of foreign firms. Federal Reserve Bank of Atlanta *Economic Review,* Summer, pp. 36–51.

A good introduction to foreign direct investment.

Meyer, Stephen A. (1986). Trade deficits and the dollar: A macroeconomic perspective. Federal Reserve Bank of Philadelphia *Business Review,* September-October, pp. 15–25.

Explains why the U.S. trade deficit exploded during the early 1980s.

Rosensweig, Jeffrey A. (1987). Constructing and using exchange rate indexes. Federal Reserve Bank of Atlanta *Economic Review,* Summer, pp. 4–16.

When the value of the dollar is said to increase, the value of the dollar increases against certain criteria known as exchange rate indexes. This article explains different exchange rate indexes.

Tolchin, Martin and Susan. (1988). *Buying into America: How foreign money is changing the face of our nation*. New York: Times Books.

Claims that foreign investment eroded American economic and political independence; states that pressure from foreign companies forced California to repeal its unitary tax of the worldwide incomes of multinationals operating in the state; and makes suggestions for change such as limiting foreign campaign contributions.

U.S. Department of Commerce, International Trade Administration. (1984). *International direct investment: Global trends and the U.S. role*. Washington, D.C.: U.S. Government Printing Office.

An in-depth study on foreign direct investment in the United States. Explains various aspects of foreign direct investment including the appeal of investing in the United States.

GLOSSARY

ability-to-pay principle An approach in taxation that suggests taxes be paid according to the ability of taxpayers to pay.

absolute price The price of a given good or service.

absolute value Value of a number without the positive or the negative sign.

ad valorem tax A tax levied on the monetary value of the tax base.

agency shop An arrangement that does not require workers to join a union but does require workers to pay union dues to stay on the job at a firm.

aggregate demand The quantity of goods and services that consumers, businesses, government, and foreign nations are willing to purchase during a period.

aggregate demand curve The inverse relation between price level and the quantity of output demanded for the entire economy.

aggregate output Total final output produced in an economy. Same as GNP. Called also aggregate supply.

aggregate supply The quantity of goods and services produced in an economy during a period.

aggregate supply curve The relation between price level and the quantity of output supplied for the entire economy.

aid in-kind Noncash aids such as housing, food, and health care.

allocative efficiency The allocation of resources in such a way that prices are lower and the quantity of output is larger. Same as economic efficiency.

antitrust laws Laws that deal with anticompetitive conduct and structure of firms.

appreciation of a currency An increase in the price of a currency in terms of other currencies.

assumption The act of taking for granted or supposing that a thing is true; or something that is taken for granted.

ATS Automatic transfer of savings, an arrangement in which if the balance of a checking account falls below a minimum required level, the deficit is automatically transferred from the person's savings account to the checking account.

automatic stabilizers Programs that reduce the magnitude of economic fluctuations by raising expenditure during a recession and reducing expenditure during an inflationary period without discretionary actions by policy makers.

autonomous consumption The portion of consumption that does not depend on the level of income.

average product of labor The quantity of output per unit of labor services, obtained by dividing the total quantity of output by the total units of labor services used to produce the output.

average propensity to consume The ratio of consumption to income at a given level of income.

average propensity to save The ratio of saving to income at a given level of income.

average revenue Total revenue divided by the quantity of sales.

average tax rate The ratio of total tax payments to total tax base.

Averch-Johnson **effect** The excessive use of capital among firms such as utility companies that are subject to rate of return regulation.

balance of payments A record of all transactions that affect the flow of a nation's currency.

balance of trade A nation's record of transactions of goods with other nations.

balanced budget multiplier effect The expansionary effect of a simultaneous increase in government expenditure and taxes, or the contractionary effect of a simultaneous decrease in government expenditure and taxes.

banker's acceptances Promissory notes issued by businesses to obtain short-term credit and accepted by a bank or other financial institution.

barriers to entry Factors such as patents and economies of scale that keep other firms from entering a given market.

barter A market arrangement in which participants exchange goods and services without using money as a medium of exchange.

basing point pricing system An arrangement in which a firm selects one or more sites for delivery called basing points, and the delivered price is quoted as the product price at the nearest basing point, plus transportation cost.

benefit principle An approach to taxation that suggests taxes be paid by those who benefit from expenditures made possible from the particular tax revenue.

big board The New York Stock Exchange.

blue chip A company, or stocks of the company, that is a leader in its industry and has a long history of dividend payment.

bond A credit instrument on which the issuer promises the bondholder to pay back the loan and make a fixed payment periodically until the loan is paid back.

bourgeoisie Capitalists who own property or capital.

brand name The name that a company chooses to call a new product.

break-even point The lowest point of the average cost curve; the point at which total revenue and total cost are equal to each other.

business cycle Recurring patterns of expansion and contraction of the overall activity of an economy.

business transfer payments Transfer payments such as scholarships and charity that are contributed by businesses.

call The option to buy a stock at a fixed price for a fixed time period.

capital Produced means of production such as machines, producers' durable equipment, and buildings.

capital account A summary of transactions on foreign direct investment and loans among nations.

capital goods Accumulated machines, equipment, and buildings.

capital inflow The flow of a foreign currency into a nation because of the deficit in the nation's current account.

capital outflow The flow of a domestic currency out of a nation because of a surplus in the nation's current account.

capitalism An economic system characterized by private ownership of property, free competition, price system, and limited government.

capture theory of regulation A hypothesis stating that the government regulates industries to protect and promote interests of the regulated industries.

certificates of deposit (CDs) Same as time deposits.

ceteris paribus All other things being equal.

change in demand Shifts in demand curve due to changes in determinants of demand.

change in quantity demanded Movement along a demand curve due to changes in the price of the product.

change in quantity supplied Movement along a supply curve due to changes in the price of the product.

change in supply Shifts in supply curve due to changes in determinants of supply.

civilian labor force The nation's labor force excluding military personnel.

classical economics A loose term encompassing economic ideas that prevailed during the eighteenth and the nineteenth centuries.

classical range The vertical portion of the aggregate supply curve.

classical school Economic ideas that are collectively called classical economics, or economists who developed and shared these ideas.

closed economy A domestic economy without foreign trade.

closed shop An arrangement that requires union membership as a condition of employment.

cogeneration An arrangement in which a privately owned manufacturing plant generates electricity for its own use and sells excess electricity to the local power company.

coincident indicators Series of economic data that historically reached their own cyclical peaks and troughs at about the same time as the corresponding turns in the business cycle.

commercial papers Financial obligations of large corporations bought and sold publicly.

common stocks Shares in the ownership of corporations.

communism A dictatorial economic and political system in which, allegedly, there are no problems of government, scarcity, or conflicting classes.

complement A good or service that is consumed together with the good or service under consideration.

completely elastic demand (supply) Demand (supply) in which an infinitesimally small percentage change in price leads to an infinitely large percentage change in the quantity of the product demanded (supplied).

completely inelastic demand (supply) Demand for (supply of) a product that remains unchanged as prices change.

conglomerate merger A merger between two firms selling products that are unrelated.

conscious parallelism A legal term meaning that an unlawful conspiracy to fix prices can be inferred in the absence of an explicit agreement if there is evidence that conduct stemmed from a tacit agreement.

conservative economists Economists who advocate a smaller role of government in the administration of economic affairs.

consumer price index Price index measuring changes in prices of a market basket of goods and services that an average consumer is likely to buy.

consumer's surplus   The difference between what consumers are willing to pay for units of a product and what consumers actually pay.

contraction   A period during which real GNP declines.

corporation   A legal entity that is owned by one or more stockholders.

corporate income tax   Same as corporate profit tax.

corporate profit tax   A tax levied on profits of a corporation.

cost   Payments that a firm makes to resource suppliers in order to attract resources away from production of alternative goods and services.

cost function   A relation between quantities of output and minimum costs of producing these quantities.

cost push inflation   Price increases originating on the seller's side because of wage push or profit push.

CPI-minus-2   An arrangement that would reduce annual cost of living adjustments on indexed entitlement programs by 2 percentage points below the increase in the CPI.

craft union   A union of skilled workers.

creeping inflation   Slowly rising prices.

cross elasticity of demand   Measures percentage changes in demand for one product in response to percentage changes in the price of another product.

currency   Dollar bills and coins that are held outside the Treasury, Federal Reserve banks, and the vaults of commercial banks.

current account   A summary of transactions of a nation's exports and imports of goods and services plus unilateral transfers.

customs valuation   The process of determining the value of imported goods by customs officers.

cyclical unemployment   Unemployment due to insufficient aggregate demand.

deadweight welfare loss   A loss to society's welfare by having a monopoly market as opposed to a competitive market.

deduction   An approach toward developing a theory by moving from development of a hypothesis to observation of facts in order to empirically prove the hypothesis.

demand   The quantity of goods and services that consumers capable of paying are willing to buy in order to satisfy their wants.

demand deposits   Checking accounts at depository institutions that do not pay interest on balances.

demand function   An algebraic statement of the relationship between the quantity of a product demanded and the determinants of its quantity demanded.

demand pull inflation   Rising prices caused by an aggregate demand that is greater than aggregate supply.

deposit multiplier   The ratio of total deposit to an initial deposit. Same as monetary multiplier.

depository institutions   Institutions at which deposits can be made such as commercial banks, savings and loan associations, and credit unions.

depreciation   The value of capital goods that decreases over time due to wear from repeated use or technological obsolescence.

depreciation of a currency A decrease in the price of a currency in terms of other currencies.

derived demand Demand for productive resources that is derived from demand for final products that these resources help produce.

devaluation A decrease in the value of a currency in terms of other currencies that results from a government's policy. Also synonymous with depreciation.

discount rate The interest rate that Federal Reserve banks charge on short-term loans made to depository institutions.

discretionary fiscal policy Tax and expenditure policies of the government that require deliberate actions by the government.

diseconomies of scale Increasing average costs of production due to problems arising from a scale that is too large for efficient management.

disposable income Personal income from which personal taxes are subtracted.

dividends Payments by corporations to their stockholders as a return for shares in the ownership of the corporations.

dumping The act by exporting countries of lowering the price of a product they sell in importing countries below the cost of production.

Dutch auction An auction in which the auction price starts very high and is reduced gradually until a person accepts the bid price.

earmarking A rule that tax receipts must be spent for specific purposes by law.

easy money policy A policy by the Federal Reserve system to accelerate money growth, lower interest rates, and make credit more easily available.

econometric methods Statistical methods applied to theoretical models of economic reality.

economic circular flow The exchange, or a diagram that shows the exchange, between sellers and buyers of final products and the factors of production needed to produce these final products.

economic efficiency Same as allocative efficiency.

economic fluctuations Significant changes in real GNP.

economic good A good, the consumption of which requires the consumer to forgo consumption of other goods and services.

economic policies Both fiscal policy and monetary policy.

economic profits Profits in excess of a normal rate of return.

economic regulation Government regulation of specific industries; also called industry regulation.

economic rent The part of the payment to an owner of resources over and above that which these resources could command in any alternative use.

economics A science in which we study aspects of human behavior that deal with the relationship between given wants and scarce resources that have alternative uses.

economies of scale Decreasing average costs of production made possible by a large scale operation.

effective tax rate A tax rate obtained when actual tax payments are divided by the tax base.

English auction An auction in which the price of an item is successively raised until only one bidder remains.

entitlements Benefits prescribed by law for all persons meeting a program's eligibility requirements.

entrepreneurship Ability to organize a business enterprise by assuming the risk.

equilibrium An equality between opposing forces.

equilibrium GNP The level of GNP that is obtained when aggregate demand is equal to aggregate supply.

equilibrium price The price that equates the quantity of a product demanded and the quantity of the product supplied.

equilibrium quantity The quantity exchanged at the equilibrium price.

Eurodollars Deposits in U.S. dollars held by individuals and nonbank businesses in banks located outside the United States.

exchange rate The price of one currency in terms of another.

excise tax A special case of sales tax in which the tax rate varies with products on which the excise tax is levied.

exclusive contracts Contracts that require the buyer not to deal with competitors of the seller.

expansion A period during which real GNP expands.

expenditures approach The process of measuring GNP by adding how much an economy spends to buy those goods and services produced as final output in an economy.

explicit costs The portion of the opportunity cost made in cash expenditures.

exports Products or the values of these products that are sold to other nations.

external benefits Positive effects of externalities of a production on those who neither produce nor consume the product.

external costs Negative effects of externalities of a production on those who neither produce nor consume the product.

external diseconomies Same as external costs.

external economies Same as external benefits.

externalities Effects of a production on those who neither produce nor consume the product.

factors of production Same as productive resources.

fascism An economic and political system that allows private ownership of productive resources but is run by one political party.

featherbedding Preserving a job no longer needed.

federal funds Funds borrowed among depository institutions on an overnight basis.

federal funds rate Interest rate charged on federal funds.

fiscal policy Deliberate changes in government expenditure and taxation in order to stabilize the economy and promote its growth.

fiscal year A 12-month period, ending on the last day of any month, selected arbitrarily for accounting of revenues and expenditures.

fixed costs Payments made in purchasing fixed inputs.

fixed exchange rate system An arrangement in which the value of a currency is fixed by government to the value of another currency or gold.

fixed inputs Inputs whose quantity remains unchanged as the quantity of output changes.

fixed investment Investment in machines, equipment and new buildings, i.e., investment minus changes in inventory.

flexible exchange rate system An arrangement in which exchange rates are allowed to fluctuate according to the forces of supply and demand in the foreign exchange market. Also called the floating exchange rate system.

floating exchange rate system Same as flexible exchange rate system.

foreign direct investment A purchase of existing businesses or information of new businesses such as new plants in other countries.

foreign exchange The currency of other nations.

foreign exchange rate The price of one currency in terms of another.

free good A good, the consumption of which does not require the consumer to forgo consumption of other goods and services.

free riders Those who enjoy consumption of goods and services but are not willing to contribute to the cost of producing these goods.

frictional unemployment Unemployment while entering the job market or changing jobs.

full employment An economy in which unemployment is mostly frictional or structural.

gainful employment Work for pay.

general sales tax Same as sales tax.

generic name The name of a type of product; in the case of pharmaceutical products, the name of the chemical compound that makes up the drug.

GNP in "constant" dollars GNP expressed in the base year prices.

GNP in "current" dollars GNP expressed in prices that prevailed.

government An organization formed for the purpose of exercising authority over individual members in a given society.

grandfathering An arrangement in which those who are holding the right at the time of change are not affected by the change.

gross investment Investment inclusive of depreciation.

gross national product The total market value of all final goods and services that are produced during a year.

gross private domestic investment Expenditures by private businesses on machines, equipment, and buildings.

gross receipts tax Same as sales tax.

hard-core unemployment The unemployment of those who cannot find a job, become discouraged, and then discontinue searching for work.

heavy industries Industries such as the steel, automobile, and oil refinery industries that require a large amount of expenditures on fixed inputs.

hemline hypothesis The proposition that stock prices go up about six months after women's hemlines go down.

horizontal merger A merger between two firms selling the same or similar products in the same market.

hyperinflation Very rapidly rising prices.

hypothesis A proposition tentatively assumed in order to extract its logical or empirical consequences and whose truthfulness can be tested against facts that are known or may be determined.

impact lag The time lag between the initiation of an economic policy such as changes in money supply and the time of the impact that these changes have on the economy.

implicit costs The portion of the opportunity cost that is not made in cash expenditures.

implicit price deflator The ratio of current dollar GNP to constant dollar GNP. Also called GNP price deflator.

import licensing The requirement of a permit as a prior condition for importing goods.

imports Products or the dollar values of these products purchased from other nations.

impure public goods Goods from which free riders are neither totally excludable nor totally desirable of exclusion.

imputation The process of developing estimates for missing or incomplete data in national income accounting. The imputed values of GNP include the rental value of owner-occupied houses, food and fuel produced and consumed on farms, and services rendered without charge by financial institutions.

income approach The process of measuring GNP by adding incomes received by all individuals for their productive services.

income elasticity of demand Measures percentage changes in demand for a product in response to percentage changes in consumers' income.

incomes policy A wide range of governmental initiatives that affect wages, prices, and real incomes in the economy.

indexing An arrangement in which wages and other future payments such as pension plans, savings accounts, and life insurance contracts are automatically adjusted in response to increases in the cost of living.

indirect business taxes Taxes that businesses pay to the government but treat as costs of producing a product and charge to consumers through higher prices. These taxes include sales tax, excise tax, property tax paid by businesses, and license fees.

induction An approach toward developing a theory by moving from observation of facts.

inferior goods Goods and services for which demand decreases as income increases.

inflation Rising prices of goods and services.

injunction A court order that requires one to refrain from doing a specified act.

institution An accepted way of doing things in a given society such as marriage, and other traditions that a society is accustomed to.

interlocking directorate An arrangement in which a person serves as a director of two or more competing corporations.

intermediate goods Produced goods that are used as inputs to produce other final goods.

intermediate range The portion of the aggregate supply curve that rises upwardly to the right.

investment The production of new machines and new durable equipment, the construction of new buildings including residential homes, and changes in inventory.

investment multiplier The ratio of an increase in GNP to the initial investment that causes the increase in GNP.

investment tax credit An amount, usually a fraction of capital investment, that firms are allowed to subtract from tax liability for the encouragement of business investment.

invisible hand A concept suggested by Adam Smith (1723–1790) that refers to the spontaneous social harmony that results from self-interested behaviors of individuals who compose the society.

involuntary unemployment Unemployment of those who are willing to work at the prevailing wage but cannot find work.

Keynesian range The horizontal portion of the aggregate supply curve.

kinked demand curve A model used to explain an oligopoly, based on the assumption that price decreases of an oligopolist are matched by rival firms in the oligopoly, but that price increases are not.

L M3 plus other liquid assets such as certain Eurodollar holdings of U.S. residents other than banks, bankers' acceptances, commercial papers, U.S. savings bonds, and short-term Treasury securities.

labor Time and effort of human beings exerted in the process of production activities.

labor force The number of persons who are 16 years of age and older, not in institutions, and actively seeking jobs.

labor force participation rate The ratio of the labor force to the working age population.

lagging indicators Series of economic data that historically reached their cyclical peaks and troughs later than corresponding turns in the business cycle.

laissez faire The philosophy that the best way of promoting economic development and the general welfare of a nation is to leave the private enterprise economy alone.

land Land in its narrow sense (the ground) and minerals not yet excavated.

large-denomination time deposits Certificates of deposit issued in denominations of $100,000 or more.

law of demand The inverse relation between the price of a product and the quantity of the product demanded.

law of diminishing returns Law indicating that as successive units of a variable input are added to fixed inputs, the marginal product that is attributable to reach additional unit of the variable input eventually declines.

law of supply The direct relation between the price of a product and the quantity of the product supplied.

leading indicators Series of economic data that historically reached their own cyclical peaks and troughs earlier than the corresponding turns in the business cycle.

liberal economists Economists who advocate a greater role of government in the administration of economic affairs.

limited liability Losses of stockholders limited to the dollar value of their stockholdings.

limited pricing Pricing method in which a new product is priced below the minimum average cost of production in order to prevent new entries to the market for the product.

loanable funds The amount of money available for loan.

lockout A situation in which an employer withholds employment.

logrolling The process in a legislative body of passing pork barrels that cannot be approved on their own merit by attaching them to significant laws that can pass on their own merit.

long run   A period of time during which all inputs vary.

loss leader pricing   Pricing method in which a product is priced below its cost to attract customers.

luxury goods   Products for which the demand is relatively elastic.

M1   The narrowest definition of money as consisting of currency, travelers checks, demand deposits, and other checkable deposits.

M2   M1 plus overnight repurchase agreements issued by commercial banks, certain overnight Eurodollars held by U.S. residents other than banks, money market mutual fund shares, savings deposits, and small-denomination time deposits at all depository institutions.

M3   M2 plus large-denomination time deposits at all despository institutions.

macroeconomics   The branch of economics that is concerned with major aggregates or averages of the economy such as total output or inflation.

managed floating exchange rate system   An arrangement in which the floating of a currency is controlled through occasional government inteference.

marginal cost pricing   The process of pricing a product according to the $P = MC$ relationship (where P is price).

marginal factor cost   The cost of hiring the last unit of a productive resource; also called the marginal resource cost.

marginal physical product of labor   The quantity of physical output that increases as one more worker is added to the productive resources that the firm already has.

marginal product of labor   Change in total product attributable to the last unit of labor services hired.

marginal productivity theory of income distribution   The theory that owners of productive resources are paid their marginal products.

marginal propensity to consume   The ratio of change in consumption to change in income.

marginal propensity to save   The ratio of change in saving to change in income.

marginal revenue   Revenue from the sale of the last unit, obtained by dividing changes in total revenue by the corresponding changes in the quantity of sales.

marginal revenue product   An increase in total revenue that results from the use of each additional unit of labor service.

marginal tax rate   The ratio of additional tax payments to changes in tax base.

market   An arrangement in which sellers of a good or service interact with buyers of the good or service.

market concentration ratio   The percentage of output accounted for by the largest four or more firms in the industry relative to the total industry output.

market demand   The quantities of a good or service that are demanded by all buyers in any given market at various prices.

market failure   The inability of a price to signal shortages and surpluses of a product in a given market.

market structure   A description of the characteristics of demand and cost conditions that are common to firms within an industry.

market supply A summation of all supply schedules of individual firms in any given market.

median voter The voter whose preferred expenditure for a given public good is at the level where the number of individuals who prefer higher expenditure is exactly equal to the number of individuals who prefer lower expenditure.

merger The purchase of the assets of a firm by another firm so that the two firms can be operated under one ownership.

microeconomics The branch of economics that is concerned with individual units within the economy such as firms or individual markets.

minimum efficient scale The smallest level of output at which a firm's long-run average cost is minimized.

mixed economy Modern capitalism in which the role of government is large.

moderate inflation Prices rising at a moderate rate.

monetarism A theory stressing the important role that money supply determines nominal GNP.

monetarists Economists who share and promote monetarism.

monetary multiplier Same as deposit multiplier.

monetary policy Discretionary changes in money supply intended to stabilize the economy and promote the growth of the economy.

money GNP Same as nominal GNP.

money market mutual funds Investment funds managed by banks or investment companies that pool investors' money and buy or sell interest bearing securities that can be bought with a large amount of money only.

monopolistic competition Markets in which a large number of firms sell products that are differentiated.

monopoly A market in which one firm produces and supplies a product that has no close substitutes, or the firm that sells the product without close substitutes.

monopsony A one-buyer market.

mortgage rates Interest rates charged on loans that are intended to purchase homes, buildings, or land.

MR = MC rule A rule stating that profits are maximized when firms produce the level of output at which marginal revenue is equal to marginal cost.

multinational corporations Firms that control and manage production establishments in two or more countries.

mutual interdependence in oligopoly Market situation in which decision on price and nonprice strategies of a firm are based on the assumption that other firms in the industry will react to these decisions.

national income The sum of all payments for productive services that were utilized in turning out final output.

national income and product accounting The process of defining, collecting, and classifying income and product data of an economy.

natural monopoly A firm for which the average cost of production declines over the entire range of market demand.

natural rate of unemployment The rate of unemployment consisting of frictional and structural unemployment. Same as the full employment rate of unemployment.

natural rate of unemployment hypothesis A hypothesis that fiscal and monetary policies cannot change the rate of unemployment over a long period of time and the rate of unemployment always returns to the natural rate.

necessities Products for which the demand is relatively inelastic.

negative-sum game An activity in which cumulative gains are smaller than cumulative losses.

net exports Total exports from which total imports are subtracted.

net investment Investment net of depreciation.

net national product Gross national product from which depreciation is subtracted.

nominal GNP GNP figures stated in current market prices. Same as GNP in current dollars.

nominal rate of interest The rate of interest calculated on current dollars.

normal goods Goods and services for which demand increases as income increases.

normal rate of return The average rate of return on investment in all (other) industries.

normative science A body of knowledge discussing criteria of what ought to be.

NOW accounts "Negotiable orders of withdrawal" checking accounts, which pay interest on account balances.

oligopoly A market dominated by a few leading sellers and characterized by mutual interdependence and barriers to entry.

open economy A domestic economy that trades with foreign countries.

open market operations Buying and selling of Treasury securities by the Federal Reserve Banks.

open shop An arrangement in which workers are not required to join a union even after being hired.

opportunity cost The amount of other products that must be forgone to produce a given product.

optimization The process of allocating scarce resources among their best uses.

option An option to buy or sell a stock at a fixed price for a fixed time period.

overnight repurchase agreements An arrangement in which banks borrow money from nonbank sources such as large corporations for short periods like overnight. Also called RPs.

over-the-counter market Telephone networks of stock brokers for the trade of stocks not listed in the New York Exchange or the American Exchange.

partnership A form of business organization existing between two or more persons who join together to carry on a trade or business.

patent The exclusive right to produce a certain product or use a certain production technology.

peak The highest level of real GNP before it starts declining again.

pegged exchange rate system An arrangement in which exchange rates are pegged to the value of another currency.

perfect competition Market conditions in which the demand for the output of every firm in a given industry is so perfectly elastic that the firm is a price taker for all quantities of output it produces and sells.

personal consumption expenditures Expenditures by individuals and nonprofit institutions on durable goods, nondurable goods, and services.

personal income All incomes received by individuals either as payments for productive services or as transfer payments.

personal income tax A tax levied on taxable incomes of individuals and unincorporated firms such as sole proprietorships and partnerships.

phantom freight Freight costs that exist only on paper.

Phillips curve A curve showing an inverse relation between unemployment and inflation.

physical science A science that deals with nonhuman objects such as atoms, superconductors, and plants, or with nonbehavioral aspects of human beings such as bones, muscles, and toothaches.

placebo A medicine void of effective chemical ingredients that is given merely to comply with the mood of the patient.

placebo effect The phenomenon that when a person believes that the placebo medicine works, it may actually work.

planned investment Business investment that excludes unintended changes in inventory.

pork barrel Appropriations by government for political patronage especially to please legislators' constituents.

portfolio investment Financial transactions that involve stocks and bonds and that have no intention of controlling the firms that issue these stocks and bonds.

positive science A body of knowledge concerning what is.

positive-sum game An activity among two or more persons in which cumulative gains are greater than cumulative losses.

predatory pricing Pricing method in which price is cut to drive competitors out of the market.

price ceilings Maximum prices that are legislated to be below the equilibrium market price.

price elasticity of demand Measures percentage changes in the quantity of a good or service demanded in response to percentage changes in the price of the good or service.

price elasticity of supply Measures percentage changes in the quantity supplied in response to percentage changes in the price of a product.

price floors Minimum prices that are imposed above the equilibrium market place.

price index A weighted average of prices for a given basket of goods and services, expressed in an index form.

price leadership The practice in which one firm in an industry initiates a price change, and other firms in the same industry follow the price leader and more or less match the price change.

price makers Firms operating under imperfect competition that have the ability to change the market place.

price takers Firms operating under perfect competition that charge the price that is determined in the market place.

prime rate The interest rate that a bank charges on the loans it makes to its most creditworthy business customers.

principle A proposition so well accepted that we do not consider challenging its validity.

private goods Goods from which others are excluded by the buyer's consumption of them.

private ownership The right by owners of property to buy, sell, and control these resources.

producer price index A price index measuring changes in the prices of selected raw materials and intermediate goods purchased by producers.

product differentiation A characteristic of monopolistic competition whereby consumers perceive two or more products satisfying the same wants to be different, and they prefer one to the other.

production The act of creating a good or service that has an exchange value.

production function The relation between the quantity of output and various amounts of inputs needed to produce the quantity of output, given the production technology.

productive resources Resources needed to produce final products such as land, labor, capital, and entrepreneurship.

profit contribution The difference between revenue from sales of a product and the variable cost of its production.

profit norm The average return on investment in any given industry.

progressive tax A tax characterized with a marginal tax rate that is greater than the average tax rate so that the portion of income that those with more income pay as tax increases as income increases.

proletariat Workers who own only their labor.

propensity A tendency or an inclination.

proportional tax A tax characterized with a marginal tax rate that is equal to the average tax rate so that the portion of income that those with more income pay as tax is exactly the same as the portion of income paid as tax by those with less income.

proposition The act of proposing something for discussion or development, or something proposed or offered for consideration, acceptance, or adoption.

proprietorship Same as sole proprietorship.

protectionism The governmental adoption of trade barriers in order to restrict imports that may compete against domestically produced products.

public goods Goods from whose consumption it is neither possible to exclude those who do not pay, nor desirable to exclude them even if it is possible to do so.

public interest theory of regulation A hypothesis stating that the government regulates industries in response to public demand for correction of market failures.

put The option to sell a stock at a fixed price for a fixed time period.

quantitive restrictions A wide range of nontariff measures restricting trade such as bans on the import or export of specific commodities as well as import and export quotas.

quantity theory of money The hypothesis that money supply is the sole determinant of changes in the price level.

random walk theory The proposition that a blindfolded monkey throwing darts at a newspaper's financial pages could select a portfolio of stocks that would do just as well as one carefully selected by the experts.

rate of unemployment The ratio of the number of unemployed persons to the civilian labor force.

rational expectationism A hypothesis that individuals are rational in the sense that they use all the available information when they make decisions.

rational ignorance effect The lack of incentive for voters to seek additional information needed to cast a more informed vote.

Reaganomics Economic policies of President Reagan in the 1980s that cut income tax rates for greater work incentives and increased military expenditure.

real balance effect The hypothesis that higher prices reduce the purchasing power of accumulated assets and the reduced value decreases public spending.

real GNP Nominal GNP adjusted for inflation. Same as GNP in constant dollars.

real rate of interest The nominal rate of interest from which the expected rate of inflation is subtracted.

real wages Money wages from which the inflationary effect is subtracted.

realized investment Planned investment plus unintended changes in inventory.

recession The state of an economy that experiences a decline in the real GNP from the previous year's level.

recovery The early months of an expansion.

regressive tax A tax characterized with a marginal tax rate that is lower than the average tax rate so that the portion of income that those with more income pay as tax is smaller than the portion of income paid as tax by those with less income.

relative price The price of a good or service in relation to the price of another good or service.

relatively elastic demand (supply) Demand (supply) in which the percentage change in quantity is greater than the percentage change in price.

relatively inelastic demand (supply) Demand (supply) in which the percentage change in quantity is smaller than the percentage change in price.

rent-seeking A case in which the profit-seeking behavior of firms or individuals in institutional settings results in social waste rather than social gain.

representative tax system A tax system that shows what the total revenue of each of the 50 states would be if every state applied identical tax rates at the level of national averages to each of 26 commonly used tax bases.

required reserve ratio The ratio of required reserves to total deposits.

required reserves The portion of deposits that depository institutions must keep by law.

respending ratio The ratio of additional expenditure to the initial spending.

retail sales tax Same as sales tax.

returns to scale Changes in output due to changes in the scale of production.

sales tax Tax in which one tax rate is levied at the retail level on a wide range of goods and, sometimes, services.

savings deposits Savings accounts that pay interest on balances but do not permit account holders to write checks against them.

Say's law The hypothesis that supply creates its own demand.

scale coefficient The ratio of changes in output to changes in all inputs.

scarcity A situation in which the available quantity of a resource is smaller than the quantity of the resource desired by humans.

science   A search to discover commonalities in the wide variety of human experience and nonhuman phenomena.

seasonal unemployment   Unemployment of those who lack work because their jobs are seasonal by nature.

securities underwriting   An arrangement in which a bank or a securities firm sells securities to the public on behalf of the firm or agency that issues the securities.

selective sales tax   Same as excise tax.

sharebuilder's plan   An arrangement by stock brokerage firms in which small amounts of money are submitted to the stock brokerage firm for the purchase of fractions of stocks.

short run   A period of time during which at least one input remains unchanged while other inputs vary.

short-term capital transfers   Financial transactions that involve financial instruments with maturities of less than one year.

shutdown point   The lowest point of the average variable cost curve; the point at which total revenue equals total variable cost.

sin tax   Tax on alcoholic beverages and cigarettes.

small-denomination time deposits   Certificates of deposit in denominations of less than $100,000.

social cost   Total goods and services that the society as a whole sacrifices to produce a given product: includes both the firm's private cost of production and externalities.

social regulation   Government regulation across industries.

social science   A science that deals with behavioral aspects of human beings.

socialism   An economic system characterized by public ownership of productive resources.

sole proprietorship   A business in which the owner is self-employed.

special interest effect   The support of special interest issues by politicians based on their judgment that their gains from supporting special interest groups will be greater than their losses from individuals who may not vote for these politicians because of their support for special interest groups.

special interest groups   Those who try to obtain significant gains for their members at the expense of a large number of individuals who suffer small losses.

speculative funds   Funds set aside for investment purposes. Called also speculative demand for money.

spillover effects   Same as externalities.

staflation   An economy characterized by concurrent stagnation and inflation.

standard   A technical specification approved by a recognized agency.

stock   A piece of paper representing a share in the ownership of a corporation.

stock split   An offering of additional shares of a given stock with an intent to lower the per-share price of the stock.

structural unemployment   Unemployment of those who lack work because of changing job requirements that these workers are not prepared for.

substantial effect doctrine   A doctrine claiming that any intrastate activity exerting a substantial economic impact on interstate commerce falls under federal regulatory power.

substitutes   Products other than a given product that can satisfy human wants almost as well as the given product does.

sunk costs   Expenditures that are already made and thus are irrelevant across alternative actions.

Super Bowl hypothesis   The proposition that stock prices rise during a given year if the winner of that year's Super Bowl is from the old National Football League, and stock prices fall if the winner is from the old American Football League.

superior goods   Same as normal goods.

supply   The quantity of a good or service that a seller is willing and able to make available for sale in the market at various prices.

supply shocks   Surprise occurrences that temporarily increase or decrease current output.

supply-side economics   A hypothesis that a cut in income taxes improves work incentives and leads to increased tax revenues as well as increased real output.

symmetry assumption   The assumption employed by Chamberlin that any adjustment of price or of product by a single producer spreads its influence over so many competitors that the impact felt by any one is negligible.

tariffs   A tax on imports or the rate at which imported goods are taxed.

tautology   A needless or meaningless repetition in close succession of an idea, statement, or word.

tax-based incomes policy   A system of tax penalties and rebates to provide incentives to businesses and labor unions so that they may voluntarily comply with wage and price guidelines established by the government.

tax capacity   The revenue that a governmental unit would collect if it applied national average tax rates to the common set of tax bases.

tax effort   A ratio of the actual tax collections of a governmental unit divided by the estimated tax capacity.

tax incidence   The final resting place of a tax burden.

theory   A hypothesis the truthfulness of which has already been proven empirically.

theory of contestable markets   The theory claiming that potential entry or competition for the monopolistic market disciplines the behavior of monopoly firms as effectively as actual competition would within the market.

tight money policy   A policy by the Federal Reserve that is intended to slow money growth, raise interest rates, and make credit less easily available.

time deposit   Savings deposits with a maturity date prior to which money cannot be withdrawn without a penalty. Called also a certificate of deposit, or CD.

total labor force   Labor force including the military personnel.

total physical product of labor   The quantity of output, measured in physical terms, produced by all workers.

total product of labor   The maximum quantity of output obtainable from a given number of workers with given capital goods that the workers use.

total revenue   Sales revenue obtained when price is multiplied by the quantity of sales.

total revenue product The sum of marginal revenue products of all workers.

trade barriers Government laws, regulations, policies, or practices that are intended either to protect domestic producers from foreign competition or to artificially stimulate exports of particular domestic products.

transactions costs Transportation, insurance, and other costs that incur in the process of a trade.

transactions funds Funds set aside for the buying and selling of goods and services. Also called transactions demand for money.

transfer payments Payments made in return for which no services are rendered at the time the payments are made.

trough The lowest level of real GNP before it starts increasing again.

tying contracts Contracts that require a buyer to purchase other products that the buyer does not want, when the buyer purchases a product from a seller.

underground economy Illegal incomes and legal incomes that are not reported. Also called the subterranean economy.

undistributed corporate profits Corporate profits from which corporate income taxes and dividends are subtracted. Also called retained earnings.

unemployed persons Those who are 16 years and over, not institutionalized, actively seek a job, but do not have a job.

union shop An arrangement that requires workers to join a union after they are hired.

unit-elastic demand (supply) Demand in which percentage changes in the price of the product are offset by corresponding percentage changes in its quantity demanded (supplied).

unit tax A tax levied on the unit of the tax base.

unlimited liability The proprietor's risking not only the assets of the business but personal assets as well.

utility Satisfaction that consumers derive from consuming goods and services.

utility companies Firms that supply public utilities such as electricity, natural gas, telephone, water, and sewer services.

value added The value that each producer adds to the cumulative value of a product upon completion of the particular stage of production.

variable costs Payments made in purchasing variable inputs.

variable inputs Inputs that vary with the quantity of output.

vertical merger A merger between two firms that are related as supplier and buyer of a product.

voluntary unemployment Unemployment of those who lack work because they refuse to work at the prevailing wage.

wages The price paid for the use of labor services.

X-inefficiency Inefficiency in utilizing resources at the firm level due to inefficient management.

yellow dog contract A contract requiring employees not to join unions as a condition of employment.

zero-sum game An activity in which the cumulative gains equal the cumulative losses.

Index

486 Index